History Matters

PROFESSOR EMERITA BRIDGET BRERETON

History Matters

*Reassembling the Fragments
of a Contested Past
In Honour of Bridget Brereton*

[EDITED BY]

HEATHER CATEAU,
RITA PEMBERTON

AND

RONALD NOEL

The University of the West Indies Press
Mona • St Augustine • Cave Hill • Global • Five Islands

The University of the West Indies Press
7A Gibraltar Hall Road, Mona
Kingston 7, Jamaica
www.uwipress.com

© 2025 edited by Heather Cateau, Rita Pemberton and Ronald Noel

All rights reserved. Published 2025.

A catalogue record of this book is available from the National Library of Jamaica.

ISBN: 978-976-640-986-9 (paperback)
978-976-640-987-6 (ePUB)
978-976-658-034-6 (hardback)

Cover image *Persistent Anthems* by Carlisle Harris.
Cover and book design by Robert Harris
Set in Gandhi Serif 10.2/14.2 x 24.

The University of the West Indies Press has no responsibility for the persistence or accuracy of URLs for external or third-party Internet websites referred to in this publication and does not guarantee that any content on such websites is, or will remain, accurate or appropriate.

Printed in the United States of America

CONTENTS

List of Tables / *viii*

Abbreviations and Acronyms / *ix*

Introduction / *xi*
HEATHER CATEAU

Part 1: The Colonial Caribbean in Transition / *1*

1 "Little England" vs "Great Britain": Barbados Slavers in the Emancipation Debate / *3*
HILARY McD. BECKLES

2 No "Gentle Glide" From Enslavement to Emancipation: The Post-Emancipation Labour Struggles in Tobago, 1838–1919 / *32*
RITA PEMBERTON

3 The Impact of Christianity on Naming Practices in Post-Emancipation Barbados / *63*
PEDRO L.V. WELCH

Part 2: Law, Justice and Empire / *85*

4 From Unicameralism to Bicameralism: Trinbago Constitutional Advances (1831–1962) / *87*
BRINSLEY SAMAROO

5 "The Thorough Knowledge of the Island and All its Departments and Instruction in Political Science": Representing the Patria in Puerto Rico's First Elections Under Spain's 1812 Constitution / *101*
JUAN GONZÁLEZ MENDOZA

6   The Crown Is Not Welcomed: Government and Politics
    in British Guiana, 1953–1957 / *127*
    JAMES ROSE

7   Eric Williams and C.L.R. James: Intellectual
    Symbiosis and Political Counterpoint / *151*
    HUMBERTO GARCÍA-MUÑIZ

Part 3: Gendered Testimonies / *177*

8   Bridget Brereton's Gendered Historiography of
    the Caribbean / *179*
    GELIEN MATTHEWS

9   Egodocuments by Women as Sources for Caribbean History:
    Three Cases from Late Colonial Suriname / *193*
    ROSEMARIJN HOEFTE

10 Imperial First Lady of Trinidad, Lady Rachel
    Hamilton-Gordon, 1865–1870 / *213*
    DANE MORTON-GITTENS

11 Slavery, Gender and the Historiography of the
    French Antilles, 1635–1848 / *233*
    BERNARD MOITT

Part 4: Engendering History: Social and Political Life in the Caribbean / *253*

12 Gender and Protest at Morant Bay and in the
    Post-Emancipation Caribbean / *255*
    GAD HEUMAN

13 Inclusion/Exclusion: Women, Citizenship and
    Political Franchise in Early Twentieth-Century
    Trinidad and Tobago / *270*
    RHODA REDDOCK

14 Gender and Nation-Building in Barbados / *293*
MARY CHAMBERLAIN

15 Ascent to Leadership: Women and the National Union of Public Workers of Barbados, 1975–1995 / *319*
RICHARD A. GOODRIDGE

Part 5: Race Relations in the Caribbean: Contested Narratives / *341*

16 "Passing for White" in Bahamian Society During the Late Nineteenth and Early Twentieth Centuries / *343*
GAIL SAUNDERS

17 It Featured a Gymkhana? Conflicting Identities in the Early Years of the Modern Crop Over Festival / *355*
MARCIA BURROWES

18 Contesting Narratives of Trinidad and Tobago's History: The Contribution of Bridget Brereton and an Exploration of the Syrian/Lebanese Narrative / *381*
FIONA ANN RAJKUMAR

Part 6: History Matters: The Historian and Her Craft / *401*

19 Bridget Brereton and the Narratives of Modern Trinidad: An Assessment of Three Volumes / *403*
MICHAEL TOUSSAINT

20 Called to Action: Caribbean Historians and the Preservation of Primary Sources for the History of the Region / *428*
JOHN A. AARONS

Selected Bibliography / *441*

Contributors / *461*

Index / *469*

LIST OF TABLES

3.1: A Schedule of the Particular Names of all ye Christian and other Stock on ye Plantaçon of Captain William Goodall Fontlaroy / *65*

3.2: Selected Moravian Slave Baptisms, Barbados, 1769–1827 / *67*

3.3: Baptismal Register, Yoy Slaves, St Philip's Parish Church, 1824 (River Plantation) / *69*

3.4: Baptismal Register, Girl Slaves, St Philip's Parish Church, 1824 (property of River Plantation) / *70*

3.5: Names of Free Coloureds, extracted from Bridgetown, Barbados, Levy Books, 1808 (selected streets) / *73*

3.6: Baptisms of Apprenticed Ex-slaves, 1834–1835 (Moravian Register) / *76*

3.7: Baptisms of Ex-slave Apprentices, St Philip's Parish Church, 1836 / *77*

3.8: Baptisms of Apprentices and Ex-slaves, Methodist Church, 1835–1839 / *79*

3.9: Sample of Marriages at St Philip's Parish Church, 1838–1839 / *82*

4.1: Constitutional Transitions, 1663–1889 / *88*

5.1: *Partidos* and Electors for 1812–1813 Elections / *103*

5.2: Results of the Parochial Elections in San German (20 September 1812) / *107*

5.3: Composition of the *Junta Electoral de Partido* / *108*

12.1: Barbados, Number of Apprenticed Labourers Manumitted, 1837 / *257*

ABBREVIATIONS AND ACRONYMS

AACC	Anglo-American Caribbean Commission
Act	Libro de Actas del Cabildo
AGI	Archivo General de Indias
AGPR	Archivo General de Puerto Rico
AHSMG	Archivo Histórico Municipal de San Germán
BACSA	Barbados Civil Service Association
BWU	Barbados Workers Union
CARICOM	Caribbean Commuity
CC	Caribbean Commission
DLP	Democratic Labour Party
FEGPR	Fondo de los Gobernadores Españoles de Puerto Rico
FWI	Federation of the West Indies
HMG	Her Majesty's Government
IBRD	International Bank for Reconstruction and Development
ILO	International Labour Organization
IMF	International Monetary Fund
NALIS	National Library and Information System Authority
n.f.	folios are not numbered
NLF	National Labour Front
NUPW	National Union of Public Workers
OWTU	Oil Workers Trade Union
PNM	People's National Movement
PPP	People's Progressive Party
RPA	Ratepayers Association
THA	Tobago House of Assembly

TTUTA	Trinidad and Tobago Unified Teachers' Association
TWA	Trinidad Workingmen's Association
UARMAC	University Archives and Records Management Advisory Committee
UDP	United Democratic Party
WICP	Women in the Caribbean Project
WIFLP	West Indian Federal Labour Party
WIRC	West India Royal Commission
WFP	Workers and Farmers Party

INTRODUCTION

[HEATHER CATEAU]

CARL CAMPBELL, A FELLOW CARIBBEAN HISTORIAN WHO HAS known Bridget Brereton for years, reflected that, "In a small West Indian society such as Trinidad and Tobago, it is not uncommon for one person in the Arts or Sciences to become particularly associated in the public's mind with a certain expertise or skill, and usually this is a well-earned reputation. So it has been with Brereton."[1] His insightful summation of the impact of her scholarship and the public interventions, with which he himself was very familiar, is reflective of the extent to which Bridget Brereton has become so much more than a lecturer and author. As suggested by the title of this volume, she has played a critical role in reassembling the fragments of the region's history. Indeed, she is regarded as a local and regional academic who can be trusted to provide academic insight into Trinidad and Tobago's past, as well as the Caribbean's. In doing this she has also raised the prominence of history, her chosen tool of analysis.

Ironically, had she been interviewed for the role that she would play in Trinidad and Tobago's and the Caribbean's history she would not have been tipped to be the successful candidate. Brereton did not start off as an insider. Born in Madras (now Chennai), her childhood was spent in England and Scotland, countries associated with aggressive colonization of the region and the creation of versions of our past that Caribbean academics are seeking to revise and expand through the recovery of the voices that have been silenced. Brereton's personal history and that of the region intersected at an opportune time and a relationship germinated, even though she had spent most of her life outside of the region. She was in the process of developing her own historical lens and the historical narratives of the region were waiting to be told. Brereton, therefore, arrived in the Caribbean at a strategic time in her own personal and academic development. It was also an important crossroads in the region's development. She became part of that amazing period in Caribbean history during which the region tackled the challenges of independence and decolonization, and as regional academics sought to frame a distinctively Caribbean scholarship at the University of the West Indies. History was an important part of these movements and by choosing to specialize in the discipline, Brereton also became part of these developments. She is also very much a product of the University of the West Indies (UWI). Her ties became cemented during her tenure as a student and as an academic staff member. She received her undergraduate degree from the Mona campus and her doctorate from the St Augustine campus. Trinidad became her home and she has resided there for most of her life (more than sixty years). She built an illustrious career at the St Augustine campus and has become a historian whose voice is respected within the society. Perhaps it is her background that in a surprising way made her well suited for the role she was to play. In interrogating the history of modern Trinidad and Tobago, and its complex social relationships, particularly race and ethnic relations, there is a need for discussions which can, at times, be politely described as uncomfortable. In such contexts, a variety of voices struggle to be heard, and often jostle for supremacy of place. The context created the background for the entry of this social historian who was, in many senses, external to the region and outwardly, not economically, politically or socially aligned. Brereton became one of the most influential voices on the Caribbean inside and outside of academia. Her voice – through her writings and scholarship – occupied a space that became valued. History, in turn, also shared that coveted space nationally and regionally.

She gained a reputation for neutrality. She used history to provide evidence-based, documented insights into the structure of our societies to help us understand our communities. She would wield her influence at the UWI as well as in the wider society, employing what Campbell described as "... a high level of improbable neutrality".[2] Much of her work serves as a demonstration of using history to provide balance. Her history, whether in the academy or public fora, is often based on bringing historical developments to our attention through a focus on actresses, actors and communities of interest. She manipulated historical events and developments in such a manner that they became the ultimate arbitrators for how the present accepted the new narratives that were being told. She immersed herself in archives which were underutilized, but also interacted closely with university students and secondary school teachers. She was also actively engaged in the public history arena. Much of this persists even today and her work continues to shape the historiography of the region and the historical narratives in our communities. Moreover, though we are commemorating a lifetime of work, Brereton is not finished by any means and shows little sign of slowing down. Her latest contribution to the history of modern Trinidad and Tobago is the recent biography of former prime minister Patrick Manning.[3] Thus, Brereton's academic career, as illustrious as it is, was merely the point from which she launched a holistic series of history-related applications in our contemporary period which are ongoing.

As professor emerita of the St Augustus campus, she is often described as a "model scholar and colleague",[4] and is still an active and much appreciated member of our history department and university. She has held numerous senior positions, such as Interim Principal, Deputy Principal and Head of Department. She was the first woman to be awarded the prestigious Vice-Chancellor's Award for Excellence for Research, Teaching and Administration (1996), and was a part of the group of female pioneers who introduced and developed women and gender studies at the UWI. Gender became one of her analytical tools and shaped the development of her methodological frameworks. However, her academic legacy extends beyond the walls of the university. She has been integral to professional bodies like the Association of Caribbean Historians, of which she served as president from 1994 to 1997. Further, her intervention has been sought at critical junctures in Trinidad and Tobago's contemporary history. She served as chair of the Cabinet-appointed committee to consider the Trinity Cross and the other national symbols and observances in 2006, and as chair of the board of the National Library and Information Service Authority (NALIS). She has been on numerous committees and is a regular columnist with the *Trinidad Express* newspaper. Her work on the social history of Trinidad and Tobago has inspired a country during a very important period of its own contemporary history and her teaching, publications and scholarship at the UWI have left their mark on the discipline of Caribbean history and the region's understanding of its past.

It is difficult to look back over the career of someone who has been not just a historian par excellence, but also a teacher, a mentor, a colleague, a leader in numerous spheres and a public figure; and decide on how best to capture and celebrate both the person, as well as her contributions to our scholarship, the UWI, Trinidad and Tobago, and the Caribbean region. To do this we turned to what we know best – history. We invited many to join us. Some took part in the conference "Reassembling the Fragments", which the Faculty of Humanities and Education held in 2011 to celebrate three of our professors: Bridget Brereton, Barbara Lalla and Ian Robertson. However, to capture all the dimensions of Brereton's work, we also turned to her colleagues locally, regionally and internationally. The chapters in this volume are all written by persons with both professional and personal connections to Brereton. Many are former students, members of staff from the UWI campuses, and colleagues from the Association of Caribbean Historians.

Brereton blazed a path in Caribbean history through her careful recounting of the history of Trinidad and Tobago as we transitioned to a modern society; and as the UWI matured and focused academic minds on the problems of the region. The period itself is of historical importance. She wrote Caribbean history, nurtured it and helped shape its development and growth through the UWI, the Association of Caribbean Historians, the History Teachers Association of Trinidad and Tobago, her articles in newspapers, her publications and her unofficial role as a public historian in the twin-island republic. This volume, therefore, is a gift of history from historians and other esteemed colleagues to someone who has fashioned our history; but even deeper than that, our epistemology and even pedagogy – be it as historians, academics, professionals or simply as citizens of the Caribbean. These biographical details and the glimpses into Brereton's life provided by the information shared foreshadow the academic discussions that follow.

The volume aims to highlight her contribution to Caribbean history, showcasing the areas covered in her work and her approach to historical enquiry and analysis. Moreover, the contributors are varied and reflect the wide spectrum of people her work has influenced. Thus, the chapters do not conform to any one approach or style. We embrace a variety of voices, just as she did. Some of the pieces are narrations that contribute to increasing our information in specific, under-researched areas where there is a dearth of information. This, too, is indicative of the type of history Brereton wrote. These pieces serve to widen the historical content and give access to more historical voices; and in other cases, analysis takes centre stage to contextualize and enhance our understanding of important areas in Caribbean history. In some cases, we are reintroduced to actors who may be already familiar to us. The volume hopes to follow Brereton's lead and weave the contributions into a historical narrative of the region, highlighting dimensions of our contested past and sharing new historical insights. Most importantly, our intention is to produce a book that will be read by the public, especially in Trinidad and Tobago, where she is well known, and across the Caribbean. The volume is also designed as a reference text for secondary level and undergraduate students, particularly those doing survey courses in Caribbean history. At the same time, some of the chapters provide specialist information and can be consulted at higher educational levels.

Brereton is very much a public historian. We hope the book is an enjoyable read and brings Caribbean history into the homes of Caribbean citizens at home and abroad. Her work impacts a very wide public, and any attempt to confine her scholarship too narrowly to a rigid set of theoretical methodologies or one style will limit the wide range of reactions to and commemorations of her contributions to academia. At the same time, the volume adds to the understanding of the history and historiography of the Caribbean, not just through the content of the chapters, but through the way in which the book is organized, its range and scope. This is achieved by placing her own work at the centre of the expositions, both in terms of the themes used and the approaches of the contributors in this volume.

In honour of the historiography shaped by Bridget Brereton, we have used her work to introduce each of the sections and themes in this book. Thus, a cursory examination of the contents page will give even the casual reader a sense of the kind of history that Brereton wrote. The chapters are collated into six sections, each with a title adapted from one of her publications. The chapters themselves reflect the historical contributions she has made through her publications and, in their progression, tell their own story of how Brereton has left her mark on our history. It seemed only fitting that we use her own words to lead us in the crafting of this historical narrative.

The book begins with the section entitled "The Colonial Caribbean in Transition".[5] The three contributions under this theme replay the details of one of the most important societal transitions in our history and include the emancipation process in the Caribbean. They reassess and add new insight into the mechanics that led to the passage of the Emancipation Act, as well as the nature and intensity of the adjustments experienced in the Caribbean, as the transition to full freedom took place against a background of strong resistance and the imposition of numerous obstacles. Together the contributors – Hilary Beckles, Rita Pemberton and Pedro Welch[6] – investigate the transition from the perspectives of British officials, the planters/slavers, as well as the enslaved and the newly freed population. Beckles examines the changing nature of the imperial relationship in "'Little England' vs 'Great Britain': Barbados Slavers in the Emancipation Debate". He positions the Barbadian planters as the "aristocracy of the imperial slavocracy", who led an active and virulent opposition to the Registration Act, the Amelioration Act and the Emancipation Act. He examines the changing perception of the slavocracy from 'Little England' loyalists (who created wealth for Britain and thus were always rewarded through policies and economic measures), to a group who felt betrayed and could no longer rely on decisions to go their way. He describes the relationship as reaching a crossroads and a transition from civilized 'Little England' to a group at the forefront of the emancipation battle, who saw themselves as the ones being persecuted. Beckles contends that they lost their place in a new conception of Britishness, which had an altered position on enslavement. The volatility was intensified by the internal revolt of the enslaved population. Barbados' initial fall from grace is demonstrated both by unexpected responses, which no longer reflected their assumed pride of place in the British imperial system, and in the denial of requests for a special compensation package. However, Beckles shows that ultimately the planters were in fact compensated twice (with money and apprenticeship), and it was the enslaved who paid more than anyone else for their freedom. Ultimately, Britain won on both sides of the Atlantic – in 'Little England' and 'Great Britain'.

The price paid by the enslaved population is taken up by Rita Pemberton in "'No Gentle Glide' From Enslavement to Emancipation: The Post Emancipation Labour Struggles in Tobago 1838–1919". Tobago was no 'Little England', but it was held up as an example of peaceful transition in the colonial project. Shattering this image, Pemberton describes a transition characterized by both confrontational and non-confrontational resistance through a close examination of both emancipation in 1838 and the decades of adjustment which followed in the often-overlooked island of Tobago. This chapter clearly demonstrates that there was no "gentle glide" in Tobago and seeks to counteract the emphasis that has been placed on the planters' ability to maintain control. In the process, she recovers the struggles of the newly freed population and positions their actions as part of the working-class struggles that would continue to plague the region. According to Pemberton, another dimension of a peculiar resistance struggle was evolving. She disrupts the idyllic image of a peaceful Tobago and in the process adds to the agency of the African working class in her re-examination of their activities from Emancipation Day to the early twentieth century.

Pedro Welch closes off this section with his chapter "The Impact of Christianity on Naming Practices in Post-Emancipation Barbados". He views naming practices as part of the attempts of the newly freed population and their descendants to fully maximize the possibilities after legal freedom. Naming, which was formerly used to strip the enslaved population of agency and identity, was consciously being used to reclaim social and family relationships. Welch demonstrates that the Church also played an important part in the naming process, particularly through conversions and baptisms. Thus, naming can also be viewed in many instances as reinforcing European norms and Judeo-Christian culture. However, Welch maintains that the naming process really demonstrated the rejection of one name and the adoption of another. Involved in this were choice, notions of legitimacy and decisions about social and family identity. He describes naming practices as "consolidating the process of emancipation". This section captures the complexity of the transition that was taking place. It challenges stereotypical ideas about emancipation and how it was accepted in the region. A dynamic picture is created of a society that was in transition in several senses and a newly free population determined to influence the nature of the changes that were taking place. Thus, in the same vein of Brereton's 1999 co-edited work on post-emancipation social and cultural history; these pieces provide novel insight into issues connected to the nature of the transition taking place in Caribbean societies in the critical early nineteenth period as we transitioned to a modern Caribbean region.

From the emancipation transition, we move to "Law, Justice and Empire" in a transition of a different nature. Brereton did not often deal directly with political developments. However, as she narrated aspects of the history of modern Trinidad and Tobago, she looked at areas such as the reform movement and the colonial career of John Gorrie, the Scottish Chief Justice who presided over Trinidad and Tobago from 1886 to 1892.[7] She described her publication on Gorrie as the work of which she was proudest. This theme builds on this and looks at the transition to self-government and elected representatives. However, the contestation uncovered by Brereton in her earlier works continues and can still be found throughout the region. The four chapters in this section grapple with the struggle to create truly democratic institutions and political frameworks in the region. Two of the contributors deal with Trinidad and Tobago, one with Guyana and the other with Puerto Rico. The section begins with the chapter "From Unicameralism to Bicameralism: Trinbago Constitutional Advances 1831–1962". The chapter is one of the last contributions to our history from Brinsley Samaroo, who died before the publication of this volume. It is indeed fitting that this piece is included in this publication in honour of his lifelong friend. The chapter also reflects an important dimension of the nature of Samaroo's contributions to Trinidad and Tobago's historiography. The piece not only puts constitutional developments into their proper context, but also does this to extend the spotlight from the past to the current reality in Trinidad and Tobago. Samaroo uses history to educate the population about the need for further constitutional development through interrogation of "how we have come to be as we are". In his own words, "At this time, when the citizens of Trinidad and Tobago are engaged in the process of constitution-making, it is necessary that we should look back at the process of governance of which we are the present inheritors." In this chapter, he critically examines the philosophy behind the proposed constitutional reforms and illuminates a psychology of control which he contends we still must break out of and make our own way. He saw this as an urgent priority for our contemporary society. The chapter deals with much more than historical details. It is also a call for devolution and decentralization.

We see a similar suppression of political evolution in Puerto Rico. Juan González Mendoza looks at the Puerto Rican context in "'The thorough knowledge of the Island and all its Departments and Instruction in Political Science': Representing the *Patria* in Puerto Rico's first elections under Spain's 1812 Constitution". Through his examination of this political development in the colonies, and the actions of the creole population, he provides insight into the nature of these political transitions during a decisive period in Puerto Rico's constitutional history. Once more we see the nature of the intricate dance staged between imperial and colonial elements in the movement towards constitutional change. Looking at the municipal and regional levels, he shows how internal autonomy was negotiated. Attempts by the creole juntas to gain interim sovereignty were further complicated by internal factions influenced by issues such as place of birth and other social, political and economic considerations. As in Trinidad and Tobago, the hold of the ancient regime was strong, creating tensions and sustaining structures that prevailed and subverted the emergence of truly representative institutions.

James Rose's chapter shows that the region was still contending with these issues in the middle of the twentieth century when constitutional reform and the first general elections in the former British territories had already taken place. "The Crown is not Welcomed: Government and Politics in British Guiana, 1953–1957" demonstrates that there was continued interference from imperial forces, not only by the former mother countries but their close ally, the United States. He recounts the swift change from constitutional reform back to what was essentially a Crown colony government in British Guiana when the political trajectory indicated by democratically held elections did not conform to the path promoted by Britain and the United States. The election of the People's Progressive Party (PPP), with its socialist leanings, could not be tolerated. Intervention took place to remove the PPP from power and to make sure its influence was neutralized. The chapter focuses on the interim administration, the attempt to justify what had taken place and policies designed to appease the population through proposed rapid economic development and social reforms. Instead, the period 1953 to 1957 was characterized by corruption and failure of development and reform plans. The central goal to undermine the PPP also failed. Intervention stunted political development and internal turmoil festered. Rose concludes that, if anything, Guiana was even further away from what was dubbed responsible government when failure and embarrassment led to the return of the democratic process.

This section ends in Trinidad and Tobago, with a look at two political personalities C.L.R. James and Eric Williams. Both were born, lived in, and were very much influenced by this convoluted and contested political and constitutional past. Each had his own vision of an indigenous political path to development. The paths were not the same and contrasted in many ways, but there were also impactful intersections. Despite difficult circumstances, these intersections provided enough fertile soil for an intriguing friendship to take root and germinate over decades. Together, they contributed to a distinctive Caribbean intellectual tradition. These men have long been subjects of historical analysis, but Humberto García-Muñiz provides a unique insight in "Eric Williams and C.L.R. James – Intellectual Symbiosis and Political Counterpoint". He looks at the interaction and the nature of the engagement between James and Williams from the 1920s to the 1980s. He draws us into a fascinating relationship that spanned decades as well as geographical spaces. He takes us from the pupil-mentor relationship that started in Trinidad; to the more mature relations and friendship that developed in Britain and the United States; and then to the complex relationship as political colleagues in Trinidad and Tobago, which also led to disaffection and separation. He describes "... an intellectual, amicable and political relationship that probably has no equal in Caribbean history and politics". A contrast is established between James, a revolutionary Trotskyist, a Pan Africanist and Caribbean activist with no university education; and Williams, an Oxford PhD; a Howard associate professor, political leader and prime minister, a pragmatist and a Caribbeanist. Both were intellectuals of the highest calibre, prolific writers with numerous publications, and both were committed to change and development for the Caribbean. He paints a picture of friends who influenced each other's work, but also very different men with dispositions that sometimes clashed. They ultimately took divergent political pathways, but both left transformative legacies and anchored Caribbean intellectual development in the twentieth century. Perhaps the most powerful element of this chapter is not just that it increases our knowledge of their contributions; but that it shares the just as intriguing and provocative nature of this, admittedly at times explosive, dimension of their interaction and friendship.

We cannot honour Brereton's contribution without looking at women and gender studies. This is the focus of the next two themes "Gendered Testimonies" and "Engendering History-Social and Political Life in the Caribbean".[8] We start Gendered Testimonies by looking at her contribution to Caribbean historiography through Gelien Matthews' "Bridget Brereton's

Gendered Historiography of the Caribbean". Matthews delineates and expounds on the nature of Brereton's contributions from her arrival at the University of the West Indies. The areas covered include the introduction of the first women and gender course, a survey of the historiography and the methodological frameworks she developed and advocated, her publications, and the work of her research students. She describes Brereton as an "educator, commentator, historical analyst, methodologist and publisher", who played a strategic role in crafting a "space for women and gender" in our history. Matthews places emphasis on Brereton's support for the application and use of gendered testimonies. She elaborates on the methodology of using egodocuments or autobiographical writings as advocated by Brereton as a means of adding the insights and observations of women to our understanding of the past. Thus, diaries, journals, letters and similar documents by women assume added importance as bona fide historical sources. This is demonstrated through the contributions of the next two contributors, Rosemarijn Hoefte and Dane Morton Gittens, who have both been influenced by Brereton.

In "Egodocuments by Women as Sources for Caribbean History: Three Cases for Colonial Suriname", Hoefte, inspired by Brereton, supports the use of similar autobiographical writings and applies the methodology to three women from Suriname's upper class whose writings span from the mid-nineteenth century to the mid-twentieth century. Through these women, we have an insight into the mindset and prejudices of the upper class, but also share in their reflections on the middle classes; servants and the enslaved; white, black and mixed-race persons; cultural, political, social and religious life; as well as the environment, climate and topography. Dane Morton-Gittens' "Imperial First Lady of Trinidad – Lady Rachael Hamilton-Gordon, 1865–1870" also applies a similar approach and we see the same themes reflected in his work. However, his focus on one woman, a very active and influential governor's wife, reveals another level of insight. He shares details of her birth, upbringing, and life in Trinidad, providing insights into how she became the governor's wife, how she saw the role, how she functioned in the role, and how the household was run. Lady Hamilton-Gordon was blunt, judgemental and critical of locals, and demonstrated all the biases expected of her station and time. However, her writings also reveal much of the reality of the era through her relationships and, in some cases, the lack thereof. Some of the surprises include appearances by Charles Kinsley, who was a close friend of her husband, and the inclusion of several examples of her own paintings. Her paintings bring her writings to life and we see representations of the characters, animals, flora, fauna and landscapes in her accounts. Both Hoefte's and Morton-Gittens' work have recurring themes of loneliness, longing for home and a sense of loss. These are women whose lives were altered – some willingly, others unwillingly – as they were thrust into the Caribbean colonial officialdom because of husbands, fathers or mothers who could not perform expected roles. The narratives they share with us, despite the lack of representation and clear prejudices, add an important dimension to our history.

Readers may now ask: And what of the enslaved and black woman? Bernard Moitt engages with this issue in the French Antilles. He provides an overview of the history of slavery in the French Antilles and places attention on work dealing with enslaved women. He cites issues such as insularity and imbalance in geographic focus, and describes French historiography as being far behind the parallel history of the anglophone Caribbean. He elaborates, however, that the problem is also ideological and maintains that a block has been created which prevents scholars from dealing with what he describes as "the ugly past of the French Antillean colonies". He stresses that the damage caused must be repaired. He therefore weaves an assessment of the degree of inclusion of women into a general critique of the historiography of slavery. He concludes that the focus on gender is still in its infancy and explores the important work that has been done. He cites as hindrances the paucity of data and the ongoing reluctance of French scholars to tackle slavery head-on.

The Theme: "Engendering History: Social and Political Life in the Caribbean"[9] demonstrates how this can be done. This section provides four examples of how the historical dialogue changes when we focus on how women contributed to national developments. Gad Heuman looks at "Gender and Protest at Morant Bay in the Post-Emancipation Caribbean". He discusses what he calls the "gendered nature of freedom", placing emphasis on apprenticeship, post-emancipation upheavals in general, and specifically the well-known case of Morant Bay. He clearly shows that although denied even the avenues afforded to black and coloured men such as voting and serving on committees, black and coloured women found outlets through which they shaped their communities, and were a force in the riots and other forms of resistance that characterized the period. Rhoda Reddock takes our discussion into the early twentieth century and looks at the struggle for women to attain the franchise in "Inclusion/Exclusion: Women, Citizenship and Political Franchise in Early Twentieth Century Trinidad and Tobago". She looks at the struggle of women within the framework of that of other groups in society and positions it within the larger national context of demands for greater representation and self-government in a country with diverse groups. She also provides for differentiations in actions and motives influenced by class, colour, ethnicity, religion, national background and the various intersections that were so visible in a country like Trinidad and Tobago. As a result, Reddock looks at various dimensions of these women's activism and shows how they shaped, and were in turn shaped by, the national context.

Mary Chamberlin follows the contributions of women into the middle of the twentieth century in Barbados where she positions them as the majority of the population and the workforce. She examines the use of often overlooked and less visible aspects of their domain, such as family life and values, which, she contends, black and coloured women steered masterfully as vehicles for more opportunities and better lives. She describes their reach as "global, strategic and long-term". She brings these women and their contributions to life through oral testimonies which provide an added level of insight. Chamberlin contends that their contributions were just as much an important part of nation-building as more organized political entities and activities, such as those of the labour movement and other contemporary associations. These women, she maintains, built their nations using an "alternative model of citizenship" and were not limited by gender boundaries. Richard Goodridge carries our examination of women into the late twentieth century in the chapter "Ascent to Leadership: Women and the National Union of Public Workers of Barbados (NUPW), 1975–1995". He starts with a historiographical outline, with a focus on what he calls the "gender factor". In his framework, he uses the start of International Women's Year and Gladwyn King's election to the presidency of the NUPW in 1994 (the first woman to do so) as key markers. Her rapid rise to power is placed within the wider national context and measures to improve the status of women in Barbados. He weaves his story between public and private spaces, and intertwines international and national arenas. King's rise is positioned within a combination of developments which include advocacy by women as well as other occurrences that created a more conducive public space.

We can make the case that almost all the pieces in this collection deal fundamentally with the issues of race and ethnicity, particularly as the region transitioned from significant historical makers like emancipation and independence. Brereton's work in this core area has inspired the next group of contributions under the theme of "Race Relations in the Caribbean: Contested Narratives". Brereton describes *Race Relations in Colonial Trinidad*[10] and *A History of Modern Trinidad*[11] as her most influential works. The chapters in this section demonstrate the important role played by race, ethnicity and culture, and look at the new lives that were forged in the Caribbean in the post-emancipation and post-independence periods. The theme of contestation (captured in the title of another of Brereton's significant works),[12] also becomes apparent as these writers examine various manifestations of race relations in Caribbean societies. Gail Saunders is well known for her contributions to the history of the Bahamas. Another valued member of the Association of Caribbean History, she died in July 2023 while this volume was still being edited. She was another lifelong friend and colleague of Brereton and we are pleased that this volume contains one of her last written contributions to Caribbean history. Saunders looked at the cultural constructions of race and identity through an intriguing examination of "'Passing for White' in Bahamian Society during the Late Nineteenth and Early Twentieth Centuries". With an emphasis on Nassau, she introduces us to the complicated and complex issue of how coloured or mixed-race persons manoeuvred appearances, parentage and public records to be "white" in a society where race and colour were defining features. She explores how an "ambiguous colour line developed . . . which allowed mixed persons to be accepted in white society", showing how what she describes as "passing" was, in fact, managed by the society. She also factors into the discussion the impact of the Bahamas' close neighbour, the United States. Her exposition is interspersed with oral testimonies and family accounts that draw us into the lives of the people she discusses.

Marcia Burrowes then takes us to Barbados with "It Featured a Gymkhana? Conflicting Identities in the Early Years of the Modern Crop Over Festival". She examines the transition from the traditional to a modern Crop Over celebration in Barbados, capturing the nature of the cultural conflict which ensued. Once again, the issues of race and class make their appearance and are associated with the local festival. Burrowes intentionally uses the term gymkhana (a sporting event usually associated with the white upper classes) in her title with an intriguing question mark. Crop Over, a cultural tradition rooted in sugar and enslavement, which originated as an African-Barbadian masquerade in a colonial space, became a festival organized by the Board of Tourism in independent Barbados with a new mandate to attract tourists. Burrowes argues that this transition was muddled "in the ideological stranglehold of conflicting agendas and identities". She recounts the ways in which the festival was disconnected from its agrarian roots and black working-class participants, and how key events which reflected aspects of this grassroots festival were now associated with the white upper class. She describes the new evolving entity as an "invented tradition" and connects these developments to a challenge to the "old constructs of Barbadian identity with the new Independence era". Crop Over evolved with a renewed focus from 1974 to 1978. However, it took until 1978 for the festival to be finally (in Burrowes' words) democratized. The change process culminated in street carnivals and Kadooment Day. This triumph was achieved primarily through the continued questioning of the population. Thus, culture remained an important and impactful avenue for resistance long after emancipation and was a critical part of forging an identity in the newly independent Caribbean states, where race and colour continued to be major influences.

Fiona Ann Rajkumar applies Brereton's focus on contested narratives to her own research on a small group who attempted to gain mobility and acceptance in the modern Caribbean: the Syrian/Lebanese in Trinidad and Tobago. In "Contesting Narratives of Trinidad and Tobago's History", she approaches this group guided by the contributions of Brereton. She uses Brereton's insights into contesting historical narratives as a context for understanding the Syrian/Lebanese community. One of the issues Brereton grappled with was the numerous ethnic narratives that had to be combined to create a holistic history, particularly in Trinidad and Tobago. As Rajkumar interrogates the Syrian/Lebanese narrative, she refines the account through details unearthed by her own research. She thus factors issues, such as the role of ethnicity and the input of the state, into the narrative of the economic success of the group. In the social arena, she examines the group's views on marriage, endogamy and integration, and the way these social facets are downplayed in the narrative created. Instead, the group focused on nation-building, a strong sense of belonging to Trinidad and Tobago, and charity work in the community. We see yet another community, albeit a smaller one, striving to create its narrative among other groups and to position itself within the larger narrative of Trinidad and Tobago.

A book in honour of Brereton would not be complete without reflecting on the legacy she has gifted us. Several of the contributors have discussed aspects of her historical narration and her methodological approaches. Indeed, *History Matters*,[13] but we cannot forget the historian. We close with theme "History Matters: The Historian and Her Craft". The context for the discussions in this section is well set by Michael Toussaint in "Bridget Brereton and the Narratives of Modern Trinidad: An Assessment of Three Volumes". Toussaint analyses Brereton's contribution to the historiography of Trinidad and Tobago with emphasis on three books: *Race Relations in the Colonial Caribbean, A History of Modern Trinidad* and *Law, Justice and Empire: The Colonial Career of John Gorrie, 1829–1892*.[14] Brereton has described the first two as her most influential and expressed her pride about the third.[15] He starts the discussion with an overview of Trinidad's historiography before Brereton made her entrance. The many varied voices involved are briefly examined. He notes, however, that though many have articulated their version of our past ". . . few have attempted to give expression to varied voices via a democratic historicity, a less skewed historicizing. Brereton is one of them." He clearly demonstrates elements of what he calls "Breretonism". If one was to attempt to create a dictionary definition of the meaning, it would read like this, "The ability to ventilate the voices of numerous historical groups and capture varying historical circumstances while weaving these contested narratives and events into one historical narrative". Of this, Brereton was the master. As Toussaint noted, no ethnic group nor any economic, political or social dimension is placed in a preeminent position in the narratives she creates. She specializes in not just illuminating the sources of contestation, but also counterbalancing them. Toussaint paints the picture of a graceful operator commandeering a battlefield laden with various historical narratives, buttressed by academic rigour and skill. Her rigour involved the use of a wide range of sources with well-thought-out methodologies. He positions her as part of a new generation of career historians who were grounded in the newly independent Caribbean region. Toussaint also notes areas like Tobago and theoretical exposition, where he felt that more could have been done. However, this in no way detracts from the value of Brereton's historical contribution. It is insignificant when one considers the complex narratives and issues that were not even ventilated, which she brought to light in her own distinctive style. His chapter clearly establishes why her body of work is so important to Trinidad and Tobago's as well as the region's historiography.

The volume closes with John Aarons' "Called to Action: Caribbean Historians and the Preservation of Primary Sources for the History of the Region". He launches this discussion by looking at Brereton's role in promoting the value and importance of archival materials. Her contributions to the preservation of historical records and her leadership role in our libraries and archives are highlighted for the part her service played in safeguarding documents for historians and social scientists. He notes that this advocacy was part of the University of the West Indies' informal mandate and focus from its very beginning, which contributed in no small way to the development of regional archives. However, he cautions that much more needs to be done and issues a warning with regard to the preservation of the documents of our post-independence societies. He points to the need for organized record management programmes, and appropriate archival facilities and policies. Aarons maintains that historians of the region, like Brereton, did their work for the pre-emancipation period. However, the contestation has not ended. Aarons closes the volume with a call for our current generation of historians to follow Brereton's example and advocate for record management policies, legislation and facilities to ensure the preservation of archival material. After all, this material is the very basis of Brereton's path-breaking contributions to our national and regional history. Aarons' contribution demonstrates that as our societies continue to grapple with development issues, contestation will continue and take on new forms.

Thus, we end as we started. We have come full circle. Guided by Brereton's work, we have used history to examine, illuminate and analyse important topics and markers as the Caribbean region moved from emancipation to independence; and ended with the challenges that remain with us in the twenty-first century. This book has been long in the making, with many starts and stops. We can only hope that we have done justice to Brereton and her contributions to our history. This volume may be even more important because it comes at a time when history and its ability to embolden, uplift and transform our people in these contested spaces is not keenly appreciated. Aarons' call to action can be widened to all of us who have been a part of Brereton's legacy to secure a new space for history in the fast-paced and constantly changing world of today.

We thank all our contributors and extend our deepest respect and appreciation for their support. The commitment to this publication reflects their understanding of how important it was to join in the celebration of Bridget Brereton and her work. We also thank the Faculty of Humanities and Education where the idea originated with a conference that captured the nature of Brereton's contribution in the title "Reassembling the Fragments". Thanks also to our students who worked as research assistants and never hesitated to make their own contributions as we worked on creating a narrative that would adequately honour the work of Brereton and would ultimately show that, as she put it, "History matters". To that, we would like to add, "The historian also matters."

NOTES

1. Carl Campbell, "Who is Bridget Brereton?" *Journal of Caribbean History* 48, nos. 1&2 (2014): 21.
2. Ibid., 24.
3. Bridget Brereton, *Manning Faith and Vision* (Port of Spain: The Leadership Firm, 2024).
4. Campbell, "Bridget Brereton," 33.
5. Bridget Brereton and Kelvin Yelvington (eds.), *The Colonial Caribbean in Transition: Essays on the Post Emancipation Social and Cultural History* (Kingston: UWI Press, 1999).
6. It is with deep regret that we inform readers that Professor Pedro Welch died when this publication was in press.
7. Bridget Brereton, *Law, Justice and Empire: The Colonial Career of John Gorrie 1829–1892* (Kingston: UWI Press, 1997).
8. Verene Shepherd, Bridget Brereton and Barbara Bailey (eds.), *Engendering History: Caribbean Women in Historical Perspective* (London: Palgrave Macmillan, 1995).

9. Bridget Brereton, *Social Life in the Caribbean 1838–1938* (Jamaica: Hodder Education, 1985).
10. Bridget Brereton, *Race Relations in Colonial Trinidad, 1870–1900* (Cambridge: Cambridge University Press, 1979).
11. Bridget Brereton, *A History of Modern Trinidad, 1783–1962* (Kingston: Heinemann, 1981).
12. Bridget Brereton, "Contesting the Past: Narratives of Trinidad and Tobago's History", *New West India Guide,* vol 81. Nos. 3&4 (2007): 169–96.
13. Bridget Brereton, *History Matters: Selected Newspaper Columns 2011–2021* (Trinidad and Tobago: Paria Publishing, 2022).
14. Brereton, "Law, Justice and Empire."
15. Patricia Mohammed, "Bridget Brereton: A Life in History," *Journal of Caribbean History* 48, nos. 1&2 (2014): 50.

[*Part One*]

THE COLONIAL CARIBBEAN IN TRANSITION

[1]

"LITTLE ENGLAND" VS "GREAT BRITAIN"
Barbados Slavers in the Emancipation Debate

[HILARY McD. BECKLES]

AT THE END OF THE EIGHTEENTH CENTURY, WHEN an organized anti-slavery force sank deep and sustainable roots into the affairs of the British parliament, West Indian slavers took cover in their ideological bunkers and prepared for political war. Barbados slavers emerged as the most aggressive and seemed most ready for discursive combat. They targeted William Wilberforce, leader of the anti-slavery campaign in the House of Commons, and justified their anger on the basis that he had launched the first missile against them. He intended, they said, to use Barbados as the subject of his career advancement, and they were his principal political adversaries.[1]

While Caribbean slavers read and understood Wilberforce's anti-slavery sentiments and agenda in general terms, the Barbadians defined him as their enemy and proceeded on the basis of a personal antipathy that became bitter and acrimonious. These aspects of their political exchange defined the first phase of anti-slavery parliamentary politics in Britain and Barbados. In so doing, they textured national and colonial ideological identity and served to shape Atlantic politics in an age of revolution and industrialism.

Jamaican slavers, in the Caribbean context, had captured the majority share of the British sugar market. In London, and beyond, they were recognized in financial terms as the top-tier absentee grandees. The Barbadians, however, considered themselves elders in the slaving business and claimed a pedigree as the pure and true aristocracy of the imperial slaveocracy. They were more endowed with official imperial titles than all other slavers. While they had less capital and chattels than the Jamaicans, their older money and manners marked them apart as the standard bearers of the Caribbean slaver consciousness and culture.

From the outset, in the mid-seventeenth century, the Barbados slavers were closer to imperial political power and took great pride in their ability to leverage these connections. They invested more time and money in acquiring prestigious official titles and sought to support and sustain social status with an empowering metropolitan education. This distinguishing asset was put into the political field in full service in the defence of slavery. In the metropole, knighthoods and peerages, academic degrees and professional offices were marshalled as a formidable social and political force.

As 'ancient' slavers the Barbadians came to believe the imperial state owed them special respect for what they had done to make Britain truly great. The empire, they said, had begun its winning ways with them. They were the men and women who had taken a small frontier island and converted it into the wealthiest economic zone of the seventeenth-century world economy. The protection of their slave-based wealth stimulated the need to sustain the nation's global naval and military supremacy. They alone, their supporters argued, first occupied pride of place as the primary creators of real wealth; they alone owned and occupied the first grand investment heartland of the imperial body.

In colonies and metropoles, these first mass enslavers of Africans projected themselves as core carriers of the corporate and cultural constructs that were the slave-based economy and society. When, at the end of the eighteenth century, the idea infiltrated the English parliament that slavery was incongruous with Englishness, and contrary to civilized consciousness, the shock to their sensibility sent shivers down their sugar plantations' spines. The pain was particularly penetrative on the old sugar estates that were established as more than business units but cultural centres. The Bridgetown Assembly felt betrayed; its members could not imagine a future in which Britain did not hold close to its bosom the business of black enslavement. The slave colony, and its hitherto nurturing 'mother', had reached a crossroads when Wilberforce declared at the end of the 1780s that his sojourn in parliament would be a tirade against the injustice of slavery. Barbados was identified as the bastion to be breached. The once-celebrated centre of imperial investors was defined as the vile embodiment of criminal enrichment and a moral abomination.

These political turns, noted David Lambert, were "particularly acute in the case of Barbados because its white colonists had long seen and portrayed themselves as the Empire's most loyal subjects – as evident in the self-description of the island as 'Little England', which gained currency in this period". While Jamaica was "the largest and economically most important of Britain's West Indian possessions", he concluded, the "original and quintessential British sugar colony was Barbados".[2] It was no empty boast that led to the self-ascription "Little England". It was a convergence of characteristics that generated an image, complex and nuanced, which, once articulated in speech and print, resonated with visitors to the colonies and residents alike. Its geography was said to conjure visions of the rolling downs of the southern counties, while its status as the most densely populated of all colonies reflected an English reality.

With the institutionally developed political system of parliamentary practices and procedures monopolized by holders of substantial property, the general cultural tendency towards social mimicry seemed complete. The temperate climate, they intimated, added to the mix, and with its "great houses" scattered across the landscape like castles among the cane, the slavers had constructed a concept that their Caribbean home was the most "civilized isle". It was, indeed, their "Little England". They had grown proud of their political legacy, which featured an early military encounter with England. The exchange of hostile words over trade law and policy led to war in 1651/52 as a declaration of political sovereignty. Demanding free trade in sugar and enslaved Africans as the basis of wealth creation, they stood up to the Protector, forcing him to deploy hundreds of his finest troops to beat them into submission. For over a century, they celebrated that moment in which they drew swords upon imperial troops. Behind it all was the perception and belief that they were English citizens with rights, and seasoned in the tradition of self-defence. In anticipation of the political battles ahead, they imagined no reason to be intimidated.

As a political elite grounded in a tradition of ideology, combat slavers allowed no one to criticize their slave society without an acerbic response. All critics, domestic and imperial, were dealt with according to the circumstances. By 1800, they were motivated with pen and podium to defend their world, especially against persons they defined as political hypocrites and born-again pretenders to moral purity. They had dealt coldly with Steele's "softer" slavery policy and were now ready to run hot against advocates of black freedom.

They were prepared to concede in 1806 that the trade in enchained African bodies was a dispensable element of their ideal world. This was entirely self-serving. By 1800, their plantations were self-sustaining in regards to enslaved labour. They were the only Caribbean slavers experiencing a boom in births and a drastic decline in the rate of deaths, producing a positive growth performance within the enslaved community. The uniqueness of this development was used as an economic tool against their trade competitors and as a political weapon against abolitionists. They defined themselves as perfect slavers, separate and apart from their Caribbean cohort.

It was impossible for them to contemplate the ending of slavery and the promotion of universal black freedom as the basis of a social order. Neither could they comprehend the idea that slavery was holding back the moral, social and economic advancement of British civilization. Slavery, they insisted, had nothing to do with the political image of the new desire of the state to project itself as a monument to human freedom and liberty. At the heart of their objection was the political attempt of abolitionists to cast their slave plantations in an unpatriotic light; places where darkness was managed by mean-spirited white men and women with money to the detriment of the nation's enlightenment. As their society was cited in the City as the model of misery, sensitivities in Bridgetown were inflamed in proportion. It was an unbearable burden for them to hear their world set apart as the symbol of the sin standing in the way of the nation's quest to be its best.

In this regard, the slavers' persistent description of their island home as Little England attracted cynicism, sarcasm and, sometimes, ridicule. Anti-slavery critics called for their political and cultural rejection as distant descendants to be shunned, shown no privileges, and directed to the back door. Objection in London to the Little England concept grew in intensity, forcing slavers to be determined in defence or retreat in defeat. Not surprisingly, they stood their ground; an attitude endemic to their fighting spirit and expressive of belief in the superiority and rightness of their thinking.[3] Some parliamentarians whose fortunes were slave generated now wanted no public linkages with the slave society. Barbados slavers were aware of the politics of disassociation and consolidated themselves as the hardcore. They believed that it was up to them, the old guard, to defend the order and to hold the feet of the "old country" to the fire.

With the ending of the slave trade, House of Commons critics and their publicly mobilized supporters turned their attention to slavery, particularly the mentality of its managers. The Barbados slavers, they asserted, were the monsters whose atrocities could no longer be ignored. "Little Englanders" took offence, and went to war with words against Great Britain. It was a battle over the fate and future of enslaved blacks in which both sides appealed to the public gallery. None was prepared to emerge a loser. The imperial state demanded radical reforms to the slave society, and ultimately its abandonment. The slavers defended the sustainability of their society and took strong objection to imperial allegations that they were sinners and criminals. The parliamentary passion for interfering in their domestic affairs, without invitation, they said, was an act of hostility. The offence, they insisted, was especially "exacerbated" because they had for two hundred years defined themselves in terms of their loyalty to king and country.[4]

The Little Englanders genuinely believed, like their southern US counterparts, that they had built a slave-based civilization worthy of worldwide respect and admiration. It was worth the spilling of blood – black, brown, and even white – in its defence. The slave society was not just an economic arrangement that facilitated wealth creation. It was an idyllic incarnation, a home honed by bonds of emotional alliances that could be placed favourably alongside any other society. Furthermore, they saw themselves as more than just slavers. They were legacy holders of ancient English innovators who deserved respect and gratitude as standard bearers within the imperial realm. Critics of their society, they concluded, were therefore deluded, ill-informed, and filled with jealousy on account of their success as social craftsmen and entrepreneurs.

The colony, however, became an easy target of the anti-slavery campaign. Slave laws were seen as brutish and implementation brutish; far from British, the critics insisted. Slavers in turn, and their agents in London, reacted "excitedly" to each attack. "What was at stake," they believed, "were their cultural status, political rights, and white identity."[5] The society they prepared to defend was based on the conversion of the human being into a legally recognized unit of property. The freehold ownership of the black body fashioned the financial and fiscal system into an economic unit. They deemed the enslaved Africans uncivilized and trapped in darkness, and now this description was being applied to them by abolitionists. England had been the trailblazer in describing and defining slavery as the key to successful economic modernity. Britain's Barbados, originally the path to national prosperity, was now branded the pariah of the empire. Slavers could not accept the popular desire for detachment from this colonial identity.[6]

The battle over slavery, then, was more than a conflict regarding the exercise of property rights held by slavers in black bodies. The imperial state – long the slavers' principal protector, and itself a major investor in the enterprise of enslavement – was shaping a new conception of Britishness. It involved meaningful mitigation of the enslaved experience, radical reform of the old slave governance laws, and the eventual elimination of all social relations that entailed property rights in humans. The first, tentative steps the state took to achieve these ends produced a rabid reaction of self-preservation among slavers from the Indies, led intellectually by the Little Englanders. It evolved into a vicious, abusive and mutually degrading political discourse. Slavers threatened, vilified and condemned the abolitionists, and described their parliamentary and public partners as political hypocrites.

In the decade after the illegalization of the transatlantic slave trade, Barbados slavers, more than others, expressed outrage at parliament's imposition of the Registry Act. This provided that they be required to prepare annual reports on the number of their enslaved persons, with full demographic details such as age, occupation, gender, place of birth and ethnicity. By this measure, the state meant to satisfy itself that efforts were being made by slavers to encourage slave breeding by means of their better treatment. The act was intended to place the burden of proof upon slavers to illustrate that there were no illegal imports and transfers of enslaved persons between colonies subsequent to the abolition of the transatlantic slave trade. The law was passed by parliament in 1814 and colonies were given a short time to report. Wilberforce, as policy leader, argued successfully that this measure was intended to protect the enslaved and to hold the slavers accountable for their use of them.

More than any other group of Caribbean slavers, the Little Englanders went on the warpath in opposition to the Registry Act, and mobilized the colonial community against its provision by publicly illustrating that it was the state's prelude to general emancipation legislation. The second half of 1815 was taken up in a political campaign, grounded in the Assembly, and let loose in the local media. They criticized what, in their opinion, was an abuse of power by the imperial state and chastised it for harbouring a clandestine plan to destroy their social order. The campaign was an intensely bitter attack focused upon the state in general, and abolitionists in particular. The tone and texture of the language in Bridgetown were considered "un-British" in London. It engendered responses that confirmed the notion that slavers believed themselves answerable to no authority with respect to their abuse of enslaved Africans.

While this crusade was moving into high gear, the enslaved population was having its own meetings in preparation to make an impactful discursive contribution. Their intervention came on 14 April 1816. It took the form of an island-wide rebellion to secure their freedom by military might, and to end the rule of slavers. Self-liberation had been achieved in Haiti in the prior decade. "General" Bussa, their leader, sought to emulate the thinking and strategies of Toussaint L'Ouverture, the Liberator. The "War of General Bussa", as it was subsequently called, became the 'text' used by Barbados slavers to demonstrate that Britain's abolitionists were guilty of mobilizing the enslaved to destroy their rule. They quickly prepared an official report into the rebellion in which the thesis of abolitionists' responsibility was laid out in stark detail. The accusation against anti-slavery elements in the parliament was printed upon every page. The blood spilt in the cane fields, the slavers insisted, was the prime responsibility of Wilberforce and his wilful, spiteful interlopers. The enslaved, they argued, were inspired by the abolitionists' reckless speeches in parliament; more than a thousand of the rebels had lost their lives. It was a massive capital loss, slavers concluded, and insisted upon property compensation from the British state.

Wilberforce, slavers argued, had planted agents and spies in the colony, who informed rebel leaders that the process leading to their legal freedom was obstructed by slavers, and that it was up to them to exert violent pressure from their end. The Registry Bill debate in 1815 – more so than the rebellion the following year – revealed their paranoia about the future. Anger and hatred permeated political postures. They spoke of British betrayal. It was the theme that identified their rage in the age of abolition. Wilberforce bravely withstood the battering from Bridgetown. He drew a line in the sand and announced his campaign to see, somewhere in the near future, an end to slavery.

Founded in 1807, the abolitionist African Institute had among its patrons George Canning, William Wilberforce, Thomas Clarkson and Zachary Macaulay. Alarmed by evidence of the illegal exportation of enslaved persons from Barbados to other colonies after 1808, it called for the total registration of the enslaved in each colony. Noting that their numbers in neighbouring Trinidad had increased by forty-four hundred between 1810 and 1813, Barbados was branded the illegal exporter. Wilberforce presented his bill in the Commons in June 1815.[7] The debate was opened in the Barbados Assembly by John Beckles, the Speaker of the House, on 14 November 1815. Predictably, Wilberforce was identified as an ardent enemy of their interest who possessed a special disrespect for them. In its official report on the rebellion, the Assembly described the event as a "convulsion" that originated:

> solely and entirely in consequence of the intelligence imparted to the slaves (which intelligence was obtained from the English Newspapers), that their freedom had been granted them in England . . . ; that these reports first took their rise immediately after the information of the proposed establishment of Registries in the British Settlements in the West Indies . . . and in the mistaken idea that the Registry Bill was actually their Manumission . . .; these hopes were strengthened and kept alive by the promises held out, that a party in England, and particularly Mr. Wilberforce . . . were exerting themselves to meliorate their condition, and ultimately affect their emancipation.[8]

An anonymous slaver, referring to Wilberforce and other members of the African Institute as a "dangerous crew", published a letter in the *Bridgetown Gazette and Barbados Mercury*, stating that they "have pierced the inmost recesses of our island, inflicting deep and deadly wounds in the minds of the black population, and engendered the Hydra, Rebellion, which had well-nigh deluged our fields with blood".[9]

The Times, holding the pro-slavery line in London, suggested that the rebellion was due primarily to the "impolite" and thoughtless interference of Wilberforce in the political business of the Caribbean slavers, those in Barbados in particular. Furthermore, it suggested:

the principal instigators of this insurrection, who are negroes of the worst dispositions, but superior understanding, and some of whom can read and write, availed themselves of this parliamentary interference, and the public anxiety it occasioned, to instil into the minds of the slaves generally, a belief that they were already freed by the King and Parliament...[10]

Further evidence of Wilberforce's commitment to the dismantling of the slave society could be seen, according to the Assembly, in his association with the cause and interest of King Henry of Haiti. This specifically enraged the slavers, particularly speaker Beckles. During the House debate, he stated: "I must confess that I was one of the many who at one time had the highest opinion of Mr. Wilberforce, and gave him the highest credit for the purity of his motives and intentions, but that is past."[11] Beckles denounced Wilberforce as a wicked man with no regard for the welfare of the oppressed sugar planter. He was driven by religious zeal, Beckles said, which was unmitigated and suspect in its moral intention.

Wilberforce was no patriot, the slavers argued. He had crossed the line and declared his support for blacks over whites. Beckles was distraught that Wilberforce had chaired a meeting at Free Mason Hall in London in early 1817 and had raised a toast to the health of "King Henry of Haiti". This, Beckles charged, was proof of Wilberforce's commitment to the proliferation of black republics in the Caribbean.[12] He asked the Assembly:

> Is it not astonishing that, in the very heart of London, in so public a meeting, any man, and especially a man holding a place under Government, should have been permitted, with impunity, to declare that King Henry of Hayti was one of the most august sovereigns in the universe, and derived his title from a more legitimate source than the monarchs of Europe, having been raised to the throne from the abject condition of a slave ... and to predict that he was the glorious founder of a new dynasty, which would in no distant time subvert the relations of the western world...?[13]

The enslaved community was informed – though not always accurately – about the content of Wilberforce's speeches and anti-slavery postures. Like their enslavers, they linked allegations of his support for Haitian freedom with their own circumstance. The local press carried a summary of the situation in Haiti which was available to the enslaved community. The report stated: "It now seems beyond all doubt that ... St Domingo [Haiti] ... that ill-fated country ... has again become the theatre of massacre and bloodshed, and the last remnants of French power almost completely overthrown."[14]

Wilberforce responded to these charges, first in parliament, and then in a letter to Babington, on 7 June 1816. Each time he spoke about ending the slave trade, he said, the Barbados slavers would respond: ". . . it is emancipation you mean; to make our slaves free; . . . . all the time denying it. At length, wonderful that not before – the slaves themselves begin to believe it, and to take measures for securing the privilege; in short, the artillery they had loaded so high against us, burst among themselves, and they impute to us the loading and pointing of it."[15]

On receiving the content of Beckles' speech, he wrote to Stephen: "The Speaker of the House of Assembly at Barbados has made a very scurrilous speech and says he now considers us very dangerous men." The Speaker, he said, was doing his best to ignore the fact that only in Barbados did the enslaved take to arms within the context of the registration legislation.[16]

The significance of Wilberforce's statement was that it served to locate slavers in Barbados centrally in the leadership of the pro-slavery campaign. Simultaneously, it repositioned the local chattels in the vanguard of anti-slavery warfare. While slavers blamed Wilberforce for creating the political opportunity for the anti-slavery revolution, abolitionists in turn suggested that Barbados slavers were the worst villains of slavery, who hid behind a fortress of hate that had to be stormed and levelled to the ground. Barbados, concluded Lambert, had assumed in British politics an "alleged status as an aberrant slave world".[17]

The brutality of Barbados slavers' reprisals in the aftermath of rebellion was used by abolitionists to illustrate the unsustainability of slavery and the disgrace it brought to emerging liberal Englishness as a global identity. Colonel Codd, who led the imperial troops against the rebels, was embarrassed by the viciousness of the slavers' militia after combat had ceased. He felt compelled to disassociate his troops from their ravages. Women and children, he said, against whom there was no evidence of guilt, were cruelly put to death. He informed the British government that "under the irritation of the moment and exasperated at the atrocity of the insurgents some of the militia of the parishes in Insurrection were induced to use their arms rather too indiscriminately in pursuit of the fugitives".[18] It was an understatement by the colonel. Hundreds of enslaved persons were randomly rounded up and massacred by the militia for simply being in their path. Codd prevailed upon the governor to put an end to the killing and to send into exile those in prison scheduled for execution. Abolitionists seized the opportunity to show that Barbados slavers had revealed themselves as a disgrace to decency. Everywhere in the empire, the colony was the source of conversations about the future of slavery. The model of stability, long imposed by means of violent militarization, was now deemed a costly failure.

The slavers struck back. Far from being management failures, they said, their members were moral, social and political leaders, representing an ancient community, but driven to self-defence by an ungrateful and uncaring imperial government. Colonel Rycroft Best of the Christ Church parish militia, broke ranks with his fellow slavers on the "blame Wilberforce" theme and suggested that the enslaved saw an opportunity to take control of their lives and the island, and used it to the best of their ability. The rebels were politically astute, Best said, and as slavers, he and his colleagues had every right to defend themselves in the heat of the battle for ownership of the colony. The blacks, he said, wanted to end white rule and create another black republic. In a subsequent revision of his position, he launched an attack on the imperial state for providing the blacks with the opportunity: "Such has been the abuse that the party in England has tried to vilify the white inhabitants with, that we should not be surprised to hear this rebellion justified by the Puritans, and we (the Barbadian) accus'd as being monsters for putting to death those whom we found with arms in their hands, those caught in the act of plundering and destroying, and those tried since and convicted of being Ring Leaders."[19]

The recalcitrant Little Englanders, then, had inadvertently ushered in the first stage of the anti-slavery campaign in British politics by moving the pendulum away from the discourse over the slave trade to slavery itself. They succeeded in dragging all Caribbean slavers deeper into the dialogue in an attempt to locate the cause of their own black rebellion within the bosom of the British parliament.

They dug in, and, oblivious of the wider Caribbean concerns, seemed obsessed with placing the match that lit the flame in Wilberforce's hand. The colony, its defendants of slavery in parliament said, was being treated like a "conquered foreign colony", rather than the first site of English pride on the hostile Caribbean frontier. They were not accorded the "well known rights and privileges of British subjects". The killing of their enslaved insurrectionists for disloyalty to their owners and empire should be seen, they argued, as a patriotic duty, and not condemned as a criminal act.[20] Wilberforce and many other parliamentarians were disgusted by this reasoning and sought to distance their conception of Englishness from that of slavers. They rejected the slavers' premise that Africans were non-humans and mere chattel, and called for legal action against them for the assertion that the mopping-up massacre was no more than a commercial loss. Wilberforce washed his hands, as an Englishman, and a parliamentarian, of the "blood that was spilt" in the cane field. The carnage, he insisted, had but one source – the "well known and celebrated intemperance of the colonists themselves".[21]

The casting of Barbados slavers as the evil enemy within the empire, and an embarrassment to Englishness, was the strategy used to great effect by the anti-slavery movement. In no other colony, said an abolitionist paper, does "slavery exist in a more unmitigated form than in the island of Barbados". These slavers, the author argued, have no right to claim an English identity. Their vengeful mass killings of blacks were without cause or good reason. Their conduct, said the paper, discredited their claim to the status of Englishmen.[22] It continued: "A thousand human lives, it seems – some accounts say two thousand – have been lost by this calamity, in the field, or by summary military execution; how justly, may perhaps hereafter appear; how merciful, the Barbadian militia can best tell. It is not so that insurrections are suppressed in England; and yet these are our fellow – subjects."[23]

Furthermore, the paper continued, it was proof of their possession of a cruel mentality, the signature of savages rather than citizens of a sophisticated state. Slavers could not comprehend this commentary. Any language in which blacks were recognized as humans, with a right to life, had been outside their governance philosophy and management rules for two centuries. In the Assembly, for example, they spoke about the British-inspired rebellion that led to the loss of nearly four hundred of the colony's "finest slaves". This political articulation went directly to the financial bottom line of the plantations. This was the logic and law upon which they had built and operated the slave economy and society.[24]

Five years on, and with Wilberforce's health waning, Thomas Buxton assumed the parliamentary leadership of the anti-slavery movement. Unlike Wilberforce, Buxton relished the battle with Barbados slavers.

He knew that in the aftermath of the Bussa Rebellion, their long-held influence within parliament had diminished considerably. It was evident, for example, that many of their Caribbean colleagues considered them excessively bullish and politically tactless. As a skilful public debater, he considered the use of irony and sarcasm effective techniques to puncture their postures. He "mocked aspects of the Barbados as Little England discourse", and proclaimed them a disgrace to civilized society. He concluded that their instinct to bask in brutality against blacks had to end if the colony was to be saved.[25]

The Little England vs Great Britain conflict was read on both sides of the Atlantic as Barbados vs Buxton. The latter won the argument in 1823 in favour of "freedom in due course", and led the campaign for general acceptance of a gradual emancipation approach. The Africans, he said, should first be converted to Christianity as an urgent reform, and prepared to embrace Christ before the path to emancipation came to an end. Missionaries, he said, should be sent out to prepare the way, and to carry out the task of African conversion that the Anglican clergy had hitherto rejected.

In 1824, Methodist missionaries entered the colony. It was at once dramatic and catastrophic. Slavers objected to their anti-slavery sermons, destroyed their church, and drove out their lead preacher. Tearing down the church that spoke to salvation for black souls made free and equal in the eyes of God was for them a simple matter. It was the clearest sign that as slavers they feared "burning in hell" less than freeing the enslaved. Speaker of the Assembly, Cheeseman Moe, told his colleagues that the presence of anti-slavery priests in their society was the result of the "diabolical falsehoods" emanating from Britain. Missionaries and abolitionists, he said, did not respect the colonial way of life and wished it gone in a "gulph of destruction". But not only did slavers tear down a "church of Christ", they burnt the goodly reverend in effigy and threatened all who endorsed his views with similar treatment.[26]

Church demolition by "the most faithful subjects" in the "ancient and loyal colony" served to cast Little England in a negative light within Great Britain. It appeared a hellish place where demons were unleashed without let or hindrance. The slavers' defenders called upon the king to acknowledge that of all his West Indian colonies, Barbados was the "most ancient and most loyal". As such, it was worthy of protection from the fanaticism of puritans within his parliament.[27] Buxton was not alone in expressing his outrage at the display of arrogance and ignorance by Barbados slavers. William Smith, a Methodist sympathizer, stated that they had wounded the "honour of this country", and the healing required remorse from the rogues. He described them, furthermore, in contrast to other Caribbean slavers, as a special breed: "There had always existed, on the part of the inhabitants of that island, the most inordinate and ridiculous ideas of their own importance. They seemed, in this instance to be clearly on the same level with the poor simple Welchman, who exclaimed, when he was about to leave the city of Bristol, "Alas! What will become of thee, poor Bristol, when I am gone?"[28]

Smith captured the general parliamentary sentiments while Buxton burnt a trail through their defences. The destruction of the church, Buxton said, emanated from the same mentality that was unwilling to accept any criticism of their slave society. Smith encouraged the abolitionists to stand up against the Barbados slavers:

> They should be taught, that however valuable to a few individuals may be the Estates they possess there, to the Empire of Great Britain, as a national possession, their island is but a toy, which, if destroyed, would in a very short time, be scarcely missed and ere long be quite forgotten: and that, instead of being one of the props of this country, as has been boasted, her conduct tended only to tease the too-forbearing Government of the Mother Country, and to bring the colonies into contempt.[29]

These slavers, he concurred with Buxton, had become an "ungovernable embarrassment" to Britain.[30]

The political crisis that followed was not simply the result of poor political leadership by the Barbados slavers. For two centuries they had been aided and abetted by the British state and civil society, and had received the full support of the established Church of England – itself a major slave owner in the colony. The intensity of the public backlash, then, was a bitter pill the slavers could not swallow, especially as it was administered by persons in politics who had benefitted one way or another from the bounty of slavery. The slavers' inability to read the changing political mood of the metropole was linked to their status as ideological owners of the black bondage brand. Attachment to slavery, Barbados slavers would admit if pushed, was not as deep with other Caribbean slavers. As pioneers, they were prepared to adopt the posture of going down with the sinking ship they had built and sailed best. Efforts were made by a moderate minority within their ranks to mediate with abolitionists, but the core of their consciousness remained adamant and obstinate. In London, and Bridgetown, diplomatic efforts were made to repair their public image, but abolitionists gave them no space to spin the evidence of their recalcitrance. Damaged irreparably, they continued with efforts to discredit the source of their pain in parliament. Blinded by their racism against Africans, their critics were deemed enemies, and treated as such.

Buxton, too, was burnt in effigy in Bridgetown. Slavers could not grasp the idea that the grip over their chattel could be loosened. "At the heart of the matter, of course," concluded Lambert, "was race" – an unyielding belief that their racial superiority was "natural" and "God ordained".[31] Ownership of the slave society brand was driving them into full confrontation with British domestic politics. The unshaken belief that as the "mother of all West India colonies" they were entitled to special treatment, shaped their final years as slavers. The West India Committee that represented them in London was now dominated by Jamaicans, and increasingly by the Guiana newcomers, such as John Gladstone. But the Little Englanders were not concerned with either numbers or relative wealth. They were the project leaders – the ones possessed of the most passion to preserve the "well constituted society".

The clash over Buxton's 1825 proposal to effect emancipation, even though with compensation for slavers, ramped up the war of words. The "most sustained criticism" of the proposed compensation methodology, and the general idea of emancipation, came from John Pollard Mayers, the bullish agent for Barbados slavers in London, and himself a substantial slaver. In London's political circles, Mayers was known for his assertive lobbying style that was generally direct and determined. Lambert described him as "one of the most active of all the West Indian agents" and "a source of information for Barbados' slaveholders and their first line of defense". He offered a spirited rejection of Buxton's thinking in specific terms, and in the process sought to foreground Barbados as entitled to a special compensation package. The colony, he said, should be addressed separate and apart from other colonies, on account of its unique historic role in the development of the slave society.[32]

Mayers' mantra was that Barbados had a greater equity in slavery than all others. They were, he said, the first to successfully breed an internal enslaved labour supply, thereby facilitating the abolition of the transatlantic slave trade. For this achievement alone and compliance with imperial policy, he argued, they should be given a special bonus in the form of a gratuity for good slavery governance. Slave-breeding success, Mayers showed, was reflected in the colony having the greatest concentration of locally born Africans. This demographic, he said, was the primary cause of their "stock" having a lower market value than colonies like Trinidad and Guiana, which were filled with African imports. These newer colonies had grown, Mayers noted, by using Barbados as a nursery for their plantations in the same way that Jamaica had benefitted in the seventeenth century. As a consequence, he proposed that these colonies "should pay a bounty to Barbados instead of receiving extra compensation".[33]

The British decision to pay compensation for the enslaved on an ad valorem basis, instead of a per capita distribution, suppressed the relative worth of the Barbados chattels. The colony had the highest density of enslaved people, which served to suppress the average unit value of the enslaved "stock" to £47; Guiana, the least densely populated colony by contrast, had an average unit value of £115. The ad valorem approach, Mayers told the British government, was unacceptable to Barbados as it was not equitable and would operate as a "bonus to those proprietors whose over production, the consequence of the severe working of the slaves, have been justly reprobated".[34] Barbados slavers, Mayers insisted, had developed a system of "kind and humane treatment", which resulted in an increased "number of their slaves and lessened their imports". They "ought to be benefitted instead of fined by such conduct". It was a battle he could not win, largely because the British state was in no mood to reward recalcitrant, boastful Barbadians. If anything, the political inclination in the country and parliament on the matter of financial compensation was their punishment for persistently embarrassing the national sensibility.[35]

Mayers instructed his clients back home, nonetheless, not to accept any official compensation policy until the government recanted in respect of a special package. Meanwhile, he trounced the treasury officials with statistics designed to illustrate and win his case. He insisted, for example, that since fifty-two hundred slave owners lived in Barbados, and 73 per cent owned enslaved persons but no land, landless slavers would be disenfranchised relative to other colonies. Government rejected his plea and posited instead that, of all the colonies in the Caribbean, Barbados was most secure, with an adequate labour force and best positioned, therefore, to manage emancipation and envision a viable, free labour economy. The Barbados Assembly followed Mayers' lead and demanded a differential compensation package. Locked into daily conflict with Barbados slavers, treasury staff spoke of the tiring nature of dealing with them, and the frustration of their not accepting the principle that all colonies had to be treated equally within the context of an applied scientific methodology. Parliament made political appeals to the office of the resident governor in Bridgetown. His response confirmed what was already known in London: that "a Barbadian [slaver] can never be brought to understand that there is any other Colony of half the value and consequence to the Mother Country that this is." Furthermore, he noted, "they would never accept in spirit the 'proposed basis for apportionment', largely because of wounded pride in being lumped together with lesser, even if 'bigger', colonies."[36]

Fairness and justice, Mayers insisted, and not further injury, was what he was insisting upon. When reports circulated in London about detailed alleged atrocities committed by Jamaican slavers during the suppression of the 1831 Sam Sharpe-led rebellion, Mayers stated candidly that they were "probably as truthful as I have heard".[37] His willingness to throw fellow Jamaican slavers to the political wolves suggests the depth of his feeling that Barbados, the mother of all slave colonies, was not getting the "deserved special treatment" in the winding-down exercise. He was adamant. "I have never allowed myself to be absent," he said, "from the shortest interval, under an apprehension that the interest of Barbados might suffer from the cupidity of those who advocate the interest of some of the neighboring colonies."[38]

Guiana and Trinidad served as salvation for some Barbados slavers, who saw in them an opportunity to expand plantation operations. In the compensation discussion, they, too, became targets. Slavers relocating to these newer colonies were allowed to take with them enslaved domestics, but not field workers. In 1828, James Stephen, who headed the slave registration process for the government, reported that: "There appear very strong grounds for suspecting that the great comparative value of slaves in Trinidad has tempted many persons to make fraudulent importations from Barbados, by attributing the character of domestics to slaves whom it was never intended really to employ in that capacity."[39] Data from Trinidad for 1827 shows that of the 266 enslaved persons imported from Barbados under licence, 204 were no longer in the employ of the persons in whose name the licence was issued. Another group of eighty-one were doing jobs that fell outside the category of "domestic".[40]

In addition, evidence reaching the Colonial Office in London indicated that Barbados slavers were deliberate in undermining official policy, subverting the gradual movement to emancipation, and seeking to profit further from the exploitation of defenceless Africans. Tensions in parliament rose as the evidence of their non-compliance mounted. Stephens believed that a case should be made against them. And, as if by intention, Franklin, a Barbados slaver, was arrested and charged in 1829 for a breach of the law.[41] The Franklin case gained notoriety throughout the empire because it symbolized Barbadian slavers' views concerning the use of imperial legislation to control and limit the intercolonial transfer of the enslaved. Franklin was described in the records as a modest Barbados slave owner. He had received various licences in order to ship fourteen of his chattels to Trinidad. They were to travel with his family. Mostly children, they were not put to domestic work. Franklin was adjudged to have violated the law, an offence for which he was imprisoned.

The trial by grand jury in Bridgetown predictably led to Franklin's acquittal. His peers took the view that a slave owner should not be presumed a criminal for altering the nature of his chattel's occupation. Empowered by the verdict, Franklin secured substantial funding to bring a suit against the magistrate who had signed the documents under whose terms he was sent to prison. Significant sections of the slaver community, many lawyers included, rallied to his aid in seeking damages to the value of £5,000 (colonial currency) for false imprisonment.[42] News of the case reached neighbouring colonies and was widely reported in the press. Franklin was described by the Barbados governor as a "man of straw" backed by men of substance whose interest it was to create a "system of intimidation" and "embarrass the Government" in order to compromise and repress the "efforts of public officials . . . in the prosecution of offenders". The Colonial Office understood all too well that Franklin was an instrument of vested interests and that the struggle "had really been waged with the Officers of Customs rather than with him".[43]

The battle, though, was much wider in scope. The field of contest was the very future of British slavery in the Caribbean. Imperial interests were still in a celebratory mode with respect to the acquisition of Guiana and Trinidad. Barbados slavers were anxious to take the lead and breathe life into the "new Eden". The frontier had obvious economic attractions. The collusion of imperial and colonial interests in this regard seemed sufficiently compelling to allow the market to determine the outcome. Abolitionists, however, had other ideas. They saw the potential in these colonies for a grand revival of investment interest in Caribbean slavery. They used the practice of intercolonial transfer of the enslaved to test the durability and depth of their support in the legislature. They won the debate and broke the Barbados resolve.

On 28 August 1833, the British parliament brushed aside as a public nuisance the persistent objections of Barbados slavers, and passed the Emancipation Law – "An Act for the Abolition of slavery throughout the British Colonies, for promoting the industry of the manumitted slaves, and for compensating the persons hitherto entitled to the services of such slaves". The act, however, was designed to secure and sustain the socio-economic dominance of the slavers, rather than liberate the enslaved. The sum of £20 million, plus the payment of interest as of 1 August 1834, was granted slavers by way of financial compensation for the loss of their human property. The 82,207 enslaved persons in Barbados, valued at an average of £47 in 1834, meant that slavers were entitled to receive £3,897,276, or 8.6 per cent of the total grant. A total of 5,349 claims were made for compensation by 1838. They held out to the end and were the last of the major slave societies to legislate black freedom in their assembly. By the time they had done so, £15 million of compensation funds had already been distributed. In the end, unlike other British Caribbean slavers, they received their payments in stock and not the cash they had preferred. They received the money with "ill grace".[44]

As political rulers, Barbados slavers never embraced the idea of black freedom and used their power – military, social and economic – to preserve as many elements of slavery as possible. In every sphere of social relations, they confronted the blacks, whom they said had been emancipated without their support. The blacks fought back; they resisted in every way they could. The depth of black resentment to persistent slaver racism was summed up in the report of a magistrate who noted that black mothers "threatened to poison their offspring in preference" to allowing them to work for their former enslavers.[45] Acrimony characterized the Buxton-Barbados war over the future of enslaved blacks. The slavers did not win the war to retain slavery, but they won critical battles that were to determine the nature of the future. The most important victory was the securing of financial compensation. This achievement placed Buxton on the defensive and positioned slavers to emerge positive about future possibilities.

By 1830 the "central economic issue of emancipation" as far as the British state was concerned was not "whether owners of slaves should be compensated", but "who should bear the costs of such compensation".[46] When the Emancipation Act was finally passed, it was determined that the enslaved and British taxpayers should pay the cost of freedom. The slavers would receive compensation in cash as "fair and just" reparation, and the enslaved would pay their share in the form of further free labour.[47] Parliament's position as specified in the act was that the enslaved should pay at least 50 per cent of the cost of achieving their freedom. Despite Buxton's description of this fiscal policy as immoral, the state proceeded to claim a major victory. Buxton remained unrelenting that the act in this regard was an ethical disgrace and a shame upon the nation. It was, he said, a betrayal of the long-suffering enslaved community in the West Indies, and a furtherance of the criminality of slavery.[48]

Sir Lionel Smith had arrived as governor of Barbados in 1833. His first assessment of the colony was that slavers were satisfied with the financial aspects of the package. He later told Lord Stanley at the Foreign Office that while the compensation was sufficient, slavers wanted more than money; they desired permanent social control over the blacks rather than the specified period of additional free labour. Slavery, he suggested, was preferred by the slavers for social and cultural reasons as much as for financial and economic benefits. In summary, he said, slavers would not accept the emancipation of blacks. The compensation package would win their political compliance, but their hearts were hardened against black freedom.[49] It was unnecessary to destroy a perfectly "beautiful" society, the Barbados slavers insisted. An attempt to punish the imperial state and its abolitionists for the audacity of emancipation would be their final ploy and posture. They meant to drain the British treasury and use the cash to rebuild a free world in slavery's image. They maintained in the coming decade the rhetorical language that their blacks were not human. Buxton's call for emancipation in 1823 presented the state with an opportunity to confront this racial and moral issue. Instead, the slavers' point of view was endorsed and embraced by parliament.[50]

Cash payment for the emancipation process eventually originated from two sources, says Fogel and Engerman; the enslaved, and the state acting on behalf of the public in the national interest. The framing of the act to allocate costs required astute actions by parliament. In effect, the political engineering to end slavery required the mobilization of the same set of racist ideologies used in its construction. Investors sought the power of the state to back their business interests; the state flexed its muscles as an investor and custodian of national wealth; and the taxpaying public was invited to recognize and enjoy the benefits.[51]

In both the construction and destruction of the slave society, the voices of the enslaved were not formally recognized. Politicians unilaterally determined that the enslaved would pay a dear price for the demise of slavery. "How could a class, as impoverished as slaves," asked Fogel and Engerman "be made to shoulder the heavy burden of compensation?" Slavers who "participated in the political councils during slavery times" saw this policy as "eminently practical".[52] When Buxton's motion to abolish slavery was laid in the House of Commons in 1823, slavers who were members were stirred to their full pro-slavery potential. Forty of them declared that they were supporters of the slave society; these were men of considerable political influence in London and the provinces. The biggest slavers in the House, such as the Marquis of Chandos, the Earl of Harewood, the Marquis of Sligo, and the Duke of Cleveland, possessed considerable political clout and intimate Cabinet connections – especially in George Canning's Foreign Ministry. They effectively corralled the state against Buxton and mobilized its power to support their camp.

The state reacted predictably. In 1831, it established a select committee to examine the slavers' compensation claim. It was a subtle strategy designed to settle the slavers' right to reparations and to create an atmosphere for an emancipation act that would secure broad political support. There was no way an act of emancipation could be passed without the slavers' endorsement, given their power and influence. They demanded three conditions for a yes vote: (1) adequate compensation for loss of property rights in the enslaved; (2) a system that allowed them further coerced access to enslaved labour; and (3) continuation of the much-maligned protective tariffs on West Indian exports to Britain.

On 10 May 1831, Stanley rose to the occasion with the first version of his plan to extract the costs of emancipation from the enslaved. He called it the "Apprenticeship". It was a crude creation in which the enslaved would work, once freed, without wages, for their enslavers for a period of twelve years. This extra time would enable the enslaved to pay their enslavers in labour for the emancipation they had received.[53] This financial strategy was sold politically to the general public as a governance instrument in the transition to freedom. It was intended, Stanley said, to serve the mutual interests of the enslaved and their enslaver. The system, he added, is "intended . . . to teach the ex-slaves industrious habits, to prepare them for their eventual freedom, and to introduce them to the system of wage labour". But the truth was, Butler has shown, that it was a deceitful way of "forcing the slaves to pay for their liberty".[54]

Buxton's advocacy of "emancipation without compensation to slavers" lost him the debate; he was pushed to the fringe of policy formulation. The slavers won, and they wanted more. A Barbados newspaper argued that the value of the eight hundred thousand enslaved in the British Caribbean was £47 million and that the slavers would be short by £27 million, given the proposed £20 million grant from the government. The acceptance of this calculation by the state was the primary cause of its decision to extract the remaining £27 million from the enslaved population.[55] Slaver Thomas Hendy, well-known in Barbados as a politically pragmatic man, argued that the full £47 million was needed to secure the future of their "beautiful society". Without the £27 million balance, he suggested, slavers would be reduced to a life of "misery and contempt", and left to "curse the day of their birth".[56] Hendy and fellow slavers lived up to their reputation as descendants of the first and most fiscally aggressive of Britain's enslavers. They were the last to sign on to the £20 million compensation package, even though it was intended to enrich and empower them. Butler's conclusion that they received the deal with "ill grace" spoke to their unrelenting social and cultural attachment to the slave society.[57]

Mayers, their indefatigable agent in London, represented them admirably. He had placed a value on their enslaved blacks at £3,897,276. They were allocated the sum of £1,721,345 by the state. This was based on an estimated average price of £47 for their 82,807 human chattels.

Inflated calculations were the order of the day as price inflation was used by slavers to extract the maximum compensation. Of the 83,149 enslaved listed for the colony, 14,732 were classified as children under the age of six, and 1,780 were "aged, diseased, or non-effective". Distrust meant that the state would make its own calculation, which resulted in widely different payment expectations.[58] Despite efforts not to be fleeced by the slavers, state officials were super generous to a degree that suggested complicity and self-rewarding. The national debt was an enormous £800 million. The £20 million represented 40 per cent of gross national expenditure for the year. The enslaved were to pay the balance – the £27 million slavers considered due to them. The state's agreement to pay £20 million represented less than 50 per cent of the total value. Apprenticeship was conceived and designed as a politically deceptive instrument to extract this sum from the enslaved population.[59]

The enslaved would pay the £27 million in free labour. In effect, noted Fogel and Engerman, the British emancipation model was designed with the "overarching" feature that "slaves were made to bear the lion's share of the direct financial cost of their freedom". This fact alone, they concluded, "helps to explain why so many of the affected slave holders eventually acquiesced in gradual emancipation", since the "burden was, for the most part, shifted to the slaves themselves".[60] British politicians intended that the enslaved would bear the greater financial brunt of the legislative intervention. The act was "designed to relieve" the state and taxpayers.

The costs that the enslaved would bear for their freedom were discernible in the calculations made by Stanley. Using the original Stanley plan of a twelve-year apprenticeship, the state transferred 71 per cent of the cost to the enslaved. The adjusted six-year period eventually agreed upon together, with extensions of working hours, ensured that they paid just about 50 per cent of the cost.[61] The decision to free all enslaved children under the age of six years, and those born during the period, shifted the cost of child-rearing from the slaver to the enslaved. All persons over the age of six were expected to work for sixty hours; forty-five of which were attributed to slavers. During this period, "Slave owners earned exactly the same average net revenue per slave that they would have earned in the absence of apprenticeship." This assumption meant that the slavers recovered "47% of the original value of the slave population" from the enslaved during apprenticeship.[62]

The British state, then, had achieved its objective. The cost of freedom would be shared almost equally between the state (British taxpayers) and the enslaved people. Fogel and Engerman stated that the government made payments to slavers of £16.7 million in 1836 and £4.1 million in 1837. Taking into account the discounted present value of the cash grant for 1834, "Compensation paid to slaveowners by the British taxpayers accounted for 49% of the estimated actual value of their slaves." "West Indian slave owners received a total of 96% of the value of their enslaved as compensation, with the enslaved themselves 'contribution' close to half of the payment."[63]

Draper accepts, in a general way, the conclusions of Fogel and Engerman, but uses a lower discounted rate for the period. He concluded that the four to six years of apprenticeship "in which at least 45 hours per week unpaid labor" was given to slavers, represented a considerable transfer of value from the enslaved to the enslaver. The £20 million, he noted, was "worth 44% of the estimated value of all the enslaved people of £45 million", and the "apprenticeship was worth a further 33–49% of the value of the enslaved people". His conclusion, then, was that "The enslaved paid a higher proportion than the slave owners, and almost as high a proportion as the British people."[64] Throughout the emancipation discourse, Draper concludes, Barbados slavers were "strikingly obdurate". "You can argue," he noted, "that it shows Barbados was less reconciled to emancipation than any other colony", suggesting "the relative attractiveness of a continuation of slavery to slave owners in Barbados". His conclusion serves to support Governor Smith's assertion that the colony's slavers were as intoxicated with their racial power over blacks as they were overstimulated by the desire to make the British state pay "through its teeth" for daring to dismantle their "perfectly constituted society".[65]

The state proceeded to describe its emancipation legislation as a moral victory, using concepts such as "enlightenment". But the facts show that it had imposed upon the enslaved the harshest conditions of freedom imaginable. The alliance between the state and slavers showed the depth and intensity of the understanding that had created the slave society two hundred years prior. The relationship was "special" in the 1640s, and had matured into a hardened racial antipathy towards Africans. It remained "special" in 1834, despite the rhetoric of conflict. Parliament skilfully engineered the ending of the old slave society. The new order was consistent with the mentalities of slavers and the state. The latter had been the slavers' patron and partner from the beginning and was expected to be loyal to the end. The state honoured its obligation to slavers and imposed upon the enslaved the punitive emancipation they politically and legally desired. These developments were anticipated by the enslaved, as expressed in their comments during the 1816 rebellion. They knew that the state would deal them a harsh hand, and they were not wrong in this regard. When the act finally came, it carried within its language and procedures all the racial and financially oppressive features mirrored in the mentality of the Barbados slavers. They were the first to pass comprehensive slave laws in 1661, and the last to pass into law the act in April 1834.

NOTES

1. Robert I. Wilberforce and Samuel Wilberforce, *The Life of William Wilberforce* (London: John Murray, 1838), vol. 4: 306.
2. David Lambert, *White Creole Culture: Politics and Identity during the Age of Abolition* (Cambridge: Cambridge University Press, 2005), 2–4. Anon., "Remarks on the insurrection in Barbados, and the bill for the Registration of Slaves" (Lon.) 1816; Anon., "Spirit of West Indian Society – Outrage in Barbados," *Edinburgh Review*, August 1825, 479–99.
3. Lambert, *White Creole*, 13; see also R. Gott, "Little Englanders," in *Patriotism: Making and Unmaking of British National Identity*, ed. R. Samuel (London: Routledge, 1989).
4. Lambert, *White Creole*, 15; see also S.H. Carrington, "West Indian Opposition to British Policy: Barbados Politics, 1774–1782," *Journal of Caribbean History* 17 (1982).
5. Lambert, *White Creole*, 35; see also Claude Levy, "Slavery and the Emancipation Movement in Barbados, 1650–1833," *Journal of Negro History* 55 (1970); C.L. Brown, "Empire with Slaves: British Concepts of Emancipation in the Age of the American Revolution," *William and Murray Quarterly* 56 (1999).
6. Lambert, *White Creole*, 40.
7. G.W. Jordon, *An Examination of the Principles of the Slave Registry Bill* (London: Cadell and Davies, 1816), 10–14.
8. *The Report from a Select Committee of the House of Assembly . . . into the*

Origins, Cause, and Progress of the Late Insurrection, April 1816 (Bridgetown: House of Assembly, 1819), 10, 12.
9. *Bridgetown Gazette and Barbados Mercury* (BGBM), 7 September 1816.
10. ibid., 5 June 1816.
11. Minutes of the Barbados Assembly, 7 January 1817.
12. ibid.
13. ibid; See also *Report from a Select Committee*, 5–15.
14. Wilberforce and Wilberforce, *Life of William*, 306; *Bridgetown Gazette*, 9 April 1805; CO 28/72, f. 91 PRO.
15. Wilberforce and Wilberforce, *Life of William*, 287.
16. ibid., 305.
17. Lambert, *White Creole*, 112.
18. Colonel Codd to Gov. Leith, 25 April 1816; CO 28/85, ff. 12, 14.
19. John Rycroft Best to Abel Dottin, 27 April 1816, Barbados Papers, New York Public Library; See also Lambert, *White Creole*, 112.
20. Lambert, *White Creole*, 115.
21. ibid.
22. ibid., 117.
23. Anonymous, *Remarks on the Insurrection in Barbados, and the Bill for the Registration of Slaves* (London: Ellerton, 1816), 8.
24. See *Report from a Select Committee*, 4.
25. Lambert, *White Creole*, 167.
26. See *Report of a Debate in Council*; Also, Minutes of the Assembly, 23 Sept. 1823, CO 31/49, ff. 128–30; J. Nelson, "An Appeal of the Wesleyan Methodists of this Island to the Public," cited in Lambert, 153; J. Barrow, "A Declaration of Inhabitants of Barbados, respecting the demolition of the Methodists Chapel" (Bridgetown, 1826, Methodist Missionary Society); *An authentic report of the debate in the House of Commons, 23 June 1825, on Mr Buxton's motion relative to the demolition of the Methodist Chapel . . .* (London: J. Hatchard, 1825); "Riot in Barbados, and destruction of the Wesleyan Chapel and mission House" (London, c.1824); J.V. Shrewsbury, *Memorials of The Rev. William J. Shrewsbury* (London, 1868); W.J. Shrewsbury, *Sermons Preached on several occasions in the island of Barbados* (London: Hamilton, Adams, and Company, 1869 edit.).
27. See G.W. Jordan, *An Examination of the Principles of the Late Slave Registry Bill and the Means of Emancipation* (London: T. Cadell and W. Davies), 13–15; Lambert, *White Creole*, 163.
28. *An Authentic Report of the Debate in the House of Commons, June 23rd 1825 on Mr. Buxton's motion relative to the demolition of the Methodist Chapel and Mission House in Barbados, and the Expulsion of Mr. Shrewsbury, a Wesleyan*

Missionary from that Island (London: J. Hatchard and Sons, 1825), 42; K. Lewis, *The Moravian Mission in Barbados, 1816–1886* (Frankfurt: Peter Lang, 1985); N.F. Titus, *The Development of Methodism in Barbados, 1823–1883* (Berne: Peter Lang, 1994).

29. *Authentic Report*, 66.
30. Lambert, *White Creole*, 168.
31. ibid., 173.
32. Lambert, *White Creole*, 177; Kathleen Mary Butler, *The Economics of Emancipation; Jamaica and Barbados, 1823–1843* (Chapel Hill: University of North Carolina Press, 1995), 28.
33. Butler, *Economics of Emancipation*, 29.
34. ibid.
35. ibid.
36. ibid., 30.
37. Lambert, *White Creole*, 185.
38. ibid., 184, 186.
39. Hilary McD. Beckles, "An Unfeeling Traffic; The Inter-Colonial Movement of Slaves in the British Caribbean, 1807–1833," in *The Chattel Principle: Internal Slave Trades in the Americas*, ed. Walter Johnson (New Haven, CT: Yale University Press, 2004), 270.
40. ibid.
41. Documents in relation to the Case: Correspondence of Attorney General, CO 28/103 PRO.
42. Stephen to Twiss, 10 March 1830; CO 28/105. PRO.
43. Lyon to Murray, 28 Sept. 1830; CO 28/105. PRO; Lyon to Soderich, 3 April 1831, CO 28/107, PRO; See also, Hilary McD. Beckles, "Emancipation by Law or War? Wilberforce and the 1816 Barbados Slave Rebellion," in *Abolition and Its Aftermath, 1790–1916*, ed. David Richardson (London: Frank Cass, 1985), 80–105.
44. Butler, *Economics of Emancipation*, 23.
45. Claude Levy, *Emancipation Sugar and Federalism: Barbados and the West Indies, 1833–1876* (Gainesville: University of Florida Press, 1980), 45. Chapter 19.
46. Robert William Fogel and Stanley L. Engerman, "Philanthropy at Bargain Prices: Notes on the Economics of Gradual Emancipation," *Journal of Legal Studies* 3, no. 2 (1974): 377–401; Stanley Engerman, "Some Considerations Relating to the Property Rights in Man," *Journal of Economic History* 33 (1973): 113–50: N. Draper, *The Price of Emancipation: Slave Ownership, Compensation, and British Society at the End of Slavery* (Cambridge: Cambridge University Press, 1980); Parliamentary Papers, 1837–38, 215,

XLVIII; Accounts of Slave Compensation Claims, Records Created and Inherited by HM Treasury, Office of Registry of Colonial Slavery and Slave Compensation Commission Records.

47. Fogel and Engerman, "Philanthropy," 377; R.E.P. Wastell, "The History of Slave Compensation, 1838–1845" (Master's thesis, University of London, 1932); Julian Hoppit, "Compulsion, Compensation, and Property Rights in Britain, 1688–1938," *Past and Present* 201 (2011): 93–128.
48. Bruce Taylor, "Emancipation in Barbados, 1830–1850" (PhD diss., Fordham University, 1975).
49. Butler, *Economics of Emancipation*, 24; Smith to Stanley, 13 July 1833 and 29 July 1833, CO 28/111; W.A. Green, "James Stephen and British West India Policy, 1844–1847," *Caribbean Studies* 13–14 (1974): 33–56.
50. Butler, *Economics of Emancipation*, 7, 21; *Parliamentary Debates*, 2nd Series, vol. 9 (1823): 274–75; 282–86; Committee of Correspondence, 13 March 1833, CO. 318/117.
51. Fogel and Engerman, "Philanthropy," 377–78; Glen Phillips, "The Changing Role of the Merchant Class in the British West Indies, 1834–1867" (PhD diss., Howard University, 1976); J.M. McPherson, "Was West Indian Emancipation a Success," *Caribbean Studies* (1964): 28–34.
52. Fogel and Engerman, "Philanthropy," 378; Claude Levy, "Barbados: The Years of Slavery, 1823–1833," *Journal of Negro History* 44 (1959): 308–45.
53. Butler, *Economics of Emancipation*, 19; Goderich to West India Body, 4 Feb. 1833, CO 318/116; *The Times*, 11 May 1833; *Parliamentary Debates* vol. 17 (1833): 1194, 1230.
54. Butler, *Economics of Emancipation*, 20; Committee of Correspondence, CO 318/117, 13 March 1833; Annual Register, 30 May 1833; Petition to the House of Commons from the West India Planters and Merchants, 18 May 1833.
55. Butler, *Economics of Emancipation*, 20, 22; Annual Register, 30 May 1833; *Parliamentary Debates* vol. 19 (1833): 1063–67.
56. Butler, *Economics of Emancipation*, 23; See also, "A Fair and Equitable Consideration: The Distribution of Slave Compensation in Jamaica and Barbados," *Journal of Caribbean History* 22, nos. 1–2 (1988): 138–52.
57. Butler, *Economics of Emancipation*, 23; *Barbados Globe and Colonial Advocate*, 20 Nov. 1834; Hendy to Stanley, 15 July 1833, CO 28/112.
58. Butler, *Economics of Emancipation*, 28; *St Jago de la Vega Gazette*, Jamaica, 13–20 July 1833.
59. Butler, *Economics of Emancipation*, 35; Barry W. Higman, "The West India 'Interest' in Parliament, 1807–1833," *Historical Studies* 13, no. 49 (1967): 1–19.

60. Fogel and Engerman, "Philanthropy," 379; Edmund Sturge, *West India Compensation to the Owners of Slaves: Its History and Results* (Gloucester: John Bellows, 1893).
61. Fogel and Engerman, "Philanthropy," 383–84; Augustus Beaumont, *Compensation to Slave Owners Fairly Considered* (London: Effingham Wilson, 1826); Nicholas Draper, "The Rise of a New Planter Class? Some Countercurrents from British Guiana and Trinidad, 1807–1833," *Atlantic Studies* 9, no. 1 (2012): 65–83.
62. Fogel and Engerman, "Philanthropy," 384, 394.
63. Fogel and Engerman, "Philanthropy," 396; Rt. Hon. Wilmot Horton, "First Letter to the Freeholders of the County of York: Being an Enquiry into the Claims of the West Indians for Equitable Compensation" (London: Edmund Lloyd, 1830).
64. Nicholas Draper, "Compensation for Barbados Slaveowners", 29th Elsa Goveia Memorial Lecture, Cave Hill Campus, UWI, 16 Oct. 2013; see also, "Slave Ownership and the British Country House: The Records of the Slave Compensation Commission as Evidence," in *Slavery and the British Country House,* ed. Madge Dresser and Andrew Hann (Swindon: English Heritage, 2013), 1–11.
65. Draper, "Compensation for Barbados."

[2]

NO "GENTLE GLIDE" FROM ENSLAVEMENT TO EMANCIPATION
The Post-Emancipation Labour Struggles in Tobago, 1838–1919

[RITA PEMBERTON]

TOBAGO'S LIMITED PRESENCE IN ACCOUNTS OF MAJOR EVENTS in the general historiography of the Caribbean has resulted in publications that have not positioned important aspects of the island's history to accurately reflect its historical experience. Until the 2008 publication of Susan Craig James' two volumes,[1] popular knowledge of the history of Tobago was limited to the European contest for possession, the 1770s uprising of enslaved Africans, the state of the sugar industry, and its union and relationship with Trinidad. These accounts have also been treated either as individual developments or from a ruling class perspective, without establishing their important linkages. The resulting narrative has presented the island as a bastion of peaceful relations between workers and plantation owners, with few noteworthy incidents and a population with a limited inclination to resist. Except for a few cursory statements, Tobago does not feature in works on Caribbean labour struggles, giving credence to the view that in peaceful Tobago there was a seamless transition from enslavement to emancipation. The notion of a placid Tobago, which fits its present tourist imagery, is historically inaccurate and was generated by the earlier writers, officials and current historians. This study presents the history of Tobago from the perspective of the freed Africans to give visibility to their struggles against ruling class control, and positions them in the narrative of Caribbean labour history. It identifies a trajectory of resistance on the island from 1838 to 1919, revealing the long struggle of Tobago's workers before an organized trade union movement emerged.

This chapter aims to show that there was no "gentle glide" from enslavement to freedom in Tobago and seeks to "counteract the emphasis on planter power . . . and make it easier to recover the struggles of working people",[2] who have not been accorded the importance they deserve. It illustrates the persistent struggle in which the freed Africans of Tobago were engaged in the effort to liberate themselves from the servile yoke that their employers sought to maintain. Through an examination of their liberation strategies, the chapter also seeks to expose the peculiar resistance culture that was developed in response to their longstanding grievances.

A brief background history of the island which establishes the context for the ensuing discussion of the various forms of resistance is followed by an examination of the literature which generates the idyllic perception of Tobago. Developments in Tobago are placed in the wider Caribbean context, with a short outline of the literature on the celebration of Emancipation Day in other Caribbean territories. This is followed by a discussion of the challenges presented in the historiography of labour regarding the question: What is to be considered resistance when there were varied manifestations of defiance from freed Africans, who refused to accept the conditions of enslavement? This study uses primary and secondary sources, but the report of the Tobago Metairie Commission of 1891[3] is particularly valuable because it provides strong evidence of planter views of workers. Up to this point, it is the only available source that gives voice to the *metayers* of Tobago, whose role in the resistance struggle should not be underestimated.

The Tobago resistance struggles, which extended from 1838 into the twentieth century, are reflected in the unrest that occurred in all the labour systems that were practised during that time. This study concludes that there was no peaceful transition from enslavement to freedom, and that the image of a peaceful island is a misrepresentation of reality. Furthermore, the island's labour struggles constitute the genesis of the organized labour movement in Tobago and form an important chapter in the island's history.

HISTORICAL BACKGROUND

The First Peoples were in undisputed occupation of Tobago until the European invasion. Archaeologists suggest that the First Peoples population migrated from Trinidad to Tobago, which was home to the Kali'nas and other First Peoples communities. Tobago functioned as a halfway station between the Windward Islands and the coastal Guianas, and was an important link in the trade between the island Caribs of the Lesser Antilles and their allies, the Kalin'as of the coastal zone of Guyana and Venezuela, and an intermediate between the South American mainland and the Lesser Antilles.[4] With support from their allies in Dominica and St Vincent, the First Peoples of Tobago strongly resisted European incursions, causing their colonizing efforts to be unsuccessful for over a century. Throughout the sixteenth century, Spanish interest in Tobago was expressed through slave-raiding expeditions sent to capture members of the First Peoples community for labour in other colonies.[5]

Beginning with the Spanish in 1614, Europeans made several unsuccessful attempts to settle Tobago during the seventeenth century. These included the Dutch (1628–1677), the English (1637–1646), the Courlanders (1639–1693), and the French from 1687, when Tobago endured a history of uncertainty as the centre of a fierce European contest and a series of short-lived European possessors, which made establishing a consensus on its ownership impossible. After the 1688 destruction of the last Courlander settlement, none existed in Tobago, although all the interested parties continued to claim ownership. The inability to establish consensus on its ownership resulted in Tobago being accorded neutral island status between 1748 and 1763.[6] During this period the indigenous population received a slight boost from reoccupation by various groups, including the Chaima and Pariagoto peoples from Cumana and the Paria peninsula, who escaped from the Capuchin mission villages on the mainland, and island Caribs from St Vincent who faced increasing conflicts with the "black" Caribs.[7]

After a series of internecine conflicts among Europeans, particularly between the British and the French, the former were formally declared owners of Tobago in 1763. They immediately sought to establish permanent possession with the development of plantations. Between 1765 and 1781, Tobago was made into a sugar plantation colony and enslaved African workers were introduced. The French retook Tobago between 1781 and 1793 when further uncertainty reigned because new laws and taxes were imposed and some British owners, who refused to swear loyalty to the French king, were dispossessed of their properties. When the island reverted to Britain in 1793, confusion about property ownership involved lengthy matters in the French courts. Eight years later, the island was again in French possession; after one year it was retaken by the British and remained a British possession until the 1962 independence in the unified colony, Trinidad and Tobago.

The island's plantation owners enjoyed a brief period of prosperity during the 1790s when there was a surge in prices and demand for sugar. Continued conflict between Britain and France and the long-term impact of the War of American Independence led to the destruction of estates, and the disruption of plantation operations and trade on the island. Under British rule in the nineteenth century, the operation of Tobago's slave system was influenced by three metropolitan movements which sought to end the slave trade; provide religious instruction for the conversion and control of the "heathen" Africans; and finally terminate enslavement. By the beginning of the nineteenth century, the Tobago sugar industry was in decline. Estates changed hands as owners sought to cut their losses. Some planters argued to be allowed to continue to import Africans to obtain a "satisfactory" supply of labour, to no avail. Planters lamented their "shortage of labour" and despite several unsuccessful attempts, they continued to articulate for immigration to keep wages low. Planter/worker tensions increased because more demands were made on the labourers while planters used their control of the island's administrative system to obstruct the development of independent workers.

The impediments included the imposition of heavy taxation on the workers' homes, deliberately hiked prices on land sold to Africans and illegal sales of land by persons without title. In addition, the freed Africans who had no voice remained under planter influence because the legislative, judicial and administrative arms of government remained planter-controlled, the cost of justice was prohibitive, and the franchise was restricted to property owners. These were classic measures used by the planters in collaboration with the island's administration to crush the ambitions of independent workers.

The island's plantation economy continued to decline across the century.

Reduced profits and increased costs of production caused plantation owners to cut their losses, but finding buyers was difficult and some abandoned their properties. The number of abandoned estates escalated after the 1846 Sugar Duties Act and the hurricane of 1847. The antiquated industry continued to produce poor quality sugar, which attracted the lowest prices on the market. Planters tried to resolve their problems through efforts to reduce their labour costs and force workers to accept low wages and poor working conditions. After attempts to introduce immigration schemes failed, recourse was made to the system of *metayage* which, from 1842, spread across the island despite the conflicts it generated. The post-emancipation years were characterized by conflict and resentment among African workers, who used confrontational and non-confrontational resistance strategies against planter domination and control.

The demise of the sugar industry which followed the 1884 crash of Gillespie and Company[8] loosened the tight hand of planter control over the island's land resources. The resulting sale of small plots led to the establishment of a landed Tobago peasantry at the beginning of the twentieth century. Relations between planters and workers on those estates that remained operational during the first half of the twentieth century did not change and this, in addition to the general dissatisfaction on the island, resulted in an eruption of workers in 1919.

THE IMAGE OF TOBAGO IN THE LITERATURE

One of the first comprehensive pieces of literature on the island was *History of Tobago* (1971), written by Henry Isles Woodcock,[9] who served as the island's chief justice from 1862 to 1867. Both as a foundation author and contemporary to a part of the post-emancipation era, Woodcock's work was widely influential on subsequent writers. While he provides details of the island's historical experiences, his conclusions are not always based on a balanced assessment of the facts. This is demonstrated regarding enslavement and emancipation in Tobago when he states: "The day was set apart as one of religious observance and peace and quiet prevailed ... evidence of the influence of religion on the minds of the peasantry, also supplying gratifying testimony in defence of the planter."[10]

And further: "The many acts of kindness which had passed between the planter and his slave, which the apprenticed labourer had not altogether forgotten to appreciate and which were recalled to the memory of the freeman, served to unite the different classes of our society in their new relations..."[11]

He suggests that good relations between masters and enslaved workers in Tobago governed their relationship during the period of apprenticeship and contributed to "... the circumstances which attended the change in August 1838". He further claimed that "under the influence of improved feelings, which had been working their silent way for many years the hand of the master had inclined the plane which safely led from slavery to freedom."[12]

Woodcock paints a picture of a smooth transition from enslavement to emancipation in Tobago, which was due to masters' kindness and good relations which unified planters and freed Africans. To stress this argument Woodcock continues: "If the slave had been the depressed creature which some would have represented him to have been, he would not, in all probability, have so gently glided from one state to the other. Indeed, many of the immunities which freedom conferred were enjoyed long before 1st August 1834."[13]

Thus, according to Woodcock, the foundation for a "gentle glide" from enslavement to freedom lay in the benign nature of enslavement on the island and the consequent good relations between planters and enslaved workers. This assessment was not based on the numerous cases of pre-emancipation resistance, those that occurred during apprenticeship, or those that erupted during the period of his tenure on the island.

Woodcock was heavily dependent on the journal of Sir William Young, whom he considers "as giving a faithful picture of the country at the time he writes".[14] Young, governor of Tobago from 1807 to 1815, owned Betsy's Hope in Tobago, Old Road in Antigua and two estates in St Vincent, which were inherited from his father. Young was an MP in the British parliament, and in 1792 he served as the agent for Tobago planters to settle their property disputes with France.[15] He was opposed to abolition and to derail Wilberforce's campaign he advocated that planters encourage missionary activity and projected the enslaved Africans as happy and contented people to eliminate the need for abolition.[16] He viewed abolition as a sacrifice of "a considerable portion of British commerce and an ultimate surrender of the British colonies" that was a dangerous step that would bring misery to both the enslaved and their masters.[17] Young was careful to advertise the good relations he had with his enslaved workers upon whom he bestowed many gifts. Unsurprisingly, he presented a rosy view of enslavement on the island. However, continued resistance by the freed Africans from 1838 belies this assertion. In his diaries, Young also provides evidence of the difficult working conditions and brutalities endured by enslaved workers in Tobago and details of their revolts on the nascent plantations in the 1770s, which did not influence Woodcock's conclusions.

After emancipation, Tobago planters adopted a combative stance against the freed African workers with a two-pronged approach. The first prong articulated a labour shortage on the island based on the claim that the workers were benefitting from the existing systems and were competitors who deprived planters of labour, rather than functioning as the labourers they were expected to be. This argument supported the second prong of convincing the authorities to support their requests for immigration, which ultimately failed. However, the notion of the happy workers of Tobago became firmly stamped in the official record and was reflected in the sentiments expressed by members of the planter class during the inquiry into the operations of the *metayage* system in 1891.

The very first individual to give evidence to the commission was plantation lessee, justice of the peace, vice president of the Tobago Agricultural Society and unofficial member of the Legislative Council, Mr John Mc Killop. He set the tone with his description of the *metayers* as people who were well off, which of course, they were not supposed to be. He stated that "the *metayers* have been able to buy a piece of land, build comfortable houses . . ."[18] In describing the *metayers*, Mr T. Blakely, merchant and owner of Alma, Burgos and other estates, stated that they are not "an impecunious class", as most were worth over £10.[19] Augustus Briggs, proprietor of Lure Estate, indicated that "The 'negro' here is as happy as he can be. They are the happiest race I know,"[20] while Maurice Rostant, manager of Mt Irvine and other estates, said of the *metayers*, "They are well off . . . too well off . . . They are in a far better position than the people in Trinidad."[21]

The notion of a happy and contented people is continued by the 1897 West Indian Royal Commission report, in spite of its description of the island as characterized by low wages, little employment, irregular payment of wages, and labourers who were forced to accept payment in kind. These conditions, along with the deplorable roads, had caused the island to have a gloomy outlook for the last twenty years. However, the report concluded that ". . . happiness is not synonymous with wealth and the condition of the people is decidedly better than the figures we have given would appear to indicate."[22] This "happiness" was attributed to their cultivation of cash and food crops; rearing poultry and animals, and the production of eggs and coconut oil.[23] After the strikes of 1919, which alarmed the administration of the island, Crown Solicitor A.B. O'Connor was pleased to report that "Tobago has resumed its *normal* (my italics) peaceful life, without any fear of it being disturbed for many a long day."[24]

In a chapter on the Trinidad labour riots of 1937, Brereton explains the absence of riots in Tobago as follows: "Tobagonians perhaps had fewer grievances than the workers of Trinidad . . . Tobago was an island of peasants; illiteracy, poverty and semiliterate servitude has always been their fate, and they were less inclined to resent these conditions than the more sophisticated workers of the larger, more developed island."[25]

However, to explain what might be perceived as a lack of worker resistance in Tobago, the Tobago Planning Team found that:

> The institution of religion more intimately affects life in Tobago than in Trinidad. The religious attachment of the bulk of the island's community bestows on it a spiritual strength which enables it to endure the material hardships associated with low level economic activity . . . What would therefore appear, in strictly material and economic terms, as a passive satisfaction with a patently mediocre way of life . . . is, in effect, a manifestation of the profound spirituality of the people.[26]

Based on the above, it might be tempting to conclude that the contented people of Tobago – whether due to their economic well-being, spiritual strength, or lack of sophistication – had little inclination to resist their difficult circumstances, but such a conclusion is not supported by the evidence of ongoing resistance across the island. A closer examination of the data will identify those forms of resistance which were manifested on the island that may have escaped the attention of these writers. Occurrences in other Caribbean territories provide a point of comparison.

Writers on the observance of Emancipation Day in the Caribbean, including Brereton, Claude Levy and William Rivere,[27] focus on its celebratory aspect, which centred on church services, without an accompanying discussion of the underlying sentiments regarding the emancipation event, and the functionality of these church services. Planters had envisaged mayhem on Emancipation Day and to prevent the anticipated retaliatory responses from the freed Africans, celebratory church services were organized. The church-oriented manipulation of Emancipation Day in 1834 and 1838 was a preventative intervention aimed at restraining the presumed naturally violent instincts of the freed Africans. Jeffrey Kerr-Ritchie explains that "the Colonial Office . . . sought to shape abolition in the image of the benevolent state"[28] and mandated that church celebrations be organized in the colonies. The response was that: "In seeking to shape emancipation in their own image, numerous colonial administrators arranged for thanksgiving celebrations overseen by Christian missionaries. Chapels, churches and places of worship were ordered to open on Friday, 1 August 1834, as colonial governors sought to enlist Christian missionaries as agents of public order."[29]

Thus, night vigils to witness the dawn of the new era were held across the Caribbean on Thursday, 31 July, and were followed by the thanksgiving services, after which the apprentices pursued their own celebrations.[30] The official position from numerous colonial officials was that the transition from slavery to apprenticeship had been "a glorious success".[31] But, as Kerr-Ritchie explains, the apprenticeship system "brought immediate tensions" because while the colonial authorities sought to create employers and employees, the planters sought "to reshape the new system in ways reminiscent of former controls" and many of the apprentices proved quite troublesome in pursuit of their own "expectations of emancipation".[32] These church diversionary celebrations do not provide a complete index of either the sentiments of the freed people or the activities that were to follow in Tobago and the rest of the Caribbean, particularly after the frustrations of the conflict-ridden apprenticeship period, 1834–1838.

The other side of the celebratory coin is raised by Gad Heuman, who observes that despite the eventless, church-based Emancipation Day celebrations in 1838, "yet all was not as well as it seemed".[33] He referred to the governor of Barbados' description of the "insubordinate spirit" on the island, and the workers who returned to work two weeks after the celebrations in Jamaica as signalling their rejection of unacceptable terms and offering "considerable resistance to the nature of freedom envisaged by their former masters and by the colonial authorities".[34] He references the strikes, fires and riots that occurred after emancipation in Barbados, Dominica, Grenada, Guyana, Jamaica and St Lucia, where there was "continued resistance and many clashes with the authorities".[35]

The notion of a peaceful transition from one legal status to another is also challenged by Henderson Carter[36] in *Labour Pains: Resistance and Protest in Barbados, 1838–1904*. Carter argues that after the celebratory church services on 1 August 1838, the formerly enslaved population engaged in a struggle against the controls of the established regime. Resistance in Barbados was expressed in strike action, cane fires, marches to government house, disruptions of court proceedings and refusals to sign contracts. These, Carter concludes, provide evidence of continuing resistance and a "persistent struggle" in post-emancipation Barbados.[37] The pattern was similar in Tobago.

LIMITATIONS IN THE HISTORIOGRAPHY OF LABOUR

The historiography of Caribbean labour focuses on the large-scale protest which stimulated the twentieth-century explosions of 1919–1920 and the 1930s, and their consequences on the development of labour organizations. In his examination of "Labour in Caribbean History", Kusha Haraksingh[38] notes the influence of "Fabian thinking on Caribbean historians, the labour movement was seen as more or less co-terminous with the rise of trade unions . . . "[39] He observes that as a result of the "Tendency to equate labour movements with trade unions . . . based on the assumption that labour is work for wages and movement represents organized activity . . . earlier activity on the part of labour was considered in dismissive terms . . ."[40]

Even though all were efforts of resistors to overcome their challenges, labour struggles are classified into a hierarchy based on whether they were isolated or general, long-lasting or short term, and have been described as uprisings, riots, strikes, fires or mobs (which are disorganized); or are dismissed as tensions, difficulties, conflicts, disturbances or plots. The persistent non-confrontational efforts of some groups or in some localities, which have no identifiable leaders, have not been recognized as part of Caribbean labour struggles. However, according to Nigel Bolland, it is important to record the activities of "The less easily identifiable people who resisted oppression [who] also contributed in myriad ways to the political culture of resistance in the Caribbean."[41]

The numbers of the protestors and their concentrations in particular locations determined what constituted a labour struggle. Large-scale confrontational episodes dominate the historiography on Caribbean labour struggles because these protests attracted researchers. Consequently, where these prevailing conditions were absent, the actions of workers have not been covered in the literature. The Tobago-freed African population of just over eleven thousand, which was concentrated on the Leeward side, with smaller numbers in the Windward areas, did not meet the size requirement of the established literature.

Despite their economic problems, planters tried to maintain their hold on the island, but their position was weakened by the demise of the sugar industry. This development did not mean automatic liberation for the workers, continued planter control efforts provoked persistent worker resistance. Although there were no large worker communities in agrarian Tobago, where estate workers also had to attend to their own plots of land, their resistance is as valid and impactful as other forms and should not go unnoticed. As Bolland indicates: "If the role of resistance is not given its true weight in Caribbean social history, we would be in danger of seeing Caribbean people merely as victims, or as faceless automations energized only by metropolitan stimuli, rather than the adaptive and creative peoples that they truly are."[42]

Discussions on labour in the Caribbean have also made distinctions between wage labourers; that is, those dependent on wages for their existence, and peasants who presumably were not wage-dependent. It was assumed that since peasants were not wage workers, they did not have labour struggles and therefore were excluded from the discourse on labour. Writing on the post-liberation period in Haiti, Mimi Sheller refers to "peasant resistance" to ruling class control, which she defines as "precisely being able to work both with and against the system at the same time, to defy power even while appearing to serve it".[43] This is well demonstrated in Tobago. Its freed African workers formed three classes: labourers about whom planters complained incessantly; *metayers* whom David Phillips cites as contributing a third of the island's sugar;[44] and the peasantry, which developed towards the end of the nineteenth century as a class of small landowners defying planter efforts to keep them landless. These were not discrete groups, for they were all in a sense labourers – the role expected of them.

The freed Africans of Tobago made maximum use of opportunities to defy the restricted labour system and they functioned in multiple capacities to extract advantages for themselves. They worked as labourers and as *metayers* on several estates. Based on the fact that special magistrates had no jurisdiction over *metayer* and planter disputes, Woodville Marshall states categorically that "the *metayer* was not a labourer".[45] However, agreements in Tobago were based on the principle that "No man was allowed to be a *metayer* except he was a labourer on the estate."[46] Planters preferred to employ wage labourers rather than *metayers*, an arrangement they considered too advantageous to the workers. As a condition for a *metayage* agreement, they insisted that the *metayer* provide labour to the estate for a wage determined by the estate. This was intended as a cost-reducing measure, to ensure that there was a plantation crop for processing.

Some freed African peasant landowners continued to work as labourers on the estates to supplement their incomes and facilitate access to land, a highly valued avenue for increased earning capacity and attaining independence. Access to land was a strategy of defiance to planter control, which Craig James refers to as the labourer's struggle for homes, lands and villages.[47] Hence, peasant cultivation and *metayage* are considered systems of labour and their resistance efforts are included as components of the labour struggles in Tobago.

It has also been acknowledged that worker grievances were long-standing issues. Brinsley Samaroo observes that the imperial authorities failed to recognize a "continuing pattern in the protest movement" in Trinidad in 1919–1920 and 1937. He noted that the 1937 protest was "the logical culmination of a longer process of struggle by a colonial people against a hated metropolitan order".[48] Of the 1919–1920 explosions, he states: "As the region moved from the nineteenth to the twentieth century, it brought along the whole burden of a colonial infrastructure that had remained fundamentally unchanged over the past century."[49] But no details are given of either the colonial infrastructure or the nineteenth-century experiences that constitute the burden, and no direct links are established between the events of the earlier period and those of the twentieth century. David Trotman notes that the Arouca riots of 1891, the water riots of 1903 and the 1937 labour riots in Trinidad "were themselves part of the problems inherent in the transition from emancipation".[50]

The long, drawn-out transitory process from 1838, which Heuman and Trotman describe, provides the setting for the resistance continuum that developed in Tobago.

Brereton questions the efficacy of established divisions in the historiography of the post-emancipation period. With reference to some writers' emphasis on "the striking continuities over the two periods", which downplays its legal significance, she states: "It may be that, in fact, this tendency has gone too far: that the argument, at least in its more extreme formulation, misses the enormous importance of the legal change for the actual lives and aspirations of the formerly enslaved (and those of others)."[51] She concludes that although "the fundamental structures were durable and transformations slow", emancipation offered new possibilities.[52]

An important one was created with the termination of apprenticeship: the ability of the freed Africans to give more open expression of their dissatisfaction than previously possible. They utilized protest actions and non-confrontational avenues, the resistance modalities of which were not recognized. Hence, emancipation stimulated the acceleration of a long-standing resistance practice that was manifested since the British imposed enslavement on Tobago. Some themes in Caribbean post-emancipation history can be treated effectively within specific time periods, but not in instances where there are continuities of action across time. This chapter positions Tobago in the historiography of Caribbean labour to counter the tendency to overlook the peculiar experiences of some territories, and argues that the creation of rigid periods in the historiography reduces the visibility and significance of some of Tobago's historical developments. The wider sweep of history illuminates previously overlooked activities in their historical context and with their linkages, and will facilitate a revision of the traditional interpretation of Tobago's history.

Existing Caribbean historiography pays scant attention to the struggles of Tobago workers, which led to the 1919 outbursts. Tony Martin, in describing occurrences in Tobago, notes: "... disturbances spread to rural Trinidad and to Tobago, in which latter place the police had fired into the crowd, inflicting several casualties, and killing one Nathaniel Williams who was then identified as the 'chief ringleader'."[53] Jerome Teelucksingh also treats developments in Tobago as an extension of the Trinidad revolts, without examining Tobago's peculiar situation and the nature of its labour problems. He asserts that the authorities conducted investigations to determine whether the Trinidad Workingmen's Association was involved in the Tobago revolts, but found no connection.⁵⁴ He admits that "the rise of the peasantry and the development of a subsistence economy constituted a significant form of resistance and challenge to the capitalist forces which dominated West Indian agriculture . . .", but makes no reference to Tobago, and cites the independent peasantry of Jamaica, Trinidad and Guyana that withdrew from the colonial plantation ". . . and thus persuasively resisted capitalist domination without the risk of violent confrontation".⁵⁵ He also mentions the establishment of an enquiry into the conditions of labour in the colony, but the rest of his discussion focuses on the development of the trade union movement in Tobago.⁵⁶

However, Craig-James mentions there were strikes on estates and in the Public Works Department, which arose from post-World War I price increases, low wages, strong anti-white feelings spawned by local conditions, newspaper reports of riots in Liverpool and Cardiff, and the heightened race consciousness of the black soldiers returning from World War I, who had suffered severe discrimination under white officers. She concludes that, in Tobago, "low wages, the rising cost of living, and race consciousness were undoubtedly factors in the situation".⁵⁷ The discussion below examines these issues.

RESISTANCE STRUGGLES IN TOBAGO

Planters' efforts to control labour stimulated the central feature of post-emancipation Tobago – the long struggle between the employers and workers. Immediately after emancipation planters' intent became very evident, and in response, the freed Africans demonstrated their determination to become independent. Though episodes varied in time and location, post-emancipation resistance in Tobago was an ongoing activity. The resistance efforts were of two types, both infused with, and strengthened by, the assertion of African culture which the ruling class did not recognize as a resistance strategy. The first was a consistent, non-confrontational movement that gnawed its way through the existing labour system and allowed the freed Africans to defy the status quo from within. Second, there were confrontational episodes, which we now discuss.

Confrontational Resistance

Wednesday, 1 August 1838 was not simply a one-day church celebration in Tobago. In addition to church services, the freed Africans organized their own celebrations. Determined to take control of their labour, the first expression of post-emancipation struggles was the workers downing tools for the rest of the week, demanding more acceptable terms of employment.[58] This was followed by strikes across the island that lasted until December on some estates. The governor reported the outbreak of strikes on thirteen estates in the Leeward district on 7 August because the workers refused to accept the reduced wages being offered. During August, the operations of estates in the northern and Windward districts were severely disrupted by workers who insisted that they should continue to occupy the houses on the plantations and resisted attempts by estate managers to eject them. Emancipation Day was the calm before the storm. While it may have passed smoothly, the workers were determined to attain a just wage and fair working conditions. The celebration could not be indicative of a smooth transition, even though the anticipated violence and reprisal actions did not occur. According to Craig-James, emancipation was not unconditional freedom but "a new order struggling to free itself from the integuments of the old".[59] This was the beginning of the long struggle to make emancipation real in Tobago.

The struggle continued in response to planters' efforts to reduce their operating costs by reducing labour costs and their unrelenting attempts to enforce the continuation of servile terms of labour. Planter pressures intensified after the passage of the 1846 Sugar Duties Act when Tobago's low sugar prices caused distress on the island. After the destruction of the hurricane of 1847, reduced wages, irregular pay and arbitrary wage stoppage were common practices. The labourers' response to planters' attempts to reduce wages was a series of strikes in 1847 and 1848.[60] The ongoing resistance was punctuated by explosive incidents such as occurred in Scarborough in 1852.

The Land Tax Riot, 1852

The Land Tax Riot, which broke out on 22 November 1852,[61] was preceded by two pieces of oppressive legislation. The 1848 trend of resident workers' withdrawal from estate housing to escape the lower paying classification as "located labour" negated planters' cost-saving measures and reduced their ability to control workers. The administration introduced the Land Tax Act of 1849, which imposed a five shillings tax on provision grounds to boost the island's revenue and force workers to work on the estates for minimal wages in order to pay the taxes. However, it was also intended to cripple workers' land acquisition ambitions, rendering them unable to save money to buy land. Next, the administration introduced a new income tax regime with the Supply Act, which imposed a tax on carts for hire and was followed by another act that permitted the use of half of the land taxes to aid immigration. A heavy tax burden was imposed on the freed Africans to frustrate their ambitions, drive wages down and enhance planter control.

The 1852 Land Tax Act imposed a four shillings per acre tax on cultivated land and sixpence per acre on occupied or unoccupied uncultivated land, with plots measuring half an acre or less to pay the same rate as for half acre. The tax was imposed on all land users – owners, tenants, *metayers* and located labourers – who were required to pay the quantum assessed for the land they occupied. The law was oppressive because many Tobago workers earned a daily wage of eight pence[62] and would have had to devote their total earnings over an extended period to raise money to pay the taxes. Additionally, workers were engaged in multiple arrangements as *metayers*, tenants, jobbers and labourers on plantation plots at various locations. The total required for taxes would be unaffordable and discriminatory because in some cases the workers were required to pay taxes for properties that they did not own. While workers faced an increased tax burden, the planters' contribution was eased by a reduction of the export duties on plantation crops. To add insult to injury, half of the penalties and the legal costs were paid to the informants, who were usually police constables.

On 22 November, armed with sticks, an angry crowd descended on Market Square in Scarborough and showed their opposition by dumping their tax forms. Missiles were thrown through the courthouse windows and the assailants fought with the superintendent of police and government officials. The crowd was only dispersed when a detachment of the garrison arrived. However, protests continued during the week when people from rural areas went to the courthouse and dumped their tax forms. To prevent further unrest, president of the Legislative Council, Henry Yeates, declared that the tax would be imposed only on employers or owners – to the chagrin of the planters. Garden lands and provision grounds were treated as uncultivated land and taxed at six pence per acre, while plots that were less than one acre were tax-free. These amendments provided limited relief to the resistors who demonstrated intolerance to the oppressive laws. Fifteen years later, another explosion occurred on the island.[63]

The Dog Tax Riot, 1867

Another confrontational episode occurred when residents of Mason Hall, discontented with the imposition of high levels of taxation while workers' wages remained low, rioted in 1867.[64] The Dog Tax Act required dog owners, primarily hunters, to pay an annual tax of six shillings per dog by May. If the tax was not paid within sixty days after the deadline, convicted owners of unlicensed dogs of any age or size would be fined twenty shillings plus costs. Convicted villagers of Mason Hall refused to pay the tax and petitioned the governor on 8 August 1867, who responded by censuring them to cease from "the disgraceful behaviour"[65] or nothing would be done.

Attempts to serve warrants on one hundred persons in the community on 12 September were met with defiance. Summoned from their gardens by a shell call and armed with sticks, stones, cutlasses and bludgeons, the villagers attacked and beat the police, who hastily retreated to Scarborough. The rioters sent strong signals of their refusal to pay and their intention to beat any collectors, including the governor himself. The authorities acted swiftly to avert an escalation and the resistors achieved some success. In 1868, the tax was adjusted, exempting dogs under six months old. It was further reduced to four shillings, with a penalty not exceeding eight shillings plus costs. In 1878 the tax was reduced to two shillings six pence when, in determined resistance, the taxpayers ignored it.[66]

The Belmanna War, 1876

The Belmanna War, which broke out on 1 May 1876,[67] was described as the most important labour protest in nineteenth-century Tobago.[68] It was caused by worker frustrations with low and irregular wages; resentment among resident workers who were earning less than those classified as strangers; arbitrary wage stoppages; the exploitative truck system in which they were overcharged for poor quality goods by deductions from their wages which left them perpetually in debt; the high costs of medical care from the despised brothers, Drs Richard and James Anderson, whose medical fees were deducted from their wages and who were eventually chased out of the area; land deprivation which was most marked in the Windward areas; and the increasing size of tasks with no equivalent increase in wages.[69]

Brereton assesses the situation as a post-emancipation protest in which "labourers were seeking to defend their rights and protect their hard-won gains".[70] The explosion was sparked by police brutality that resulted in the death of Mary Jane Thomas, a Barbadian woman, and injury to a Barbadian man. In revenge, the crowd, armed with cutlasses, sticks, stones and missiles, disarmed and beat the policemen. The perpetrator, Police Corporal James Henry Belmanna, was killed, and several other officers were injured. The Roxborough courthouse was stoned and wrecked, cane fields were burnt and the megasse house on the Roxborough estate was set on fire. Strike action also occurred on several other estates, including Goldsborough and Richmond in the Windward districts, and some in the Leeward district. Seventy people were arrested, sixteen were convicted for Belmanna's murder; six were imprisoned for life and ten were given twenty-year penal servitude, while thirty were convicted of rioting. The HMS *Angus* arrived from Barbados with Barbadian policemen and English soldiers to restore order. Brereton concludes that the Belmanna War was "a significant act of protest by both immigrant and creole labourers in Tobago against longstanding grievances and oppressive conditions on the estates".[71] It is significant that in both instances, the protesters vented their anger on the courthouse, the symbol of oppression and injustice on the island.

The island's officials were so terrified that they called for the establishment of a system of government that would provide them with the security they felt they needed against the labourers. The police force was immediately increased from twenty to fifty men, with two corporals in Scarborough and one in Windward, eight officers and three sergeants.[72] The result was the Tobago Constitution Act 1876,[73] which dissolved the functions and privileges of the House of Assembly, demonstrating planters' fear of the potential strength of the black labouring class. The big planters, to their detriment, played into the hands of the imperial government and willingly surrendered their power in exchange for support against the black labouring class. The next episode was even more terrifying for the ruling class.

The 1919 Labour Struggle in Tobago

At six o'clock on the morning of 6 December 1919, the eruption of a riot in Scarborough alarmed the authorities, who swiftly galvanized their defence resources to contain its spread. The riot began with cartmen, carpenters and labourers employed in the Public Works Department striking for better wages.[74] They were joined by other workers and took possession of the town, flatly refusing to entertain entreaties from officials to return to their homes and rejected the offer of the warden to meet with a deputation of labourers to discuss their grievances.[75] The resistors gathered in the uptown business area, where they armed themselves with bottles, sticks and stones, and went around forcing the closure of businesses. The protest action was taken to the commercial buildings, where strikers forced workers to exit the buildings and owners or managers to close their doors. They then directed their attention to government buildings – the courthouse, telephone exchange and wireless building.[76]

Officials, including the warden and the Inspector General of the constabulary, who sought to defuse the situation, were struck by missiles and beaten from the commercial area to the police station and back around the marketplace. While reading the Riot Act, the warden was stoned. Initially, the Acting Magistrate Warden Mr Sorzano, downplayed the explosion as "an exaggeration . . . because it was over so quickly,"[77] but later admitted that the strikers took possession of the town up to 10.30 a.m. The Inspector General stated that "he could not cope with the eruption because it was a difficult mob both in composition and expectations". When the situation appeared to be getting out of control, the Sub Inspector asked for reinforcements to deal with what he described as "serious disturbances"[78] on the island. There were strikes by estate labourers on several estates and in particular, the tense situation at Friendship Estate required the presence of a patrol of marines to maintain order.

Special constables, including plantation owners, government officials, members of the clergy and a group of World War I veteran volunteers, were appointed to help restore order. The authorities claimed they were forced to arm the police who were "forced" to fire into the crowd "to defend their lives". Nathaniel Williams, aged twenty-five, a porter of Mt Marie, died of gunshot wounds. Injured were Henry Niblett, Samuel Emmanuel, Sylvester Chevalier, Cyril Gordon, and domestic workers May Mc Kenzie and seventeen-year-old Albertha Critchlow. Twenty-three people were arrested.

Sensing the mood of workers and amid fears of further disruption, the magistrate/warden requested the Sub-Inspector to leave the twenty reinforcements for an additional period to guard the courthouse and wireless and telephone buildings, which would need protection after the departure of the marines. They remained in Tobago until 19 December 1919. He also asked for a permanent unit of the force to be stationed in Tobago.[79] Officials agreed that economic factors caused the outburst; wages were low and escalating prices made life difficult for the workers. The daily wage was twenty-eight cents; salt fish sold at eighteen cents per pound and rice six cents.[80] Officials were not convinced that the outburst was racially motivated because the returned war veterans (primarily black) volunteered their services to assist to restore order and were of good conduct.[81]

The Sub-Inspector of the constabulary agreed that wages were largely responsible, but insisted on an outside influence from "agitators [who] came over from Trinidad and stirred the population up".[82] He identified three suspects who appeared on the island; F. Hinds a bookseller from Port of Spain, as well as Victor Sylvester and J.T. Parris, who appeared at Kings Bay. As a security measure, a rule was implemented that all ships leaving the island must be checked before leaving and no ship would be allowed to sail after dark. However, the Governor Chancellor reported that there was no evidence to support the claim that a Trinidad influence was at work as a check of the passenger list of the *Belize* failed to establish a link with the Trinidad Workingmen's Association (TWA).[83] He conceded that, "The state of unrest prevailing among the 'negro' population was enough for developments in Trinidad to influence the population and bring discontent to a head."[84]

The response of employers was a clear admission that the riot was caused by the prevailing economic conditions, in particular, low wages.

The Public Works Department issued an instruction that workers be informed that all employees, including those involved in task work, would receive a bonus of 25 per cent, an increase from the normal 10 per cent, from 1 January 1920. Planters across the island also immediately increased the wages of labourers from thirty-six to fifty cents per day.[85]

Thus, while an undisguised attempt was made to appease the workers, these measures provided no resolution to the underlying problems that caused the upheaval. Low wages, high costs of living, the absence of any mechanism to protect the interests of workers, and continued exploitation by employers remained unaddressed. While this eruption shows that worker dissatisfaction in Tobago included the skilled and the unskilled, government employees, private sector and estate workers, it is evident that confrontational resistance resulted from some level of organization.

Non-Confrontational Resistance

The uprisings represent a part of the struggles of Tobago workers. Ongoing non-confrontational resistance occurred before, during and after these heated episodes, providing evidence of the practice, described by Sheller, in which resistors working within the system extracted benefits for themselves while undermining it. One of the most noticeable features of the freed Africans in Tobago was their desire to own land as the means to attain both independence and social mobility. Their landowning ambitions were evident immediately after emancipation and in response, the planter community imposed several obstacles to frustrate their landowning efforts. The strategies used to achieve their aims constitute an important feature of the workers' struggle in Tobago.

A significant portion of the non-confrontational resistance strategies displayed by workers employed on the estates related to their landowning efforts. Given the extent of planter control of the island's administration and land resources, their determination to prevent black land ownership and the limited employment opportunities available to the freed Africans, it was imperative that workers utilize strategies to challenge the system from within. Hence, throughout the post-emancipation era, the most common resistance strategies were land-related. While some freed Africans saved their earnings and were able to buy land during the early post-emancipation period, even at the prohibitive price of £20 per acre, many had to continue working on the estates. Their eagerness to buy land was demonstrated by the existence of 966 freeholders on the island in 1854, despite the experiences of those in the Middle[86] district who had purchased poor quality, inaccessible land with no title. The arbitrarily measured plots were not the size stipulated at sale.[87] Those who were unable to purchase land engaged in a variety of means to gain access to it, with the ultimate aim of becoming landowners. Access to land was critical to the ability of the free population to offer an effective challenge to the system of exploitation. It is therefore essential to examine the *metayage* system – which was dominant in post-emancipation Tobago – in any discourse on non-confrontational resistance among workers in Tobago.

The system, which was first introduced on two estates in 1842,[88] was intended to address the shortage of credit that planters faced. The *metayage* arrangement was expected to guarantee a supply of labour to the estates and permit the maintenance of cashless plantation operations. It was not immediately popular because workers were wary of the potential to be exploited at a time when their main objective was to attain their independence. Those who were unable to buy land would rent a house spot and, as homeowners, they could rent land and pasture from the estate and engage in agricultural pursuits. Some formed or joined jobbing gangs, while others worked as non-residential labourers, all with the intent of increasing their earnings and independence. Workers were able to take advantage of those planters who sought to attract workers by offering higher wages than their neighbours, even though they were bound to offer their labour to the estates at the end of the year when their own crops demanded their time. In addition, in 1854 the shortage of imported food caused an increased demand for locally produced food, which the African workers were able to exploit.[89] The introduction of the *metayage* system by cash-strapped planters provided the avenue for workers to operate a system of resistance within it.

By 1852, of the 892 estate workers, 208 were also *metayers* who cultivated two hundred acres of estate lands in the Windward district and were gradually withdrawing from estate labour.[90] Despite its rapid spread to estates across the island and the claim by David Phillips that ". . . as late as 1870 Tobago was the only island on which this system of cultivation could be regarded as successful,"[91] there was an underbelly of resentment and resistance in the system of *metayage,* which was replete with workers' struggles against exploitation from the time of its introduction. As Brereton has indicated "despite its popularity, *metayage* was a source of conflict between *metayers* and owners and unrest was always below the surface."[92] These conflicts were related to wages, and hours and terms of work, and were revealed in the large number of cases (164) that were brought before the courts in 1890.[93] In the evidence presented at the enquiry, the *metayers* indicated how planters flagrantly disregarded the terms of the agreement and introduced new arrangements which relieved them of the cost burdens of sugar production, while they increased those costs for the *metayers.*[94]

Metayers were required to bear the costs of planting, reaping, carting, grinding and manufacturing the cane and for pasturage if they kept animals on the estate. They were also charged rents for provision grounds which were traditionally given rent-free[95] as an incentive to encourage labourers to participate in the system. Over time, planters shifted their responsibilities onto the *metayers,* who complained about spite-stimulated delays in grinding their canes, which resulted in losses,[96] and if a labourer chose to stop working on an estate, their canes cultivated as part of the *metayage* agreement would be confiscated. They reacted by wresting advantages from the system. Their resistance measures included interplanting potatoes and corn in the canes in defiance of the planters and with great benefit to themselves.[97] Senior justice of the peace and planter Sladden's evidence indicates that the *metayers* "could earn $13.50 each from potatoes and corn on one cane bank even before the planter made an ounce of sugar".[98]

Malingering was also a common strategy[99] and planters constantly complained about the slow rate of work and low levels of production.[100] They said workers gave priority to their own concerns, paid little attention to estate cultivation, left canes in weeds, and would abandon their estate responsibilities to attend weddings, funerals and other activities.[101] They often refused to respond to the call to work when it was raining[102] and they entered into *metayer* arrangements with several estates.[103] This increased their access to land, with some gaining access to as much as ten acres.[104] The shortage of cash on the island led to payments in kind and usually this facilitated access to land. While it complicated the arrangement and generated conflicts of its own, it provided *metayers* with considerable opportunities to increase their earnings and to protest in a non-confrontational manner.

They engaged in several income-generating practices on their *metayer* pieces and on rented land.[105] They cultivated and sold cocoa and sugar cane[106] as well as food crops, and used the additional rented land to expand their cultivation.[107] They reared animals, for example, horses, cows, goats and sheep, which served as their banks since there was none on the island.[108] When conflicts arose, they refused to give up the land.[109] Some made use of the option of seasonal migration to Trinidad, where wages were higher.[110] Despite the injustices they encountered, workers did not seek redress in the courts because that option was unaffordable. One *metayer* said they invested in animals rather than the expensive process of taking the planters to court, which required hefty lawyer fees. He said the lawyers ". . . take the milk but they don't give milk".[111] In addition, they squatted on estate land, especially in Charlotteville and Speyside;[112] negotiated their own terms for service to the plantations;[113] engaged in a range of other resistance activities, such as writing petitions, and complaints to the governor and magistrates, and conducted other supporting economic activities, such as fishing and hunting. In this way, the *metayers* were able to defy the restrictive laws, and some emerged not only as landowners but estate owners.[114] Recognizing that the system was being used against them, planters preferred to employ full-time labourers, but though pressured, the *metayers* refused to become full-time labourers who earned less and were under greater planter control.[115]

However, *metayage* was not a single system. In addition to the formal planter-organized *metayer* system, three other labour arrangements were instituted by the workers, which functioned under the umbrella of *metayage*. Firstly, some of the *metayers* were also employers who hired labourers to cultivate their pieces, and secondly, *metayers* made use of "return labour" also called "len 'han", an ancestral tradition that became a cultural institution on the island. *Metayers* gave assistance to each other to complete assigned tasks and in return, the recipient gave an equal amount of time to those who assisted them. In addition, they reintroduced family labour and used their women and children to assist in cultivation. These strategies facilitated management of the cultivation of the multiple pieces of land to which the *metayers* had access. Thirdly, jobbing gangs created by the *metayers* were organized by a headman, who recruited teams of workers to perform tasks obtained through contracts from the estates. Planters objected to negotiating with workers with whom they had other arrangements, whom they continued to view as their labourers. Despite their abhorrence, the planters' need to keep their estates operational left them no option but to embrace the system in which they were hiring the very people with whom they were in conflict, and on terms which they were unable to dictate. The jobbing gangs functioned in parallel, both competing with the *metayage* system, which planters were fighting to make more beneficial to themselves and complementing the efforts of the *metayers* to use the system to their advantage. To make matters worse, jobbers were paid twice as much as labourers on the plantations for similar jobs. Plantation labourers were paid eight pence (sixteen cents) per day, compared to jobbers at one shilling and four pence (thirty-two cents).[116] Planters complained bitterly about their inability to hire labourers for estate work, and in their desperation, came to depend on jobbers; but that was not without its share of conflicts. The combination of jobbing with *metayage* brought added turbulence to labour relations in Tobago, but permitted the erosion of planter control of the labour force, which ultimately corroded the system of *metayage* and reduced its effectiveness as a mechanism to counteract the shortage of credit that planters faced.

With increased earnings and the facility to buy land in instalments, Africans became landowners, despite the restrictive measures of the ruling class. Some acquired small parcels of land, while others became estate owners. These included Brutus Murray, who owned Pembroke and Cardiff Estates; Daniel Gordon, who bought Adventure and Roselle Estates and owned considerable properties in Plymouth, and shops at Plymouth and Black Rock; Paul Tobago, a shopkeeper in Buccoo, who owned Prospect Estate, and J.B. Swalls of Moriah, who became a merchant and proprietor.[117] Planters' dissatisfaction with the system is reflected in their vain attempts to institute laws to control its operation. In 1884, the Tobago Agricultural Society established a commission to enquire into the operation of the *metayage* system, where planters aired their concerns and expressed the desire to implement a legally controlled, more favourable system. As a result, the 1888 Ordinance was passed, but was never implemented. Union occurred the following year and with it came the intervention of Justice John Gorrie, whose tenure on the island facilitated the demise of the *metayage* system.[118] What is striking is that despite the restrictions, the number of landholders on the island increased even before the ultimate crash of the sugar industry in 1884. Thus, the *metayage* system presented a challenge that the *metayers* resisted, and opportunities that they utilized as part of their struggles within the system. Metayage continued from its inception in the second half of the nineteenth century into the twentieth.

CONCLUSION

The period of change from enslavement to emancipation was a time of turbulence in planter/worker relations in Tobago. Despite their penurious situation, planters maintained their hold on the arms of government and the island's land resources, and continued to dictate the terms of labour because employment opportunities were very limited. Since worker ambitions for independence and real freedom clashed with employer desires for maintaining a cheap, controllable labour force, there was a protracted struggle by the freed Africans to circumvent the legal and other impediments imposed on them by the ruling class to establish themselves as independent landowners. The freed African workers engaged in organized confrontational resistance, but their most enduring strategies were rooted in the peculiar labour system planters devised to alleviate their labour and credit problems. The system of *metayage* and the shortage of cash on the island provided openings through which both resistance and labour could occur simultaneously, and access to land was widely used as a liberating strategy across the island. The *metayage* system contributed to the development of a cultural tradition of len' han' and an esprit de corps which characterized the Tobago population in the twentieth century and allowed its survival, despite the lingering apparition of the planter. Through this method, many *metayers* became landowners, despite the strong-armed planter preventative mechanisms that led to Lieutenant Governor Usher's observation in 1874 that *metayage* was "effete and obsolete" and "planters are gradually being ruined by it".[119] Although Tobago's conflicts are not mentioned in the historiography of Caribbean labour, these struggles demarcate an important phase of the island's history as a prelude to the development of trade unionism there. They also provide evidence that contradicts the perception that the population of Tobago was disinclined to resist and that it was a place of peaceful tolerance of the ignominy of employer exploitation of workers. As indicated above, like any other Caribbean colony, Tobago faced upheavals in its post-emancipation labour relations that indicate that there was no gentle glide from enslavement to emancipation for the freed Africans of Tobago.

NOTES

1. Susan Craig-James, *The Changing Face of Tobago, 1838–1938: A Fractured Whole, Volume I, 1838–1900. Volume II, 1900–1938* (Arima: Cornerstone Press, 2008).
2. Kusha Haraksingh, "Labour Movements in Caribbean History," in *General History of the Caribbean Volume VI: Methodology and Historiography of the Caribbean*, ed. B.W. Higman (London: UNESCO Publishing/Macmillan Education, 1999), 290.
3. *Report of the Tobago Metairie Commission*, 1891, Appendix I, Proceedings and Evidence.
4. Arie Boomert, *The Indigenous Peoples of Trinidad and Tobago: From the First Settlers Until Today* (Leiden: Sidestone Press, 2016).
5. ibid., 115.
6. ibid., 115, 127.
7. ibid., 127.
8. Rita Pemberton, Debbie Mc Collin, Gelien Matthews, and Michael Toussaint, *Historical Dictionary of Trinidad and Tobago* (Lanham, MD: Roman and Littlefield, 2018), xxvii.
9. Henry Isles Woodcock, *A History of Tobago* (London: Frank Cass, 1971).
10. ibid., 87–88.
11. ibid., 88.
12. ibid., 88.
13. ibid., 88.
14. ibid., 62.
15. Sir William Young, 2nd bart. Profiles and Legacies Summary 1749–10 January 1815. Accessed 1 July 2021. https://www.ucl.ac.uk/lbs/person/view/2146632174(q.v.).
16. "Members 1790–1820, Published in 1986," *The History of Parliament: British Political, Social & Local History*, accessed 1 July 2021, https://www.historyofparliamentonline.org/volume/1790-1820/member/young-sir-william-1749-1815.

17. Parliament, "Members 1790–1820."
18. *Report of the Metairie Commission*, Appendix I, 13.
19. ibid., 26.
20. ibid., 165.
21. ibid.
22. *Report of the West India Royal Commission* (London: Printed for HM Stationery Office, by Eyre and Spottiswoode, 1897), 40.
23. ibid.
24. Report by the Crown Solicitor, Enclosure No. 5 in Trinidad Dispatch, Confidential, 24 January 1920.
25. Bridget Brereton, *A History of Modern Trinidad, 1793–1962* (Oxford: Heinemann International, 1989), 178.
26. Trinidad and Tobago Government, *Report of the Tobago Planning Team, Part 4, 11* (Port of Spain: Central Statistical Office Printery Unit, 1964).
27. See Bridget Brereton, "A Social History of Emancipation in the British Caribbean: The First 50 Years," in *August First, the Celebration of Emancipation Day*, ed. Patrick Bryan (Kingston: Fredrich Ebert Stifrung and The Department of History, UWI, 1994); William Rivere, "Labour Shortage in the British West Indies after Emancipation," *Journal of Caribbean History* 4 (May 1972); and Claude Levy, *Emancipation, Sugar and Federalism in Barbados and the West Indies 1833–1876* (Gainesville: Florida University Press, 1980).
28. Jeffrey Kerr-Ritchie, *Rites of August First: Emancipation Day in the Black Atlantic World* (Baton Rouge: Louisiana State University Press, 2007), 17.
29. ibid., 17.
30. ibid., 18.
31. ibid., 25.
32. ibid., 26.
33. Gad Heuman, "'Is This What You Call Free?' Riots and Resistance in the Anglophone Caribbean," in *Contesting Freedom: Control and Resistance in the Post-Emancipation Caribbean*, ed. Gad Heuman and David Trotman (Oxford: Macmillan Caribbean, 2005), 105.
34. ibid., 105.
35. ibid., 110–113.
36. Henderson Carter, *Labour Pains: Resistance and Protest in Barbados, 1838-1904* (Kingston: Ian Randle Publishers, 2012).
37. ibid., 85–96.
38. Haraksingh, "Labour Movements," 283.
39. ibid.
40. ibid., 284.

41. Nigel Bolland, *The Politics of Labour in the British Caribbean: The Social Origins of Authoritarianism and Democracy in the Labour Movement* (Kingston: Ian Randle Publishers, 2001), 18.
42. ibid., 17.
43. Mimi Sheller, "'You Signed My Name, But Not My Feet': Paradoxes of Peasant Resistance and State Control in Post-Revolutionary Haiti," in *Contesting Freedom: Control and Resistance in the Post-Emancipation Caribbean*, eds. Gad Heuman and David Trotman (Oxford: Macmillan Caribbean, 2005), 90.
44. David Phillips, *La Magdalena: The Story of Tobago 1498–1898* (New York: iUniverse, 2004), 292.
45. Woodville Marshall, "Metayage in the Sugar Industry of the British Windward Islands 1838–1865," *Jamaica Historical Review* 3, no.1 (May 1965): 28–29.
46. *Metairie Commission Report*, 99.
47. Craig-James, *Changing Face*, 88.
48. Brinsley Samaroo, "The Trinidad Disturbances of 1817–20: Precursor to 1937," in *The Trinidad Labour Riots of 1937: Perspectives 50 Years Later*, ed. Roy Thomas (Trinidad: Extra Mural Studies Unit, University of the West Indies, 1987), 21.
49. ibid., 22.
50. David Trotman, "Capping the Volcano: Riots and their Suppression in Post-emancipation Trinidad," in *Contesting Freedom: Control and Resistance in the Post-Emancipation Caribbean*, ed. Gad Heuman and David Trotman (Oxford: Macmillan Caribbean, 2005), 141.
51. Bridget Brereton, "Recent Developments in the Historiography of the Post-Emancipation Anglophone Caribbean," in *Beyond Fragmentation: Perspectives on Caribbean History*, eds. Juanita De Barros, Andre Diptee, and David Trotman (Princeton: Marcus Weiner Publishers, 2006), 187.
52. ibid., 187.
53. Tony Martin, "Revolutionary Upheaval in Trinidad, 1919: Views from British and American Sources," *Journal of Negro History* 58, no. 3 (July 1973): 323.
54. Jerome Teelucksingh, *Labour and the Decolonization Struggle in Trinidad and Tobago* (New York: Palgrave Macmillan, 2015), 35.
55. ibid., 5.
56. ibid., 55–79.
57. Craig-James, *Changing Face*, 92.
58. ibid., 66–67.
59. ibid., 69.
60. Brereton, "Post Emancipation," 111.

61. Craig-James, *Changing Face*, 103.
62. ibid., 98.
63. ibid., 249.
64. ibid., 249.
65. ibid., 249.
66. ibid., 250.
67. ibid., 140.
68. Brereton, "Post Emancipation," 112.
69. ibid.
70. ibid., 110.
71. ibid., 121.
72. ibid., 120.
73. Pemberton, Mc Collin, Matthews, and Toussaint, *Historical Dictionary*, xxvii.
74. CO295/523 Confidential letter from Governor Chancellor to Secretary of State Viscount Milner, 24 January 1920.
75. CO295/523 Enclosure II Report by the Sub-Inspector of the Constabulary, 8 December 1919.
76. CO295/523 Chancellor to Milner, 24 January 1920.
77. CO 295/523 Enclosure I Report by Ag Magistrate Warden of Tobago, 7 December 1919.
78. CO295/523 Enclosure II Report by the Sub-Inspector of the Constabulary, 8 December 1919.
79. CO 295/523 Enclosure III Report of the Sub-Inspector of the Constabulary, 11 December 1919.
80. ibid.
81. CO295/523 Chancellor to Milner, 23 January 1920.
82. CO 295/523 Enclosure III.
83. The Trinidad Working Men's Association was formed in 1897 to articulate on behalf of workers for better working conditions, higher wages and to obtain a voice in the administration of government of the colony.
84. CO 295/523 Chancellor to Milner, 24 Jan. 1920.
85. ibid.86 Tobago was divided into three districts – Leeward, Middle and Windward. The Middle district included the more populous areas in the parishes of St Andrews and St George, Scarborough and its environs, Mason Hall, Moriah, Mt St George and Parlatuvier on the north coast.
87. Craig-James, *Changing Face*, 89.
88. ibid., 101.
89. ibid., 89.
90. ibid., 91.

91. Phillips, *La Magdalena*, 292.
92. Brereton, "Post Emancipation," 112.
93. *Metairie Commission Report*, 12.
94. ibid., 49.
95. ibid., 71.
96. ibid., 104, 156.
97. ibid., 25.
98. ibid., 162.
99. ibid., 169.
100. ibid., 24, 164.
101. ibid., 25, 160.
102. ibid., 160.
103. ibid., 93.
104. ibid., 167.
105. ibid., 53.
106. ibid., 18, 54.
107. ibid., 26, 52.
108. ibid., 158.
109. ibid., 113.
110. ibid., 52.
111. ibid., 158.
112. ibid., 117.
113. ibid., 153.
114. *Metairie Commission Report*, 158. Paul Tobago was one *metayer* who, through multiple *metayer* arrangements, was able to purchase the 500-acre Prospect Hall Estate.
115. ibid., 26, 168.
116. Craig-James, *Changing Face*, 163.
117. ibid., 165.
118. ibid., 177.
119. Phillips, *La Magdalena*, 282.

[3]

THE IMPACT OF CHRISTIANITY ON NAMING PRACTICES IN POST-EMANCIPATION BARBADOS

[PEDRO L.V. WELCH]

IN PRACTICALLY ALL SOCIETIES, NAMING PRACTICES HAVE AN identifying function that assists in connecting individuals to locations, kinship, occupational or ethnic groups, among other social configurations. The particular function served by naming practices is largely determined by the norms peculiar to a given society. In some cases, naming practices perform the function of identifying social status, or even ascribing that status. In the context of post-emancipation Caribbean societies, naming practices have not been the subject of a major investigation, nor is the coverage of naming practices among the enslaved in pre-emancipation Caribbean society significantly more encouraging, the work of Jerome Handler and Jo Ann Jacoby notwithstanding.[1]

This chapter makes a modest attempt at an investigation of naming practices in one Caribbean territory, Barbados. It does so with the hope that this will assist in charting more fully the response of the formerly enslaved and their descendants to the social possibilities that came with the legal enactment of freedom in 1834. The documentary base for the study is baptismal records and plantation records that cover both the pre- and post-emancipation periods.

The study also looks at the case of one family for whom the documentary record is particularly rich in the post-emancipation period. Some attention is also placed on the naming practices of some churches in the Caribbean context. Finally, some tentative conclusions are offered about the expectations of ex-slaves on the question of naming. We begin by addressing the issue of pre-emancipation antecedents in the evolution of naming practices in the Barbadian and wider Caribbean case.

PRE-EMANCIPATION ANTECEDENTS

It is clear that in the early phase of the slave system in Barbados and other Caribbean territories, many of the enslaved brought and kept with them the names that had been bestowed on them in Africa. Thus, as Richard Dunn informs us, "... The island slaves bore a strange medley of names in the seventeenth century. Some blacks imported into the Caribbean kept their native names; others were given new names by their masters [and mistresses]."[2] In this context, we find the origins of a duality in naming practices which was fairly common throughout the region. That is, the enslaved often received new names from their owners while some, in the earlier years of the plantation system, may have retained their African names. Where African names might have been retained, however, it must not be assumed that this concession represented any respect for African custom on the part of the enslavers. Rather, this might well have reflected a decision to permit the retention of names where these might fit, even if loosely, within the context of European phonetic conventions. In any case, over time, the assault on African identity meant that, in most cases, African names gradually disappeared.

Thus, we might summarize the evolution of naming practices as follows: Enslavers most likely had some difficulty in pronouncing some African names and might have selected names that emanated from their own familiar cultural norms. Additionally, renaming the enslaved with European names probably reflected an attempt to impose a European cultural orthodoxy, or to facilitate a process of de-culturation that was intended to further control the existence of the enslaved. Another aspect of the renaming might have been rooted in the influence of the Christian church. Table 3.1 illustrates the patterns that characterized naming practices in the plantation culture of Barbados in the formative years of the slave system.

One of the issues that might be detected in table 3.1 is the association of European names with surnames with a Christian identification. Over time, one of the distinguishing elements in the further development of a racist culture appears in the differentiation between the enslaved and the

Table 3.1: A Schedule of the Particular Names of all ye Christian and other Stock on ye Plantaçon of Captain William Goodall Fontlaroy

Christian servants	Women Negroes
William Gould	Abaca
Irish Thomas	Abara
Benjamin Asinoman	Aolu
John Jr Taylor	Bussa
Sarah, a maidservant	Cullabulla
John Hawltey	Cumba
Irish Richard	Hagar
Irish Will	Jappa
David Baylie	Jecina
William Clark	Jocka
Frolise and Eustace	Jug
	Leamo
	Maria
	Mary
	Wombo

Source: Extracted from Deed (RB 3/3/869-870), 15 October 1654, Barbados Department of Archives (BDA)

free (European) on the basis of an ascription that equated whiteness with Christianity, and therefore, with freedom. In this context, the naming of Africans with "Christian" names represented an assertion of superiority over African religious traditions. Additionally, the general absence of surnames in the lists of Africans in various plantation inventories probably represented another aspect of the attempted negation of the enslaved. In short, in a system in which the role of the African male as a social parent was partially subjugated to that of the male enslaver, the absence of the patriarchal marker reflected the legal position of the enslaved as a species of property.

The experiences faced by many of the enslaved may well be represented in the experience of Olaudah Equiano. James Walvin, in commenting on Equiano's autobiography, noted that he had been given a variety of names by different white people, notwithstanding his strong desire to retain his African name. If Equiano was not successful in this retention, he hoped, at least to retain the name Jacob, which had been given to him by whites at one time. After "a flurry of blows", he was forced to accept the name Gustavus Vasa, which he kept until his autobiography was published. Walvin observes that ". . . This renaming process involved more than a change of name. It involved, from the slave-owner's viewpoint, a stripping of African identity."[3] Whatever the enslaved might have felt about this process, it is clear that the reality of the slave owners' capacity for extreme sanction often forced an unwilling acceptance. The experience of another slave, Jeffery Brace, shipped from Africa to Barbados, and thence to North America, illustrates the brutality which might have forced slaves to acquiesce in their own subordination.[4]

The influence of the church might have been important in the naming process. Various baptism records which survive from the eighteenth century reflect a theology that viewed the baptism process in terms of an assertion of European norms. Table 3.2 reflects that influence while illustrating the perseverance of some African naming patterns up to this period.

The data, extracted from the Moravian baptism records for the period 1769–1827, provides the new name and the former (sometimes African) name. A comparison of this list with Handler and Jacoby's list for baptized slaves (in the Anglican Church) on the Codrington Plantations in 1741 suggests that Moravian practice was probably reflected in the other denominations. Certainly, the first Moravian converts in Barbados, in 1768, experienced a name change at baptism.

The list illustrates that some African names, for example, Quashy, Quamy and Coffy (all Akan names), were still relatively common among the enslaved, prior to baptism. Additionally, it shows the influence of the church on the naming selections. Most of the new names were biblical. Moreover, a review of Moravian baptisms for the period just after emancipation shows a consistency in which some of the enslaved with the same names (imposed in the pre-emancipation period) received the same "converted" name. Thus, the name Caroline replaced that of Coobah, even for those enslaved females of different plantations and with no identifiable connection with each other. This, inferentially, is highly suggestive of the influence of the Moravian minister in name selection, and of some commonality in the naming practices of such ministers. The clear inference is that quite apart from the owners' contribution, or that

Table 3.2: Selected Moravian Slave Baptisms, Barbados, 1769–1827

Baptismal name	Former name	Plantation/ owner	Nation	When baptized
John	Jack	Mrs Alleyne	Creole	1769
Abraham	Fortune	Dr Bannister	Papaa	1770
Joseph	Quashy	Devonish	Creole	1775
Joseph	Quashy	Mission of the Brethren	Mandingo	1788
Nathaniel	Quamy	John Spooner	Creole	1789
David	Kitt	Mr King, the plumber	Coromante	1788
Steven (mul)	Joseph	Beamans	Creole	1791
Tobias	Primus	Mt Wilton	Creole	1792
Jonas (mul)	Packet	Blowers	Ebo	1792
Lewis	Rhode Island	John Cobham	Creole	1794
Daniel	Coffy Mool	Lord Harwood	Creole	1795
Jacob	Coffy	John Lewis	Creole	1796
Charles	Clark	Yorkshirehall	Coromante	1795
Samson	Sambo	Spooners	Creole	1819
Daniel	Daniel	Blowers	Guinea	1826
John (partner, Palase at Mt Wilt.)	John Groom	Mt Wilton	African	1826
Henry (partner Mary at Mt Wilt.)	Handy	Mt Wilton	Barbadian	1828
Philip (partner Margaret at A'seat)	Phil Sandy	Mr Taylor at After seat	Barbadian	1828
Dauphny (partner, Lovely at C'hams)	Dauphny	Cobhams	Guinea	1827

Source: Compiled from Moravian Baptismal Registers, Department of Archives (Barbados)

of the enslaved, to naming practices, it is important for us to factor into our analyses the impact of Christianization.

Later, as we turn our attention to the post-emancipation experience, it might be noted that the influence of the church grew over time and had an even more profound effect on the norms of the formerly enslaved and their descendants. The practice identified among the Moravians of

Barbados may be identified in other Caribbean territories. For example, in 1734, the first Moravian missionaries changed the name of the first convert in St Thomas, in the Virgin Islands, from Camel Orly to Joshua. In 1736, three other converts were "given the names of early disciples, Andrew, Peter, and Nathanael in the hope that they would become the nucleus of the Lord's followers among the slaves".[5]

Mass baptisms of the enslaved by the Anglican Church in Jamaica and Barbados might also shed some light on the prevailing attitudes toward the naming. In Jamaica, it is reported that planters in the area of Devon, anxious to prevent the Moravians from establishing themselves in the locality, asked the Anglican priest to baptize their slaves. On those occasions, "... the slaves being all assembled, generally in the mill-house, the minister went around... carrying a basin of water and naming each slave by a new name, while he sprinkled the water on them".[6] It is not clear what these new names might be but if the example of the St Philip Parish Church in Barbados is typical, it appears that Anglicans were a little less anxious to change names if they already fitted European standards of phonology. Thus, where names were close enough to a European pattern, they were simply repeated on the baptismal record. If they departed from these norms, it is likely, then, that they might be changed. Again, as in the case of the Moravian baptisms, the evidence shows that some, albeit few, African names had survived the "Europeanization" of creole culture.

In attempting to uncover the church's contribution to naming practice in the Caribbean, we might also note that those of the Methodist and Presbyterian churches among the Indian immigrants, mirror similar attitudes of the Anglicans and Moravians among the enslaved. We can identify, for example, the renaming of Ann Gill, one of the first converts to Methodism in Barbados, as Sarah Ann Gill. (She was later to be listed under that name among the national heroes of Barbados.) We note, also, the 1871 baptisms of Annajee and Balam, two Hindu converts to the Presbyterian faith, as Joseph Annajee and Thomas Balam respectively.[7] In this case, the Indian names were kept as surnames, while they were given names "appropriate" to their Christian status. There are similar suggestions in the baptisms of John Kanyapa and Margaret Terude Kanyapa into the Presbyterian faith in that same year.[8]

As seen in tables 3.3 and 3.4, a few names have some obvious African connections, such as, for example, Coobah Margaret, Mimbah Rose, Betty

Table 3.3: Baptismal Register, Yoy Slaves, St Philip's Parish Church, 1824 (River Plantation)

Name of slave	Description	Owner	Name of slave	Description	Owner
Willdo	Boy	River Pltn.	Pyramis	Boy	River Pltn.
Prince Henry	"		Homer		"
Will Daniel	"		Zachariah	"	
Judge James	"		James Thomas	"	
Frank Robin	"		Joseph	"	
Jack Gift	"		Thomas King	"	
Minimus	"		Paul	"	
Isaac Christmas	"		James William	"	
Pompey	"		Mingo	"	
Harry	"		Nelso	"	
Ned Thomas	"		Felix Elcock	"	
York	"		Adam	"	
Joe Richard	"		William Francis	"	
John Apsey	"		John James	"	
Frances	"		Joshua Bowland	"	
John Hope	"		Andrew Pierce	"	
John Edward	"		Henry Thomas	"	
Isaac Thomas	"			"	
Chance	"			"	
John Henry	"			"	
Ben Thomas	"			"	
Harry	"			"	
William Green	"			"	
William Bowland	"			"	

Source: Barbados Department of Archives

Table 3.4: Baptismal Register, Girl Slaves, St Philip's Parish Church, 1824 (property of River Plantation)

Name of Slave	Description	Owner	Name of Slave	Description	Owner
Delia Patience	Girl	River pltn.	Pamelia	Girl	River Pltn.
Ancilla	"		Mary Ann	"	
Joan	"		Threcy Ann	"	
Mary George	"		Violet	"	
Sarah Phillis	"		Eley Hope	"	
Peggy	"		Melly	"	
Polly Ann	"		Betsey	"	
Susana	"		Margaret Ann	"	
Thomasin	"		Charlotte Hester	"	
Juddy	"		Honesty	"	
Anabella	"		Henry Hope	"	
Betty Mercy	"		Cripsy Ann	"	
Betty Hester	"		Patience Rose	"	
Phythy Ann	"		Betty Anna	"	
Elizabeth	"		Gracey	"	
Mary Ann	"		Beck	"	
Hannah Grace	"		Sarey	"	
Juddy Ann	"		Charlotte Rose	"	
Nelly Patience	"		Betty Lubbah	"	
Lucinda	"		Thisby	"	
Mimbah Rose	"		Jenny Grace	"	
Sally Pathena	"		Elizabeth Ann	"	
Hannah Christmas	"		Coobah Margaret	"	
Louisa	"		Hannah Lucy	"	

Source: Barbados Department of Archives

Lubbah, Mingo and Betty Affey. In most of these cases, the African names are linked with an English name. This linkage might be used in cases where more than one slave had the same African name and the English name might have served as an identifier. Additionally, it should be noted that while there might be the occasional hint of a surname, most of the enslaved in Barbados did not receive a surname at baptism. Handler and Jacoby note that in some plantation lists slaves had double names, some of which "were possibly or probably surnames".[9]

The pattern of listing the enslaved without a surname on plantation lists is also replicated on the lists of small slaveholdings. For example, in the inventory of Susannah Ostrehan, a free biracial slave-owner of Bridgetown, Barbados (1809), we see the listing: William (a man), Joannah, Present, Henny, Nancy, Charlotte, Bettey Will, and Sarah Hannah (women), James (a boy), Ann Rose, Louisa, Patty, and Anna Bell (girls). The only hint of a possible surname is in the case of Bettey Will, although the cases of Sara Hannah, Ann Rose, and Anna Bell might also suggest a precursor to the acquisition of a surname. Another inventory, that of James Allen (1792), lists twelve enslaved with only the barest hint of a surname in the name of one man, Cuffee-George.

Given our observations on the influence of the church in the evolving naming traditions of Caribbean slave societies, we need, also, to note that not all of the enslaved were baptized and that the choice of a European name by some of the enslaved might have more to do with the prevailing norms of the dominant culture than any conversion, nominal or not. In any case, it is important to recognize that for many of the enslaved, the badge of freedom lay in adoption of aspects of that dominant culture. In much the same way that freed men and freed women owned slaves as an expression of their own freedom, some of the enslaved might have chosen European names as their way of asserting a persona. Indeed, if we take note of the evidence from Saint-Domingue, whereas some of the enslaved escaped from their bondage, many of them chose to retain or to adopt European names.

Jean Fouchard's discussion of Maroon naming practices in Saint-Domingue represents an important contribution to our understanding of acculturation in Caribbean slave societies. He observed several ways used by enslavers in choosing slave names, including "names of saints, names from the calendar, names descriptive of character or special traits, names related to geography, history, or mythology, invented names or whimsical ones, structured first names, diminutives, and ... creole and African names".[10] Additionally, some surnames might be bestowed in cases where it was necessary to distinguish between slaves with the same names, often from the same plantation.

What is of particular interest to our own study is the fact that most of the enslaved in Saint-Domingue, once freed, abandoned the names given on the plantation, and adopted the names of their European oppressors. Fouchard observes, further, that ". . . As for the purely African name, the newly freed slave dropped it with alacrity." Fouchard speculates on these issues and asks: "was [the newly freed] tempted . . . to establish his personality and his new status by presenting himself in his new life with a solid French name, more suitable from his point of view for marking his elevation and for symbolizing with legitimate vanity both satisfaction and prestige?"[11]

Fouchard's observations for Saint-Domingue may hold true for the Barbados experience. Indeed, as we look at the free coloureds there, we discover a practice that might well have informed some aspects of slave naming. All around them, the enslaved could see kin who were former slaves like themselves. In many cases, free coloureds expressed their keen awareness of slave kin and it is not unlikely that where the enslaved named themselves and their offspring after free coloured kin, this reflected an equal awareness of such family connections.

In all cases where free coloureds are listed in the local records, the names have largely lost any African connections and this Europeanized pattern might also have been adopted by some enslaved kinfolk. Its adoption suggests that the freed man and his enslaved "cousin" had analyzed the conditions of their existence and had come to the conclusion that one clear signal of the freed condition was the adoption of the naming practice of the dominant white classes. In this connection, Andrew Miller's study of naming practices in Barbados shows that the shift away from African names was in direct proportion to the levels of exposure to English culture and the educational system of the whites.[12] Table 3.5 lists the names of free coloureds in Bridgetown, where the majority of this community lived. Many of these names could be found in slave communities. Indeed, where free coloureds and whites were involved in manumission exercises, the enslaved that were to benefit from such action might be identified

Table 3.5: Names of Free Coloureds, extracted from Bridgetown, Barbados, Levy Books, 1808 (selected streets)

Cheapside St	Elizabeth Wood	Pinfold Street	Charlotte Barrow	John Eversley
John Leary	Janet Cowes	Lemon Braid	Back Church St	Patience Luke
Sarah Rogers	High St and Roebuck	Samuel Game	Hannah Gill	Charlotte Warner
Sarah Carter	Jacob Branch	Princess Pinheiro	Samuel Adams	Mary Toney
Richard Lee Sisnett	John Fercherson	William Husbands	John Cogan	William King
Prince William Henry Street	Sussanah Thorne	Canary Street	George Gill	Rebecca Lee
Elizabeth Grasset	Joseph Cummins	Nancy Clarke	Elizabeth Hoyte	John Springer
Hannah Green	Christian Hackett	Niles Sampson	Lemon Love	Thomas Moll
Christopher Denny	Jacob King	Fort Alley	James Chaplain	William Black
Christian Millington	William Bourne	William Gowdy Joslyne	Frances Blackman	Jane Walrond
Richard Lucas	Thomas Brewster	John Greene alias Free Jackey	Rebecca Bootman	Reed Street
Mary Clarke	John Springer	George Street	Mary Kennedy	Sally Simons
John Crichlow	Ann Blenman	Betty Pinder	Mary Lemon	Rebecca Hall
Amelia Barrow	Matty Sargeant	Catharine Carvallo	Susey Niles	Nelly Simmons
William Welch	Thomas Belgrave	Benjamin Alleyne	Frank Briggs	Sarah Adamson
John Gill	Robert Thorne	Church Street	Elizabeth Grace	Mary Jordan
Betty Lemon	Joseph Belgrave	Thomas Green	Phoebe Aplin	Elizabeth Dales

Table 3.5 continues

Table 3.5: *(Cont'd)*

William Weekes	Phillip Millar	John Thomas	Henrietta Moore	Thomas Carter
Marle Hill St	Mariah Conliffe	Mary Harper alias Aboab	Benjamin Bibby	London Niles
Brooks Blackman	John Thurbane	Elizabeth Goodwin	John Leary	Sally Townsend
Amey Savery	Matty Ryan	Ann Jordan	Susanna Gill	James Ball
John Martin	James Mascoll	Mary Bosden	Nancy Yard	Thomas Thompson
Richard Lucas	Prescilla Donnell	Kathy Ann Carter	John Solomon	The Bay
Sarah Ryan	James Street	John Grogan	Mary Wiles	James Humphrey
Renn Jordan	Molly King	Sarah Kirton	Jane Thompson	Maria Johnstone
Kitty Sealy	William R. Jordan	Hannah Valverde	Tudor Street	Nathaniel Bovell
Amaryllis Collymore		John Gill	Jacob Briggs	Ann Fisher
Elizabeth Vaux		Grace Yard	Mary Roach	Molly Hester

Source: St Michael's Vestry, Levy Books, 1808, Barbados Department of Archives

with an alias or with a surname descriptor that tied him or her into the lineage of the former.

It may be noted that the free coloureds listed in table 3.5 have surnames, a feature that reflects several influences. In some cases, surnames were acquired through marriage with other free coloureds; in other cases, surnames were adopted from white or free coloured lovers and benefactors, in which cases, the names were often adopted directly from enslavers. In yet other circumstances, such names were adopted from kin who either had acquired these names after manumission or held them by right of descent from a free ancestor. Of some interest is the fact that some surnames, for example, Carvallo, Pinheiro, Valverde, are influenced by the Sephardic Jewish community which was resident in Bridgetown. Whatever the origin, it is useful to note that in many cases these surnames were acquired by the recently manumitted, a fact which might say something about the expectations of the enslaved with respect to naming once they were freed.[13]

Against the background that we have explored in the preceding paragraphs, we are facilitated in exploring naming practices as an adjustment to the new possibilities brought about by emancipation. The formerly enslaved had generations of an acculturative practice during which naming models had been developed. What we must avoid at all costs as our attention is shifted to the post-1834 situation is any accusation that the forebears of the current Afro-Caribbean population had sold out their birthright by adopting European naming norms.

POST-EMANCIPATION NAMING PRACTICES

The immediate post-emancipation years presented a period of adjustments for the ex-slaves. In particular, we will note that there were opportunities for re-constituting family relationships. In many cases, the formerly enslaved sought to legitimize concubinage relationships by marriage. In some of the denominations, marriage was only permitted if the partners were members of the church. Thus, adult baptisms were common. The baptisms provided an opportunity for persons to acquire new names or to have old ones recorded and legitimized. However, it must be noted that in the first years of freedom, old practices died hard and baptisms were conducted in some cases without surnames being adopted or recorded. It appears that in the dominant Anglican tradition, there was more adherence to the old folkways in the immediate post-emancipation years than in the Moravian and Methodist churches. Tables 3.6, 3.7 and 3.8 illustrate some of the issues which have been introduced here.

As the data in the tables is analyzed, several things begin to emerge. In the first place, it may be noted that family relationships are being defined more closely. In tables 3.6 and 3.8, the father is identified in a way that was rare on the slave plantation. Moreover, the surnames adopted or held by the father are being applied to sons and daughters. In table 3.6, for example, Jack Thomas is being defined in relation to his son, John Thomas. Similarly, Edward Haynes Bledman is connected to his father, William Bledman. In table 3.8, the naming protocols of the slave period appear to predominate; however, surnames are beginning to appear with greater frequency.

Table 3.6: Baptisms of Apprenticed Ex-slaves, 1834–1835 (Moravian Register)

Name	Mother	Employer	Father	Employer	Year of Baptism
Edward Simon	Catharine	Wests	Joe	Arthur Seat	1834
William Alleyne	Charlotte	Moores	Sam	Harding	1834
Samuel Richard	Catharine	William Mayers	Henry	Welches	1834
Thomas Daniel	Christiana	Padmore	Renn Thomas	Straker (Yorkshall)	1834
Henry William	Molly Lilly	Jackson	Acrow	Jackson	1834
George	Priscilla	Mr Gilks	Matt	Clifton	1834
Richard Thomas	Priscilla	Mr Gilks	Matt	Clifton	1834
Joseph Sampson	Priscilla	Mr Gilks	Matt	Clifton	1834
Benjamin Richard	Philo Ann	Mt Wilton	Will John	Mt Wilton	1835
William Thomas	Mercy Catharine	Cliften	Anthony Robert	Seaill Savory (free)	1835
Henry James	Matilda	Warrens	Quaco Niblet	Lodge	1834
John Thomas	Ruthy	Warrens	Jack Thomas	Poole	1835
Daniel Jones	Charity	Mt Wilton	Daniel	Mt Wilton	1835
Renn Thomas	Agnes	Warrens	Anthony	Whites	1835
Jacob Isaac (twins)	Tina	Bagatelle	Quash	Bagatelle	1835
Edward Haynes Bledman	Mary Isabella	Mt Wilton	William Bledman	Mt Wilton	1835

Source: Extracted from the Moravian baptismal register, Barbados Department of Archives

Table 3.7: Baptisms of Ex-slave Apprentices, St Philip's Parish Church, 1836

Name	Parent's Christian name/ surname	Abode	Quality/trade or Profession
John Crawford	Adult	Miss Crawford	Apprenticed labourer
William	Adult	Miss Crawford	Apprenticed labourer
Richmond	Adult	Groves	Apprenticed labourer
William	Adult	Mr William Lord's	Apprenticed labourer
Henry	Adult/Gittens	Mr William Lord's	Carpenter
John Richard	Adult	Mr J.F. Woods	Apprenticed labourer
William Edward	Anna Maria	Chapel	Apprenticed labourer
Louisa Newsam	Fanny Frances	Chapel	Apprenticed labourer
William Henry	Rachael	Chapel	Apprenticed labourer
Francis Augustus	Robert and Rossana/ Elder	Chapel & Mt Pleasant	Apprenticed labourer
Elizabeth Rose	Mary Thomas	Hampton	Apprenticed labourer
Sarah Elizabeth	Lubbah	Oughterson	Apprenticed labourer
Edward Muller	Polly Ann	Oughterson	Apprenticed labourer
John King	Adult	Summer Vale	Apprenticed labourer
Joanna	Adult	Congo Road	Apprenticed labourer
Christopher Frances	Flower	Mt Pleasant	Apprenticed labourer
Frances Jane	Jezebel	Carrington	Apprenticed labourer

Table 3. 7 continues

Table 3.7: (cont'd)

Name	Parent's Christian name/ surname	Abode	Quality/trade or Profession
Sarah Mary	Jezebel	Carrington	Apprenticed labourer
Rose Ann	Susannah	Oughterson	Apprenticed labourer
Samson Stanley	Hannah Rettah	Mr J. Gooding	Apprenticed labourer
Cato	Thomasin	Mr J. Gooding	Apprenticed labourer
Thomas Isaac	Maria	Little Diamond	Apprenticed labourer
Rebecca	Maria	Little Diamond	Apprenticed labourer
Mary Rebecca	James Thomas and Suckey Rinah	Halton	Apprenticed labourer
James Forte	Bacchus & Dido Eve	Sunbury	Apprenticed labourer
Daniel	Adult	Summer Vale	Apprenticed labourer
Easter Crawford	Adult	Miss K.R. Crawford	Apprenticed labourer
Henry Quash	Adult	Summer Vale	Apprenticed labourer
Elizabeth	Maria	Little Diamond	Apprenticed labourer

Source: Extracted from St Philip's Parish Church baptismal records, Barbados Department of Archives

The Impact of Christianity on Naming Practices in Post-Emancipation Barbados

Table 3.8: Baptisms of Apprentices and Ex-slaves, Methodist Church, 1835–1839

Child's name	Parents	Surname	Abode/year of baptism
James (son of)	Paul and Nanny	Spencer	Speightstown/1835
Dorothy Jane (daughter of)	Goodridge Haw and Cumberbatch		Speightstown/1835
Mimba	Belgrave	Adult	Speightstown/1835
Mary	Scantlebury	Adult	Speightstown/1835
Maria	Croydon	Adult	Speightstown/1836
Thomas	Chandler	Adult	Reeds Bay/1838
Charlotte (daughter of)	James Hayes and Dutchess Cornwall		Bridgetown/1838
Alphaeus	Chandler	Adult	Reeds Bay/1838
Ann	Gilkes	Adult	Mullins/1838
Margaret	Bearcroft	Adult	Hammonds Estate/1838
Mary Ann	Gibbons	Adult	Hammonds Estate/1838
Peter	Gibbons	Adult	Hammonds Estate/1838
Samuel (son of)	Richard and Kelly		Speightstown/1838
Hagar	Farley	Adult	Speightstown/1839
Maria	Niles	Adult	Speightstown/1839
Samuel Francis (son of)	Peter and Joanna	Archer Ward	Speightstown/1839
John Edward (son of)	Edward and Joanna	Lawrence (deceased) Ward	Speightstown/1839

Table 3.8 continues

Table 3.8: (cont'd)

Child's name	Parents	Surname	Abode/year of baptism
William Henry (son of)	Edward and Joanna	Lawrence Ward	Speightstown/1839
Maria	Gibbons	Adult	Hammonds Estate/1839
Lilly	Coulthurst	Adult	Walley's Estate/1839
Mary Ann	Maloney	Adult	1839
George	Boyce	Adult	1839
Kate		Adult	1839
Elsy	Gibbons	Adult	1839
Thomas Henry	Cumberbatch	Adult	1839
Amelia Ann	Sandiford	Adult	1839
Polly Kitty	Porter	Adult	1839

Source: Extracted from the Methodist Church baptismal records, Barbados Department of Archives

In table 3.8, under the heading 'Parents', names are listed in the baptismal record for adults, which might represent the acquisition of a surname, or an attempt by the formerly enslaved to identify parents by surnames. In many cases, however, for all of the denominations represented, a single name is often recorded for both the baptized and for parents. The full acquisition of Christian forenames with surnames as identifiers took some time to achieve commonality, and in marriage and baptismal records up to the 1880s may be found remnants of the naming practice which had characterized the slave period. In some families, as the following case study illustrates, individuals took decisive steps to establish their identities through the acquisition of surnames and to consolidate the process of emancipation.

The genealogical line which links Thomas Henry Drakes and his wife, Catharine Jane, to a contemporary Barker clan (the clan to which yours truly belongs on the maternal side of my family) might well be typical of the Afro-Barbadian family after emancipation.[14] Thomas Henry was born as a slave in the parish of St Andrew sometime around 1809. Like many other enslaved kin, he had never had his name regularized or recorded in the local registry. However, in 1851, just thirteen years after legal emancipation, he planned to marry his sweetheart, Catharine Jane. There was one obstacle: he needed to have his name legalized and to connect with the Anglican Church where the marriage was to take place. Thus, on 1 March 1851, in an event listed as an "adult christening", he received official, legal confirmation of his name.[15] It is not clear why he had chosen the name Drakes, but the proliferation of the name Drakes in the baptismal records of the parish of St Andrew and the neighbouring parish, St Thomas, in the period between 1850 and 1881 is strongly suggestive of a kinship structure with its ancestral roots in those locations.

Thomas Drakes' wife, Catharine Jane, is not listed with a surname at the time of the marriage, a feature which, again, reveals the influence of the pre-emancipation naming protocols. However, in later documents which name the children of this couple, her maiden name is given as West. A thorough search of the baptismal records did not turn up a baptism in the name of Catharine Jane West, which might fit her profile. However, a Catharine Jane West was baptized in 1806, the daughter of an Ann West and a Reynold Pittekins in the parish of St John. The baptismal record indicates that the birth took place out of wedlock. The date of the recorded names of the parents, the absence of a racial descriptor and the location (by the early 1800s most poor whites lived in St John or Bridgetown) suggest that this couple was of poor white origin. In that case, Catharine Jane of 1806 might well be the parent of our Catharine Jane of 1851. Oral tradition among the descendants of Thomas Henry Drakes records that his wife was "almost white".

The union of Thomas and Catharine Jane produced seven children, Phyllis Jane (1852), Sarah Jane (1854), John William (1856), Elizabeth Jane (1857), Benjamin (1858), Joseph Henry (1860), and Catharine (1862). In each case, the child is baptized with the surname Drakes, thus, irrevocably, linking the Drakes name with this clan. However, the saga does not end there. Elizabeth Jane Drakes had a child christened as Angelina Drakes in 1874, four years before she marries James William Bishop. When Angelina marries Samuel Christopher Barker in 1898, she lists her surname as Bishop. In turn, her husband lists his surname as Barker, although the baptismal register shows that he was baptized as Samuel Christopher Hall and that his mother had never married a Barker. In this case, oral history sources show that both Samuel Christopher and one sister, Catharine Elfrida Hall, were born out of wedlock to Mary Frances Hall and a Samuel

Christopher Barker (senior). Later, Mary Frances had other children christened with the surname Hall, before her marriage to William Frances Sharpe, for whom she had three children registered as Sharpe. In respect of Angelina and Samuel (junior), there was a deliberate attempt to claim their paternal surnames and to have them registered for posterity. By the time their son, Frank Herbert Barker, was born in 1906, the Barker name had been tied, fully, to the descendants of this couple.

The experience of Thomas Henry Drakes and Catharine Jane West is repeated too many times in various records to be accidental. For example, in the marriage records for the St Philip, St George, St James and St John parishes, for the period between 1838 and 1844, several marriages are recorded in which the bride has no prior surname. In the majority of cases, the bridegroom has adopted a surname, a fact which is highly suggestive of a solution devised under the auspices of the church. It is quite possible that the wedding is preceded by a baptism or, at the very least, the bridegroom has chosen a surname for the purpose of satisfying the norms of a church wedding ceremony. Thus, in the following representative sample of weddings at the St Philip parish church, we see the pattern from 1838 to 1839. However, by the 1840s, marriages with both partners reporting surnames had become more common:

Table 3.9: Sample of Marriages at St Philip's Parish Church, 1838–1839

Bride-groom	Bride	Date of marriage	Bride-groom	Bride	Date of marriage
Frank Saunders	Lucy Ann	23/7/1838	Quashey Wall	Louisa	18/7/1839
Richard	Madame	28/7/1838	Anthony Payne	Rosanna Edgehill	23/7/1842
Issac Nile	Bella	18/8/1838	Joseph Clarke	Mary Chaplain	28/7/1844
Richard Moore	Leonora	01/9/1838	Thomas Thornhill	Elizabeth Bryant	30/7/1844
James McCartney	Margaret Dottin	28/2/1839	Joseph Ashby	Sarah Gooding	02/8/1844

Source: Compiled from St Philip's marriage register, Barbados Department of Archives

REFLECTIONS

In each of the cases discussed above, the church appears to have a major role in the renaming exercise which characterizes the post-emancipation period. Through baptismal and marriage ceremonies, the church is helping to consolidate the dominant Judeo-Christian culture – one which had contributed to the norms and mores of creole society. The names that were chosen by the formerly enslaved and their descendants were common to English and Western European Christian culture. The adoption of these names shows, perhaps, more than anything else, the effect of acculturation on the descendants of the enslaved Africans. There were still some remnants of that African culture among Afro-Barbadians, but with respect to naming practices, this has largely disappeared. What seems clear is that the naming and kinship models which characterized the pre-emancipation period disappeared slowly over time. Thus, in the baptismal register of St Luke's Anglican Church in 1844, we find the following: Thomasin, daughter of Hariett; Lucy Francis, daughter of Leonora; Nancy June, daughter of Henrietta; Pallas Grace, daughter of Hariett; James Prescod, son of Resa; and John Robert, son of Isabel. In many of these cases, the acquisition of a surname and the acknowledgment of paternity came later, at marriage, when either a bride or a bridegroom adopted the paternal surname. In all of these cases, the naming practice adopted may represent, on the part of the formerly enslaved and their descendants, an assertion of their right to an identification associated with free status. Additionally, naming practice in the post-emancipation period might well represent an effort to restore family and kinship links that enslavers had attempted to negate in the earlier pre-emancipation period.

NOTES

1. Jerome S. Handler and JoAnn Jacoby, "Slave Names and Naming in Barbados, 1650–1830," *William and Mary Quarterly* 53, no. 4 (1996): 685–728.
2. Richard Dunn, *Sugar and Slaves* (Kingston: University of the West Indies Press, 2000), 252.
3. James Walvin, *An African's Life: The Life and Times of Olaudah Equiano, 1745–1797* (New York: Cassell, 1998), 31.

4. Brace's experiences are found in a narrative entitled the "The Blind African Slave", apparently dictated by this slave in his old age to Benjamin Franklin. The manuscript is the property of the University of North Carolina at Chapel Hill and may be extracted online at http://docsouth.dsi.internet2.edu/neh/brinch/brinch.html.
5. The baptisms of these persons are reported in J. Taylor Hamilton and Kenneth G. Hamilton, *History of the Moravian Church: The Renewed Unitas Fratrum, 1722–1957* (Pennsylvania: International Board of Christian Education, Moravian Church in America, 1967), 47, 48.
6. See S.U. Hastings and B.L. MacLeavy, *Seedtime and Harvest: A Brief History of the Moravian Church in Jamaica 1754–1979* (Kingston: Moravian Church Corporation, 1979), 27.
7. Sarah E. Morton, ed., *John Morton of Trinidad: Pioneer Missionary of the Presbyterian Church in Canada to the East Indians in the British West Indies* (Toronto: Westminster, 1916), 78–80.
8. ibid.
9. Handler and Jacoby, "Slave Names," 721.
10. Jean Fouchard, *The Haitian Maroons: Liberty or Death*, trans. A Faulkner Watts (New York: Edward W. Blyden Press, 1981), 181.
11. ibid., 185.
12. Andrew L. Miller, "Naming in Barbados: Proper Names, A Historical and Philosophical Analysis of Personal and Place Names in Barbados, 1627–2000" (unpublished research paper, University of the West Indies, Cave Hill, 2001), 47.
13. Neville Hall's discussion of naming practice among the free coloureds of the Danish West Indies suggests that in naming themselves after Europeans, the freed man might well have been expressing some defiance towards the conventions that whites sought to impose. See Neville A.T. Hall, *Slave Society in the Danish West Indies* (Kingston: University of the West Indies Press, 1992), 148. A useful source for following the practice among free coloureds in Barbados is Jerome Handler, Ronald Hughes, and Ernest Wiltshire, *Freedmen of Barbados: Names and Notes for Genealogical and Family History Research* (Charlottesville: Virginia Foundation for the Humanities, 2007).
14. The genealogical data for this family is extracted from the birth and baptismal, marriage and death records of the Barbados Department of Archives.
15. Baptismal record, St Andrew Parish Church, Barbados Department of Archives.

[Part Two]

LAW, JUSTICE AND EMPIRE

[4]

FROM UNICAMERALISM TO BICAMERALISM
Trinbago Constitutional Advances (1831–1962)

[BRINSLEY SAMAROO]

"BUT WHY, IT MAY BE ASKED, SHOULD TRINIDAD not govern itself as well as Tasmania or New Zealand? Why not Jamaica, why not all the West Indian islands? . . . Responsible government in Trinidad means government by a black parliament and a black ministry."[1]

At this time, when the citizens of Trinidad and Tobago are engaged in the process of constitution-making, it is necessary that we should look back at the process of governance of which we are the present inheritors. In this, we shall look at the philosophy which propelled the process. The British Empire was not created by chance; from the time of conquest there were clear directions which drove the whole process. The nineteenth century was particularly important for the setting out of these directives; hence, a good deal of our time will be devoted to British ontology at that time. As the empire moved into the twentieth century, the nineteenth-century way of seeing became more entrenched. As circumstances in the colonies changed, there were variations on the theme, and when the Colonial Office gradually gave independence to these colonies from the 1960s, they hobbled these new nations with constitutions rooted in one hundred years of colonial control. The psychology of that control is what we must understand if we are to break out of the box into which all Caribbean governments have been locked.

Early British colonization during the sixteenth and seventeenth centuries operated on the premise that colonies were extensions of the home country and should therefore be governed as the metropolis was constructed. Therefore, early colonial government was called the Old Representative System (ORS) in which there was representative government, that is, legislatures in which elected members formed the majority in law-making assemblies, generally presided over by the governor who represented the monarch. As table 4.1 shows, most Caribbean governments were devised in this manner, including Tobago, which obtained its elected assembly in July 1778, appropriately named the Tobago House of Assembly (THA). This honeymoon between mother country and distant colonies could not last forever. The revolt of the American colonies during the late eighteenth century was the first rude shock which started a change in metropolitan thinking. After this uprising of "ungrateful" American colonists, the colonial office determined that more stringent controls were needed. The government of Trinidad had to be devised at the time when there was another cataclysmic event taking place in the Caribbean, namely the revolution in St Domingue. In framing a government for new colonies such as Trinidad and St Lucia, Mr George Canning, a major policymaker in the British parliament, warned

Table 4.1: Constitutional Transitions, 1663–1889

Colony	Old Representative System	Crown colony	Remarks
Jamaica	1663	1866	
St Kitts	1663	1866	
Montserrat	1663	1866	
Tobago	1768	1877	1874: reduced from a bicameral legislature to a unicameral legislature 1877: Crown colony 1889: united administratively with Trinidad 1889: made a ward of Trinidad & Tobago
Grenada	1766	1875	
St Vincent	1766	1877	
St Lucia	Nil	1803	
Trinidad	Nil	1803	
British Honduras	1853	1870	

Source: Adapted from Hume Wrong, *Government of the West Indies* (Oxford: Clarendon Press, 1923); reprinted (New York: Negro University Press, 1969), 80–81.

his colleagues of the danger that had to be met: "Would the moral danger be best guarded by having established a new Negro colony by increased importations from Africa? One would have to dread the population as much as the enemy; a population which, while you defended it with one hand, you must keep it down with the other."[2]

In order to keep the black population under control, therefore, the myth was created that democratic government was the prerogative of white English settlers in the first instance. When sufficient numbers of these could not be found, other white Europeans from central and northern Europe or Iberia could be allowed to shore up the white population, as in the cases of Canada, South Africa, Australia and New Zealand. As in the case of slavery, it was necessary to salve the consciences of doubting Thomases. Some of Britain's most eminent nineteenth-century scholars felt obliged to fill this gap. The English essayist Anthony Trollope, a well-respected guru among the validating British elite, visited Trinidad in 1859 as part of a Caribbean tour and was very pleased to see the operation of Pure Crown colony there: "They have no House of Commons or Legislative Assembly, but take such rules or laws as may be necessary from the Crown . . . One does see clearly enough that as they are French in language and habits and Roman Catholic in religion, they would make even a worse hash of it [representative government] than the Jamaicans do in Jamaica."[3]

Trollope hoped that providence would save his Trinidad friends from assemblies as "would be returned by French Negroes and hybrid mulattoes".[4] After the Indian revolt of 1857, the British attitude toward non-white colonies hardened. On 26 July 1858, the Earl of Newcastle told the House of Lords that responsible government, that is, government in which ministers or heads of department are responsible to an elected majority, was applicable only to colonists of the English race. In 1906, Walsh Wrightson, Director of Public Works, after whom a major Port of Spain thoroughfare had been named, gave his take on the suitability of colonials to participate in government: "The people of Port of Spain and of the colony generally are not fitted by their personnel qualities, character and education to exercise such an important privilege of self-government on English lines . . . It would appear that in the tropics the great mass of the people have not that energy, self-reliance and determination to be masters of their own destiny which characterized the people of Great Britain."[5]

On his visit to Trinidad in 1888, James Anthony Froude, Professor of Modern History at Oxford University, a training ground for British officials, scoffed at those Trinidad radicals who wanted representative government. He was happy, he wrote, that Trinidad was a pure Crown colony and had hitherto escaped the introduction of the election virus, "If for the sake of theory, or to shirk responsibility we force them to govern themselves, the state of Hayti stands as a ghastly example of the condition into which they will then inevitably fall."[6]

Froude was one of the major influences on Joseph Chamberlain, Secretary of State from 1895 to 1906, during which time the Port of Spain City Council was shut down and replaced by nominated town commissioners. But these cogently argued strictures against the exercise of governance by non-white people in the Caribbean, Africa, Fiji, Mauritius and India did not apply to the white-ruled colonies. Between 1850 and 1855, responsible government was given to Upper and Lower Canada, Nova Scotia, Prince Edward Island and Newfoundland. During the 1850s, New South Wales, Tasmania, South Australia and Victoria were granted representative assemblies, followed by New Zealand and British Columbia. The opposite route was followed in the case of the non-white colonies. The majority of these colonies, which had earlier been granted assemblies under the Old Representative System, reverted to Crown colony status once a pretext could be found. The 1865 Morant Bay rebellion in Jamaica, for example, was a perfect excuse, and in the case of the Windward and Leeward Islands, black unrest, such as the Belmanna riot in Tobago in 1876, and the need for administrative efficiency, were convenient excuses. By the end of the nineteenth century, only Barbados, the Bahamas and Bermuda remained under the Old Representative System. Barbados, for its part, would have preferred to part company with a black Caribbean. In 1884, it sought union with Canada, which itself was wary about a black influx into its borders.

During the nineteenth century, Trinidad was held up as a model of Crown colony government, which set the tone for the abolition of legislative assemblies in the Windward and Leeward Islands, hence the detachment of Tobago from the Windward Islands Federation in 1889 and its attachment to Trinidad. Tobago had a bicameral legislature since July 1778, but this was gradually whittled away, first in 1874 when one chamber was removed; then three years later, even that was abandoned as Tobago was made a Crown colony. We must also bear in mind that what was happening in the Caribbean during that period was part of an international scenario, often described as the heyday of imperialism. During the last quarter of the nineteenth century, Europe, bolstered by the achievements of the Industrial Revolution, was carving out spheres of influence throughout the tropical world, with major inroads into China, India, Malaya and the Philippines. The year 1885 witnessed the partition of Africa by European overlords, who sat in faraway Berlin in front of maps and shared out the continent – without any regard for cultures that spanned both sides of a river or a mountain. These very arbitrary decisions would cause serious havoc in Africa during the twentieth and twenty-first centuries. The bard of British poets, Rudyard Kipling, urged fellow white men to persist in these efforts, despite the opposition of the victims, who were "half-devil and a half-child":

Take up the White man's burden –
And reap his old reward:
The blame of those ye better,
The hate of those ye guard –
The cry of hosts ye humour
(Ah, slowly!) toward the light: –
"Why brought ye us from bondage,
"Our loved Egyptian night?"[7]

The celebrated English essayist and public philosopher, Thomas Carlyle, was among those whose support was courted for justification of British racism. In a published and republished pamphlet on "The Nigger Question", he claimed that he had nought but deep sympathy for "poor Quashee", who "alone of wild men can live among men civilized". He now, "lives and multiplies and evidently means to abide among us, if we can find the right regulation for him".[8] While he could accept the principle of one man, one vote, he could not envisage equality between the vote of a "Demerara nigger" and a Chancellor Bacon. Whites should always rule over blacks because they could not stand the heat of the tropics. The fortunate black man was much better off than the less fortunate white man of those tropical "localities".[9] This inability of white persons to work in tropical climates was another popular nineteenth-century argument to justify white dominance and to keep the labouring population away from education, which might encourage them to aspire for jobs above their station.

Having widely dispersed these arguments through their control of the media, the European governments moved to other devices to establish political control. Most significant in this regard was the policy of divide and rule, along lines of the ancient Roman mode, *Divide et Impera*. The Indian revolt of 1857 taught a salutary lesson to the British, who had come close to defeat because of the unity between Hindus and Muslims. From thenceforth, every effort was made to keep Muslims apart from Hindus, even to the extent of allowing communal representation on state assemblies on the subcontinent. The success of the policy was amply demonstrated in the 1947 partition of India, accompanied as it was by rivers of blood and the never-ending conflict with what is now Pakistan. The same policy was used in West Africa, Cyprus and Fiji, where "Race relations were a reflection of British colonial policy, viewing and treating ethnic Fijians and Indo-Fijians differently and minimizing contact between the two groups."[10]

In Trinidad, that policy of divide and rule predated 1857. In 1806, the Governor's Council of Advice counselled the Colonial Office to continue to encourage labourers, with the exception of those who were black, to immigrate to the colony after the arrival of 194 Chinese in that year. These Chinese would be useful as a counterpoise to the Africans, thus forestalling the "baneful and destructive" consequences of the "establishment of the Black Empire of Haiti and St. Domingo".[11] In 1897, a Trinidad planter was totally frank in informing the Royal Commission of that year that he needed more "coolies" to be a counterpoise to black uprising. In 1919, Trinidad and Tobago's leading white oligarch, George Huggins, headed a petition to the Crown lamenting the end of Indian indentureship, since the Indians could have been used as a counterpoise, but "now, they may even join the black mob".[12]

While they kept the races apart, the rulers portrayed themselves as impartial referees between the major sparring groups. They "bowed" to the black demand for representation in the wholly nominated legislature by appointing a Cedros-born lawyer, C.P. David, to the legislature in 1904. When the Indians complained, one of their lawyers, George Fitzpatrick, was appointed in 1912. During the discussion leading to the drawing up of the 1946 Trinidad and Tobago constitution, the validating white elite did all in its power to exclude the Indian population from participating in the electoral process by insisting on English language tests for all prospective voters. Despite strong protests from local groups, such as the trade union movement, and Colonial Office persuasion, the local oligarchy persisted in its efforts to debar another non-white group from participating in power relations. It was only through the insistence of the Secretary of State that the English language requirement was dropped.[13]

This then was the theoretical framework that formed the backdrop for constitutional change in Trinidad and Tobago during the twentieth century. Before going on to the actual process of change, I will share my insights into what I suggest are the major features of the 'pure' Crown Colony system which had evolved here for more than a century. Its major features, which have persisted to the present day, were the following:

a. Strong, centralized, undemocratic control exercised by the governor who, in C.L.R. James' view, was father, son and Holy Ghost. From 1962, Eric Williams became the new 'governor', in a sense, ruling with a paternal but firm hand until his death in 1981. His successors followed suit; that was the only tradition to which they were accustomed. Lloyd Best called it "Doctor politics".

b. The population came to accept a strong leader, who was expected to be in total control, micromanaging the affairs of state. From the time of conquest in 1797, the population was socialized into an acceptance of maximum leadership.

c. There was also the indigenization of the Westminster model to conform to existing cleavages in the society. In places like Cyprus, Fiji, Trinidad and Tobago, and British Guiana, the previously encouraged ethnic antagonism fostered by *divide et impera* led naturally to the formation of ethnic or communal parties, despite the best efforts of enlightened leaders to break this mould. In Guyana, Cheddi Jagan, fully aware of the ethnic tensions, sought to create a united nation by stressing class rather than ethnic solidarity. In India, Gandhi did his utmost to unite Hindus and Muslims, only to be assassinated by a Hindu fanatic; and Williams initially made serious efforts to heal the breach in Trinidad and Tobago. After some years, realizing the depth of the cleavage, he gave up and further cleavage occurred. History has been stronger than noble intentions.[14]

THE EVOLUTION OF CENTRAL GOVERNMENT

As figure 4.1 shows, Trinidad – as a separate colony from Tobago – was initially administered by the Spanish *cabildo,* presided over by a governor. Upon conquest in 1797, the island was first ruled by a British governor up to 1803, when a Council of Advice was installed. In 1831, the first legislature, called the Council of Government, was introduced. This council consisted of nominated officials, such as the Chief Justice, Colonial Secretary, Colonial Treasurer, Attorney General, Collector of Customs and the Protector of Slaves, who was replaced after 1845 by the Protector of Immigrants. These same officials constituted the Governor's Executive Council, created in 1831. Very soon, however, the Council of Government underwent quantitative changes. In response to agitation by the local elite for a share in governance, a window was opened up in the Council of Government for unofficial, that is, non-governmental employees to participate at a high colonial level.

This opening up was achieved through the inclusion of increasing numbers of merchants and planters over the decades. While this concession was given to Britain's tropical colonies, it was granted under the strict and

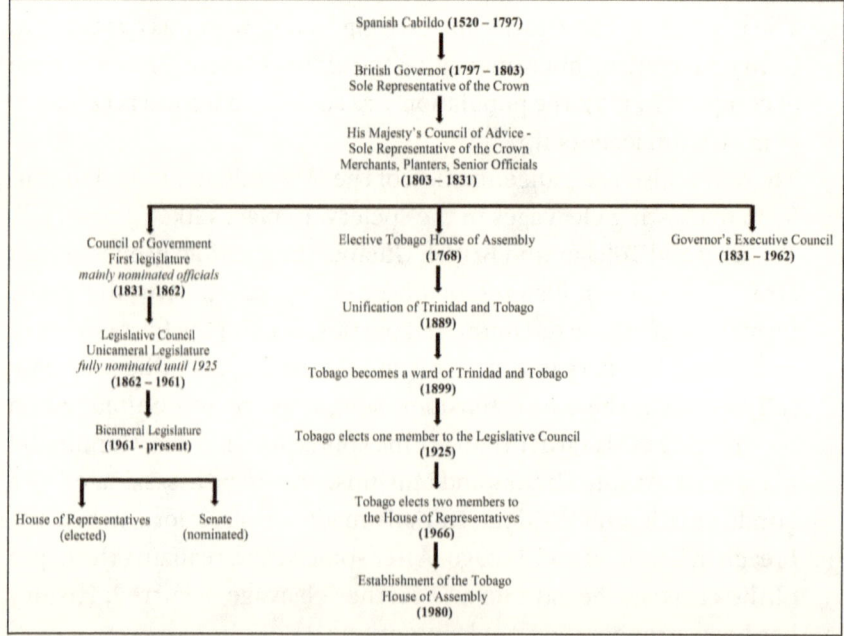

Figure 4.1. The Evolution of Central Government in Trinidad and Tobago

often repeated condition that should the unofficials ever band together to oppose the government, efforts would be made to increase the number of officials so as to avoid disruption of the wishes of the government. As late as October 1956, just over a century after its introduction in Trinidad, the Colonial Office was cautioning the governors of the Windward and Leeward Islands, British Honduras, British Guiana and Mauritius to maintain Crown control by avoiding "so close a balance between the government and opposition so as to make the operations of government difficult".[15] In the meantime, Trinidad and Tobago had to tread the tortuous route of strict colonial control. From 1831 to 1862, there were six officials and six unofficials, with the governor as presiding officer holding an original as well as a casting vote, ensuring state dominance. In 1863, two unofficials were added, giving them a majority, but with the warning that if they voted as a bloc, officials would be added. With the accession of Tobago in 1889, one Tobago unofficial was added and two officials were appointed, one of whom was to be the Commissioner for Tobago. By the end of the nineteenth century, it was found that after the addition of French Creoles[16] and coloured proponents of reform, that unofficials were banding together to oppose the government. Therefore, one official was added in 1898 to counter this tendency. Thus, there were now ten officials and eleven unofficials, with the governor having two votes.

As late as the first election of 1925, the Legislative Council consisted of twelve officials and thirteen unofficials (seven now elected) with the governor as arbitrator. As the number of elected unofficials was increased after that time, and the number of officials reduced, the power to govern was increasingly shifted to the governor and the Executive Council. The 1940s and 1950s were years of intense political activity, and one of the issues at the forefront was the ending of the appointment of nominated persons to the legislature. But such a concession could not be granted to a non-white tropical colony. In 1949, Secretary of State Arthur Creech Jones informed the politicians that at "this stage in the development of Trinidad and Tobago", the nominated element could not be dispensed "without seriously disturbing confidence in the economic and financial stability of the colony". By 1956, in the view of the Colonial Office, this situation had not changed.[17] Nominated members were to be maintained so as to "strengthen experience and knowledge of the Council in dealing with the complex issues of government".[18]

THE FINAL STRUGGLE FOR BICAMERALISM

On 22 September 1961, the unicameral legislature of the colony was dissolved, 130 years after its initiation in 1831. In his report for September 1961, Governor Solomon Hochoy noted: "And so ended the life of the legislature which, by the enactment of many far-reaching measures, contributed substantially to the constitutional, political, economic and social advancement of the people of this territory. It also marks the end of the uni-cameral system and the dawn of the era of full internal government."[19]

The first senate of the bicameral parliament met on 29 December 1961. This historic landmark, however, was not easily achieved. The colony had, over its long period of pure Crown colony government, become so used to the paternal, dominating hand of the Crown that change was hard to accept. The *Trinidad Guardian* in July 1955 argued that it was pointless to change a system to which people have grown accustomed, particularly on the eve of federation. Crown colony government, too, had allowed the hardening of vested interests, particularly in oil and sugar, and these interests were fearful of a change in their status. A constitutional reform committee set up in January 1955 had recommended the retention of unicameralism with more elected members and ministers, and the retention of nominated officials and unofficials with the strictures which we have previously discussed. This conservative tide was reversed and public opinion was galvanized through a vigorous campaign waged by Eric Williams during the months of July and August 1955. From the middle of July to the beginning of August, the People's Education Movement of the Teacher's Economic and Cultural Association hosted no fewer than eight public meetings in places such as Sangre Grande, Couva, Arima, Fyzabad and Point Fortin. To a people whose opinions were hardly ever canvassed by politicians, these university-type lectures were enthusiastically received. In these lectures, the historian traced the evolution of democratic systems from the time of the Greek city-state to the present. He pointed out that in the United Kingdom, the mother of parliament, bicameralism was the norm and the framers of the 1776 American Constitution had opted for two chambers. Most pertinently, he cited a 1957 British Guiana Constitutional Commission Report submitted by three prominent British academics, which had recommended a bicameral legislature for that colony.[20]

The reasons for that recommendation were effectively used by Williams as he argued his Trinidad and Tobago case. Among these were the provision of a pool of experienced persons in various areas of endeavour, who could rise above the political fray in matters of national interest; the enabling of the expression of the public will by the removal of the nominated element from the elected chamber; and in place of the irritant of a nominated block, the upper chamber could provide a constitutional check through its delaying powers. Two chambers would also provide a deep pool of potential Cabinet members and could be the basis for further evolution of democratic self-government. With his usual thoroughness, Williams circulated a petition, signed by thousands, to the Colonial Office calling for the institution of a bicameral legislature. Williams' senate was to be a sixteen-member chamber made up of the following elements:[21] oil, sugar, commerce, cocoa, shipping, and local industries – six members; religious heads: Roman Catholic, Anglican, Hindu, Muslim, and one for other faiths – five members; three ex officio members: the Chief Justice, the Colonial Secretary and the Attorney General; two men or women of distinction appointed by the governor.

The Colonial Office, in the short term, decided not to go with Williams' recommendation of bicameralism, but rather with that of the 1955 Constitution Reform Committee. Therefore, the 1956 elections were fought on the basis of a single chamber comprised of twenty-four elected members, five nominated unofficials and two officials. It was only after the victory of his People's National Movement (PNM) that Williams was able to put into effect the movement for bicameralism.[22] Ensconced in office, the PNM appointed a select committee in 1958, consisting of a majority of the PNM legislators. This committee recommended a bicameral legislature, with the senate consisting of the same elements that Williams had proposed in 1955. In 1962, the final composition was to be twenty-four members. Based on the criteria used, thirteen were selected from the ruling party and four from the Opposition.

The senate did not have the power to delay money bills, but could delay other bills for no more than one year or two consecutive sessions. It must be noted that the prime minister now obtained a Crown colony dominance over the senate, similar to what he had over the elected chamber. As Hamid Ghany points out, the office of the Governor-General on the independence of the nation "was the weakest that had been created in the Commonwealth up to that time".[23] But in a region in which the Crown colony mentality had permeated deeply into the society, this was an ideal model. As Ghany further informs us, it was copied by Barbados (1966), Belize (1981), Grenada (1974), St Lucia (1979), and Antigua and Barbuda (1981).

The senate was introduced as part of the constitutional monarchy established in 1962 and was retained when the nation moved to republicanism in 1976. At the present time, the senate comprises thirty-one members, of whom sixteen are appointed by the president on the advice of the prime minister, six by the president on the advice of the Leader of the Opposition, and nine by the president at their discretion. During this half-century it has worked well. As Williams had accurately prescribed, its members have been chosen from among those who had opted out of electoral politics, but possessed competence in many areas of national life. The fact that the ruling party could choose ministers from among its senators has been an added advantage in a small nation with limited expertise. The president's nominees (the independents), with no overt political affiliation, have, by and large, spoken independently and learnedly. The ruling party and the opposition have used the senate as a training ground for future candidates in the electoral process and this has been beneficial to the nation. The power to delay non-money bills has also served as an effective brake on hasty legislation. As the nation now embarks on the debate about constitutional change, an institution like the senate needs to be retained to give balance to the parliamentary process. But this must be done against a different, non-colonial background. At the present time, too many vestiges of Crown colony government persist in the society. The system now needs to be opened up, allowing for more devolution and decentralization. Our authoritarian structures will have to make way for more participatory government, catering to the heterogeneous mixture of cultures that inhabit this world on two islands. The process of the indigenization of the constitution has to be an urgent priority.

NOTES

1. James Anthony Froude, *The English in the West Indies, or, The Bow of Ulysses* (Illinois: Scribner, 1888), 87–88.
2. W. Cobbett, ed., *The Parliamentary History of England*, Vol. 36, 1820. Col. 869.
3. Anthony Trollope, *The West Indies and the Spanish Main*, 4th ed. (London: Chapman and Hall, 1860), 220.
4. ibid.
5. *Hansard*, Trinidad and Tobago, 1906, 97–98.
6. Froude, *English*, 81.
7. Rudyard Kipling, *Complete Verse* (New York: Doubleday, 1939), 322.
8. Trollope, *West Indies*, 311.
9. ibid., 307.
10. Carmen Voigt-Graf, "Twice migrants' relationship to their ancestral homeland: The case of Indo-Fijians and India," *Journal of Pacific Studies* 27, no. 2 (November 2004): 180.
11. British National Archives CO 295/13. Enclosure with Hislop to Windham, 26 October 1806.
12. British National Archives CO 295/522. Enclosure with Best to Milner, 7 August 1919.
13. British National Archives CO 295/630. Stanley to Clifford, 27 March 1945.
14. This is the author's own analysis, gleaned from his own political experience.
15. British National Archives CO 1032/102. Nominated members of the Legislative Council.
16. Bridget Brereton, *Race Relations in Colonial Trinidad 1870–1900* (Cambridge: Cambridge University Press, 1979), 3, stated that "A 'French Creole' was a person of European descent, usually French, but also Spanish, Irish, English, Corsican and even German, who was born in the island and who considered himself, and was considered by others, to be a member of the French Creole group. He might possibly have ancestors of African descent, but in order to be accepted as a member of this group, he would have to be regarded as of 'pure white' descent. Sometimes people not actually born in Trinidad but possessing the other necessary criteria, were 'adopted' as French Creoles."
17. British National Archives CO 1032/102. Nominated members of the Legislative Council.
18. Ibid.
19. CO 1031/3719 Monthly Intelligence Reports, 9 October 1961.
20. Eric Williams, *Constitution Reform in Trinidad and Tobago*, Teachers

Economic and Cultural Association, Public Affairs Pamphlet No. 2, 1955: 23.
21. ibid., Appendix.
22. This account is drawn from Hamid Ghany, "*Constitution Making in the Commonwealth Caribbean with Special Reference to Trinidad and Tobago*" (PhD diss., London University, 1987), 136f.
23. ibid., 160.

[5]

"THE THOROUGH KNOWLEDGE OF THE ISLAND AND ALL ITS DEPARTMENTS AND INSTRUCTION IN POLITICAL SCIENCE"

Representing the *Patria* in Puerto Rico's First Elections Under Spain's 1812 Constitution[1]

[JUAN GONZÁLEZ MENDOZA]

THIS CHAPTER IS PART OF A BROADER RESEARCH project on how Puerto Rico's creole patriots, to use D.A. Brading's term, imagined a blueprint for the island's development and how they justified their position as legitimate representatives of their *patria* (homeland) in the imperial and colonial spheres.[2] These issues came to the fore during the final decades of the eighteenth century and the implosion of Spain's American empire that followed soon after the Napoleonic invasion of 1808. Puerto Rico's colonial elite forged its political project in the crucible of the economic and social transformations that characterized the eighteenth century and the Atlantic revolutionary storms unleashed by North American independence, the French and Haitian Revolutions, and the crisis of sovereignty that paralysed the Spanish monarchy and led to independence in most of Hispanic America.[3]

The 1812 elections have not been thoroughly examined at the regional and municipal levels, so this preliminary study aims to fill part of the historiographical gap. Our attention will centre on Puerto Rico's first (and only) elections during the very brief period 1812 to 1814. The 1812 Constitution defined the peninsular and American political landscape, and among other things, deemed the American possessions to be provinces of a single nation.[4] It is a straightforward narrative of the electoral process as it unfolded in the island's second electoral circumscription or *partido* between 20 November 1812 – when parochial electors were chosen in San Germán – and 6 February 1813, when, after Governor Meléndez's annulment of Don Nicolás de Quiñones as Provincial Elector, the *Junta de Partido* conducted new elections to fill the resulting vacancy in the Provincial Junta.[5]

As we shall see, San Germán played a key role in the events following 1808 and the first constitutional period. In the case under consideration, it was head of the second electoral *partido* (see table 5.1 below). At that time its jurisdiction was one of the island's most populated and its creole elite had a long history of active participation in insular and imperial institutions, particularly after the Seven Years' War had provoked a series of military, economic and social reforms, which the Crown had inaugurated in the conflictive Caribbean frontier.[6]

As already mentioned, the 1812–1813 electoral process occurred under the shadow of a profound crisis of sovereignty and representation. Although the 'junta explosion' (*eclosión juntera*) of 1808 did not take hold in Puerto Rico, the colonial authorities would confront and survive several anxious moments.[7] In July 1808, a group of wealthy *vecinos* or residents (including Ramón de Castro, former Captain General and hero of the 1797 British incursion) petitioned Governor Toribio Montes to convene a junta similar to those active in the peninsula. Probably more troubling was the fact that Bishop Juan Alejo de Arizmendi sided with the petitioners. Montes demurred, however, and the whole affair came to nought.[8] In Cuba, Captain General Someruelos took a different tack and sympathized with Francisco Arango y Perreño's plan to establish a *Junta Gubernativa* in Havana. However, the idea faced bureaucratic and elite opposition and had to be scrapped. According to Michael Zeuske, its opponents feared "a reduction in their departments' expenditures" and the loss of the *situados*.[9] Salvador Meléndez (1809–1820), Montes' successor, would prove even more hostile to the sector of the Puerto Rican creole elite that promoted a more autonomous relationship with Spain.[10] This should come as no surprise since he would have to deal with the formation of a junta in Caracas and, later, with its declaration of independence, while supposed imitators in San Germán contrived to establish a similar junta in Puerto Rico; and finally, the issues of slavery and the slave trade had been debated in the Constituent Cortes, which apparently inspired a slave

Knowledge of the Island and All its Departments and Instruction in Political Science 103

1er Partido	Citizens	2o Partido	Citizens	4to Partido	Citizens	3er Partido	Citizens	5to Partido	Citizens
San Juan	907	San Germán	551	Aguada	662	Coamo	210	Arecibo	529
Vega Baja	45	Yauco	276	Aguadilla	712	Juana Díaz	129	Utuado	305
Toa Alta	85	Cabo Rojo	325	Moca	449	Ponce	712	Tuna	405
Corozal	83	Mayagüez	685	Rincón	520	Peñuelas	185	Manatí	775
Vega Alta	150	Total:	1,837	Pepino	518	Cayey	88	Total:	2,014
Toa Alta	273	Electors:	12	Total:	2,861	Cidra	84	Electors:	15
Bayamón	560			Electors:	15	Guayama	66		
Gaynabo	98					Patillas	112		
Río Piedras	69					Yabucoa	174		
Cangrejos	13					Total:	1,760		
Trujillo	93					Electores:	11		
Loiza	92							Citizens:	12,919
Luquillo	48							Electors:	76
Fajardo	352							% electors:	0.59
Naguabo	216								
Humacao	352							Inhabitants 1812	183,014
Maunabo	66							% citizens:	7.06
Barranquitas	149							% electors:	0.04
Las Piedras	55								
Juncos	133							Inhabitants 1812 (SG)	16,523
Caguas	504							% citizens:	3.33
Hato Grande	104								
Total:	4,447								
Electors:	23								

Source: 1812 Census in AGPR, FGEPR, CR, c. 12 and Cruz Monclova, Vol. I (1970) conspiracy led by *mulatos* and free blacks, some of whom were enlisted in the island's militias.[11]

Members of San Germán's elite and *cabildo* would play a crucial role during this critical juncture. When the Junta Central in Spain called for American representation in the Junta, the *Villa's* municipal body met on 7 September 1809 and accepted Aguada's proposal to establish a junta that would consider the instructions the *cabildos* had to forward Ramón Power, the island's elected delegate to the junta in Spain.[12] We do not know if the Captain General got wind of this invitation, but it is easy to see that he would have construed the proposed meeting of *cabildos* as the first step in a scheme that could easily slide into proclaiming a junta to govern in Fernando VII's name. The proposed meeting did not materialize, so San Germán commissioned its *Régidor Alferez Real*, Dr Felipe de Quiñones, and Dr Nicolás de Quiñones, lawyer for the *Real Audiencia de Distrito*, to compose Power's instructions. Unfortunately, we have no idea of how the document was drafted nor are there extant copies of the minutes of the meeting that debated their draft prior to the *Instrucciones*' final approval. Be that as it may, several disquieting ideas were expressed in the text that was formally sent to Power. Among them was the idea that sovereignty would devolve to the island, should the legitimate sovereign be lost:

> [The Cabildo] must firstly protest that this Villa recognizes and subjects itself to the Supreme Junta now and as long as it governs in the name of Our much Beloved, August and Dignified King, our lord don Fernando the Seventh and his Dynasty; but if by Divine Will (may God never allow it) the [Junta] should be destroyed and the Spanish Peninsula lost, may this Island rest independent and free to elect the best means to assure the conservation and subsistence of its inhabitants in peace and Christian Religion.[13]

No less troubling was the second instruction that proposed the creation of a provincial junta in the capital to be composed of the Captain General, the bishop and deputies from the five *cabildos* then in existence: "to be presided by the former and that will decide all issues by plurality in case of discord". The third instruction described the body's functions: "that the proceedings of said Junta shall deal with all matters concerning the welfare of the Nation and State, the welfare and utility of the Island and its inhabitants, *fusing together all Superior Governmental, Military and Intendancy provincial authority, including the faculties of the District's*

Royal Audiencia".[14] San German's proposal placed interim sovereignty squarely in creole hands, and in all probability, contributed to Meléndez's hostility towards the patriots' aspirations to legitimate representation and autonomy.

Dr Nicolás de Quiñones would play a key role in the electoral drama that unfolded between 1812 and 1813, since the central issue of the election in the second *Electoral Partido* was precisely the annulment of his election by the Captain General. Don Nicolás' salient role in the events that unfolded between 1809 and 1812 were sufficient reason for the governor's alarm and his efforts to thwart Quiñones' vocal and articulate participation in the election of the island's *Diputado a Cortes*. The clash of wills between the two men and Quiñones' backers in the *Junta de Partido* would bring several crucial issues to the fore. Salient among them was the question of who could rightfully represent the best interests of the *patria*. Puerto Rico's creole patriots were very clear as to what the answer should be. But their right of representation was disputed by other interests such as the bureaucracy, some *peninsulares* and the growing number of émigrés that had found refuge from revolution and war in Santo Domingo and Venezuela.[15] Besides this issue, the political give and take that occurred during the election would also precipitate other issues, such as hostility towards things French, the exclusion from political participation of *pardos* and other undesirable groups, among others.[16]

THE 1812–1813 ELECTIONS

Title 3, chapter 1 of the 1812 Constitution established the procedure to determine the number of electors who would choose the provincial deputies to the Spanish Cortes; while article 34, chapter 2 specified that deputies were to be elected in a three-tiered system consisting of electoral juntas at the parish, *partido* and provincial level.[17] In Puerto Rico, the process to set up the first elections under the new constitutional system was commissioned to a preparatory junta that included the Captain General, Bishop Arizmendi, *presbítero* Antonio Sánchez, Francisco Pimentel, Francisco Antonio Hernández and Alonso Cangas Llanos.[18] This body presented its final resolutions on 21 August 1812. The island was divided into "forty-five (45) parishes and five *partidos* (5), with an electoral body consisting of thirteen thousand five hundred forty-seven citizens (13,547)".[19] As table 5.1 shows, the Constitution limited political participation to a few and granted an "institutional recognition [to] the superiority of the wealthiest citizens, identifying them as the more able, who had the right of political participation, through property qualifications for the vote".[20] The citizen is the touchstone of the new political system but in America, further restrictions were imposed as persons of African origin, among others, were excluded from citizenship. As we have indicated elsewhere, a faction of the creole elite would later suggest the political necessity of including in the body of citizens those to whom the constitution extended a tenuous hope in its twenty-second article.[21]

Hotly contested, the 1812/1813 election was conducted "at a very slow pace due not only to lack of experience, a large number of illiterates and poor means of communication, but, above all, to the marked antagonism that characterized the conduct of liberals and conservatives."[22] Both factions tried to get the upper hand by presenting "numerous pleas for annulment, *limpieza de sangre*, and constitutional infractions to ensure the electoral triumph of their candidates, who were, respectively doctor don José María Quiñones and *presbítero* don Miguel de Andino".[23] As would be seen later on, all these strategies were utilized during the elections for Provincial Elector that were held in San Germán between 18 and 20 September 1812, and finalized in February 1813 (see table 5.2 for the first phase of the election).

As table 5.2 shows, eight (47 per cent) of the seventeen electors were or had been active in the militias or administrative posts and three (18 per cent) were members of the regular clergy. Two of the electors, whose profession or activities were not determined at the time, had held posts in San Germán's *cabildo*, Antonio Ramírez de Arellano (*Alcalde de Segunda* in 1802 and *de primera* in 1803) and José Monserrate Jusino (*Regidor Llano* between 1810 and 1812).[24] Regarding the electors' origins, everything suggests that they were creoles. References are also included as to how some electors were classified in the *aviso reservadísimo*, prepared after the conspiracy of 1811 was unearthed in San German.[25] As we shall see, this incident would be a major issue in the election of the *partido*'s Provincial Elector and contributed to Nicolás de Quiñones' disqualification by Captain General Meléndez.

The *Junta Electoral de Partido* met on 14 November 1812 under the

Table 5.2: Results of the Parochial Elections in San German (20 September 1812)*

Elector	Votes	Conspiracy of 1811
Captain of Grenadiers Faustino del Toro	60	Mentioned
Militia Captain (retired) José de Quiñones	51	Suspect
Tente. à Guerra (retired) José Antonio de Sepúlveda	46	In good standing
Sargent Major of Urban Miltias (retired) Germán Pagán	43	
Antonio Ramírez de Arellano (2º 1802; 1º 1803)	42	
Subdelegado de la Marina Francisco Antonio Ramírez de Arellano	40	Suspect
Andrés Manuel del Toro	39	
Presbo. Beneficiado [Manuel] Pizarro	38	In good standing
Juan Vélez Borrero	37	
Presbo. Cura Tente. Buenaventura Barrientos	30	Implicated with his brother
Tente. a Guerra José Ortiz de Peña	30	
José Monserrate Jusino (Regidor Llano retired)	30	
Captain of Urban Militias Juan Manuel de Seda	27	
Presbo. Cura Tnte. Antonio Vélez	26	
Dr Nicolás de Quiñones	26	Suspect
José Barrientos	25	
José Monserrate Ramírez	25	

*AHMSG, Act. 2, {1812} ff1-2. The Parochial Junta would pick the electors who would be part of the *Junta de Partido* that would then choose the Provincial Elector corresponding to the *partido* de San Germán; see Table 5.1 for the electoral *partidos*.

presidency of Captain don Faustino del Toro, San Germán's *alcade de primera*. The junta met two days later to name a secretary, two *escrutadores* (ballot counters) and to choose the commission that would scrutinize the credentials of the partido's electors, as required by the Constitution. Juan Fons y Mañer, Cabo Rojo's curate, was chosen secretary, while Dr Nicolás de Quiñones and Manuel Pizarro, San Germán's *Sacristán Mayor*,

Table 5.3: Composition of the *Junta Electoral de Partido**

Name	Position	Parish
Faustino del Toro	President, *Alcalde primero*, Captain of Grenadiers	San Germán
Manuel Pizarro	*Sacristán Mayor*	San Germán
Buenaventura Barrientos	*Cura Teniente*	San Germán
Dr Nicolás de Quiñones	Lawyer *Audiencia* of Puerto Príncipe, Auditor interino province of San Francisco de Paula	San Germán
Juan Fons [y Mañer]	*Cura*	Cabo Rojo
Tomás Ramírez de Arellano	*Teniente a Guerra*, Lieutenant Captain	Cabo Rojo
Joaquín Ramírez de Arellano	*Alcalde primero*	Mayagüez
Mateo Peña	*Síndico Procurador General, Subdelegado de Correos* (from Maracaibo, Venezuela)	Mayagüez
Dr Félix García de la Torre**	Lawyer, Native of Habana	Mayagüez
Yldefonso Sepúlveda	*Cura teniente*	Añasco

*AHSMG, *Act. 2, {1812} ff4-4v.*
**After settling* in Mayagüez, don Félix became one of its pioneer coffee *hacendados* during the 1820s and 1830s. According to Pedro Tomás de Córdova, he had contributed 2,000 pesos towards the construction of the road linking Furnias (a coffee-growing ward) to the port of Mayagüez in 1825, he "also assisted for a long time with 40 peons, he gave impulse and direction to the task, being it admirable that this was undertaken before the new plantation s were harvested". *Memorias geográficas, históricas, económicas y estadísticas de la Isla de Puerto Rico*, 6 vols. (1831; San Juan: Editorial Coquí, 1968), II: 214. He was commercial representative for major St Thomas concerns and also had commercial contacts in Martinique, from where he procured slaves in exchange for coffee. His dealings were not limited to Mayagüez and extended to Cabo Rojo and San Germán. See Juan R. González Mendoza, "TheParish of San Germán de Auxerre in Puerto Rico, 1765–1850: Patterns of Settlement and Development" (PhD diss., SUNY at Stony Brook, 1989), note 96, 385–86.

were chosen to count the ballots. Buenaventura Barrientos, Captain Tomás Ramírez de Arellano, Cabo Rojo's *Teniente a Guerra*, and Joaquín Ramírez de Arellano, Mayagüez's *Alcalde primero*, were picked to inspect the electors' credentials.

The first round of disqualifications began during the meeting when Dr Nicolás de Quiñones insisted on the removal of Mateo Peña, a Venezuelan émigré and one of Mayagüez's three electors. Although not directly expressed in the meeting's minutes, it is evident that Quiñones invoked article 22 of the Constitution to disqualify Peña. In other words, he claimed Peña was a *pardo* and, therefore, should be barred from the Junta. A vote was taken and Peña's exclusion was decided nine votes in favour and two opposed.[26] Once this matter was settled, the Junta proceeded to elect Dr Quiñones as Provincial Elector and dissolved itself. As mandated by the Constitution, its former members participated in the religious ceremony that followed the electoral procedure.[27]

The Venezuelan's rejection would, however, bring further complications, and on 26 January 1813, the Junta reconvened to consider Brigadier Meléndez's order, which was received eight days before. The order informed the Junta that "D.D. Nicolas de Quiñones has been suspended from his duties as Elector de Partido since criminal charges have been brought against him and others, so it is necessary to name another candidate."[28] After Meléndez's order was duly read, Don Joaquín Ramírez de Arellano produced an *auto* (order or opinion) issued by the Captain General on 19 January that recognized the "quality, *pureza de sangre* alleged by D. Mateo Peña" and, hence, restored his rights as a Spanish citizen. Furthermore, the document stated that Peña had reserved the right "that may assist him to present cause, how and when the time arises, against the person or – those others – that promoted the unjust and false repudiation that he suffered at the hands of the Junta Electoral de Partido".[29] The Junta, however, did not admit the document and submitted the matter to a vote. A tie resulted, so lots were drawn, and in the end, Peña was readmitted.[30]

Once this issue was settled, it was decided not to proceed immediately with the new election as Meléndez had instructed, since "a new difficulty had arisen regarding the correctness of the Recommendation made by said superior order". Therefore, the Junta "resolved ten votes in favor and one adverse to postpone the election and that his Lordship should be informed that [the Junta] would like him to indicate who are the various subjects implicated in the judicial procedures so that [the Junta] may correctly proceed with the selection of a new Elector Invested with the required qualities".[31]

This dilatory tactic may have served various ends. Since some members of the Junta had been implicated in the criminal case cited by Meléndez (see table 5.2), it would be wise to know which members of the electoral body were under suspicion. Secondly, the Junta could perhaps get a sense of which of the probable candidates enjoyed the Captain General's preference, and therefore, pick among them an elector favourable to creole interests. And finally, as would be seen later, to give Dr Quiñones sufficient time to prepare a defence of his good standing and mount a new attack against Peña.

In response to the Junta's decision, the Captain General issued a communiqué (dated 30 January 1813) that compelled the Junta to reconvene on 6 February 1813. In no uncertain terms, Meléndez expressed his dissatisfaction with the election's postponement and insisted on the exclusion of Dr Quiñones. Regarding the names of the co-conspirators, the governor alleged that he had to abstain from involvement in the judicial process, and could also not inform the Junta as to who were the other suspects implicated in the case.[32] Unable to procrastinate further, the Junta proceeded with the new election. Before the voting, however, the president asked if there were any objections to the proceedings. Nicolás de Quiñones seized this opportunity to insist on the illegality of his separation from the Provincial Junta and presented additional testimonies related to the 16 November 1812 meeting that had rejected Mateo Peña on Don Nicolás's insistence.

QUIÑONES' RESPONSE: WHO REPRESENTS THE *PATRIA*?

Quiñones began his counter-offensive by objecting to Peña's reinstatement without Meléndez first hearing the *Junta de Partido*. The governor's resolution was illegal because article 70 of the Constitution specified that "there should have been no appeal to [the Junta's] decision".[33] The Junta, therefore, should not have authorized Peña's reinstatement "with the vote of the same Electors that had previously voted for his exclusion during the Junta that was reconvened on the past twenty sixth of January".[34]

This constitutional objection was followed by an accusation of criminal wrongdoing that included the Venezuelan and Mayagüez's *alcalde de primera*. Quiñones implicates the latter as "one of the principal accused in the case that was signed by the *Oidor Fiscal de Real Hacienda*, don Jose Ygnacio Veldelluli,[35] acting as Commissioner for the *Intendencia*'s tribunal regarding the unauthorized sale of some seized French [prizes]". Peña was also involved "because he clandestinely bought some of [the prizes], for which reason both should be stripped of their citizen rights and cannot serve as electors." Quiñones' attack was extended to don Juan López, the junta's member from Añasco, because "a judicial procedure is followed against him for slapping Dn. Jose Ma. Ramirez, Officer of [Añasco's] Militia Regiment, which case has not been concluded".[36]

Quiñones then proceeded to deflect any doubts as to his motives for pursuing the matter of his exclusion. He began by stating it was his duty to defend his honour and expressed his confidence that in time his name would be cleared. He questioned whether he should let the issue pass: "[even] if my duties as Father, Husband, and member of my Family would require that I defend the honor and fidelity that have been questioned, and the confidence, that my conscience inspires and is insured by God's Universal Justice, would silence my voice and reduce my worries to let time reveal my innocence and punish malignity."[37]

Rather, he added, his acts responded to higher principles. "It is not my case that I want to bring forth, it is the honour of this *Partido*, the peace of this Island, and the interests of all the Spanish Monarchy, that push me to bring forth a fact that has lain hidden up to now." An affair of personal honour is thus transmuted into a cause that extends from the *Partido* to the island and, beyond it, the whole Spanish monarchy.

Having presented local and personal issues in his defence, Don Nicolás then fixed his sights on Brigadier Meléndez. He equated the publication of the election results in the *Gaceta* of 12 December with the Captain General's approval as an acknowledgment of the election's legitimacy. Besides, he pointed out, on the 19 December, "I presented myself before this gentleman and he manifested the clearest testimonies that my election was not annulled."[38] Quiñones added that a letter sent from Mayagüez informed him that Peña had travelled to the capital to intervene in the electoral procedure after the results of the contest had been published.[39] Once there, Peña supposedly alleged that the junta had omitted the second ballot count mandated by Article 74 of the Constitution. Quiñones concluded that the end result of Peña's "sad ploy should have been the petition's dismissal as impertinent, or that the omitted formality should have been verified so that I would continue to receive the honors and distinctions conferred by our Gral (General) during the days when the Junta Provincial had to be deferred because Coamo's elector had taken ill and had to be replaced".[40] After exposing Meléndez's duplicitous behaviour, Quiñones accused him of attempting a crass manipulation of the election.

In the first place, his reference to Coamo's elector insinuates that the latter's substitution was a concerted plan to rig the composition of the Provincial Junta.[41] Quiñones avers that since don José Colón, the new elector, "is from Coamo it may be supposed that he is subject to the opinions of his Lodger and companion, past Vicar and at present *Racionero* D. Tiburcio de Esminas."[42] A graver accusation follows. On 15 January 1813, the electors of Aguada and San Juan had accompanied don Nicolás to a consultation with the Captain General. During the meeting, the governor dropped the hint that he favoured "the election of *Racionero* D. Miguel Andino as Provincial Deputy, which expressions we reminded him were Co[ntrary] to artcl. 97 of the Constitution, because he] . . . was employed by the Government, and received his salary from public funds". It was thus clearly insinuated that the failure of Meléndez's ploy was behind the removal of Quiñones as Provincial Elector.[43]

Quiñones ended this tale by expressing his perception of the political factions at work within the Provincial Junta. According to him, Coamo's substitute elector was allied to don Emidio Andino, first cousin to Menéndez's favourite (Andino), and also the Plaza's Adjutant. This group, Quiñones calls the bi-headed council (*"concilio bicápite"*). Even as the junta's president, Menéndez could not ensure his faction's success, since "there remained three votes, that it was necessary [for them] to whittle down to two so that the decisions of the Junta could be reduced to two against one [vote], how could this be achieved? *by using a person foreign to the Patria*, from the Province of Caracas, *of unknown quality* and now disqualified by this Government".[44] Finally, the crucial question was posed: Who rightfully represents the *Patria* and, therefore, should decide who would be the island's representative in the Cortes? Even if Peña was not a *pardo*, as Quiñones had asserted, he should still be excluded. Above all, he should not be chosen over a native son who could clearly demonstrate his "renowned service to the Patria, his profound knowledge of the Island and all its Departments, and instruction in Political Science".[45]

After this volley, Quiñones went on to question the legal basis of his exclusion, objecting that the alleged criminal case against him was patently illegal: "They refer to a criminal process, when they should refer to an extrajudicial proceeding in which I participated out of my free, and spontaneous will, and only to inform the mind of the Gral. and that he should be on guard against the traps of evil-sayers, this confusion can only be the product of wretched minds."[46] The doctor is apparently referring to an incident contained in the *aviso reservadisimo* (confidential advisory) of 1812. According to this section of the report, Don Bernardo Pabón Dávila, Don Francisco Antonio Ramírez, Don José Quiñones and Don Nicolás Quiñones travelled to San Juan after finding out, through Don Vicente Ramírez's note to Don Francisco Ramírez, "that summary proceedings were underway in the Villa of Sn German about various particulars that pointed to the Quiñones and Ramirez families, and having found out also that Juan Varea had visited the homes of several neighbors to warn them that the Quiñones and the Ramirez were trying to conspire against the Europeans." According to the document, the quartet's objective had been:

> to have the [Captain General] see the calumny and imposture that was devastating their esteem and conduct, and that, as good and loyal subjects of the King and Patria, they could not tolerate nor permit that their reputation be stained, and, for said reason, they asked that [the examiners] query people who had a fair idea of their dealings, so that such affronts would unravel, and that they did not doubt that in the Villa de San German there were those that did not love them well because, as people of character and strong opinions, they tried to curb some of the abuses and disorderly procedures that were committed by some in the government of said Villa, that the Meetings they held in Guánica served the purpose of supervising and dividing the cattle they had in their *hatos* and *haciendas* since their Father's testament was still under review; and to amuse themselves hunting; adding that Dn Franco. Anto. Ramírez had retired to the place of Guánica to establish himself and farm, for his welfare and that of his large family, since he did not possess greater assets, that ever since he has remained working there, trying only to prosper, without dealing with anyone, outside of business, and procuring the greatest ease possible.[47]

Behind the accusations that undermined his honour and rights as a citizen, Quiñones saw the machinations of the *junta bicápite* and alluded to his interview with *fiscal* Maroto when the investigation into the 1811 conspiracy was underway.[48] So as not to attack the governor directly, Quiñones insinuated that Colón and Andino were as corrupt as those courtesans who, in the past, had profaned the will of kings and added that the Cortes would be scandalized "if they saw the honor and reputation of a vassal subject to the dictates and proclamations of two Individuals bereft of instruction and only authorized to find out, along with three others, about the bribes and other wrongdoings, disregarding the claim that he [Quiñones] made regarding this Constitutional rule".[49] Therefore, he asked that the *Junta de Partido* should annul any other elector's appointment, except his, and that his protest be included in the minutes of the meeting. Furthermore, he presented the junta with certifications obtained in Cabo Rojo, Añasco and Yauco that purported to show that Don Mateo Peña was reputed to be *pardo* (black) in Maracaibo.[50]

Once Quiñones stated his case, it was Peña's turn to object. He argued that the renewed attempt to exclude him violated the Constitution, and furthermore, was "a manifest contravention of the Superior [government's] declaration that [reinstated him as a citizen]; and is a seditious procedure, and a formal disobedience to the high standing of the Governor's Tribunal, since this contradiction cannot be merely resolved by the simple reports of the *Ayuntamientos* (municipal councils) of Añazco, Cabo-Roxo, and Yauco on which my opponents base my expulsion".[51] He also suggested that all the machinations against him were a product of Quiñones' suspension and the profound animosity against his person that it provoked in Quiñones. Furthermore, Peña tried to squash his representation as *pardo*, arguing that the municipal authorities and his adversary had plotted against him because Quiñones was their fellow countryman (*paisano*). He went on to dismiss the testimony of two of Don Nicolas' witnesses by claiming that one of them only proffered testimony against him because he was Peña's debtor, while the other alleged that Peña was the brother of a so-called Simeón Peña simply because they bore the same surname. Peña summed up his rebuttal by declaring that the junta lacked the authority to reconsider an issue already settled by the island's supreme authority.

After both sides had presented their case, the junta debated whether it should expel Mayagüez's *Síndico Procurador* and *Alcalde de Primera* together with Don Juan López from Añasco, as Dr Quiñones had petitioned. Clergymen Pizarro and Fon were of the opinion that the junta should accept Peña, while Dr Félix García de la Torre argued that both Peña and Ramírez de Arellano should continue in the junta, lest Mayagüez be shorn of two of its three electors.[52] The junta finally decided to exclude Peña and Ramíriez de Arellano, but concluded there was no motive to exclude López, Añasco's elector. Since it was already too late to celebrate the mass of the Holy Spirit called for by the Constitution, the junta proceeded with the election without this formality. However, before the votes could be cast, *présbitero* Buenaventura Barrientos presented an objection against Dr García de la Torre, charging that the latter had been denied permission to settle in the island due "to his French education" and that, contrary to official procedure, García de la Torre had then obtained his residency directly from the governor.[53] García de la Torre retorted that this was an unfounded accusation since "once he arrived at the Island's Capital from Cuba, he presented himself to the Captain General who, after consulting with the *Asesor* [advisor] and *Fiscal* [prosecutor], and (without any misgivings) granted him the lic. [licence] he had petitioned to settle in Mayagüez, where he had since married after presenting his Excellency the Bishop the required documents that gave proof of his birth and other circumstances".[54] After concluding these proceedings, he presented all his documents in San Gemán. The junta resolved to dismiss the complaint against García de la Torre and proceeded with the election. After two rounds of voting resulted in a tie, lots were cast and Don Yldefonso Sepúlveda, Añasco's parish priest, was selected Provincial Elector.[55]

Thus concluded a contentious and prolonged process that allows a glimpse into the opposing interests that surfaced with greater intensity during the imperial crisis that characterized the closing years of Charles IV's reign and provoked, among other things, the inauguration of a new political regime that altered the rules of representation and, hence, political practices. The new electoral process also sheds light on the tensions that resulted from the persistence of the *Ancien Régime* and the emergence of the new order, particularly when the actions of Brigadier Meléndez are viewed from the standpoint of Quiñones and the other creole patriots. According to these political actors, the Captain General was willing to circumvent, or put to advantageous use, those features of the 1812 Constitution that shored-up his authority while, at the same time, blocking creole aspirations for self-government. Thus, Meléndez would exploit his position as governor in an attempt to influence the elections, while also availing himself of those opportunities afforded him by the Constitution, since provincial governors were constitutionally set up as presidents of the Provincial Electoral Juntas.

Meléndez's manoeuvring was an effort to preserve his prerogatives in the midst of a political context that had undermined traditional claims to authority and whose final resolution was very much uncertain. Puerto Rico's governor tackled the conundrum that other metropolitan authorities had faced in the years after 1808 and which had swept many of them from power. This was precisely the case with his antecessor Montes in Venezuela. As Halperin Donghi has perceptively observed, the crisis transformed the institutional relationship between the metropolis and the colonies:

> because the local magistrates knew that they were dealing with a superior authority that needed them more than in the past [to maintain the colonial bond]: the first consequence of this state of affairs was a tendency [of the Junta Suprema] to extend the sphere of its loosely defined attributions and even to exceed them. As the effects of this new attitude accumulated, the supreme authority had to play its traditional role as arbitrator between the [imperial] authorities and local forces (all of them acting in an increasingly decentered way) in a progressively biased manner.[56]

This helps explain the Captain General's insecurity and even hostility to the growing participation of Puerto Rico's patriots in imperial and colonial affairs. It did not help at all that Caracas had declared independence, a supposed conspiracy to establish "the system of Caracas" had been unearthed in San Germán in 1811, and a conspiracy (involving persons of mixed origin, white and black – some from the militia, free blacks and enslaved Africans) was uncovered in the capital's environs in 1812. All of this occurred during his anxious watch.[57]

Similar fissures occurred in Cuba in 1808, when Arango y Parreño (spokesman for the emerging *sacarocracy*) outlined a plan for a *Junta Gubernativa* with the support of the marquis of Someruelos, the island's Captain General. As Zeuske has shown, the majority of the Habanero oligarchy "opted for a pact with imperial absolutism over an uncertain autonomy".[58] Although the similarities with Cuba must be nuanced, the actors and factions that disputed Puerto Rico's 1812–1813 elections were very similar to Cuba's. We must not forget that the idea of convening a *Junta Gubernativa* had also cropped up in Puerto Rico in 1808, and that it was precisely San Germán's *cabildo* that had suggested the establishment of just such a junta in its *instrucciones*. As we have already seen, the proposed body would enjoy "all the Superior Governmental, Military and

Intendancy authority of the Province". Although the island's governor and bishop would be included, representation in the junta by the five existing *cabildos* would annul any power the Captain General may have enjoyed in the new provisional government. We have also seen that Dr Nicolás de Quiñones was among the authors of San Germán's *instrucciones* and was probably the mastermind behind the idea – further reason for the governor's hostility.

Puerto Rican historiography has generally described the quarrels unleashed by the elections begun in 1812 as "the antagonism that characterized the behavior of both liberals and conservatives" or a battle framed by the opposition *criollos* versus *peninsulares*.[59] These conclusions should be reconsidered upon closer examination of both the process leading to the election of Puerto Rico's deputy to the 1810 Constitutional Cortes, and the municipal political contests that occurred under Spain's first constitution. Firstly, it is not evident that political labels, corresponding to a politics centred on individualism and fully modern political discourse, could be readily applied to the participants at this particular juncture. The political actors, whose opinions have been labelled liberal or conservative by historians, oscillated between the traditional political paradigm of neo-patrimonial monarchy and the novel paradigm of citizenship and constitutionality, according to what political necessity dictated.[60] Thus, in some instances they would present themselves as loyal vassals pleading an audience with a paternal monarch while, on other occasions, they would deploy the language of popular sovereignty and insist on the construction of an able body of citizens to ensure the island's representation in the new national politics. They would also employ traditional terms such as *condición, casta, reputación, estado,* all of which were out of tune with political concepts such as the equal status of citizens. Thus, Dr Quiñones' disqualification of Peña centres on the place the Venezuelan occupied in the hierarchy of *castas* and is backed by witnesses that refer to Peña's *reputación* in Maracaibo.[61] The 1812 Constitution was only the starting point of this paradigmatic shift and, as is well known, it never had the opportunity to consolidate a new political universe. Neither could we strictly differentiate between *criollos* and *peninsulares* in this contest, as is attested by the opposition to Mateo Peña and don Félix García de la Torre. After all, Peña was from Maracaibo and García de la Torre was born in Cuba. Nowhere in the *actas* are they labelled *peninsulares*, so they were most probably *criollos*, but not from Puerto Rico, and this was precisely the point that Quiñones, and others like him, were stressing.

All these issues await further in-depth study of municipal politics and, also, Puerto Rico's elites and how they were constituted. Particularly since they retained the privilege of traditional representation characteristic of the *Ancien Régime* and during the brief constitutional periods that Fernando VII was compelled to tolerate during his reign. What, if any, was the role played in the clash of public opinion by "the knowledge of Political Science" that Dr Quiñones presented as his credential to represent patriotic interests in the political order recently installed? What role was assigned to familial and other ties, to the clienteles mobilized by the oligarchy, which had to be divested of their traditional roles so as to play a part in the new politics of citizenship?

These, and other matters, were crucial concerns for Puerto Rico's creole patriots and their efforts to ensure representation both at the imperial and local levels. They were also essential for the concretion of the blueprint they had designed for the advancement of their *patria* and part of politics writ large. But what about what Pocock has labelled "sub-political activities" or Domínguez refers to as pre-political phenomena, such as social banditry, tax or subsistence riots, peasant uprisings?[62] The elite had to respond to this prodding from below and, somehow, incorporate the demands of the lowly or, at least recognize their existence as members of society. How did plebeians, to use E.P. Thompson's term, interpret events that transcended narrow, insular contexts and forcefully linked the island to the wider realm of a monarchy that straddled both shores of the Atlantic? There is no space to ponder these issues now. However, it is important to remember that several social stages could have allowed the intersection of elite political concepts and popular conceptions of a shared, albeit differently interpreted, reality. One has only to think of the mulatto and free black sailors who travelled the Caribbean or the close contacts between elite officers and plebian militias, or the billiard halls and *pulperías* (rural stores) (maligned centres of rumour and socially improper interactions, whose evil influence the municipal authorities so often deplored) to realize that the boundaries between high and low politics were not impermeable. In large measure these and other questions are still awaiting proper study.

NOTES

1. This chapter constitutes a revised version of the paper that I presented during the Association of Caribbean Historians' 46th Annual Meeting in Martinique (May 2014). I have to thank Universidad Interamericana de Puerto Rico, Recinto de San Germán for granting the sabbatical leave that allowed me to conduct part of the research necessary to complete this text. This essay is also part of the project directed by José Raúl Navarro "El peso de las reformas de Cádiz (1812–1838). La reformulación de la administración colonial en Puerto Rico," Escuela de Estudios Hispanoamericanos. Consejo Superior de Investigaciones Científicas, Spain.
2. D.A. Brading, *The First America: The Spanish monarchy, Creole patriots, and the Liberal state 1492–1867* (Cambridge: Cambridge University Press, 1991). The eighteenth century was crucial in the emergence of a creole identity, according to Brading (see chapters 19–21). Some of these issues I deal with in *"Hombres incultos, desagradecidos, inconstantes y desaplicados autores particulares de la destrucción de su Patria*: los agregados puertorriqueños como cimiento endeble de la patria'," *Colonial Latin American Review* 7:2 (1998), 224–50 and "Puerto Rico's Creole Patriots and the Slave Trade after the Haitian Revolution," David Geggus, ed., *The Impact of the Haitian Revolution in the Atlantic World* (Columbia: University of South Carolina Press, 2001), 58–71.
3. Spain's imperial crisis began before Napoleon's invasion. According to José A. Piqueras: "The symptoms of Spanish and American decay became evident after the first war with England (1796–1801) consumed resources and levies. Atlantic traffic was one of its first victims when [war] interrupted the promising commerce between the monarchy's ports... The commercial disconnection between Spain and its possessions provided the latter sudden and intense opportunities of exchange with other nations and offered practical demonstrations of the advantages of free commerce or, at least of the benefits of shaking off Spain's official monopoly." José Antonio Piqueras, *Bicentenarios de libertad: La fragua de la política en España y las Américas* (Barcelona: Ediciones Península, 2010), 122. I must thank José Antonio for his generosity in providing me a copy of his book. See also Tulio Halperin Donghi, *Reforma y disolución de los imperios ibéricos 1750–1850. Historia de América Latina* 3, Nicolás Sánchez Albornoz, dir. (Madrid: Alianza Editorial, 1985) and Jeremy Adelman, *Sovereignty and Revolution in the Iberian Atlantic* (Princeton and Oxford: Princeton University Press, 2006), 177–80.
4. *Constitución de 1812* http://www.congreso.es/docu/constituciones/1812/ce1812.pdf English version: http://www.cervantesvirtual.com/obra-visor/

the-political-constitution-of-the-spanish-monarchy-promulgated-in-cadiz-the-nineteenth-day-of-march--0/html/ Chapter 1, Article 1. "The Spanish nation is the re-union of all the Spaniards of both hemispheres." Accessed 31 July 2015.

5. The Constitution established a three-tiered system of elections for provincial deputies to the regular Cortes. Parochial electors would choose electors to the *Juntas de Partido* (five in 1812); the *Juntas de Partido* would vote on a Provincial Elector; and, finally, the Provincial Junta would elect the Cortes' deputy.

6. The Bourbon reforms had integrated the Cuban and Puerto Rican elites in the military reforms that ensued soon after the Seven Years War. They had also favourably responded to the economic demands of those elites, particularly of the sectors that were interested in plantation development and the liberalization of the slave trade. Some examples may suffice: Puerto Rico's deputy to the Constitutional Cortes, Ramón Power y Giralt's first experience in the Royal Navy occurred during the siege of Toulon (1793); this was followed by actions against the British during the battle of Cabo San Vicente and in the waters near Cadiz. When the Junta Central decided to include American delegates in 1809, Power was in Santo Domingo as commander of the flotilla that transported the expeditionary force that defeated General Ferrand in Palo Hincado on 7 November 1808. Other members of the colonial elite had commanded the ethnically mixed Disciplined Militias during Abercromby's siege of San Juan in 1797. Closer to San Germán, Dr Nicolás Quiñones had distinguished himself during the British incursion on Mayagüez in 1804. Quiñones was also an active lawyer in the Audiencia de Puerto Príncipe, Cuba, had served as *Teniente a Guerra* in Mayagüez and, in 1809, was *Auditor Interino* of San Francisco de Paula Province. Besides presiding over the Junta Electoral de Partido, Captain of Grenadiers, Don Faustino del Toro would also be San Germán's first Constitutional Alcalde, while Puerto Rico's deputy to the 1813 Cortes was Don José de Quiñones, who had been *Oidor* in the *Audiencia de Caracas*. For Cuba's elite participation in the Bourbon reforms, see Allan J. Kuethe, *Cuba, 1753–1815: Crown, Military, and Society* (Knoxville: University of Tennessee Press, 1986); Power's naval career in Piqueras, *Bicentenarios de libertad* (Barcelona: Peninsular, 2010), 251–53; Quiñones' role in the defence of Mayagüez in Lido Cruz Monclova, *Historia de Puerto Rico: Siglo XIX, Vol. 4* (Río Piedras: Editorial Universitaria, 1970), I: 109. Anderson has suggested that creole experience in imperial bureaucratic careers contributed to the development of a universal sense of identity (Americans), while also strengthening regional identities; the same regionalisms that generated

the nationalisms that inspired the diverse independence movements. See chapter 4 of Benedict Anderson, *Imagined Communities: Reflections on the Origin and Spread of Nationalism*, rev. ed. (London: Verso, 1991), 47–65.
7. See Manuel Chust, coord., *1808 La eclosión juntera en el mundo hispano* (México: Fondo de Cultura Económica-El Colegio de México, 2007), particularly Michael Zeuske, "Las capitanías generales de Cuba y Puerto Rico, 1808–1823," 356–404.
8. Piqueras, *Bicentenarios de libertad*, 264–66.
9. Zeuske, "Las capitanías generales," 371. Contact between Cuban, Venezuelan and Puerto Rican elites was frequent. Puerto Rico had no university, so the elite had to go to the Peninsula, Cuba or Venezuela to complete superior studies. The University of Havana was established in 1725 and the University of Caracas in 1728. Links between Venezuela and Puerto Rico had strengthened during the eighteenth century. Don Domingo de Barrios from Maracaibo had been San German's *Regidor Alcalde Provincial* from 1797 to 1804. In 1804, the *Audiencia* ordered Barrios to return to Maracaibo, where he had a wife and family. However, he was reinstated by the governor in 1805. He was still *regidor* in 1811 and was classified among the people of good standing during the 1811 conspiracy. Venezuelans represented a high proportion of settlers in San German during the eighteenth century. See Juan R. González Mendoza, "Demografía y sociedad en San Germán: siglo XVIII," *Anales de Investigación Histórica* IX, nos. 1–2 (1982): 1–64. See also note 5 above.
10. See María de los Ángeles Castro Arroyo, "La lealtad anticolonial: Ramón Power en las Cortes de Cádiz," in *Las Antillas en la era de las Luces y la Revolución*, ed. José A. Piqueras (Madrid: Siglo XXI Editores, 2005), 277–300.
11. Documents dealing with San Germán 1811–1812 in AGI, Ultramar, 450, "Aviso reservadísimo de 21 de enero de 1812. Sobre conspiracion contra el Gobierno, de la Villa de San Germán. Audiencia de Santo Domingo. Puerto Rico." Courtesy of Héctor Feliciano Ramos. Regarding the 1812 conspiracy, see Guillermo Baralt, *Esclavos rebeldes: Conspiraciones y sublevaciones de esclavos en Puerto Rico (1795–1873)* (Río Piedras: Ediciones Huracán, 1981).
12. AHMSG, Act. 2, ff 46v–47. A communique was received from the *alcalde de primera* of the Villa de Aguada (1 September 1809) "to the effect that, if this Body approve, it should name some of its Individuals that together, at some specified meeting place, could meet to consider the Instructions that have to be given his Most Excellent Sir Dn. Ramon Power ... to insure the most laudable correctness and utility of the Country (*País*)." Coamo's *cabildo* also agreed to the junta, but the plan fizzled when Arecibo's municipal body opted out.

13. Aida Caro de Delgado, *Ramón Power y Giralt: Diputado puertorriqueño a las Cortes Generales y Extraordinarias de España 1810–1812*, (Compilación de Documentos) (San Juan, 1969), 123–24. When the instructions were written the junta had already dissolved, but the news had not yet arrived in Puerto Rico.
14. Caro de Delgado, 124. (my emphasis)
15. The 1812 Constitution was of no help, since it proposed a unitary nation with equality among all citizens. Hence, no preference could be given to particular citizens because of their residence. Western Puerto Rico was home to a large proportion of these recent arrivals. Complaints were frequent as to the deleterious effect of their presence in San Germán's *cabildo* meetings between about 1790 and the time of the elections.
16. This was not such a clear-cut issue, as a sector of the creole elite (precisely those proposing a plantation economy with slave labour) showed itself willing to extend citizenship to at least some *mulatos* and free blacks. See González Mendoza, "*Puerto Rico's Creole Patriots and the Slave Trade*."
17. *Constitución de 1812* http://www.congreso.es/docu/constituciones/1812/ce1812.pdf English version: http://www.cervantesvirtual.com/obra-visor/the-political-constitution-of-the-spanish-monarchy-promulgated-in-cadiz-the-nineteenth-day-of-march--0/html/. Article 22, however, is omitted in this translation.
18. Sánchez and Pimentel would be members of Puerto Rico's first *Diputación Provincial* (1813–1814). See Cruz Moncolva, *Historia*, I: 53. In 1836, Pimentel, then San Germán's Vicar, was listed as one of the *partido's hacendados*. AGPR, FGEPR, SG, c. 555 "Villa de San Germán. Lista de los sugetos blancos de 25 años arriba."
19. Cruz Monclova, *Historia*, Vol. I: 52.
20. Miguel Artola, *La Burguesía Revolucionaria (1808–1869), Historia de España Alfaguara V* (Madrid: Alianza Editorial-Alfaguara, 1973), 35.
21. "Those Spaniards that through whatever line are considered and reputed as originating in Africa can aspire to citizenship through the open door of virtue and merit. In which case, the Cortes will grant a letter of citizenship to those who have offered qualified services to the Patria, or those who distinguish themselves through their talents, assiduousness, and conduct, on condition that they be children of free Parents linked by legitimate marriage; that they should be married to a free woman, and *avecindados* in the Spanish dominions; and that they exercise a profession, trade, or industry with their own capital." *Constitución de 1812*, f6. (My translation. All translations are mine, except where otherwise noted. The English translation cited for some unknown reason omits this article.) González Mendoza, "Puerto Rico's Creole Patriots and the Slave Trade."

22. Cruz Monclova, *Historia* Vol. I: 52–53.
23. ibid.
24. The same pattern was typical of the elections held in the rest of the empire, since, as Piqueras argues, the whole process was designed to limit the consultation to the elite. Hence potential candidates were scarce and "the best-known names corresponded to the ecclesiastical dignitaries, the military, royal officials and lawyers". Piqueras, *Bicentanarios de libertad*, 292–93.
25. AGI, Ultramar 450. "Aviso reservadisimo." As we have seen, San Germán's instructions to Ramón Power, Puerto Rico's deputy to the Junta Central and later to the constituent Cortes, had included a petition to establish a junta in San Juan, so the government's suspicions were not entirely unjustified.
26. From what would transpire in the 6 February 1813 meeting, we may infer that these two votes were cast by Mayagüez's *alcalde de primera* and Juan López. Quiñones would petition the junta to exclude both men during that meeting of the Parochial Junta. Although one of the votes favourable to Peña could also have been that of Dr García de la Torre, Peña's fellow elector from Mayagüez.
27. AHMSG, *Act. 2* {1812} ff5–6.
28. AHMSG, *Act. 2* {1812} ff7–7v. Present at the meeting were Faustino del Toro, Manuel Pizarro, Buenaventura Barrientos, Juan Fons y Mañer, Tomás Ramírez de Arellano, Joaquín Ramírez de Arellano, Mateo Peña, Félix García de la Torrre, Yldefonso García, Joaquín de los Reyes, Juan López, and José Julián de Torres. Fons y Mañer was named Secretary, while Pizarro and García de la Torre were chosen as *escrutadores*, (8–8v).
29. AHMSG, *Act. 2* {1812} ff9–9v.
30. AHMSG, *Act. 2* {1812} n. f. "As a conseq[uence] the discussion was opened as to whether or not elector D. Mateo Peña, repulsed in the previous Junta, should be readmitted, opinions having resulted in a tie, lots were cast and [Peña] was readmitted." Unfortunately, the minutes do not include the contrasting opinions and who emitted them.
31. AHMSG, *Act. 2* {1812} n.f.
32. AHMSG, *Act. 2* {1812} f10v.
33. Article 70 states the following: "On that day [of the election] with the parochial electors congregated, the reports about the qualifications shall be read, and if some objection be raised against any of them, or of the electors due to the absence of some of the required qualities, the *Junta shall definitively and immediately resolve, and what it resolves will be without appeal*" (My emphasis.) Constitución de 1812, f18.
34. AHMSG, *Act. 2* {1812} f11v–12.

35. During the elections ordered by the Junta Central in 1809, José Ignacio Valldejuli was selected by San Juan to be the island's deputy. The other four *cabildos* chose Power y Giralt. Piqueras, *Bicentenarios de libertad*, 266. Quiñones was making good use of his connections, since he had been active in the proceedings dealing with Power's election and was one of the minds behind the San German's instructions to Power.
36. AHMSG, *Act. 2* {1812} f12v.
37. AHMSG, *Act. 2* {1812} f13. It not surprising that his "political rivals should call him the *Prince*, because of the favors showered on his friends and colleagues," and we may add because of his pride. Cruz Monclova, *Historia de Puerto Rico*, I: 109.
38. AHMSG, *Act. 2* {1812} f12.
39. This is what Quiñones stated in the *Junta de Partido* (26 February 1813) when he declared that Peña presented himself to the Junta Provincial during the installation ceremony to promote Quiñones' disqualification because "of the part I played in [Peña's] exclusion as elector, and my role as ballot counter (*escrutador*) during the first act of this Junta." AHMSG, *Act. 2* {1812} f12.
40. AHMSG, *Act. 2* {1812} f13–13v.
41. That Quiñones focuses on Coamo is interesting, since that *partido* is mentioned in the documents relative to the 1811 conspiracy. According to the *aviso* Coamo's *Regidor Alguacil Mayor* had lodged with Don Francisco Ramírez de Arellano, first cousin to Nicolás Quiñones and *alcalde* during the conspiracy. Francisco Quiñones was the son-in-law of Don Ramón Ramírez de Arellano, *Regidor Alguacil Mayor*, and also one of the alleged plotters. As we have seen, Aguada's *cabildo* had suggested a meeting to discuss the composition of Power's instructions. San Germán and Coamo had agreed, but in the end, Arecibo was not willing to participate and the plan fizzled.
42. AHMSG, *Act. 2* {1812} f14.
43. AHMSG, *Act. 2* {1812} f13v.
44. AHMSG, *Act. 2* {1812} f14. (my emphasis)
45. AHMSG, *Act. 2* {1812} f15v.
46. AHMSG, *Act. 2* {1812} f14–14v.
47. A.G.I. Ultramar 450. "Aviso reservadísimo" written on the margin. f132 and subsequent.
48. A.G.I. Ultramar 450. Meléndez had consulted Don José Joaquín Maroto, *Fiscal* of Quito's *Audiencia*. Maroto had recommended prudence "in consideration of the innumerable testimonies that had yet to be discovered, and that, if this case were to adopt the forms prescribed by our laws, what would follow

was a mound of complaints, the implication of subjects of high standing (*carácter*), the necessity of placing a multitude of people under suspicion of their grievances which would only result in igniting hate among families without any good arising from it. Rather it would be certain that this would ignite, among the majority of the Island's inhabitants a contentious combustion, that far from assuring Justice would be the fountainhead of irreparable damages and chaos and confusion; [and] he was of the opinion that judicial procedures should be dropped, and to only try to tighten the security of the Island, which happily has been achieved." The only persons sent to prison in this affair were José Vicente González, Sergeant Felipe Nazario and Tomás Cardoso "exiled in said Island for the preceding Revolution in Caracas" and arrested for proffering injurious words at the royal commissioner. González and Cardoso were categorized as *pardos* or *mulatos*. Don Pedro Benito Vidal and Don José Costa y Gali, *Oidor* (judge) and *Fiscal* (prosecutor) respectively of Caracas' *Audiencia*, and in transit through Puerto Rico, had disagreed with Maroto's recommendations. The *Audiencia* of Quito had experienced the formation of a junta to govern in the name of Ferdinand VII between August and December 1809. Many of its members, like the marquis of Selva Alegre, the junta's president, belonged to the Quiteño aristocracy and creole elite. See O. Rodríguez and E. Jaime, *The Independence of Spanish America*, Cambridge Latin American Studies 84 (Cambridge: Cambridge University Press, 1998), 67–69.
49. AHMSG, *Act. 2* {1812} f15–15v.
50. AMSG, *Act. 2* {1812}. Testimonies about Peña's lowly status ff18–24.
51. AHMSG, *Act. 2* {1812} f24v.
52. AHMSG, *Act. 2* {1812} f26v–27v.
53. Opposition to the French and things French were generalized in the Peninsula and America. Rodríguez O., *The Independence of Spanish America*, 51–52. As Eastman points out: "The entire French nation had become an enemy of Spain rather than a few impious individuals representing seditious causes." In America, as in Spain, "anti-French epithets became synonymous with atheism and hostility towards the Catholic church," and were also used to demonize political rivals. Scott Eastman, *Preaching Spanish Nationalism across the Hispanic Atlantic, 1759–1823* (Baton Rouge: Louisiana State University Press, 2012), 132.
54. AHMSG, *Act. 2* {1812} 28.
55. ibid., 30.
56. Tulio Halperin Donghi, *Reforma y disolución de los imperios ibéricos 1750–1850. Historia de América Latina 3*. Nicolás Sánchez Albornoz, dir. (Madrid: Alianza Editorial, 1985), 116.

57. See the references to the 1811 conspiracy already cited, and for the 1812 slave conspiracy, Baralt, *Esclavos rebeldes*. As already mentioned, the latter was sparked by debates regarding slavery and the slave trade in the Cortes of 1810, and rumours that slavery had been abolished, but freedom was being withheld by the colonial authorities and the slave owners.
58. Zeuske, "Las Capitanías Generales," 371. Jorge I. Domínguez explains Cuba's permanence in the Spanish orbit by adducing a mixture of racial fear and economic interest, since the Crown favoured the modernizing enterprise of Arango and his fellows. *Insurrection or Loyalty: The Breakdown of the Spanish Empire* (Cambridge: Harvard University Press, 1980), 160–63.
59. Cruz Monclova, Historia, Vol. I: 53.
60. Regarding political paradigms see, J.G.A. Pocock, "Languages and Their Implications: The Transformation of the Study of Political Thought," in *Politics, Language & Time: Essays on Political Thought and History* (Chicago: University of Chicago Press, 1989), 3–41. The term neopatrimonial as described by Domínguez, *Insurrection or Loyalty*, 11–15.
61. On these terms, see Ramón María Serrera, "Sociedad Estamental y Sistema Colonial," in *De los Imperios a las Naciones: Iberoamérica*, coord. A. Annino, L. Castro Leiva, and F.X. Guerra, Forum International des Sciences Humaines (Zaragoza: IberCaja, 1994), 51. This ambivalence also characterized the framers of the Constitution.
62. Pocock, "Languages," 22; Domínguez, *Insurrection and Loyalty*, 46–58.

[6]

THE CROWN IS NOT WELCOMED
Government and Politics in British Guiana, 1953–1957

[JAMES ROSE]

IN RECOGNITION OF THE STATE OF UNDERDEVELOPMENT IN the colony of British Guiana (Guyana), and the fertile ground which this provided for social disaffection and political agitation, Her Majesty's Government (HMG) undertook to provide a period of rapid economic development and social reforms in the wake of the October 1953 invasion, which ousted the democratically elected People's Progressive Party (PPP) government after only 133 days in office. Whitehall hoped that conspicuous economic progress and social reforms would defuse colonial anger resulting from the suspension of the constitution and the dismissal of the PPP representatives. In order to ensure that the programme met with as little resistance as possible, while providing local support for the governor and officials as well as a semblance of democratic coverage for continuing colonial autocracy in the colony, a select group of middle-class representatives was nominated to the Executive and Legislative Councils. In reality, a Crown colony administration was imposed on Guyana in place of what had, but a few months earlier, been hailed as one of the most advanced constitutional forms in the Anglophone Caribbean.

This chapter focuses on this interim administration and its efforts to promote the programme of economic development and social reforms. Attention will also be directed at the various forms of responses to the administration, the emergence of an opposition to it, and the eventual decision to return to democratic institutions in British Guiana.

THE INTERIM ADMINISTRATION

When Whitehall undertook to move troops into British Guiana, the Secretary of State secured royal assent for three documents which authorized the suspension of the Waddington Constitution, proclaimed a state of emergency in the colony and varied the Constitution to introduce Crown rule in the occupied territory.[1] Ministerial appointments were suspended and the membership of the Legislative and Executive Councils was purged.[2]

The governor was granted full discretion in the exercise of all the powers conferred on him by the altered Constitution. Whereas in the 1953 Constitution he was required to act on the advice of the Executive Council, this was no longer a requirement. Subsequent royal instruments augmented these powers still further by providing him with extensive authority, subject only to consultation with the Secretary of State and the assent of the queen.[3] But in addition to these powers, the declaration of a state of emergency and the presence of British soldiers in the colony significantly increased the autocracy of Governor Alfred Savage.

The broad outlines of the administrative structure to be implemented in the colony had been enunciated both in the initial correspondence informing the governor of the proposed intervention and during the parliamentary debate of the state of emergency. In subsequent discussions between the governor and the Colonial Office, the administrative structure was further defined. They agreed on the exclusion of members of the PPP from both the Legislative and Executive Councils.[4] Additionally, the governor argued that service in the interim government would jeopardize the political future of members of the smaller parties and the potential leaders of reasonable and responsible elements in the colony, so they were to be excluded as well.[5] The Legislative Assembly was to be comprised of twenty-four members, with a Speaker appointed by the governor from outside the House.[6] He proposed the appointment of a wholly nominated Executive Council consisting of seven to ten members. Three or four seats were to be allocated to the ex officio members, while the others were to be given to reliable members of the Legislative Council.

Whitehall did not support an arrangement in which nominated members were fitted out with ministerial portfolios, so soon afterwards elected ministers were dismissed and the governor's initial proposal was rejected when it was made in September.[7] Subsequently, Whitehall conceded a very limited experiment in which not more than two such members would be given ministerial posts [referred to as members, rather than ministers], but on the very clear understanding that their function was advisory and not executive. The governor, appreciating that Whitehall intended to reintroduce Crown rule in the colony, accepted this stipulation.[8]

The new government was announced on 27 December 1953.[9] The three ex officio members from the former council – Chief Secretary John Gutch, CMG, OBE; Attorney General Frank Holder, QC and Financial Secretary; and F.O. Fraser, OBE – along with seven others made up the Executive Council.[10] The Legislative Council was comprised of Sir Eustace Woolford, OBE, QC, who retained his appointment as Speaker of the Legislature, and the ten members of the Executive Council. They were joined by five of the six minority members in the former legislature and six of the nine members of the former State Council. As had been agreed, no member of the PPP was considered for appointment, even though one, Jai Narine Singh, was reported to have declared himself available.[11]

While several of the leading personalities of the United Democratic Party (UDP) refrained from serving in the interim government, eight members of the executive remained in the Legislative and Executive Councils. Seven members of this legislature had been defeated in the 1953 election; five by humiliating margins. There were eight merchants, four barristers-at-law, three trade union officials, two rice millers, two public servants, a minister of religion, a teacher and a managing director in the legislature. From an ethnic point of view, the remodelled Executive Council was made up of three Africans, one Indian, two of mixed racial heritage and one European, while the Legislative Council was comprised of five Africans, eight of mixed racial heritage, six Indians, two Chinese and three Europeans. In spite of the number of Indians among the appointees, the peasant rice farmer or the sugar worker could not identify with any of them. It was apparent that the councils had recaptured the old middle-class complexion that was defeated in the 1953 election.

THE FAILURE TO PRODUCE DEVELOPMENT AND REFORMS

The immediate criticisms of the composition of the interim administration did not unsettle Whitehall, committed as it was to direct Crown rule and the use of non-representative political personalities in the administration of the colony. Whitehall was, however, concerned that the administration be seen to be advancing HMG's programme of economic development and social reforms in the colony. Economic development, so long neglected, had at last become a priority concern but, in so doing, it presented problems which Whitehall had not originally foreseen and now found extremely difficult to resolve.

When, in February 1954, Sir Alfred Savage announced his development plan envisaging the expenditure of GYD$66 million, the PPP scoffed at its pretensions.[12] The plan undertook to spend as much as GYD$46 million in the first two years. This was $11 million more than the International Bank for Reconstruction and Development (IBRD) had earmarked for a similar period, and 50 per cent in excess of what the bank had anticipated spending in its five-year plan. The party's dissatisfaction stemmed from the fact that this plan, like the 1947 one, was premised on a "quasi-inducement approach" to economic development.[13] This approach was seen as inevitable in colonies like British Guiana, where the colonial economy was dominated by private capital, which exercised considerable influence in the constitutional assemblies of the colony. This was their preferred pattern because the revenue base of the colony was very small due to the limited range of taxes levied which, in turn, restricted public investments. In the circumstances, various inducements were offered to attract foreign investments. The nationalists criticized this arrangement because very often the ordinary gains to the colony were frittered away either in concessions to private companies or by the exportation of company profits.[14]

Two very serious problems affected the implementation of the programme: the first was an absence of development finance, and the second, a critical shortage of technical and administrative personnel.[15] Whitehall was optimistic that development finance could be located for the projects earmarked for the colony, but very little could be done about staff recruitment. Only a limited number of officers was available in the empire and with colonial development being promoted everywhere, the personnel were not sufficient to service all the projects. What was more, those available tended to gravitate to the more economically advanced colonies where salaries were normally more attractive. This, however, was not only a British Guiana problem.[16]

Savage had been very concerned about both shortages and the manner in which they were likely to affect HMG's commitment to economic development and social reform in the colony.[17] Since the war, it had been the experience of both the previous governors in British Guiana that Whitehall's promises seldom matched Whitehall's performance.[18] As if to justify the governor's apprehension, in December 1953, just two months after the white paper's promise of development, he experienced his first disappointment when Whitehall rejected an application for development funding.[19] Savage then travelled to London to discuss an application for GYD$46 million to fund the two-year development plan approved by Whitehall.[20] He had requested an initial commitment to an advanced line of credit for GYD$36 million, pending a decision on the method by which funding would be provided.

Savage argued that Guiana's development plan would lose its priority once the emergency had slipped the attention of the international press and HMG's opposition in parliament. Even before this happened, however, he did not expect funding to be provided easily so he was prepared to have Whitehall dictate what portion of the total was to be treated as a grant, and the rest a loan. But Whitehall refused to offer a line of credit to the governor, promising instead to provide assistance in raising loans on the London money market and new Colonial Development and Welfare funding at a later date.[21]

Savage experienced other disappointments as well. Immediately after the intervention, he submitted a list of expatriate staff required for executing the development programme.[22] He stressed the urgency with which technical and administrative personnel were needed and the extent to which the success of the plan depended on their recruitment. He never received the staff requested.[23] Then in July 1954, a few months after the discussion on funding for the development programme, two of the most senior officers tasked with arranging development finance for British Guiana engaged in a discussion which effectively reduced the urgency of economic development in the colony. N.L. Mayle, a principal officer in the Colonial Office, argued that an unproven theory claimed the absence of economic development and social reforms were responsible for nationalist protests in colonies like Guiana.[24] He found no evidence to support the thesis, and warned against pursuing policies like those preferred by the United States, in which development was unrelated to the ability of the colony to fund the upkeep of the projects once the United States had withdrawn. P. Rogers, who shared an office with Mayle, reasoned that the dependence so created made it almost impossible for the colony to ever achieve real independence. They agreed and the urgency first attached to a development programme for British Guiana was dealt a very severe blow. In actual fact, there was but one reasonable explanation of the contradiction between the public statements made by the Secretary of State and the hopes of Governor Savage on the one hand, and the official view in Whitehall: it lay in the fact that limited imperial resources were constantly outstripped by competing colonial demands.

Initially, Whitehall also wanted to reform the conditions governing the landlord-tenancy relationship. The PPP had attempted to effect similar reforms and had incurred the wrath of the land-holding class. Rogers once described the land owner-tenant relationship as most unsatisfactory, but anticipated vigorous opposition from powerful landlords, "the old gang", long accustomed to having their own way and receiving official protection.[25] Since this class was represented in the Executive Council, the opposition to reforms was expected to be most vigorous, necessitating unwavering commitment and resolute action from the governor. But the interests which had moved Whitehall to suspend the constitution could not be dealt with in an arbitrary manner and in the end the landlords were left secure with their privileges.

There were other areas of similar sensitivity. Both the police and civil establishments were to be reorganized to avoid the discontent which made the PPP so attractive to the junior officer ranks. Housing, for so long neglected, was in an appalling state and demanded an aggressive construction programme in both rural and urban areas. But the efforts to have sugar accelerate its programme for housing its workers failed, as did the administration's attempts to locate funding for an urban housing programme.[26]

Training for the assumption of public office was another of the key areas requiring urgent attention. Reforms of the local government system on which this training programme depended therefore became a priority area, both as a means of improving local administration and as training for a career in politics.²⁷ But since these reforms included the introduction of adult suffrage, it was feared that the PPP would obtain control of the reform councils. Local government reforms therefore conflicted with the emergency which sought the exclusion of the PPP from power. At the same time graft and corruption had become serious problems since the interim administration had taken office thus increasing the need for trained public officials.

The failure of the proposed development and reform packet was significant, but it did not have the same effect as embarrassments experienced at other levels. A major run on the Post Office Savings Bank soon after the interim government assumed office suggested that the depositors did not trust them to administer their savings.²⁸ The colonial administration complained that the PPP had created the impression that local savings would be used to pay for the upkeep of British troops in the colony and since the invasion lacked support among the people, they withdrew their deposits. The colonial administration had described an earlier run as indicative of a lack of confidence in the PPP administration.²⁹ They were now reluctant to see the subsequent run as indicative of a similar lack of confidence – this time in themselves.

The second issue was of far greater significance. When the rumour of a military intervention first surfaced, assurances were obtained that the colony would not be burdened with its cost.³⁰ Three months later, Her Majesty's Treasury ruled that since colonial governments were responsible for their own internal security, when it failed to the extent that HMG's troops were required to intervene, HMG's War Office expected to recover the costs governing the movement and upkeep of such troops from said colony.³¹ The bill for garrisoning British troops in Guiana to 31 March 1955 was put, in the first instance, at £400,000.³² The Colonial Office countered that even if British Guiana could, no colonial government would ever vote that sum for such a purpose. It argued that British Guiana could not afford such a bill and doubted whether the Executive and Legislative Councils, though wholly nominated bodies, would support a bill of that nature. However, by the end of 1956, the Colonial Office had given up its attempt to make the Treasury pay and the colonial administration, under a new governor, was instructed to honour the bill with great dispatch.³³

To make matters worse, the interim administration never seriously attempted to gain the respect of the electorate. It reversed the liberal legislation of the PPP and reintroduced the ban on Caribbean nationalists.[34] Communist literature was once again outlawed, while the Trade Union Council was placed under the control of the British trade union movement. Thereafter, British and US trade unionists determined the credibility of the working people's representatives.[35] They also distanced the entire labour movement in the colony from the Caribbean Labour Congress and the World Federation of Trade Unions, both of which had been deemed communist. Utilizing a special vote of £3,000, the British Trade Union Council provided the services of Messrs George Woodcock [General Secretary of the British Trade Union] and Andrew Dalgleish in what one parliamentarian described as "the best thing that has happened in British Guiana for a very long time".[36] The statement, ironic in a way, was indicative of the prevailing insensitivity of British colonial policy since the invasion.

But the credibility of the local administration suffered an even greater setback when the nominated members of the interim administration undertook to raise their salaries.[37] The governor and the Colonial Office argued that members had, in October 1953, agreed to serve at a stipulated salary and were shocked when they not only voted to increase their salary by between forty and fifty-six per cent, but chose to make the increase retroactive to 1 January 1954.[38] The report reaching the Colonial Office illustrated the extent of the increases.[39] Nominated members in the Executive Council with portfolio moved from GYD$7,200 to GYD$10,000 – an increase of 45 per cent; Executive Council members without portfolio moved from GYD$3,600 to GYD$5,040 (a 40 per cent raise), and Unofficial Members of the Legislature from GYD$1,900 to GYD$3,000 (a 56 per cent increase).

One senior officer, in a fit of exasperation, complained that over the months since their nomination, the interim government had insulated itself from the shocks of public opinion and the increases in their salary so soon after taking office on acceptance of a proposed salary was a clear indication of that tendency.[40] They were outraged that not only had the members chosen to increase their salary, but that they had actually made the raise retroactive. It was a gross abuse of office, they complained. They argued that the increases could not even be justified by a corresponding rise in the cost of living, a revelation which considerably increased Whitehall's embarrassment. Officials could only lament the absence of a sense of service or self-sacrifice on the part of the local legislators. The Secretary of State, now totally embarrassed, lamely wondered why he had not been consulted on the matter.[41]

The press condemned the pay hikes as immoral, while some sections of the conservative community castigated the move as disgraceful.[42] Anthony Tasker, a senior executive of Booker Brothers, described the measure as suicidal.[43] It was, in his opinion, appallingly bad public relations by a group of non-representative persons, who seemed to have lost touch with the reality of the politics of the colony. In a private letter to the Minister of State, one Guianese described the move as thoroughly disastrous and excessive for legislators who had neither constituencies nor extra-parliamentary duties. The correspondent disclosed that within business circles the move had only served to increase the contempt in which the interim administration was held locally.[44]

The Daily Argosy, the newspaper supportive of the sugar interests in the colony, condemned the measure and pointed to other weaknesses in the administration. It noted over-confidence, over advertising, scarcely justifiable trips abroad, touches of arrogance and reluctance to let the public into members' confidence, to name but a few.[45] The paper remarked on the high note of confidence, the spirit of urgency and self-dedication that prevailed at the time the interim administration assumed office; and wondered how, in the short time they had been in office, they could have lost it all and forget that they were the focus of public attention.

By mid-1955, Governor Savage had become totally disillusioned and on 22 July he withdrew with as much grace as the situation allowed. No one believed that ill-health was responsible for his resignation and credibility was accorded this disbelief when it was announced, soon after, that Savage was accepting another post.[46] Even before his resignation, it had been widely rumoured that economic interests, particularly sugar, which the governor had frequently criticized, had exerted pressure in Whitehall, demanding his recall.[47] While Savage never endeared himself to the Guianese public, his departure nevertheless exposed the level of disagreement which characterized the relationship between him and his superiors in Whitehall.

Governor Patrick Muir Renison was appointed 29 September 1955, but took up his appointment on 25 October. Upon succeeding Savage, he immediately expressed disappointment with progress in the colony.[48] He pointed out that land development schemes in progress during the tenure of the PPP government had ground to a halt. The responsible officers had resigned and the replacements promised to his predecessor had not materialized. Local government was at a complete standstill, with nothing done about the reforms recommended by the British expert, A.H. Marshall, which had been accepted by the Colonial Office.[49]

Renison was despondent enough to have complained that six months after he had asked for help to implement reforms in the conditions affecting housing, land development, local government and roads, he had received none. Renison was an ambitious colonial administrator who believed himself equal to the challenge which British Guiana presented and was therefore intolerant of the failure to provide development and reforms in the colony since October 1953. He bitingly complained that Whitehall's criticisms about the administration's lack of enterprise and the slowness of progress rang hollow and that ". . . nothing visible has happened for nearly a year in a project which you thought so urgent and important that you instructed that it was to go ahead before . . . it had been considered by legislature."[50] The Colonial Office shared the "disappointment and sense of discouragement about our complete failure" in Guiana, but then rationalized the situation by suggesting that they had pitched their hopes too high and needed more time if they were to be helpful.

CRITICISMS OF THE INTERIM ADMINISTRATION

In view of negative reports and statements emanating from the colony right from the very beginning, and due to serious misgivings within the Colonial Office, the Minister of State, Henry Hopkinson, was sent on a familiarization visit to the colony in October 1954. He displayed a special interest in the functioning of the organs of the interim administration and the reception they were accorded locally.[51] He also received complaints about the reinstatement of the discredited "old brigade". From deliberations he had with them, he concluded that they had little hope of establishing any rapport with PPP constituencies. Hopkinson was also perturbed that the process of training in, and preparation for, public life was being wasted on the incumbents, as few had any political future beyond the interim administration. He therefore suggested that the nominated members be encouraged to cultivate constituencies, a process which, if successful, would enhance their performance at electoral politics. He also suggested that since, as constituted, the interim administration could not be used as a training ground for participation in representative institutions, the local government system which had fallen into disuse should be rehabilitated.[52]

In his 1955 New Year's message, the Archbishop of the West Indies declared that the situation in Guiana had worsened since the intervention of the British. He argued that fifteen months after the withdrawal of representative government, there was little to show, except the British troops and an overpowering anger among the people. The colony was saddled with an administration remarkable for bribery, corruption and nepotism, which sapped the resolve of the honest and stifled the opportunities of the dedicated. He lamented that: "The mighty wave of discontent with existing conditions which swept the PPP into power remains as strong as ever."[53] The society remained a cauldron in which powerful combinations of wealth and influence oppressed the weak. He reported unhappily, "The sense of empty frustration and agonising bitterness has become accentuated."[54]

This was a biting criticism of colonial policy. It was all the more remarkable since it attacked the emergency programme which HMG undertook to provide in the wake of the suspension of the Constitution. The archbishop recognized that the administration was unsatisfactory, but he also admitted that the policies were ineffective. He denounced the weaknesses of the society, but he also recognized the social and economic disequilibrium which informed nationalist discontent and encouraged radical thought and action. *The New Commonwealth* discovered a scapegoat at hand and hinted that the time had come for a new administrator. Savage had done his best, but British Guiana was going nowhere and getting there very fast. In the enlightened opinion of this journal, British Guiana needed an all-powerful dictator – with authority unfettered by memories of failure – to secure loyalty and cooperation and win over the Guianese people to the concept of good government.[55] The weaknesses of the interim administration were also criticized in a discussion which George Woodcock, the British trade unionist, assigned to the task of reinvigorating the Manpower Citizen Association, had with an official of the Colonial Office. After a short stay in the colony in which he met most of the nominated members, Woodcock concluded that P.A. Cummings, the member responsible for Labour, Health and Housing in the Executive Council, and Rahaman Gajraj were self-seekers, lacking in any party spirit, policy and the capacity for organization. Woodcock reported that members were regarded as "stooges" and would never acquire political credibility. He predicted that they would soon be squabbling among themselves.[56]

THE MOVEMENT FOR CONSTITUTIONAL REFORM

Disappointment with the performance of the interim administration, particularly its inability to effect economic development, and the ethical and political poverty of the membership, aggravated the frustrations felt by Colonial Office staff over the obvious failure to restrict the militancy or reduce the influence of the PPP.[57] It was increasingly apparent that the Colonial Office was becoming reconciled to the fact that their efforts to seduce the membership of the PPP or to crush the party were more difficult than originally imagined.[58]

At this point the problems with which Whitehall were confronted were the results of three distinct failures by the interim administration: its failure to effect the promised colonial economic transformation; its inability to win over the Guianese electorate and its lack of success in reducing the political influence of the PPP. It was, however, easier to identify these shortcomings than to formulate solutions for the problems they created. It was also clear that the period of marking time, because it had been so obviously unproductive, could not be prolonged much longer.[59] This conclusion was the more serious because the very state of emergency and the process of political repression had prevented the new parties from recruiting new membership.[60] On the one hand, the suspension of the electoral principle had caused the politically uncommitted to mentally distance themselves from electoral politics.[61] It was difficult to stimulate serious debate about party politics outside the PPP constituencies and the new parties did not dare engage in such discussions within PPP constituencies. While the political activity of the PPP was proscribed, it was unhelpful to permit others to organize politically, since this exposed them as politicians favoured by the oppressor.[62] Frustrated by the impasse, the new parties grumbled that for so long as the emergency regulations were in force, only the PPP had a commanding platform.

The politically ambitious needed to present themselves openly to the electorate before public recognition could be won, and this was virtually impossible once political assemblies were outlawed by the emergency regulations. Lionel Luckhoo and others therefore demanded a relaxation of the state of emergency to permit political organization and public assemblies.[63] Whitehall recognized the soundness of the case presented by the colonial politicians and discussed the issue.[64] Realizing this, Renison presented Whitehall with a formula to cope with the political impasse in the colony. He suggested that the Emergency Regulations be varied so as to allow for party political activity by all, while the communists remained restricted. Political meetings would be permitted but the leaders of the PPP, due to their restrictions, would be banned from such activities.[65] The plan was well received in the Colonial Office but, in actual fact, it was not easy to implement. For one thing, as was suspected by most local politicians, it provided the PPP with further evidence of "political gerrymandering". This was a potent charge which, once levied, instantly discredited the opponents of the PPP, who were revealed as recipients of political patronage.

The Secretary of State, in his reply, pointed out that HMG was not satisfied that representative government could be restored in Guiana without the risk of a further breakdown in the Constitution. Referring to a split in the PPP in 1955, HMG considered it premature to assess the impact of this development on the true nature of representative politics in the colony. It was apparent that Whitehall was still hesitant about the feasibility of constitutional restoration in British Guiana and, in particular, the pace of any considered concessions. Whitehall argued that a halfway return to responsible government was difficult to arrange and highly undesirable in Guiana. The imperial government was particularly concerned about the staging of an election which could possibly return the PPP to office with an extended majority due to fears that the administration could once again be confronted with a hostile group that was democratically elected to the legislature.

One month later, the Colonial Office admitted that the interim government was a mistake which could not be tolerated much longer. It was, in the estimation of Secretary of State Lord Lloyd, inefficient and undoubtedly corrupt.[66] Yet the prospect of a return to democratic institutions in the colony alarmed some and worried most. In Lloyd's assessment, the PPP would win any election held under adult suffrage and the administration would be forced to decide on its relations with Janet Jagan and other radicals in the party. Whitehall considered removing Janet Jagan from the coastal zone, but that was hardly likely to contribute to HMG's credit and would ultimately be exploited by the PPP. They concluded, however, that a general relaxation of the Emergency Regulations to enable political forces to demonstrate their standing was unavoidable. In the House of Commons, the question put to the Secretary as to whether he was now willing to concede the possibility of holding an election in British Guiana received a cautious response. HMG was committed to preparing British Guiana for a return to democratic processes, but doubted the time was right to hold an election. The governor was assessing the situation and would report on the prospect of making further concessions.[67]

CONSTITUTIONAL REFORMS

Sometime later, in his specific recommendations for constitutional reforms, Renison suggested that a general election be held around March or April 1957, and that the Legislative Council be comprised of: a Speaker, elected from outside the Legislative Council with a casting vote; four officials; seven or eight nominated members; twelve elected representatives; and a Deputy Speaker selected from within the House. He further recommended an Executive Council comprising the governor, four officials, one nominated member from the Legislative Council and five elected members from the Legislative Council. Finally, he argued that universal adult suffrage and the twenty-four-seat constituency should be retained.[68]

Renison insisted on an elected preponderance in the House because it reduced the possibility of deadlocks and other conflicts which tended to unsettle the economy and of which investors tended to be afraid. The Secretary of State seemed relieved to accept the proposals but cautioned prudence.[69] The modifications were to appear as a rudimentary alteration of the interim Constitution to make allowance for elected members and the governor was advised to remind the colony that HMG still stood firmly by her intention to prevent the emergence of a communist state in Guiana.

The proposed reforms were unpopular and no political organization in the colony supported them.[70] This was obviously another major setback for Whitehall, but particularly so for the governor. Even the moderates sponsored by Whitehall confessed that while as individuals they were inclined to support the proposals, as politicians in the field they could not do so and face the electorate.[71] The criticisms were discussed in the Colonial Office and it was agreed that the ratio between the nominated and the elected elements was not large enough to avoid constitutional deadlocks. It was therefore decided to increase the elected representatives from twelve to fourteen.[72] This was a concession of considerable proportion, but it did not satisfy the political actors in the colony.[73]

Renison complained that the parties were fearful of being outdone by the PPP and therefore became involved in the extremism and extravagance normally associated with the PPP.[74] This allegation was rejected by Luckhoo, who in a meeting recounted by Mayle, revealed his disappointment with the proposals. He confessed that while he was normally reluctant to criticize Whitehall's policy, he was forced to do so because the constitutional proposals were limited.[75] Luckhoo did not associate his organization with the all-party grouping, but after consultation with Whitehall, he publicly condemned the proposals.[76]

Whitehall had still not become fully reconciled to the return of the Jagans to nationalist politics in the colony. The matter was discussed once again and Renison pointed out that they could not be ignored for appointment to the Executive Council if the PPP emerged with the greatest influence, even though they were unlikely to change their political beliefs or commitments.[77] Whitehall conceded the point but, given the circumstances, were concerned about Washington's attitude to the return of the Jagans and the PPP to power. It was agreed that all plans for a return to constitutional governance in the colony were dependent on the reception they were accorded in Washington.[78]

In an effort to persuade Cabinet that it was time for the return to constitutional government in British Guiana, a Cabinet paper on constitutional development was presented to the Colonial Policy Committee that spoke of the significant changes in colony.[79] These included the split in the PPP, the emergence of Linden Forbes Sampson Burnham as a serious contender for the leadership of the party, and the development of moderate parties with serious political potential capable of challenging the PPP. The paper argued that the time was appropriate to experiment with a return to constitutional government in the colony since it secured the initiative for HMG in containing further political demands and in determining the measure and pace of subsequent reforms. To delay might force Whitehall, at some inconvenient moment, to make immoderate concessions in response to colonial pressure. Continuing, the paper observed that recent events in the colony indicated that the Jagans might be more inclined to cooperate with HMG than previously. This was a welcome development, especially as the performance of the PPP at the election might warrant their appointment to the Executive Council. The paper concluded by arguing that constitutional advance in British Guiana should be supported, since it was a very important first step to providing the opportunity for continued stability, the acquisition of political and administrative experience in the art of self-government, and further and accelerated reforms in the future. The election date was fixed for 12 August 1957 and the necessary variations in the Emergency Regulations were made to accommodate an election campaign.[80]

THE RETURN TO PARTY POLITICAL MOBILIZATION

With the announcement of the date of election, the political atmosphere in the colony was electrified and the governor reported on the quickening of political activity.[81] He was filled with optimism about the political future of the colony, particularly since he was also able to report another split in the PPP and movements towards a coalition of the parties among the moderates. He hoped that HMG's continued determination to oppose the communists would not only encourage the opposition to unite to challenge the PPP, but would persuade the electorate to support the new parties.[82] Although agreed upon, the actual date of elections was withheld from the public so that, if necessary, it could be varied to coincide with the most advantageous moment for the moderates. The governor was instructed to facilitate the effectiveness of the moderates.[83]

More than anything else therefore, what Whitehall wanted was a party offering a strong rural challenge to the PPP. With the United Democratic Party (UDP) set to relieve the PPP of its urban predominance, the expectation was for the National Labour Front (NLF) to perform a similar function in the rural constituencies.[84] When Renison's strategy seemed destined for failure, efforts were made to create a coalition of the three parties – the NLF, the UDP and the Burnham faction of the PPP. Burnham rejected the idea, reasoning that both parties could win only a single seat in the city, and he was quite capable of taking that seat himself.[85] Furthermore, Luckhoo was a political liability with whom he did not savour a relationship since he would lose credibility with the electorate. Faced with this rebuff, the governor scaled down his plans to create a coalition. He was satisfied, however regretfully, to have them opposing the PPP severally.[86]

Whitehall would have preferred to have concentrated on the UDP, but between June and August 1955, two Colonial Office assessments of the UDP were unfavourable.[87] Radford dismissed its chances against the PPP, claiming that it was ineffectively organized and that John Carter's middle-class background and leadership style would prove detrimental in any contest with the PPP. Whitehall was therefore forced to look elsewhere for a party to replace the PPP.

The most vociferous of those possessing an interest in party politics was Lionel Luckhoo who, in 1956, formed the NLF. Originally organized as a liberal foil to the reactionary UDP, the party was really the brainchild of Jock Campbell, the influential spokesman for sugar, who was afraid that the conservative UDP could not mount a serious challenge to the PPP and suggested a more progressive organization. The NLF was therefore patterned after the British Labour Party, with its welfare policies and programme,[88] which included national independence, the creation of a welfare state, land reforms and redistribution, full employment and industrialization.[89] But irrespective of the support offered by the administration, none of the parties formed during this period demonstrated the capacity to become really serious contenders at the election, and by nomination day 1957, several had disappeared.[90] Whitehall assessed the chances of each and in the end concluded that recourse would once again have to be made to an Executive Council in which the influence of the PPP was overwhelming.

Between October 1953 and 1957, HMG embarked on a deliberate programme to undermine the influence of the PPP in British Guiana. In this pursuit, the constitution, the military and an undemocratic administration were employed. Utilizing emergency regulations, an attempt was made to dislocate the party's leadership and frighten its membership, but in the end, the failure of that programme was admitted. Whitehall was unhappy with the result, especially as the PPP seemed to have emerged, in spite of two splits, as strong as it had been in 1953. What was more, the October invasion, the performance of the interim administration and Whitehall's own failure to produce reforms had provided the party with an altogether stronger nationalist platform.

The 1957 election was therefore likely to be very important, not least because the PPP was expected to be returned to office, but also because it was returning to office under an even more restrictive Constitution than the one it had protested against in 1953. Since no other alternative could be devised, Whitehall was forced to accept the challenge which the return of the PPP entailed. Significantly, due to the absence of dialogue with the PPP, since October 1953, Whitehall had been uncertain of the attitude of the party's leadership to taking office under a limited Constitution, and was reduced to hoping that the burden of office would moderate the radicalism of the PPP when it returned to office in 1957.

NOTES

1. CO.1031/1167. These instruments were obtained on 4 October 1953 and became active on 8 October. They were: the British Guiana (Emergency) Order-in-Council, 1953; the British Guiana (Constitution) (Amendment) Order-in-Council, 1953, and the Royal Instruments (Additional). See CO.1031/319, Savage to the Secretary of State, No. 108, 13 October 1953; D.G. Gordon to F.W. Holder, 14 October 1953; and the Secretary of State to OAG, No. 23, 7 January 1954.
2. *British Guiana Official Gazette*, 9 and 10 October 1953; CO.1031/319, Secretary of State to OAG, No. 23, 7 January 1954; CO.1031/1167, British Guiana (Constitution) (Amendment) Order-in-Council, 1953, and Great Britain, Suspension of the Constitution (London: HMSO, 1953), p. 12 para. 44.
3. *British Guiana Official Gazette*, 9 October 1953; CO.1031/1167. Royal Instruments (Additional) Order-in-Council, 1953.
4. CO.1031/406, Savage to the Secretary of State, No. 237, 11 December 1953, and Secretary of State to Savage, No. 226, 22 December 1953.
5. CO.1031/319, Savage to the Secretary of State, No. 58, 27 September 1953, and CO.1031/406, Rogers to Savage, 16 November 1953.
6. Savage to the Secretary of State, No. 58, 27 September 1953 and No. 63, 29 September 1953.
7. CO.1031/319, Savage to the Secretary of State, No. 58, 27 September 1953; CO.1031/319, Secretary of State to Savage, No. 173, 31 October 1953.

CO.1031/315, Savage to the Secretary of State, No. 188, 2 November 1953, and CO.1031/315, No. 247, 18 December 1953.
8. Savage to the Secretary of State, No. 118, 2 November 1953.
9. CO.1031/416, Savage to the Secretary of State, No. 253, 23 December 1953, and No. 256, 26 November 1953, and 741D.00/1-1254, Maddox to the Dept. of State, No. 230, 12 January 1954. These documents contain interesting biographical information on those nominated to the various organs. The section which follows depended to a large extent on these documents.
10. Speaker, Sir Eustace Gordon Woolford.

The Executive Council
President, Governor, Sir Alfred Savage

Ex-Officio
The Chief Secretary, John Gutch, The Attorney-General, F.W. Holder, Financing Secretary. W.O. Fraser.

Nominated Members
Sir Frank Mc David, Member for Agriculture, Forest, Land & Mines,
P.A. Cummings, Member for Labour, Health & Housing,
W.O.R. Kendell, Member for Works & Communication,
G.A.C. Farnum, G.H. Smellie, R.B. Gajraj, R.C. Tello and W.J. Raatgever.

The Legislative Council
Nominated Officials
W.J. Lord, J.I. Ramphal, T. Lee, W.A. Phang, L.A. Luckhoo, W.A. MacNie, C.A. Carter, E.F. Correia, Rev D.C.J. Bobb, H. Rahaman, Miss Gertie Collins, Mrs Esther Day, Dr H.A. Fraser, Lt Col E.J. Harewood, R.B. Jailall and Sugrim Singh.

11. CO.1031/1187, Savage to the Secretary of State, No. 100, 10 October 1953, and CO.1031/1174, Savage to the Secretary of State, No. 196, 10 November 1953.
12. *Economic Proposals, British Guiana* (London: Hansard, UK Parliament, 1954) 5, 9–18. The entire plan is reproduced on pages 9–18.
13. W. David, 345.
14. Clive Thomas, *The Poor and the Powerless: Economic Policy and Change in the Caribbean* (New York: Monthly Review Press, 1988), 60–73; Denis Benn, *Ideology and Political Development: The Growth and Development of Political Ideas in the Caribbean 1774–1983* (Kingston: Institute of Social and Economic Research, UWI, 1987), 84–106.
15. CO.1031/38, Secretary of State to Savage, No. 404, 30 October 1953, and CO.1031/1687, Renison to the Secretary of State (Personal for Rogers) No. 316, 3 July 1956.

16. For a balanced discussion of this issue as it affected colonial development throughout the empire, see D.J. Morgan, *The Official History of Colonial Development: A Reassessment of British Aid Policy, 1951–1965* (London: Macmillan, 1980), vol. 5: 236–70.
17. CO.1031/38, Secretary of State to Savage, No. 404, 30 October 1953.
18. CO.537/2245, "The Future of British Guiana: A Personal View." Enclosed, Lethem to Secretary of State, 27 June 1949.
19. Secretary of State to Savage, No. 229, 24 December 1953.
20. CO.1031/1329, Mayle to Rogers, 2 February 1954.
21. HCD, 523, 8 February 1954. 827–32.
22. CO.1031/829, Secretary of State to Savage, No. 163, 28 October 1953.
23. Internal memoranda by Mayle and H.T. Bourdillon, 8 December 1953, and Minutes of a Colonial Office Meeting, 10 December 1953. Present were Rogers, Mayle and Bourdillon.
24. CO.1031/1355, N.L. Mayle, Head, West Indian Dept., to P. Rogers, Assistant Under-Secretary of State, 1 July 1954, and Rogers to Mayle, 2 July 1954.
25. CO.1031/1432, Note on Colonial Policy for British Guiana by Rogers, 15 July 1955.
26. "Housing Development," *British Guiana Report*, 1954–57.
27. CO.1031/1432, Note on Colonial Policy for British Guiana by Rogers, 15 July 1955.
28. CO.1031/1183, Savage to the Secretary of State, No. 120, 20 November 1953.
29. CO.1031/38, Savage to the Secretary of State, No. 120, 15 October 1953. The figures released were of the order of: Deposits = 988,987, Withdrawals = 2,688,709, Net withdrawals = 1,699,722. In 1953, the Post Office Savings bank carried deposits equal to the sum of G$16 million on its books.
30. CO.1031/1436, Rogers to Savage, 22 May 1954, and Savage to Rogers, 16 July 1954.
31. B. Melville to A.E. Drake (Her Majesty's Treasury), 9 February 1954.
32. HMG estimated that the extra cost up to 31 December 1953 of moving the troops was about £100,000 and the cost of maintenance at about £2,000 a week. HCD, 523, 1 February 1954, col. 14.
33. F. Kennedy to Renison, 4 October 1956.
34. CO.1031/961, Savage to the Secretary of State, No. 205, 17 November 1953, and No. 206, 18 November 1953.
35. *The Thunder*, 31 December 1955.
36. HCD, 524, 1955–56. Col.1211. J.K. Vaughan-Morgan, 21 June 1955.
37. CO.1031/1491, Governor's Deputy to the Secretary of State, No. 73, 4 July 1955.
38. Secretary of State to OAG, No. 32, 14 September 1955.

39. Governor's Deputy to the Secretary of State, No. 73, 4 July 1955.
40. CO.1031/1433, G.F. Sayers to Mayle, 5 October 1955.
41. Secretary of State to OAG, No. 32, 14 September 1955.
42. *The Daily Argosy*, 24 June 1955. Reuter dispatch carried the PPP's response, 8 July 1955.
43. Tasker to Campbell, 30 June 1955.
44. John Vaughan-Morgan to Rt Hon Henry Hopkinson, Minister of State, 8 August 1955.
45. *The Daily Argosy*, 3 July 1955.
46. CO.1031/1433, Sayers to Mayle, 5 October 1955.
47. PREM.11/827, Sweany (private secretary to the Secretary of State) to Prime Minister, attached the Minister of Colonial Affairs' Hopkinson Report to the Secretary of State on his visit to British Guiana, 28 September to 5 October 1954. But the most damning document is Secretary of State to Prime Minister, No. 35, 22 June 1955 (Secret), reporting on the circumstances leading up to the withdrawal of the Governor. The Secretary of State noted that the decision would be unpopular, particularly among the Governor's Labourite friends, but he would nevertheless be withdrawn. Savage was subsequently employed, post-resignation as Governor of British Guiana, as Second Crown Agent for Overseas Governments and Administrations. For the local reactions, see *The Daily Argosy*, 3 July 1955, and *The Thunder*, 4 July 1955.
48. For information on both the resignation of Savage and the appointment of Renison, see CO.1031/2222, Dabny to Revell, 8 October 1955. For the governor's expression of disappointment, see CO.1031/1355, Colonial Office discussion of the general policy to be applied in British Guiana, 19 September 1955. Those present were Renison, Rogers, Mayle, Windsor and Radford.
49. A.H. Marshall, *Report on Local Government in British Guiana, 1955* (Georgetown: Government Printery, 1955) (*The Marshall Report 1955*) and *British Guiana, Local Government Reorganisation on The Implementation of The Marshall Report* (Georgetown: Government Printery, 1957). The Colonial Office did not get around to locating Marshall until late 1954, when he was appointed by the Secretary of State, *to enquire and report on all aspects of local government in both rural and urban areas of the Colony and to make such recommendations as may be practicable and desirable*. Marshall arrived in the colony on 15 February 1955 and left on 5 May. Even though the Colonial Office accepted his report, no serious effort was made to implement its main aspects.

50. CO.1031/1687, Renison to the Secretary of State (Personal to Rogers), No. 316, 3 July 1956.
51. CO.1031/1355, Minutes of a Special Meeting between the Minister of State and Officials in the Executive Council, 5 November 1954.
52. CO.1031/1415, Report of the Minister of State, Mr Henry Hopkinson, on his Visit to British Guiana, October 1954.
53. The full speech was carried by Reuter's Telegram, 12 January 1955. For extracts, see *The British Guiana Diocesan Magazine*, January 1955.
54. ibid.
55. *New Commonwealth*, 24 January 1955, 54.
56. CO.1031/1357, Note by Radford, 14 February 1955.
57. Minutes of a Colonial Office Meeting, 19 September 1955. Present were Rogers, Mayle, Windsor, Radford and Renison.
58. CO.1031/1355, Report of the Minister of State on His Visit to British Guiana, October 1954, 5 October 1954.
59. This fact had been recognized as early as September 1955. CO.1031/1432, Jakeway to Rogers, 1 September 1955. But nine months later, the governor was forced to reiterate them for the edification of the Colonial Office. Renison to Mayle, 22 June 1956. See also CO.1031/1355, Minutes of a Colonial Office Meeting on General Policy in British Guiana, 19 September 1955. Present were Rogers, Mayle, Windsor, Radford and Renison.
60. CO.1031/1541, Note by Vaughan-Morgan, 3 January 1955; OAG to the Secretary of State, No. 319, 27 June 1955; and Minutes of a Colonial Office Meeting on General Policy in British Guiana, 7 October 1955. Present were Lloyd, Mayle, Rogers, Radford and Renison.
61. Minutes of a Colonial Office Meeting on General Policy in British Guiana, 7 October 1955. Present were Lloyd, Mayle, Rogers, Radford and Renison.
62. OAG to the Secretary of State, No. 319, 27 June 1955, and Reuters Dispatch, 18 April 1956.
63. CO.1031/1541, Reuters Dispatch, 18 April 1955; OAG to the Secretary of State, No. 319, 27 June 1955; and Minutes of a Colonial Office Meeting on General Policy in British Guiana, 19 September 1955. Present were Rogers, Mayle, Windsor, Radford and Renison.
64. Minutes of Meeting on Constitutional Development in British Guiana, 24–25, February 1956, and Minutes of Colonial Office Meeting with Renison, 19 March 1956. Present at both meetings were Rogers, Kennedy, Radford and Renison.
65. Minutes of a Colonial Office Meeting on General Policy in British Guiana, 19 September 1955. Present were Rogers, Mayle, Windsor, Radford and Renison.

66. 7 October 1955.
67. HCD, 546, 30 November 1955, 211.
68. CO.1031/1355, Renison to Rogers, 5 January 1956.
69. Secretary of State to Renison, No. 8, 23 January 1956.
70. Reuters Dispatch, 2 May 1956.
71. Renison to the Secretary of State, No. 27, 28 April 1956, and No. 41, 11 July 1956.
72. K.W.A. Scarlett to Kennedy, 30 August 1956.
73. CO.1031/1355, Press Release of 3 August 1956, which was carried in the dailies on 4 August 1956, and *The Thunder*, 6 August 1956.
74. Renison to the Secretary of State, No. 27, 28 April 1956, and No. 358, 31 July 1956.
75. Internal memorandum, Mayle to Rogers, 2 July 1956.
76. Renison to the Secretary of State, No. 41, 11 July 1956.
77. Renison to the Secretary of State, No. 358, 31 July 1956.
78. Report of a Colonial Office Meeting with Renison, 19 March 1956. Present were Renison, Rogers, Kennedy and Radford.
79. CO.1031/1355, Draft Memorandum on British Guiana Constitution prepared for presentation to The Colonial Policy Committee, 6 April 1956. See also, CAB.129/80, British Guiana: Memorandum by the Secretary of State for the Colonies, 17 April 1956&PREM.11/1727, Proposed Amendment to British Guiana Constitution, 17 April 1956. Attached see, Copy of Proposed Amendment of the Constitution.
80. CO.1031/2246, Colonial Office, Paper on "Political and Constitutional History of British Guiana," (n.d.).
81. Renison to the Secretary of State, No. 358, 31 July 1956.
82. CO.1031/1355, Minutes of a Colonial Office Meeting on British Guiana Constitution, 19 March 1956. Those present were Rogers, Kennedy, Radford and Renison.
83. CO.1031/1355, Memorandum on British Guiana Constitution for Presentation to Colonial Political Committee Meeting. 6 April 1956, and CAB.129/80, British Guiana: Memorandum of the Secretary of State for the Colonies, 17 April 1954.
84. See also, CO.1031/1542, The National Labour Front. Note prepared by Radford on the NLF, 7 June 1956.
85. CO.1031/2482, Minute of a Meeting between A. Kershaw and Mr Burnham, in Kershaw to Profumo, 15 March 1957.
86. CO.1031/1719, Renison to Rogers, 4 June 1956.
87. CO.1031/1539, R.E. Radford reports on a Meeting with John Carter, Leader of the United Democratic Party, 5 August 1955. See also CO.1031/1431, A Note by Radford, 28 June 1955.

88. Cheddi Jagan, *The West on Trial: My Fight for Guyana's Freedom* (London: Michael Joseph, 1967), 176–77.
89. CO.1031/1542, See Reuter Report on the National Labour Front formed by Luckhoo, 6 March 1956, and Renison to the Secretary of State, No. 38, 29 May 1956.
90. Several leaders of political parties contested the election as members of another party. These included P.A. Cummings, Charles Carter and J. Fernandes, while D. Debidin did not contest at all.

[7]

ERIC WILLIAMS AND C.L.R. JAMES
Intellectual Symbiosis and Political Counterpoint

[HUMBERTO GARCÍA-MUÑIZ]

"James, as an intellectual . . . is a much broader figure than Williams – but of course as a politician he is a much narrower one. James talked about the world and how to make it better but he never *did* anything about it. They were very different."
—S.W. Mintz[1]

NO BOOK ON CARIBBEAN HISTORY HAS CAUSED A greater intellectual commotion than *Capitalism and Slavery* by Eric Williams, the first professional historian of the region and a key figure in the political world of Trinidad and Tobago and the Caribbean from 1956 until his death in 1981. The classic analyzes the contribution of African slavery in the British Caribbean colonies to the industrial revolution inBritain. However, the origin of this argument comes not from Williams, but from his academic mentor, friend and political ally turned adversary, C.L.R. James. Yet the relations between these two men of letters and political actors are much deeper, complicated and extensive.

My concern in this chapter is to weave the history of James' presence and influence in Williams' early education, intellectual development and political praxis from the 1920s until their falling out in the 1960s. I start with their lives and early connections in Trinidad and Tobago. Then I follow their relationship to Great Britain in the 1930s, when James developed as a writer and anti-colonialist spokesperson, an influential revolutionary thinker and a Pan-Africanist man of action; while Williams pursued his doctoral studies and defended a controversial dissertation at Oxford University. In the 1940s, both are in the United States, where

Williams emerged as the leading Caribbeanist of the academic world, and James was submerged in the left political debates and "the Negro question" in the United States. The 1950s found Williams back in Trinidad and Tobago, as a high official in a metropolitan-dominated organization with regional aims and projects, and then becoming the main successful pro-independence leader of the British Caribbean. Meanwhile, deported to Great Britain in 1953, James returned five years later – after a twenty-six-year absence – to Trinidad and Tobago to collaborate with Williams and the People's National Movement (PNM). The chapter ends in the mid-1960s when *realpolitik* rekindled their ideological differences within the context of party politics, destroying irreparably an intellectual, amicable and political relationship that probably has no equal in Caribbean history and politics.

ORIGINS IN COLONIAL TRINIDAD AND TOBAGO

The family history of Eric Eustace Williams (1911–1981) is well known. He was the firstborn of a Catholic family of twelve children, living in the poor wards of the predominantly black capital, Port-of-Spain, with a "dark brown" father employed in the postal services, and a mother of "French-Creole"[2] descent, selling cakes in the vicinity, whose social and economic ambitions rested on his academic performance.[3] His godfather was Grenada's T.A. Marryshow (1887–1958), an anticolonial politician, recognized as the "father of West Indian integration".[4] Williams was the recipient of several scholarships enabling him to study in the best primary and secondary schools. He won one of the three Island Scholarships, given by the colonial government, to complete his university studies in Great Britain. Against his authoritarian father's insistence that he study medicine, Williams applied and was accepted into St Catherine's College, Oxford University, to complete a Bachelor of Arts in Modern History. Among his letters of recommendation, the one by Trinidad's Director of Education, J.O. Cutteridge, stands out: "Mr Williams is not of European descent but is a coloured boy, although not black. He comes from a good family, and bears an excellent reputation as to his character and conduct in this Colony."[5]

Ten years older than Williams, C.L.R. James (1901–1989) was born in Caroni and raised in Tunapuna in a family of Barbadian origins. His father worked as a teacher and school principal, while his mother, a housewife, was a voracious reader. At the age of nine, James became the youngest boy ever to win an exhibition to Queen's Royal College, the only government secondary school. James did not care about the family pressures, or his failure to attain an Island Scholarship. After graduation, he taught at QRC and other schools. He met Williams during this period: "I have known Dr Williams since he was about ten or eleven years. I taught him."[6]

Young James joined the small world of letters of the colony with contributions to journals. Among these were a review of an autobiography of Mahatma Gandhi and a critique rebutting an article by Dr Sidney Harland on the biological differences of the races.

In March 1932, James travelled to Great Britain in pursuit of a literary career. He settled in the city of Nelson, Lancashire, to stay at the home of his friend, the cricketer Learie Constantine. James found employment as a cricket reporter. While there, he published two of the three manuscripts he brought from Trinidad and Tobago. The first, *The Life of Captain Cipriani: An Account of British Government in the West Indies*, is his first book-length venture into "the relationship between a leader and a broad social or political movement".[7] Leonard Woolf, husband of Virginia the writer, asked that it be abridged to publish it as a criticism of British colonialism in the Caribbean. *The Case for West Indian Self-Government* came out in 1933, and as a result, James became the first popular speaker in support of the independence of British Caribbean colonies.[8] The pamphlet elicited the first review of a publication by James in an academic journal. In *International Affairs*, F.G. Pratt described the work as "a bitter indictment of the Crown Colony system of government in the West Indies".[9] That year, he served as ghost-writer for Constantine's autobiography, *Cricket and I,* of which he said, "To the West Indians it was the first book ever published in England by a world-famous West Indian writing as a West Indian about people and events in the West Indies."[10]

In London, in 1934, James became one of the first British Caribbean novelists when *Minty Alley,* his third manuscript, was published. He also wrote *Toussaint L'Ouverture*, a dramatic piece, with Paul Robeson playing the leading role in its first stage presentation in 1936. These were his last two literary works because, as he explained in his autobiography, "Literature was vanishing from my consciousness and politics was substituting itself."[11] For James, politics came to mean not only researching and writing history and political tracts, but also organizing Trotskyite political discussion groups, and frequent protests and public speaking, all under government surveillance.[12] Also in 1934, George Padmore (1903–1959), a childhood friend of James and now an experienced political organizer, arrived in London from Moscow. His ideological differences with Soviet communism centred on the primacy of the racial issue. He and James joined forces in the anti-imperialist uproar that resulted from the Italian invasion of Ethiopia in 1934, by forming the International African Service Bureau and its journal, *International African Opinion*.

For his part, in 1932, Williams disembarked in an economically depressed Great Britain, with fascism taking hold of Italy and Germany, and Stalinism in the Soviet Union. During his studies, Williams was always short of money, even though he received scholarships from the Trinidad and Tobago colonial government, the university itself and particular British entities. He found Oxford's tutorial system, "much to my taste ... admirably suited my temper ... I took a very independent line."[13] His performance was superb, obtaining the highest marks: Honour School of History (first in the First Class). It gave him the opportunity to avoid returning home to work in the Education Department. St Catherine College's principal wrote to the relevant colonial authorities that Williams was "a man capable of advanced academic work, such as teaching teachers, not boys".[14] With his scholarship extended, he registered to read politics, economics and philosophy, and also aimed for a fellowship in All Souls College. He failed at both, allegedly partly for reasons of racial discrimination.[15]

In 1936, Williams opted for a PhD in history, under the tutorship of Vincent Harlow. At that time, colonial history was relegated to second place at Oxford. Reginald Coupland, Professor of Colonial History, had the main position. In October of that year, Williams obtained a £50 one-year scholarship from Leatherseller's Company for research work. In Williams' autobiographical writings and later academic work, Coupland is referred to as the major exponent of the popularly accepted proposition that slave emancipation in the British Caribbean was due to the campaign by the humanitarian movement known as "The Saints". The demolition of that view was Williams' aim in his dissertation and for this, he gave greater emphasis to the economic factors. According to Williams, he selected as his theme "the very beginning of modern society in the West Indies, the abolition of the British West Indian slave system".[16]

During his studies in Great Britain, Williams managed two contrary currents in terms of historical schools and personalities, which he kept separate from one another. On the one hand were the British, white, racist Oxford academic world and professors with an imperialist mindset, not sympathetic to his proposed line of research; and on the other were his Afro-Trinidadian leftist, anti-imperialist friends in radical London. He periodically met with them, read their publications and discussed his academic plans as well as contemporary affairs.

About his relationship with Williams, James has pointed out the occasions upon which they conversed and spent time together, even talking about his dissertation topic and research. He recalled that Williams advanced that he was going forward to the doctorate and inquired: "What shall I write on?" James remembered his reply: "I know exactly what you should write on. I have done the economic basis of slavery as it was in France. But that has never been done in Great Britain . . . A lot of people think the British showed goodwill. There were lots of people who had goodwill, but it was the basis, the economic basis that allowed the goodwill to function. . . . I sat down and wrote what the thesis should be with my own hand, and I gave it to him".[17]

In 1938, the same year Williams defended his thesis, James published *The Black Jacobins: Toussaint L'Ouverture and the San Domingo Revolution*. Two scholars of Haiti praised the author and the book in academic journals. W.G. Seabrook commented that James "has rendered the public a service for which he merits the attention due to a scholar who blazes the way in an all but neglected field".[18] Noting the author was "British, Negro, and Marxist", Ludwell Lee Montague asserted that James "finds his way in both Haiti and France, achieving clarity where complexities of class, color and section have reduced others to vagueness and confusion".[19]

James received accolades for his Caribbean publications as well as his writings siding with Trotsky in his dispute with Joseph Stalin. In a review of James' *World Revolution 1917–1936: The Rise and Fall of the Communist International*, E.H. Carr asserted, "Mr James has written a decidedly useful book. It is the first attempt outside of Trotsky himself to tell the story of the Russian revolution from the Trotskyist standpoint."[20] Another book James published in 1936, *History of the Negro Revolt*, was not commended, despite the issues and events discussed, such as the Haitian Revolution, revolts in Africa, the case of Marcus Garvey and contemporary black movements.[21]

It is not surprising that Williams, with his insatiable appetite for knowledge, continued in Great Britain the pupil-mentor relationship with James. He must have been impressed by James' meteoric metamorphosis, without university studies and affiliation, from a cricket reporter and writer to a respected intellectual and revolutionary Marxist-Trotskyist and Pan-Africanist activist, whose writings gained praise in British and US academic journals. Between March 1932 and October 1938, the number and quality of James' literary, historical and political publications, his leadership in political organizations, as well as his editorship of political publications was, as Robert Hill affirmed, "by anyone standards, a monumental achievement".[22]

James' *The Black Jacobins* and Williams' dissertation research coincided, so in all probability they exchanged sources and ideas, and served as sounding boards for each other. For Williams, witnessing James' research methodology and process of writing *The Black Jacobins* must have been a learning experience. James consulted relevant primary and secondary sources in the French archives and libraries,[23] and also consulted Haitian archival sources, mailed by Dr Jean Price-Mars, author of *Ansi parle l'oncle* (1928).[24]

However, James admitted that Williams, "in pursuit of material of the slave trade and the West Indies", had visited the archives of Bordeaux and Nantes before he did.[25] Christian Hogsbjerg argued that for *The Black Jacobins* section on the prevalence of economic factors over humanitarian motives of William Pitt the Younger, "James had doubtless been helped more than he acknowledged by Williams, who spent two years undertaking doctoral research in the Public Record Office, Parliamentary Papers, Hansard Records, Colonial Office papers, Foreign Office papers and the Chatham papers."[26]

With regard to political militancy, Williams met with James and Padmore but never affiliated or participated in any of their organizations or events. Williams attended only the meetings of the West Indian African Students Union and an Indian nationalist student group, the Majliss Society.[27] Only the Italian invasion of Ethiopia in 1934 took him out of Oxford to attend a demonstration at Aggrey House, an accommodation house sponsored by the Colonial Office in London. For him, later, the rejection extended to the publication of his dissertation when the leading leftist publisher told him: "... are you trying to tell me that the slave trade and slavery were abolished for economic reasons? I would never publish such a book, for it would be contrary to British tradition."[28]

His reticence to identify publicly with James and Padmore took a back seat, up to a point, when he completed his doctoral degree. In his first article, "Child Labour in the West Indies", in the *International African Opinion*, Williams denounced the exploitative conditions of the children and asserted "no reform contrary to the interests of the employing class can be expected until full self-government is achieved."[29] It was followed by his first book review, *Glory Dead*, by the British journalist Arthur Calder-Marshall, which he considered critical of the Crown colony system and of the loyalty of West Indians towards the British Empire.[30] It must have been gratifying for James to see his pupil complete a path-breaking dissertation at Oxford, denounce colonial class exploitation in his first publication, and call for self-government in the British Caribbean.

With the doctoral diploma in hand, in August 1939 Williams travelled to the United States to take up an appointment as Assistant Professor of Social and Political Science at Howard University in Washington, DC. His first academic assignment was a new course on the evolution of civilization that would be a requirement for all incoming students. He turned to James, who had arrived in the United States in November 1938 for support. The result was a three-volume, mimeographed compilation of readings, published later, under Williams' name, without any mention of James' input.[31]

One reason Williams did not recognize James' contribution was his reticence to be associated with a leftist who was in the United States illegally, with an expired visa and presumably already under FBI surveillance.[32] Responding to a request from Trotsky, who was then in Mexico, James came originally to the United States for a series of lectures about the European situation and to participate in the Trotskyite movement about "the Negro question". After lecturing on the east coast and in midwest industrial cities, he arrived in California and at one of his speeches met Constance Webb, a white eighteen-year-old model, aspiring actress and Socialist Party militant. He married Webb in 1946. His trip ended in Mexico where he held discussions with Trotsky to develop a coherent position on "the Negro question", although he acknowledged that he had never faced the type of segregation practised in the United States. Upon his re-entry to the United States, James continued his political work, in a state of semi-concealment, on what became known as the "Johnson-Forest tendency" in the US left and ended in the early 1950s with the study of US culture.[33]

Yet again, the lives of these two Afro-Trinidadians coincided in a metropolitan country, again with different routes and goals. In the next few years, their relationship evolved from pupil-mentor to one of friendship between two intellectual-cum-political actors. In April 1944, in his first mention of Williams to Webb, James expressed a parental-like pride and understanding: "I have a son you know . . . he is not my son really. He is a scholar of repute . . . For nearly 12 years now, I have watched him come along. He sometimes is very thoughtless and selfish. But I don't mind. Seeing him develop pleases me."[34]

As in Great Britain, both were well apprised of the need to conceal their relationship or keep it to close friends and family. James was aware that his revolutionary left-wing politics might be detrimental to Williams' budding university career and activities in metropolitan-controlled international organizations. As such, he was protective of Williams: "I did not want him to get into unnecessary trouble."[35] Also, James was mindful that Williams did not sympathize with his politics, as will be seen by his reaction to the latter's first book, *The Negro in the Caribbean*.

In his first years at Howard, Williams earned two grants for research on *The Negro in the Caribbean*. According to his own perception, the book, published in 1942, "established my reputation" and "laid the foundations for my emergence as intellectual spokesman of the Caribbean peoples".[36] By that time, Williams had travelled to Cuba, Puerto Rico, Haiti and the Dominican Republic. In the first two places, he conducted archival research and met with the most important intellectuals. His list was impressive: Fernando Ortiz (Cuba) and Jaime Benítez (Puerto Rico), the latter connected to the University of Puerto Rico. In Haiti, he met Dr Jean Price Mars, and in Trujillo's Dominican Republic, "The silence of the tomb reigned everywhere, disturbed only by the sound of army boots."[37]

The Negro in the Caribbean started with his definition of the region that added the Guianas (British Guiana, Surinam and French Guiana) and British Honduras to the Antilles' archipelago: "For reasons of convenience they may well be considered together with the Caribbean islands to which they are similar in economy as well as the racial character of their population."[38] In the book, Williams made "an out-and-out attack on colonialism in the Caribbean" – economic and political.³⁹ On the economic side, his criticism of the effects of the plantation as monoculture drew the ire of British sugar interests. Williams stole a page from US plans by proposing a federation of Caribbean territories.⁴⁰ He said: "An economic federation of all the areas will considerably strengthen their bargaining position in the world market. It would take a federation of democratic governments to settle the land question and introduce that program of diversification so necessary to a sound and healthy economic structure."⁴¹

The Negro in the Caribbean received laudatory reviews for its wide-ranging research and interpretations. One reviewer affirmed that "Williams is the greatest living authority on the Negro in the Caribbean."⁴² The only critical review came from one "W.F. Carlton", a pseudonym used by James. I quote him *in extenso* to calibrate their opposing political and ideological views, which are a prelude to later confrontations. According to James:

> The evidence is all the more valuable because Williams is no Marxist. But approaching the facts from the point of view of the Negro, i.e., from the point of view of labour, his mastery of his material forces upon him an inevitable pattern, economic necessity, class struggle, etc. He is sure of the past, clear as to the present, but the future demands more than Williams has. It needs a conscious theory. He is a sincere nationalist and a sincere democrat, but after so sure a grasp of historical development as he shows in this history of four centuries, he displays an extreme naivety in his forecasts of the future.
>
> Williams' immediate demands, federation, national independence, political democracy, are admirable, but he commits a grave error in thinking that these will end or even seriously improve West Indian mass poverty and decay. But for this lapse, his book is a little triumph, admirably planned and very well written. . . . It is in its bourgeois way a short but instructive study of capitalist beginnings, maturity, decline . . .⁴³

One can surmise that James did not read *The Negro in the Caribbean* prior to publication. In terms of the British Caribbean, it was novel that Williams' federation project was inclusive of other European and US colonies as well as independent countries. The year before, in 1941, Williams had called for "A Pan Antillean Federation based on democracy, self-government, racial cooperation . . . such would seem to be a long view of the future development of the Caribbean."⁴⁴ Williams avowed that in the federation,

"The leading place should be taken by Cuba, not so much for reason of its size as by virtue of its intellectual contributions which are a conspicuous oasis in the desert of intellectual sterility which sugar has created."[45] For Williams, Fernando Ortiz was "the greatest scholar of the Caribbean".[46]

By this time, Williams was engaged in creating his own personal network inside and outside of academia in Washington, DC, Harlem, and the Caribbean. He took advantage of Howard to call on outside interests and gain access to them. For example, for a conference on the Caribbean economic future held at Howard in 1943, he invited, among others, sugar magnate Charles W. Taussig and Sir John Huggins, the US and UK representatives of the Anglo-American Caribbean Commission (AACC) respectively.[47]

Williams was eager to participate in the commission and got his first job, as consultant, in that organization thanks to Taussig, a FDR (Franklin D. Roosevelt) brain truster, "the live wire of the Commission", and someone "who knew all about *The Negro in the Caribbean*".[48] It speaks well of Taussig, having seen the sugar industry attacked in the book and he himself belittled in the bibliography, that he considered Williams of value.[49] But being wartime, the Caribbean, under siege by Axis submarine attacks, could have grown restless and hindered the war effort. Williams also had wide knowledge of the region and could be of use in dealing with the British.

In 1942, Williams had started to revise his dissertation for publication. One important difference between his dissertation and the book was his analysis of the role played by British capital in establishing the slave system in its Caribbean colonies and how the profits derived from this system contributed to the economic growth of Great Britain. This time, in the bibliography, Williams acknowledged his intellectual debt to two studies that discuss "in a general way" the capitalism-slavery connection: "The more important is C.L.R. James, *The Black Jacobins, Toussaint L'Ouverture and the Santo Domingo Revolution* (London, 1938). On pages 38–41 the thesis advanced in this book is stated clearly and concisely and, as far as I know, for the first time in English."[50] James linked the French Industrial Revolution and the slave trade stating, "Nearly all the industries which developed in France during the eighteenth century had their origin in goods or commodities destined either for the coast of Guinea or for America. The capital of the slave-trade fertilised them: though the bourgeoisie traded in other things than slaves. Upon the success or failure of the traffic everything else depended."[51] James attributed the insight to the French academic-socialist politician, Jean Jaurès, who "saw the full influence of the colonial trade in the rise of the French bourgeoisie and his chapter on it, profound and brilliant, has formed the basis of the corresponding chapter in this book".[52] Williams was au courant with Jaurès' work, having consulted it for his dissertation to make the point of France's dominance of the sugar market.[53] The second study to connect African slavery and capitalism was a Howard master's thesis by Wilton E. Williams entitled "Africa and the Rise of Capitalism".

Moreover, Williams and James remained in touch during the process of publication of the book. While revising the manuscript's proofs, James made a key recommendation which gave principal agency to the slaves.[54] Williams wrote to the University of North Carolina Press that "a friend" pointed out that the chapter on the slave revolts must be analyzed "as a reflection of the growing economic dislocation" and asked to submit a new chapter.[55]

On 14 June, James wrote to Webb that, "By late fall, my friend Bill Williams's book will be out – I have read the page proofs – a masterpiece."[56] A month after he told her: "There is Bill Williams. He is a PhD of Oxford. He has already written and published some brilliant work and this fall will appear a *superb* work on Capitalism and Slavery."[57] Later, in a letter dated 25 February 1945, James commented that "Bill is bourgeois but thinks of his books and his ideas and principles *first*."[58] Williams visited in 1946, when he was already attached to the Caribbean Commission.[59]

Anthony P. Maingot posited that the historiography of James and Williams showed their differences in ideology and political paths. *The Black Jacobins'* main concern was with "revolutionary populism, direct action of the masses led by men who spring from the masses, and keep an organic relationship with them", while *Capitalism and Slavery* dealt "with shifts in elite behaviour caused by economic changes".[60] Yet he noted that their one feature in common was that "they interpreted and wrote history as part of a wider political activism".[61]

Shortly after *Capitalism and Slavery*, Williams involved himself in a public policy project, instigated by the appointment of a British commission to study the needs of higher education in its Caribbean colonies. In his report, he expressed the view that a university in the British Caribbean should be unitary and with no external affiliation, such as the University of Puerto Rico. The book came out in 1950, with a foreword by Dr John Dewey.[62] James read the unpublished manuscript and wrote to Constance Webb: "Bill was up for the weekend. Already he has a superb piece of work done.... and a great victory is at the end for us."[63]

The intimacy of the relationship can be further apprehended when on 3 September 1948, James wrote to his then-separated wife, that "... we haven't any friends except Bill."[64] Previously, on 4 January 1944, James wrote to her, stating that she understood him well, without "my explaining too much, like my friend Bill Williams".[65] In April 1949, their first and only child was born and Constance recorded in her diary: "Eric (Bill) Williams came down from Washington, D.C., a few days before the baby was due to be of help in case we needed him."[66]

Williams settled in Trinidad and Tobago in 1948, taking over as deputy chairman of the Caribbean Research Council at the Caribbean Commission's headquarters.[67] By resigning his position at Howard, he walked away from a promising academic career. In a period of nine years (August 1939–June 1948), Williams published three books, thirteen articles and eight book reviews – all in scholarly journals. Also, he edited two books, organized an academic conference, worked for the AACC and its outgrowth, the Caribbean Commission, conducted research in the Caribbean, and delivered numerous lectures in the United States and the Caribbean. All these accomplishments were in the open, making Williams a scholar to be reckoned with in any activity relating to the Caribbean.

It is difficult to think that Williams took the momentous step of accepting the position at the CC and moving to Trinidad and Tobago without talking to James. Their relationship had grown from one of procuring intellectual advice from James to friendship among their families. Later, James expressed approval of Williams' work in these regional organizations, as they "made him acquainted in the most comprehensive and intimate manner with the West Indian economy. ... Williams now had an opportunity as no other West Indian politician ever had of constant study and coordination of the West Indian, in fact the Caribbean economy, taken as a whole."[68]

Working in the Caribbean Commission from 1948 to 1955 was not easy. There was no way for him to advance professionally to higher positions. The CC had lost its initial integration momentum. In 1953, his personal life was shattered by the death of his Chinese-Trinidadian wife, Evelyn Suilan Moyou. He had to care for his two-year-old daughter, Erica. Yet, neither leaving Howard nor working in the CC meant that Williams reneged on his commitment as a professional historian. In 1950, he took over the presidency of the Trinidad and Tobago Historical Society and published the first-ever journal of regional history, the *Caribbean Historical Review*. The journal was a one-man show. In a letter to Sidney Mintz, he wrote; "I am the Society. I have no staff, no clerical or editorial. I have no funds."[69]

Also, Williams forged cooperative links with the University of Puerto Rico that culminated in the publication of one volume of primary documents of Caribbean history.[70] Previously, Williams had harboured plans to affiliate himself with the University College of the West Indies. But it was not to be: ". . . every effort was made to keep me out of the West Indian University".[71] Still, from 1949 to 1954, Williams edited the book, *Documents on British West Indian History, 1807–1833*, and published twelve academic articles.

In June 1955, with institutional academia and metropolitan-regional organizations closed, Williams announced his break with the CC in Woodford Square, and thrust himself into politics. In October, he met with his friends, James, Padmore and W. Arthur Lewis in London to discuss the programme and constitution drafts of a political party to be named the People's National Movement. The PNM was an immediate success in the 1956 elections, winning thirteen of twenty-four seats. Williams was appointed premier with 39 per cent of the votes.

Meanwhile, in 1952, McCarthyism caught up with James, who was deported from the United States to the United Kingdom, after detention on Ellis Island. While sick with duodenal ulcer, he wrote *Mariners, Renegades, and Castaways: The Story of Herman Melville and the World We Live In*, which he published himself.[72] Kent Worcester suggested that during his fifteen-year US sojourn, "James combined revolutionary activism, philosophical study, and an enthusiasm for popular culture and in an energetic and iconoclastic fashion."[73] But missing were his activities and writings about things Caribbean, which he recaptured in Great Britain by starting his autobiography. Outside the United States, James could not maintain the same level of contact with his political group. Somewhat isolated in London, his contacts with Padmore restarted, but the latter left for Ghana in 1957 as advisor on African affairs to President Kwame Nkrumah.

That year, on 2 October 1957, James wrote to Williams, now premier, about a project that may "expand the material base of the party paper". Complaining when he received no answer, he sent a handwritten note: "Take care of yourself, Bill. I feel you are overwhelmed, pressed hard. That is why I should come and come soon."[74] James had taken the initiative in proposing his return to Trinidad. With Padmore as an advisor to Nkrumah, what could be more challenging than to join with his prized past pupil, intellectual companion and friend, presently leader of a mass anti-colonialist, nationalist party at the moment that the British Caribbean was moving towards federation?

On 10 December, James wrote identical letters to Williams (as premier), Norman Manley (Chief Minister of Jamaica) and Grantley Adams (Chief Minister of Barbados), which stated: "It is fitting that I place before you my desire that I (and my wife) should be formally invited to the Federation celebrations."[75] On 17 March, Williams penned a letter to James, informing that the invitation was on and that "we can arrange for your continued stay for the purposes you have outlined".[76] He apologized for his late reply by enumerating the "pressures of Budget", and "the election campaign".[77] The latter, the first election for the House of Representatives of the Federation of the West Indies (FWI), was foremost in his mind. He ended saying: "The campaign is in full swing and our bulldozer is flattening out the inane resistance of the opposition."[78] Williams' elation was short-lived. On 28 March, the federal Democratic Labour Party (DLP) defeated the West Indian Federal Labour Party (WIFLP) in Trinidad and Tobago, winning six seats to four.

In April 1958, James returned at the invitation of the Governor General to witness the opening of the parliament of the FWI. The PNM executive supported the invitation, but not unanimously. Williams appointed him editor of *The Nation*. A bit later, James was named WIFLP secretary. For his part, James had no objection to joining an anti-colonial, nationalist party and he agreed to moderate his views according to the PNM programme. At that conjecture, the goal was the independence of the British Caribbean colonies under the FWI, but no one expected that Chaguaramas and the Jamaica referendum would complicate that initial aspiration. Williams' long-term federation aims referred to a wider Caribbean than the British. James stated: "If you listen carefully to Williams in ordinary conversation you will note that he speaks of Cuba, Puerto Rico, Martinique, etc, as if they were one of us."[79] One gets the impression that Williams' federation was more inclusive than James'.

At this time, their relationship changed. Williams was the head of a disciplined mass party and the nationalist movement, but was wounded locally due to the unexpected defeat at the federal polls. James was now in a subordinate position as editor of the PNM's organ, an unusual position for him. Both were treading on new ground. Leftist James, unknown to most PNM members, was considered a liability by several high-ranking party members, Great Britain and the United States.

At the risk of oversimplifying their relationship, I will analyze the James-Williams break within the context of Chaguaramas and the party issue. The history of this US Navy base and the recommendation as one of the best locations for the capital of the FWI originated in the 1941 destroyer-for-bases agreement between the United States and Great Britain. In 1957, Williams' real involvement started because of his reading the still-classified documents relating to the 1941 Leased Bases agreements.[80] He had examined them in James' "rooms in Central London", and made remarks like "James, listen to this!" and similar comments. James declared: "A lot of people believe that I told him to go and attack Chaguaramas. I never did."[81] So suffice it to say that originally Williams, supported by James in the *Nation*, demanded the exit of the US Navy from Chaguaramas, but for reasons of internal politics and geopolitics, he was forced to moderate his claim.

First, Williams could count on the Afro-Trinidadian majority supporting the PNM, but not the Hindu/Indo-Trinidadian sector – a third of the population – most of whom backed the DLP, whose official position was against Williams regarding Chaguaramas. Ashford Sinanan, leader of the opposition in the federal parliament, and Simboonath Capildeo, a DLP leader, met on 10 July 1959 with Philip Habib, US consul general, and attacked Williams' Chaguaramas position, noting that the premier, with "the communist C.LR. James" planned to introduce "totalitarianism".[82]

Earlier that month, officials of several US agencies, such as the State Department, the Central Intelligence Agency and the military services, held a meeting where it was said that "we have agreed to certain measures to undermine Dr Williams's position" and instructed US consul E. Moline to meet informally with him "in order to provide a useful 'cover' while we are engaged in the process of attempting to bring down Williams".[83]

The covert operation had difficulties due to the "reluctance" of Great Britain.[84] The hard line towards Williams came from the US Navy, which saw itself as custodian of the Panama Canal and the nearby sea-lanes. Eventually, after meeting with Williams, Moline reported that a resolution was possible, but it would be "buying the right to stay".[85]

Williams was relentless in using history to disseminate his policies. From 22 January to 6 February 1960, he published in *The Nation* six articles under the title "The History of Chaguaramas, Authorized Version, U.S.A."[86] Also, James, in *The Nation*, reckoned that the British and the Americans "are so eaten up with prejudice and superiority to a colonial people of colour that they are determined to put them in their place and keep them there".[87]

On 17 March 1960, President Eisenhower, at a National Security Council meeting, supported a better treatment of Trinidad and Tobago, as "Cuba should be a warning to us".[88] He grasped that the lessened strategic value of Chaguaramas was not worth having a falling out with an oil-producing British Caribbean country headed for independence. The situation in British Guiana, still not resolved, was enough trouble, and the geopolitical crisis in the area was boiling due to the events in Cuba. On 8 May 1960, Cuba and the Union of Soviet Socialist Republics (USSR) established diplomatic relations. Twenty-two days later, on 30 May, the pragmatic and reformist Williams aligned Trinidad and Tobago with the United States: "If the Iron Curtain is the great divide separating the two camps, then it is axiomatic that we are West of the Curtain and not East of it."[89]

Contrary to other British Caribbean leaders, Williams was cognizant of the US historical automatic reflex of "intervention – direct or preventive", which "is the guiding thread to the labyrinth of American diplomacy"; worse yet, when the word communism entered the picture.[90] He knew about the British military intervention in British Guiana in 1953 and was probably aware of US covert operations after Cheddi Jagan's party won the 1957 election. There is no proof that he was aware that the DLP was meeting with US officials, but he did put the US consul general under surveillance![91]

By late 1960, Trinidad and Tobago agreed to the continued use of Chaguaramas by the US Navy, subject to mutual agreement regarding duration and economic aid. The row continued for almost two more years as Williams fought for better terms. On 9 March 1962, Governor General

Solomon Hochoy called on the US consul general to say that Williams might flirt with Fidel Castro and communism. That broke the impasse as the Kennedy administration made a new financial offer and other terms acceptable to Williams.[92] The agreement stipulated a phased US withdrawal across seventeen years.

By that time – depending on the source – James had resigned, or been expelled, from the PNM and had flown back to London in August 1960. Relations between the two had broken down as James was charged with offences against the PNM programme and misappropriation of funds given to spend on *The Nation*. James saw Williams' accommodation of the United States regarding Chaguaramas as capitulation. As he wrote to A.N.R. Robinson, a PNM official, on 28 March, "The general opinion among all persons who take any political interest in affairs is that Chaguaramas has been sold out."[93] He informed Robinson of his leaving, even though he was "besieged on all sides to stay here, enter into the coming elections and organize a labour and socialist party".[94] He added: "It is recognized that for the first time there is on the island someone who is perfectly able to take care of Williams in debate, public authority and political competence. That person is myself."[95]

Apparently, they were not on speaking terms. Two days before, on 26 March 1960, James wrote to Williams: "Too many people seemed to have forgotten or never knew that I am a person with definite political principles and attitudes. I have subordinated myself to the P.N.M. completely. I can do so no longer."[96] A final letter of notice came on 14 July: "You have had my resignation now for a long time, Bill . . . This time now is final . . . Put any date you want on the resignation."[97] James explained that the reason was "fundamentally political . . . with a strong personal bias" as he proposed to link *The Nation* to a reorganized party, something that Williams was not inclined to do.[98] Their final exchange of words came when Williams curtly responded to a telephone call from James, saying, "There is nothing to discuss!"[99] In *Inward Hunger,* he said that James, expelled after refusing to answer the charges, explained his position in a mimeographed document that was finally printed with the title *Party Politics in the West Indies*.[100]

James' role in the PNM was to establish a party organ of high standard to compete with and simultaneously counterattack the anti-Williams campaign by the newspapers with the largest circulation, the *Trinidad*

Guardian and the *Port of Spain Gazette*. James' editorship contributed to the PNM's smashing win in the 1961 elections, with a 57 per cent vote and an absolute majority of parliamentary seats. Williams took the country to independence on 31 August 1962, and in commemoration, published *History of the People of Trinidad and Tobago*. However, he relegated James to the bibliography and only a second recommendation for information about Cipriani at that: "On Capt. Cipriani, the best material is in the Legislative Council and the files of the Government. There is also a *Life of Captain Cipriani*, by C.L.R. James, 1932."[101]

Much acrimony remained between the two. In February 1964, James signalled from Scotland his return to take on Williams: "If I go, I am running for the constituency that the Premier has chosen himself."[102] He arrived in March 1965 to cover the England and West Indies cricket test match for British newspapers. Williams placed him under a six-week house arrest due to continuing labour instability and the publication of the report of the commission of inquiry into subversive activities, which concluded it had no evidence "to support the view that a revolution was planned at this time by Mr. James".[103] An attempt by James and Stephen Maharaj to control the Hindu-Indo Trinidadian DLP failed, so they resorted in October 1965 to establish the Workers and Farmers Party (WFP). The party strategy aimed to unite the Afro-Trinidadian oil workers, and the Indo-Trinidadian sugar workers and cane farmers. In the 1966 election, ethnic mobilization prevailed again. The PNM won 52 per cent of the votes and the DLP 34 per cent. All WFP candidates lost their deposits. After the results, James flew immediately to London, returning sporadically to Trinidad.

James and Williams never talked or met again, ending as bitter adversaries a relationship of friendship and mutual intellectual enrichment, which in Great Britain in the 1930s was probably more two-sided than usually acknowledged. Due to James' maturity and achievements, he was the one to lead the way. In the United States, the intellectual symbiosis turned more one-sided in Williams' favour as he became a recognized scholar, reworked his dissertation into *Capitalism and Slavery* and wrote *Education in the British West Indies*, all with James' collaboration. There is no written evidence of Williams confiding in James about the Anglo-American Caribbean Commission or the Caribbean Commission, but he must have, since James was aware of his Caribbean-wide research projects. On the other hand, there is no indication of Williams' interest or participation in any of James' political or cultural endeavours. On the contrary, in terms of politics, James acknowledged that Williams was a bourgeois, nationalist democrat and no Marxist, but still took good care to assist and protect him because he valued his friendship and principled, high-standard academic work. Probably to his surprise, James later realized that, with his return to Trinidad and Tobago in the late 1940s, Williams further developed his wider Caribbean integration project because of his work in the CC. During this period (1948–1955), Williams was totally engulfed in his regional work and historical research and publications, all Caribbean-centred.

Inside the metropolitan-dominated CC, Williams developed into a nationalist-regionalist, anti-colonial and anti-imperialist political persona. After entering politics, it is no surprise that he welcomed James, his old mentor, intellectual advisor and friend, but also an experienced editor of political newspapers, to take over the party paper and assist in federation affairs. For reasons of *realpolitik*, as Chaguaramas flared up during one of the Cold War's peaks, and PNM's issues, their relationship came to a crashing halt in 1960. The ensuing electoral encounter of 1966 exacerbated the tensions between them.

From the late 1960s onwards, a self-exiled James was invited to teach and lecture in universities throughout the United States, Europe and the Caribbean. For several years, he was appointed "Star Professor" at the Federal City College, University of the District of Columbia. He lived for a time in Trinidad and Tobago as a guest of the Oil Workers' Trade Union (OWTU). Wide recognition came from all quarters before and after his death in London in 1989.

On the contrary, Williams found academic forums closed to him after the 1970 February Black Power Revolution. It did not matter that Henry Kissinger called *From Columbus to Castro* "a standard work on the history of the Caribbean" five months after publication.[104] Gradually, he became reclusive, until he died, alone, of an undiagnosed diabetic coma in 1981. Williams won five elections and governed for twenty-five consecutive years, with (Afro-Trinidadian) mass support. Yet, he felt disappointed by the few advances in Pan-Caribbean integration after CARICOM's establishment. He was the only statesperson in power in Caribbean history to push it forward. In his solitude, he returned to historical research. Plans to do a book entitled *The Search for Caribbean Identity* got nowhere.[105] The year of his death, he completed a book of his major speeches.[106] Postmortem, a manuscript, *The Blackest Thing in Slavery Was Not the Black Man*, which he completed in 1976, has been discovered and published recently.[107]

The estrangement of these two different intellectual-political personas might have become unavoidable just as soon as Williams decided to participate actively as a leader in the formal colonial and postcolonial politics of the US-dominated Caribbean. James exhibited flexibility with Williams while he was in the academic world, but in the national or regional political arena, a clash was to be expected because, in the final analysis, their political views were mutually exclusive, with Williams an anti-colonial, pragmatic nationalist, aware of his weakness in the wider geopolitical conjuncture, and James, an open-minded socialist, giving primacy to the anti-imperialist struggle.

In terms of their achievements, Williams and James wrote classic books on Caribbean history, published numerous articles, and lectured and delivered speeches extensively. Williams was Caribbean-centred as a student at Oxford, an academic at Howard, a metropolitan-regional official at AACC and CC, and as the prime minister of Trinidad and Tobago. James' interests radiated farther than the Caribbean to literature and literary criticism, socialist militancy and thought, aesthetics, philosophy, popular culture, cricket and other fields. Yet, Williams' classic, *Capitalism and Slavery*, written with James' collaboration, is currently "the framework for the reparations case" for Caribbean slavery, certainly a well-deserved recognition that history writing was part of their wider political praxis.[108]

NOTES

1. Charles V. Carnegie, "The Anthropology of Ourselves: An Interview with Sidney W. Mintz," *Small Axe* 19, no. 19 (2006): 137.
2. Bridget Brereton, *Race Relations in Colonial Trinidad 1870–1900* (Cambridge: Cambridge University Press, 1979), 3: "A 'French Creole' was a person of European descent, usually French, but also Spanish, Irish, English, Corsican and even German, who was born in the island and who considered himself, and was considered by others, to be a member of the French Creole group. He might possibly have ancestors of African descent, but in order to be

accepted as a member of this group, he would have to be regarded as of 'pure white' descent. Sometimes people not actually born in Trinidad but possessing the other necessary criteria, were 'adopted' as French Creoles."
3. Eric Williams, *Inward Hunger* (Chicago: University of Chicago Press, 1969), 26.
4. See "Inward Hunger: Early Drafts", EWMC, folder 139.
5. J.O. Cutteridge to Sir E. Sadler, Oxford, 8 January 1932, EWMC, folder 2.
6. *The Nation*, 7 August 1959, quoted in Walton Look Lai, "C.L.R. James and Trinidadian Nationalism", in *C.L.R. James's Caribbean*, ed. Paget Henry and Paul Buhle (Durham: Duke University Press, 1992), 192.
7. Bridget Brereton, introduction to C.L.R. James, *The Life of Captain Cipriani: An Account of British Government in the West Indies, with the pamphlet The Case for West Indian Self-Government* (Durham: Duke University Press, 2014), 24.
8. See Christian Hogsbjerg, *C.L.R. James in Imperial Britain* (Durnham: Duke University Press, 2014), 56–57.
9. F.G. Pratt, "Review of *The Case for West Indian Self-Government*, by C.L.R. James," *International Affairs* 12, no. 5 (1933), 674.
10. C.L.R. James, *Beyond a Boundary* (London: Hutchinson of London, 1963), 124; See Learie Constantine, *Cricket and I* (London: P. Allan, 1933).
11. James, *Beyond a Boundary*, 124.
12. James was under surveillance by UK and US authorities. See C.L.R. James Portal, http://www.clrjames.uk/works/c-l-r-james-security-file-1/.
13. Williams, *Inward Hunger*, 41.
14. ibid., 44.
15. ibid., 45–49.
16. ibid., 49, 50.
17. Quoted in Selwyn Ryan, *Eric Williams: The Myth and the Man* (Kingston: University of the West Indies Press, 2009), 24.
18. W.G. Seabrook, "Review of *The Black Jacobins*, by C.L.R. James", *Journal of Negro History* 24, no. 1 (1939): 126.
19. Ludwell Lee Montague, "Review of *The Black Jacobins: Toussaint L'Ouverture and the San Domingo Revolution*, by Cyril Lionel Robert James," *Hispanic American Historical Review* 20, no. 1 (1940): 130.
20. E.H. Carr, "Review of *World Revolution: The Rise and Fall of the Communist International, 1917–1936*, by C.L.R. James," *International Affairs* 16, no. 5 (1937): 819–20.
21. See C.L.R. James, *A History of Negro Revolt* (London: Fact, 1938).
22. Robert Hill, "In England, 1932–1938," in *C.L.R. James: His Life and Work*, ed. Paul Buhle (London: Allison and Busby, 1986), 62.

23. Author of *Retour de Guyane* (Paris: Jose Corti, 1938).
24. Hogsbjerg, *C.L.R. James in Imperial Britain*, 86; see Jean Price-Mars, *Ainsi Parla L'Oncle* (Port-au-Prince: Imprimerie de Compiègne, 1928).
25. James, "A Convention Appraisal," 345.
26. Hogsbjerg, *C.L.R. James in Imperial Britain*, 176.
27. See Williams, *Inward Hunger*, 53.
28. ibid.
29. Quoted in Mathew Quest, "George Padmore's and C.L.R. James's *International African Opinion*," in *George Padmore*, ed. Baptiste and Lewis, 121.
30. Quoted in Quest, "George Padmore," 121; Arthur Calder-Marshall, *Glory Dead* (London: Michael Joseph, 1939), 255.
31. See Eric Williams, ed. and comp., *Documents Illustrating the Development of Civilization*, 3 volumes (Washington, DC: Kaufman Press, 1947–1948).
32. On 19 October 1939, a Chief Constable, Special Branch, added that the trip was taken also "to assist JAMES to recuperate from a recent illness". C.L.R. James Portal, Security Service Record KV 2_1824_Page (42), http://www.clrjames.uk/works/c-l-r-james-security-file-1/, accessed 30 August 2022.
33. See Grace Lee Boggs, "C.L.R. James: Organizing in the U.S.A., 1938–1953," in *C.L.R. James: His Intellectual Legacies*, ed. Selwyn R. Cudjoe and William E. Cain (Amherst: University of Massachusetts Press, 1995), 163–72.
34. C.L.R. James to Constance Webb, 8 April 1944, Grimshaw, ed., *Special Delivery*, 103.
35. James, "A Convention Appraisal," 341.
36. Williams, *Inward Hunger*, 68.
37. ibid., 66.
38. Eric Williams, *The Negro in the Caribbean* (Washington, DC: Associates in Negro Folk Education, 1942).
39. Williams, *Inward Hunger*, 68.
40. In 1942, President Roosevelt told a British official that all Caribbean islands could be combined in a vague federation to be "watched by the various nations concerned as trustees". William Roger Louis, *Imperialism at Bay: The United States and the Decolonization of the British Empire, 1941–1945* (New York: Oxford University Press, 1978), 182.
41. Williams, *Negro in the Caribbean*, 104.
42. W.M. Brewer, "Review of *The Negro in the Caribbean*, by Eric Williams," *Journal of Negro History* 28, no. 2 (1943): 238.
43. C.L.R. James, pseudonym W.F. Carlton, "The West Indies in Review. Recent Developments in the Caribbean Colonies, June 1943", in Marxists Internet Archive, https://www.marxists.org/archive/james-clr/works/1943/06/westindies.htm, accessed 30 August 2022.

44. Eric Williams, "The Impact of the International Crisis upon the Negro in the Caribbean," *Journal of Negro Education* 10, no. 3 (1941): 543.
45. ibid., 543–44.
46. Williams, *Negro in the Caribbean*, 117; Fernando Ortiz, *Cuban Counterpoint: Tobacco and Sugar* (New York: Alfred Knopf, 1947).
47. See Eric Williams and E. Franklin Frazier, eds., *The Economic Future of the Caribbean* (Washington, DC: Howard University, 1944).
48. Williams, *Inward Hunger*, 81. Taussig was president of American Molasses (its subsidiary the refinery Sucrest), with interests in Barbados, Cuba and Puerto Rico.
49. In the Notes of *The Negro in the Caribbean*, Williams described an article by Taussig in the *Survey Graphic* as "a superficial treatment by a writer apparently easily impressed by 'paper' policies" (117).
50. Williams, *Capitalism and Slavery*, 268.
51. James, *Black Jacobins*, 35.
52. James, *Black Jacobins*, 320; see Jean Jaurès, *Histoire Socialiste de la Révolution Française*, tome I, *La Constituante* (Paris: Éditions de la Librarie de L'Humanité, 1927), 62–84.
53. Eric Williams, *The Economic Aspect of the Abolition of the West Indian Slave Trade and Slavery*, ed. D. Tomich and W. Darity (New York: Rowman and Littlefield, 2014), 50.
54. Ryan, *Eric Williams*, 43.
55. ibid.
56. "Nello to Constance Webb, 14 June 1944," Grimshaw, ed., Special Delivery, 124.
57. ibid.
58. "Postmark 24 July 1945," Grimshaw, ed., *Special Delivery*, 217. Italics in the original.
59. See "[Summer 1945]," Grimshaw, ed., *Special Delivery*, 209, and "[1946]", 272.
60. Anthony P. Maingot, "Politics and Populist Historiography in the Caribbean", in *Intellectuals in the Twentieth Century*, vol. 2, *Unity and Variety: The Hispanic and Francophone Caribbean*, ed. Alistair Hennessy (London: Macmillan Caribbean, 1992), 149.
61. Maingot, "Politics and Populist," 148.
62. Eric Williams, *Education in the British West Indies* (Port of Spain: Teachers' Economic and Social Association, 1950).
63. "[February 1945]," in Grimshaw, ed., *Special Delivery*, 203.
64. "[Postmark, 3 September 1948]", ibid., 332.
65. "Nello to Constance Webb, 4 January 1944," ibid., 88.

66. Constance Webb, *Not Without Love: Memoirs* (Hanover: Dartmouth College and Lebanon, NH: University Press of New England, 2003), 234.
67. The Netherlands openly opposed his appointment and Great Britain did so in a covert way.
68. James, "A Convention Appraisal," 342–43.
69. Eric Williams to S.W. Mintz, 19 April 1955, EWMC, folder 192.
70. See Eric Williams, *Documents of West Indian History, vol. I: 1492–1655* (Port of Spain PNM Publishing, 1963).
71. Eric Williams, "My Relations with the Caribbean Commission," in *Eric E. Williams Speaks*, 127.
72. See C.L.R. James, *Mariners, Renegades and Castaways: The Story of Herman Melville and the World We Live In* (New York: privately printed, 1953).
73. Kent Worcester, *C.L.R. James: A Political Biography* (Albany: State University of New York Press, 1996), 113.
74. C.L.R. James to Eric Williams, 2 October 1957, C.L.R. James Papers, Columbia University, Series 1, Box 3, Folder 4.
75. James to Williams, 2 October 1957, ibid.
76. Eric Williams to C.L.R. James, 17 March 1958, ibid.
77. Williams to James, 17 March 1958, ibid.
78. ibid. The PNM was only an associate member of the WIFLP because it was not socialist, like the others. The Hindu-Indo Trinidadian Democratic Labour Party (DLP) joined the federal party of the same name and although winning in their island, the WIFLP won twenty-five to the DLP's nineteen seats.
79. James, "A Convention Appraisal," 342, 343, 346. This presentation of Williams by James at a PNM convention in May 1960 is the best exposition of his relationship with Williams.
80. See Palmer, *Eric Williams*, 85.
81. C.L.R. James, "A National Purpose for Caribbean Peoples (1964)," *At the Rendezvous of Victory* (London: Allison and Busby, 1984), 151
82. Palmer, *Eric Williams*, 117.
83. Steven High, *Base Colonies in the Western Hemisphere, 1940–1967* (New York: Palgrave Macmillan, 2009), 180–98.
84. ibid., 186–87.
85. ibid., 190.
86. See Eric Williams, "The History of Chaguaramas, Authorized Version U.S.A", in *People's National Movement, Major Party Documents* (Port of Spain: PNM Publishing, n.d.), 195–215.
87. *The Nation*, 19 April 1960, quoted in Rosengarten, *Urbane Revolutionary*, 118.

88. Quoted in Spencer Mawby, *Ordering Independence: The End of Empire in the Anglophone Caribbean* (London: Palgrave Macmillan, 2012), 136.
89. Williams, *Inward Hunger*, 223.
90. Eric Williams, "Manifest Destiny of the United States: Review of *The Caribbean Policy of the United States, 1890–1920*, by W.H. Calcott," *Journal of Negro Education* 12, no. 1 (1943): 85.
91. See Mawby, *Ordering Independence*, 132.
92. ibid., 138.
93. Quoted in ibid., 137.
94. C.L.R. James to Arthur [A.N.R. Robinson], 28 March 1961, C.L.R. James Papers, Columbia University, Series I, Box 2, Folder 31.
95. James to Robinson, 28 March 1961, ibid.
96. Ryan, *Eric Williams*, 362.
97. C.L.R. James to Eric Williams, 14 July 1960, C.L.R. Papers, Columbia University, Series I, Box 3, Folder 4.
98. James to Williams, 14 July 1960, James Papers, Columbia University, Series I, Box 3, Folder 4.
99. Boodhoo, *Elusive Eric Williams*, 168.
100. See Williams, *Inward Hunger*, 268; See Gordon K. Lewis, "The Trinidad and Tobago General Election of 1961," *Caribbean Studies* 2, no. 2 (1962): 2–30.
101. Eric Williams, *The History of the People of Trinidad and Tobago* (Port of Spain, PNM Publishing, 1962), 288.
102. James Millette, "C.L.R. James and the Politics of Trinidad and Tobago," in *C.L.R. James: His Intellectual Legacies*, 328–47.
103. *Report of the Commission of Enquiry into Subversive Activities in Trinidad and Tobago* (Port of Spain: Government Printery, 1965).
104. See Eric Williams, *From Columbus to Castro* (London: Andre Deutsch, 1970). "Background Information for Pres. Ford 2-21-75, Meeting with Eric Williams, Prime Minister of Trinidad and Tobago," 21 February 1975, 1, *Declassified Documents Reference System*, Document Number: CK3100288455, accessed 2 October 2004.
105. See Andre Deutsch to Eric Williams, 3 February 1971, EWMC, folder 87.
106. See Paul Sutton, comp., *Forged from the Love of Liberty: Selected Speeches of Dr. Eric Williams* (Port of Spain: Longman Caribbean, 1981).
107. Brinsley Samaroo, ed., *The Blackest Thing in Slavery was Not the Black Man: The Last Testament of Eric Williams* (Kingston: University of the West Indies Press, 2022).
108. Hilary McD. Beckles, *Britain's Black Debt: Reparations for Caribbean Slavery and Native Genocide* (Kingston: University of the West Indies Press, 2013), 4.

[*Part Three*]
GENDERED TESTIMONIES

[8]

BRIDGET BRERETON'S GENDERED HISTORIOGRAPHY OF THE CARIBBEAN

[GELIEN MATTHEWS]

THE CONTRIBUTIONS OF PROFESSOR EMERITA BRIDGET BRERETON TOWARDS securing an autonomous space for the study of women and gender in Caribbean history have been phenomenal. She established, developed and taught a full-fledged women and gender history course and constructed a much-needed Caribbean historiographical survey of the scholarship involved in the engendering process. She also advanced the women-authored text approach as a sound methodology for making women visible in the region's history. Additionally, she published several scholarly treatises carefully tracing the experiences and roles of Caribbean women in the past, and has supervised a number of MPhil and PhD graduate history students who successfully completed gender-centric dissertations. Consequently, to deepen the understanding of, and appreciation for, Caribbean women and gender history, while paying homage to Brereton's critical contribution to this internationally growing academic field, her achievements will be closely scrutinized in this chapter.

WOMEN AND GENDER IN CARIBBEAN HISTORY

When Brereton began her career as a lecturer in history at the University of the West Indies' St Augustine Campus in 1973, none of the faculties had developed courses that included women and gender studies in their programmes. Brereton was greatly perturbed by this exclusion and expressed the view that St Augustine, as a tertiary-level institution of learning, was trailing behind.[1] She just could not accept the state of affairs at the UWI St Augustine campus in light of international developments. These included the formal struggle for equal rights and respect for women in the United Kingdom and the United States, which had been ongoing since the mid-nineteenth century, as well as the fact that from the 1960s in both countries, tertiary-level institutions had taken steps to recognize the critical importance of gender studies. Coincidentally, 1973 was the very year that Oxford University, credited as the pioneer tertiary institution of women and gender studies, graduated its first women and gender student, Sheila Robotham, whose groundbreaking doctoral dissertation was entitled "Hidden from History: Three Hundred Years of Women's Oppression". Brereton was determined to bring about the much-needed curriculum revision at St Augustine, armed with the conviction that gender is "a hugely important part of Caribbean history and a way of understanding the evolution of our societies".[2] Thus, early in her career, along with other gender-conscious academics, such as Marjorie Thorpe and Verene Shepherd, Brereton campaigned for women and gender to be taught as an autonomous academic discipline.

The first fruit of the gender lobby was the 1979 launch of an informal league called the Women and Development Study Group, with units on the three main campuses of the UWI – Mona, St Augustine and Cave Hill. It was through this body that Brereton and her colleagues at St Augustine designed and co-taught the interdisciplinary gender course, Introduction to Women's Studies. This was an important, initial step in searching for the "invisible women" of the Caribbean's past. Further strides were made in 1990 when Brereton introduced an undergraduate third-year history course, Women and Gender in the English-speaking Caribbean, which located women and gender at the centre of historical analysis. The course interrogates the gender systems governing the lives of those who inhabited the English-speaking Caribbean during different eras, such as the Tainos and Kalinagos, Europeans, Africans, Indians, Chinese and various mixed-race groups. The course also examines ideologies of gender domination and subordination in various aspects of social life, including education, employment, trade unionism and politics in the Caribbean. The course is built on the scholarship of such gender-conscious Caribbean historians as Lucille Mathurin Mair, Verene Shepherd, Hilary Beckles, Bernard Moitt, Barbara Bush, Mary Butler, Trevor Burnard, Marysa Navarro, Marietta Morrisey, Rhoda Reddock and Brereton herself. The course, Women and Gender in the English-speaking Caribbean, has been expanded significantly and has resulted in a revision of the study of Caribbean history. It continues to be an important offering of the History Departments of three of the five campuses of the UWI. One of its most glaring shortcomings, nevertheless, is that it is silent on the history of women and gender in the non-English Caribbean. It is now possible, however, to fill this yawning gap by referring to the work of Arlene Gautier and Jessica Pierre Louis on the French Antilles, Margo Groenewoud on the Dutch, and Lorraine Bayard de Volo on the Spanish West Indies, thereby expanding the geographical parameters of the course.[3]

SURVEY OF CARIBBEAN WOMEN AND GENDER HISTORIOGRAPHY

Brereton has been astute in mapping the evolution of gender discourses in Caribbean history. To date, she has published four articles on the subject: "Searching for the Invisible Woman", "Gender and the Historiography of the English-Speaking Caribbean", "Recent Developments in the Historiography of the Post-emancipation Anglophone Caribbean", and "Women and Gender in the Caribbean (English Speaking) Historiography: Sources and Methods".[4] The most comprehensive of these surveys is her 2002 article (republished in 2019) entitled "Gender and the Historiography of the English-Speaking Caribbean". In this work, Brereton clearly identifies both the thematic advances and gaps evident in women and gender historiography of the region by the dawn of the new millennium. She notes, for example, that the first major breakthrough in engendering Caribbean history was Lucille Mathurin Mair's 1974 PhD dissertation, "A Historical Study of Women in Jamaica, 1655–1844". Verene Shepherd and Hilary Beckles have since edited, added an introduction to the dissertation and secured its publication in 2006 with the University of the West Indies Press. This work, Brereton observes, was "the first full-length work on Caribbean women's historical experience" and "the first to explicitly raise issues about slavery and gender".[5] While it interrogates the lives of the three major ethnic groups of women inhabiting the Caribbean during the slavery and post-slavery periods (that is, the black, brown and white women), Brereton draws attention to its limitation in only covering the colony of Jamaica. This is a valid observation, underscoring the need to take Caribbean historiography beyond research on Jamaica as well as Trinidad, Guyana and Barbados to include the lesser-studied histories of territories such as St Vincent, St Lucia, Montserrat and Nevis. With regard to Mair's pioneering scholarship, nevertheless, Brereton affirms that it is an invaluable contribution to the reconstruction of the Caribbean's past because Jamaican women's experiences were in many respects representative of other women in the region.[6]

Brereton and other Caribbean gender pioneers also consider *The Rebel Woman in the British West Indies During Slavery*, by Lucille Mair, published in 1975, and "Women Field Labourers in Jamaica During Slavery", the title of her Elsa Goveia Lecture, presented at the UWI's Mona campus in 1986, to be invaluable. *The Rebel Woman* compelled historians to confront squarely Mair's revolutionary construct of gynaecological resistance. Mair proved convincingly that while both enslaved males and females fought against slavery, enslaved women adopted resistance strategies that were peculiar to their gender, owing to their physiological makeup.[7] Similarly, her "Women Field Labourers" revised Caribbean historiography by insisting that contrary to the traditional view, particularly from the end of the eighteenth century in the midst of the British-led campaign to abolish the trade in enslaved Africans, enslaved females rather than males dominated the work gangs in the sugar cane fields. Enslaved men had more work options than their female counterparts. While both men and women performed field and domestic work in the Great House, men dominated employment in the factory and as skilled artisans. Enslaved women had far less diversity in the performance of servile duties on the Caribbean plantations.[8] Brereton was insightful in noting that, collectively, Mair's publications pioneered a novel approach to reconstructing the Caribbean's past. It marked a significant departure from the gender-blind tradition set by androcentric colonial writers such as Richard Ligon of Barbados, Edward Long of Jamaica and John Stedman of Suriname.[9] Moreover, Mair's scholarship infused Caribbean history with sufficient, appropriate sensitivity to the past experiences of women and the influence of gender.

Brereton's historiographical survey also acknowledges the indirect but critical contribution of the research of historian Barry Higman in adding women and gender to Caribbean history. Higman's work,[10] Brereton declares, "elucidated the basic parameters of the enslaved woman's existence . . . birth, death, fertility, reproduction and infant and child mortality . . . and laid the groundwork for more ambitious studies of enslaved Caribbean women".[11]

Brereton has also highlighted in her survey of gendered publications in Caribbean history that ". . . the slavery era has been the major focus of research on Caribbean women and gender history".[12] For example, Brereton contends that Arlette Gautier, Hilary Beckles, Barbara Bush and Marietta Morrissey[13] "have given us a solid picture of the historical experience of enslaved women especially in the later decades of slavery"[14] in the areas of labour organization, population stagnation and resistance experiences. Despite the proliferation of gendered sources, however, Brereton remains dissatisfied in general with the extent to which the past experiences of women have been included in mainstream Caribbean historiography. She urges that more research needs to be conducted regarding free women (indigenous, European, African, and mixed race) during the period of slavery, as well as Caribbean women's inclusion in politics and religion in the decades following the abolition of slavery. She posits, nevertheless, that while the post-slavery history of the Caribbean is under-explored, "There is a rapidly growing body of work scattered widely in one or two books and many articles, conference or seminar papers and theses."[15] Simultaneously, Brereton laments the dearth of historical studies on the smaller immigrant communities of Chinese, Portuguese, Syrian, Lebanese and Jewish women of the post-emancipation era. She reiterates that from a specific women's history or gender history perspective, most of the work accomplished thus far concentrates heavily on Jamaica, Barbados and Trinidad, while relatively little is written about Guyana, Belize, the smaller English-speaking islands, or the Spanish, French and Dutch Caribbean.[16]

METHODOLOGICAL APPROACHES

Central to Brereton's engendering of Caribbean history is her analysis of five major methodological approaches to the discipline. She points out that historian Rosalyn Terborg-Penn has offered an Afrocentric methodology to make women visible in historical writing.[17] The approach is useful in Caribbean history, Brereton admits, since people of African descent dominated most Caribbean populations during the slavery and post-slavery periods.[18] Nevertheless, Brereton cautions that one cannot ignore the obvious limitations of an approach to history that is blind to the varied, multi-racial historical experiences of our Caribbean region.[19] What Brereton perhaps overlooked was the fact that Terborg-Penn's emphasis on black women grew out of her groundbreaking research which revealed that black women in the United States were deliberately omitted from the history of the suffragist movement in that country.[20]

Gender specialist Patricia Mohammed pioneered a second methodology. She advocates that past relationships between Caribbean men and women can be gauged by assessing the extent to which women accepted, negotiated with and challenged patriarchy.[21] While Mohammed applied her schema exclusively to women in the Indian diaspora, Brereton believes that it has the potential as an analytical tool to critically interrogate Caribbean gender systems from as early as the Taino and Kalinago era.[22]

Thirdly, regarding Blanca Silvestrini's oral history method,[23] Brereton embraces the possibilities that can be wrested from oral sources, both for solving the problem of inadequate sources on women and gender, and for yielding first-hand information about the past. However, Brereton notes that an obvious and serious drawback of Silvestrini's method is that it can only be employed to retrieve accounts of the fairly recent past.[24]

Brereton credits the American historian and feminist Elizabeth Fox-Genovese[25] with the fourth methodology in Caribbean gender history – the creative writing source approach. Fox-Genovese argues that literary works inspired in part by historical events are authentic sources of historical research. Brereton, however, cautions that while many literary reconstructions are at least in part founded on actual historical occurrences, the historian must exercise due care in separating fact from fiction, which can be easily blurred in these sources.[26]

Brereton is a strong advocate for and ardent practitioner of a fifth methodology, the gendered testimony approach, which can be used both to make women visible in history and to analyze their gender roles in relation to men. Brereton insists that while diaries, journals, memoirs, autobiographies and private letters produced by women who have lived in and written about the Caribbean are small in number, previously ignored and sometimes even scorned, they are dynamic repositories of gendered testimony.[27] She delineates this methodology in her bibliographical survey of texts written by or about nine women: Mary Prince, Mrs A.C. Carmichael, Frances Lanaghan, Mary Seacole, Elizabeth Fenwick,

Janet Schaw, Lady Maria Nugent, Yseult Bridges and Anna Mahase.[28] Their records span the pre- and post-emancipation periods. The voices represented in these largely private texts are indeed rich and varied, representing the four major ethnic identities of Caribbean women – European, African, Indian and racially mixed. The selected texts are also diversified in terms of social classes – the lowest classes, descendants of the enslaved Africans and migrant workers from India, the middle-class mixed race and the wealthy upper class. The geographical range encompasses several of the Leeward and Windward islands of the English-speaking Caribbean. These are the texts of women who lived, visited or worked in Trinidad, St Vincent, Jamaica, Barbados, Antigua, St Kitts, Bermuda, and Turks and Caicos. With regards to Mary Seacole, the text provides useful insights into her adventures in Panama, the United States and Europe. In terms of the subject matter, the collective work of these female authors represents a trove of invaluable information – all from a woman's perspective – on slavery, antislavery, Indian indentured labour and other post-emancipation experiences. Such variety makes possible a historiography based on a diverse interrogation of the history of women and gender systems of the region. The only major group that Brereton's survey does not include is the First Peoples. This is understandable, considering that Brereton's agenda was to search out female-authored texts. The First Peoples of the Caribbean, both males and females, left no written records and the surviving documented texts of their past were penned primarily by European male observers. In terms of geography, however, as previously noted, Brereton's selection overlooked the non-English Caribbean territories.

GYNOCENTRIC LIBERATION

Brereton's methodology of utilizing gendered testimony is critical to the liberation of researchers from the strangling monopoly that male authors exercised over Caribbean records prior to the scholarship of Lucille Mathurin Mair. The monopoly was in the hands of such writers as Richard Ligon, Edward Long, Bryan Edwards, Matthew 'Monk' Lewis, Thomas Thistlewood and John Stedman.[29] Brereton observes that while these androcentric texts are very useful primary sources of Caribbean history in general, they are problematic for scholars who wish to come to terms specifically with Caribbean women and gender history. At best, they are desultory in capturing womanhood in the seventeenth, eighteenth and nineteenth centuries, while their commentary on gender systems is sparse. The list of female-authored private texts that Brereton has proffered goes a long way, and will continue to do so, in filling the gaps that male writers left. This demonstrates that it is time to give even more agency to 'herstory' from the gynocentric perspective.

Of course, Brereton does not dismiss out-of-hand male narratives of the past. On the contrary, her gendered testimony is intended to widen the range of materials at the historian's disposal. Nevertheless, she questions the androcentric bias of earlier Caribbean historical writings, insists on revisionism and engenders a Caribbean historiography that is cognizant of women and gender experiences. Brereton's commentary on the limitations of male-authored texts on the history of the Caribbean also raises important questions about other kinds of sources that have been overlooked. These include perspectives of African, Indian and Chinese-descended writers, for example, whose reflections on Caribbean women and gender systems may not have been recorded in the English language or, for that matter, in texts, but in songs, paintings, sculptures and prayers. Such a consideration strengthens Brereton's observation that the earlier, male-dominated scholarship was deficient, since it did not include alternative texts from supposedly 'non-literate', subaltern sources. Brereton was, therefore, right in concluding that the traditional sources were far from complete in offering comprehensive narratives of the sexes and gender relations in the Caribbean.

WOMEN AND GENDER PUBLICATIONS

As previously indicated, an important avenue through which Brereton fuelled the advancement of women and gender studies in Caribbean history is her scholarly publications in this variant of historical studies. Her most critical contributions to the field include "Family Strategies, Gender and the Shift to Wage Labour in the British Caribbean".[30] In this article, Brereton reexamines the theme of exodus from the plantations of the English Caribbean in the first decade following emancipation. Using gender as the primary analytical tool, she interrogates the extent and timing of the withdrawal of formerly enslaved females from the estates, and their use of family strategies to secure autonomy and economic security, and she evaluates the role of gender ideologies in women's removal from the estate labour force.[31] Brereton is also a contributor to the two major texts that currently feed the study of women and gender historiography in secondary schools in the region and at three of the five major campuses of the UWI. The first of these texts, *Engendering History: Caribbean Women in Historical Perspective*, for which Brereton also served as an editor with Verene Shepherd and Barbara Bailey, was published in 1995. The work emerged out of the 1993 International Symposium on Caribbean Woman and was the first collection of essays by historians writing primarily through the lens of women and gender. The second work is *Engendering Caribbean History: Cross Cultural Perspectives*. Brereton's scholarly expertise on the labour and social experiences of enslaved females, as well as on the lives lived by the free coloured, white women and other ethnic groups – during and after slavery – are evident in these publications.

SUPERVISION OF GRADUATE THESES

Brereton's successful supervision of MPhil and PhD history candidates at the UWI St Augustine campus is yet another manifestation of her sterling contribution to the development of women and gender study in the Caribbean. In Shameen Ali's 1993 MPhil in history dissertation entitled "A Social History of East Indian Women in Trinidad since 1870", Brereton guided the student in her quest to uncover the ways in which her subjects adapted to the historical experience of immigration and settlement in a New World society.[32] Under Brereton's tutelage, Bronty Liverpool Williams completed her MPhil in history with a dissertation entitled "A Historical Study of Women in Twentieth Century St Vincent and the Grenadines". Brereton assisted her student in giving voice to numerous hitherto voiceless Vincentian women, who helped shape the history of their country in the areas of education, trade unionism, politics, protest and resistance, and in the development of the women's movement on the island. In her acknowledgements, Liverpool Williams expressed heartfelt gratitude to Brereton for stimulating her interest in the field of women's studies.[33] Nicole Phillip, a Brereton PhD student who submitted her dissertation titled "Women in Grenadian History from Slavery to People's Revolution 1783–1983" in 2002, went on to publish it with the University of the West

Indies Press in 2010 under the shorter title *Women in Grenadian History 1783–1985*. Phillip indicated that Brereton planted the seed in her mind to become a serious academic and was critical to her completion of the first full-length history of women in Grenada, an island that is relatively under-researched in comparison to territories like Trinidad, Jamaica, Barbados and Guyana.[34] Brereton's fourth graduate history student whose area of research was gender centred was Karen Eccles. Her dissertation was entitled "Trinidadian Women and World War II". The degree was awarded in 2013. The study includes a discussion on prostitution in Trinidad during World War II. Brereton encouraged her student not to overlook the history of local prostitutes on this island. She invited Eccles to delve into the complex nuances of their relations with American servicemen within the context of dire economic circumstances, condemnation, ridicule and scorn, which culminated in hostility and violence against them. Other themes which Brereton's student uncovered in her research were the roles of middle- and upper-class women as uniformed members of the British war effort, and by forming guilds and organizations that operated out of clubs, halls and their homes on behalf of Britain's role in standing up to Hitler and his allies. During the war, the study reveals, women from Trinidad engaged in fundraising for the British Empire, securing food for the servicemen, tending to British casualties of war and hosting social events to entertain them. Brereton also pushed her students to consider how the skills that the Trinidad service women acquired during the war were locally employed in the immediate post-war era.[35]

CONCLUSION

As an educator, commentator, historical analyst, methodologist and well published author, Professor Emerita Bridget Brereton has been strategic in crafting an autonomous space for women and gender in Caribbean history. In the early years of her academic career at the UWI, she was instrumental in inserting the discipline into the curriculum. As the number of scholars working in this area of academic study increased, Brereton surveyed their work and reported on the state of the scholarship. She remained vigilant, critiquing the different methodologies used in the research, and writing about women and gender history. She also offered her own creative approach to this relatively new field of academia. She published her research and co-edited a substantial volume upon which the discipline can stand firmly. She also mentored and supervised a number of young, promising scholars who have pursued specialized research in this academic field. Bridget Brereton, Professor Emerita of the History Department of the UWI, continues to champion gender pedagogy as an indispensable analytical tool of Caribbean history.[36]

NOTES

1. Interview with Bridget Brereton, St Augustine, 2015.
2. ibid.
3. See Arlette Gautie, *Les Soeurs de Solidtude: La Condition Feminine dans l'esclavage aux Antilles du XVIIe as XIX e siècle* (Paris: Editions Caribbeenes, 1985); Jessica Pierre-Louis, "Free Women of Colour and Property Donations in Martinique (1806–1830)," *Clio. Women, Gender, History* 2 no. 50 (2019): 109–23; Margo Groenewoud, "Hidden Strengths: Intellect and Ideology behind the Women's Movement in Curacao and Aruba, 1946–1995," in *Handbook of Gender Studies in the Dutch Caribbean*, ed. Rose Mary Allen and Sruti Bala (Boston: Brill, 2024), 114–33; Lorraine Bayard de Volo, *Women and the Cuban Insurrection: How Gender Shaped Castro's Victory* (New York: Cambridge University Press, 2019).
4. Bridget Brereton, "Searching for the Invisible Woman," *Slavery and Abolition* 132, no. 2 (1992): 86–96; "Gender and the Historiography of the English-Speaking Caribbean," in *Gendered Realities: Essays in Caribbean Feminist Thought*, ed. Patricia Mohammed (Kingston: University of the West Indies Press, 2002), 129–44; "Recent Developments in the Historiography of the Post-Emancipation Anglophone Caribbean," in *Beyond Fragmentation: Perspectives in Caribbean History*, ed. Juanita De Barros et al. (Princeton: Wiener Publishers, 2006), 187–209.
5. Bridget Brereton, "Gender and the Historiography of the English-Speaking Caribbean," *Clio. Women, Gender, History* 2 no. 50 (2019): 211.
6. ibid.
7. Lucille Mathurin Mair, *The Rebel Woman in the British West Indies during Slavery* (Kingston: Institute of Jamaica, 1975).
8. Lucille Mathurin Mair, The 1986 Elsa Goveia Memorial Lecture: Women Field Workers in Jamaica During Slavery (Kingston: Department of History, University of the West Indies, 1986), 7–9.

9. Richard Ligon, A True and Exact History of the Island of Barbados (London: Humphrey Moseley, 1657); Edward Long, The History of Jamaica or, General Survey of the Antient and Modern State of the Island: With Reflections on its Situation Settlements, Inhabitants, Climate, Products, Commerce, Laws, and Government in Three Volumes (London: T. Lowndes, 1774); John Gabriel Stedman, Narrative, of a Five Year's Expedition Against the Revolted Negroes of Surinam, in Guiana, on the Wild Coast of South America, from the year 1772 to 1777 (London: J. Johnson and J. Edwards, 1796).
10. Barry Higman, "Demographic Trends," in The Cambridge World History of Slavery, ed. David Eltis, Stanley Engerman, Seymour Drescher, and David Richardson (Cambridge: Cambridge University Press, 2017), 20–48; "Demography and Family Structures," in *The Cambridge World History of Slavery*, ed. David Eltis and Stanley Engerman (New York: Cambridge University Press, 2011), 479–511; *Slave Populations of the British Caribbean 1807–1834* (Baltimore: John Hopkins University Press, 1984).
11. Brereton, "Gender and the Historiography," 132.
12. ibid., 133.
13. Arlette Gautier, *Les Soeurs de Solidtude: La Condition Feminine dans l'esclavage aux Antilles du XVIIe as XIX e siècle* (Paris: Editions Caribbeenes, 1985); Hilary Beckles, *Natural Rebels: A Social History of Enslaved Black Women in Barbados* (New Brunswick: Rutgers University Press, 1989); Barbara Bush, *Slave Women in Caribbean Society 1650–1838* (Kingston: Ian Randle Publishers, 1990); Marietta Morrissey, *Slave Women in the New World: Gender Stratification in the Caribbean* (Kansas: University Press of Kansas, 1989).
14. Brereton, "Gender and the Historiography," 139.
15. ibid.
16. ibid., 138.
17. Rosalyn Terborg Penn, "Through an African Feminist Theoretical Lens: Viewing Caribbean Women's History Cross Culturally," in *Engendering History: Caribbean Women in Historical Perspective*, ed. Verene Shepherd, Bridget Brereton, and Barbara Bailey (New York: St Martin's Press, 1995), 3–19.
18. Brereton, "Gender and the Historiography," 130.
19. ibid.
20. Rosalyn Terborg Penn, *African American Women in the Struggle for the Vote, 1850–1920* (Indiana: Indiana University Press, 1988).
21. Patricia Mohammed, *Gendered Realities Essays in Caribbean Feminist Thought* (Kingston: University of the West Indies Press, 2002).
22. Brereton, "Gender and the Historiography," 130.

23. Blanca Silvestrini and Maria de los Angeles Castro Arroyo, "Sources for the Study of Puerto Rican History: A Challenge to Imaginative Research," *Latin American Research Review* 16, no. 2 (1981): 156–71.
24. Brereton, "Gender and the Historiography," 131.
25. Elizabeth Fox Genovese, *Within the Plantation Household Black and White Women of the Old South* (North Carolina: University of North Carolina Press, 1988).
26. Brereton, "Gender and the Historiography," 131.
27. Bridget Brereton, "Text, Testimony and Gender: An Examination of Some Texts by Women on the English Speaking Caribbean from the 1770s to he 1920s " in Verene Shepherd (ed) *Engendering Caribbean History Cross Cultural Perspective* (Kingston: Ian Randle Publishers, 2011) 733–53.
28. Mary Prince, *The History of Mary Prince, A West Indian Slave. Related by Herself* (London: F. Westley and A.H. Davis, 1831); A.C. Carmichael, *Domestic Manners and Social Condition of the White, Coloured, and Negro Population of the West Indies* (London: Whittaker, Treacher, 1833); Frances Lanaghan, *Antigua and the Antiguans, Vol. 1&2* (London: Saunders and Otley, 1844); Mary Seacole, *Wonderful Adventures of Mary Seacole in Many Lands* (London: James Blackwood Paternoster Row, 1857); A.F. Fenwick, ed., *The Fate of the Fenwicks: Letters to Mary Hays, 1798–1828* (London: Methuen, 1927); Janet Shaw, *Journal of a Lady of Quality Being the Narrative of a Journey from Scotland to the West Indies, North Carolina and Portugal in the Years 1774–1776* (New Haven: Yale University Press, 1921); Maria Nugent, *A Journal of a Voyage to, and Residence in the Island of Jamaica from 1801 to 1805 and of Subsequent Events in England from 1805 to 1811 in two volumes, Vol. 1* (London: T. and W. Boone, 1839); Nicholas Guppy, ed., *Child of the Tropics, Victorian Memoirs* (London: Collins and Harvill, 1980); Anna Mahase, *My Mother's Daughter: The Autobiography of Anna Mahase Snr 1899–1978* (Claxton Bay: Royards, 1992).
29. Richard Ligon, A True and Exact History of Barbados . . . (London: Humphrey Moseley, 1657); Edward Long, The history of Jamaica . . . (London: T. Lowndes, 1774); Bryan Edwards, History, Civil and Commercial, of the British Colonies in the West Indies in Three Volumes (London: Stockdale, Piccadilly, 1801); Matthew Gregory Lewis, The Journal of a West Indian Proprietor Kept During a Residence in the Island of Jamaica (London: John Murray, 1834); Trevor Burnard, Mastery, Tyranny and Desire Thomas Thistlewood and His Slaves in the Anglo Jamaican World (Chapel Hill and London: University of North Carolina Press, 2004); John Gabriel Stedman, Narrative, of a Five Year's Expedition . . . (London: J. Johnson and J. Edwards, 1796).

30. Bridget Brereton, "Family Strategies, Gender and the Shift to Wage Labour in the British Caribbean," in *Engendering Caribbean History Cross Cultural Perspectives*, ed. Verene Shepherd (Kingston: Ian Randle Publishers, 2011), 499–521.
31. Bridget Brereton, "Family Strategies," 499.
32. Shameen Ali, "A Social History of East Indian Women in Trinidad since 1870" (MPhil diss., University of the West Indies, St Augustine, 1994), ii.
33. Bronty Liverpool Williams, "A Historical Study of Women in Twentieth Century St Vincent and the Grenadines" (MPhil diss., University of the West Indies, St Augustine, 2002), i–ii.
34. Nicole Laurine Phillip, "Women in Grenadian History from Slavery to People's Revolution 1783–1983" (PhD diss., University of the West Indies, St Augustine, 2002), iii–iv.
35. Karen Eccles, "Trinidadian Women and World War II" (PhD diss., University of the West Indies, St Augustine, 2013), ii.
36. An earlier abridged version of this article was published in History in Action 5 no.1 (2016). This is the journal of the History Department, University of the West Indies, St Augustine.

[9]

EGODOCUMENTS BY WOMEN AS SOURCES FOR CARIBBEAN HISTORY
Three Cases from Late Colonial Suriname

[ROSEMARIJN HOEFTE]

IN HER ELSA GOVEIA MEMORIAL LECTURE, BRIDGET BRERETON emphasized the importance of personal documents left by women as a "key source for women's history, a channel for the transmission of their own voices".[1] Since official historical records are most often created and administered by men, letters, diaries, travelogues, memoirs and autobiographies by women are indispensable sources to reveal information about their lives, family relationships and domesticity. In her lecture, Brereton explored personal or egodocuments "as sources of gendered testimony" for anglophone Caribbean history.[2] She discussed five autobiographies, three memoirs, three diaries, and three sets of letters by respectively Mary Prince, Mary Seacole, Yseult Bridges, Anna Mahase, Sr Olga Comma Maynard, Maria Nugent, Amelia Gomez, Adella Archibald, Elizabeth Fenwick, Sarah Morton and Susan Rawle. These egodocuments were produced in the nineteenth and the first half of the twentieth century.

Inspired by Brereton's work, I look at the egodocuments of three women who lived in late colonial Suriname: Anna de Savornin Lohman, Cato Idenburg and Grace Schneiders-Howard. My scope is thus considerably more limited, not only in number but also in the backgrounds and experiences of these women. Two of them, Anna de Savornin Lohman and Cato Idenburg, were governors' daughters and thus Dutch outsiders who lived in Suriname for only a short period of time, while the third, Suriname-born Grace Schneiders-Howard, originated from the colonial white upper class. Bearing in mind that their letters and memoirs are clearly culturally, ethnically and socially determined, it is highly questionable that these egodocuments will reveal many new insights into the lives of Caribbean women in general. These documents, however, do inform us about the position and lives of these writers' (expected) gender roles, and perspectives of upper-class women in this Dutch colony. I will look at how these women describe their own inner circle, that is, their family and the house staff, paying special attention to their relationships with the most important men in their lives; social life in the colonial capital of Paramaribo; the lives and circumstances of other women in the colony; tropical nature and its effect on them; and, finally, their relation to the home country. In the writings of these three women, colonial politics play an important role, with the governors' daughters defending their fathers, and Grace Schneiders-Howard being a politician in her own right, but this will be of marginal interest here. But first, let me introduce the three protagonists.

Catharina Anna Maria (Anna) de Savornin Lohman (1868–1930) was born in the agricultural north of Holland to an aristocratic and well-to-do family.[3] She was the only daughter in a family with four sons. She did not receive extended schooling as she was expected to marry a suitable partner who would take care of her. After the death of one of her sons, her ailing mother, Florentiana Johanna Alberda van Ekenstein, turned to orthodox Christianity, which had a great influence on Anna's upbringing. She was no longer allowed to go out and reading became her only pastime. As she stated later, "I had no youth."[4]

When her father, Maurits Adriaan de Savornin Lohman, became governor of Suriname in 1889, the family moved overseas. Within a few months, however, her mother passed away and twenty-one-year-old Anna assumed the role of First Lady. Her father soon ran into a number of political conflicts and, eventually, a popular uproar ended his career in Suriname.[5] In 1891, the former governor and his daughter returned to Europe, destitute and disillusioned.[6] The family refused to support them, and Anna was forced to take a job teaching German and French at a small girls' school in Scotland. Later, she moved with her father to Batavia (present-day Jakarta), the capital of the Netherlands East Indies, where she began a successful writing career. She authored essays, newspaper articles, translations and twenty-eight novels.[7] Lohman was applauded and vilified for her audacity and agnosticism. The influential Dutch historian

Annie Romein-Verschoor[8] characterized her as a "trouble maker and an *enfant terrible*", but also as a courageous woman who dared to speak her mind. Feminist historian Mineke Bosch called her "eccentric".[9] In 1909, Lohman published her memoirs entitled *Herinneringen* (Memories); about one-fifth of the volume is devoted to her time in Suriname.

Catharine Jeanette (Cato) Idenburg (1885–1970) was one of the three surviving children of the prominent politician Alexander Willem Frederik Idenburg and Maria Elisabeth Duetz. Her father was thrice colonial minister, governor of Suriname and governor-general of the Netherlands East Indies. Later, he served as personal advisor of Queen Wilhelmina and Minister of State for more than a decade.[10] In 1905, twenty-two-year-old Cato sailed with her parents, sister Rosine, and brother Piet to the West. Her correspondence (1905–1908) detailed her life in Suriname. When her mother had to return to the Netherlands due to ill health, she became head of the gubernatorial household and hostess on official occasions. Her letters had strong religious overtones. Her father was a member of the *Anti Revolutionaire Partij* (Anti Revolutionary Party), which represented orthodox tendencies within the Dutch Reformed Church. In her letters, Cato presented herself as even more orthodox than her father, as she eschewed any form of "modernity" in religion. She later married Leo Middelberg, the son of a well-known Dutch politician, and later a politician himself.

Grace Howard (1869–1968) was the only child of an impoverished Barbadian planter, Alfred Ernest Howard, and Helena Sophia van Emden, who was part of the Surinamese elite. Grace told Dutch journalist and writer Johan van de Walle[11] that she had enjoyed a "fantastic" childhood and how she was taken to school in a large carriage, like "a little queen". What she did not mention was that her parents separated when she was two, and she and her mother moved to the Netherlands. Family matters became even more acrimonious in the early twentieth century, when her mother, who was under psychiatric care, and Grace asked the colonial authorities in Suriname to commit Alfred to the local mental asylum.[12] In 1893, Grace married Wilhelm Schneider, a German, in Dover, England. The family, including their three children, returned to Suriname in 1902. Except for occasional trips abroad, Grace Schneiders-Howard stayed in Suriname and remained socially active well into her seventies.

THE INNER CIRCLE

In her 1994 Elsa Goveia lecture, Bridget Brereton stated that the private sphere plays a much larger role in the lives of, and thus the writings by, women. Cato Idenburg is an example of this observation, as she gave the clearest insight into the life of her family. She described a close-knit unit, with their fixed daily routines and a certain distance from the outside world. In her first letter to her grandmother, her main correspondent, she drew in detail the layout of the official and private quarters of the gubernatorial palace, including the bedroom she shared with her sister, Rosine. The bedroom of their ten-year-old brother, Piet, doubled as a guest room. "Our house is very cozy and our first impression of everything, also of the servants is very pleasant, especially the garden is very beautiful."[13] A week later, she described the family's daily routine. They got up at 6 a.m. and after morning prayers, her father and other family members took a walk around Paramaribo. After breakfast at 7 a.m., her father worked till 2 p.m. Her mother was in charge of the household; Rosine taught Piet; and Cato sewed. After the afternoon rest, they drank tea at 4 p.m. Father walked again through town before they had sandwiches at 7 p.m. In the evening, the governor worked, while the women read or did needlework.[14] This evening routine changed when they started to read to each other. In a "small town such as Paramaribo, the conversation is narrow minded, and it cannot hurt to learn."[15] The family delighted in receiving newspapers and journals from Holland, "because it allows you to imagine yourself living in a civilized world for a few days".[16] Sunday afternoon, after church, was reserved for writing letters. Cato complained that her friends in Holland did not write back. In Paramaribo, Cato and Rosine made some acquaintances by joining the tennis club, but certainly in the beginning they did not play often because of the heat.[17]

Piet, who was much younger than his sisters, was home taught by Rosine and later, his mother, as the schoolchildren in Paramaribo were considered not "very moral". In the afternoon, a "Jewish-Christian" head teacher took over. In her letters, Cato described Piet as rather carefree and playful, and noted that only his father was able to keep him on the straight and narrow. He had some playmates who came over, but his parents would not allow him to play at other homes: "Although there are some very respectable families, considering Papa's position we cannot let him play with the one and not the other. That would cause jealousy." Within a few months the family noted that Piet was becoming lonely, with all "these old people" and by not attending a regular school.[18] After a year, the homeschooling stopped as Piet was missing classmates. He was sent to a local school, but to avoid the "immoral" influences of the other boys, he sat at a separate desk and was not allowed to go to school by himself.[19] In 1907, however, Piet returned to Holland to continue his education.

To give herself "something useful to do" and to prepare for her return to the Netherlands, Cato started a self-study programme in English language, in the hope that it would help her to find a job as a teacher at a Dutch school. Her father actually wanted her to return to Holland to study, but given the expenses involved, she elected to stay in Suriname.[20] Cato diversified her social activities. She soon declined to join the walks around town, as she found them "not very amusing" and "boring". She and her sister started making their own dresses, as "the seamstresses here are not very good", but "of course, nobody is supposed to know this".[21] A more modern hobby was photography, and after ordering a small camera in the United States, Cato started to send pictures of, for example, her father or her parrot.[22] She also started gardening and took singing lessons with Mrs De Vries-Robles, "an extremely nice Jewess".

The family dynamics changed when first Rosine departed for the Netherlands and then her mother and Piet; only the governor and Cato remained in Paramaribo. They spent most of their spare time reading and Cato was now managing the household. After some initial problems with the kitchen staff, "who tried to pull Mama's leg, but she was prepared for this to happen", the servants "didn't trouble us much, fortunately".[23] At first, Rosine and Cato took weekly turns to support their ailing mother in running the household. Cato admired her mother for figuring out months in advance "how many tins etcetera" she needed to order.[24] Cato was in charge of making puddings as "our kitchen maid isn't very good at it". After a few months, she prepared puddings and flowers for an official dinner. Despite her mother's hesitation, all went well.[25] One year after her arrival, Cato assumed full responsibility for official functions, while her mother created the menus. "Now I understand why Mama is so nervous, as one constantly is in fear of forgetting something and to make sure everything is all right. Fortunately, our servants have had a long training and know how things work."[26]

Cato repeatedly complained how difficult and tiring it was to be a hostess, even though there were fewer official functions due to her mother's ill health.[27] Apparently, Cato's complaints prompted her future mother-in-law to rebuke her as Cato replied that her letter has woken her up, and that it was good that she was reminded of her duties. She stated that she was not efficient and that she found it "terribly difficult" to "handle Negroes", whom she considered lazy. According to her, it was incomparable to problems with Dutch servants. "But of course I always try to adopt a serious and dignified attitude."[28]

In her first sentences in the chapter entitled "Suriname", Anna Lohman introduced herself as "a hothouse plant, rich girl", whose parents raised her in a "dream world", detached from reality.[29] She described her time in Suriname as an extremely unhappy one, as it was there that her mother was buried and her father found his political Waterloo. To her the gubernatorial palace remained the place where her mother's funeral had been held in the reception room. "Through my sincere tears I saw the fake grief on the Pharisee faces of the authorities."[30] In fact her memoir on Suriname is a long defence of her father's beliefs and policies, as well as an apology, explaining that she truly did not understand what was expected of her, "I was a *child*, a completely inexperienced *child*,"[31] and "I was the last person suitable for an official position, on account of my character, my education, my decided convictions."[32] These self-ascribed character traits got her into trouble socially and politically. After her first reception one of her "few" good friends, advised her not to express herself "so loudly, honestly, and unreservedly".[33] In the midst of the uproar against her father, the Surinamese attorney general informed the colonial minister about "his Excellency's daughter who habitually is rude to highly placed ladies, yes offends them".[34] Her book does not offer any insights into her daily routine or her relations with the staff.

Grace Schneiders-Howard was an avid correspondent, but in her letters, she revealed little about her private life. This may be due to the fact that the main recipients of her archived letters were officials in Paramaribo and the Hague. Her main concerns were political developments, health care and sanitation, and social conditions in Suriname. After her return to her country of birth, Grace became socially active. In contrast to other white women, she did not join philanthropic organizations, but became a "casual employee", cleaning yards in Paramaribo, and later served as a contractor for garbage collection and she also arranged funerals for the indigent.[35] In 1914, she informed Colonial Minister T.B. Pleyte that she sometimes inspected yards from 7 a.m. to 3 or 4 p.m.[36] She also became involved in efforts to unionize Indian labourers (in Suriname known as British Indians or Hindostani). Between 1919 and 1937, she was active in the sanitation movement.[37] In 1926, she wrote, "If I were a man I would like to be Medical Inspector for three months."[38] That was not to be; in her letters she described how hard she worked. "I sometimes leave at 6.30 a.m., only to return at 7 p.m. Rain or shine."[39] And she repeatedly informed the colonial and Dutch authorities that she walked forty kilometres every day.

In the early 1930s, Grace expressed her ambition to become politically active. "Unfortunately, women cannot become a member of the Koloniale Staten. I would definitely be in! And I would speak on behalf of public health."[40] In 1938, after a legislative change, she was the first woman to be elected to the *Koloniale Staten* (Colonial States), even though women still did not have the right to vote. In a letter to Governor J.C. Kielstra (1933–1944) she explained that she has a very modest office, "so that the poor will feel at home" and that she sometimes gave her last cent to famished labourers, as "hunger is a dangerous counselor".[41]

As said, Grace did not write much about her family or household, but she gave an interesting glimpse when her oldest son, Charles, got into trouble because of his association with a so-called *transporté*. In a letter to Governor D. Fock, she explained that two escaped *déportés* from French Guiana lived in her house, and that one of them turned out to be "a known pederast" and she called for the governor's help to arrest the man. Interestingly, she stated, "I wished mister Idenburg or mister Staal was here, as Charles would no longer go secretly to [the *déporté's*] room."[42] The apple of her eye was her youngest child, Hein, whom she supported through medical school. Again, she called upon the governor for assistance – this time to prevent a new doctor from setting up his practice near Hein.[43]

FATHERS AND PARTNERS

Both Cato Idenburg and Anna Lohman were great admirers and supporters of their fathers, their policies and their Christianity. Anna was a staunch defender of her beleaguered father, who was absorbed in his work and who allowed her to lead the life she wanted.[44] She praised his "independent, tough honesty" and his "sincere religiosity", which made him "utterly unfit" for the governorship.[45] She bitterly concluded that even though he was the "first true Christian governor", he received little support from his fellow Christians in the Dutch government. Meanwhile, major colonial civil servants pretended to help him but were conniving against him, "to *deliberately* alienate him from the Surinamese and the Koloniale Staten and the most influential men in the colony, in order to be able to fish in troubled waters".[46] "I imitated my father because I was young and inexperienced. I proudly held my hands behind my back when I was presented to a person I didn't like or when I knew he frustrated my father."[47]

Cato described her father, "Papa", in numerous letters as a devout Christian, courageous and steadfast.[48] "Everyone who comes into contact with Papa has to feel how he is guided by a holy endeavour."[49] When the other family members were back in the Netherlands, and the two of them remained in Paramaribo, they grew closer. "I am not the perfect housekeeper, but Papa doesn't complain and we have a good time together [*gezellig*]. [We read much.] We understand each other so much better." Later she wrote that Papa was caring and attentive, and longed for domesticity and coziness, but he was not showing it.[50]

Despite the complicated relationship with her father, Grace was proud of her Howard roots: "I am a Howard and a thoroughbred is not a carthorse."[51] When her superior accused her of writing anonymous letters, she stated that she would never do so as that would be cowardly. "And we Howards were never cowards! [. . .] I think it is a terrible insult!"[52] In the late 1930s, her son Hein's sympathies for Benito Mussolini and his aversion to democratic politics were duly noted, but his mother was upset when Hein insulted the British, "while forgetting that his grandfather is a Howard".[53] Nevertheless, Hein remained the most important man in Schneiders-Howard's life.

Cato Idenburg was the only one who wrote about her (future) partner. In Suriname, she got engaged to Leo Middelberg, a Dutch engineer who was involved in the construction of a railroad in the interior. He stayed up to ten weeks in the forest before returning to Paramaribo for a week or so. As she explained in a letter to her future mother-in-law, the engagement was announced rather unexpectedly, as "it is impossible to keep a secret in Paramaribo", and to her grandmother she wrote, "Paramaribo is watching us with Argus' eyes."⁵⁴ Cato described Leo as the "most lovely and very best boy in the whole world", but she was not sure about the sincerity of his religious beliefs.⁵⁵ Her doubts were such that she broke off the engagement, but later reconsidered and married him anyway.

SOCIAL LIFE IN PARAMARIBO

In her letters Cato Idenburg continuously expressed her discomfort with her life as the daughter of the governor. "It is terribly annoying to think that you are not invited because of who you are, but because of your father's dignity."⁵⁶ She intensely disliked the weekly dinners and receptions, and she did not fail to describe how "terribly boring" she considered them, when she constantly encountered the same people. She pointed to two problems: the small size of Surinamese society and racial segregation. Cato painted a picture of a backward, tranquil colony: "Outside Paramaribo there is almost nothing, and Paramaribo itself is such a terribly small place", it was not surprising that people become "sedated and petty". She underscored how important it was not to create envy between (coloured) "Surinamese", blacks and colonial Dutchmen. Even the last group felt slighted at "things that only exist in their imagination".⁵⁷ These groups did not mix and "the Dutch don't want to be saddled with the Surinamese, as one has to be terribly cautious about what one says."⁵⁸ After six months in Suriname, she concluded, "We are becoming bores who are losing ability to talk about anything important. I am glad I still have my studies."⁵⁹ Cato used dinners and receptions to testify about her religious beliefs. She wondered "why the Lord has brought us here".⁶⁰

She clearly felt isolated as she was not free to do as she pleased and "there are few suitable girls" to socialize with. Moreover, they only talked about parties, dresses and the tennis club. She also remarked on their "velvet little tongues" when gossiping about everyone and everything in Paramaribo. She described their vulnerability to "vicious chitchat", so Rosine and Cato preferred to keep their socializing to a minimum.⁶¹ "Everything here is fuss and humbug."⁶²

Anna Lohman agreed that Paramaribo is "Oh such a small town; every liaison, every on dit, every spicy affair, even from long times past is chewed over, disentangled, fleeced and reported to the highest local authority."⁶³ Only later did Anna realize that the "so-called *Christian* circles in The

Hague are not any better or different, because it is the same everywhere in the world, in hypocritically pious England, in openly immoral Paris – and in the wilderness of the jungle – every place where people live – man wants a woman, and a woman a man, and behind the varnish of decency and civilization, law and church they hide their unfulfilled desires."[64]

Anna, however, was also critical about her own behaviour. In her own words, she derided "the ladies in their old-fashioned dresses, speaking broken Dutch" and the antique top hats of the gentlemen, but forgot how "unkind" it was and how these elderly men "*had* to bow and be polite, *because* I was the governor's daughter". Only later did she realize how much they disliked her because of her attitude. Suriname was "the school of hard knocks".[65] After the death of her mother, she suddenly was a "principal player in a small, very faraway corner of the world" and she did not know how to cope with this new situation.[66] When Grace Schneiders-Howard returned to Suriname after a two-year holiday in the Netherlands, she noted that the return was not an easy transition. "It is so terribly narrow minded here. I was shocked by the people's attitude."[67]

Another important aspect of most women of the higher classes was philanthropy. Grace Schneiders-Howard, of course, did paid social work; Anna Lohman did not write about it. Cato Idenburg, however, frequently described the work of Moravian missionaries – men and women. She admired their dedication to the Protestant Christian cause. She was especially taken by the work of Mrs Pigott, the wife of the British consul, for the Protestant leprosy asylum, Bethesda. She even arranged for her sister's future mother-in-law, Mrs Rutgers, to start a sewing circle in the Netherlands to support the asylum.[68] There are no indications, however, that Cato herself was actively involved in these philanthropic projects.

COLONIAL WOMEN

How did these three women view other women in the colony? We have seen that Rosine and Cato Idenburg disapproved of the young women in their own social group and their female guests at official functions, and how they viewed their relations with the household staff. Cato also expressed some strong views on women outside of their household or social network. She fully supported some of the "moral laws" (*zedelijkheidswetgeving*) designed by her father within two months of his arrival in Suriname, such as the one that prohibited women from selling liquor in pubs, and the idea to return all "idle Javanese women" to their home country. According to Cato, Queen's Day in Paramaribo, the colony's major holiday, was "more decent" than a regular funfair in the Netherlands, "because Papa had decided that no liquor could be sold to women". She argued that the anti-liquor laws had a positive effect as there were far fewer "drunken hussies" (*meiden*) in the streets at night.[69] In general, Cato had little hope for women in the colony, as "almost all women lead immoral lives." Mrs Pigott "shed tears" when, after eight years of teaching a bible class to girls, she had made no difference. Only the Roman Catholic nuns, who had been in Suriname for more than fifty years, said that they were slowly noticing a difference, "but oh so little".[70]

Anna Lohman, too, decried the immorality in the colony, but she aimed her arrows at the small middle and upper classes by stating that many men lived with a "permanent housekeeper" (a term she at first took literally), while pretending to be moral, upright human beings, and their families acted as if nothing untoward was happening. She explicitly mentioned "Dutch, distinguished, decorated, highly-positioned gentlemen, who sometimes have a wife and children in Holland" yet openly lived with another woman who needed to be treated with the utmost respect.[71] She resented that young men treated Surinamese coloureds as inferior, but accepted everything from these women, "even the *most* intimate".[72] She also remarked on the biological consequences of these practices, as mothers "of sons and daughters who receive a thoroughly European education and therefore move in the upper circles, are consequently pushed to the background, because her face is not white enough to be shown. Beautiful, very beautiful Surinamese girls are embittered, when their dark, curly, extraordinary fine frizzy hair, even though it looks good on them, undeniably reveal Negro blood". According to Anna Lohman, these blood lines explained the disdain and animosity of the Surinamese upper class towards the coloureds and blacks. She called the European man equally immoral as he set a bad example because he "uses the colonial women [...] he commandeers and dominates them".[73]

Anna also questioned some of the moral policies of the Christian churches. "Needless to say, the Surinamese natives will live with as many women as they want before their conversion," but after becoming Christian they were forced to marry only one woman. Anna pointed out how doctrine and Christian clemency were at odds here. She explained that the Catholics followed Roman doctrine and demanded the sending away of women other than the legal spouse. The Moravians, however, preferred a middle road where the newly converted man chose one legal spouse, while taking care of the other women and their children, even letting them live in his house. Personally, Anna believed that the Moravians were right, even though their practices would not lead to a more moral society, as it was clear to her that the majority of the converts would continue to have sexual relations with the "illegal concubines".[74]

NATURE AND ITS CONSEQUENCES

It is customary for egodocuments by newcomers to mention the heat, humidity and natural abundance of Suriname. Native Grace limited her observations to the dust and dirt in town; Cato also noted that the dusty roads in the dry season were an assault on the respiratory system and the eyes.[75] It was Anna who wrote most poetically about the colony's environment. She readily admitted that when in Suriname, she did not have an eye for the beauty of the country: the "strangely beautiful orchids" or "the setting of the tropical sun over the river."[76] "I remember well how I hated, positively hated, the stiff, motionless palms on the waterfront. How I longed for one day of glazed frost on the trees [. . .] and how I disdained the orchids and the garishly coloured tropical flowers."[77] "In the tropics everything is so overwhelming, so big, so too much [. . .] the sun is *too* bright; the foliage *too* dense; the rain pelts down with *too* much force and *too* heavy drops; the flowers' colours are *too* bright; the woods are *too* impenetrable because of the parasitic plants."[78]

Cato's observations were fairly standard, remarking on the huge rivers and the abundant flora she saw while making trips to the east, west and south of the colony. But she also mentioned the effect of the hot, humid climate on the household. Mama frequently suffered from the heat and humidity, and even had to repatriate to recover in a sanatorium. Within a month of their arrival she reported that the humidity also ruined their books as they got stained and the leather became mouldy.[79] After half a year she wrote, "Anything that can grow mouldy is thick under all kinds of creepy yellow, green, and white mould layers." During the rainy season, the wooden floor of one of the rooms had become completely moulded, while in the dry season the house was caked in layers of dust.[80] Cato remarked that in the dry season it was so hot that it seemed that at noon, "Nature is dying, everything droops and it is stock still."[81]

HOME SWEET HOME

Given their experiences in Suriname, it is not surprising that both Cato and Anna longed for home. After seven months in the colony, Cato wrote that she enjoyed meeting people from the Netherlands, but that "we all long so much for the Fatherland". She believed that her father was too busy to think about it, but he "too will be happy when he can say goodbye to this beloved Suriname." Three months later she expressed the same sentiment, emphasizing that the family felt strange and would probably remain outsiders forever.[82] When Rosine returned to the Netherlands, these feelings became more pronounced, as she envied her sister for being able to leave this environment "and lives there where living with God is so much easier".[83] Cato was counting the days in late 1906: "1 year +3 days after our arrival [...] 2 more years, dear grandma."[84] Similar, and perhaps even stronger, were the sentiments of Anna, who "longed to get away – away, regardless" as Suriname was "for me the place of disillusionment".[85]

Only Grace wrote of her unconditional love for the colony. "I've been here for so long. And I love Suriname [...] the disappointments don't change me."[86] However, in many letters, she testified to her belief that a strong Dutch hand – including Dutch judges, lawyers and military – was needed to rule the colony. During World War II, she worried about anti-Dutch sentiments.[87] Some three decades earlier, however, Anna wondered, with a sense of melancholy, "What are we actually doing here? By what right are we here? Why? Why?"[88]

CONCLUSION

It is obvious that the three women discussed in this chapter were not representative of women in the Caribbean. The writings of all three show how class, cultural and ethnic background informed their insights and observations. Cato Idenburg and Anna Lohman were young Dutch women transplanted to the colony on account of their fathers' career, while Suriname-born Grace Schneiders-Howard and her family chose to return to "the West" when she was in her thirties. I do not know whether the three ever knew each other. In the case of Lohman and Idenburg, it is rather unlikely; given the age difference between the two it is doubtful that they met before Lohman left for Suriname and after her return, she moved to Germany, Scotland and the Dutch East Indies. Lohman had left the colony before Schneiders-Howard's return. Schneiders-Howard and Idenburg could have met socially; and Schneiders-Howard wrote that "she loved [governor] Idenburg", and she claimed to have had a good relationship with him.[89] And there is another minor connection between the two women, as Schneiders-Howard stated in 1939 that "she loved Mrs Rutgers" with whom she occasionally had a cup of coffee.[90] Mrs Rutgers was Rosine, Idenburg's sister, who returned to Suriname as the wife of Governor A.A.L. Rutgers (1928–1933).

Lohman and Idenburg arrived in Suriname as daughters of the governor, but because of the respective death and illness of their mothers, they were thrust into the role of First Lady. Their egodocuments show that they both had trouble coping with this new situation. Their letters and memoirs not only display an almost existential loneliness and a longing for home in Holland, but also a rather aloof attitude towards the Paramaribo social circles they moved in and their official obligations. To be sure, the writings of these women are very different in character and tone, as Lohman wrote her memoirs eighteen years after leaving Paramaribo. The advantage of hindsight and experience of life make the chapter on Suriname a long apology for her immature and uncouth behaviour. Idenburg's letters to her grandmother reveal little sympathy for most people she encountered, a great distaste for official functions and everything that came with her father's position, and Christian zealousness. Her ultimate yardstick for judging other individuals was Protestant orthodoxy. Lohman, in retrospect, also displayed more understanding for the complicated racial/ethnic, social and gender relations in the colony in general, and the subordinate position of women in particular. She was openly critical of male conduct with regard to family life and sexual relations. These memoirs almost literally justify Romein-Verschoor's qualification of Lohman as an *enfant terrible*, but also show her as an observer with an eye for extant conditions and insights into the position of women in colonial society.

Schneiders-Howard's letters are also very different in tone because the great majority of them that are still available were directed towards policy makers, including governors and colonial ministers, in Suriname and the Hague. She regularly commented on conditions in Suriname, but her letters lack the insights that mark Anna Lohman's memoirs. Her discussions repeatedly take personal and gossipy turns, by accusing superiors, politicians and other well-known individuals of all kinds of untoward behaviour, including adultery and fraud. Schneiders-Howard's letters seem to confirm Idenburg's and Lohman's observations about prattle and scandal-mongering in Paramaribo.

Idenburg adhered most closely to the expected gender role of an upper-class woman. She loved her family, adored her father, and later wrote in glowing terms about her fiancé. Her correspondence shows the central role of "Papa" in decisions regarding education, personal relationships and religious matters. Her activities included sewing, managing the household, organizing social functions, and an interest in philanthropy. Schneiders-Howard was almost her opposite as her paid work made her an exceptional, and often controversial, case in the colony.[91] If she revealed anything about her family life, it was an aside, not a major topic. In her memoirs Lohman made clear that she did not conform to her expected role as she was unprepared and inexperienced, in mourning and gauchely defending her controversial father.

Not surprisingly then, Idenburg's rather ordinary letters reveal most about the day-to-day affairs of the gubernatorial family, the health of the family members, and life for Suriname's upper class. According to Bridget Brereton, "One of the greatest insights of women's history is that no sharp rift exited (or exists) between women's 'public' and 'private' lives and that the 'private sphere' has been much more central to the lives of women than of men in most human societies".[92] Idenburg's letters are a case in point, but Schneiders-Howard's much less so. This difference may be partially explained by the recipients of these letters: an overseas family member, and colonial and Dutch dignitaries respectively.

Notwithstanding the fact that the content and tone of the letters and memoirs of Idenburg, Schneiders-Howard and Lohman are determined by the class, cultural, religious and ethnic background of these women, they provide a gendered texture to upper- and middle-class life in late colonial Paramaribo that official documents often lack.

NOTES

1. Bridget Brereton, *Gendered Testimony: Autobiographies, Diaries and Letters by Women as Sources for Caribbean History*. The 1994 Elsa Goveia Memorial Lecture (Kingston: University of the West Indies, 1994). This lecture was later published in *Feminist Review* in 1998.
2. The Dutch historian Jacques Presser coined the term 'egodocument' to refer to autobiographical writing, including diaries, memoirs, letters and travel accounts. To be sure, oral history is also vital to reconstruct (women's) history, but this is beyond the scope of this chapter.
3. For brevity's sake I will call her Anna Lohman.
4. Anna de Savornin Lohman, *Herinneringen* (Amsterdam: P.N. van Kampen, 1909), 5. All translations are mine. Occasional italics and underlines in the quotations are in the original.
5. See for an analysis of de Savornin Lohman's governorship; Hans Ramsoedh, "Politieke Strijd, Volksopstand en Antisemitisme in Suriname Omstreeks 1890," *Tijdschrift voor Sociale Geschiedenis* 18 (4) (1992): 479–501.
6. Ernestine van der Wal, "Lohman, Catherina Anna Maria de Savornin", Digitaal Vrouwenlexicon van Nederland (2015) (http://resources.huygens.knaw.nl/vrouwenlexicon/lemmata/data/Lohman, accessed 9 June 2015). It is unknown how and why her father lost his fortune.
7. Tineke Steenmeijer-Wielenga, "Savornin Lohman, jonkvrouw Catherina Anna Maria de," in *Biografisch Woordenboek van het Socialisme en de Arbeidersbeweging in Nederland*, ed. P.J. Meertens (Amsterdam: IISG, 1992), 238–41. (See also: http://hdl.handle.net/10622/BB269D5E-8945-47C8-9819-996DD5F7F076, accessed 5 June 2015); See also Ernestine van der Wal, "Lohman, Catherina Anna Maria de Savornin," Digitaal Vrouwenlexicon van Nederland, 2015 (http://resources.huygens.knaw.nl/vrouwenlexicon/lemmata/data/Lohman); and Inge de Wilde, "Tegen het feminisme uit 'modezucht': Anna de Savornin Lohman (1868–1930) – een eigenzinnige freule," *Spiegel Historiael* 7/8, no. 40 (2005): 330–53.
8. Annie Romein-Verschoor, *Vrouwenspiegel* (Nijmegen: SUN, 1977, orig. 1935), 72.
9. Mineke Bosch, *Aletta Jacobs 1854–1929: Een onwrikbaar geloof in rechtvaardigheid* (Amsterdam: Balans, 2005), 301.
10. C. Fasseur, "Idenburg, Alexander Willem Frederik (1861–1935)," in *Biografisch Woordenboek van Nederland*, 2013 (http://resources.huygens.knaw.nl/bwn1880-2000/lemmata/bwn1/idenburg, accessed 25 June 2015).
11. Johan van der Walle, *Een oog Boven Paramaribo: Herinneringen* (Amsterdam: Querido, 1975), 45.

12. Gemeentearchief Ede, the Netherlands, inv. nr 1103, nr 14, brief 14 October 1904; Nationaal Archief (NA) Paramaribo 4536.
13. National Archives (NA), The Hague, 2.21.232 Collectie 295 Familiearchief Middelberg (1820–1960), inv. nr 222, Cato Idenburg to grandmother, 19 November 1905. I want to thank Irene Rolfes for her assistance in researching the files in the Middelberg archive.
14. NA, The Hague, 2.21.232, inv. nr 222, Cato Idenburg to grandmother, 26 November 1905.
15. NA, The Hague, 2.21.232, inv. nr 222, Cato Idenburg to grandmother, 18 February 1906.
16. NA, The Hague, 2.21.232, inv. nr 222, Cato Idenburg to grandmother, 24 December 1905. Other reading materials included political-religious works.
17. NA, The Hague, 2.21.232, inv. nr 222, Cato Idenburg to grandmother, 26 November 1905.
18. NA, The Hague, 2.21.232, inv. nr 222, Cato Idenburg to grandmother, 24 December 1905.
19. NA, The Hague, 2.21.232, inv. nr 222, Cato Idenburg to grandmother, 26 November 1905 and no date [late November 1906].
20. NA, The Hague, 2.21.232, inv. nr 222, Cato Idenburg to grandmother, 24 December 1905. Her mother later took up English lessons with Mrs Pigott, the wife of the British consul, as so many Anglophone guests attended dinners and receptions in the colony.
21. NA, The Hague, 2.21.232, inv. nr 222, Cato Idenburg to grandmother, 4 March 1906.
22. Unfortunately, these pictures are not included in the Middelburg family archive.
23. NA, The Hague, 2.21.232, inv. nr 222, Cato Idenburg to grandmother, 26 November 1905.
24. NA, The Hague, 2.21.232, inv. nr 222, Cato Idenburg to grandmother, 6 August 1906.
25. NA, The Hague, 2.21.232, inv. nr 222, Cato Idenburg to grandmother, no date [mid-July 1906] and 2 August 1906.
26. NA, The Hague, 2.21.232, inv. nr 222, Cato Idenburg to grandmother, no date [mid-November 1906].
27. NA, The Hague, 2.21.232, inv. nr 222, Cato Idenburg to grandmother, 26 February 1907 and 9 April 1907.
28. NA, The Hague, 2.21.232, inv. nr 222, Cato Idenburg to Mrs Middelberg, 20 November 1907.
29. *Lohman, Herinneringen*, 87.
30. *Lohman, Herinneringen*, 115. Anna Lohman did appreciate the voluntary

wakes and singing by the Roman Catholic and Moravian servants, whom she considered 'truer Christians' than the Hague aristocracy (*Memoires*, 130–31).

31. Lohman, *Herinneringen*, 102.
32. ibid., 89–90.
33. ibid., 89.
34. Ramsoedh, "Politieke strijd, volksopstand en antisemitisme in Suriname omstreeks 1890," 497.
35. NA, Paramaribo, 1599, 17 May 1924, and 362, 29 January 1919.
36. NA, The Hague, 2.21.142, inv. nr 19, Grace Schneiders-Howard to T.B. Pleyte, 21 November 1914.
37. Rosemarijn Hoefte, "The Lonely Pioneer: Suriname's First Female Politician and Social Activist, Grace Schneiders-Howard," *Wadabagei* 10, no. 3 (2007): 87.
38. NA, The Hague, 2.21.142, inv nr 19, Grace Schneiders-Howard to L.M. Rollin Couquerque, 4 April 1926.
39. NA, The Hague, 2.21.142, inv nr 22, Grace Schneiders-Howard to L.M. Rollin Couquerque, 30 April 1934.
40. NA, The Hague, 2.21.142, inv nr 21, Grace Schneiders-Howard to L.M. Rollin Couquerque, 20 April 1930.
41. NA, The Hague, 2.10.18, inv. nr 85, Grace Schneiders-Howard to J.C. Kielstra, 11 November 1939.
42. NA, Paramaribo, Grace Schneiders-Howard to D. Fock, 3 September 1909. Gerard Jan Staal was Idenburg's government secretary and right-hand man. Grace Schneiders-Howard's youngest child, Hein, was the son of the other *déporté* living in her house.
43. NA, The Hague, 2.10.18, inv. nr 85, Grace Schneiders-Howard to J.C. Kielstra, 31 July 1939.
44. Lohman, *Herinneringen*, 90–91.
45. ibid., 93.
46. ibid., 117, 91–92, 94, 119–21.
47. ibid., 97.
48. See also Hans van der Jagt, "Aan tafel bij een *fijn* gezin: Gouverneur A.W.F. Idenburg door de ogen van zijn dochter," *Tijdschrift voor Biografie* 2, no. 1 (2013): 53–61.
49. NA, The Hague, 2.21.232, inv. nr 222, Cato Idenburg to grandmother, 22 July 1906.
50. NA, The Hague, 2.21.232, inv. nr 222, Cato Idenburg to grandmother, 26 June 1907 and 25 September 1907; Cato Idenburg to Mrs Middelberg, Paramaribo, 20 November 1907.

51. NA, The Hague, 2.21.142 inv. nr 21 Grace Schneiders-Howard to L.M. Rollin Couquerque, 13 May 1930.
52. NA, The Hague, 2.21.142 inv. nr 21 Grace Schneiders-Howard to L.M. Rollin Couquerque, 20 May 1930.
53. NA, The Hague, 2.10.18, inv. nr 85 Grace Schneiders-Howard to J.C. Kielstra, 26 August 1939.
54. NA, The Hague, 2.21.232, inv. nr 222, Cato Idenburg to Mrs Middelberg, 20 and 30 January 1907.
55. NA, The Hague, 2.21.232, inv. nr 222, Cato Idenburg to grandmother, no date [late 1906 or early 1907]; 6 January and 3 February 1907.
56. NA, The Hague, 2.21.232, inv. nr 222, Cato Idenburg to grandmother, 18 February 1906.
57. NA, The Hague, 2.21.232, inv. nr 222, Cato Idenburg to grandmother, 24 December 1905 and no date [1905].
58. NA, The Hague, 2.21.232, inv. nr 222, Cato Idenburg to grandmother, no date [fall 1906].
59. NA, The Hague, 2.21.232, inv. nr 222, Cato Idenburg to grandmother, 26 May 1906; see also 14 October 1906 for a similar analysis.
60. NA, The Hague, 2.21.232, inv. nr 222, Cato Idenburg to grandmother, 22 July 1906.
61. NA, The Hague, 2.21.232, inv. nr 222, Cato Idenburg to grandmother, no date [November or December 1905].
62. NA, The Hague, 2.21.232, inv. nr 222, Cato Idenburg to grandmother, 13 May 1906.
63. Lohman, *Herinneringen*, 111.
64. ibid., 112–13.
65. ibid., 101, 97–99.
66. ibid., 102.
67. NA, The Hague, 2.21.142 inv. nr 21 Grace Schneiders-Howard to L.M. Rollin Couquerque, 16 February 1933.
68. NA, The Hague, 2.21.232, inv. nr 222, Cato Idenburg to grandmother, 13 May 1906; 22 July 1906; 19 May 1907. Mrs Rutgers is the mother of Abraham (Bram) Rutgers, who was to become governor of Suriname in 1928.
69. NA, The Hague, 2.21.232, inv. nr 222, Cato Idenburg to grandmother, 21 January 1906; 2 August 1906; 14 October 1906. Notwithstanding her pioneering role in politics and society, Grace Schneiders-Howard was not a feminist.
70. NA, The Hague, 2.21.232, inv. nr 222, Cato Idenburg to grandmother, no date [early April 1907].
71. Lohman, *Herinneringen*, 107–9.

72. ibid, 112.
73. ibid., 125–27.
74. ibid., 135–36.
75. NA, The Hague, 2.21.232, inv. nr 222, Cato Idenburg to grandmother, 30 September 1906.
76. Lohman, *Herinneringen*, 113.
77. ibid., 139–40.
78. ibid., 140.
79. NA, The Hague, 2.21.232, inv. nr 222, Cato Idenburg to grandmother, no date [November 1905].
80. NA, The Hague, 2.21.232, inv. nr 222, Cato Idenburg to grandmother, no date [November 1905], 27 May 1906, 10 October 1906
81. NA, The Hague, 2.21.232, inv. nr 222, Cato Idenburg to grandmother, 28 October 1906.
82. NA, The Hague, 2.21.232, inv. nr 222, Cato Idenburg to grandmother, 10 June 1906 and 6 August 1906.
83. NA, The Hague, 2.21.232, inv. nr 222, Cato Idenburg to grandmother, 28 November 1906.
84. NA, The Hague, 2.21.232, inv. nr 222, Cato Idenburg to grandmother, no date [November 1906].
85. Lohman, *Herinneringen*, 116.
86. NA, The Hague, 2.21.142, inv nr 20, Grace Schneiders-Howard to L.M. Rollin Couquerque, 15 March 1929.
87. NA, The Hague, 2.21.142, inv nr 21, Grace Schneiders-Howard to L.M. Rollin Couquerque, 27 August 1930, 14 September 1930; inv. nr 26, Grace Schneiders-Howard to L.M. Rollin Couquerque, 27 March 1916; NA, The Hague, 2.18.10, 2.2.5.1.2 inv. nr 570, Grace Schneiders-Howard to Edmund van Duiven, 27 October 1943.
88. Lohman, *Herinneringen*, 140.
89. Earlier Colonial Minister Idenburg, however, believed that Schneiders-Howard "had lost her wits", NA, The Hague, 2.10.36.04, inv.nr 919, notitie Afdeling B, 23 April 1912.
90. NA, The Hague, 2.10.18, inv. nr 85, Grace Schneiders-Howard to J.C. Kielstra, 26 August 1939.
91. Hoefte, "The Lonely Pioneer," 93–98.
92. Brereton, *Gendered Testimony*, 4.

[10]

IMPERIAL FIRST LADY OF TRINIDAD
Lady Rachel Hamilton-Gordon, 1865–1870

[DANE MORTON-GITTENS]

THERE HAVE BEEN FEW STUDIES ON GOVERNORS' OR officials' wives in the English-speaking Caribbean. Those that exist, like *Lady Nugent's Journal* or *The Letters of Margaret Mann*, provide similar observations and comments.[2] The wives discussed their loneliness, their struggles with domestic affairs, their observations and opinions on the climate, flora and fauna, and the people. By applying methodologies honed by Bridget Brereton, this discussion positions these women as sources of valuable information, which not only gives us insights into the lives of these women, but also first-hand observations on life at that time. We must admit that, at times, the recollections seem aversive, but to sanitize them would mean tampering with the narrative. Lady Rachel Hamilton-Gordon presents us with a unique opportunity to observe the life of a woman from the highest levels of British society occupying the highest position in society in Trinidad. Lady Gordon was the wife of one of Trinidad's more productive governors, Sir Arthur Hamilton-Gordon,

Potrait of Lady Rachel Hamilton-Gordon[1]

who was of noble birth. He was the son of the fourth Earl of Aberdeen and became the first Lord Stanmore (1893) after his wife's death. As the wife of a nobleman, Lady Gordon felt entitled to critique people of every class and race in Trinidad. She lived during the Victorian Age, and her behaviour and attitude unsurprisingly reflected all its values, including racism, paternalism, subordination of women and patriarchy. As a governor's wife, she ran the domestic household, was a good hostess and the role model whom many colonial women followed. Lady Gordon also enhanced and contributed to the governor's career and status via her roles as wife, mother, homemaker, preserver of European civilization, arbiter and pillar of social hierarchy in Trinidad.[3]

Her correspondence provides a wealth of information about aspects of Trinidad's culture and societal makeup, as well as the interactions, idiosyncrasies and characteristics of particular individuals and groups. She was also very liberal with her judgements and comments, and this provides us with insights into how the groups were comparatively valued and, by extension, treated from her viewpoint. These observations also reflect her complex character and personality, which were representative of British women of her position. Information on Rachel Gordon comes mainly from correspondence preserved in the Stanmore papers (Hamilton-Gordon) and the biography *A Strong Supporting Cast: The Shaw Lefevres 1789–1936*.[4] The Stanmore papers have been sourced for information on her husband; however, Lady Gordon's correspondence, found within the Stanmore collection, has been relatively untouched as a source for primary evidence.[5] Brereton advocates for the value of the insights that can be gleaned from such documents if they are properly used and contextualized. This chapter applies this methodology by showing how Lady Gordon's letters can add to the historical accounts of Trinidad in the second half of the nineteenth century.

Lady Gordon was born in 1828, the daughter of Sir John Shaw-Lefevre, liberal Member of Parliament for Petersfield, and the former Rachel Emily Wright. She was a sickly child and barely recovered from scarlet fever when she was a baby. She was educated at home, probably by a governess or her parents. As her mother was sickly and Lady Gordon was the eldest daughter, she was required to supervise her six siblings. This may have influenced the pragmatism that is often reflected in her letters. She was neither interested in charitable pursuits nor had the enthusiasm of her sisters for the arts.⁶ In 1861, she spent some time in Quebec as a companion to the governor's daughter. This was her first taste of colonial life. In June 1864, she met Arthur Hamilton-Gordon at a dinner party given by a family friend.⁷ The two grew close and eventually married on 20 September 1865, at St Martin-in-the-Fields, London, a few months before travelling to Trinidad.⁸ Lady Gordon was thirty-seven, older than her husband by one and a half years, which would have been unusual in those times.

She suffered at least two miscarriages just before coming to Trinidad. The after-effects were so bad that for seven months she remained weak and sick.⁹ Her husband organized to have her sister, Madeleine, join her for the trip to Trinidad and a few months following so she would be able to recover and have company. In Trinidad, she suffered her third and fourth miscarriages. A doctor recorded that the third caused her serious injury. On her sixth pregnancy (Willson reports she may have had a possible fifth miscarriage) in early 1868, she was ordered to return to England where she was able to have their first child, Nevil, a daughter.¹⁰ Their second child, George, was born in 1871, soon after the family left Trinidad. Her advanced age and the stress of living in the colony could have contributed to her enduring so many difficulties in having children.

The Shaw-Lefevres' wealth can be described as "new money", whereas the governor's family, the Hamilton-Gordons, were heirs to the Lord Aberdeen title, and established nobility. Willson argues that Lady Gordon was very comfortable with herself and her background. Her family was very close – by all accounts – and her marriage into a higher status family did not change her attitude, since the deciding factor of people's worth was their behaviour in her judgement (at least concerning people of her own class, colour and creed). However, it seems as though her husband's family believed her attitude should have changed since she needed to recognize and respect the great privilege of having joined their important clan. This difference in values may have made her somewhat unsure and very defensive, especially of her position. According to Willson, her attempts to appease them, common in a time when social status equalled worth, according to contemporary literature, could often make her appear to view all groups in the colonies as beneath her and to hold them in contempt.¹¹ Yet, at twenty-one, Lady Gordon was deemed "very warm hearted and affectionate, very amiable and merry, full of fun and clever too".[12] She maintained this reputation throughout her life, even under what would have been considered as most 'primitive' conditions in Fiji when she lived there in her late forties. A distant kinswoman of Gordon's who visited them there said she was "as lovable and gracious as she was pleasant to the eye – the very ideal of a comely British matron and happy wife and mother".[13] As one official put it: "I would trust anything to her perfectly good sound sense and tact. I have never seen her in the least out of temper, and she is on the best terms with the whole household ... She always makes the best of things, and is luckily not nervous."[14]

Her letters, whose contents extend far beyond what could be gleaned by observers, provide a treasure trove of information. As previously stated, her accounts are historically important because of the information they provide about Trinidad between 1866 and 1870. Moreover, her correspondence was mainly with family members and in this environment, she felt free to record her attitudes and feelings about everything she experienced. Thus, as Willson says, they reveal a great deal about her character and personality. Her letters, he states, were written over days and weeks as she waited for the next steamship to arrive, thus her topics and moods change from page to page[15] and give us real-time insight into them, and through them, her character and personality. Willson states that her writing shows distraction, as she switched suddenly from a serious point in one paragraph to a triviality in another. He also elaborates that her letters reflect: "... one with a sound grasp of the language but without any elegance of expression. Her descriptions are readable, her comments are often sharp though never witty, her emotional sincerity is unquestionable."[16]

After a short time as the governor's wife in New Brunswick, Lady Gordon reprised the role upon her husband's second appointment to Trinidad in November 1866. Her early feelings towards Trinidad were equally optimistic and cautious. She hoped that they would become comfortable, but when they arrived, she found the heat overbearing. She had to change six times a day. The island was too "leafy" and the wind drafts were too strong.[17] The people were "so poor" and the prices of things were "very dear". Lady Gordon was dissatisfied with the fruit of the island, especially the banana, which she felt was "an acquired taste", and when given a pineapple from the Botanic Gardens, she wrote that it "was the most beautiful one I ever saw – but the taste was disappointing".[18]

Reading her correspondence might lead one to conclude that they contain a lot of opinions, complaints, regrets and anxieties. However, even though they are filled with complaints, Willson notes that these were "related to the simple fact that she did not really want to be away from England" and her close personal circle.[19]

However, by 1870, Lady Gordon had softened her stance, probably having acclimatized. She described the flowers of the island as beautiful, especially the poinsettia. Trinidad had become, in her estimation, a pleasant place; she enjoyed its "perpetual summer" and said, "It is really very pleasant here now. There is a delicious cool breeze most of the day, and sometimes it feels chilly at five in the morning."[20] Readers travel through Trinidad and experience the island from her eyes. On a trip with her husband to Arima, Lady Gordon found the trees and vines fascinating, and after drinking a coconut, she commented it was refreshing and tasted like ginger beer.[21] During their final months in Trinidad, Lady Gordon was out exploring the island with her husband. Charles Kingsley, the famous writer who visited Trinidad in 1869, recorded in *At Last: A Christmas in Trinidad* that Lady Gordon had visited the Pitch Lake with them and was carried over the lake in a chair, while they walked on planks placed across the lake.[22] On another trip, this time to Maracas Falls, they travelled by horse.[23]

Yet, Lady Gordon felt that colonies like Trinidad were not only backward and uncomfortable, but survival there was difficult. Such feelings were shared by even those considered by their contemporaries to be the strongest, most adventurous Europeans of the time.[24] Away from family, friends and the society she was accustomed to, Lady Gordon found Trinidad a lonely place. The only person she could talk to was her husband, but he was always working. Happily, however, Willson notes that after five years in Trinidad, "Lady Gordon was thoroughly familiar with the obligations of office and was able to take a cool and critical view of them."[25]

In her correspondence, Lady Gordon recorded her criticisms as well as her appreciation strongly, but one must remember she was communicating with close friends and family, and therefore would be blunt with them in ways she would not in more formal relationships. Thus, the private nature of her comments adds another layer to their value. She seemed to judge people by demanding, arbitrary standards. However, her background helps us understand the positions she takes in her letters. In several instances, Lady Gordon showed general dislike and contempt for colonial people. This revealed the impact of the strict social hierarchy and structure of the times, which would have been further reinforced by her husband's family.[26] To her, colonials violated the established societal norms and she therefore deemed them impolite, uncivilized and inferior. On the other hand, she was "hostile to anyone who 'pulled rank'" and she also disliked when people behaved artificially; she considered such behaviour to be in poor taste.[27] She highly objected to people whose only reason for meeting her and her husband, she believed, was to advance their positions. Perhaps this was influenced by the fact that her family's fortunes can be described as 'new money'.

A complex, ambivalent relationship with both the colony and the colonists at all levels of the society is revealed. Her remarks about the previous owners of Government House, the Manners-Suttons, were not positive. She judged them very "dirty people" who left the house "filthy" and "disgusting".[28] They had been so "dirty", she wrote, that a new bed from England had to be ordered for her and her husband. She did not care for the ladies of the island and found the men only a little better.[29] A few colonials did not like her either. In 1867, the auditor general said that, although she was a good wife for a leader, she was "forward and haughty" in relation to his wife.[30] In reply, Lady Gordon complained seemingly somewhat hypocritically that neither of them understood her character, and wrote about his wife: "I don't think she is exactly jealous but I fancy she made up her mind from the first that I was going to be 'very fine' ... My opinion of her is that she is narrow, colloquial in mind and not a perfect lady. The fact is she has been spoilt and made so much of all her life..."[31]

Even friends did not escape her judgement and traits she considered faults seemed to disturb her even more. Charles Kingsley and Governor Gordon were very close. She wrote that both Gordon and Kingsley had the same love of nature and thought with "the same mind".[32] Yet, when Kingsley and his daughter, Rose, visited them in 1869, she expressed her disappointment with changes in him: "I like Kingsley ... in many ways very much. I feel that I ought to like him more – but – between ourselves I don't think he is quite so nice as he used to be. He has got rather spoilt by adulation, and is slightly affected and very conceited in manner

(I wish he wouldn't call me 'My Lady'!) and he likes to talk and lay down the law and doesn't care to hear others speak."[33]

She was even critical of church laymen who did not come from the upper classes. Willson argued that Lady Gordon's strong religious upbringing made her intolerant of what she saw as the social unfitness of churchmen. In January 1870, her comment about the new Church of England's bishop of Trinidad was, "It's bad enough to be Low Church, but worse to have a Bishop who is not quite a gentleman. I will never get on with it."[34]

When Lady Gordon wrote positively about people it reflected deep and sincere appreciation for their service to her and her husband. The Rushworths were considered pleasant and gained her high regard as they seemed always ready to serve. Her opinion was shaped by the fact that they had prepared Government House for them and provided everything they needed, despite having their own responsibilities.[35] Captain Hallows, Gordon's aide-de-camp, was a great companion who, if he ever left, the Gordons believed it would render them incapacitated.[36] Another officer of the household, known as Crickham, was described as an attractive man as a result of his good manners and because he knew his orders, and was pleasant to have around.[37] Lady Gordon apparently came to depend on Mrs Jones, a servant she described as a "mulatto". She relied on her for domestic responsibilities as well as her opinions. By 1868, Lady Gordon wrote that she prized Mrs Jones' opinion about her appearance more than her husband's.[38] Everywhere Lady Gordon went, Mrs Jones was recorded as being by her side; she would go nowhere without her. When in October 1869 they received the news that Mrs Jones had died of yellow fever, Lady Gordon wrote: "No one can tell what a loss she is to me and I know I shall feel it more and more – I so entirely depended on her in every way and had become so fond of her. I feel that I have lost a friend as well as a servant who I can never replace."[39]

Lady Gordon has also left glimpses into the leisure activities of her group. She was not always guided by what was deemed popular at the time. She and her sister Madeleine's hobbies generally exemplified the common pursuits of elite Victorian women. She wrote to her sister, Jane, in July 1867 that she could not force herself to like botany, which many in Trinidad raved about.[40] She enjoyed walking and riding although, due to her miscarriages, she was not strong enough to do either for quite some time. She had recovered enough by 1867 though, and in fact, she started to ride Arthur's horse, Citron, but preferred Madeleine's pony, Bobby.[41]

Another pastime, reading, was made difficult without a sitting room at Government House and she had to resort to sharing Gordon's.[42] When she was feeling better, she and Madeleine took walks every morning before breakfast. They would also sketch and paint. Lady Gordon commented in 1870 that her artistic skills were diminished since her miscarriages, with "one [drawing] worse than the other".[43] Although she lacked confidence in her artistic skills, she captured some realistic and impressive images of people, flora and fauna. Kingsley, too, disagreed with her and used one of her sketches of the cocoa fruit in his book, *At Last*.[44]

Her position gave her access to different groups in the society and her accounts provide a mirror into domains of which we seldom get glimpses in historical accounts of Trinidad. She adored Indian cloth and jewellery (bangles, bracelets and rings). Her husband and his aide-de-camp wore bangles and she wanted some as well.[46] On many occasions, she travelled with Mrs Jones to barter for these items. On one occasion, she travelled with Rose Kingsley to a nearby Indian village to buy "coolie" scarves.[47] On another visit to Arima in April 1867, Arthur warned her not to wander off by herself without a male escort, but she defied him and went walking around looking for jewellery with Mrs Jones.[48] Here,

Lady Gordon's Paintings entitled *Orange Grove* and *Cocoa*. The latter was used in Charles Kingsley's book *At Last*. "Annai" 1867 (William Reese Company).[45]

again she demonstrated an independent and perhaps headstrong streak. She loved displaying her trophies on her body to shock local elite women when they visited her. She stated: "They say I have turned Coolie, for I have got bangles on both arms and only want a ring to be complete. No one else ever thought of wearing these and they look surprised when I pull up my habit sleeves and display a row of bangles."[49] In March 1868, when her bangles needed repairing, she called an Indian peddler to come up to Government House to fix them. Lady Gordon wrote that this man came with his own coal pot and tools, which he had made himself, and that she had him fix them outside her room where she could watch him.[50]

Political views from women in that period are difficult to locate. They provide insights into the women themselves as well as this male-dominated arena where few female voices have been officially recorded. Women were expected to keep to their spheres of influence – domestic and social work – and a governor's wife would be expected to enhance his position by being a good hostess and model wife. Victorian men, especially political figures like Sir Arthur Hamilton-Gordon, would never expect or allow their wives to enter politics. Lady Gordon followed this pattern; she was not interested in politics, and even if she had been, her husband never talked to her about it.[52] Nevertheless, within the pages of her correspondence with family, Lady Gordon expresses opinions

Lady Gordon's Paintings of the Flowers of Trinidad, 1867
(William Reese Company).[51]

about her husband's political life. She once told Madeleine: "How utterly unfit he is to be the Governor of a Constitutional Colony . . . He cannot sit down and lead an easy life and submit to be dictated to . . . and know that measures that he disapproves of are being passed, in which he is not allowed a voice."[53]

A month after their arrival in Trinidad, Lady Gordon commented that her husband's work was much harder than what he had had to do in New Brunswick, but acknowledged that he enjoyed it and could never have enough of it.[54] In January 1870, close to their departure date, Lady Gordon reported that only when Arthur had settled the issues dealing with his education scheme would they be able to leave the island.[55]

We are more familiar with women's activities in the domestic sphere and Lady Gordon was no exception. In this arena, her frankness shows us the society and its innate conflicts through a new lens. While in Trinidad, Lady Gordon administered her household, taking notice and charge of every aspect as was proper for a woman of status in the Victorian era. In nearly every letter to family and friends, she commented on troubles she was having with the servants or some other aspect, thus giving us insights into a governor's household. On arriving in Trinidad, she started to organize Government House, which she described as an "agglomeration of detached huts".[56] They retained the Manners-Suttons' servants, in spite of reservations about the household they ran, including a coachman, a footman, boys, cooks (whom she noted were all black), a "mulatto" house maid, carpenters, two orderlies, two messengers and a number of "coolie convicts".[57] The only problems with settling in were her illness, which prevented her from doing more, and their cutlery and china were yet to arrive. When she recovered, Lady Gordon turned her attention to her staff and the menagerie of animals she and her husband kept. This, she recorded, included six monkeys, four parrots (including one that spoke French) and an ocelot,[58] as well as regular farm animals, such as chickens imported from Grenada, and seventeen cows. The funniest moment, Lady Gordon wrote, was when a chicken laid eggs in the governor's armchair.

Other things also dissatisfied her. She lamented that even with so many cows, they could only get two quarts of milk because they were said to be nursing calves.[60] She also complained that the cost of running Government House in Trinidad was far greater than in New Brunswick; for example, mutton cost 30¢ a pound in Trinidad but only 10¢ in New

Madeleine Shaw-Lefevre's Paintings of Granny the Dog and a Macaw done in 1867 at Government House, Trinidad (William Reese Company).[59]

Brunswick.[61] She fretted because her clothes, especially her dresses, constantly needed cleaning as the place was always damp and mildew settled quickly. Madeleine had to discard a number of pairs of new gloves because of mildew.[62]

As she described aspects of her everyday life, Lady Gordon documented some instances, routines and topics she found of interest, capturing her lifestyle and aspects of life in Trinidad at the time. She and Madeleine met weekly with local black and mixed dressmakers from Port of Spain about dresses for dinners, balls and public occasions.[63] She enjoyed having rare and exotic fresh flowers brought in every morning as they brightened the place. Chicken was the meat most frequently served with meals and Lady Gordon soon tired of it. At the Christmas dinner of 1866, she commented that she was fed up and wished for the day she could eat turkey.[64] She was fascinated with ice and its delivery to the Government House. She wrote in more than one letter that it was brought from the iwce house in Port of Spain, which was also operated as a restaurant by an "old black Frenchwoman" named Madame Lucille who was a "jolly old creature".[65] It was flavoured with guava and cost a shilling a block. Sometimes, Lady Gordon added, Madame Lucille would bring extra for the servants. The ice was used at meal times and also placed in jugs in different rooms.[66]

Most of Lady Gordon's time was spent around the servants on whom she commented regularly. Again, the complexity and multifaceted nature of her interactions with them, as well as within their own interrelationships, become apparent from her letters. The household she gives insight into reflects the numerous racial, ethnic and national groups that co-existed in the space. Their jostling to carve out individual spaces is depicted in these letters in ways that could not be captured in any official or secondary historical account. She enjoyed the company of her mulatto maid, Mrs Jones, and appreciated the physical attributes of the "Coolie boy" Matthew, who did all the odd jobs around the house.[67] The rest of her staff seemed to constantly cause her trouble; she was always lamenting that her household was in disarray due to them. In one letter she wrote, "They all hate each other, get involved in conflicts and carry news, which I try to ignore, but they disrupt the house."[68] The issue of race, in her estimation, seemed to play an integral role in many of the disputes. She commented that if a servant remarked about another servant's race, it caused arguments, fights and confrontations. In January 1870, she wrote:

> My household is still in rather an uncomfortable state, I have too many different races to get on well, Welsh, Scottish and Portuguese, white, black, coloured and Coolie, they each hate and despise the others. Mrs. Graham has got the upper hand and rules Mrs. Jones, who is afraid of her. She is most disagreeable to the blacks... "you hear what I say you nigger" to the footman Francis. She is a good and valuable servant but if I were going to stay, I doubt I could keep her...[69]

In spite of this show of concern, Lady Gordon, like most Europeans of the time, saw all other races as inferior servants, regardless of the law. She described a black, "wooly haired" child being christened alongside a white child (Mrs Rushworth's) with surprise.[70] In one letter, she used the term slave to describe a black girl who was a servant, even though there had been no slaves since 1838. Her bluntness could offend: "We have given Mrs Jones a little nigger as her slave. We give her no wages except clothes, and of course, she has to be taught everything but is of the greatest use."[71] She saw the Afro-creole population as savages and had no problem expressing her dislike for them. In October 1867 she wrote to her sister:

> The more I see of the black servants the more I hate them – they are all alike – thinking liars, great cowards – only befit in order and fear – hurriedly quarrelsome among one another ('please mame the cook and me is not on terms'). If you are kind to them, they despise you, as they think you have a motive. Their only gratitude (as can be said of them) is for favours to come...[72]

Even though she also considered Indians inferior, Lady Gordon preferred them to Africans and, surprisingly, had relatively nice things to say about them. She described them as dark-skinned but handsome and with splendid eyes. About the Indian servant, Matthew, she wrote, "I am getting rather fond of Matthew, the Coolie boy, he is very dark, but a gentleman-like looking boy – very good looking and rather vain."[73] She and Gordon liked him so much they were planning to take him to England with them when they left Trinidad. On the other hand, Lady Gordon had no love for creole whites or mixed people. She felt they did not know their place. In October 1867, they held a ball and she wrote that six ladies arrived, "one very deeply coloured!"[74] She was apparently offended that a mixed woman would come to the ball as an equal. It had rained the whole night and she scoffed when these ladies had to go home on horseback in their ball dresses. Such behaviour to her only solidified her view that the local elite carried themselves with "an aristocratic air about everything", but were inferior because they did not observe the accepted mores of social hierarchy.

It was only in March 1867 that Lady Gordon was recovered enough from her miscarriages to attend parties. These were mostly held at the Prince's and Furness buildings. She wrote that she and Gordon had a heavy schedule that month, with four dinners a week and a number of balls.[75] At one ball held in their honour at Prince's Building, more than five hundred people attended, and the ballroom was impressively illuminated. The place was decorated in streamers and candles, but no people of interest to her were there, except the Danish Council.[76] Lady Gordon liked being admired. In January 1868, at a grand dinner held at Government House, she recorded her pleasure in everyone's approval of her: "The ball dress looked beautiful, as it should, and I liked it much more than I expected. I was most effective and extensively admired. Arthur liked it very much and Mrs. Jones, who decided guests' appearances at times, was delighted when she saw me come in it, and said I looked just as a Governor's wife should."[77]

At the end of November 1866, the Hamilton-Gordons opened the house twice a week on Mondays and Wednesdays from 3 p.m. to 5 p.m. to visitors from the local elite – mainly whites.[78] On the first day, no one arrived because people thought there would have been a rush, but the mad rush happened on the second day, with Lady Gordon reporting that up to forty people had come. Visitors, she wrote, drove up in their carriage and presented their cards to the footman to be passed to Captain Hallows, who then introduced them.[79] By 1868, Lady Gordon was getting sick of these "tiresome affairs". Horseracing events also amused her but she wrote that she had trouble getting dresses made for these social occasions.[80]

Willson writes that Lady Gordon was not one to pioneer charitable causes,[81] but in Trinidad she did become patron to a few. In 1866 she adopted a "Coolie" school, which Lady Manners-Sutton had originally adopted.[82] The school was located in Port of Spain and was run by a couple referred to as Mr and Mrs Richards. She would read stories, distribute buns and make clothes for the girls. By 1868, she was visiting the school twice a week. She maintained that it was important to treat the children like all other children and that they needed to be "coaxed and petted" or they would not attend.[83] She was also patron to Port of Spain's only Meal Society which, she wrote, provided meals to forty people every fortnight at 2 p.m. The inmates, as she called them, included old, infirm blacks and a few "Coolies", and the meal consisted of soup with rice.[84]

As a primary source for historical information, letters and personal correspondence are a treasure trove of a person's true feelings and emotions. Lady Gordon's are no different. Her illness must have given her the space and time to write such extensive and descriptive letters. We must keep in mind, however, that it may have also influenced her own feelings, as well as those about Trinidad, the people and the society. She was frustrated by her miscarriages, which left her weak and sick. She regularly complained about her back pains and incapacitation. She tried many remedies, including a tonic of warm milk in the morning, and vanilla beans, which she swore got her through her last "sickness". She

Madeleine Shaw-Lefevre's Paintings, *Trinidad* and *Lizard*, 1867 (William Reese Company).[85]

noted, however, that vanilla was expensive in Trinidad.[86] By April 1867, her condition was taking a toll on Arthur too. She said he sulked about it and kept himself busy so he would not have to worry. He suggested to her that she visit Monos, a small island off Trinidad's northwest coast, to recover.[87] Lady Gordon, however, was worried that the trip would make her worse. In one letter to her sister, she confided that she was fearful that she would never be able to have a child.[88] All this changed when she returned to Trinidad in the latter part of 1869 with Nevil, her first child. Her correspondence afterwards was full of happy moments "with baby". The baby was "pretty", "chubby", "dances and jumps" and "spoilt by Arthur".[89] In fact, Willson states that the last few months in Trinidad with the baby were their happiest.[90]

Lady Gordon constantly felt lonely in Trinidad. She felt there was no one to talk to, of like mind and emotion,[91] aside from her husband, who was constantly working. She felt so miserable that in one letter to her family, she wrote how odd it was to be left alone with the servants so much, and quarrelled that she believed Gordon liked leaving her alone. Once, when he went to Monos with friends, she confided that she would have liked to have gone but "That is not my function!"[92] However, later, she says he seldom went away and complains instead that they spent time together, but doing exactly the same things every day, such as taking walks together twice around the savannah in the evening.[93] Even so, they were seldom at odds with each other or distant,[94] and Lady Gordon cared deeply for her husband. In 1869, when she returned from England, Arthur confessed that he had contracted yellow fever and had kept it from her;[95] she was very upset with him and scolded him for not having told her. She wrote that he never really got over it and afterwards looked five years older. Lady Gordon never seemed to really feel settled or to even like the places she and her husband were stationed until it was almost time to leave, if at all, but she performed her duties admirably, according to contemporary accounts.

This biographical reflection not only adds to the body of knowledge, that is, Trinidad's history, but reveals it through the eyes of a woman at the top ranks of society, as recognized at that time. Her correspondence gives us a good picture from her point of view of race and social relations, people, places, flora and fauna, and the daily routine of elite white women in Trinidad. Lady Gordon clearly perpetuated the paternalism and colonial domination of British rule, including the view that British civilization was far superior. She is very much reflective of her social group and adhered to most of the norms, values and expectations of the society. She did what was necessary to support her husband and her own station obtained through marriage to him. Though we would definitely condemn her attitude today, we cannot let this detract from the value of her letters. Lady Gordon was strategically placed to provide a privileged view of Trinidad in the late nineteenth century. Her vantage point, her bluntness and the intimate nature of her correspondence all coalesce to provide an intimate, rare and gendered insight into Trinidad. She saw all social classes and races on the island as inferior to her, in accordance with the manner in which she would have been socialized. Lady Gordon continued to perpetuate and reinforce the typical stereotypes of her class and gender, but she was neither weak nor submissive when we put her in the context of her time.

She had interesting and outstanding characteristics. Her artistic portrayals of Trinidad, though something many Victorian women did, have a quality that has stood the test of time and are snapshots of history we can now view. Her good opinion of her "mulatto" servant, Mrs Jones, as well as her dependence on her, are especially surprising, given her background and status. Her letters also reveal other examples of the depth of her appreciation when people did things for her, especially without wanting favours for themselves, like the Rushworths. At the same time, she could be very particular and intolerant, like most of her era and status. Lady Gordon was clearly not only an interesting character because of the position she held as wife of a governor, but also in her own right. She was a complex woman about whom too little is known. However, the little insight that we do have is intriguing and gives perspectives from an insider into various aspects of Trinidad at the time of her residence, particularly its social and cultural history.

NOTES

1. J.K. Chapman, *The Career of Arthur Hamilton Gordon: First Lord Stanmore 1829–1912* (Toronto: University of Toronto Press, 1964).
2. Danielle Delon, ed., *The Letters of Margaret Mann: With the Cazabon-Mann Watercolours of 19th Century Trinidad* (Port of Spain: National Museum and Art Gallery of Trinidad and Tobago, 2008), Print.
3. Margaret Stroble, "Gender and Race in the Nineteenth- and Twentieth-Century British Empire," in *Becoming Visible: Women in European History*, ed. Renate Bridenthal, Claudia Koonz, and Susan Stuard (Boston: Houghton Mifflin Company, 1987), 376–89.
4. F.M.G. Willson, *A Strong Supporting Cast: The Shaw Lefevres 1789–1936* (London: Athlone Press, 1993).
5. Sir Arthur Hamilton-Gordon, November 1866–May 1870, *Collection of Private Papers of Sir Arthur Hamilton-Gordon*, MS Stanmore Papers: XXX–LXXIII: Add MSS 49228–49271, London: British Library.
6. ibid., 198.
7. ibid., 195.
8. "The Peerage, 22 Nov 2004, Arthur Hamilton-Gordon, 1st Baron Stanmore," *The Peerage.com – Person Page 2472*, accessed 23 October 2007: http://thepeerage.com/p2472.htm#i24712.
9. Willson, *Strong Supporting Cast*, 202.
10. ibid., 273.
11. ibid., 274.
12. ibid., 198.
13. ibid., 275.
14. Alfred P. Maudslay, *Life in the Pacific Fifty Years Ago* (London: George Rutledge and Sons, 1930), 83–84.
15. Willson, *Strong Supporting Cast*, 198–99.
16. ibid., 198.
17. Sir Arthur Hamilton-Gordon, *Collection of Private Papers of Sir Arthur Hamilton-Gordon;* Lady Gordon to Lady Shaw-Lefevre, 8 November 1866, MS Stanmore Papers. LXXIII: Add MSS 49, 271 (London, British Library) 54–55; Lady Gordon to Madeline Shaw-Lefevre, 10 March 1870, MS Stanmore Papers. LXXIII: Add MSS 49, 271, 127.
18. Lady Gordon to Lady Shaw-Lefevre, 8 November 1866, MS Stanmore Papers. LXXIII: Add MSS 49, 271, 55.
19. Willson, *Strong Supporting Cast*, 279.
20. Lady Gordon to Madeline Shaw-Lefevre. 10 March 1870. MS Stanmore Papers. LXXIII: Add MSS 49, 271. 127.

21. Lady Gordon to Dear G, 21 April 1867, MS Stanmore Papers. XXX: Add MSS 49, 228, 139.
22. Charles Kingsley, *At Last: A Christmas in the West Indies* (London: Macmillan, 1871), 95–97.
23. Lady Gordon to Dear G, 6 February 1870, MS Stanmore Papers. XXX: Add MSS 49, 228, 240.
24. Willson, *Strong Supporting Cast*, 272.
25. ibid., 273.
26. ibid., 274.
27. ibid.
28. Lady Gordon to Lady Shaw-Lefevre. 8 November 1866, MS Stanmore Papers. LXXIII: Add MSS 49, 271, 53–54.
29. Lady Gordon to Mary Shaw-Lefevre, 22 November 1866, MS Stanmore Papers. LXXIII: Add MSS 49, 271, 60.
30. Lady Gordon to Dear G, 21 April 1867, MS Stanmore Papers. XXX: Add MSS 49, 228, 143.
31. ibid.
32. Lady Gordon to Lady Shaw-Lefevre, 24 December 1869, MS Stanmore Papers. LXXIII: Add MSS 49, 271, 120.
33. Willson, *Strong Supporting Cast*, 273.
34. ibid., 276.
35. Lady Gordon to Lady Shaw-Lefevre, 8 November 1866, MS Stanmore Papers. LXXIII: Add MSS 49, 271, 54.
36. Lady Gordon to Dear G, 2 March 1867, MS Stanmore Papers. XXX: Add MSS 49, 228, 95.
37. Lady Gordon to Lady Shaw-Lefevre, 7 January 1870, MS Stanmore Papers. LXXIII: Add MSS 49, 271, 122.
38. Lady Gordon to Dear G, 3 January 1868, MS Stanmore Papers. XXX: Add MSS 49, 228, 176.
39. Lady Gordon to Dear G, 24 October 1869, MS Stanmore Papers. XXX: Add MSS 49, 228, 206.
40. Willson, *Strong Supporting Cast*, 276.
41. Lady Gordon to Madeline Shaw-Lefevre, 10 March 1870, MS Stanmore Papers. LXXIII: Add MSS 49, 271, 127.
42. Lady Gordon to Lady Shaw-Lefevre, 8 November 1866, MS Stanmore Papers. LXXIII: Add MSS 49, 271, 55.
43. Lady Gordon to Mary Shaw-Lefevre, 22 November 1866, MS Stanmore Papers. LXXIII: Add MSS 49, 271, 58–59; Lady Gordon to Lady Shaw-Lefevre, 7 January 1870. MS Stanmore Papers. LXXIII: Add MSS 49, 271, 122.

44. Kingsley, *At Last*, 155.
45. William Reese, 1866–1870, Rachel Gordon and Madeleine Shaw-Lefevre. Album: Nineteen Mounted Watercolor Drawings of the Flora and Landscape of Trinidad, most initialled "R.H.G." on Mount. William Reese, accessed 10 August 2011, http://www.williamreesecompany.com/shop/reeseco/WRCAM34100.html.
46. Lady Gordon to Lady Shaw-Lefevre, 8 November 1866, MS Stanmore Papers. LXXIII: Add MSS 49, 271, 63.
47. Lady Gordon to Madeline Shaw-Lefevre, 6 February 1870, MS Stanmore Papers. LXXIII: Add MSS 49, 271, 126.
48. Lady Gordon to Dear G, 21 April 1867, MS Stanmore Papers. XXX: Add MSS 49, 228, 140.
49. Faith Smith, *Creole Recitations: John Jacob Thomas and Colonial Formation in the Late Nineteenth-Century* (Charlottesville: University of Virginia Press, 2002), 116.
50. Lady Gordon to Dear G, 8 March 1868, MS Stanmore Papers. XXX: Add MSS 49, 228, 191.
51. William Reese, 1866–1870.
52. Willson, *Strong Supporting Cast*, 276.
53. ibid., 201.
54. Lady Gordon to Lady Shaw-Lefevre, 24 December 1866, MS Stanmore Papers. LXXIII: Add MSS 49, 271, 68.
55. Lady Gordon to Dear G, 11 January 1870, MS Stanmore Papers. XXX: Add MSS 49, 228, 239.
56. Lady Gordon to Lady Shaw-Lefevre, 8 November 1866, MS Stanmore Papers. LXXIII: Add MSS 49, 271, 53.
57. ibid., 55.
58. Lady Gordon to Lady Shaw-Lefevre, 24 December 1866, MS Stanmore Papers. LXXIII: Add MSS 49, 271, 68.
59. William Reese, 1866–1870.
60. Lady Gordon to Lady Shaw-Lefevre. 8 December 1866. MS Stanmore Papers. LXXIII: Add MSS 49, 271. 63.
61. ibid., 64.; Lady Gordon to Madeline Shaw-Lefevre, 10 March 1870, MS Stanmore Papers. LXXIII: Add MSS 49, 271, 127.
62. Lady Gordon to Lady Shaw-Lefevre, 8 December 1866, MS Stanmore Papers. LXXIII: Add MSS 49, 271, 64.
63. Lady Gordon to Dear G, 19 November 1867, MS Stanmore Papers. XXX: Add MSS 49, 228, 168; Lady Gordon to Lady Shaw-Lefevre, 7 January 1870, MS Stanmore Papers. LXXIII: Add MSS 49, 271, 122.
64. Lady Gordon to Lady Shaw-Lefevre, 8 December 1866, MS Stanmore Papers. LXXIII: Add MSS 49, 271, 67.

65. Lady Gordon to Mary Shaw-Lefevre, 22 November 1866, MS Stanmore Papers. LXXIII: Add MSS 49, 271, 60; Lady Gordon to Lady Shaw-Lefevre, 8 December 1866, MS Stanmore Papers. LXXIII: Add MSS 49, 271, 64.
66. ibid.
67. Lady Gordon to Dear G, 16 October 1867, MS Stanmore Papers. XXX: Add MSS 49, 228, 156.
68. ibid., 157.
69. Lady Gordon to Lady Shaw-Lefevre, 7 January 1870, MS Stanmore Papers. LXXIII: Add MSS 49, 271, 124.
70. Lady Gordon to Mary Shaw-Lefevre, 22 November 1866, MS Stanmore Papers. LXXIII: Add MSS 49, 271, 61.
71. Lady Gordon to Lady Shaw-Lefevre, 8 December 1866, MS Stanmore Papers. LXXIII: Add MSS 49, 271, 66.
78. Lady Gordon to Dear G, 16 October 1867, MS Stanmore Papers. XXX: Add MSS 49, 228, 157.
79. ibid., 156.
80. Lady Gordon to Dear G, 9 October 1867, MS Stanmore Papers. XXX: Add MSS 49,228, 155.
81. Lady Gordon to Dear G, 2 March 1867, MS Stanmore Papers. XXX: Add MSS 49, 228, 96.
82. ibid., 97–98.
83. Lady Gordon to Dear G, 3 January 1868, MS Stanmore Papers. XXX: Add MSS 49, 228, 176.
84. Lady Gordon to Mary Shaw-Lefevre, 22 November 1866, MS Stanmore Papers. LXXIII: Add MSS 49, 271, 60.
85. ibid.
86. Lady Gordon to Lady Shaw-Lefevre, 24 December 1867, MS Stanmore Papers. LXXIII: Add MSS 49, 271, 71.
87. Willson, *Strong Supporting Cast*, 198.
88. Lady Gordon to Mary Shaw-Lefevre, 22 November 1866, MS Stanmore Papers. LXXIII: Add MSS 49, 271, 59.
89. Lady Gordon to Dear G, 22 February 1868, MS Stanmore Papers. XXX: Add MSS 49, 228, 186.
90. Lady Gordon to Mary Shaw-Lefevre, 22 November 1866, MS Stanmore Papers. LXXIII: Add MSS 49, 271, 60.
91. William Reese, 1866–1870.
92. Lady Gordon to Dear G, 21 April 1867, MS Stanmore Papers. XXX: Add MSS 49, 228, 104, 110.
93. ibid., 114, 128.
94. ibid., 109.
95. Lady Gordon to Dear G, 24 October 1869, MS Stanmore Papers. XXX: Add MSS 49, 228, 207.

[11]

SLAVERY, GENDER AND THE HISTORIOGRAPHY OF THE FRENCH ANTILLES, 1635–1848

[BERNARD MOITT]

SLAVERY IN THE FRENCH ANTILLES, WHICH BEGAN WITH the colonization of Martinique and Guadeloupe in 1635, and lasted until 1848, has been the subject of numerous studies, but the historical literature is at best limited and spotty; the quality of the scholarship highly uneven; and the treatment of race, gender and the harsh, degrading experience of the enslaved, minimal and largely unsatisfactory. This assessment also applies to the general historiography of the French Antilles. An overview of the historiography of the French Antilles, with particular emphasis on slavery, is the primary objective of this chapter. With regard to the literature on gender, the examination will pay particular attention to the work on enslaved women in the French Antilles, who have not been the subject of the kind of intellectual inquiry into slavery in the Caribbean that they merit. Thus, it is important to emphasize that although gender made slavery different for both sexes, it was virtually obliterated under slavery, as women were required to do the same work as men for the most part, and pursued complementary strategies in dealing with bondage. Viewed through the lens of most enslaved people in the French Antilles, enslavement was a condition that was worth fighting against, which women as well as men did. However, the invisibility of women in the historical literature persisted until recent decades, as we shall see.

THE HISTORIOGRAPHY OF THE FRENCH ANTILLES

In reference to the historiography of the Caribbean, Gordon K. Lewis was correct when he noted that the "literature is immense, covering a historical time span of nearly five centuries".[1] But although he made reference to Charles de Rochefort's *Histoire naturelle et morale des Antilles*, in his treatment of the seventeenth and eighteenth-century literature of the French Antilles, he confined himself, of necessity, mostly to Jean-Baptiste (Père) Du Tertre's *Histoire générale des Antilles habitués par les Français* and Jean-Baptiste (Père) Labat's *Nouveau Voyage aux isles de l'Amérique*.[2] Lewis was faced with the absence of a good variety of historical studies of the French colonies, itself the result of the paucity and unevenness of the data. This situation has persisted and has led to an over-reliance on too few sources. Most of the studies have focused on the Ancien Régime – the period before 1789. The period from 1789 to the abolition of slavery in 1848 constitutes another major block in the historiography, but there are relatively few studies upon which to draw. There are fewer still of the post-slavery period. The tendency has been to deal with major blocks of time, a century or more, for example. Indeed, it is rare to find a study that deals with slavery within a specific, limited time frame, such as 1800 to 1848. Thus, Victor Schoelcher's *Histioire de l'esclavage pendant les deux dernierès anneés* stands out as one of the few such studies.[3]

Lucien Abénon was well aware of these difficulties. In *La Guadeloupe de 1671 à 1759*, he noted that it was particularly hard to study the Ancien Régime due to lack of documentation and antiquated studies of the French Antilles geared to popularization rather than sound, critical treatment of the subject matter. In 1987, Abénon stated that despite the publication of a few serious works during that decade, scholars stuck to precise themes, such as the sugar economy and currency, much to the neglect of a general historical treatment that could serve as a basis for research-specific historical problems. He stated that the works published in the nineteenth century were heavy on historical facts and often given to great digressions that had nothing to do with history. Therefore, the historian was faced with numerous studies of a diverse nature, but rarely with a solid reflection based on supportive evidence.[4] A conscientious historian, Abénon knew the sources well. His stark assessment is valid and helpful in understanding the burden that the contemporary historian faces in writing about French historiography on slavery. It was not meant to discourage; it was a dose of reality. Even so, Abénon overlooked other hindrances.

French historiography on slavery in the French Antilles is also marked by insularity and a great imbalance in geographic focus. Certainly, the lack of a regional perspective, though difficult to achieve because of differences in evolutionary patterns and political developments in all of the French colonies, remains glaring. Elsa Goveia must have faced similar hurdles when researching and writing *A Study on the Historiography of the British West Indies to the End of the Nineteenth Century*, but she produced a work that constitutes essential reading and remains a central cornerstone in the historiography.[5] No one has produced such a work for the French Antilles. And there is no counterpart to Gordon K. Lewis' *Main Currents in Caribbean Thought*, which the author describes as "a descriptive and critical analysis of the total complex of ideas, sentiments, outlooks, attitudes, and values that, in the fullest sense of the word, constitute the ideology of the groups that have figured in the Caribbean story".[6] There is no anthology on the level of Shepherd and Beckles' *Caribbean Slavery in the Atlantic World*, which is now used in many university courses. Indeed, it is difficult to foresee the development and publication of a series such as UNESCO's multi-volume *General History of the Caribbean*.[7]

Insularity and the lack of a regional perspective have resulted in more concentration on the histories of Martinique and Guadeloupe, and much less on Saint-Domingue (now Haiti), and French Guiana. In the case of Haiti, much of the historical writing revolves around the Haitian Revolution, which means that knowledge of Haiti is virtually confined to the period from the outbreak of the revolution in 1791 to the achievement of independence in 1804. Thus, Lucien Abénon's comment about the absence of a work of synthesis on the history of Saint-Domingue is still valid.[8] As for French Guiana, it has all been but forgotten until recent years, thanks largely to the many works published by Ibis Rouge.

French historiography has also been disappointing with regard to the lack of detailed and specific studies that portray the experience of the enslaved from their perspective, particularly with regard to the valiant ways in which the enslaved, particularly women, resisted slavery. In these and many other instances, French historiography on slavery lags far behind that of the anglophone Caribbean. Why is this so? Are there other factors besides those related to the lack, and fragmentary state of, the data, and the difficulty with reading French archival sources, especially seventeenth and eighteenth-century manuscripts on microfilm that are hard to decipher? There are, indeed. The French colonies, like other colonies ruled by Europeans, were, and still are seen as a peripheral part of metropolitan France. As such, the control exerted over the colonies by the imperial power manifested itself in writings mostly by imperial scholars, who set the agenda and tone, and wrote about slavery from their perspective. This was facilitated by the location of French publishing houses that scholars indigenous to the Caribbean would have found difficult to access. And if they did, they would have been expected to carry on the imperial traditions. In recent times, most of the studies on the French Antilles have been published by L'Harmattan and Karthala in Paris; few have been published by Presses Universitaires de France. When Alex Roy-Camille created the publishing house *Éditions Caribéennes* in Paris in 1978, he provided a very useful outlet to scholars of the French Antilles. Indeed, Jacques Adelaïde-Merlande wrote fondly of this development and attributed the writing of his *Histoire général des Antilles et des Guyanes* to conversations he held with Roy-Camille.[9] *Éditions Caribbéennes* published many notable works, such as Arlette Gautier's *Les Soeurs de Solitude*, the first comprehensive study of women and slavery in the French Antilles – but the establishment that Roy-Camille founded did not survive his death in 1993.[10] To be sure, Roy-Camille played the role that Ian Randle Publishers and Ibis Rouge Editions now play in Jamaica and Martinique respectively.

The large number of works that Ibis Rouge Editions has published in a relatively short period, a few by historians, suggests both a pent-up demand for works by indigenous scholars and the need to repair damages of old. In addition to the publishing houses, the local journals in the French Antilles have played a pivotal role in advancing the historiography of slavery. The *Société d'histoire de la Martinique* and the *Société d'histoire de la Guadeloupe* have published regular bulletins with work on slavery that has advanced the historiography. They have also republished and made available to the public invaluable scholarly works such as *Code Noir*, without which scholars doing research on slavery would have a more difficult time.

Above all, however, the major problem regarding French historiography on slavery is ideological, since French scholars of all ethnic backgrounds are hesitant to confront what Sue Peabody calls "the ugly past of the French Antillean colonies".[11] Indeed, in a work that deals with the histories of race in France, Sue Peabody and Tyler Stovall note that in a public debate on French and US racism, some Guadeloupeans argued that when all is said and done, both forms had the same effect, despite the obvious differences in their manifestations – conformity and assimilation to French cultural norms that lead to humiliation in one case, and open, direct racism in the other. They point out that: "The French universal curriculum for secondary students makes no mention of slavery or race, thereby making them appear irrelevant to the lives of some of the poorest residents of former French colonies. To many of these black French citizens, the American 'multicultural' model of education appears enviable."[12]

To be sure, Louis Sala-Molins' condemnation of the French *Code Noir* as "the most monstrous judicial text in modern times", and his statement that the official state thinking which lay behind it caused the "Afro-Antillean genocide" is rare.[13] In a more nuanced treatment of these issues with specific reference to French Guiana, Serge Mam Lam Fouck has stated that: "Guianese society has imposed upon itself a blackout on slavery for more than a century and has only recently rediscovered the memory of her origins in the 1950s. In essence, one had to wait for more than a century after the abolition of slavery for Guianese society to acknowledge the fact that slavery is an element that determines the people's actions."[14]

Similarly, in a review of literary works on slavery, Lydie Ho-Fong-Choy Choucoutou noted that "unlike the literature of the United States and the Caribbean, Guianese literature is devoid of the memory of slaves".[15] The collective loss of memory to which Mam Lam Fouck and Choucoutou refer is not accidental, according to Miraim Cottias. Indeed, she argues that it was fostered by the French state and local politicians, and used for political ends.[16] In *Slavery in the Caribbean Francophone World*, Doris Kadish sought to jog this loss of memory by bringing together twelve interdisciplinary essays aimed at bringing enslaved people in the Francophone Caribbean principally, and those associated with them – whites and mixed-race individuals – out of anonymity. Tilted largely on the literary side, the study sought to listen to and capture the voices of the enslaved – a worthy scholarly pursuit – but the authors were hampered by the scarcity of primary source material that made their objective difficult to achieve, despite its many fine qualities.[17]

THE HISTORICAL TEXTS AND SLAVERY

There is material about slavery in the general studies of the French Antilles dating back to the seventeenth century, but as Arlette Gautier has pointed out, only fourteen books on slavery in the French Antilles were published in France before 1980.[18] Material can also be found in colony-specific studies of the region. However, specific studies of slavery came much later. Du Tertre's *Histoire génénal* provides useful information about the lives of slaves in areas such as work, family life, law, nourishment, accommodation and resistance in the seventeenth century. A keen observer, Du Tertre provided information about the enslaved and the slave system that have served as a basis for future research. But he is virtually silent on the treatment of the enslaved by their owners.[19] In this regard, Gordon K. Lewis saw Du Tertre as "the Catholic humanist, deeply religious, full of compassion for the plight of both the African slave and the Carib Indian in the manner of Las Casas, yet incapable in the final resort of openly challenging the system that oppressed them".[20] Lewis paints a different picture of Père Labat, whom he deemed insensitive toward the enslaved, and accepting of the slave system. But the difference is really a matter of degree. According to Lewis, Labat wrote about "the onerous working hours of the field slave, but without comment". As Lewis continues:

> He describes seeing freshly embarked blacks handsome enough to inspire an artist; but the aesthetic feeling did not lead him, as it did Du Tertre, to that sense of generous pity which almost makes the unfortunate appear to the reader in an illusive, almost ideal aspect. So, while Du Tertre prays masters in the ameliorative fashion, to be merciful to their slaves, Labat suggests that slavery is a legitimate means of redeeming Negroes from superstition; indeed, Labat regards the Negro as a natural child of the devil, a born sorcerer, and evil spirit wielding occult power. He is remarkably free from religious bigotry, as his attitude to employing heretics on his ecclesiastical plantation shows. But he is the epitome of racial bigotry.[21]

While the early studies were all-encompassing in their attempts to describe everything in sight, those that followed have been more circumscribed. However, they did not necessarily provide great insights into slavery. In fact, slavery sometimes received minimal coverage. For example, the edited work, *Histoire general des Antilles et de la Guyane*, contains 482 pages, but only twenty-one are dedicated to slavery – a chapter written by Gabriel Debien. Here, Debien's treatment of slavery is very general, and most of his examples are taken from Saint-Domingue, the colony he knew best, and which became the focus of his innumerable studies. Curiously, Debien opened the chapter by stating how paradoxical it was to engage in writing about the enslaved when, during slavery, few observed their lives, and those who did were whites – planters, plantation and colonial administrators, and on occasion, travellers. He urged caution in using the limited sources available and hinted at the frightening prospect of scholars falling into a state of silence, much like the enslaved themselves.[22]

Other examples of general histories include works by Jacques Adelaïde-Merlande and Paul Butel. Adelaïde-Merlande's *Histoire Général des Antilles et des Guyanes* was aimed at satisfying the needs of high school teachers, who wanted to include Caribbean history in their teaching, while catering to the demands of students seeking knowledge of the area. The fact that Adelaïde-Merlande cast his net even wider is revealing about the state of the historiography of the French Antilles in 1994, when he published this work. Indeed, he hoped that the work would also interest politicians, administrators, the media and lay people who wished to be informed or impart the history of the French Antilles to others. To this end, he included a number of primary documents in French and English, and chronological tables that instructors could use as teaching aids. Adelaïde-Merlande's *Historie Général* was the first attempt by a French scholar to engage in a broad comprehensive treatment of the history of the Caribbean, not just the French Antilles. In this respect, it seems certain that he adopted the approach that Eric Williams took in *From Columbus to Castro*. But the work lacks the critical tone that Williams brought to his work. For example, slavery is given a factual treatment, and this includes the many forms of resistance mentioned. Certainly, the enslaved do not come to life in this work.[23]

The treatment of slavery in Paul Butel's *Histoire des Antilles françaises* is much the same, that is, a factual account. However, Butel also discusses cruelty to the enslaved by their owners, and the response of the enslaved. Interestingly, his emphasis is on administrative action. He gives an example of a white planter who was banished from Guadeloupe in 1743 and prohibited from owning enslaved persons for a period of five years, after he was found guilty of excessively whipping those he owned. He emphasizes the fact that cruelty to the enslaved was not universal, and that in spite of the criticisms levelled at slavery by abolitionists, a milder form of slavery prevailed in the French colonies by the end of the eighteenth century. Butel's book offers a very non-critical and reactionary treatment of slavery. The statement that the Western world justified slavery as a means of saving the Africans from barbarity and idolatry is not followed by any corrective. Overall, the French administration and the white planter class come off very well in this 2002 publication.[24]

Among the colony-specific studies worthy of note are works by Afred Martineau and L. May, C.A. Banbuck, Phillipe Blérald, Lucien Abénon, Armad Nicolas and Serge Mam Lam Fouck.[25] Martineau and May are good on historical chronology, dates of events and biographical highlights about administrative personnel and historically important figures such as Louis Delgrès, who led the fight against the French forces sent by Napoléon Bonaparte to reestablish slavery in Guadeloupe in 1802. Banbuck deals with slavery mostly from the point of view of law, but notes, "Slavery, or better yet, black skin, was quite shameful."[26] Therefore, he considered it useless to list the litany of acts of cruelty meted out to the enslaved by their owners. He does not take the white planter class to task for these acts. Was slavery not a pretext for reducing men who had nothing else against them except weakness and helplessness, he asked? So, while he seems critical of the ideal that slavery was meant to Christianize the African, he does not condemn the slave system.

Blérald's book on the history of Guadeloupe and Martinique begins with slavery, the first section of the text tracing from 1635 to 1945 in fewer than one hundred and fifty pages. In the few pages he dedicates to slavery, Blérald focuses mainly on the plantation economy. But in drawing upon the work of the French abolitionist Victor Schoelcher, he ventures that the whipping of the enslaved was a symbol of the terrorism and totalitarianism that characterized the slave system. In drawing attention to the short lifespan of the enslaved, the arduous tasks that they performed, and the work-to-death policy of the enslavers, Blérald's short, succinct treatment of slavery is effective. But in employing a class analysis to determine who benefitted from the surplus produced by the enslaved in colonies that were integrated into the world economy, a certain level of abstraction sets in.[27]

With regard to Guadeloupe, scholars have found Auguste Lacour's multi-volume work *Histoire de la Guadeloupe* informative for the period up to the early nineteenth century. This includes his reconstruction of the struggle that the enslaved in Guadeloupe waged to stave off the re-establishment of slavery in May 1802. However, a major weakness in the work is its lack of citations. First published in Guadeloupe between 1855 and 1858, much of the book hinges upon Lacour's personal communication with individuals whose involvement in the revolutionary struggles gave the work authenticity. The charge of lack of citations can also be levelled at Oruno Lara's *La Guadeloupe dans l'histoire*, even though Lara, like Lacour, viewed the enslaved as actors in their own right.[28]

Abénon's two-volume work on the history of Guadeloupe was the first critical, comprehensive and well-documented study. By stating early on that "We have very little information about the mentality of the slaves during the early colonial period", he indicated that he was not prepared to go beyond the data.[29] As an historian, he cannot be faulted for that, but he *could* have been more imaginative and probing. Aside from a small section on *marronnage*, there is relatively little material on slavery in his work. Nicolas provides a much more extensive treatment of slavery in his *Histoire de la Martinique*, but he thrives on generalities. The work lacks a critical and rigorous academic approach. After highlighting a number of abuses that the enslaved suffered at the hands of their oppressors, the author rightfully concludes that three years before the abolition of slavery, the Mackau Law of 1845 still attempted to regulate whipping. He also noted that in 1847, innumerable acts of cruelty against the enslaved came to light, but that slaveowners were usually acquitted or were given very light fines. "Never was a master condemned to severe penalties," he wrote, "for having mutilated or killed his slaves."[30] He does not reflect on what this says about the slave system.

As for the specific studies of slavery in the French Antilles, Lucien Peytraud's *L'esclavage aux Antilles françaises* was one of the earliest.[31] Published in 1897, this work is a very detailed, comprehensive and useful study. It begins with chapters on the establishment of the French colonies, slavery and slave trading in Africa, and the Atlantic slave trade. The author dedicates several chapters to slavery, covering such areas as religion, customs, social condition, punishment and resistance. But this broad coverage is heavy on law, particularly the *Code Noir*, and the African is seen as an inferior being. Christianizing the blacks was the best means of introducing them to "a superior civilization", Peytraud wrote. It is little wonder that he was content with merely describing the slave system without comment or analysis.

Gaston-Martin's *Histoire de l'esvclavage dans les colonies françaises*, also describes the process and conditions of enslavement. He believed that it was not possible to understand the collective mentality of the enslaved, unless it was viewed in relation to those who owned them. In other words, the enslaved could not be studied collectively in their own right. He painted the enslaved African as docile and malleable, and wrote about the "primitive mentality of the servile population".[32] One would expect more recent works to counter this image of the enslaved, but Lémy Lémane Coco's is a general treatment that lacks a critical edge.[33]

Antoine Gisler's *L'esclavage aux Antilles françaises* was motivated by the need to determine how sound the claims that Victor Schoelcher made about the suffering of the enslaved in the French colonies during the last years of the institution were.[34] Schoelcher criticized contemporary missionaries for inaction, who, along with moralists, remained silent in the face of atrocities committed against the enslaved. Gilser's study reinforces Schoelcher's findings, but he attributes the silence of the missionaries to pressure from civil authorities. Given this point of departure, Gisler's book constituted a major departure from the old views of enslavement. He engaged in a detailed study of the *Code Noir*, and gave detailed examples of cases of abuse of the enslaved and their resolution. The end result is a richly documented study that brings out the difference between the theory and the practice of slave laws, and a conclusion that slavery could not be humanized. The laws governing slavery in the French Antilles are also taken up in a recent study that focuses broadly on social control. In *La Police des Noirs*, Hurard Bellance concentrates on the various dimensions of policing, the mechanisms of control, and agencies involved in policing the enslaved. Bellance's work is general in many ways, as it addresses such issues as the role of Christian missionaries, African cultural forms such as dancing, slave resistance and regulations governing interracial unions, and manumission acquired through concubinage. However, the work highlights a good example of the severity of punishment that a woman in Saint-Domingue endured for cutting her owner with a knife in 1786. Under Article 33 of the *Code Noir* of 1685, this was an act punishable by death. In this case, the slave woman was maimed, placed on a wheel with her face facing the sky and roasted alive in public.[35]

Bellance made no judgement about the slave system, but Victor Schoelcher's Histoire *de L'esclavage pendant les deux dernières années* is a major indictment of the institution, even in its last throes. Schoelcher was often dismissed as an overzealous abolitionist, but the work contains excellent material, including detailed and specific cases of the interface between the enslaved and their owners. For example, there is very good material on the struggle waged by enslaved women to free themselves and their children through litigation. The work also contains good information about *marronnage* from the French colonies to British ones such as St Lucia, Dominica and Antigua. Schoelcher did not attempt to write a gendered history, but much useful information about enslaved women *can* be culled from his work.

In addition to these major, general studies, at least a few others are geared towards the school system. One is René Belnus' *L'esclavage en Guadeloupe et en Martinique*; another is *Le grand livre de l'esclavage*, the work of Gérard Thélier and Pierre Alibert.[36] Both are similar in terms of coverage and presentation, especially in the use of text and accompanying photographs depicting various views of slave life. The latter is a more serious endeavour, but both are useful, despite the non-critical approach that they adopt in dealing with slavery. Also, they are too general in tone, and this makes it difficult to view the enslaved as real persons. Specific and detailed examples of lives of enslaved people could have enhanced these books.

Many such examples abound in the works of Gabriel Debien, one of the few scholars to concentrate on the enslaved as a group. Were it not for his monumental scholarly contribution, it *would* be considerably more difficult to reconstruct the lives of the enslaved in the French colonies. Debien spent much of his life working on slavery in Saint-Domingue and drew most of his examples from this colony as a result. But his principal work, *Les esclaves aux Antilles françaises*, takes a regional approach, and remains the sole treatment of its kind since its publication a little more than four decades ago.[37] In addition to tapping traditional sources, such as material from the French national archives, Debien collected data from private archives and papers in the possession of families whose relatives had owned plantations in Saint-Domingue. This made it possible for the researcher to get as intimate a view as possible of slave life. Debien's contribution, which the University of the West Indies at Cave Hill (Barbados) acknowledged when it awarded him an honorary doctorate in 1978, lies not so much in the analysis he bought to his work, but in his wide-ranging and often detailed exploration of slavery from every possible angle. Debien, a pioneer, did not focus on gender, but it has been possible to extract a great deal of information about the lives of women from the rich historical legacy he has left us. He inspired many of the studies on slavery in the French Antilles, and the magnitude of his intellectual contribution is reflected in an issue of *Bulletin de la société d'histoire de la Martinique*, which listed two hundred and thirty of his publications.[38] As he published some of his work in obscure outlets, the journal could not account for all of them. In many ways, the edited work *Esclaves et les plantations* – homage to the French scholar, Pierre Pluchon, whose works advanced the study of slavery and the slave trade – is a collection that would please Debien. It covers most of the areas dealing with the lives of the enslaved, as Debien did, but it contains at least one chapter by Arlette Gautier that deals with women.[39]

More recently, Josette Fallope has published a well-researched and detailed study of enslaved and free persons in Guadeloupe that complements Debien's work. In *Esclaves et citoyens*, she explains that she wrote the book to get a better grasp of Caribbean history, and its African dimensions in particular. She takes the position that the enslaved population in Guadeloupe experienced "a situation of permanent aggression for the first two centuries of colonization".[40] Also, she argues that racism was used to justify slavery and protect the colonial order.[41] However, the specific ways in which this racism was manifested in the daily lives of the enslaved is not given concrete treatment.

Although much of the writing on Haiti has been the work of anthropologists, political scientists, religious scholars and journalists, the literature on slavery in France's most prized colony of Saint-Domingue is among the best in the region. This may well be due to the fact that Haiti bears the distinction of being the only example in world history of an enslaved people who rose up against their owners, destroyed the slave system and declared themselves independent. Thus, Jean Fouchard's *Les marrons de la liberté* is the only full-length treatment of *marronnage* in the French Antilles and remains popular, despite its lack of citations.[42] The concentration on resistance and, in particular, the Haitian Revolution has been marked. One of the most notable studies is C.L.R. James' *The Black Jacobins*, translated into French as *Les Jacobins noirs*. James used his sources well, at a time when few in the Anglophone Caribbean could boast proficiency in French. Although slavery underpinned every aspect of *The Black Jacobins*, James spent very little time on it. James' vision of the African showed his lack of knowledge of the African continent and its peoples, but he described the oppression they faced in Saint-Domingue in stark terms. He also highlighted what slave owners of all persuasions must have known – that the Africans were humans. As he wrote: "The difficulty was that though one could trap them like animals, transport them in pens, work them alongside an ass or a horse and beat them both with the same stick, stable them and starve them, they remained, despite their black skins and curly hair, quite invincibly human beings; with the intelligence and resentments of human beings. To cow them into the necessary docility and acceptance necessitated a regime of calculated brutality and terrorism..."[43]

In *The Black Jacobins*, James displayed his critical analytical skills, not only in dealing with the revolutionary war, but with the social stratification and racism that characterized society in Saint-Domingue. Carolyn Fick has followed up with an excellent study of the revolution, which brings out the interrelationships between various local groupings and leaders, and gives the revolution a human face. The works of David Geggus, whose expertise and concentration on the Saint-Domingue revolution is well acknowledged and duly respected, has no doubt encouraged others to follow in his footsteps and share the field. This development has been fruitful, considering the substantial and solid work that a young scholar like Laurent Dubois has already published.[44]

No discussion of the historiography of slavery in the French Antilles should ignore the contributions of scholars whose work focus on gender. This area of study is still in its infancy. For many years, Arlette Gautier's *Soeurs de Solitude* – a pioneering and significant study about the lives of enslaved women in the French colonies – remained the sole reference, even for those who could not read French. Gautier's book, though quite general, was a very important beginning, and the author deserves credit for blazing the trail. The work brought to light aspects of the slave woman's condition that remained hidden from view. The participation of the slave woman, Solitude, in one of the last battles that the enslaved of Guadeloupe fought against the emperor Napoleon's forces in 1802 when they were trying to stave off the restoration of slavery, was as illuminating as ever. Similarly, even though they had no direct access to the courts, the acts of litigation in which slave women engaged, using official intermediaries and Article 47 of the *Code Noir,* which prohibited the breakup of the slave family as long as the family was owned by the same individual and the children were minors, that is, under the age of fourteen, revealed an aspect of women's resistance to slavery that expanded the boundaries of investigation and enriched the historiography measurably. Gautier has continued this line of research.

Sixteen years after the publication of Gautier's book, I published the first comprehensive treatment in English or French of enslaved women in the French Antilles, entitled *Women and Slavery in the French Antilles, 1635–1848.*[45] The number of reviews the book has undergone, irrespective of their content, speaks of the significance of this study. Certainly, it opened up the French Antilles to English readers and laid bare the difference that gender made in the condition of enslavement. It highlights the fact that women outnumbered men in the field gangs, where they spent most of their working lives, and performed proportionately more hard labour than men, even though women were fewer in number than men over the lifespan of slavery. The text also illuminates areas of women's resistance to slavery that have not been traditionally studied. For example, women banded together and formed associations that circumvented the slave system.

Karol Weaver's *Medical Revolutionaries* has made a significant contribution to the historiography of women's resistance to slavery. In an original and path-breaking study, Weaver uses historical ethnomedicine to show how enslaved women healers, while providing medical care for themselves and their white owners, helped to inspire and lead the Haitian Revolution. These healers included herbalists, veterinary practitioners and nurses. She argues convincingly that they emerged as significant leaders of slave communities through a process of cultural retention, assimilation and creation; profited economically from their healing practices; and initiated and implemented an ideology of resistance through sabotage and the destruction of human (mostly other enslaved people) and animal life. According to Weaver, because enslaved women occupied authoritative positions within the slave occupational hierarchy, one cannot fully understand the origins of the Haitian Revolution without due consideration of the magnitude of their role. The importance of women's roles in these areas is amplified in Caroline Oudin-Bastide's *L'effroi et la terreur: Esclavage, poison et sorcellerie aux Antilles*. The text is particularly enlightening about initiation ceremonies and secret societies.

The role of women in resistance is also central in Gilbert Pago's *Les femmes et la liquidation du système esclavagiste à la Martinique, 1848–1852*. Based largely on secondary sources, Pago has cleverly highlighted the ways in which women of colour – enslaved and free – rallied and worked together, especially in the months leading up to official emancipation in May 1848 to hasten the end of slavery. The first part of the book deals mostly with the events in the 1840s; the second part focuses on the aftermath of emancipation. According to Pagot, slaveowners in Martinique were surprised at the number of slave women who challenged the authority of their owners following the passage of the Mackau law of 1847, which prohibited the whipping of women. Women were also at the forefront of the struggle for the rights of free coloureds. Although there were no distinct women's movements, free women of colour were very active on many fronts. They mobilized enslaved people in urban areas. They also organized petitions for the return of Cyrille Bissette – a free mixed-race activist who agitated intellectually on behalf of free coloureds in Martinique in the 1820s. As a result, Bissette was condemned in 1824, branded with a hot iron, imprisoned and subsequently deported. Pago's book does not provide new insights into the activities of enslaved women. Even so, it fills a gap in the historiography, especially for the period after 1848.[46]

The number of studies of woman and slavery in the French Caribbean remains insignificant. In 2009, Arlette Gautier could only identify five published books (in French and English) dedicated to women and slavery in the French Antilles.[47] There is no indication that this situation will change in the foreseeable future, given the difficulties associated with the paucity of data and the ongoing reluctance of French scholars to tackle slavery head on. What one is more likely to see is the publication of articles and chapters in edited volumes on slavery which *should* be encouraged.

NOTES

1. Gordon K. Lewis, *Main Currents in Caribbean Thought* (Baltimore: Johns Hopkins University Press, 1983), 29.
2. Jean-Baptiste (Père) Du Tertre, *Histoire Générale des Antilles Habitées par les Français*, 4 vols. 1671, reprint Fort-de-France, Éditions des horizons caraïbes, 1973; Jean-Baptiste (Père) Labat, *Nouveau Voyage aux Isles de l'Amérique*, 6 vols., Editeurs G. Cavelier et P.-F. Giffard, Paris, 1772; Charles de Rochefort, *Histoire Naturelle et Morale des Antilles de l'Amérique* (Rotterdam, 1658). The English translation of this work by John Davies is *History of the Caribby Islands* (London, 1666).
3. Victor Schœlcher, *Histoire de l'Esclavage Pendant les Deux Dernières Années*, Vol. I and II (Pointe-à-Pitre: Émile Désormeaux, 1973, reprint of 1847 edition).
4. Lucien-René Abénon, *La Guadeloupe de 1671 à 1759: Étude Politique, Economique et Sociale* (Paris: L'Harmattan, 1987), Vol. 1, 7.
5. Elsa V. Goveia, *A Study of the Historiography of the British West Indies to the End of the Nineteenth Century* (Mexico City: Instituto Panamericano de Geografia e Historia, 1956).
6. Lewis, *Main Currents*, ix.
7. Verene Shepherd and Hilary Beckles, *Caribbean Slavery in the Atlantic World* (Kingston: Ian Randle Publishers, 2002); B.W. Higman, *UNESCO General History of the Caribbean*, 6 vols. (New York: Palgrave Macmillan), 2003.
8. Abénon, *La Guadeloupe*, vol. 1: 7.
9. Jacques Adelaîde-Merlande, *Histoire Générale des Antilles et des Guyanes: des Précolombiens à nos Jours* (Paris: Editions Caribéennes, 1994), préface.
10. Arlette Gautier, *Les Sœurs de Solitude: La Condition Féminine dans l'esclavage aux Antilles du XVIIe au XIX siècle* (Paris: Éditions Caribéennes, 1985).
11. Sue Peabody, "A Point of Comparison: Enslaved Women in France's Caribbean Colonies," H-Net Review (H-Caribbean), May 2002: 1. http://www.h-net.msu.edu/reviews/showrev.cgi?path=68181022698382.
12. Sue Peabody and Tyler Stovall "Introduction," in *The Color of Liberty: Histories of Race In France*, ed. Sue Peabody and Tyler Stovall (Durham: Duke University Press, 2003), 4.
13. Louis Sala-Molins, *Le Code Noir ou le Calvaire de Canaan* (Paris: Presses Universitaires de France, 1987), 9–10.
14. Serge Mam-Lam-Fouck, *L'Esclavage en Guyane entre l'Occultation et la Revendication* (Cayenne: Ibis Rouge Editions, 1998), 7. See also Serge Mam-Lam-Fouck, *La Guyane Française au temps de l'Esclavage: de l'or et de la Francisation* (Petit-Bourg: Ibis Rouge, 1999).

15. Lydie Ho-Fong-Choy Choucoutou, "Littérature et Esclavage: Quelques Considérations," in *De l'esclavage aux Réparations*, ed. Serge Chalons, Christian Jean-Etienne, Suzy Landau, and André Yebakima (Paris: Karthala, 2000), 21.
16. Myriam Cottias, "Le Triomphe de l'oubli ou la Mémoire Tronquée?" in *De l'Esclavage aux Réparations*, 96.
17. Doris Y. Kadish, ed., *Slavery in the French Caribbean world: Distant Voices, Forgotten Acts, Forged Identities* (Athens: University of Georgia Press, 2000).
18. Arlette Gautier, "Genre et Esclavage aux Antilles Françaises: Bilan de l'Histographie," in *L'Esclave et les Plantations: De l'Etablissement de la Servitude à son Abolition*, ed. Philippe Hrodĕj (Rennes: Presses universitaires de Rennes, 2009), 163.
19. See Du Tertre, *Histoire*, vol. 2 :398–501.
20. Lewis, *Main Currents*, 63.
21 ibid., 66.
22. Gabriel Debien, "Les Esclaves," in *Histoire des Antilles et de la Guyane*, ed. Pierre Pluchon (Toulouse: Privat, 1982), 141–59.
23. Jacques Adelaïde-Merlande, *Histoire Générale des Antilles et des Guyanes: Des Précolombiens à nos Jours* (Paris: Editions Caribéennes, 1994), 116–80; Eric Williams, *From Columbus to Castro: The History of the Caribbean, 1492 to 1969* (London: André Deutsch, 1970).
24. Paul Butel, *Histoire des Antilles Françaises, XVIIe-XXe Siècle* (Paris: Editions Perrin, 2002), 165–78.
25. Alfred Martineau and L. May, *Trois Siècles d'Histoire Antillaises: Martinique et Guadeloupe de 1635 à nos Jours* (Paris: Société d'histoire des Colonies Françaises, 1935); C.A. Banbuck, *Histoire Politique, Economique et Sociale de la Martinique sous L'Ancien Régime, 1635–1789* (Paris: Librairie des Sciences Politiques et Sociales, 1935); Alain-Phillipe Blérald, *Histoire économique de la Guadeloupe et de la Martinique du XVIIe à nos jours* (Paris: Karthala, 1986); Lucien Abénon, *La Guadeloupe*; Armand Nicolas, *Histoire de la Martinique: Des Arawaks à 1848* (Paris: L'Harmattan, 1996).
26. Banbuck, *Histoire*, 309.
27. See Blérald, *Histoire*, 24–36.
28. Auguste Lacour, *Histoire de la Guadeloupe*, 4 vols. (Basse-Terre: Editions de Diffusion de la Culture Antillaise, 1976); Oruno Lara, *La Guadeloupe dans l'Histoire* (Paris: L'Harmattan, 1979).
29. Abénon, *La Guadeloupe*, vol. 1: 56.
30. Nicolas, *Histoire*, vol. 1: 173.
31. Lucien Petraud, *L'Esclavage aux Antilles Françaises Avant 1789* (Paris: Hachette, 1897).

32. Gaston-Martin, *Histoire de l'Esclavage dans les Colonies Françaises* (Paris: Presses Universitaires de France, 1948).
33. Lémy Lémane Coco, *Histoire de l'Esclavage dans les Colonies Françaises* (Chevilly-Larue: Éditions Monde Global, 2008).
34. Antoine Gisler, *L'Esclavage aux Antilles Françaises XVIIe-XIXe siècles* (Paris, Karthala, 1981).
35. Hurard Bellance, *La Police des Noirs en Amérique (Martinique, Guadeloupe, Saint-Domingue) et en France aux XVIIe et XVIIIe Siècles* (Matoury, Guyane: Ibis Rouge Editions, 2011), 88.
36. René Belénus, *L'Esclave en Guadeloupe et en Martinique du XVIIe au XIXe Siècle* (Pointe-à-Pitre: Editions Jasor, 1998); Gérard Thélier and Pierre Alibert, *Le Grand Livre de l'Esclavage: Des Résistances et de l'Abolition* (Réunion: Les Editions Orphie, 1998).
37. Gabriel Debien, *Les Esclaves aux Antilles Françaises, XVIIe-XVIIIe Siècle* (Basse-Terre: Société d'histoire de la Guadeloupe, 1974).
38. *Bulletin de la Société d'histoire de la Martinique*, no. 27 (1988–1991): 7–27.
39. Philippe Hroděj, ed., *L'Esclave et les Plantations: De l'établissement de la Servitude à son Abolition* (Rennes: Presses Universitaires de Rennes, 2008).
40. Josette Fallope, *Esclaves et Citoyens: Les Noirs à la Guadeloupe au XIXe siècle* (Basse-Terre: Société d'histoire de la Guadeloupe, 1992), 11.
41. ibid., 16.
42. Jean Fouchard, *Les Marrons de la Liberté* (Paris: Editions de l'école, 1972).
43. C.L.R. James, *The Black Jacobins: Toussaint L'Ouverture and the San Domingo Revolution* (New York: Random House, 1963), 11–12.
44. Carolyn Fick, *The Making of Haiti: The Saint Domingue Revolution from Below* (Knoxville: University of Tennessee Press, 1990); David Geggus, *Slavery, War and Revolution: The British Occupation of Saint-Domingue, 1793–1798* (London: Oxford University Press, 1982); David Geggus, ed., *The Impact of the Haitian Revolution on the Atlantic World* (Columbia, SC: University of South Carolina Press, 2001); David Geggus, ed., *Haitian Revolutionary Studies* (Bloomington: Indiana University Press, 2002); David Geggus and David Barry Gaspar, eds., *A Turbulent Time: The French Revolution and the Greater Caribbean*, 1997); Laurent Dubois, *Avengers of the New World: The Story of the Haitian Revolution* (Cambridge, Mass: Belknap Press of Harvard University Press, 2004).
45. Gautier, *Sœurs de Solitude*; Bernard Moitt, *Women and Slavery in the French Antilles, 1635–1848* (Bloomington: Indiana University Press, 2001).
46. Gilbert Pago, *Les Femmes et la Liquidation du Système Esclavagiste à la Martinique, 1848-1852* (Pointe-à-Pitre: Ibis Rouge, 1998), 43–131. On Bissette, see Bernard Moitt, "In the Shadow of the Plantation: Women of Color and

the *Libre de Fait of Martinique and Guadeloupe, 1685–1848*," in David Barry Gaspar and Darlene Clark Hine, eds., *Free Women of Color in the Americas* (Bloomington: Indiana University Press, 2004), 44.
47. Gautier, "Genre et esclavage," 165.

[Part Four]

ENGENDERING HISTORY:
Social and Political Life in the Caribbean

[12]

GENDER AND PROTEST AT MORANT BAY AND IN THE POST-EMANCIPATION CARIBBEAN

[GAD HEUMAN]

IN EXAMINING RIOTS AND PROTESTS IN THE ANGLOPHONE Caribbean after 1834, it is important to examine the role of gender. It is clear that freedom was experienced differently by black men and women, and that gender inequality continued after the abolition of slavery. In the Caribbean, men generally had access to citizenship; and, assuming they met the franchise requirements, they could vote. In Jamaica, they could also sit in the House of Assembly and on local vestries and juries. None of these possibilities were open to women. As Diana Paton and Pamela Scully have noted, women "were political minors in the post-slavery landscape".[1]

Yet, despite their different experiences of freedom, both men and women protested the terms of emancipation. They sometimes did so in different ways, reflecting their varied experiences of emancipation. This chapter will highlight the role of women in these movements, while also devoting some attention to men. It will also discuss the gendered nature of freedom more generally.

APPRENTICESHIP

Although the enslaved were declared legally free on 1 August 1834, they were obliged to serve a period of apprenticeship to their former masters. This meant that ex-slaves were legally obligated to work without compensation for their former masters for up to forty-five hours per week. Their term of continued compulsory labour depended on their status: former field slaves (praedials) were to be apprenticed for six years, while skilled apprentices and domestics (non-praedials) were to be fully free after four years. Beyond the time required by law for the apprentices to serve their former masters, ex-slaves were free to negotiate conditions of work and wages with their former masters or with another employer. Moreover, the legislation establishing apprenticeship sought to protect the apprentices by prohibiting former masters from punishing their former slaves. Instead, special magistrates were appointed, largely from England, to adjudicate disputes between masters and their former slaves.[2]

One of the provisions of the apprenticeship legislation was to allow for the compulsory manumission of the apprentices. Apprentices, therefore, had the right to purchase the remaining time of the apprenticeship period, even against the will or without the consent of the owner. However, the method of appraising the value of the apprentice's labour favoured the former owners. Tribunals consisted of a stipendiary magistrate, but also two colonial justices, local people who may well have had an interest in apprenticed labour themselves. Despite this obstacle, many apprentices were able to buy themselves out of apprenticeship and, importantly, the overwhelming majority were women.

In table 12.1, it is possible to get a sense of the type of apprentices most likely to be manumitted. For Barbados, there were considerably more females than males and more non-praedials than praedials. Neither of these figures is surprising, especially considering the preponderance of females as domestics among the apprenticed population. Most of them went through the process of appraisement, the official route for manumission, but a significant proportion were discharged by mutual agreement of the master and the apprentice. A high proportion was also freed voluntarily, that is, without payment.

Where possible, then, many women sought to be fully free. These women often stopped working as field labourers, preferring instead to do domestic work or trade as hucksters. Moreover, women also protested against the apprenticeship system generally. The authorities repeatedly complained about the women apprentices; for example, Governor Sligo wrote home that "it is notorious that they [the women] are all over the Island the most troublesome". Nor did their activities cease in 1834.[3]

There were repeated cases of trouble among women apprentices during the period of apprenticeship. More than a year after the system had been established, one of the special magistrates in British Guiana, A.M. Lyons, reported on the "insubordination" of women apprentices. According to

Table 12.1: Barbados, Number of Apprenticed Labourers Manumitted, 1837

District	M	F	Praed	Non-Praed	By Appraise	By Agree	Volun	Mag	Total
A-Town	155	268	75	348	36	146	241	2	425
A-RURAL	62	71	41	92	56	42	35	2	135
B-RURAL	65	98	59	104	70	31	62	–	163
C-RURAL	70	109	98	81	129	21	29	–	179
D-RURAL	20	26	31	15	45	1	–	–	46
E-RURAL	72	115	78	109	91	36	60	4	191
F-RURAL	22	23	30	15	40	5	–	8	53
G-RURAL	–	2	–	1	1	–	2	–	2
Total	466	712	403	775	467	282	429	16	1,194

Source: CO 28/122, General Return of Appeals of Apprenticed Labourers from the Praedial to the Non-Praedial Class, Barbados, 14 June 1838. Reproduced as in original.

Lyons, on plantation Kitty: ". . . about twenty-five women, apprenticed labourers, conducted themselves in a most unruly manner, in attempting to rescue four men convicted by me of conspiring not to perform their work, and sentenced to be punished by whipping."[4] Asked whether this was part of a conspiracy or combination, Lyons reported that "on plantation Kitty, the women have attempted to set all authority at defiance; the whole have combined together not to perform their work."[5]

Later in the same year, there were complaints elsewhere in British Guiana about "idle and disorderly apprentices", most of whom were women. In early 1836, special magistrate Lyon again reported on the behaviour of women on two plantations. On one, the women were very rude to those in authority and, on the second, some of the pregnant women pretended to be ill and would do no work. In another case, the whole gang of women refused to work "in consequence of some women having been required to go to their work after having been discharged by the medical attendant".[6]

Similar cases were also reported in Jamaica. Two observers who were sent by the Society of Friends to assess apprenticeship, John Sturge and Thomas Harvey, reported on a series of abuses of women apprentices.

In one incident, on an estate near Falmouth, police were called to quell a disturbance among the nursing mothers. The women had refused to come to work before breakfast, "as it was very wet, and they were obliged to carry their children into the fields with them".[7] Brought before the special magistrate, the apprentices were sentenced to work six extra Saturdays. They explained the difficulties this would cause, as the women devoted Saturdays to tending their provision grounds and "without their Saturdays, they had no means of obtaining subsistence. For their contumacy, they were sent to the workhouse for three days, and will still have to work the six Saturdays."[8]

As Mimi Sheller suggests, Sturge and Harvey used such cases to demonstrate how planters exploited apprentices generally and women in particular. The British visitors were particularly sympathetic to the plight of these female apprentices, in part because some of their own support came from metropolitan, middle-class women, many of whom had been involved in anti-slavery campaigns. As Sheller concludes: "The incident demonstrates the women's concerted efforts to resist the plantation labour regime by stopping work, presenting justifications in terms of their need to protect and feed their children, and protesting their lack of subsistence and free time, both of which they had formerly depended on to support their families.[9]

There were good reasons, then, why women were so prominent in the resistance to apprenticeship. As Thomas Holt has pointed out, female apprentices formed the bulk of the field labouring force on the plantations, just as they had during slavery.[10] Regulations about hours and about working practices would therefore have affected women more directly than men. When Golden Grove Estate in Jamaica employed workers on nine-hour shifts, for example, it was women who were the leaders in protesting about these arrangements. The special magistrate for the district reported that "the women always foremost protested against such mode of labour the ringleader of whom I felt obliged to punish by sentence of one month's hard labour."[11] In this particular case, the magistrate released the woman on the promise of good behaviour by the other workers on the estate.[12]

However, the explanation for the role of women as ringleaders against apprenticeship is more complicated than simply numerical predominance. In her article, Mimi Sheller discusses women's role in Jamaica during this period as both workers and mothers. As Sheller suggests, "Unlike their male counterparts, female field labourers could make claims for improved working conditions not simply as free workers, but specifically as mothers who were struggling to support their families." The planters' withdrawal of privileges during apprenticeship impinged directly on women, specifically, those affecting pregnant women, women with children, and the role of elderly matriarchs. "Female apprentices were punished in large numbers for trying to assert and protect the limited rights they had won as mothers of the slave labour force . . ." In the end, the harsh treatment of women rebounded against the planters and helped to discredit the whole apprenticeship scheme and led to its premature abolition in 1838.[13]

POST-EMANCIPATION RIOTS AND RESISTANCE

In the aftermath of emancipation, gender differences were significant. Unlike women, men could become citizens. They could take part in politics. As Sheller has suggested, this was part of expressing their "masculine citizenship".[14] In the case of Jamaica, the franchise requirements remained relatively low until the late 1850s. Although the House of Assembly sought to raise the minimum requirements for the vote, the Colonial Office in London repeatedly disallowed the legislation. The result was that, after 1838, some former enslaved men had the vote and could significantly affect elections to the House of Assembly. This helps to explain the election of brown and black men to the assembly in the post-emancipation period.[15]

Although women did not have the vote, this did not exclude them from expressing their views publicly, and participating in riots and demonstrations during this period. One of the areas that women occupied spatially in the Caribbean was the street. They dominated the markets and many also worked as domestics in towns and cities. As a result, women "played an important part in the development of a politically-active Afro-Jamaican public . . . and filled the streets and squares during popular political mobilizations or demonstrations."[16]

One example of this was women's participation in the John Canoe riots of 1840 and 1841. The riots were in response to the mayor of Kingston attempting to suppress Christmas celebrations centred on cultural practices carried over from slavery. When the police seized the people's drums and made arrests, men and women resisted. One description by a magistrate highlighted the particular role of women: "I saw many stones thrown and glass bottles. They flew about me like hail... I saw women with stones tied up in their petticoats. They supplied the mob with them and threw them themselves."[17] As Swithin Wilmot has noted, other observers described the women as the most violent members of the crowd, who threatened "blood for blood and to lick down the police".[18]

Similarly, women were involved in the Antigua riots of March 1858, which resulted from a confrontation between dockworkers from Antigua and Barbuda. The Antiguans regarded the Barbudans as rivals, taking their jobs at a time of severe economic stagnation. Hundreds of Antiguans in the capital, St John's, joined the riots. They attacked Portuguese Madeirans who had been imported to work on the sugar plantations after emancipation, as well as white planters, and black and mixed-race policemen.

Black women were very involved in the riots. As Natasha Lightfoot has observed, "Women allegedly led angered crowds about the streets, brandished weapons, attacked their designated antagonists, and appeared in their comportment and dress to be 'like men'."[19] Antiguan women attacked Barbudan women and destroyed some of their homes because the Antiguans were concerned about competition from the Barbudans in the markets and for jobs as domestics. Like the men, the women also threw stones at the police station in an unsuccessful attempt to seize arms stored inside. For Lightfoot, then, the women were not bystanders in the Antiguan riots but essential to its spread. They also paid a heavy price for their participation; a few were among the eight people killed, and more than fifty were arrested. Moreover, the description of women acting "like men" was not unique to Antigua. This symbolic masculinization of women was part of the gendered discourse of slavery and the post-emancipation period.[20]

One of the concerns of both free men and women after emancipation was the possibility of re-enslavement. This was the motivating force behind the riots in Dominica in 1844, in response to the authorities' decision to organize a census that year. As Russell Chace has noted, "Almost every affidavit and piece of testimony taken after the protest... points to the same conclusion: that the freed persons firmly believed that they were to be re-enslaved, and that many of them were prepared to resist to the point of death."[21] Initially, free people attacked the census enumerators, then estate property and managers. Although the riots were dominated by men, women also abused the enumerators. As in the cities of Kingston and St John's, women in the capital, Roseau, were involved as well.

Another significant issue for free men and women in the aftermath of emancipation was the problem of low wages and the often-irregular payment of wages. These concerns help to explain the outbreak of the Belmanna riots in Tobago in 1876. The riots occurred on the Roxborough estate, which was owned by a Barbadian who employed many of his compatriots. Some of these workers were apparently involved in arson attacks on the estate. However, when the police arrived to arrest the alleged arsonists, a crowd, including many women, resisted. Corporal Belmanna fired into the crowd, killing a Barbadian woman. He was set upon by the crowd and badly beaten, with the women described as among the "most prominent" of his attackers. Although those arrested for his subsequent death were mostly men, a woman was also found guilty.[22]

Writing about the Belmanna riots, Bridget Brereton has identified low wages as central to understanding the riots. For Brereton, "the complex of grievances that centred on wages, stoppages, and estate shops" were "the common sources of friction behind many post-emancipation disturbances in the Caribbean".[23] This included the Belmanna riots, where a type of debt peonage had been created as a result of the truck system in which many estates had their own shops and planters arbitrarily deducted debts incurred there from wages. For women, whose domestic responsibilities would have included being in charge of the household, these problems would have been severe. It helps to explain their active participation in these riots.

Low wages were also an important element in the riots which occurred in St Croix in 1878. Plantation workers there regarded the labour law that had been established thirty years previously at the time of emancipation as a new form of servitude. When wages for the plantation workers fell below that stipulated in the labour ordinance and far below the wages paid at a new central factory opened in 1878, the workers rioted. Their first target was the police in Frederiksted and then the homes of the most prominent inhabitants in the town. The riots then spread to the countryside. The damage to homes and plantations was extensive and the loss of life very high. At least eighty-four blacks were killed and three whites. Immigrant workers were prominent among the leaders of the "Fireburn", as it was known, one of whom was Mary Thomas from Antigua. Known as Queen Mary, she has been immortalized in song and legend in St Croix for her participation in the riots.[24]

THE MORANT BAY REBELLION

As in St Croix, Tobago and Antigua, many of the same issues were present at Morant Bay. Rebels in this town in the parish of St Thomas, Jamaica, were angry about low wages and the possibility of re-enslavement. In addition, they were bitter about the lopsided and partial judicial system, and not being given access to their provision grounds if they did not pay rent. In the period leading up to and during the Morant Bay Rebellion, men and women protested, often together but sometimes separately.

Men clearly dominated the meetings held just before the outbreak of the rebellion. At one in St Thomas in the East, a rebel leader, James McLaren, protested about the paltriness of wages and how impossible it was to be a man and look after his family: "Why cause me to hold this meeting; myself was born free, but my mother and father was slave; but now I am still a slave by working from days to days. I cannot get money to feed my family, and I am working at Coley estate for 35 chains for 1s., and after five days' working I get 2s.6d. for my family. Is that able to sustain a house full of family?"[25]

The paper owned by George William Gordon, *The Jamaica Watchman and People's Free Press*, had a similar message and exhorted men to act as men: "You are no longer Slaves, but Free men. Then, as Free Men, act your part at the meeting." As Mimi Sheller has observed, this was an example of freedmen's masculinity being "appealed to as a personal and political identity that must be performed actively".[26]

At some of these meetings, McLaren and Bogle sought to recruit men to march into Morant Bay. Men often took an oath at these meetings. Although the oath differed from place to place, one report maintained that it was "to pay no taxes and to kill every buckra in Jamaica".[27] Men were clearly drilled ahead of the confrontation at Morant Bay; moreover, it was clear that McLaren and Bogle expected a violent confrontation between the authorities and the men they were organizing.

When the police sought to arrest Bogle at Stony Gut the day before the rebellion, they saw men acting like soldiers. Although the police had a warrant for Bogle's arrest, he refused to go and shouted for help. Immediately, upwards of three hundred men, armed with cutlasses and sticks, appeared out of the nearby cane fields and the chapel in the village. They then handcuffed the police, who reported witnessing three of Bogle's lieutenants drilling their individual gangs. The men carried sticks, cutlasses and lances, and practised marching in the village. Before being freed, the police learned that Bogle and his men would be coming to Morant Bay the following day.

Before marching to Morant Bay, Bogle and his allies sent a petition to Governor Eyre, complaining about the injustice of the warrants issued against them and proclaimed their innocence. Moreover, they said: "We, therefore, call upon your Excellency for protection, seeing we are Her Majesty's loyal subjects, which protection if refused to will be compelled to put our shoulders to the wheel, as we have been imposed upon for a period of 27 years with due obeisance to the laws of our Queen and country, and we can [no] longer endure the same . . ."[28] The petition was clearly expressed in threatening language. Moreover, the rebels understood freedom in a particular way. They felt "imposed upon", something which they believed should not have been the experience of free men.

When the largely male crowd marched into Morant Bay the following day, they were highly organized. The men marched four abreast, with the women on their flanks. As one observer noted, they "came in rows . . . they were well packed together close behind each other, but not at all straggling; they advanced slowly and deliberately."[29] Though dressed in ordinary labourers' clothes, they looked more like troops than an irregular mob. This was also the case after the burning of the courthouse at Morant Bay. Bogle and his men marched, again in a military fashion, to the district police station to liberate the prisoners in the gaol. Accompanying Bogle were three companies of ten men each, led by three captains. They were ordered to stand guard in various parts of the town.

In the days after the outbreak, Bogle was seen in various places, usually marching with his forces. Nearly a week afterwards, he and several associates signed a document that was a call to war: "It is time now for us to help ourselves. Skin for skin, the iron bars is now broken in this parish, the white people send a proclamation to the governor to make war against us . . . Blow your shells, roal your drums, house to house, take out every man, march them down to Stoney Gut, any that you find in the way takes them down with their arms; war is at us, my black skin, war is at hand from to-day to tomorrow."[30]

Bogle envisioned a battle to be fought by black men against the whites. Moreover, the rebels sought – in vain – to get the backing of the Maroons, whose skill in using guns and tracking their opponents would have been crucial to the success of the rebellion. But while men saw themselves as the soldiers, they did not act alone. Women were also central to the uprising.

Their role in the rebellion was apparent on the march into Morant Bay. Women not only formed part of the crowd proceeding to Morant Bay, but they also encouraged the men along the route. One observer heard women along the road crying out "Flog them John's Town", referring to marchers from a settlement on the way.[31] At Morant Bay, the officials and the militia confronted a stone-throwing crowd in front of the courthouse. As the custos of the parish attempted to read the Riot Act, a volunteer observed a woman he knew named Geoghegan throw the first stone, followed by a hail of stones from other women in the crowd. The members of the militia, as well as the parish officials, retreated into the courthouse but, eventually, the crowd decided that the best method of attack was to burn the building down, and force the volunteers and vestrymen to come out. It is likely that women were responsible for this plan. One witness claimed that a woman named Rosanna Finlayson "said they must go and get a fire stick and trash, and set the school-room on fire. She said the white people were locked up in the courthouse, and if they set fire to the school room the whole people would be burnt up alive."[32] Five minutes later, the school house was on fire. It was adjacent to the courthouse and it was not long before that building began to burn as well.

Women were also instrumental in encouraging the men in the crowd to continue their attack on the courthouse. After the volunteers had fired at the crowd, some men had withdrawn. But women on one of the roads leading into the town reportedly told the men: "Now, you men, this is not what you said in the mountain. You said you would come to the Bay and do so and so, and now you leave all this work to the women; go to the Parade and see what the Volunteers do to the men there."[33]

Women were instructing men to do their manly duty: to act as men and fight the militia who had attacked the rebels at Morant Bay. Women also helped to determine the fate of Charles Price, a prominent black builder who was caught by the crowd after the burning of the school house. They debated what to do with him, largely because of his colour. The women made their point of view very clear, saying, "We work for him on the road and he not pay us, and we burn bricks for the church at Morant Bay, and he not pay us. You need not keep him till before day."[34] Price was then beaten to death, despite offering £200 for his life. These women were reacting to the problem that plagued free people in the aftermath of emancipation: low and irregular pay.

While many women were clearly prominent in the rebellion, others behaved very differently. Some actively helped injured men at Morant Bay. James Moore Ross was a volunteer who, although wounded, tried to escape to the wharf. A woman was helping him when Bogle appeared and threatened to kill Ross. The woman shouted to Bogle, "Don't kill him. He is nearly dead already." Ross managed to get to the wharf and onto a boat and to safety. This was not an isolated incident. For instance, another volunteer, W.W. McGowan, had been badly hurt and left for dead. The crowd had removed his boots, shirt and money. He remained on the ground until the next morning, when a member of the mob came across him, realized he was not dead, and threatened to behead him. A woman whom McGowan did not know offered him a glass of water, but the man threatening the volunteer knocked it out of her hand. She then offered 4s. for McGowan and another wounded volunteer, saying that McGowan was her brother.[35]

In the aftermath of the rebellion and in the face of personal danger, black women sought to protect whites. At Serge Island estate in St Thomas in the East, a headwoman of one of the gangs, Jane Messam, was able to protect the manager, William Miller. As a group of about twenty-five people approached the estate armed with cutlasses, sticks and a gun, Messam hid Miller in a garret. Although the crowd had come "to take Mr Miller's life", she convinced them to return later to deal with him. The crowd turned back, allowing Miller time to escape to Kingston.[36] Elsewhere in the parish, another headwoman, Diana Blackwood, was able to protect the white women and children on Hordley estate. Blackwood hid them in a cane field when the estate came under attack and then took the women and children to her own house the following day. This put Blackwood herself in danger when the crowd realized what she had done.[37] In both of these cases, it was headwomen who helped to save the lives of whites. Class allegiances may help to explain the role of elite blacks in protecting white managers and their families. But this alone did not account for the actions of many women who responded in a similar way during the rebellion.

In the end, women paid a high price for their involvement in the rebellion. Seven were hanged, including Geoghegan, who threw the first stone at Morant Bay. As in Antigua in 1858, women were demonized for their role in the rebellion. This suggests a deep-seated fear of their potential political influence.[38] However, women suffered in other ways as well as a result of the Morant Bay Rebellion. Jenny Jemmott has documented the extreme trauma suffered by women who lost sons, husbands and fathers. Women not only suffered the emotional trauma of losing kin, but also the severe economic consequences of life without the main provider in the family. Since more than a thousand houses were destroyed, many women lost their homes and, often, all their material possessions. In light of the severity of the repression in the wake of the rebellion, it is not surprising that some women were also raped. Jemmott rightly suggests that rape would have been used as a punitive measure in suppressing the rebellion.[39]

Ultimately, patriarchy remained dominant. Unlike women, some men could participate in politics and enjoy the fruits of citizenship. This meant not only voting and serving on juries, but also petitioning the authorities, as in the case of Bogle and the other rebel leaders. Women were denied these rights in the post-emancipation Caribbean. Yet, in their own way, as Swithin Wilmot has suggested, freed women "played an important part in the politics of the black community, thereby maintaining the tradition they had established in slave society as 'persistent rebels'".[40]

NOTES

1. Pamela Scully and Diana Paton, eds., *Gender and Slave Emancipation in the Atlantic World* (Durham, NC: Duke University Press, 2005), 3.
2. The most comprehensive treatment of apprenticeship remains W.L. Burn, *Emancipation and Apprenticeship in the British West Indies* (London: Jonathan Cape, 1937). See also William A. Green, *British Slave Emancipation: The Sugar Colonies and the Great Experiment, 1830–1865* (Oxford: Clarendon Press, 1976); and "The Apprenticeship in British Guiana, 1834–1838," *Caribbean Studies* 9 (1969): 44–66; Thomas C. Holt, *The Problem of Freedom: Race,*

Labor, and Politics in Jamaica and Britain, 1832–1938 (Baltimore: Johns Hopkins University Press, 1992); Douglas Hall, "The Apprenticeship Period in Jamaica, 1834–1838," *Caribbean Quarterly* 3 (December 1953): 142–66; Swithin Wilmot, "Not 'Full Free': The Ex-Slaves and the Apprenticeship System in Jamaica, 1834–1838," *Jamaica Journal* 17 (1984): 2–10; W.K. Marshall, "Apprenticeship and Labour Relations in Four Windward Islands," in *Abolition and Its Aftermath: The Historical Context,* ed. David Richardson (London: Frank Cass, 1985), 203–24; Demetrius L. Eudell, *The Political Languages of Emancipation in the British Caribbean and the U.S. South* (Chapel Hill: University of North Carolina Press, 2002); Diana Paton, *No Bond but the Law: Punishment, Race, and Gender in Jamaican State Formation, 1780–1870* (Durham, NC: Duke University Press, 2004).

3. CO 137/194, Sligo to Spring Rice, 9 December 1834, no. 91.
4. British Parliamentary Papers (hereafter PP), 1836 (166-II), Part III, vol. 49, Smyth to Glenelg, 12 November 1835, no. 249, encl: Epitome of the monthly reports from special magistrates in British Guiana for October 1835.
5. ibid.
6. Smyth to Glenelg, 13 December 1835, no. 255, encl: Epitome of the monthly reports from special magistrates in British Guiana for November, 1835; Smyth to Glenelg, 28 January 1836, no. 257, encl: Epitome of the monthly reports from special magistrates in British Guiana for December 1835.
7. John Sturge and Thomas Harvey, *The West Indies in 1837* (London: Hamilton, Adams and Company, 1838), 200.
8. Sturge and Harvey, *West Indies in 1837,* 201.
9. Mimi Sheller, "Quasheba, Mother, Queen: Black Women's Public Leadership and Protest in Postemancipation Jamaica, 1834–1865," *Slavery & Abolition: A Journal of Slave and Post-Slave Studies* 19 (December 1998): 95.
10. Holt, *Problem of Freedom,* 64
11. CO 137/194, Sligo to Spring Rice, 9 December 1834, no. 91.
12. ibid.
13. Sheller, "Quasheba, Mother, Queen," 93–94. See also the important discussion of this issue in Bridget Brereton, "Family Strategies, Gender, and the Shift to Wage Labour in the British Caribbean," in *Gender and Slave Emancipation,* ed. Pamela Scully and Diana Paton (Durham, NC: Duke University Press, 2005), 143–61.
14. Mimi Sheller, "Acting as Free Men: Subaltern Masculinities and Citizenship in Postslavery Jamaica", in *Gender and Slave Emancipation,* ed. Pamela Scully and Diana Paton (Durham, NC: Duke University Press, 2005), 86.
15. Gad J. Heuman, *Between Black and White: Race, Politics and the Free Coloreds in Jamaica, 1792–1865* (Westport, CT: Greenwood Press, 1981), 117–20.

16. Sheller, "*Quasheba, Mother*, Queen," 103.
17. Swithin Wilmot, "Females of Abandoned Character? Women and Protest in Jamaica, 1838–65," in *Engendering History: Caribbean Women in Historical Perspective*, ed. Verene Shepherd, Bridget Brereton, and Barbara Bailey (Kingston: Ian Randle Publishers, 1995), 287.
18. Wilmot, "Abandoned Character," 287.
19. Natasha Lightfoot, "'Their Coats were Tied Up like Men': Women Rebels in Antigua's 1858 Uprising,'", *Slavery & Abolition: A Journal of Slave and Post-Slave Studies* 31 (December 2010): 528.
20. Lightfoot, "'Their Coats were Tied Up," 530, 536.
21. Russell Chace, Jr, "Protest in Post-Emancipation Dominica: The 'Guerre Negre' of 1844," *Journal of Caribbean History* 23, no. 2 (1989): 129.
22. Bridget Brereton, "Post-Emancipation Protest in the Caribbean: The 'Belmanna Riots' in Tobago, 1876," *Caribbean Quarterly* 30, nos. 3/4 (1984): 114.
23. ibid., 115.
24. George F. Tyson, "'Our Side': Caribbean Immigrant Labourers and the Transition to Free Labour on St. Croix, 1849–79," in *Small Islands, Large Questions: Society, Culture and Resistance in the Post-Emancipation Caribbean*, ed. Karen Fog Olwig (London: Frank Cass, 1995), passim; for Mary Thomas, 149.
25. PP, 1866 (3683-1, XXXI, *Report of the Jamaica Royal Commission, Part II, Minutes of Evidence and Appendix* (hereafter JRC), Evidence of William Anderson, 165.
26. Sheller, "Acting as Free Men," 90.
27. Gad Heuman, *The Killing Time: The Morant Bay Rebellion in* Jamaica (London, Macmillan Caribbean, 1994), 82. The following discussion is taken from *The Killing Time*.
28. PP, 1866 (3683), XXX, JRC, 14.
29. Heuman, *Killing Time*, 3.
30. CO 884/2, Confidential Print, no. 2: Papers Relating to the Insurrection in Jamaica, October, 1865, Printed for the Use of the Cabinet, December, 1865, 23.
31. JRC, Evidence of Arthur Warmington, 57–58.
32. PP (3682), XXX, Papers Laid before the Royal Commission of Inquiry By Governor Eyre (hereafter Papers), In the Special Commission, 7 March 1866; The Queen v. Bogle and Henry Theophilus and others for Felonious Riot, Evidence of Charlotte Carter, 360.
33. JRC. Evidence of Cecilia Gordon, 180.
34. Papers, Statement of Arthur Warmington, 168.

35. Heuman, *Killing Time*, 12–13.
36. JRC, Evidence of Jane Messam, 972; Evidence of William C. Miller, 62, 919.
37. JRC, Evidence of Joseph Wood, 846; Evidence of Diana Blackwood, 847.
38. Sheller, "Quasheba, Mother, Queen," 111.
39. Jenny M. Jemmott, *Ties That Bind: The Black Family in Post-Slavery Jamaica, 1834–1882* (Kingston: University of the West Indies Press, 2015), chapter 5.
40. Wilmot, "Abandoned Character," 292.

[13]

INCLUSION/EXCLUSION
Women, Citizenship and Political Franchise in
Early Twentieth-Century Trinidad and Tobago

[RHODA REDDOCK]

THE STRUGGLE FOR THE FRANCHISE IN TRINIDAD AND Tobago can never really be examined separately from the struggle for representative government. Indeed, in the colonial post-slavery/post-indentureship context, such struggles were part and parcel of wider battles for citizenship, national self-government and self-determination. The struggle for women's franchise was, therefore, part of a complex interweave of identity politics through which women of different classes, colours and ethnicities sought to claim their limited rights of citizenship within the colonial context of the early half of the twentieth century. This struggle traversed a tortuous route, eventually coming into being as part of a package of welfare-oriented reforms in the post-World War II period. This contradictory offering came into conflict with local women's movements' demands for their economic autonomy, based on a tradition where the housewife role was not as fully developed and universally accepted. The result was the imposition of a notion of citizenship that contrasted greatly with women's aspirations. During the early twentieth century, nationalist sentiment in the Anglophone Caribbean combined a commitment to the "West Indies" with an identification with Africa or India at a time when these two continents were also under colonial rule. As noted by Kumari Jayawardena, for other parts of the colonial world at this time, movements for women's emancipation "were acted out against a background of nationalist struggles" aimed at "political independence, asserting national identity and modernizing society".[1]

One of the newer settlements of the British Empire, Trinidad (not Tobago), unlike its counterparts in other parts of the British Caribbean, was established as a "pure" Crown colony and had never been granted an elected system of government. Conquered by the British in 1797, after close to three hundred years of Spanish rule, it had a relatively small population of Spanish colonialists and capuchin monks, who extracted labour from the mainly indigenous population and did not have a developed plantation system. Large-scale French Catholic migration of planters and slaves from French colonies[2] was encouraged through a 1783 Cedula of Population, which provided lands previously occupied by indigenous peoples. Tobago, on the other hand, was settled much earlier by the British, although it changed hands on many occasions among them, the French and the Dutch. A representative system of government had existed since 1768, a situation which continued until 1877, when a Crown colony system, similar to that established in Trinidad, was instituted.[3] Due to economic difficulties, the impact of the Belmanna Riots and the prerogatives of the British colonists, Tobago was made a ward of the colony of Trinidad and Tobago by an 1898 Order in Council, a situation that was deeply wounding to most Tobagonians.[4]

The use of the term "representative government" to describe the system of assemblies in the British colonial territories is problematic. Certainly, women could not be members of these assemblies, but the majority of the population was also excluded. In relation to Tobago, for example, Bridget Brereton noted that, unlike Trinidad, Tobago had enjoyed the "dubious blessings" of a "British constitution". After cession to Britain in 1763, an assembly had been established, elected by the white landowners, and this assembly had survived into the post-emancipation decades. The reality of this, however, was that:

> A small, impoverished island supported nine privy councilors, seven members of the legislative council (the nominated 'Upper House') and sixteen elected representatives in the assembly. But the electorate was a minute fraction of the population; in 1857 it only numbered 102 people; after franchise reform in 1860 the grand total of 215 was reached. Exactly ninety-one people voted in the 1860 elections and two representatives (for St. John and Plymouth) were returned by one voter each. Clearly, the old representative system was a farce in a society like Tobago . . .[5]

Yet, based on the experience of the more prosperous colonies, such as Jamaica and Barbados, the British administrators had become weary of the powers of these local assemblies. By the late nineteenth century, attempts were being made to bring them more in line with the Crown colony system, which was implemented in its pure form in newer colonies like Trinidad. Indeed, in Tobago, which would later become a sister colony to Trinidad at the turn of the century, the battle to preserve the assembly was intense, but the Tobago House of Assembly was abolished by 1876.[6] This proved to be a major issue of concern in relations between Trinidad and Tobago, and a matter of great inconvenience for Tobagonians, especially being made a ward. Many of its heroes – James Biggart, A.P.T. James and others – were advocates of administrative autonomy for Tobago, and from its inception, Tobago's wardship was the basis of numerous petitions.[7]

James believed strongly that Tobago, though disadvantaged by years of neglect by the British government and the central government in Trinidad, was an equal partner in the union and not a subordinate dependent adjunct. He contended that Tobago should have separate representation and a separate voice on all issues and in all forums, even in the parliament of the British West Indies Federation.[8]

The Crown colony system was based on direct rule by the British imperial government through Orders in Council. In anticipation of the onset of emancipation in 1831, a purely nominated legislative council was established in Trinidad, which lasted with few changes until 1924. Until then therefore, no one in Trinidad and Tobago had the franchise and no residents could be elected to public office, except in municipal bodies. This new council comprised "official" members – that is, leading public officials and "unofficial" members – private citizens nominated by the governor from among the "principal proprietors of the colony".[9] Between 1832 and 1862, the number of officials exceeded that of unofficials, thereby ensuring the governor's control over the council's decisions.

One justification for the maintenance of the Crown colony system in Trinidad and Tobago was its diverse character. This was reported by the 1921 Wood Commission, which described it as ". . . more difficult than . . . any other colony", because of the racial complexity and divisions in the society.[10] In addition to its prior history of settlement by the First Peoples, Spanish colonists, French white and coloured planters with small numbers of enslaved Africans; British officials, planters and enslaved Africans were added at the end of the eighteenth century. In the nineteenth century, new labour migrations introduced Chinese and Portuguese (Madeirans) indentured labourers, free Africans who were in the minority, and Indian[11] indentured labourers, who were in the majority. In discussing this diversity, Tobago's relationship with Trinidad is often omitted. However, this also complicated governance in the Crown colony. As a newer plantation economy also, it attracted continuous streams of migration from other British Caribbean territories, especially Barbados and Grenada, as well as neighbouring Venezuela. At the turn of the century, *The Trinidadian* newspaper was published in three languages – English, French and Spanish. In this context, state efforts to establish British (over French) cultural and English language hegemony were reflected in a strong anglicizing policy in many areas of life. This diversity was, of course, extremely hierarchical and as a former slave society, notions of unequal access to citizenship were accepted. Struggles for reform always took place within the context of this diversity, with discourses on who should be included and excluded, and on what basis. Efforts to extend the franchise to women and specific groups of women, therefore, occurred alongside those of other groups, and sub-groups, all seeking recognition as citizens. Additionally, women of different groupings – class, colour, ethnicity, religion, national background, and intersections of these – were very unevenly located.

THE REFORM MOVEMENT

While there is evidence of women's interest in the movements for reform of the Crown colony system in the late nineteenth and early twentieth centuries, the issue of franchise for women was seldom publicly entertained. Male reformers, "French and British creoles", and coloured and black professionals, attacked their non-representation on the council and its facilitation of narrow planter/merchant interests.[12] This mobilization was heightened around the period of the 1887 Royal Franchise Commission, set up to "consider whether Trinidad was ready for elected members in the council and if so to recommend a suitable franchise". A majority recommendation for the introduction of a limited franchise with high property qualifications and a literacy test in English for persons over forty was rejected by the Colonial Office. Instead, a concession was made to limit the term of unofficials to five years instead of life. This recommendation, if accepted, would have resulted in an electorate of less than 6 per cent of the total population.[13]

The reform movement continued with petitions, public meetings and delegations to London. The organizations involved included the early Workingmen's Association and Workingmen's Reform Club, operating initially under the umbrella of the Ratepayers Association (RPA) and later, the Legislative Reform Committee (LRC). With the exception of the Trinidad Workingmen's Association (TWA), which had the long-term goal of widening the franchise, the aims of this early reform movement were quite moderate. According to Brereton, the reformers all opposed universal adult suffrage and did not envisage a fully elected council. One of the main leaders of the 1890s, Henry Alcazar, stated in 1897: "It had not been proposed to place power in the hands of the working classes, but only in those of the wealthier middle classes".[14]

While the main public actors were men, evidence shows that women members of these organizations, especially the labour-oriented TWA, were very much involved. One source suggests that due to the influence of the Pan-African Association of Henry Sylvester Williams, which paid much attention to the mobilization of women, increasing numbers of them began attending meetings of the RPA.[15] For example, a secret police report of a mass meeting held by the TWA in the Queen's Park Savannah on 16 October 1912, noted that among the two thousand-strong crowd, there were "a fair number of coolies, and 50 or 60 women respectably dressed".[16] Another confidential dispatch, dated 21 November 1921, included a list of people who attended an important meeting on representative government at the Prince's Building in August 1921. This list included names of a number of middle-class women, including Mrs and Miss Jeffers, as well as that of Miss Husbands, an active member of the TWA.[17] It is interesting the ways in which persons who were not even being considered for inclusion in the proposed reform process were mobilized in its cause. One of the best examples of this was the Water Riots of 1903.

THE 1903 WATER RIOTS

Working-class women contributed significantly to the reform process – overtly in working-class organizations such as the Trinidad Workingmen's

Association and the Negro Welfare Cultural and Social Association (NWCSA), but also in indirect but no less forceful ways as in the Water Riots of 1903, which dealt a major blow against Crown colony government.

Dissatisfaction with this system was heightened in 1899 with the abolition of the Port of Spain Borough Council. The capital and seat of the legislature was also the main location of the reform movement activities. In the wake of this demise, the Ratepayers Association was formed to monitor the government's spending of taxpayers' money. The water issue was mainly of concern to the wealthy classes since the majority had no access to running water. Most people accessed water free of charge from surrounding springs or, for the fortunate few, a communal standpipe.

Efforts by the Director of Public Works to introduce a new Waterworks Bill were the latest attempts to control water use by the "better classes" of the city. The proposed imposition of new controls was seen as yet another imposition of Crown colony government, and mobilization against the proposed bill took place in the *Port of Spain Gazette,* which made it a common cause with all classes, including those who would not be affected. According to one source, informal lobbying of domestics, cooks and washers by employers fuelled the public fear of the impending legislation. This was confirmed by the Commission of Enquiry into the riots, which found that many of the poor, including the washerwomen – working class women who would "take out" washing and return them cleaned, starched and ironed for a fee – had been led to believe that their water supply would be reduced and those who paid less than $4 per month in rent would get no water.[18]

Public mass meetings on this issue were held and by 23 March 1903, the day the bill was due to be read in the council chamber, riots broke out. Symbolically, it was during these riots that the original Red House, the seat of the legislature and symbol of Crown colony government, was destroyed by fire. From all reports, working-class women and their children were the main participants in these riots. Numerous reports provide different versions of the riots being started by women. According to an eyewitness: "Coming up the street between the Building and the square was a moderate crowd of women and children dancing and singing. As they reached the cross street, they began throwing stones at the Audit Office windows, which they succeeded in breaking."[19]

The Honourable H.A. Alcazar, in his evidence before the commission of enquiry into the disturbances, disclosed that: "... the first people who threw stones were a number of women and boys. Who were these women and boys? I submit you can come to no other conclusion than that the women and boys who threw stones were people who derive their living from washing clothes and people who were highly indignant at the conduct of the government" (Minutes of the Commission 1903, 1036).[20]

While the "respectable classes" were debating in the council chamber, the working classes were fighting their battles outside in the streets. By 2:30 p.m. the Red House was on fire. All the council members managed to escape. The Riot Act was read and the police and their reinforcements began to shoot. In the end, sixteen persons (four women) were killed and fifty-one injured. Of the wounded admitted to hospital, eleven were women, all members of the working classes and independent trades,[21] those considered by the reformers as "uneducated and irresponsible".

Although this was never publicly acknowledged by the colonial authorities, it was generally felt that these riots moved the battle against Crown colony rule one step further. A year later, the governor, Sir Alfred Maloney, and the Colonial Secretary were recalled, and the commission of enquiry recommended greater municipal control over water and sewerage.[22] The governor was also advised to consult more with the unofficials and, in 1904, a black reform activist, C.P. David, was made an unofficial member of the Legislative Council.[23] Indeed, it is in response to this report that Secretary of State Joseph Chamberlain declared his agreement with the recommendation that "... gradually, and at no distant date, there will be not only nominated but also elected members on the Board [Borough Council]."[24] It was truly interesting the ways in which working-class women facilitated a process within which they were never seriously considered to be possible participants.

But this promise was still long in coming. In 1905, conservative members of the Legislative Council rejected the governor's proposal for the phased introduction of an elected borough council over a period of four years. After much agitation, and support from an increased number of reform-minded unofficials in the local legislature, in 1913, the colonial government agreed to restore an elected borough council to Port of Spain. This was a victory for the reform movement. The majority report's recommendations of high property and income qualifications were incorporated into the 1914 Ordinance, which re-established an elected Port of Spain Borough

Council. Women, if qualified, could vote, but were not eligible for election.

From here, the struggle continued for elected representation in the Legislative Council. This was fuelled by increased working-class agitation through the TWA; the now racially conscious soldiers who had returned after World War I; the influence of African-nationalist organizations, such as the Pan-African Association (PAA), started in Trinidad by Barbados-born, Trinidad resident Henry Sylvester Williams;[25] the Garvey movement; and the revolutionary inspiration of the 1917 Bolshevik revolution.[26] Another important influence was the emerging women's movement, which was making its voice heard within the nationalist and labour-oriented organizations, as well as in its own organizations.

In spite of this, however, as late as 1921, the governor was still not convinced and could state the following in a dispatch to the Secretary of State for the Colonies:

> ... the Government of the colony was of the opinion that the demand for direct representation lacked popular support, as it held the view that the great bulk of the people were peasants or agricultural labourers who neither understood nor agreed about the meaning of the change proposed by the gentlemen ... [It] pointed out that the demand was supported by the Creole Negroes and coloured people, many of whom have no settled occupation. They are represented by the educated men of their race and it is the latter who have organized the agitation for a change in the form of government; some of them being actuated simply by racial feelings. The government also asserted that the demand was opposed by the important merchants and planters, especially by the old established French families.[27]

Due to continued representations by those supporting reform, including delegations to Britain by members of the TWA, which was affiliated with the Fabian Society and British Labour Party, in 1921–22, Under-Secretary of State for the Colonies, E.L.F. Wood, visited Trinidad to evaluate the demand for elected representation. Submissions to the Wood Commission reflected the differing class and ethnic interests of the society. In his report, Wood remarked on the political underdevelopment of the area, highlighting the diversity of Trinidad's population and the absence of a "homogeneous public opinion". The population of three hundred and sixty thousand, he reported, included "French creoles", Spanish elements, Chinese, approximately "130,000 East Indians, mainly illiterate", and

African and coloured elements.[28] He noted the absence of a leisured class, which could take an active part in public life.

While the groups associated with the Legislative Reform Committee – including the TWA and the north-based Young Indian Party – supported elected representation, others, such as the Chamber of Commerce, the Agricultural Society and according to Kelvin Singh, the majority of elite south-based Indians and members of the East Indian National Association (ENIA), opposed it: "They argued that the society was a heterogeneous one; that the 'many races resident differed in thought and temperament. The majority of the East Indian community were not sufficiently educated to participate in political affairs, and their rights and privileges would be prejudiced by the election of men who could not appreciate and interpret their desires.'"[29]

They, therefore, preferred to maintain the existing Crown colony system. But there were other Indian groups, such as the central-based, East Indian National Congress (EINC), which, while supporting electoral representation, were of the opinion that: "The communal or proportional form of representative government provides the most adequate safeguards against the danger of East Indians being swamped by West Indians (Malik 1971, 72), by guaranteeing that there would be members of the Legislative Council who would represent the interests of Indians."[30]

While also opposed to a more democratic Constitution, the Tobago Planters Association called for their island to be administered through a commissioner and not a warden. This was rejected by Wood on the grounds that this was an internal matter to be addressed by the Trinidad and Tobago government.[31]

Wood concluded that while the demand for elective representation was far less than its champions professed, it would be unwise not to allow it. He noted that the demand for representative government had a long history and that a considerable proportion of the population was of mixed stock, which, "although coloured in appearance, possess a large fusion of European blood . . ." He reasoned that because there was an acceptance of the British way of life by the Negroes of the West Indies, it would be wise "to build upon the foundations of the remarkable loyalty to the throne".[32] In other words, Trinidad and Tobago's colonials' eligibility for citizenship in the British Empire was evaluated based on their European ancestry. As a result of these recommendations, a Royal Franchise Commission was established in 1922, and following this, the 1924 Constitution, which allowed limited franchise for the first time, came into being. Key issues of debate in the commission's deliberations were the imposition of an English language literacy test and the extension of the franchise to women. The former was seen as an attempt to disenfranchise Indians who qualified, while the latter, after heavy resistance, was accepted by a split decision, but with a higher age qualification. According to Kelvin Singh, the two issues also came together: "There was considerable controversy about whether females should be given the franchise. The chief opponent, A.G. Bell, was apparently motivated by traditional male prejudices against female participation in politics. But the realization that several Indian women who owned small parcels of land in the countryside would be enfranchised was also an undisguised consideration."[33]

Under this Constitution, men over twenty-one, and women over thirty who qualified in their own right were allowed to vote. This was in keeping with UK legislation in 1919, which introduced a similar discriminatory age qualification. Although women were eligible to be voters, as with the Borough Council, they could not be candidates. Voters also had to satisfy the registering officer that they understood spoken English.[34] In addition to the income, property and residence qualifications, candidates had to be male, able to read and write the English language, and registered as a voter.[35] Under this new Constitution, only 6 per cent of the population was eligible to vote in the first national elections after 128 years of colonial rule.[36]

REPRESENTATION, SOCIAL REFORM AND WOMEN'S CITIZENSHIP

It was in this climate of reform that the governor received a delegation of women in September 1925 to discuss the issue of votes for women.[37] But it was not until 1927, however, that at the municipal level, the issue of women's participation in public life really emerged. The mobilization and organization of women for charity and for what could be termed women's interests was evident since the early twentieth century. One example is the late nineteenth to early twentieth century women's self-help movement, comprised mainly of white and "highly coloured" ladies, wives and relatives of colonial officials, merchants and proprietors of the upper classes. These women combined charity with self-help at a time when charitable works brought much prestige to those who could afford to be so involved.

By the early 1920s, organizations of middle-class black and coloured women emerged in Trinidad as well as in other parts of the region. These organizations, influenced by the black nationalist movement of the time, in many ways, saw the advancement of their "race" and sex in the acquisition of the best characteristics of the colonizers. The most important of these in Trinidad and Tobago was the Coterie of Social Workers, founded in 1921 by Audrey Layne Jeffers, a member of a prosperous, landowning black family in St Clair, an elite residential area in the capital. Jeffers had received higher education in England, where she had been one of the founders of the Union of Students of African Descent, later, the League of Coloured Peoples. During World War I, she had served among the West African troops and started a West African Soldiers Fund.[38]

Although a charitable organization of women aimed at women, the Coterie's activities reflected the feminist concerns of its founder and members. These included: day-care centres for children of wage-earning mothers; "breakfast sheds" – a system of school feeding throughout the country for poor children; a tired mothers' rest – a beach rest facility for women (where no men or children were allowed!); working women's hostels in Port of Spain; petitioning; and lobbying for education for girls, and legislative reform such as the Bastardy Ordinance. The Coterie collaborated with the Fabian socialist oriented TWA, benefitting greatly from the support of its leader, Captain Arthur Andrew Cipriani, then mayor of Port of Spain. For example, in 1936, just one year after the protracted seven to eight-year battle for women (who fulfilled the high qualifications) to be eligible for election to the Port of Spain Municipal Council,[39] Cipriani hosted a visit by Susan Lawrence, former member of the British parliament, and organizer of the National Federation of Women Workers in Britain, as a guest of the TWA. In welcoming Lawrence at a mayor's reception, Cipriani noted that: "Only within the past twelve months has it been made possible for women to obtain a seat around this table. I hope your presence will put a new spirit and a new sentiment in these women and they will realize that there is plenty good valuable work for women today around this table."[40]

In her response, Lawrence urged women to take advantage of the opportunity offered. She stated, "I was introduced to Councillor after Councillor, and I looked for another woman and I could not find any" and went on to express her hope that when she returned this situation would have changed.[41]

Also in 1936, the First Conference of British West Indies and British Guiana Women Social Workers was hosted by the Coterie in Trinidad and Tobago to mark its fifteenth anniversary. Held in April, and attended by delegates from British Guiana, Barbados, Grenada and St Lucia, it was hailed as the "First Intercolonial Conference of Women in the West Indies" and culminated with the formation of the British West Indies and British Guiana Women Social Workers Association. Throughout the conference, a speaking ban was placed on all men who attended. It was temporarily lifted for one evening when Jeffers announced that "men will be permitted to say a few words" but would not be allowed to ask questions.[42] The speeches made at the conference reflected the concerns of the women for recognition, and social and political rights. Their concern for the poor and the centrality of social work to their political ambitions was always evident.

In her opening address, Jeffers called for a regional federation of women social workers to form closer intercolonial bonds in matters of educational, political and social interest and for loosening insular ties. Beatrice Greig, white feminist and labour activist, in her speech entitled "The New Age and Women's Place Within it", highlighted the fear of the power of women's minds in modern society, as typified in the writings of Schopenhauer and his followers, but concluded that it was only the influence of the woman's mind, when put to use for the good of humanity above self that could ensure the future of the human race.[43]

In her presentation, Mrs George Masson, wife of the Medical Officer of Health, noted that up to the present, the women of Trinidad and Tobago had not shown themselves to be politically minded, but this was not surprising, as up till then they had no political background. She called on women to lay the foundation for future generations of women. Concretely, she called for the inclusion of women on the Housing Commission as "no one was more directly interested in the home than the housewife"; for the voting age of women to be lowered from thirty to twenty-one, as for men; and for women to be eligible for seats on the Legislative Council as they were now eligible for seats on the City Council.[44]

The two-week conference ended with a call for the greater participation of women not only in welfare activities but also on official committees and boards, and municipal and legislative councils. The *Sunday Guardian*, while acknowledging the conference's success in "making the public aware that women in the colonies have other ambitions besides those of darning socks and cooking", hoped that it would encourage them to take a more active part in political and social work. Indeed, women were even blamed for the fact that no women councillors were on the Legislative Council.[45] As we would see, however, it would be some time before this came to pass.

THE MOVE TO UNIVERSAL ADULT SUFFRAGE AND THE INTRODUCTION OF THE WELFARE STATE

Between 1925 and 1946, the majority of the population were unable to vote in national elections. Nevertheless they "influenced elections by disrupting meetings, heckling opponents and cheering popular candidates, especially in Port of Spain, and through the leadership and organization of the TWA".[46] They were also able to affect developments through their actions on the estates and the streets as in the labour disturbances of 1934 and 1937. Labour and related activism during the post-World War I depression culminated in mass upheavals in the south and north in June 1937, led by Tubal Uriah "Buzz" Butler and his British Empire Workers and Citizens Home Rule Party in the south, and the Negro Welfare, Cultural and Social Association (NWCSA) in the north. Throughout the region labour disturbances were taking place in that decade, first on Trinidad's sugar estates in 1934, and culminating in Jamaica in 1938.

From 1938 to 1939, therefore, the West India Royal Commission (WIRC), led by Lord Moyne and popularly known as the Moyne Commission, travelled throughout the region with the mandate to "investigate social and economic conditions . . . and matters connected herewith and to make recommendations".[47] Unlike other royal commissions, this WIRC included two women, Dame Rachel Crowdy and Dr Mary Blacklock, who raised questions related to women during the interviews. Among the memoranda received by the Moyne Commission was one from women's organizations led by the Coterie of Social Workers. In a document entitled "The Problems of Women and Children of the Colony", three main areas were emphasized

– girls' education, women's employment, and colour discrimination and political rights. They began: "We, the women of Trinidad associated with the Coterie of Social Workers and various organisations, wish to call the attention of the Royal Commission to the undermentioned subjects pertaining to the welfare of women and children of the island . . ."[48]

They went on to call for the establishment of a girls' college (secondary school) with qualified teachers, at which girls could be more adequately prepared to compete for the Island Scholarship; an independent girls' scholarship at a lower intellectual standard for those who wanted to pursue specialized nursing, music, secretarial work, domestic science, farming and scientific dressmaking; the institution of a school of home economics for women who had had no previous opportunity to acquire this valuable education; and a vocational school for girls. In relation to employment, they called for some mechanism, such as examinations or a board to prevent colour discrimination in the appointment of female teachers; improved wages and conditions for shop assistants and clerks; improvement in the status of local nurses (vis à vis the British nurses who usually occupied the senior positions); the protection of the independent trades of women – dressmaking and laundering; and expressed concern over the problem of homeless young women, calling for women police to operate as rescue workers. They reiterated their call for the Bastardy Ordinance to compel fathers to support their illegitimate children. In the area of political rights, they called for the removal of the prohibition of women on the Legislative Council; for women to be appointed as jurors in cases where women were on trial; and for women to be appointed on all boards in connection with housing and the welfare of children.[49]

Also making submissions to the WIRC on franchise and representation issues were the elected members of the Legislative Council. In their memorandum they recommended the following: that all unofficial members of the Legislative Council be elected; that electoral districts be re-divided to permit an increase in the number of representatives; that officials comprise no more than the existing number; that women be eligible as candidates for election to the legislature on the same terms as men; and that qualification for voters should be reduced by at least 50 per cent and progressively, with the view to instituting adult franchise.[50] The Negro Welfare, Cultural and Social Association,[51] a socialist-oriented, pan-Africanist, working-class organization with a significant female membership, for its part, prepared its own constitution in 1938, which was submitted as a memorandum of constitutional reform to Malcolm Macdonald, Secretary of State for the Colonies. Signatories to this document included two women, Elma Francois, organizing secretary, and Adelaide Harrison, financial secretary. This memorandum received no response from the colonial powers. It had called for the widening of the franchise and the removal of non-elected members.[52]

The commission, in its report, generally agreed with the principle of universal adult suffrage. The commissioners, however, could not agree on whether it should be immediate or gradual. They also recommended the establishment of a fully representative local franchise committee to consider the extension of the franchise for both local and central government. They proposed that: "Such committees should keep in close touch with their counterparts in other West Indian colonies, and should consider carefully whether, as is strongly desirable, that their recommendations would assure substantial equality as between the sexes."[53]

In the section on the "Status of Women", the commissioners reported that women could take little part in the administration of the Caribbean colonies, as few of them met the income and property qualifications to vote. Additionally, they noted that in three colonies, eligible women exercised the vote at an older age than men, and up to that point, only one woman was a member of a municipal council.[54] They concluded:

16. In this connection the position of women should come under review. At present, in some Colonies women are debarred from registration as electors, while in others the age at which women become eligible for the vote differs from that prescribed for men.

17. All such discrimination between the sexes should certainly be abolished but even the grant of votes to women on the same terms as men would not, in the circumstances prevailing in the West Indies, result in the enfranchisement of any large number of women. This is one of the considerations which have influenced the members of the Royal Commission who advocate the immediate introduction of universal suffrage. Those of us who dissent from that proposal consider that the situation can be met to some extent by the grant of a vote to the wives of registered voters.[55]

In relation to increasing women's representation in the Legislative Council, the commissioners suggested that one way to do so was for governors to make "wise use of the power to nominate members to Council". They noted that: "Women are just beginning to take part in the public affairs in the West Indies and as will be clear from other passages in this report, many reforms are needed on which their advice might be of considerable value. Where representation of those interests has not been secured through elections to the Legislative Council, the Governor should bear in mind the possibility of nominating a woman to that body."[56]

The Moyne Commission and the subsequent Colonial Development and Welfare Programme (introduced in the 1940s) were the key mechanisms through which the welfare state operations of post-war British governance were introduced into the Anglophone Caribbean. The tension identified by Carole Pateman as "Wollestonecraft's Dillemma" was very evident in its recommendations. Pateman argues that the patriarchal understanding of citizenship did not allow for the special needs of women – for example, as mothers in the family – to be combined with participation in public life. Therefore, the welfare state, as it was conceived and institutionalized, was unable to grant full citizenship to women and simultaneously take care of their special 'welfare' needs as mothers.[57]

The demands of the women's organizations, however, did not reflect much of this tension. The Coterie, in its welfare activities, sought to relieve women of much of their childcare responsibility, and indeed was more concerned with making women economically self-sufficient than with making demands for special provisions to facilitate their family responsibilities. While the Moyne Commission represented a positive force in its recommendation for the expansion of the franchise, through its other recommendations, it encouraged the establishment of a welfare state system based on the premise that women were dependents and housewives, located primarily in the family.

Due to the exigencies of World War II, the final report was published in 1945. In the meantime, however, summary recommendations were made available. In May 1941, a local Franchise Committee, made up of thirty-three members, was established "to investigate . . . the desirability of the extension of the franchise and . . . the reduction in the margin between qualification for registration and election to the enlarged house".[58] In the meantime, a few changes were made to the composition of the Legislative and Executive Councils to increase the number of elected members. Of the thirty-three members of the Franchise Committee, four were women – Marceline Archibald, Ada Atherly, Audrey Jeffers and Mrs R.M. Scott; four trade union representatives; and four labour-oriented members. The majority were conservative unofficials, for example, the chair, L.A.P. O'Reilly. The committee's deliberations lasted three years, with much debate and manoeuvring in relation to the various and intersecting concerns of race, class and gender, which confronted the colony at that time. Its report was finally presented in 1944.

The majority report recommended the immediate granting of adult suffrage to all adults twenty-one years and over, not legally incapacitated and able to understand spoken English. This motion was carried by a majority of one. A minority report, of the sixteen who voted against, which included the chair, recommending income and property qualifications was also submitted. Two of the four women on the committee voted against universal adult suffrage. They were Audrey Jeffers and Marceline Archibald. In this regard, Jeffers' famous words were "We must hasten slowly", an example of the class contradictions that affected women of Jeffers' class. While she had advocated on behalf of women and developed welfare services for the poor among them, it is clear that her relationship with the latter was more one of charity than solidarity. This is only one instance where her class concerns outweighed her interest in welfare and democracy.

In 1924, the main debate emerging from this report related to the inclusion of the English language test. This was perceived by the majority of the Indian population as aimed at their disenfranchisement. An Indian member of the Franchise Committee, Adrian Cola Rienzi, felt particularly betrayed by his labour counterparts, some of whom had voted in favour of this condition. He denounced this as a deliberate effort to disenfranchise older Indians, who had not had opportunities for formal education. This recommendation was vigorously opposed by Indian activists locally and in petitions to the colonial government. Public meetings were held and Indian-oriented publications, such as *The Observer*, raised the issue. *Al Azan*, described as "An Organ Devoted to the Cause of Islam", edited by the Islamic reformer Moulvi Ameer Ali, highlighted the impact on rural women:

> The Majority Committee recommended that Adult Franchise should be granted to the people of the Colony; but it is regrettable and to their utter shame, the Committee included in their report a clause which has come to be known

as the Language Test. In other words, the recommendation that every man or woman who is a British subject will have the right to vote, providing that he or she can understand the English Language when spoken. Why has this clause been inserted? The answer is readily given by the reaction to it by the Indian community . . . If this method of franchise were to be introduced here, the Indian section, particularly the women of rural villages, would be mostly affected through no fault of theirs.[59]

After much debate and protests, the Secretary of State for the Colonies instructed the governor to use his reserve power to pass the legislation without the language test. In 1945, through a special Order in Council, the language requirement was removed and universal suffrage granted to all adults in Trinidad and Tobago over twenty-one, but income and property qualifications were maintained for candidates.[60]

In 1946, the first general election under adult suffrage was held. With this, Trinidad and Tobago[61] entered into the era of mass electoral politics and 46 per cent of the population registered as voters. For the first time since the Audrey Jeffers campaign for the Port of Spain City Council in 1936, the women's vote was actively pursued. Politicians made it their business to elicit the support of prominent women, especially those in women's organizations, to arrange meetings at which they could speak. From all reports, they participated actively in the campaigns. In addition to organizing meetings, they spoke on political platforms, raised funds and did other behind-the-scenes tasks. On election day, women were the focus of attention, with the *Trinidad Guardian* reporting the day after that: ". . . Women showed equal interest with men in yesterday's first polling under universal adult suffrage . . . Hitherto women did not vote on equal terms with men, they had to be 30 years old before they could exercise the franchise." Now, "[it exulted] everybody votes at 21 and there is no discrimination on account of sex."[62]

However, no candidates were women. This was remarked upon by a letter writer to the *Sunday Guardian*, "Interested", who remarked that "It must occur as something significant that women are not represented in the new Legislative Council, having regard to the role played by women in the polls."[63] It was in anticipation of this that the WIRC report had proposed that in such an eventuality, the governor should use his prerogative to nominate a woman to the council. This was done, and in 1946, Audrey Jeffers was nominated by Governor John Shaw to the first Legislative Council in the era of adult franchise, the first woman to serve in this position.

Six months after being sworn in, Jeffers was able to give her strong support to the resolution moved by Roy Joseph for "equal pay for equal work" for women teachers. In her contribution she asserted that women of Trinidad and Tobago, like women all over the world, had fully justified their claims, adding that no education system was complete without women teachers. She contended that compared to men, women "do more work, better work and more dependable work", and concluded by advising those members of the council who owed their successful election campaigns to women's votes in the first adult franchise election to show their gratitude by supporting this resolution.[64]

REFINING THE CONSTITUTION

Almost immediately after the 1946 election, dissatisfaction with the 1945 constitutional amendments surfaced. In response, a twenty-five-member Constitutional Reform Committee was established, comprising mainly unofficials of the Legislative Council and L.A.P. O'Reilly again as chair. Three of the twenty-five members were women – Audrey Jeffers, Beryl Archibald-Crichlow and Mrs R.M. Scott. The issue of self-government or 'home rule' was uppermost in the minds of many people, especially those in the working-class organizations of the time. These included the NWCSA, but also Butler's British Empire, Workers and Citizen's Home Rule Party, which had led the disturbances of the 1930s.

The 1948 majority report of the committee signed by most of the unofficials, including the three women, did not recommend home rule or 'responsible government'. In a minority report, Patrick Solomon, a liberal/socialist, attacked the conservative composition of the committee, including the three women, and described them using Jeffers' terminology as "undisguised supporters of the status quo and the notaries of the 'hasten slowly' cult".[65] Through his Caribbean Socialist party, he campaigned for the rejection of the report. One such meeting held in Woodford Square was reported to have been attended by "a huge crowd including many women . . ."[66] In another minority report, Ranjit Kumar, while agreeing that the committee was unrepresentative, did not advocate immediate responsible government. As a member of a minority group, he felt that the Crown and the nominated principle were needed as a buffer between the two ethnic groups. He was fearful of self-government by a party of the majority ethnic group.[67]

Working class and labour-oriented resistance to the new Constitution was substantial. Working-class women activists, such as Christina Lewis, a member of the Butler Movement who later founded the Caribbean Women's National Assembly, joined with others to condemn it. On the issue of the Constitution, she had this to say:

> As a woman and West Indian I feel happy at times to see two members of my sex on our local Legislatures, but I often feel ashamed when the vote is taken to find them voting against the elected representatives of the people. Given the opportunity I will return poor and hardworking persons who know the pains of labour into the Legislature... most of the Intellectuals we voted to represent our views have joined hands against the interest of the working-class.[68]

This expression brings home the sharp differences of opinion among women activists, based here on class contradictions. Both Audrey Jeffers and Christina Lewis were fighters for women's rights who combined concerns about women's welfare with their activism. The contexts of their work, however, were quite different. Jeffers, a property owner from a wealthy black family with numerous rental properties, in many ways, represented a kind of feminist conservatism which, while seeking to change the system, had difficulty in overcoming her class prejudices and interests. A position aptly summed up in her famous phrase, "We must hasten slowly".

CONCLUSION

Issues of inclusion and exclusion were central to debates and the struggle for 'responsible government' and adult franchise in early twentieth-century Trinidad and Tobago. This was similar to other situations where, as noted by Kumari Jayawardena: "The movement for women's emancipation [in the Third World] was acted out against a background of nationalist struggles aimed at achieving political independence, asserting national identity, and modernizing society."[69] In Trinidad and Tobago, this was, and continues to be, very much the case. The contradictions of race/ethnicity, class and colour continue to be important to feminist activism and the conceptualization of a feminist vision of an alternative. An understanding of this past is central to developing a new praxis for the future.

NOTES

1. Kumari Jayawardena, *Feminism and Nationalism in the Third World* (New Delhi: Kali for Women, 1986), 3.
2. Mainly royalists and loyalists fleeing Grenada, Guadeloupe, Haiti and Martinique after the Haitian and French Revolutions.
3. A Tobago House of Assembly was reinstated with the adoption in parliament of the Tobago House of Assembly (THA) Act No. 37 of 1980 on 23 September 1980. The THA elections and the inaugural meeting of the Assembly on 4 December 1980 followed this.
4. Bridget Brereton, "Contesting the Past: Narratives of Trinidad & Tobago History," *Nieuwe West-Indische Gids* 81, nos. 3&4 (2007): 179–82. See also, Susan E. Craig-James, *The Changing Society of Tobago, 1838–1938: A Fractured Whole, Volume II: 1900–1938* (Arima: Cornerstone Press, 2008), 251.
5. Bridget Brereton, *A History of Modern Trinidad: 1783–1962* (Kingston: Heinemann Caribbean, 1981), 154.
6. Craig-James, *Changing Society of Tobago*, 240–42. After years of struggle for greater autonomy, a new Tobago House of Assembly was established in 1980.
7. Learie Luke, *Identity and Secession in the Caribbean: Tobago versus Trinidad, 1889-1980* (Kingston: University of the West Indies Press, 2007), 125.
8. ibid., 168.
9. Brereton, *History of Modern Trinidad*, 126.
10. Craig-James, *Changing Society of Tobago*, 93.
11. India, at that time, comprised what are currently the countries of India, Pakistan and Bangladesh. Therefore, this group is elsewhere referred to as South Asians. Historically, however, in Trinidad and Tobago they are known as Indians.
12. Brereton, *History of Modern Trinidad*, 142.
13. ibid., 142–44.
14. ibid., 144.
15. Brinsley Samaroo, "Constitutional and Political Development of Trinidad 1898–1925" (Unpublished PhD diss., University of London, 1969), 71.
16. Colonial Office Record (CO 295/ 496; 35762. Vol. 4).
17. Colonial Office Record (CO 318/365; 61923).

18. *Port of Spain Gazette*, 15 May 1908, 4.
19. K.O. Lawrence, ed., "The Trinidad Water Riot of 1903: Reflections of an Eyewitness," *Caribbean Quarterly* 15, no. 4 (1969):12.
20. Lawrence, "Trinidad Water Riot," 12.
21. Rhoda Reddock, *Women, Labour and Politics in Trinidad and Tobago: A History* (London: Zed Books, 1994), 102–3.
22. Michael Anthony, *The Making of Port of Spain: Volume I: 1757-1939* (Port of Spain: Key Caribbean Publications, 1978), 83.
23. Brereton, *History of Modern Trinidad*, 151.
24. Anthony, *Making of Port of Spain*, 91.
25. Samaroo, "Constitutional and Political Development," 69–71.
26. Reddock, *Women, Labour and Politics*, 107–8.
27. Yogendra K. Malik, *East Indians in Trinidad: A Study in Minority Politics* (London: Institute of Race Relations, Oxford University Press, 1971), 70.
28. Report by Parliamentary Under-Secretary, the Hon. E.L.F. Wood, on his visit to the West Indies and British Guiana, Cmd.1679 (1922): 22.
29. Kelvin Singh, *Race and Class Struggles in a Colonial State: Trinidad 1917–1945* (Kingston: University of the West Indies Press, 1994), 49.
30. Singh, *Race and Class Struggles*, 50.
31. Craig-James, *Changing Society of Tobago*, Vol. II, 93
32. Report by Parliamentary Under-Secretary, the Hon. E.L.F. Wood, on his visit to the West Indies and British Guiana, Cmd.1679 (1922): 22.
33. Singh, *Race and Class Struggles*, 67.
34. Interestingly, it emerged in the debates on the institution of a language test that in some West Indian colonies a language test existed for women and not for men (Singh, *Race and Class Struggles*, 65).
35. Singh, *Race and Class Struggles*, 67.
36. Brereton, *History of Modern Trinidad*, 166.
37. "Almanack," *Trinidad Mirror*, 1925.
38. Olga Comma-Maynard, *The Brierend Pattern: The Story of Audrey Jeffers O.B.E. and the Coterie of Social Workers* (Port of Spain: Busby's Printerie, 1971), 2.
39. For more on the campaign for seats for women on the Port of Spain Municipal Council, see Reddock, *Women, Labour and Politics*, 174–78.
40. Tony Martin, "Vote for a Woman! Audrey Jeffers and the 1936 Entry of Women into Trinidad Politics," in *Before and After 1865: Education, Politics and Regionalism in the Caribbean*, ed. Brian Moore and Swithin Wilmot (Kingston: Ian Randle Publishers, 1998), 154.
41. Martin, "Audrey Jeffers," 154.
42. *Trinidad Guardian*, 20 May 1936.

43. *Trinidad Guardian*, 5 May 1936, 11.
44. *Trinidad Guardian*, 9 May 1936.
45. *Sunday Guardian*, 10 April 1936, 4.
46. Brereton, *History of Modern Trinidad*, 167.
47. West India Royal Commission Report, Cmd 6607, HMSO, 1945.
48. The Moyne Papers, Memoranda presented to the West Indian Royal Commission, 1938–39, and Notes made for the Report of the Commission, London, housed at the Institute of Commonwealth Studies.
49. ibid.
50. ibid.
51. Popularly known as the NWA.
52. Bukka Rennie, *History of the Working-Class in the 20th Century – Trinidad and Tobago* (Toronto: New Beginning Movement, 1973), 128–35.
53. West India Royal Commission Report, London, HMSO, Cmd 6607, 1945: 25.
54. ibid., 217.
55. ibid., 381.
56. ibid., 377.
57. Carole Pateman, "The Patriarchal Welfare State," in *Defining Woman: Social Institutions and Gender Divisions*, ed. Linda McDowell and Rosemary Pringle (Cambridge: Polity Press in association with Open University, 1992), 236.
58. John Gaffar La Guerre and Cherita Girvan, "The General Election of 1946 in Trinidad and Tobago," *Social and Economic Studies* 21, no. 1 (1972): 184.
59. *Al Azan, An Organ Devoted to the Cause of Islam* 1, no. 1 (1944): 25.
60. Brereton, *History of Modern Trinidad*, 193–94.
61. Susan Craig-James argues: "Constitutional Change for Tobago before 1946 owed more to ...broader national and regional political movements than to the initiatives of organizations and spokesmen within Tobago" (*Changing Society of Tobago*, 95).
62. *Trinidad Guardian*, 2 July 1946, 2.
63. *Sunday Guardian*, 7 July 1946, 8.
64. Comma-Maynard, *Brierend Pattern*, 42.
65. Patrick Solomon, Minority Report of the Committee on Constitutional Reform (Port of Spain, 1948), 3.
66. *Port of Spain Gazette*, 16 October 1948.
67. Selwyn Ryan, *Race and Nationalism in Trinidad and Tobago* (Toronto: University of Toronto Press, 1972), 82–83.
68. *The People*, 26 March 1949.
69. Jayawardena, *Feminism and Nationalism*, 3.

[14]

GENDER AND NATION-BUILDING IN BARBADOS[1]

[MARY CHAMBERLAIN]

"Feminist history... becomes not the recounting of great deeds performed by women but the exposure of the often silent and hidden operations of gender that are nonetheless present and defining forces in the organization of most societies."[2]

ERROL BARROW, AS HE RAISED THE FLAG OF Barbados on 30 November 1966, was not just building on what Hilary Beckles termed the "ancestors" (Bussa, Prescod, Green, Payne, Barrow), who had hewed the road to independence.[3] He was drawing on a reservoir of social cohesiveness and consciousness, developed around the kitchen tables and on the street corners of Harlem and London, around the standpipes and in the fields of rural Barbados, and in the everyday subjectivities of women (and men) who sought to improve and make sense of their lives.

In the period from 1937 to 1966, women were the majority of the population in Barbados and of workers in the largest employment sectors. They were also heads of households and often the sole breadwinners. They predominated in villages, and maintained and replicated a set of family and neighbourhood values. They raised generation after generation in conservative religious beliefs, but also gave them empowering faith practices, which served to differentiate them from the racism of formal, European Christian church organizations, and reinforced a togetherness, a kind of "covert manifestation of identity", as Donna Bonner has observed.[4] They displayed ingenuity and resourcefulness in the pursuit of family welfare, and emphasized mutual support. Committed to community, they were the moral police of the neighbourhood, and judge, jury and executioner of the moral economy. They circumvented the daily humiliations of racism and colonialism, and taught their loved ones to hold a pride in themselves as its antidote. They sent off their children to Panama, Cuba, New York or London (and many stops in between), bringing up their children's children to facilitate the mobility of the family, and replicating in the next generation their own values.[5] Their vision was global, strategic and long-term. These social structures, which governed the organization of family life, the principles of behaviour, and the primacy given to particular values, were invisible and gendered.

This social history was just one important element in the making of a nation, but it is sometimes absent from the foundational narratives. These children who migrated, numbering in the tens of thousands, were also part of that story. They gave Caribbean nationalism its particular, peculiar flavour of black internationalism. Without a nation to call their own, they used, in Derek Walcott's words, their imagination.[6] One of the most distinguishing features of Caribbean nationalism has been the force of the diaspora as an organizing intellectual principle.[7] It also gave it its grounding in home and families. The (West Indian) scholar Ira Reid was one of the first to point out that West Indian identities overseas were linked as much to the region as to the individual islands, and established small, island-based or interest-based organizations that functioned in part as friendly societies and mutual associations, as well as ways in which island identities could be reinforced. Like West African secret societies, these collectives functioned partly as ways through which social life could be organized, support provided and education imparted.[8] This operated against the backdrop of race – at home and abroad.

Long since the defining ingredient of the Caribbean social world, race and colour permeated every nook and cranny of the body and its psyche; notions of racial inferiority and superiority, as Fanon so skilfully explicated, were internalized and normalized.[9] How could self-autonomy be contemplated, if the contemplators had no faith in themselves? The response was multi-faceted: the pan-African movement had shown the way, taken up and elaborated upon by Marcus Garvey, to affirm black pride, acknowledge and celebrate an African heritage, and form agencies of solidarity with Africans across the diaspora. It transposed the black experience into black political action. In many ways, this was partnered with the creation of a unique black voice, which was to manifest itself in the poetry, literature and music of Africa and its diaspora, from the Harlem Renaissance in the 1920s to *presence Africain* and the International Congress of Negro Writers and Artists in Paris and Rome in the 1950s. This black voice emerged also from within the Caribbean, as writers and artists began to reflect the region's unique social forms within new and vigorous cultural expressions. These cultural manifestations were, equally, outpourings of defiance, nurtured in the alternative cultures of the villages, in the myriad ways in which poor, black people learned to survive spiritually and materially, and circumvent the doctrinal racist attitudes that controlled the judicial, political and economic worlds of the islands. Nowhere was this more so than in Barbados, where the challenges were faced daily, but where defiance was as much (if not more) about subversion and deception as open confrontation. Race and poverty may have been all-powerful, but they did not crush the black Barbadian's spirit.[10] Mechanisms and defences – some public, some secret – were in place to survive, and to link the society in silent solidarity. Passive resistance may not have been dramatic, but was no less powerful for that.

The structures of survival were also those of subversion and were to emerge as articulators of national and transnational belongings. In time, the parallel social world in which black Barbadians lived their lives came to be celebrated as distinctively Barbadian. These concealed currents running through Caribbean and Barbadian society – the stuff of everyday life – were the resources that a burgeoning state could draw upon, what Elsa Goveia might term the "adaptive responses" writ large. They remained immune to the interference of local and colonial legislators who attempted to impose an alternative vision of nation. Their nation-building efforts brought little imagination to bear but, rather, attempted to mould the region into a pale image of itself. It riled against family life and the seemingly amorphous villages, preferring to impose a domestic and social order on the region that mirrored the models of English family life, and villages whose heart and social hierarchies could be readily identified. It pronounced on the need to develop manufacturing and industry, but invested in an infrastructure that continued to bolster sugar, and with it, the old regimes. It denounced the poverty and ills of the region, but was too timid and too parsimonious to introduce progressive social measures. It despaired of the character and the loyalty of the "negro", but was reluctant to invest in anything more than rudimentary education. It condemned the morals of the "negro" and sought to redirect their moral compass with the injection of British culture. It despised the influence of the United States, but was prepared to surrender to them the interests of the region for its own security. And when the tide of independence became unstoppable, it sought to divest itself of the region as cheaply, and rapidly, as it could.

With the exception of Patricia Mohammed, Verene Shepherd and Rhoda Reddock, there have been few Anglophone Caribbean historians who have examined, through gendered eyes, the grand enterprise of the nation.[11] Yet, most national projects derived from, and relied upon, particular definitions of masculinity and femininity, "manhood" and "womanhood".[12] British ideas of citizenship, for instance, were contingent on strong families and homes where men and women performed separate roles, in which the independent, public male sphere of activity stood in contrast to the private, dependent, domestic and presumed inactive world of women.

Many accounts of the transition from West Indian colony to Caribbean nation run through the chronologies – riots, federation, independence.[13] The histories of decolonization and nation-building, which prioritize activism and the labour movement in the struggle for independence, also tell a limited – and gendered – story, for trade union membership was not a mass membership. In 1946, in Barbados, union membership stood at 5,600, rising to 12,500 in 1950, but dropping to 8,751 in 1954 (4.7 per cent of the population). A similar story could be told about Jamaica and elsewhere.[14] Trade unions focused on the heartland of industry: docks, oil (in the case of Trinidad), bauxite (in Jamaica and British Guiana) and so forth. This accorded with labour movement orthodoxy of the period, which saw industrial, urbanized workers in the vanguard of the struggle. But in the Caribbean, and in Barbados in particular, the majority of workers were employed in agriculture, domestic work or as hucksters. None of these areas was targeted, at least initially, by the burgeoning unions, and for two reasons. First, there was a lingering shame about rural labour, which dated back to slavery, and this, coupled with contemporary labour orthodoxy, relegated rural workers to the backseat of the historical struggle. Second, the majority of workers in agriculture, domestic work and huckstering were *women*. No revolution had been led by women from the countryside.

While the insurgency of the 1930s was a critical watershed in decolonization, not least because it signalled to the British that the region was potentially ungovernable, it could, nevertheless, obscure our understanding of the process of nation-building by emphasizing the role of labour activists – predominantly male – or the constitutional processes, negotiated by a male, educated elite, identifying the *noise* at the expense of the *quiet* social capital without which no nation could cohere.

There is, then, another dimension to the story of nation-building that could be found in the thoughts, habits and institutions of women who were not part of the labour movement, whose strategies for survival and patterns of resilience formed a subterranean current that flowed below the radar of organized political life. Studies of nation-building that focus on structure and activism would miss these alternative dynamics in the enterprise of nation.

The majority of the black population in Barbados were rural workers, or in cognate occupations, such as hawking. The census of 1921 (there was no census in 1931) records that out of the total population of 156,312, plantation labourers totalled 32,728, or 21 per cent, of whom 12,387 were male and 20,341 (or 62 per cent) were female.[15] The second largest group were domestic workers. Totalling 25,255, or 16 per cent of the population, the overwhelming majority (88 per cent) were women: 22,247 were female and 3,008 were male.[16] Next were hawkers and peddlers, also dominated by women: of 6,799 hawkers and peddlers, 94 per cent or 6,423 were women.[17] By 1939, it had been estimated that a total of 37,500 people were engaged in estate work – almost double those working in commerce or manufacturing.[18]

As plantation labourers and domestic workers, women's wages were consistently lower than men's. Agricultural workers in Barbados were the lowest paid in the Anglophone Caribbean, as the 1930 Report of the West Indian Sugar Commission confirmed. Wages remained more or less the same by the time the Deane Commission reported in 1937, when the average for a male labourer was thirty cents (or one shilling) a day.[19] For women and children, of course, who comprised two thirds of the labour force on the plantations, the wages were even lower – sixteen or eighteen cents a day.[20] It had been unchanged for a hundred years.[21] Centuries of slavery had inured the planter class to the naturalization of black poverty.

Levels of unemployment, intermittent and under-employment were high. Of the 37,500 people engaged in estate work in 1939, only about 18,574 were working at any one time.[22] Most labourers could not find work all year round; for the most part, they subsisted on a mixture of waged labour and horticulture, growing provisions for their own consumption or as a cash crop.

Impoverishment was compounded by over-population, one solution to which had been migration. But this altered the demography of the island. At emancipation, the sex ratio, while favouring women, was broadly balanced, with 86.3 males per one hundred females,[23] or 116 females to every hundred males. Although women also migrated, the majority of nineteenth- and early twentieth-century migrants were male. As a result, since 1871, the preponderance of women over men in the black and mixed-race community grew dramatically from 121 in 1871 to 148 in 1921.[24]

With the exception of St Kitts and Nevis, Barbados had, by far, the highest excess of women in the eastern Caribbean. This demographic profile contributed significantly to rural workers' low pay. Women, even in first-class labouring gangs, were paid less than men for the same work. Moreover, this imbalance in the sex ratio began early, peaked for the 30–39 age cohort, and though it declined in later years (to rise again for the 70+ cohort, where women's longevity contributed to their excess), it did not even out.[25]

Poverty was, therefore, gendered and generational. The female/male ratio was highest precisely at the time when childbearing and rearing was at its most intense, and when women were also at their peak employment. Moreover, mother-headed households, in which the woman was the main or sole wage earner, was a predominant feature of Barbadian (and Caribbean) family structures.[26] Elderly women were also among the most impoverished, and in many cases, were also bringing up grandchildren. Life, as one informant brought up by his grandmother, recalled, was "so poor. To study those thing, man, I don't like to talk about it. No, it's too hard, it was."[27]

Infant and child mortality were at devastating levels. In 1921, the rate for children under one year was 270 per thousand births (the UK rate was 82.9 per thousand).[28] Infant mortality in 1938 was 221 per thousand live births, the highest in the Caribbean.[29] Garfield Alleyne stated that: "I don't have no sisters. My mother had five children . . . The sister to me dead. Another brother, the sister to him dead and an odd sister, and she died too . . . at birth, as they born actually. None ain't grow. I know neither one. They die small."[30] Malnutrition was rife, the diet deficient in fat, protein and vitamins:[31] "Mother was so poor she couldn't feed us as she like, and some nights you go to sleep hungry because small wages she getting, and many of us, she couldn't feed us as we like, so we did hungry, and that's that."[32]

Children were inadequately clothed and housed. Child labour was common. Even though from 1938 it was illegal to employ children under twelve, employers breached the law, and families needed their children's wages. Angela began work on the plantation in 1943 when she was ten:

> I work in the field. I roll trash. I drop cane plants . . . they had the cane plants in a big ditch soaked with . . . white lime, so on mornings you come and you take the plants out of the water and then you'd get a . . . basket . . . and packed them so and so . . . and then you'd get a lift and you put up on your head . . . we had to drop manure [too] . . . but rolling the trash was the worse . . . burned like pepper.[33]

These problems – of poverty and unemployment – were exacerbated by the concentration of nearly half the population in the parish of St Michael, with its close proximity to Bridgetown. Housing was substandard, and overcrowding rife. The slums of Bridgetown were the worst in the region.[34] For the destitute, the only resource was the Poor Law. Parochial statistics paint a devastating picture. In the first six months of 1931, for instance, 45,516 cases were given some form of Outdoor (mostly medical) or Indoor Relief.[35] In 1937, 21,754 individuals received some kind of Poor Relief (the number of cases is not given). Low wages and no unemployment benefits meant that other members of the family subsidized kin in times of hardship, an additional expense that aggravated their own impoverished conditions – an excuse that had little mileage with the Poor Law Board, which required family members to subsidize less fortunate members, making no distinction between "natural" dependency (such as childhood, old age or childbearing) or "manmade dependency" (such as injury, disease, unemployment or underemployment).[36]

When the means-tested pensions were introduced in 1938 for everyone over the age of seventy (and in the teeth of opposition from the Legislative Council), there was no accurate information on how many people could or would qualify.[37] Those under seventy could claim Parish Relief, and pensions were given to those who could claim destitution – mainly widows, orphans or the sick. Neither the relief nor its distribution was standardized, and the amounts granted, and those claimants deemed to qualify, varied from parish to parish. More particularly, no provisions were made for unemployment, and the able-bodied unemployed had no resource to draw on or claim from. Those who were members of a friendly society were able to claim (short-term) benefits, and Barbados had some of the highest rates of friendly society membership in the region.[38] For the most part, low wages were the primary cause of poverty. In the absence of health and welfare provisions, the results were cataclysmic.

The planters had a monopoly on local employment, controlled access to poor relief and pensions, owned most of the land on which the rural workers rested their houses or grew their provisions, and until universal suffrage in 1951, governed the island in their own interests. For the majority of black Barbadians, it was a relationship of almost total dependency, and rural life was lived in relation to the plantation. It was a relationship that gave the planter the maximum potential for exploitation. Rural workers – predominantly women, as we have seen – were vulnerable to the vagaries of the planter at the micro level, and the world market at a macro level. When they also rented land or a house spot, their vulnerability was compounded. Rural workers were trapped on or by the plantation system and economy. On the face of it, they were resigned to the inequities of the situation and engaged in risk adverse behaviour – reinforced by those who were also peasant proprietors (in 1939, there were 3,905 with holdings of between one and three acres[39]) – which, as the Deane Commission noted, was "a revolution which has introduced a valuable element not only of political but of economic stability".[40] The seemingly powerless, however, did not lack power. The strategies for survival that women adopted also undermined the hierarchy and authority of the planter society.

Although it was common for plantation labourers to work in gangs, by the 1920s two other forms of employment had been successfully negotiated: task work and farming. Task work was done mainly by men who would be paid a fixed rate for fixed work. It favoured individual activity; it could be divisive; and the potential for unreasonable practices was high, but it could also be financially rewarding, so long as the tasks and the rate were fair. Farming was essentially piece work. An area of land would be allocated to labourers to work in their own time. Farming was almost exclusively done by women, and was the labouring work of choice. Gang work for women was poorly paid, hard and inflexible. "When you in a gang," as one labourer explained, "you got . . . a superintendant behind, to drive you . . . you got to keep going."[41] Farming, for women, offered an opportunity to earn more, at times more favourable to them. It fitted into the household routine, enabled them to grow produce on their own or rented land and was, crucially, distanced from the regulation of plantation labour. It was possible for women to make a living separate from the plantation, even if, in many cases, such as carrying water or selling bread and other foods to the field labourers, it was a parasitical relationship. Indeed, this need to separate from the plantation had practical, as well as moral, imperatives. Jasper's maternal great-grandmother, a "located" labourer, in the late nineteenth century, baked bread which she sold, making sufficient profit to buy land and with it, the family's release from the plantation. "There is a corner," he explained, "known as Lola's corner, which has been handed down in the family . . ."[42] The land was at once a symbol of the family's success and of resistance to the plantation. Other avenues to earn money included domestic service and home-based industries, such as huckstering, sewing and straw plaiting.

The small plots yielded a variety of crops for home consumption and for sale. The cash crop of choice, however, was sugar. "It was like your bank account," one informant commented and another explained: "When you had a good crop of sugarcane you could depend financially on the returns every year. The plantations would . . . take what was theirs but if you contracted bills at stores, shops, hardware stores, anything, they were sure that when you reaped your gains they would get every cent that you owed them . . . the sugarcane, when you had a spot of sugarcane you had money, so to speak."[43]

Access to land was a crucial component of the calculations for subsistence. If sugar was the preferred crop, a pig, or other stock, was an equally viable investment. The advantage of a pig was that it could be killed and the profits reaped at any time (unlike sugar, which was seasonal). A pig, moreover, did not require grazing land, could be kept by landless workers, and did not involve labour. It was often kept by women. As Angela explained, "you can always sell them and help to buy the schoolchildren things . . . *You don't have to depend on nobody*."[44] Her sentiments were replicated by Avalene who "kept a pig, a mother pig. I had a sheep [too], yes, all those sorts I had to help me with my children."[45] For the most part, the whole village benefitted from the pig: "If the neighbour kill a pig, the whole village get a piece of that pig."[46]

The rural labourer looked at both the overt control of the plantation and the covert symbols of survival and resistance – dependency and independence. This struggle was based on a strong moral code which, because of its inflections of race and status, was also, inherently, political. Overall violations of this moral code would be resisted and redressed, and were necessarily political in intent and effect.

E.P. Thompson's insights on the "moral economy of the poor" in the eighteenth century and James C. Scott's comparable insights into the peasantry of South East Asia in the first half of the twentieth century could be applied in some measure to the conditions and responses of rural workers in Barbados in the same period. In all cases, the "right to subsistence" constituted the cornerstone of the moral economy, from which emerged a range of social adjustments that constituted village life. This life and the adjustments to survival were premised on values of solidarity and communitarianism which, in turn, became one of the cornerstones of the nation.

A recurrent theme in memories of rural life was village cooperation. Childcare, certainly, was a village responsibility. "It took a village to raise a child," Wesley recalled:

> So you had to be very careful to say good morning and good evening to everybody you met and that sort of thing. Cause . . . that person to whom you didn't say good morning or good evening, was quite entitled to give you a little touch on your head and say, 'Now you behave yourself' and that sort of thing.[47]
>
> Neighbours around . . . sort of keep an eye, you weren't their children, but . . . *you were their responsibility*.[48]
>
> You had to be careful, even . . . although you were away, out of your parents' sight, you know, there were still people there, sort of keeping an eye to make sure that you didn't do anything that you shouldn't be.[49]

The repetitions in accounts of childhood that stress the community involvement are striking, suggesting not only a shared memory, but also prescriptions for appropriate behaviour and mutual responsibility. Children were watched over and as a result enjoyed considerable autonomy. The care of children would be shared within the family – it was not uncommon for one (or more) children to be brought up by a grandparent (usually grandmother) or aunt for part or all of their childhood, particularly (but not exclusively) if a parent died. In any case, the principal carers were women. Destitute children – and formal adoption – were rare.[50] Children were taught to respect others, and implicit in those lessons were principles of reciprocity. If children were taught that respect was due to those more senior, they also knew that they would be afforded, in return, a measure of concern and protection.[51] Everton recalled: "We were always brought up ... as kids ... to give respect ... *Both sides had to give respect*, and we as kids had to give that respect, and if we didn't give it, no matter what status the person had in the village ... I would get really chastised for it. It's a very interesting sort of reverse of it."[52]

When all were living at the level of subsistence, family and neighbours ensured that no one fell too far below the poverty line. Food and services were, as a result, exchanged and circulated. "Everybody shared what they had."[53] "Anything you had additional, you would share with others."[54] Informants refer, over and over again, to examples of exchange and reciprocity: "We had a neighbour ... and her husband that used to work in the fishing area, so when they have overplus sell of fish, she would always share with my mother some, knowing that it was she alone with the children, so that we were able to get something to eat."[55] Another informant shared: "My mother was always a person that loved to share and I grew up loving to share so if I have something more than some person, we always give some persons who helped me some too."[56]

Giving required a return: "If you will give to somebody, they will give you too" – whether the donor was a neighbour, where the returns would be more immediate, or family, where they could be delayed.[57] Angela put the case succinctly: "They [the children] come first. I could make do. So, now, they provide for Mummy and I get payback for what Mummy have done."[58] Vere's story was particularly poignant. His neighbour, a tailor, was shot in the leg during the 1937 riots. His mother dressed the wound and nursed him. He said: "He can't pay her ... So, after my mother died, he came to me and he asked me if I would like to live [with him], cos it's the only thing he knows, the only thing he can repay my mother ... so I went with him and learn [tailoring]."[59]

Such behaviour derived from a set of values that stressed mutual aid and reciprocity, provided an alternative model of citizenship to that proposed by the colonial authorities, premised on British middle-class values and behaviours, and profoundly hierarchical in both concept and practice. As Karen Fog Olwig points out:

These communities consisted of complex webs of relations of mutual rights and obligations based on notions of kinship or friendship and tended to valorize the significance of general sociability and mutual help rather than the individual achievement and socioeconomic mobility. The British missionaries and educators regarded these ways of life as presenting uncivilized, debased forms of existence that needed to be combated, and they therefore came to be seen as counter to the development of proper citizenship in the colonial society.[60]

In terms of employment, the principle of reciprocity was more abstract, but nonetheless adhered to. A good day's work required a fair wage, and vice versa. Angela, who was brought up in the countryside, took these values with her when she worked in the hotel industry. She said: "We were taught, This is your work. This is your bread and butter. That's the people's money. They're who are paying you. You don't have to let them walk in your face, but be courteous . . . that's the meaning of understanding."[61] Avalene, who worked as an agricultural labourer and a domestic servant, espoused the same moral values: "I do my work perfect . . . I went to work and I do it . . . Whatever job I had to do I always tried to do it correctly and not incorrect. You understand what I mean? *You pay me, and I give you your work.*"[62] (emphasis added)

Reciprocity – giving and sharing – were core moral values. No one was exempted. The moral values enshrined the right to subsistence, which metamorphosed into duties for those further up the social hierarchy. Portia, for instance, was the daughter of a teacher in a country village, where the people "looked up to this headmaster, the reverend and so on, and sought their advice, and my father was like a welfare person in that district, you know?"[63] Such respect, nevertheless, had to be reciprocated. As Portia recalled: ". . . he [father] would . . . look for the children who hadn't come to school and if they needed something he would try to help provide for them, and in this way he'd help. And in the community, he was the only one who had a car and many a night someone who was ill knocked on our door . . . and he would take them to the hospital or the doctor or whatever."[64]

But the person in the village hierarchy regarded as having the greatest duty of care was the planter. Not only was he expected to give a fair wage for a fair day's work, but he was expected to help in a variety of contexts. The distribution of food grown on the plantation, for instance, was not only the hallmark of a good manager, but an expected requirement, as Rupert explained: "When they take the food, they would always give the labourer some so it could balance up with the little money they get. You get it?"[65] Angela put the fairness principle more sharply. Work, she argued "was really tough then . . . Working hard and somebody [else]'s drawing the benefits".[66] Under those conditions, it was only fair that a labourer had access to such provisions.

The planter was also expected to redistribute wood for cooking, which was also essential to survival. When it was not available, or unaffordable, planters would "let us pick some . . . go in the cane . . . go in the canefields and try to get some dry rotten cane, you know".[67] Similarly, the planters were expected to provide lumber or loans for housing repairs. They emphasized these responsibilities in the debates surrounding the repeal of the Masters and Servants Act in 1937, and in their reports to the Deane Commission. It was to the planters' advantage to stress their responsibilities and obligations, for repeal of the act would remove the last vestige of control over the location of their labourers. But the planters failed to acknowledge or, even recognize, the logic of the situation, for what they deemed kindness was, to the labourer, a *right*. Indeed, it was their only right in a context which had, historically, denied them all others.

Given the particular economic, social and political context of Barbados, which had effectively been able to resist all but the most basic reforms in the century after emancipation, and left the dependent relationship between the labourer and the planter virtually unchanged, the moral economy remained the only basis for a viable partnership. However, as James Scott argues, "Peasants expected of elites the generosity and assistance that they imposed within the village on their better-off neighbours; social rights were, in this sense, village morals writ large."[68] Indeed, the complex family structures and village organization in the Caribbean are premised on a communitarian philosophy of society and act as metaphors for approved social behaviour.[69] Violations of the moral order would not be tolerated, and women were at the forefront of endorsing the code of conduct as both recipients and providers. At village level, breaches in the moral code incurred displeasure, and even sanctions. Those who did not comply or conform to the village norms found 'trust' (in the local shop) and other mechanisms of social support crucial for survival withdrawn. "You have to be a good paying person," Eurita explained.

"So, if you're a person that would pay, you can trust... Like my mother with her family, she would get trust. But you have to make sure that at the end of the week you pay back what you owe, because if you don't pay that, you cannot get next week."[70]

The higher up the hierarchy, however, the greater the returns expected. Thus, planters and other employers would find themselves regularly penalized for breaches in expected behaviour. Avalene, for instance, argued: "If you have a servant who have to cook your food, keep your place clean, will you treat them like a two-foot doll or four-foot doll? I think you should respect who has to handle your food and keep your place clean like that."[71]

If an employer breached his side of the contract (by behaving badly, imposing unfair conditions and so on), the ultimate sanction – withdrawal of labour – would be imposed by the employee. Pearl began work as a domestic servant for a white lady, but "I didn't like it there because I felt that I was more or less like a little slave ... and I hated it [and left]..."[72] A bad manager – such as one who denied labourers plantation perks or who "come and give you the work hard"[73] – could well find themselves penalized. In crop time, for instance, the plantations needed extra labour, a requirement that was given an added urgency by deadlines set by the sugar factories. A bad employer would suffer the very real sanction of having a shortage of labourers at a critical time. As quoted in *Renters and Farmers*: "Well, the workers knows good from bad, you understand? ... You see, if a plantation is a good plantation, like the manager is genuine, the people are genuine, well, the people will clamour to work such a place ... because you get help ... the plantation dig yams, and give you some cut ones, all that kind of thing ... If the manager's good, the plantation will be good..."[74]

Lack of "morality" (as one informant described it) on the part of the employer could result in them being forced to hire labourers themselves lacking in "morality" – to the detriment of both productivity and labour relations. But with the odds between the planters and the labourers stacked so systematically in favour of the planters, breaches in the moral code resulted in a more direct home-grown redistributive justice. Planters – or their managers – who denied labourers perks such as cut yams would find themselves the victim of a rough and ready redistribution. "They go in the plantation ground and [get] the sprout potatoes. That's when the manager don't sell the food and we get cross that he sell the sprout," explained Editha. Then, "You dig the sprout to find the potato."[75] "Well, they had to," corroborated Ivy. "People used to steal the potatoes. They'll go at night and come out in the day . . ."[76] Equally, if a manager was suspected of short-changing the labourers, the latter would take justice into their own hands. "I remember my father and my mother," Angela recounted, "put by some yams and different stuff [so] in the dead of night . . . we would go with them [to fetch them] . . . mostly they used to give, like, the cut ones . . . but of course, you have to have some hidden back that they can have later on . . ."[77]

By far, the greatest problem for the planters and the government was praedial larceny, whose prevalence was remarked upon even in the Colonial Office.[78] Given that the right to subsistence lay at the basis of the rural workers' moral economy, and that the planters on some level were seen to control the key to this subsistence, it is not surprising that high levels in the rates (or, rather, convictions) of praedial larceny coincided with moments of economic distress. Thus, from 1929 to 1931, during the worldwide recession, levels of praedial larceny were almost double those that followed in relatively less tumultuous years. They climbed again in 1937, which was also the year of riots in Barbados, peaking again during the early 1940s, when the privations of war began to bite. The rates thereafter remained more or less steady, with fluctuations of 10 to 20 per cent until 1955 when, again, they rose after the destruction caused by Hurricane Janet.[79]

The peaks in praedial larceny, however, were not just confined to moments of economic despair. They were linked also to sentiments of injustice, as evidence to the Deane and Moyne Commissions demonstrate. Many of the customary perks of sugar labourers – sweet liquor from the boiling house, allowances of sugar and molasses, access to grazing facilities after the crop – had been lost to modernization so "that labour have been Completely (sic) thrown to the wolves".[80] In addition, many smallholders felt that their sugar crops were being unfairly weighed in the factories and sold at "unfair prices", as the Deane Commission observed.[81] Country people had taken matters into their own hands on these occasions – a factor implicitly recognized by the Deane Commission, which observed that: "the lawless acts committed in the country were more purposive than those committed in Bridgetown; and it would appear that hunger, or the fear of hunger, coupled with the news of the disturbances in Bridgetown, were the chief causes of the outbreaks [of rioting] in the country districts."[82]

For the Deane Commission, however, hunger was sufficient an explanation for the lawlessness in the countryside. Yet, as E.P. Thompson reminds us, we should be cautious of so "simple [a] response to economic stimuli. It is insufficient to mention a bad harvest or a downturn in trade and all requirements of historical explanation are satisfied."[83] Rural workers were operating within a context of hunger, but also a sense of fairness that had been violated. The right to subsistence had been fundamentally challenged by both low wages, and unemployment and underemployment, as well as mechanization and, for many, unfair pricing of their sugar crop. The lawlessness at the time of the riots in 1937 may have appeared random and uncoordinated, particularly in the rural areas, but nevertheless should not be seen as irrational or lacking in agency. "Lawlessness", coupled with the increase in praedial larceny, may be seen as a collective political response to what was a violation of the moral order on the part of the planters and their agents. Indeed, this point was made firmly by Ulrick Grant, who was imprisoned for ten years for sedition, in his evidence to the West India Royal Commission: ". . . conditions here are very, very bad . . . It is . . . essential that such recommendations made by this Royal Body should be powerfully enforced, in order *to extricate the poor from this great mass of unfairness and injustice*."[84]

The upsurge in praedial larceny in 1940 and 1941 could be interpreted similarly. Once again, the sense of moral justice was challenged as labourers felt that they were assuming too great a share of wartime privations. Governor Waddington wrote in his report of 30 September 1940: "Though . . . many . . . believe . . . that whilst they are suffering considerable hardships due to the war, the capitalist and white classes continue to enjoy their pre-war mode of life . . . There can be no doubt that there is considerable distress due to undernourishment . . ."[85]

By the following March, the cost of living was 25.42 per cent above the pre-war figure,[86] borne primarily by the working classes (predominantly women and their dependents) and praedial larceny peaked once again. "It is true to say," wrote Sir Grattan Bushe to the Secretary of State, "that the richer section of the population have not had to make any harsh sacrifices, while the poor are suffering considerably."[87] It was not regarded as a crime but as redistribution: "It wasn't theft," insisted Everton, "not the sort of theft as we know it today".[88]

Labourers saw themselves as equal moral partners in a relationship dominated by brute economics, which provided legitimacy for more subtle forms of retribution. At a base level, the inequalities between the labourers and the owners of production were seen as inherently unfair and ripe for redistribution. While praedial larceny might have peaked at moments of anger or outrage, its levels were consistently high, suggesting a continuous redistribution or rebalancing of the subsistence odds.

Such redistributive practices were also employed beyond the plantation. Ena's father, for instance, was a tailor. His suits "took a lot of precision, a lot of thinking, a lot of time and a lot of goodwill . . . because often people didn't have the money to pay . . . and he wouldn't say that he wasn't going to do it. He would do it."[89] If goodwill operated at one end of the arrangement, it was amply compensated by exploitation at the other. Ivy, for instance, was a shoemaker and explained, "You had to work for the rich and you had to work for the poor. And the rich man going to pay the big money, and coming to the poor man, we would get the thing to do a little cheaper . . . "[90] The "rich people", she elaborated, were, "the whites". "Cause you, like, charge the whites more than you would charge the coloured. . . . what you can charge the white, you can't charge the coloured. So, the white would always put on top. And the poor man, he stayed down."[91]

Given how close to the margin most Barbadians lived, such redistributive practices were a necessary part of the package for survival. Equally prominent were the mechanisms for self-help, another established part of Barbadian society, based once more on exchange and reciprocity, and for the most part, negotiated by women. 'Trust' at the local shop was a regular way of raising credit; delaying the rent another. For instance, Angela's aunt with whom she lived, "didn't like to pay, cause they always come knocking for the rent, and the bailiff would come to get at her. And she would say to me, 'Don't you open that window if anybody call.' I was intelligent enough to peep through the holes [in the walls]."[92] 'Meeting turns' or 'sou-sou' were a way of raising small amounts of capital. "Ten dollars," explained Avalene "to help with the children's clothes and things."[93] "From the time I can remember," Angela said, "I draw sou sou up . . . That pay for certain things then. You always like a lump sum."[94] Based, again, on the principles of reciprocity and trust, and usually organized by a female neighbour, meeting turns represented a small but significant opportunity for (mainly) women to plan for the medium term in a context where basic decisions had to be made hand to mouth, day by day.

Other forms of self-help such as the landship movement[95] (started in 1863 and was initially open only to men), credit unions, savings schemes or lodges, were more visible and more formal. For instance, in 1939, 191 friendly societies were formally registered, with a membership of approximately 55,000 and dependents approximated at 128,000, providing members with a Christmas bonus, relief in sickness and funeral expenses.[96] These organizations formalized the informal relations of trust and reciprocity, which characterized village existence. They also provided another lesson in the advantages of cooperation and collective action and, as such, were an important political model.[97]

The dominance of women in village and family life, and the culture of a moral economics, undoubtedly provided one explanation for the prevalence of non-violent resistance which characterized conflict in Barbados. This is not to say that women did not participate in the conflagrations that did erupt – in 1816, 1875 and 1937 – but it may account for the relative infrequency of violence.

Barbadian society was not, however, a feminized society, nor were gender relations equal. Patriarchal forms and attitudes were dominant and visible, whether in politics, popular culture or in the diaspora. The social capital required for a newly emerging nation was, however, being banked quietly elsewhere, alongside alternative practices of citizenship. The overlap of domestic and communal space, what might be termed the private and public sphere, has a long history in the Caribbean. Women, in particular, consistently negated gender roles and flaunted gendered space. While white and colonial authorities saw appropriate gender ordering as a mark and condition of citizenship, endorsed by the brown and black elites as evidence of their suitability and maturity; black working-class women – by far the majority – had no option but to cross the gender boundaries. As heads of households, they worked and made choices for themselves and their families. While poverty provided little autonomy, women did have sovereignty over their own domain. This could be (and often was) challenged by men, who entered as members of the household, but that membership was always contingent. If economics eroded the gendered division of labour, and destabilized the hierarchies within the home; the home itself was part of a wider, public domain. The functions of a family – to reproduce, support and socialize the next generation – considered to the European eye as the sacred terrain of private, feminized, domestic space, had been franchised out to other family members and to the broader village community. It was they who controlled the morals of the young, guided them away from unsuitable influences, collectively transmitted values and culture, and supported them when they went abroad. The world of the village was a holistic one, and the roles that women performed within it multifaceted. Women's sovereignty was not vested in a single individual nor in a single geographic space, but was dispersed throughout the village.

The first breach in colonial authority came at village level, when the public/private sphere was violated and with it a particular model of political authority, in which the male, public world held sway over the female and the private. In the villages, citizenship was not vested in particular practices of participation in the formal institutions of state, or in a particular set of instrumental behaviours, but was indicative of a moral relationship of responsibility and reciprocity between one individual and the group. As such, it represented an alternative model of political authority in which citizenship was dispersed rather than concentrated in a particular group, was inclusive in membership and performed a range of social activities, which were accountable to the group. If the moral economy was "independence in action", village morality was citizenship in action. Both were well suited to embrace participatory politics when they emerged in 1951.

Moreover, in their support of migrants, either by raising the funding for travel or by caring for their children, or in the collection and execution of remittances, or in the maintenance of family goals and relations across the diaspora, women forged an alternative diasporic politics that was rooted in gender, and the island. Women, too, were migrants.[98] Home or abroad, their imagined nations were formulated by family connections and needs, where mobility was as much a requirement as connectedness, where fluidity and adaptability necessarily challenged the concept of settlement or fixity, and where they acted as the conduit for money and love. If federation failed to capture the imagination at home, it could be that women's trajectories of family were more linear, vertical and tangible than the multiple, horizontal and theoretical connections presupposed by a federal state, and advocated by migrants abroad. Indeed, this federal state endorsed an idea of a nation state, borrowed from imperial memory, in which the particular global strategic visions of its women orientated to family welfare had little echo in the rhetoric of sovereignty by its male advocates.

Women, always a majority of the population, and the three major employment sectors, also proved to be the most assiduous at the polls. They outnumbered men by approximately 25 per cent in the voting booths – even accounting for the demographic imbalance, this still showed a predominance of women – and have continued to outnumber them.[99] At independence, poverty was beginning to be addressed and undoubtedly one explanation for the high turnout at election time, and the predominance of women in the voting booths, was the impact of poverty on their families and on themselves as the bearers and 'rearers' of children. Education, health, welfare and maternity provisions were all issues of direct concern to them.

There have been many narrative routes to nationhood, and there will be more, for they are sites also of continuing struggle. Important as the role of protest and the actions of a politicized elite are, we should be aware that these accounts are gendered, and favour the activities of one gender over another. We should not elevate the majesty of industrial muscle at the expense of the humbler – and often less visible or audible – processes of village life, in which women are the dominant actors.

NOTES

The following abbreviations have been used.

BM – Barbados Migration, interviews conducted by M. Chamberlain 1993–95, archived in the British Library, London.
BN – Barbados Nation, interviews conducted by M. Chamberlain, 2004–6, archived in the Oral History Collection, University of the West Indies, Cave Hill.
Caribbean Families, interviews conducted by Dwaine Plaza 1997–98, Qualidata Archive, University of Essex.

1. This article is based on the chapter "Gender and the Moral Economy" in *Empire and Nation-building in the Caribbean. Barbados, 1937–66* (Manchester: Manchester University Press, 2010).

2. J.W. Scott, *Gender and the Politics of History* (New York: Columbia University Press, 1988), 27.
3. H. Beckles, *Chattel House Blues: Making of a Democratic Society in Barbados, from Clement Payne to Owen Arthur* (Kingston: Ian Randle Publishers, 2004).
4. D. Bonner, review of Walter F. Pitts' *Old Ship of Zion: The Afro-Baptist Ritual in the African Diaspora, American Anthropologist* 98, no. 2 (1996): 452–53.
5. See M. Chamberlain, *Narratives of Exile and Return* (New Brunswick: Transaction Publishers, 2004 [1997]).
6. D. Walcott, *The Star Apple* (New York: Farrar, Strauss and Giroux, 1977).
7. B.H. Edwards, *The Practice of Diaspora. Literature, Translation and the Rise of Black Internationalism* (Cambridge, MA: Harvard University Press, 2003).
8. The classic work on this is F.W. Butt-Thompson, *West African Secret Societies. Their Organisation, Officials and Teaching* (London: Witherby, 1929). See also S. Greenbaum, "Economic Cooperation among Urban Industrial Workers: Rationality and Community in an Afro-Cuban Mutual Aid Society, 1904–1927," *Social Science History* 17, no. 2 (1993): 173–93; S.L. Ishemo, "From Africa to Cuba: An Historical Analysis of the Sociedad Secreta Abakuá (Ñañiguismo)," *Review of African Political Economy* 92 (2002): 253–72; B.M. Kuyk, "The African Derivation of Black Fraternal Orders in the United States," *Comparative Studies is Society and History* 25, no. 4 (1983): 559–92.
9. Frantz Fanon, *Black Skin, White Masks* (London: Paladin, 1970).
10. See J.C. Scott, *Domination and the Arts of Resistance. Hidden Transcripts* (New Haven: Yale University Press, 1990).
11. Verene Shepherd, Bridget Brereton, and Barbara Bailey, eds., *Engendering History: Caribbean Women in Historical Perspective* (Kingston: Ian Randle Publishers, 1995); Verene Shepherd, *Women in Caribbean History* (Kingston: Ian Randle Publishers, 1999). Patricia Mohammed, *Imaging the Nation* (Basingstoke: Macmillan Caribbean, 2007); Rhoda Reddock, *Women's Movements and Organisations in the Process of Revolutionary Transformation: The Case of Grenada*, presented at ISS/FLACSO Seminar on "The Objectives and Margins of State Intervention", Quito, Ecuador, 5–12 September 1982; *Elma Francois: The NWCSA and the worker's struggle for change in the Caribbean* (London: New Beacon Books, 1988); *Women, Labour and Politics in Trinidad and Tobago* (London: Zed Books, 1994). There is a considerable historiography on the role of women in slavery and in resistance to slavery, but the record becomes progressively slimmer as it approaches the twentieth century. Historians, in this regard, are behind their colleagues in sociology, anthropology and development studies.
12. See C. Hall, *Gendered Nations: Nationalisms and Gender Order in the Long*

Nineteenth Century (Oxford: Berg, 2000); N. Yuval-Davis, *Gender and Nation* (London: Sage Publications, 1997); N. Stepan, *The Hour of Eugenics: Race, Gender and Nation in Latin America* (Ithaca: Cornell University Press, 1996); A. McClintock, A.R. Mufti, and E. Shohat, *Dangerous Liaisons: Gender, Nation and Post-Colonial Perspectives* (St Paul: University of Minnesota Press, 1997); R. Roach Pierson, ed., *Nation, Empire, Colony: Historicising Gender and Race* (Bloomington: Indiana University Press, 1998); F. Anthias and N. Yuval-Davis, eds., *Woman-Nation-State* (Basingstoke: Macmillan 1989); Kathleen Canning and Sonya O. Rose, *Gender, Citizenships and Subjectivities* (Oxford: Blackwell, 2002); T. Mayer, ed., *Gender Ironies of Nationalism;* A. Davin, "Imperialism and motherhood," *History Workshop Journal* 5 (1978): 9–66.

13. Both L. Lynch, *West Indian Eden: The Book of Barbados* (Glasgow: Robert Maclehouse and Company, 1959) and A. Hoyos, *The Rise of West Indian Democracy: The Life and Times of Sir Grantley Adams* (Bridgetown: Advocate Press, 1963) offer a foundational story, but the result is a hagiography either of the island or of Sir Grantley Adams. More recent scholarly accounts are H. McD. Beckles, *A History of Barbados* (Cambridge: Cambridge University Press, 1990); *Great House Rules: Landless Emancipation and Workers' Protest in Barbados 1838–1938* (Kingston, Ian Randle 2004); *Chattel House Blues: Making of a Democratic Society in Barbados, from Clement Payne to Owen Arthur* (Kingston, Ian Randle 2004). Multi-disciplinary analysis of nation-building can be found in T.A. Carmichael, ed., *Barbados – Thirty Years of Independence* (Kingston: Ian Randle Publishers, 1996); G.D. Howe and D.D. Marshall, eds., *The Empowering Impulse: The Nationalist Tradition of Barbados* (Kingston: Canoe Press, 2001).
14. G.T. Daniel, "Labor and Nationalism in the British Caribbean," *Annals of the American Association of Political and Social Sciences* 310 (1957): 162–71.
15. TNA, CO31/107 census 1921, appendix B, 152.
16. TNA, CO31/107 census 1921, appendix B.
17. TNA, CO31/107 census 1921, appendix B.
18. *Annual Report on the Social and Economic Progress of the People of Barbados, 1938–39* (London: HMSO, 1939), 18. No census had been taken in Barbados since 1921.
19. Deane Commission report, 244; see also evidence of H.A. Vaughan, 10.
20. A point reiterated by Charles W. Taussig, *Report of the United States Commission to Study Social and Economic conditions in the British West Indies, appointed by the President of the United States on November 13, 1940*, p.32.
21. TNA, CO 950 612. H.A. Vaughan, Memo of Evidence, West India Royal Commission.

22. *Annual Report on the People of Barbados.*
23. *West Indian Census, 1946 – Barbados,* xix. See also B. Higman, *Slave Populations of the British Caribbean 1807–1834* (Kingston: University of the West Indies Press, 1995), 116.
24. *West Indian Census, 1946.*
25. TNA, CO321/107, Documents laid at Meeting of Assembly of 22 November 1921, 97.
26. See Mary Chamberlain, *Family Love in the Caribbean. Migration and the Anglo-Caribbean Experience* (New Brunswick: Transaction Publishers and Kingston: Ian Randle Publishers, 2006).
27. Interview with Reginald Franklin for Barbados Tenantry Project, 1990.
28. TNA, CO31/107, Report on Marriages, Births and Burials for year ended 31 December 1920.
29. *Annual Report on the People of Barbados,* 7.
30. Interview with Garfield Alleyne, Barbados Tenantry Project, 1990.
31. *Report of the Committee appointed to consider and report on the Question of Nutrition in Barbados,* 1936. Laid as a supplement to the *Official Gazette,* 7 October 1937, p.8. See also evidence presented to the West India Royal Commission 1938. TNA, CO 950 572, Office memorandum: labour questionnaire, 1938–39.
32. BM, B4.
33. BN27.
34. BA, GH3/6/10 Mis/G/51. Report on 22 November 1937 of interview between Secretary of State and Grantley Adams in which Adams reported that, "The Bridgetown slums which Professor Macmillan had described as among the worst he had ever seen, were regularly discussed at election times, but no action ever resulted." See also *Royal Commission Report – Medical and Public Health – Barbados.* From Chief Medical Officer to Colonial Secretary, 23 March 1940, TNA, CO 318 444 18.
35. BA. Srl 11 Barbados. *Annual Report on Poor Relief.* By Dr. E.A. Seagar, Chief Medical Officer, for the year 1931.
36. Richard Titmuss, "The Social Division of Welfare: Some Reflections on the Search for Equity," in *The Philosophy of Welfare* (London: Allen and Unwin, 1987).
37. See Debates in the Legislative Council, 18 October 1937 and 23 November 1937.
38. BA, Pam C27; J. Henry Richardson, *Report of Inquiry into Social Security in Barbados,* Bridgetown, 1954.
39. *Annual Report on the People of Barbados,*12.
40. Deane Commission report, 272.

41. Quoted in Mary Chamberlain, "Renters and farmers: the Barbadian plantation tenantry system 1917–1937," *Journal of Caribbean History* 24, no. 2 (1990): 216.
42. Quoted in Mary Chamberlain, *Narratives of Exile and Return* (London and Basingstoke: Macmillan Press, 1997), 53–54.
43. BN31.
44. BN 27. Emphasis added.
45. BN7.
46. BN11.
47. BN24.
48. "Family Structure and Social Change of Caribbeans in Britain" research project, ESRC Award Number L315253009, (hereafter Caribbean Family). BK 080/1/A/8.
49. Caribbean Family, BK 080/1/A/8.
50. TNA, CO 950 566, West India Royal Commission. *Questionnaire on Certain Matters Connected with Social Welfare,* 11. This point was also made by Thomas Simey, although he also referred to the homeless children "who obtain their living by begging and petty theft". Simey, *Welfare and Planning,* 15–16.
51. For a fuller discussion of this, see Mary Chamberlain, *Family Love in the Diaspora.*
52. BN1.
53. BN15.
54. BN1.
55. BN8.
56. BN9.
57. Chamberlain, "Renters and Farmers," 221.
58. BN27.
59. BM, B5.
60. Karen Fog Olwig, *Caribbean Journeys: An Ethnography of Family and Home in Three Family Networks* (Durham: Duke University Press, 2007), 30.
61. BN27.
62. BN7.
63. BN25.
64. BN25.
65. BN18.
66. BN27.
67. BN11.
68. Scott, *Moral Economy,* 184.
69. See Chamberlain, *Family Love in the Diaspora.*

70. BN8.
71. BN7.
72. BN12.
73. Chamberlain, "Renters and Farmers," 208.
74. ibid., 209.
75. BN11.
76. BN14.
77. BN27.
78. BA, C42/S5/12, Macdonald to Waddington, 12 April 1940.
79. BA, Srl 99 *Barbados Criminal Statistics*, 1938–1960.
80. TNA, CO 950 582 Israel Lovell, Memorandum of Evidence, West India Royal Commission (submitted to the WIRC from Glendairy Prison, where he was serving a sentence of five years on four counts of sedition arising from the "disturbances" of 1937).
81. Peasant holdings and sugar plantations without factories represented 26 per cent of arable land. Deane Commission report, 246, 247.
82. Deane Commission report, 240
83. Thompson, "Moral Economy," 185.
84. TNA, CO 950576. Olrick (sic) McDonald Grant, Memorandum of Evidence to West India Royal Commission. Written evidence sent from Glendairy prison.
85. BA. GHQ/C20. Vol. 1. Intelligence Reports, 30 September 1940.
86. BA. GHQ/C20. Vol. 1. Intelligence Reports, 31 March 1941.
87. TNA, CO 875/5/17. Sir Grattan Bushe to Secretary of State for Colonies, 19 May 1942.
88. BN1.
89. BN31.
90. BN14.
91. BN14.
92. BN27.
93. BN7.
94. BN27.
95. A unique form of Barbadian traditional masquerade in which the performances are based on the passage of ships through rough seas. Such performances are symbolized by parades, jigs, hornpipes, maypole dances, and other music and dance types. The ship's crew wears uniforms that similar in style to those worn in the navy. They are also trained and disciplined in the manner of the military.
96. *Annual Report on the People of Barbados*, 25.
97. For a discussion on this, see K. Hunte, "The Struggle for Political Democracy:

Charles Duncan O'Neal and the Democratic League," in Howe and Marshall, *The Empowering Impulse*, 133–48.
98. For a broad discussion of gender and migration, see Patricia Ruth Pessar and S.J. Mahler, "Transnational Migration: Bringing Gender," *International Migration Review* 37, no. 3 (2003): 812–46.
99. www.caribbeanedu.com/elections/bb07.asp.

[15]

ASCENT TO LEADERSHIP
Women and the National Union of Public Workers of Barbados, 1975–1995

[RICHARD A. GOODRIDGE]

THE 2010s BROUGHT AN UNUSUAL BUT WELCOME DEVELOPMENT in the trade union movement in Barbados: the general secretaries of the country's two biggest unions were women. In 2014, Toni Moore, currently an elected member of the Barbados parliament, was appointed to the post at the Barbados Workers Union (BWU), the country's oldest union; and between 2015 and 2020, Roslyn Smith, and then Delcia Burke, held the position at the National Union of Public Workers (NUPW), the main representative of public sector employees. Smith's departure was controversial, amid claims and counterclaims of retirement and wrongful dismissal, in August 2021, Kimberley Agard was elected president of the NUPW. While the general secretary of the BWU has traditionally been its most powerful office-holder, the president still wields great power within the NUPW. So, in the mid-1990s, when Gladwyn Ophelia King (née Campbell) became the first woman to be elected president of the NUPW, this, too, was seen as a moment of triumph for women unionists.

King's election was a most significant development and this was not only because it meant that a woman held the highest office in the union for the first time in its fifty-year history. It may be said to have marked the culmination of the movement to ameliorate the lives of women, which had been given impetus with the declaration of 1975 as International Women's Year (IWY) and the United Nations Decade for Women (1975–1985). During this period, the Barbados government pledged to improve women's lives in every way and to improve the level of participation by women in the public, professional and private spheres; a pledge that clearly influenced developments within the NUPW. In spite of the pledge, and the evident elevation of the status of Barbadian women, it should not be assumed that it was plain sailing for them within the NUPW.

This chapter seeks to examine the position of women and women's interests within the NUPW in the two decades starting from the launch of International Women's Year to King's election to the presidency. It focuses, for example, on the question of equal treatment within the union and the country, while considering the measures which actively sought to promote the position of women. The approach is at once to consider the general and the specific. In this regard, the paper examines such issues as the workings of the Women's League within the NUPW, while considering the specific quest for equality with respect to the provision of passages for spouses. Similarly, while discussing the national campaign to improve the status of Barbadian women, the chapter will focus on the campaign by which King became union president. The chapter suggests that these were parts of the same broad process in which socio-economic forces are central to its understanding.

The first part of the chapter attempts to demonstrate the context in which developments are understood. This is followed by a brief survey of the relevant literature, followed by an examination of some of the major issues affecting women within the NUPW. The last section is devoted to the emergence of Gladwyn King and her campaign for the post of president.

BRIEF SURVEY OF LITERATURE

The work carried out by Cheris Kramarae – following the earlier work of Edwin Ardener – on muted group theory suggests that women and others who occupy the low end of the totem pole are discounted in society.[1] For this reason, women have been overlooked in the discussions on organizations and institutions in society. The literature covering women in trade unions is extensive, but most focus on women in Europe and the industrialized world, and Asia. One of the earlier studies, in 1920, dealt with women and trade unions in Britain. Barbara Drake's *Women in Trade Unions* focused on such issues as obstacles to organization, trade union restrictions on female labour, and equal work for equal pay. Later, in *Governments and Trade Unions: The British Experience, 1964–1979,* Denis

Barnes and Eileen Reid investigated the critical question of the relationship between government and trade unions, especially the consequences of the growth of trade union power for government's macro-economic policies, but this work was not concerned with specific women's issues. A major study on women and trade unions in industrialized countries[2] considered the policies of governments and trade unions towards women in the historical and cultural contexts. A critical essay by Elaine Gubin and Valerie Piette concluded that women's militant trade unionism first developed in sectors with a predominantly female workforce, before gaining a hold in other sectors. The Fabrique Nationale strike of 1966 in Belgium, over the issue of equal pay for equal work, was the turning point in female trade unionists' militancy as the event forced trade unions to consider both women's place in trade unions and the need to review forms of militancy, including seeking more active leadership roles.

Few major studies of the organized labour movement in Barbados or of the place of women's interests therein have been attempted. Francis Mark's 1966 study of the Barbados Workers Union was an early effort that focused on the industrial relations process, and given the time it was published, ignored women and women's interests.[3] A full quarter-century elapsed before the next major study by Lawrence Nurse, which again emphasized industrial relations practices.[4] Nurse's subsequent efforts – whether individually[5] or in collaboration with Dwayne Devonish[6] – have had as their focus the extent or level of participation by members in the trade union, but the gender factor has been absent from the analyses. Early Barbados trade union activity had been characterized by the unions working individually, although there were instances of informal support for each other's actions. This was to change dramatically in the early 1990s.

Although the unions representing public sector employees had worked closely together in the late 1980s during salary and wage negotiations with the government, the transformation of an informal alliance into a formal coalition of unions that posed a militant challenge to the 1991–1992 structural adjustment programme marked the apogee of the labour movement in Barbados. The rise of Gladwyn King cannot be understood except in the context of this new militancy. The labour coalition would come to constitute one part of the tripartite social partnership that emerged to offer possible solutions to the economic malaise haunting the country and which recognized the adverse socio-economic consequences upon women. Yet, when Minto Coy examined the origins of the Barbados social partnership she focused on structures and ignored both individuals and gender.[7]

While there is a growing body of literature on gender and women, limited attention has been paid to the work and place of women in the (Caribbean) labour movement, especially in public sector employment. An effort by N.M. Riccucci[8] attempted to assess the issues of race and gender in public service unions in the United States. In the Caribbean context, Rhoda Reddock has analyzed the efforts of women in the Trinidad labour movement[9] and provided a case study of the activities of politician-cum-unionist Elma Francoise. Of greater relevance to us is her work on women and the Trinidad and Tobago Unified Teachers' Association (TTUTA), a public sector quasi-union, which is treated within the broader discussion of women in the Trinidad labour movement.

Reddock found that women were not elected to executive positions; that, in spite of its relatively large female membership, the union's leadership remained "predominantly male"; and that within TTUTA the leadership expressed little concern about the practice of wage inequality that favoured men. To support her claims, she cites several specific examples to show how women's issues were marginalized.[10] Lynn Bolles' work on female trade union leaders concludes that the movement in the Anglophone Caribbean had been led by middle-class men, and consequently, "the organizing principles follow the prescribed notions of gender relations, i.e. the dominant ideology of female insubordination".[11]

Not surprisingly, Bolles contends that gender inequality was reinforced by the organizational structure of the trade unions. Together, the structure and inequality restricted, devalued and subordinated women's activities and aspirations. Ultimately, concludes Bolles, the reality of women trade unionists includes a lack of recognition and impediments to their progress within the organization. Following Howard L. Smith and Mary Grenier,[12] Bolles argued that women's progress in trade unions may be explained by the dynamic intersection of women, power and organizations, and by understanding the three sources of power – namely, centrality, control of uncertainty and access to resources.

Before Reddock and Bolles, the Women in the Caribbean Project (WICP) was a major investigation into the condition of women in the Anglophone Caribbean. Roberta Clarke's study of women's organizations and how they worked to advance women's interests constituted one section of the WICP.[13] Yet, Clarke did not consider trade unions among her list of organizations, preferring instead to concentrate on governmental machinery for women; political parties; church associations; national organizations of women; and "Non-Governmental Organisations, whose projects are aimed specifically at women, though not necessarily being women's organisations".

In 2004, I produced the first study of women in public sector unionism in Barbados.[14] In that piece, I examined the place of women in the NUPW – initially called the Barbados Civil Service Association (BACSA) – in the three decades between its formation in 1944 and the International Year of Women. The present chapter will advance that work by examining the situation up to 1995. We turn next to examine the context in which the chapter is undertaken.

CONTEXT

At the start of the period covered by this chapter, the situation with respect to Barbados women was under review due to international pressure as well as the desire of the Barbados government to address several legal and practical inequalities between men and women. In outlining the situation, it seems appropriate to consider the position of women in Barbados in general, and their position in the public service in particular. In this regard, the chapter draws heavily on the report of the enquiry into the status of women, but the international context ought not to be ignored.

The declaration by the United Nations of 1975 as the International Year of the Woman had as its objective the promotion of equal rights and opportunities, and to integrate women into the development process. Yet, the United Nations had itself not done enough internally to advance the cause of women, according to a statistical assessment of the gender of those who had chaired the seven sub-committees of the UN General Assembly. The Fourth Committee, which dealt with trusteeship matters, had two women as chair, while the Third Committee (social, humanitarian and cultural matters) had ten women as chair. However, the other committees – First (political matters); Second (economic and development issues); Fifth (administration and finance of the United Nations itself); Sixth (legal questions) and Seventh (a special political committee) – had never been chaired by women. It was, perhaps, poignant that this statistical review had been produced by Helvi Sipila, who was tasked with the responsibility of coordinating matters pertaining to International Women's Year (IWY) and the planned World Conference.[15]

A 1979 report from the International Labour Organization (ILO) found that the ratio of men to women in executive positions in the Anglophone Caribbean was 3:1,[16] and this male domination of executive posts manifested itself in the Barbados public service. Indeed, the authors of a commission appointed to investigate the status of Barbadian women had much to say about this. The commission was appointed in November 1976, held its first formal meeting in January 1977, and presented its report to the attorney general (that is, the minister responsible for women's affairs) in May 1978. The commission received submissions of memoranda; held meetings with men's and women's organizations; and also hosted fourteen public hearings. The subject matter discussed in these hearings ranged from the constitutional rights of women to the effects of garbage collection and disposal.

Under its terms of reference, the commission had been appointed to enquire into and report upon the following:

(a) the citizenship and immigration laws, policies and practices so far as they affect women;
(b) the position of women in the civil and criminal laws, especially the laws governing matrimonial property, marriage and divorce;
(c) income tax and estate and succession duty legislation in so far as the same affect women;
(d) labour laws in their application to women and their role in the labour force;
(e) the employment, placing and promotion of women in the public service and the private sector;
(f) the cultural and historical attitudes which lead to discrimination and prejudice against women, making it difficult for them to realize their full potential;
(g) the mental and physical health of women, including all aspects of family planning and its application to women;
(h) education, including its availability to girls and women at all levels of the educational system;

(i) the one-parent family, with special reference to women's roles therein;
(j) laws and practices concerning the political rights of women;
(k) and such other matters in relation to the status of women in Barbados as may appear to the commissioners to be relevant.

Term of reference (e) is of particular relevance to this chapter and the commission found solid evidence of glaring inequality in the public service.[17]

It is incredible to think that forty years ago, no women were employed as customs officers in Barbados. This was one significant omission which highlighted women's situation in the Barbados public service. Between 1977 and 1978, only 16.5 per cent of those holding appointments on the boards of statutory corporations or committees of management were women; and a quarter of them were appointed to boards belonging to the Ministry of Education. In addition, women were entirely absent from some boards, including those responsible for the Industrial Development Corporation and the Barbados Development Bank. Similarly, in the years 1974 to 1976, of the 287 public servants who received overseas training, only fifty-seven of them were women.[18] The situation for women at the higher echelons of the public service was so dire that the prime minister was prompted to assuage concerns expressed by women public servants about their future prospects, and to assure them that their advancement to the very top was but a matter of time.

In 1917, the first woman to enter the public service was a clerical officer and until the late 1950s, the few women who were recruited were confined to this grade. A specific policy of recruitment of women into the general grades of the public service was adopted as a result of an agreement between the Barbados Civil Service Association (BACSA) and the government that 10 per cent of all civil service jobs should be allocated to women. This quota was subsequently raised to 20 per cent and then 25 per cent, but was eventually abandoned "in favour of the general principle of appointment based on qualifications". Moreover, the 1957 agreement negotiated by BACSA had called for the special recruitment of six female administrative cadets who were to be groomed for top administrative positions. However, five of them left the civil service twenty years later. It is true that by 1977, when Prime Minister J.M.G.M. "Tom" Adams addressed the annual conference of the NUPW, women held about 48 per cent of all posts in the public service; 130 out of 616 posts in "higher categories" and 29 per cent of the senior posts below permanent secretary, that is, those posts ranging from executive officer to senior assistant secretary. Crucially, however, all the permanent secretaries were men.[19]

This detailed outline of the positions of women in the public service has been presented because of the historical linkage between holding a leadership position in the public service and aspiring to the highest office in the public sector trade union. Up to the mid-1970s, the starting point for this chapter, all those persons who had ascended to the office of president of BACSA/NUPW had been drawn from the most senior ranks of the public service. Since women had been left out of the senior echelons of the service, it was unlikely that they could have become president of a trade union. The Commission on the Status of Women in Barbados made recommendations to improve their standing in the public service and to ameliorate their overall position so that they might challenge historical prejudices and realize their full potential.

The commission recommended, inter alia, that a special effort be made to explore the possibility of retaining the services of highly trained women by offering part-time employment opportunities; that there ought to be an increase in the number of women in the public service who received overseas training; and called for the revival of the administrative cadet system in an effort to increase the intake of promising young women for training for entry into the administrative section of the public service. Generally, the commission hoped that the Public Service Commission would energetically publicize, through its recruitment procedures, "the fact that women are eligible for appointment in all occupations and professions"; recommended that some statistical report be annually presented to parliament to provide information on women's progress in the public service; and called upon the Cabinet to issue a policy statement to all ministries in which would be outlined the official position on the question of equality of employment, training and promotion opportunities for women, and the specific measures by which these were to be achieved. The commission also made recommendations on specific conditions of service brought to its attention,which continued to fester until the early 1990s.[20]

WOMEN AND LEAVE PASSAGES

The commission recommended to the government that steps should be taken to review the then extant pensions legislation, with a view to ensuring that there would be no difference in the provisions made for public officers on the basis of gender. Of greater relevance to our discussion was the succeeding recommendation: "113. The Commission recommends that the Leave Passage Legislation be so amended as to allow females to enjoy the same privilege as males in the same grades, and the amendment be worded in such a way as to avoid duplication of leave passages."[21]

It should be emphasized that in March 1974, the House of Assembly debated the question of leave passages but mainly to make certain adjustments: to substitute the words six weeks for two months, and four weeks for six weeks. Given this focus, it is not surprising that the ensuing discussion remained centred on opposition to the payment of leave passages. At no time in the debate was the discrimination in favour of male public servants addressed.[22] Retaining the benefit of a leave passage had been one of the earliest priorities of the BACSA, but the denial of this fringe benefit did not sit well with some women in the public service, who made it a point to bring it to the attention of the commission on the status of women.

In a memorandum submitted to the commissioners, Frances Chandler and June Roach fulminated against the practice – sanctioned by Chapter VI of the General Orders – which entitled certain male public service officers to payment of return passages for themselves and spouses within or outside the Caribbean, according to rank. As Chandler and Roach averred, no mention was made of female officers being entitled to payment of leave passages for their husbands, and this ought to be modified. In keeping with the tenor of their brief memorandum, the pair concluded: "In our opinion, the leave passages are fringe benefits which go with the post and since in cases where a MAN holds the post, he is allowed at least 2 passages (for HIMSELF AND HIS WIFE) then a WOMAN holding the SAME POST should qualify for the same number of passages i.e. at least 2 passages for HERSELF and HER HUSBAND."[23] (Original emphasis)

This opinion was endorsed by the commissioners. In addition to the summarized recommendation quoted above, they made more detailed comments in the main body of the report as follows:

Leave passages which benefit dependants at present is only granted to males. There is no provision for females whose husband might not be an employee of the Government. We are not asking that leave be duplicated, but that where a female Civil Servant is at a grade which grants leave passage, then the female officer be granted the same terms which would apply to males. It must be emphasised that we are not asking for any one person to benefit twice from this regulation, but that it be so worded that all discrimination would be removed.[24]

This campaign for equality of treatment for women public officers with respect to the award of leave passages continued for another fifteen years. This is not the place to provide a detailed exposition of the campaign, but a few pertinent comments are in order. The matter was constantly drawn to the attention of the NUPW leadership; indeed Denis Clarke, who recently retired as general secretary, recalls that the matter was unfailingly brought up at the union's annual conferences. The records of the Women's League of the NUPW suggest that the matter was given some ventilation.[25] Yet, when I questioned several informants about women being granted leave passages, they recall that the issue was regularly raised, but struggle to remember the persons who brought it up! It seems that this was an uncomfortable issue for both the leadership and the membership. On the one hand, gendered discourse conflicted with the reluctance to grant equal treatment; and on the other, class must have been a factor because the union drew increasingly larger numbers from outside the traditional civil service cadres. For those in the lowest ranks of the public service, the payment of leave passages must have appeared to be elitist. In this regard, they had the support of Frank Walcott who – in the aforementioned parliamentary debate of 1974 – had considered the granting of leave passages to Barbadians as but an unwelcome relic of the country's colonial past. At that time, Walcott had recognized that granting leave passages to Barbadians was introduced about twenty-five years earlier to offset the clear discrimination against local civil servants, since expatriates were granted leave passages. However, Walcott did not believe that the granting of leave passages could be justified in the 1970s, since the government was expending significant sums on the overseas training of civil servants. Walcott never addressed the discrimination against women civil servants in respect of leave passages.[26]

Yet, the campaign to abolish discrimination on the grounds of gender in the matter of the leave passage reached a happy conclusion when Prime Minister L.E. Sandiford in 1990 introduced a Resolution to approve the Civil Establishment (Leave Passages) (Amendment) Order, which received support from all three political parties. The three main reasons that the legislation was supported were: firstly, failure to grant the women public officers' payment of leave passages for their husbands constituted a breach of the ILO's Conventions on Discrimination, Employment and Occupation, and the Convention for the Elimination of Discrimination against Women, which Barbados had long ratified. Secondly, there was a sense that "times were changing"; that the reforms introduced in the aftermath of the 1978 report into the status of women in Barbados had had the desired effect. Finally, the pressure brought to bear by the NUPW was acknowledged.

In his contribution to the debate on the resolution, the Majority Opposition Leader, Dr R.C. Haynes, highlighted the contribution of the NUPW general secretary. While we ought not to discount the fact that Joseph Goddard was then linked to Haynes's party and would later stand as a candidate in the general election, it is reasonable to suggest that Haynes was being sincere when he posited, "It is also important for us to record that the General Secretary of the NUPW has also been foremost in the fight to ensure that this disability was removed." Similarly, Sandiford had recognized the efforts of the union, acknowledging that since 1981, the NUPW had been raising the matter "from time to time" on the basis that female officers should be eligible to claim leave passage for their husbands, just as male officers did for their wives.[27]

While Goddard and the union's leadership received public recognition for their role, we must explain why they had championed the case for equality of treatment regarding leave passages. Essentially, the answer lies in the inter-relationship of several factors and actors – actually, actresses. The union could not ignore the declaration of International Women's Year and government reforms, which both sought to improve the conditions and status of women in Barbados. Moreover, IWY and the legal reforms served to embolden and empower women. Into this situation stepped the likes of Marva Alleyne, who combined her official position as a member of the Bureau of Women's Affairs, which was set up by the government to oversee the post-1978 changes, with activism in the NUPW.

In a public lecture delivered to commemorate the seventieth anniversary of the founding of the NUPW, it was suggested that the union's record on women's issues had been far from stellar.[28] However, Alleyne challenges such assertions. In this context, she is keen to emphasize the fact that in the aftermath of IWY, the NUPW leadership embraced change, and she and others helped to introduce programmes designed to raise awareness of women's issues and to make the union more conscious of and sensitive to its treatment of its women members and their issues. Moreover, Alleyne is convinced that the union took on board the complaints raised by women members and actively fought to protect and promote women's interests as part of its day-to-day activities. One avenue through which this sensitization process was carried out was the Women's League of the NUPW.

Formed in January 1972 by the male-dominated council of the NUPW, the Women's League has had a torturous existence. This is not the place for a full account of its numerous travails, but one may note the low attendance at meetings and events organized by the league, as well as the resignations of senior officers. Thus, for example, Annice Dalrymple, who would later become campus bursar at the Cave Hill campus of the University of the West Indies, resigned as secretary with immediate effect in September 1978 because "my involvement at this present time does not afford me the time to function in this post with the efficiency which my principles demand".

Nevertheless, I contend that the league contributed to greater awareness of issues affecting women in the union and the public service. Thus, three years after resigning as secretary of the NUPW Women's League, Dalrymple was invited by the Bahamas Trade Union Congress, in her capacity as a member of the steering committee of the Caribbean Women Trade Unionists, to attend a triennial congress in June 1981. This congress drew up a programme of continuous training of women trade unionists in the Dutch- and English-speaking Caribbean.[29] Such programmes ultimately contributed to the elevation of women to the NUPW council, although most did not owe their elevation to electoral success, but were appointed as representatives of their respective divisions. Yet, by the early 1990s, there had been progress.

Patsy Crichlow, a staff nurse, had served as chair of the Women's Affairs Committee and had been a member of the NUPW council since 1980. Similarly, Katherine Hutson served as secretary of Division II of the NUPW from 1990 to 1992, and was also elected Deputy General Treasurer for the same period. Hutson eventually became Assistant Secretary/Treasurer of the Women's Affairs Committee after 1992. The NUPW executive from 1990 to 1992 counted Joan Glasgow as Second Vice-President and Joyce Sealey as Third Vice-President. It is significant that all four had been active in the Women's League and this lends support to our claim that it must have helped to engender an atmosphere in which the talents and views of women were being given recognition. It was the election of Gladwyn Ophelia King to the top post of president in 1994 that marked the real ascent of women to leadership positions.

ASCENT TO LEADERSHIP

The rise of King to the presidency cannot be understood without reference to the tumultuous events and drama of the early 1990s, in which public servants were central. At this juncture, we turn to briefly explore the causes of the economic crisis affecting Barbados and how the measures adopted to deal with the situation adversely affected public servants, but conversely contributed to the rise of Gladwyn King.

Whatever the underlying structural defects of the Barbados economy, it is recognized that the economic crisis of the early 1990s was due to internal fiscal deficits as well as an unfavourable international economic environment, which coincided with a loan repayment schedule – including one for thirty million pounds sterling to Barclays de Zoete Wedd – that was, at best, unfortunate in its timing. The various economic, fiscal and financial indicators made plain the extent of the crisis, and the critical coalescence of these indicators in 1991 was to have dramatic consequences. The roots of the fiscal crisis lay in the income tax concessions promised by the Democratic Labour Party in its election campaign of 1986, which had been implemented almost immediately after they won.[30] Thus, Barbados' debt was $50.2 million at the end of 1976, but $1,079.7 million at the end of 1989; and the cost of servicing that debt had risen from $85.3 million in 1983, to $187.2 million by 1986, and stood at $303 million in 1990. Similarly, a Statement of Current Revenue for the Ten-Year Period 1983–84 to 1992–93 showed that for the first time, in 1990–91, current revenue did not increase from the year before.[31] Moreover, the *Bulletin of the Barbados Statistical Service* and the *Economic Review of the Central*

Bank of Barbados for June 1991 both highlighted the economic malaise: exports of manufactured goods were "sluggish" and even weaker than 1990; sugar receipts were "small"; and the balance of imports over exports had risen sharply.[32]

In light of the deteriorating economic situation and the growing fear of a currency devaluation in the face of adverse terms of trade, the government indicated, in early July 1991, its intention to seek assistance from the International Monetary Fund (IMF) and to negotiate a structural adjustment programme (SAP). Given the paranoia and anxiety associated with SAPs and dealings with the IMF, the then Opposition spokesman on economic affairs, Owen Arthur, introduced a resolution in parliament which "urge[d] Government to submit for our consideration before implementation or ratification, any proposals incorporating monetary, fiscal and other measures designed to arrest and correct the continuing decline of our economy, to entrench its stability and growth and to protect and strengthen the value of our currency".[33]

The period July to October 1991 saw the government propose a series of measures to deal with the crisis. Essentially, the options available were increased taxes, job retrenchment, issuance of national bonds to public workers, devaluation, and a pay cut. The government abandoned the idea of bonds in the face of opposition from the unions and ultimately rejected currency devaluation; but increased taxes, introduced layoffs and reduced emoluments of public servants. It was the last which helped to propel Gladwyn King to national prominence.

In a nationally televised address in early September 1991, Sandiford iterated the government's intention to terminate any discussion on bonds and to move instead to reduce the emoluments of all public servants. It is worth pointing out that in the parliamentary debate on the Appropriations Bill, members of the governing party had affirmed their opposition to salary cuts and the implementation of measures to undermine the social benefits which accrued to the population. Yet, the seeds for cutting public servants' salaries and wages were clearly sown in the 1991 Appropriations Bill when, for example, trade unionist Robert Morris highlighted the growing public sector wage bill. According to him, the figures were $408 million for 1989–90, $416 million for 1990–91, and a projected $476 million for 1991–92; or what Morris termed "a rapid and relatively massive increase". Perhaps he should have alluded to the increase in ministers' salaries, following the passing of Order No. 10 of 18 March 1991, "to move the passing of a Resolution to approve the Ministers and Parliamentary Secretaries (Remuneration and Allowances) Order 1991".

In a statement to Parliament on 17 September 1991, Sandiford outlined how the deteriorating fiscal and economic position had resulted in a revenue shortfall and a foreign exchange deficiency, which had placed pressure on the ability to maintain the exchange rate of the Barbados currency against others. In these circumstances, he argued, the government had no choice but to legislate a reduction in pay for public servants for the period October 1991 to March 1993, and withhold increments for a specified period. The Public Service Reduction of Emoluments Act, 1991 was passed by an eleven to ten majority, with two abstentions. Significantly, the two who abstained were paid employees of trade unions, one a high-ranking official of the NUPW. The passing of the act was, in the view of the government, "legitimated" by a plebiscite in which public servants were asked to choose between the salary cut and a devaluation of the Barbados currency, and the majority who voted opted for the pay cut.[34]

In the immediate aftermath of the passing of the bill, the trade unions (now organized into an informal Coalition of Trade Unions and Staff Associations of Barbados) sought confirmation of an earlier opinion that the act was unconstitutional. Indeed, Patrick Frost, general secretary of the Barbados Secondary Teachers Union, recalls that "the unions were already in possession of legal advice to the effect that any attempt to reduce salaries through legislation would be unconstitutional".[35] Even two decades earlier, Henry Forde had raised the matter during a debate on the Protection of Wages (Amendment) Act, 1975 because he observed that nothing was said in the legislation about whether the act affected the government or not. Forde opined that it was short-sighted at a time when the government and "quasi-public boards" were becoming the biggest employers, and the Crown as employer had reserved the right to hire and fire, in some instances, without adequate notice and without redress in the courts. Forde, who would later serve as attorney general from 1976 to 1981, concluded somewhat prophetically: "There is no reason why the Crown should be exempted from legislation such as this. I think that workers in many instances need as much protection both in relation to wages and otherwise against the Crown as they do against any other persons."[36]

In 1992, the Chief Justice ruled on a case brought in the name of

Gladwyn Ophelia King against the attorney general on the constitutionality of the 1991 legislation. Simply put, King argued that the act represented an unlawful seizure of property, without reasonable compensation.

King's team argued, inter alia, that:

(a) in passing the Public Service Reduction of Emoluments Act, 1991, the Barbados parliament had acted *ultra vires*;
(b) salary was property and property constituted one of the fundamental rights protected by the Constitution;
(c) a distinction existed and ought to be made between altering the remuneration of an officer as opposed to the remuneration of that officer;
(d) Gladwyn King's employment was a contractual one "and the nature of the contract was such that an increment could only be withheld by the Public Service Commission if she were being disciplined".

In return, the attorney general countered that a public servant's position was one of status, not contract, and even if it were contractual, that contract *could* be unilaterally altered by the Crown. Furthermore, Parliament had acted within its powers and in the national interest.

In rejecting King's application, Chief Justice Williams opined that the Barbados Constitution specified which officers (including judges!) could not have their salary and conditions of service altered without their consent, and any officer not so specifically mentioned was not entitled to similar protection. Furthermore, the terms under which King was employed stated that the Crown had the right to unilaterally adjust her emoluments, as had happened under the Public Service Reduction of Emoluments Act. Consequently, concluded the learned judge, King's constitutional property rights had not been breached. King unsuccessfully appealed the decision. In a two-to-one decision, the Court of Appeal held:

(i) that the 1991 Act was an effective exercise of the jurisdiction vested in Parliament to determine the emoluments attached to offices in the public service. Section 112 of the Constitution (which protected the salaries and terms of office of certain specified public officers) was inconsistent with the claim that all public officers were entitled to the protection expressly conferred by that section on specified office-holders (of whom the appellant was not one) and there was no implied term attached to service in public office that the emoluments attached to such office would never be reduced;

(ii) that the appellant had no right to a minimum salary and, accordingly, no right protected by sections 11 or 16 of the Constitution; her only right was to the payment of such emoluments as the Minister under the Civil Establishment Act or as Parliament in the exercise of its legislative powers from time to time attached to her office. Her emoluments had been lawfully reduced by the 1991 Act.

King eventually took her case to Barbados' highest court at the time, the Judicial Committee of Her Majesty's Most Honourable Privy Council. Here I simply quote the conclusion of that most august body: "The emoluments of the appellant were lawfully reduced by the 1991 Act. Sir Denys Williams, C.J., sitting in the High Court, and the Court of Appeal (Smith and Moe, JJ. A.; Husbands, J.A. dissenting) came to the same conclusion. Their lordships will humbly advise Her Majesty that this appeal ought to be dismissed. The appellant must pay the costs of the Attorney-General before their lordships' Board."[37]

The trade unions had clearly expected to win their appeal before the Privy Council and NUPW correspondence demonstrates both the anticipated success and the dejection following the failure. That the unions had a strong case is borne out by the following comment delivered by Professor Simeon McIntosh in the immediate aftermath of the Privy Council ruling: "The Privy Council has delivered of itself a judgement in the 'Ophelia King Case' so wretchedly poor in its analysis that it has virtually silenced the claims of critical reason and hermeneutic reflection, and hardly merits a mark of *elagantia juris*."[38]

KING LOST THE LEGAL BATTLE, BUT WON RECOGNITION

The late legal luminary Simeon McIntosh once affirmed that "the *Gladwyn Ophelia King* case has proved to be one of the most important cases – if not the most important case – in Barbados (post-independence) history."[39] While McIntosh addressed the defamation suit brought by the Chief Justice over a local newspaper's reporting of the public reaction to his ruling in favour of the attorney general and against King, it is clear that the significance of the case really lay in the legal and constitutional ramifications of her challenging the actions of the sovereign Barbados parliament; a challenge with implications for the constitutional development of the Anglophone Caribbean. Recognition would also come in the form of support for her candidacy for president of the NUPW in 1994.

As King tells it, she initially neither sought to be the person who challenged the attorney general nor to be president of her trade union. However, she was sure that something had to be done about the injustice of the pay cut, especially in light of the fact that the very parliamentarians who voted in favour of the 1991 act had voted themselves a pay increase some months prior. Thus, when the trade union coalition asked for a list of those willing to challenge the pay cut, King was quick to put her name down and then constantly followed up with the union leadership to see what progress was being made. King acknowledges that she was no radical, but had attained a level of consciousness which made her chafe at all types of injustice, and the unilateral reduction of her pay was one of the worst forms of it. This level of social consciousness she attributes to her study of history and to the teachings of her history teachers, Anthony Wiltshire and, especially, the late Leroy Harewood.[40]

It is possible to suggest that King was somewhat piqued by the treatment she received once she had put her name forward with a view to ensuring that her rights prevailed in 1991. Such was the intimidation and harassment – even from members of the public service – that the NUPW was forced to issue a press release on 25 February 1992, asking for an end to the derogatory remarks and threatening telephone calls being made to King. Added to this, she was not initially informed of the outcome of the Privy Council ruling, although she was assured that she would be invited to attend when the trade union movement met with the lawyers for a debriefing.[41] King made the decision to seek the highest office in the NUPW simply because she felt she had something to contribute.

King recalls that she felt she could "make a difference" to a trade union whose membership had been savaged by the structural adjustment programme of 1991–93; and which was undermined by the belief that union leaders were playing politics and not providing adequate representation. Yet, King did not pitch her campaign on the level that members should vote for her because she was a woman and the time had come for a woman to take the reins. While she *did* believe these perspectives, she was careful to emphasize that the SAP and the government's measures to resuscitate the economy had had a greater negative impact on women, while simultaneously highlighting the need for the leadership of the

NUPW to be more aggressive in its defence of workers' rights. King, therefore, sought to build an alliance across all divisions of the NUPW, and was successful in the 1994 election when she defeated the incumbent, Cedric Murrell.

CONCLUSION

The election of King to the presidency of the major public sector union in 1994 was accompanied by the sweeping away from office of the Sandiford administration following the September general election. As a further postscript, it must be pointed out that the Barbados Constitution was amended in 1995 to protect the emoluments of public servants and that legislation was introduced to facilitate the repayment of the 8 per cent of their salary that public servants lost through legislative action in 1991. Still further, King would end up working in the library of Parliament!

The two decades between the declaration of International Women's Year and Gladwyn King's election as NUPW president were characterized by attempts – official and otherwise – to ameliorate the status and condition of women in Barbados. The chapter has shown the intertwining of the official with the private, whether in the form of the National Commission on the Status of Women or women in the NUPW fighting to improve their position on various subject matters, including the award of leave passages. Until Gladwyn King became the face – or was it the name? – of public workers' legal challenge to the government of Barbados, she was relatively unknown. Her ascent to leadership of her trade union was rapid, but it was facilitated by reforms initiated by the government for women in the society at large, and by an NUPW that was persuaded by women of the need to advance their issues within and beyond the trade union.

NOTES

1. Shirley Ardener, "Ardener's 'Muted Groups': The Genesis of an Idea and its Praxis," *Women and Language* 28 no. 2 (Fall 2005): 50–54, 72.
2. A. Cook, Val Lorwin and Arlene Kaplan Daniels, eds., *Women and Trade Unions in Eleven Industrialized Countries* (Philadelphia: Temple University Press, 1984).
3. Francis Mark, *The History of the Barbados Workers Union* (The Barbados Workers Union, 1966).
4. Lawrence Nurse, *Trade Unionism and Industrial Relations in the Caribbean: History, Contemporary Practice and Prospect* (Westport, CT: Greenwood, 1992).
5. Lawrence Nurse, "Different Faces of Participation in Trade Union Activity in Barbados – A Research Note," *Social and Economic Studies* 53, no. 3 (Sept 2004): 111–25.
6. Lawrence Nurse and Dwayne Devonish, "Worker Participation in Barbados: Contemporary Practice and Prospects," *The International Journal of Human Resource Management* 19, no. 10 (2008): 1911–28.
7. Indira Minto-Coy, "The Grit that Makes the Pearl: Collaborative Problem Solving in the Midst of National Crisis," *Systems Research and Behavioral Science* 29 (2012): 221–26.
8. N.M. Riccucci, *Women, Minorities and Unions in the Public Sector* (New York: Greenwood, 1990).
9. Rhoda Reddock, *Women, Labour and Politics in Trinidad and Tobago: A History* (London: Zed Books, 1994).
10. Reddock, *Women, Labour*, chapter 3.
11. A. Lynn Bolles, "Claiming Their Rightful Position: Women Trade Union Leaders of the Commonwealth Caribbean," (University of Maryland College Park: Department of Spanish and Portuguese Working Papers No. 13, 1992), 22.
12. Howard L. Smith, and Mary Grenier, "Sources of Organizational Power for Women: Overcoming Structural Obstacles." *Sex Roles* 8, no. 7 (1982): 773–846.
13. Roberta Clarke, "Women's Organisations, Women's Interests," *Social and Economic Studies* 35, no. 3 (1986):107–55.
14. Richard A. Goodridge, "Women in Public Sector Unionism in Barbados 1944 to 1975," in *New Gender Studies from Cameroon and the Caribbean*, ed. J. Endeley et al. (Buea: University of Buea, 2004), 113–33.
15. Sipila's findings were gladly seized upon and highlighted by those investigating the status of women in Barbados.
16. Bolles, "Claiming Their Rightful Position," 22.

17. Government of Barbados, *Report of the National Commission on the Status of Women in Barbados,* Bridgetown (laid in Parliament, September 1978).
18. ibid., 404–9.
19. ibid., 184–97.
20. ibid., 396–99.
21. ibid., 398.
22. House of Assembly Debates (official report), First Session of 1971–76. Tuesday, 5 March 1974.
23. Government of Barbados, *Report of the National Commission on the Status of Women,* 57.
24. ibid., 406.
25. See NUPW 75/22, a multi-volume file, for the minutes/records of the Women's Affairs Committee.
26. House of Assembly Debates (official report), First Session of 1971–76.
27. The discussion draws heavily on the House of Assembly Debates (Official Report), First Session 1986–1991. Tuesday, 14 August 1990.
28. Richard A. Goodridge, "Understanding the Past to Change the Present: The history of the National Union of Public Workers since 1944," lecture delivered at Horatio Cooke Auditorium, Dalkeith, St Michael, Barbados, to commemorate the seventieth anniversary of the NUPW (January 2014).
29. NUPW 75/22, vol IV.
30. The most recent discussion on the subject is by Clyde Mascoll, "Modelling Two Caribbean Economies with a Fiscal Emphasis: Barbados and Jamaica 1973–2010" (PhD diss., University of the West Indies, 2014). I also had an interview with Mascoll on 26 August 2015. He worked at the Central Bank of Barbados in the early 1990s and has been a spokesman on economic affairs for the two leading political parties in Barbados over the last twenty years.
31. During the parliamentary debates over the period 1990–1994, various figures were cited, as politicians from each side attempted to demonstrate that the other side was responsible for (worsening) the crisis.
32. "Exports fall by $6.8m in 1990," *Daily Nation,* 16 July 1991, p.11.
33. House of Assembly Debates (official report), 1st Session, 1991–96. Meeting of 23 July 1991.
34. Research suggests that some public servants did not complete the option forms; others received the forms after the deadline or never received them. This clearly casts doubts on the idea that a majority of public servants voted for the pay cut.
35. Personal interview with Mr Frost, 2011; also see "The Public Service Reduction of Emoluments Act, 1991 and its Implications" by Patrick Frost. Unpublished memo, September 1992.

36. House of Assembly Debates (Official Report), Second Session of 1971–76. 20 May 1975. See pages 5083–93.
37. The three cases may be followed at a) King vs Attorney General [High Court. Civil Suit No. 1878 of 1991 (Williams, C.J.) May 15, 1992]; b) King vs Attorney General [Court of Appeal Civ. App. No. 19 of 1992 (Husbands, Smith and Moe, J.J.A, 9–13 Nov 1992, 18–19 Jan 1993 and 24 May 1993]; c) King v Attorney General [Judicial Committee of the Privy Council. On Appeal from Barbados. Appeal No. 1 of 1994 (Lords Templeman, Brownne-Wilkinson, Mustill, Slynn of Hadley, and Woolf) 3 May 1994].
38. Simeon McIntosh, "A Wretched Judgement," *Barbados Advocate*, Monday, 16 May 1994.
39. S.C.R. McIntosh, *Fundamental Rights and Democratic Governance: Essays in Caribbean Jurisprudence* (Kingston: Caribbean Law Publishing, 2005), 127.
40. R. Worrell, "Leroy Harewood Pan-African Humanist," *IDEAZ* 1, no. 2 (2002): 29–35. See also, R. Worrell, "Leroy Harewood: Pan-African Humanist," in *Pan-Africanism, Pan-Africanists, and African Liberation in the 21st Century*, ed. H. Campbell and R. Worrell (Washington, DC: New Academia Publishing, 2006), 81–145.
41. Correspondence dated 1994-04-21 – and other information – may be found at NUPW Personal Grievance No. 3879; Campbell, formerly King, Gladwyn Ophelia.

[Part Five]

RACE RELATIONS IN THE CARIBBEAN:
Contested Narratives

[16]

"PASSING FOR WHITE" IN BAHAMIAN SOCIETY DURING THE LATE NINETEENTH AND EARLY TWENTIETH CENTURIES

[GAIL SAUNDERS]

BAHAMIAN SOCIETY, LIKE THE CARIBBEAN GENERALLY, WAS DEEPLY divided by race and class. Racism, an important legacy of slavery, meant that the majority of Caribbean people who were of African descent were considered racially and morally inferior by local and metropolitan whites, who considered themselves superior to non-whites. These racist attitudes persisted into post-emancipation years, dominating Caribbean societies in such a way that non-whites internalized feelings of inferiority, despising anything African.[1]

Class stratification was also important and closely related to racial divisions. Caribbean societies (which included the Bahamas) were generally divided into three major "sectors in descending order of power and status: the white upper class, the colored mixed stratum and the black masses who just had been freed".[2] The three-tier class/race structure persisted in Caribbean societies until the 1930s and 1940s, and even longer in the Bahamas. In Nassau, the capital, located on New Providence Island, an intermediate coloured or mixed-race class held an ambiguous position in the strictly stratified society between the white elite at the top and the black labouring class at the bottom. It comprised free coloureds who had emerged out of slavery and were products of European and African ancestry, and those who were born in a free society. By the turn of the nineteenth century, the coloured or mixed-race community of Nassau comprised a highly complex parentage.[3]

Class lines were not as clearly demarcated in the widely scattered

Out Island settlements where the majority of the population lived. Out Islanders were usually extremely poor in material terms, most living at the same economic and social level. Yet, despite their poverty, intense racial feelings and deep prejudice kept the two races apart.

Colin Hughes argued that the Bahamian experience differed from the norm of the British Caribbean and asserted that M.G. Smith's distinction of five dimensions of colour concept – structural colour – is the most important for political change in the Bahamas. Hughes contends that in the categories which define and constitute the social framework, "wealth has had pre-eminent place in the Bahamas". Wealth attracted power and authority, and therefore in the Bahamas racial differences were linked to economic relationships. Racial, rather than class, difference "... determined the predominant features of social, economic, and political relationships".[4] Until the 1920s, many of the white elite were far from rich, but prospered during the Prohibition years.

Gordon Lewis also maintained that the development of the Bahamas and Bermuda, although shaped by most of the forces which moulded the rest of the Caribbean, was fundamentally different from that of the region. The absence of the sugar plantation made for this difference. Early in their history, both colonies developed economies that were maritime and commercial in character, thus separating them from the rest of the Caribbean. Their commercial rather than agricultural economies; close ties with the United States; isolation and poor communications; larger white populations; retention of the old representative system combined with the protracted political dominance of the white mercantile elite; and a weak middle stratum (at least in the case of the Bahamas) made for significant social and political differences.[5]

An ambiguous colour line developed in the Bahamas and was particularly evident in Nassau. Certain persons were acknowledged as white and moved into white society, but were clearly of mixed descent. This was in contrast to the United States with its legalized segregation (Jim Crow), where a person known to have African blood was socially a 'negro' in America, although a small number of very light-skinned persons "passed" for white.[6] In the Bahamas, as in the Caribbean generally, many light-skinned non-whites, some with straight hair and European features, because it was to their advantage, "passed" for white and were accepted by the white elite.

Charles Ives, an American author of an early travel book, expressed the ambiguity of the Bahamian whites' 'purity' in 1880: "It is true that the blood of a portion of the 'gentry' is said to be perfectly pure, but it is difficult in some cases of mixture to accurately draw the colour line, and it is wise to ignore and ask no questions of one's partner in a voluptuous waltz, which might result in banishing the inquisitor from high-toned society. It is at times injudicious to scrutinize closely hair that appears straight or nearly so."[7]

English stipendiary magistrate L.D. Powles, in his book, *Land of The Pink Pearl*, published in London in 1888, also commented on Bahamian whites and those who were passing for white:

> Although there is plenty pure unspotted white blood scattered throughout the Bahamas, a good deal of that upper crust of Nassau Society is decidedly mixed, and in truth many of the so-called white families owe their right to that title to an old statute which enacts that every person who is more than three degrees removed from African shall rank as white. Though the skins of most of them are fair enough to pass for pure white anywhere in Europe, their African blood would at once be detected by any Southerner or West Indian.[8]

Nassau society was segregated in almost every aspect. Colour separated the races in housing, education, occupation and in social intercourse. In some of the biracial Out Islands, the separation of races was more stringent. This chapter attempts to analyze the reasons why the Bahamas', particularly Nassau's, social system, which more resembled that of the United States than the Caribbean situation, tolerated 'passing'.

Bahamians, particularly non-whites from Nassau, suffered pernicious discrimination, humiliation and oppression. They endured offensive treatment from whites and were discriminated against by the leading religious denominations, barred from some private schools, such as Queen's College, St Francis Academy and St Hilda's; theatres, clubs and restaurants; and certain exclusively white residential areas. At the J.P. Sands shop, located in downtown Nassau, non-whites were relegated to a separate line and had to wait for all whites to be served before they were. Most whites had membership in the Anglican, Methodist and Presbyterian churches. The Anglican Christ Church Cathedral's congregation in 1911 was two-thirds white, and by paying pew rents, they commanded the better seats in the church. Segregation was so rigid that, in the 1950s, two Sunday schools existed at Christ Church – one held on Saturday for whites, and the other on Sunday for non-whites.

The latter were encouraged to worship at St Mary's in the western suburbs, formerly a chapel of Christ Church, and at St Agnes in Grant's Town, a black section of Nassau. Trinity Methodist Church, located in central Nassau, until 1889 catered mainly to the well-to-do white families, many of whom left the church because it welcomed a poorer class of whites and "a few respectable light-skinned coloreds". Ebenezer, the eastern Methodist Chapel, was mixed, and Wesley Chapel in Grant's Town catered almost exclusively to a black congregation.[9] However, the two races entered by separate doors. The Presbyterian Church's congregation was almost wholly white, but held a separate Sunday school for non-whites.

Boy Scout and Girl Guide Companies were strictly segregated in the 1920s. Only light-skinned girls and boys from middle-class families were admitted into certain Girl Guide Companies and Boy Scout troops. When Lord and Lady Baden-Powell, Chief Scout and Chief Guide, visited the Bahamas in early 1930s, they were appalled to find that the two races in the Guides were segregated, even in their passing out parades. By the 1950s, the Second Nassau Girl Guide Company accepted a few light-skinned girls from middle-class families. However, when darker-skinned girls were introduced, white parents removed their daughters from the company. Even when non-whites attended predominantly white schools, joined Girl Guide companies and Scout troops, or attended churches with a mainly white congregation, they rarely socialized with them.[10] The white elite, many of whom were related and socialized together, had a firm grip on the economy and political machinery, and controlled social life. Many whites owned shops on Bay Street in Nassau and hired only whites as clerks in their businesses. Wealth and power came to be equated with race.

Some light-skinned, mixed-race people from Nassau and those migrants from Long Island, Abaco and Eleuthera especially resented the prevailing discrimination and the denial of certain privileges. Skin colour and shade were important. There was a distinction between black and coloured. Methodist Minister Reverend Stewart Denyer admitted in 1947 that "the definition of a colored person varies greatly among our people. The white people say 'that any man with a tincture of colored blood in him is a colored person' – we do not use the term 'black' here of anyone . . ." However, he added, "The colored people either go just as far in the opposite direction and call a man with a tincture of white blood in him a white person, or else, more often and more accurately . . . a mulatto, or yellow person, or a bright skinned man."[11] British Methodist ministers were often startled at having to reclassify persons in the church or in Queen's College whom they considered "predominantly black" (but obviously with white ancestry), as those "who consider themselves white".[12] In many cases, the explanation for a dark skin was an Indian ancestor, which was considered much more acceptable than an African. Reverend Denyer stated that some also belonged to a "finer group", referred to as "the pale-skinned children" who were allowed to go to Queen's. The coloured children attending Queen's College belonged to a group "who are predominantly white, but have a slight mixture of color of which we are aware". He added that the latter did not presume to mix too freely with those who were aware of their colour. However, they got on well with "those who consider themselves white, whatever they may actually be".[13]

With the expansion of tourism in the 1920s and the introduction of American 'Jim Crow' in certain establishments, for example, the New Colonial Hotel, came the hardening of racial barriers. American Frank C. Munson of the Munson Steamship Line, described as a "viciously prejudiced man", was partly responsible for heightened discriminatory policies and the deeply prejudiced feelings of whites against brown and black Bahamians. Munson, on acquiring the New Colonial Hotel, introduced a strict whites-only policy. By barring all non-whites from the hotel, he upset a few near-white men, such as a leading photographer, Fred Armbrister, who in spite of his mixed-race pedigree, had moved among the white society in Nassau. Armbrister found this hotel ban to be a most disturbing experience which, as Benson McDermott indicated, was to haunt him for the rest of his life. In fact, Armbrister died a tragic death in the Nassau Asylum in the mid-1950s.[14]

Another young, light-skinned Bahamian, a member of the Smith family, who belonged to a predominantly white Boy Scout troop, was devastated during an overnight stop in Miami, en route to a Scout World Jamboree in Washington, DC in 1937. In Florida, the white Scouts were accommodated in a hotel, while the non-whites stayed with black families. The young scout, on reaching Washington, started "acting strangely" and his friend, Basil North, who was mixed-race and had also stayed with a black family, was asked by the white Scout leader to look after him. Soon after his return from the United States, Smith committed suicide. North's mother, who was from Key West, but had married a Bahamian, had warned him of the segregation he would experience in the United States.[15]

In addition to having a light complexion, straight hair, "association with the right people", wealth and political power were also important to those who were passing for white. Roland T. Symonette, later knighted, became the first premier of the Bahamas. He was born in December 1898 at the Current, Eleuthera, and was registered as mixed, and never changed his racial category. A son born to the wife (a current native) of his first marriage was registered as mixed. His second and third marriages were to white women and their children were registered as "E", that is, white. Having actively participated during Prohibition, he bought an interest in a Nassau wholesale liquor business known as Rost-Symonette (the predecessor of Robertson and Symonette) in 1922. Using his profits to establish a boatyard on Hog Island (renamed Paradise Island), he was able to build the Rozelda Hotel in 1929, later known as the Carlton House in downtown Nassau. Over the years he developed an extensive business in real estate, construction and road building. As far as colour was concerned, he associated only with whites and considered himself as such. Apparently, money 'whitened'![16]

Symonette became a member of the nouveau riche group. Prohibition had a pervasive effect on Bahamian society. Before the 1920s, an entrenched mercantile white elite had little real capital. Their colour, rather than their wealth, had separated them from non-whites. Bootlegging profits – augmented by those from the land boom – brought quick money into Nassau, creating a new moneyed class that was mostly white. Prohibition provided, as Gordon Lewis stated, the "financial foundation of their status as the social and political ruling class of the island...".[17] To consolidate his position and wealth, Symonette entered politics in 1925 and was elected to the House of Assembly that year. In less than a generation, he and his family were accepted by the white community.

A number of light-skinned families, realizing the great advantages being offered to whites, gradually disassociated themselves from their non-white acquaintances. Changing racial sides was accomplished primarily by having racial categories changed on their birth certificates, going abroad or through marriage to someone of European origin. An example of this was the non-white W.E.S. Callender family from British Guiana. Originally friends of the middle-class, mixed-race North family, the Callenders, through marriages to white women, were accepted by the white elite within one generation.[18]

Why was it so important for light-skinned non-whites to pass? They still believed in European superiority and looked down on people of African descent, many of whom were poor, lived in modest housing, worked in menial occupations or were unemployed. Some mixed-race persons also were convinced that life was much easier for white people as they were accorded what is known as white privilege.[19] The Bahamas' proximity to the southern United States, with its rigid colour line, did not help matters. Blacks and mixed-race persons were denied certain privileges. Some light-skinned, mixed-race persons separated themselves completely from blacks and non-whites, even from within their own families. Two cousins of Basil North migrated to the United States and England. They never returned to the Bahamas, refusing to see any of their family – "hiding their mixed racial heritage, they melded into the white populations of England and the United States and, for all intents and purposes, they disappeared".[20]

Similarly, Iris Marie Tynes, who descended from the settlement of Pompey Bay, Acklins, where the Hanna, Heastie and Tynes families had settled, related a story about her father's sister, who had migrated to Miami. The Hanna, Heastie and Tynes families were descended from British families and had intermarried for generations. Most were light-skinned and were referred to as "white people". However, they also married out of their settlement to people of African descent, and by the mid-twentieth century, they could be classified as mixed-race. Mrs Tynes stated that her aunt, Ethel Tynes Lewis, was very "light-skinned and had straight black hair and greenish eyes". Ethel migrated to Miami and had five children. Four were light skinned; one was dark. When Mrs Lewis rode the bus, she sat in the white section. One day, she had her darker child with her and was mortified on being asked to move to the back of the bus. She died in Miami and her death certificate gave her race as Caucasian. Her brother, also very light-skinned, lived in Key West. He passed for white by shaving his hair. When he was hospitalized in Miami, family members looked for him in the coloured section, but failed to locate him there. He was on the white ward.[21]

Shade was also important among people who were passing. As Powles also observed about the capital:

> In Nassau, anyone who passes for white, though he may be unable to converse intelligently on any rational topic outside of his business, is considered fit to sit down to table with any lady, whilst his next-door neighbor, well read, intelligent, and an agreeable companion, is tabooed because he is considered to belong to the coloured race. Yet the latter is often scarcely a shade darker than the former, and the former's black ancestor is well remembered by many persons still alive.[22]

Despite this knowledge, some light-skinned Bahamians found a way to remedy what they considered a hindrance. Numerous affidavits in the Registrar General's Department (also known as the Registry) in Nassau relating to births and the changing of racial categories have been preserved. Until the early 1960s, a person's race was recorded in the Registrar General's Office in Nassau, and sub-offices on the Out Islands. Their race was also written on birth certificates. The categories of colour or race were: E for European (white), M for Mulatto (Mixed) and A for African (black). Up to the late 1950s, most births took place at the family home. Each district had sections; for example, New Providence was divided into the East, the City, the West and Over-the-Hill (St Agnes), over which a registrar presided. The population was fairly small, numbering 130,220 in 1963.[23] The registrars did not ask the parents their racial category as they knew the backgrounds of the persons in the area. Registrars, therefore, determined each child's category. Light-skinned near-whites registered as M sometimes disagreed with the registrar, and had the category changed from mixed to European. Parents of such children desired them to attend private schools, some of which were segregated. Adult mixed-race persons also changed their racial categories for various reasons. They knew of the discrimination in Florida, the South and other parts of the United States and wished to stay in the white-only hotels, and for their families to mix with the "right (that is white) people". Some lived their lives as white people, as did some Americans who passed in the United States.[24]

Light-skinned persons from Long Island and Eleuthera were eager to change their racial categories for various reasons. Some needed such information to apply for certain positions; others for more personal reasons such as marriage or migration to the United States. Uriah T. Knowles, son of Stanley and Clotilda Knowles of Long Island, both registered as M at birth, was also designated mixed-race. Uriah married Olga Cade of Middlesex, England. Knowles served in the British Intelligence Service, headquartered at the Royal Victoria Hotel in Nassau, before being transferred to the Colonial Office in London. Returning to Nassau, he was appointed as aide de camp to Lord Ranfurly, then governor of the Bahamas. In 1957, Knowles was offered and accepted a post as an Official Secretary of the Government in Nigeria, where he served for almost eight years. Senior posts in the Colonial Service were customarily occupied by Europeans. In October of 1957, Knowles' brother and sister swore an affidavit declaring that both their parents were of European descent, and that the birth certificates of their children registering them as M were incorrect.[25]

It appears that Sylvia Hall's racial category was questionable. An affidavit signed on 10 July 1944 by her mother asserted that "Sylvia Valeria Hall is of the European race".[26] Another affidavit signed by Josephine Elizabeth Hall, Sylvia's grandmother, swore that Charles Randolph Hall, Sylvia's father, formerly of the Current, Eleuthera, but at present living in Nassau, was born on 24 April 1904, and "is of the European race".[27] This documentation was important for Sylvia as she applied for a marriage licence in the very segregated Dade County in Miami on 17 May 1948. She was married there four days later to Maurice R. Cole, a white Bahamian. Their race, registered as W for white, was inserted next to their names on the marriage licence.[28]

There are many other examples of light-skinned persons who had their birth certificates amended or corrected, changing their racial category from M (mixed) to E (European), including numerous residents of George Town, Exuma.[29] Evans W. Cottman, in his book, *Out Island Doctor*, stated: "There is another thing I noticed particularly about George Town. A larger percentage of the people were almost white than any other place I visited, and far more conscious of it, proud of their white blood while bitterly resenting the mixture."[30]

Light skin colour, "good" hair and sharp features were important to those people who were passing for white. Such people were perceived as less threatening and often had better chances of obtaining job opportunities. Lawrence O. Graham, writing about the United States' black upper class, cited a study by the Russell Sage Foundation in 1995, which concluded that "whites feel more comfortable around light-skinned blacks . . ."[31] This was probably also true of the Bahamas. In some families, the lighter child was more highly valued and many passed into the white society by distancing themselves from black family and friends, joining all-white clubs and societies, attending predominantly white schools (for example, Queen's College) and churches, and even relocating to another country. As Nicolette Bethel describes in her poem, "Aunt Selma's Dilemma", skin colour and quality of hair were very important considerations in Bahamian class and colour structure:

> Aunt Selma's dark skin mars her appearance so;
> White skin is far more practical socially.
> Aunt Selma's long fingers test the
> Texture of grandchildren's hair – ambition.
> Aunt Selma's forebears: "Indian" immigrants.
> (Straight hair outweighs one's face of mahogany.)
> Just who they were, no one is sure – still,
> Mystery ancestors whiten black skins.
> Her children all too early were taught her creed:
> White skin is good; ask God to deliver it.
> "Bleach us, and grant fair girls for marriage,
> Lighten our darkness, we pray, O Father."
> Old proverb; "Blood will out." An unfortunate
> Truth. Selma's light-skinned grandchildren let her down.
> Blond Nordic looks grew dark as time passed,
> Curling majestically. Negro blood reigns.[32]

NOTES

1. Christine Bolt, *Victorian Attitudes to Race* (London: Routledge and Kegan Paul, 1971), 134–37; Bridget Brereton, "Society and Culture in the Caribbean, The British and French West Indies, 1870–1980," in *The Modern Caribbean*, ed. Franklin Knight and Colin Palmer (Chapel Hill, NC: University of North Carolina Press, 1989), 88.
2. Brereton, "Society and Culture," 88; See also Lloyd Braithwaite, "Stratification in Trinidad," in *Slaves, Free Men, Citizens. West Indian Perspectives*, ed. Lambros Comitas and David Lowenthal (New York: Anchor Press, 1973), 212–39.
3. G.S. Northcroft, "Sketches of Summerland Giving Some Account of Nassau and the Bahama Islands," *Nassau Guardian*, 1912, 62.
4. Colin Hughes, *Race and Politics in the Bahamas* (St Lucia: University of Queensland Press, 1981), 25–26.
5. Gordon K. Lewis, *The Growth of the Modern West Indies* (New York: Monthly Review Press, 1968), 308.
6. Deborah Gray White, *Too Heavy a Load: Black Women in Defense of Themselves, 1894–1994* (New York: W.W. Norton, 1999).
7. Charles Ives, *The Isles of Summer or Nassau and the Bahamas* (New Haven: Self-published, 1880), 292.
8. L.D. Powles, *The Land of The Pink Pearl: Recollections of Life in the Bahamas* (London: Samson Low, Marston, Searle and Rivington, 1888), 120–21.
9. Gostwich to McDonald, Nassau, 10 February 1898, Wesleyan Methodist Missionary Society (WMMS), School of African and Oriental Studies, London.
10. Personal reminiscences.
11. Stewart Denyer to Noble, Governor's Harbour, Eleuthera, 10 April 1947, Wesley Methodist Missionary Society (WMMS), Correspondence, Bahamas.
12. ibid.
13. ibid.
14. Benson McDermott, *Bahamas Handbook, 1983* (Nassau: Etienne Dupuch Jr Publications, 1983), opposite page 22. See also *Nassau Tribune* (editorial), 16 December 1983. Fred Armbrister's grandfather was mixed-race and had married a woman of colour.
15. Interview with E. Basil North and Audrey V. North, Nassau, 10 August 1984.
16. Hughes to Geddes, 26 June 1922, C.O. 23/292, Misc.; Grant to Churchill, 31 August 1922, Confidential, C.O. 23/291, 215; Nellie Symonette to Devonshire, 29 December 1923, C.O.294; *Nassau Tribune*, 10 December 1930; Michael

Craton and Gail Saunders, *Islanders in the Stream*, 2 (Athens and London: University of Georgia Press, 1998), 240 and 338.
17. Gordon K. Lewis, *Growth of The Modern West Indies* (New York: Monthly Review Press, 1968), 311.
18. Interview with E. Basil North and Audrey V. North, Nassau, 10 August 1984.
19. Interview with George Heastie, Nassau, 5 March 2015.
20. Jacquelyn D'Aguilar, *Thicker Than Blood: The DeGregorys of the Bahamas – An Island Family Story* (Nassau: Media Enterprises, 2014), 26.
21. Interview with Iris Marie Tynes, Nassau, 13 November 2014.
22. Powles, *Land of the Pink Pearl*, 122. Those who could not pass "like to say they are of Indian descent". Letter, from Lenora North to her son, Bert, 30 June 1943.
23. *Report on The Census of The Bahama Islands, Taken on 15 November 1963*, Nassau, 1965.
24. Lawrence Otis Graham, *Our Kind of People: Inside America's Black Upper Class* (New York: Harper Collins Publishers, 1999), 376–93.
25. Affidavit correcting Uriah Theophilus Knowles' name from Ralph to Uriah T. Knowles and declaring that our parents are both of European descent and the "M" in the race column is wrong and should be corrected to "E" (European/white). Signed by Hubert F. Knowles and Ethel Harris (nee Knowles), 11 October 1957 before the Assistant Registrar and Justice of the Peace.
26. Affidavit relating to the birth of Sylvia Cole-Tierney. Registrar General's Office, Book R-15: 377–78.
27. Affidavit relating to the birth of Charles Randolph Hall. Registrar General's Office, Book P-15: 407.
28. Copy of Marriage License, Central Bureau of Vital Statistics, State of Florida, Dade County, 21 May 1948; Certificate of Marriage, 25 May 1948.
29. Interview with George Heastie, 5 March 2015. Mr Heastie produced a list of those persons who had their racial category corrected from mixed to Caucasian or European.
30. Evans W. Cottman (with Wyatt Blassingame), *Out Island Doctor* (London: Hodder and Stoughton, 1987), 201 (first printed in 1963).
31. Graham, *Our Kind of People*, 378.
32. Nicolette Bethel, "Aunt Selma's Dilemma". A poem originally published in *Junction: An Anthology of Bahamian Poetry and Prose*, ed. Eunice Bethel Humblestone (London: Macmillan Caribbean and Bahamas Poetry Society, 1987), and in *Lignum Vitae* vol. 1, Nassau, 1992.

[17]

IT FEATURED A GYMKHANA?
Conflicting Identities in the Early Years
of the Modern Crop Over Festival

[MARCIA BURROWES]

THE YEAR 1974 MARKED THE REINTRODUCTION OF THE Barbadian festival known as Crop Over; a plantation experience that had emerged during slavery. Entangled in the celebrations were the experiences of sugar and oligarchic privilege, enslaved and freed plantation labour, and African-Barbadian masquerade in the colonial space.

Traditional Crop Over had been one in which individual plantations organized their celebrations according to their rituals when their final loads of canes were cut. Hence, festivities occurred throughout the island anytime between April and August, with plantations placing emphasis on rituals that had evolved within the localized plantation space. Modern Crop Over emerged as a festival organized by the Board of Tourism, with a central committee and a fixed calendar of events. It was based on preliminary research that, in turn, was based on a few reports of plantation histories. Promoted as a tourist event, the activities were centred in Bridgetown[1] and its hotels, prime sites for viewing by tourist voyeurs.

This chapter will argue that from inception, the modern version of the Crop Over festival found itself in the ideological stranglehold of conflicting agendas and identities. It was not seen as a celebration of agriculture and the contribution of the African-Barbadian labour force to the development of the newly independent nation. Indeed, little effort was made in the formative years to take the festival into the areas where sugar cane was grown, and the labourers lived. Rather, the primary emphasis became one of spectatorship, not participation for the Barbadian public, as key events marginalized the majority. When Crop Over was placed in the hands of the Ministry of Education, there was significant change, but the battle of identities continued, as organizers struggled to give birth to a festival that would reflect the new nationalist agenda.

AN INVENTED TRADITION

In coining the term 'invented tradition', what Eric Hobsbawm referred to were those deliberate acts of creating a tradition in the present that claimed an authentic stake in the past. It did not matter whether the past was a moment in time or a period. What defined them for Hobsbawm was their fictitious claim on this past: "However, insofar as there is a reference to a historic past, the peculiarity of 'invented' traditions is that the continuity with it is largely factitious. In short, they are responses to novel situations which take the form of reference to old situations, or which establish their own past by quasi-obligatory repetition."[2]

I find this theory a most appropriate one for this discussion. When the Board of Tourism reintroduced the tradition of Crop Over in 1974, the African-Barbadian cultural practices that were integral to the festival were relegated to the margins, as emphasis was placed on the planter elite. The board claimed that Crop Over's roots lay in a medieval practice known as "Harvest Home", an English festival brought to Barbados by English planters. There was even a projection that it had been introduced in the early days of enslavement: ". . . as long as sugar cane has been grown in Barbados, and that is over 300 years – there has been Crop Over". Anthropologist Jerome Handler quickly put the inaccuracy to rest, stating that the historical evidence did not support "this common assumption", adding, "I would doubt that the holiday during the slave period was ever as idyllic as is implied in Gordon's article."[3]

Evidence revealed that its first appearance was in 1782 at Newton plantation. Moreover, by the time of its introduction, a rich African-Barbadian cultural heritage already existed, which encompassed, for example, masquerade and drumming traditions, song and dance, rituals of birth and death, and constructs of worldviews by the enslaved that reclaimed and reinvested in their humanity. This African-Barbadian heritage *predated* the late eighteenth-century introduction of Harvest Home and served to challenge any misconception that the medieval festival had been deposited in a cultural *tabula rasa*.[4]

Furthermore, through the process of creolization, these traditions of the enslaved and then freed labourers had significantly transformed the medieval festival and had become the core components of plantation Crop Over. Indeed, it remains unclear as to what aspects of the medieval practice, other than the ceremonial presentation of the last crop of the harvest, actually gained a foothold in Barbados. The board opted to rely heavily on the oligarchic narrative that focused on the plantation yard, with the planter sponsoring the feast. This deliberate omission of African-Barbadian cultural practices served, as Hobsbawm would point out, the purpose of fixing the past and of casting Crop Over into a predictable, unchanging mould. It called upon a formalized practice of oligarchic privilege, and upon ritual through the lens of Englishness and colonialism. Further, the notion of repetition of a single tradition, not innovation or creation of new or creolized traditions, was imposed upon the festival, in the modern space.

Why 1974 though? Independence had been granted in 1966, so it was an event of the new era. Yet, its occurrence signals more than this. This example of bringing back a tradition indicates a certain angst in the society, such as one that would occur "... when a rapid transformation of society weakens or destroys the social patterns for which 'old' traditions had been designed, producing new ones to which they were not applicable."[5]

In the case of Barbados, independence had provided that potential change in the fabric of society. Though certainly not rapid nor drastic in character, what independence did bring with it was a challenge to the old constructs of Barbadian identity and to the old institutions of power. For example, the immediate years after 1966 witnessed the advent of what could be considered 'white flight', as significant numbers of white Barbadians migrated to countries such as Australia, Canada and South Africa. It was said that they were unsure about the future and their role in an independent Barbados led by Barbadians of African ancestry.[6]

Yet, independence does not fully account for the invention of this particular tradition of Crop Over. What needs to be acknowledged is the ideological space and cultural confidence that independence encouraged, as traditional notions of Barbadian identity were challenged. For example, these early years of independence witnessed a growing concern over the practice of utilizing art forms deemed to be the instruments of colonization. Also noted was the lack of national acknowledgement of cultural practices arising from an African-Barbadian heritage.[7] Consequently, the immediate post-1966 era witnessed the birth of key movements within the arts, as a surge of creativity propelled the evolution of new cultural narratives. The Barbados Dance Theatre Company was formed, as well as the National Independence Festival of Creative Arts. In addition, Yoruba House was launched, advocating an Afrocentric philosophy for the examination of Barbadian identity in the independence period.

Yoruba House was created by a group of artists, led by Black Power advocate Elton Elombe Mottley. Its performance arm specialized in the teaching of African performance culture while its research arm pursued a policy of recording village cultural practice.[8] Yoruba House also represented a rejection of the notion of the very anglicized and colonized Barbadian. Being an active member of Yoruba House, or just a member of the audience at a performance, would lead to being labelled a rebel, one who rejected Barbadian norms.[9]

When this concept of an actively creative cultural space is coupled with the advent of independence, it becomes clearer why the 1974 Crop Over emerged in the way it did. In reviving the festival, the members of the elite and middle classes opted for a cultural entity with which they were familiar. These "Back-to-Africa" manifestations sharpened their awareness of the changing narratives of Barbadian identity that were emerging with independence. Thus, they reached for the narrative of the medieval official feast for the revived Crop Over. Such a feast preserved the world order and was a "consecration of inequality". Rank and hierarchy were evident as the oligarchy sponsored the activities and determined its form and content.[10] Reviving Crop Over in this manner was one way of controlling the manifestations of Barbadian culture at the time.

The opportunity for the restaging of the familiar was provided through tourism. Charged with the responsibility of increasing visitor traffic, the board was in a state of near-desperation over the significant fall in visitor numbers between the months of May to August. Hence the following statement in the 1975 annual report: "The Board had long recognized the fact that more summer business was needed. The month of June, being the least active, was thought to be the best time for the event. The objectives of the festival are (a) to increase visitor traffic to Barbados in June – a long-term objective, and (b) to establish the festival as an indigenous Barbadian institution – the short-term objective."[11]

Note that the board determined that the *primary* purpose of the festival was to "increase visitor traffic", while the secondary purpose was to "establish the festival as an indigenous Barbadian institution – the short-term objective".[12] But Crop Over had already been established and celebrated in villages and plantations for at least *one hundred and fifty years*! The plantation festival continued into the 1960s, though significantly reduced in practice.[13] Hence, the primary purpose significantly outstripped the secondary.

Nevertheless, when faced with criticism over the decision to reintroduce the festival, the tourism board maintained that Crop Over was built on the historic past and this would give it a stamp of authenticity. Critics quickly reminded the board that the historic past was plantation slavery and enslavement of the African labourers. The vast majority of Barbadians were of African descent and would not want to be reminded of the enslaved past.[14] One critic argued that plantation Crop Over had died ". . . a natural death. If it died at a time when racial consciousness and the dignity of labour was being drummed into the ears of the working class, it should not be surprising. To my mind, the working classes seem to have relegated the festival to the place where it belonged – out of their minds."[15] The board disagreed.

With tourism given as the main reason for the reintroduction of the festival, the battle lines were clearly drawn. At a time when there was avid interest in the reshaping of African-Barbadian identity, the Crop Over festival was cast in the role of portraying Barbadian culture at its most superficial level, through the lens of tourism. One observer commented: "The idea having come from 'above' where time, resources, organisational skills, drive etc. are possessed in abundance, presto! Crop-Over Festival arrives, lock, stock and barrel."[16]

CROP OVER RETURNS

In 1974, Crop Over magically reappeared. The narratives regarding the question of who recovered the memory of the plantation festival and proposed its revival are contradictory. Officially, Julian Marryshow and Peter Morgan have been accorded credit for orchestrating the revival. Marryshow, a Grenadian citizen, had come to Barbados via Trinidad, to work with the Trinidad-based advertising company Norman Craig and Kummel. Marryshow was put in charge of the Barbados branch and renamed it Marryshow Advertising. The company won a competition sponsored by the Board of Tourism with a project entitled "Project T – Tourism Needs You, You Need Tourism".[17] Marryshow then became the public relations officer for the board, expressly at the time it was reorganizing its structure for the new tourism initiative.[18]

In 1951, Peter Morgan, a British citizen who would become a naturalized Barbadian, came to Barbados and purchased the St Lawrence Hotel. He quickly became known as the white hotelier who did not succumb to the rabid discriminatory practices that so marked Barbados at the time, and accordingly, "He turned his hotel into a place where Blacks and Whites could meet and have a drink."[19] A popular figure, Morgan was thrice president of the Barbados Hotel Association, became a senator and eventually was awarded the CBE (Commander of the British Empire). He contested a seat in the national elections as a member of the party led by Prime Minister Errol Barrow and in 1972, became the representative for Christ Church, the lone white parliamentarian. He was given the portfolio of Minister of Tourism.[20]

Thus, it has been argued that it was the Marryshow and Morgan duo who successfully pushed for the rebirth of Crop Over.[21] These were the faces of the Crop Over enterprise when it began, a reality that elicited this response: "Let's face it – historically cropover was a people's celebration, a natural climax to the end of crop season.... Crop Over today is essentially a bourgeois exercise – a massive, money-making venture, masterminded by non-Barbadians and conceived solely for the purpose of filling somebody's coffers with tourist-dollars."[22]

Yet, a counter-narrative has always existed as to where the idea for the rebirth of Crop Over emerged. Al Gilkes has argued that it was Yoruba House who had unearthed the evidence of the festival: "The Barbados Tourist Board decided they needed something to boost arrivals during the summer programme. Before that Elombe Mottley, then known as Elton Mottley, had been proposing the revival of the Crop-Over festival which had traditionally marked the end of the sugar harvest, but had been abandoned in the 1940s during World War II."[23]

Gilkes, a journalist who had been actively involved in the entertainment industry at the time, confirmed that he had no knowledge of the festival until he heard Mottley speak of it some two years before the official tourism announcement. And Mottley maintains that Marryshow, with his Grenadian background, had little knowledge of Barbadian culture. He was a regular visitor to Yoruba House and was a beneficiary of their research.[24]

It is my argument that with Mottley, the Black Power activist, actively campaigning for new constructs of Barbadian identity that featured an African heritage, it was inconceivable that the Tourist Board, mainly composed of the elite who represented the old guard, would sanction him to lead the charge. Moreover, the festival was, as Jeanette Layne-Clarke declared, a "bourgeois . . . massive, money-making venture" that the board had designed to attract white tourists to Barbados.[25] An African-Barbadian focus with a Yoruba House slant would have been seen as intolerable. The Marryshow/Morgan duo was deemed more suitable to the enterprise.

As secretary of the special Crop Over Festival Committee, Marryshow established a committee chaired by Straker of The Merrymen.[26] What the committee conceived for the first year became its template for three years to follow. Bridgetown was to be the central focus for most activities, key entertainers were to be imported and individual events were earmarked for the elite, separate from the masses. Finally, the festival would not end with a carnival-style masquerade, but with a cultural activity suited to its tourism mandate.

It is intriguing to note that a festival based on a sugar heritage was centred in Bridgetown, where sugar was *not* grown. Also, that at a time when a national performance culture was actively emerging, emphasis was placed on the importation of performance troupes. The outright rejection of the African-Caribbean masquerade that was symbolic of the festivals of the region must also be noted. This anti-carnival sentiment was strong among members of the board and the committee, partially because previous attempts to stage a carnival in Barbados had garnered limited success. There was also the ever-present cultural rivalry between Trinidad and Barbados.[27] Furthermore, as the elite saw themselves as responsible for shaping the ideal Barbadian, the behaviour arising from bacchanalia could not be tolerated. Consequently, Kadooment, the masquerade finale for which the festival became known, was only created some *four* years after Crop Over was reintroduced.

On 1 June 1974, the festival was officially opened. In another perplexing move, the board opted *not* to advertise the festival to potential visitors overseas for its first two years, aiming instead to showcase it to the few visitors who happened to be on the island, as well as the local populace.[28] The latter responded with apparent enthusiasm: "In Broad Street, the main street of the capital, Bridgetown, on the first of June, a crowd of some 20,000 people converged upon a parade of decorated donkey carts, landship groups, Beauty Queen contestants and steel bands. Independence Square, during the barge shows in the Careenage, was filled with crowds never before equalled except during election campaigns."[29]

The 1974 festival began with a decorated donkey cart parade, a tourism-oriented construct of the old plantation tradition. In traditional Crop Over, the plantation labourers placed the last load of canes on a donkey cart decorated with flowers. They then led the cart around the plantation yard. In the tourism version, hotels such as the Hilton and the Holiday Inn sponsored the event and the hotel owners, or managers, along with the hotel staff, paraded the carts around Bridgetown. Few to no plantation labourers were involved. Even the carts were specially constructed for the occasion, raising calls from the public for real donkey carts, that is, functioning models with their owners, to be included in the festival.[30] A competition was held for the best decorated cart, which, for the first two years, was won by the Hilton Hotel.

Though some tourists did view the opening of the first festival, the vast majority of the twenty thousand onlookers were Barbadians. Stunned by the overwhelming response, both the Minister of Tourism and the chair of the Tourist Board reflected on the meaning of the numbers, opting, ironically, to place emphasis on the festival's Barbadian heritage. Morgan called it "a people's festival", noting that Crop Over was more than a carnival: "It is something natural to our country, and our way of life."[31] And the chairman spoke of the need for greater involvement from the community. Thus, the board found itself in the contradictory stance of publicly embracing the national text, while advocating that tourism was the primary beneficiary.

Another 1974 event that sent the committee and the board scrambling to the reorganizing table was the Plantation Fair. It was the only event that put full focus to the plantation and the African-Barbadian masquerade heritage, and was specially earmarked for the masses. It called upon the tradition in which the planter paid for a feast and a band to play the music for the official plantation activities.[32] Only two fairs were scheduled over the three-week period on plantations estimated to comfortably hold the few visitors and curious Barbadians. Once again, the committee and the board were overwhelmed by the response.

The first fair was held on 8 June at Springhall Plantation in St Lucy, with the affordable entrance fee of one dollar. Entertainment was provided by troupes depicting traditional masquerade, such as Stiltmen, the Bum Drum characters and the Landship BLS *Director*, with its maypole dance. Also included were El Verno del Congo and his drumming performances and the Barbados Dance Theatre, who portrayed traditional plantation dances. Carmeta Fraser, the advocate known for her promotion of Barbadian foods, had a booth sponsored by the Agricultural Development Corporation.

More than 10,000 people were crammed into Springhall to participate in the event, with the majority in the plantation yard. Trees, walls and all vantage points were used to view the activities. John Wickham reflected as follows: "There was something ironically appropriate in a Crop Over fête being held in a cemetery of the sugar industry amid ruins and relics of a past glory."[33] Stunned by the response, the Director of Tourism announced at the Springhall event that the second fair would not be held at its appointed venue of Fairy Valley, Christ Church. That plantation would have been unable to accommodate the large number of attendees. Instead, the fair would be held at Spencers Plantation in Christ Church, a much larger venue.[34] Again, this fair was well attended.

However, there were times when the response of the populace was not welcomed in this modern version of Crop Over, especially when the event was marked for the tourist gaze. Broad Street, the central street in Bridgetown, was closed to vehicular traffic between Monday and Friday for fifteen days over a period of three weeks. Toasted as a key feature of the festival, a pedestrian mall was created. However, chaos reigned as the closing of this main street proved to be a traffic nightmare. The many thousands who turned out for the mall provided an unwelcome sight for some Barbadians: "It became a loafers or limers' mall, not the pedestrian mall that it was hoped. More tourists were insulted by the same loafers or limers than ever before for the simple reason that the loafers who hang out elsewhere concentrated on this area where they met more tourists who do not frequent their other jaunts."[35]

One critic called the hundreds of young Barbadians who came to the mall ". . . the rag tag and bobtail rabble that cavorted in the street . . . How many visitors are likely to consider this a reason for taking a trip to Barbados to see and join?"[36] This time the committee listened to the critics and scrapped the mall the following year.

However, it was the importation of entertainment that brought the loudest outcry from some Barbadians. Local theatre and dance companies were actively performing their work for the public. The Cuban group Conjunto Folklorico Nacional – comprising folk dancers, singers and drummers – was invited to perform at the Marine House. The group gained much coverage in the press and were even included on a 1975 commemorative stamp edition. The Ambakaila Dancers of Trinidad, with a full cast of fifty-eight dancers, singers, musicians, drummers, were also invited, along with the Trinidadian 1973 steelband champions. On 30 June, the final night of Crop Over, the American troupe Folk Music USA closed the festival.[37]

Almost immediately afterwards, the committee received complaints about the inclusion of what was seen as "foreign culture". Arguments such as they "should keep it, if possible, strictly Bajan" became a rallying cry.[38] And calls were made for Barbadian theatre companies, such as Writers Workshop, to be more involved. Moreover, the lack of confidence in featuring Barbadian cultural acts for the tourist gaze and the choice of acts were also noted. For example, the show "Ambakaila" was seen as an example of a flawed enterprise, due to the directive to cater to metropolitan audiences: "It is for this reason that it should be viewed as a prostitution of artistic talent. It is when producers of shows and festivals are guided by the expectations of foreign audiences rather than by what they genuinely believe about themselves that artistic expression is prostituted."[39]

WHOSE CROP OVER?

In 1975, the committee was sent back to the drawing board with a mandate from some members of the public to include the community in the festival. Calls were also made to give further emphasis and respect to its agricultural roots: "If this festival is to be a meaningful activity, it is essential that it be centred firmly around those already employed in agriculture so that these workers may feel a sense of pride in their work and the community at large may show interest in and respect for those who are the backbone of a vital industry and contribute far more to the economy than any wage can adequately reward."⁴⁰

However, an editorial in *The Advocate News* had reminded its readers just two days before of the intended focus of Crop Over: "The festival is not seen so much as a local spree but is intended to attract visitors to our shores at a time of year when something is needed to encourage more people to seek us out as a tourist destination. This must be borne in mind."⁴¹ The *Tourism Newsletter* had created a different perspective of the 1974 launch as it celebrated the "encouraging response by Barbadians" and made no mention of the challenges of the first year. It noted that the board would be "casting the net wider in the community" in an effort to increase visitor traffic and "pave the way for invitations to be issued to relations abroad, friends and visitors to 'Come Over for Crop Over' in '76".⁴² Hence, the primary objective of attracting visitors was maintained, as *The Advocate News'* editor had cautioned.

With its visitor mandate back on track, the board continued much as before. The practice of importing the featured entertainment resumed, despite public protest. In 1975, Tshira, the Apollo Stars and the Apollo Dancers, the performing group from the visiting *Apollo* yacht were the guest artistes. Straker still remembers that he was especially criticized for inviting the Apollo dancers to a Barbadian festival.⁴³ The Guyanese troupe known as All Uh We had a series of shows but, though usually well received due to their riveting performances and as a Caribbean entity, the performers found themselves caught up in the tensions surrounding the choice of acts for the festival:

> Why must we import entertainment like Ken Crosbie and the Guyana Players, the Apollo Troupe, Paco, T'Shura and others? Last year was bad enough, we imported the whole Ambakailla Show lock, stock and barrel. What is wrong with our local dancers, singers and actors? Are they not good enough? . . . One wonders where was our spouge, the only thing in the way of music that we can call ours. It was sickening to see a so-called Barbadian festival with the music of almost every country in this part of the world portrayed except our own. Our spouge should be synonymous with Crop Over as Calypso is with carnival.⁴⁴

These pleas fell on deaf ears as the committee continued to stick to their formula. In 1976, they organized a show entitled "International Night", which was held over three nights on the penultimate weekend of the festival. The performances included artists from Germany, Britain, Canada, Venezuela and Trinidad. As part of the marketing strategy, the Hilton Hotel placed an 11ft wooden globe on its roof. With a diameter of 8ft, the globe was built to withstand winds up to 80 miles an hour, presumably in case it was hit by a hurricane. Ironically, fire, not wind, turned out to be the enemy as the props caught afire on the Old Fort stage.[45] The show continued, nevertheless.

However, though actively pursuing what many saw as an elitist agenda, the committee did try to stage a few more events for mass participation. A babes and kiddies festival allowed children to have their moment. Talent shows at a few communities outside of Bridgetown provided a measure of response to the accusations that the festival was too centralized. In addition, an 'ole mas' competition was staged, in which participants were invited to "Get out your old clothes and enter the competition for the big cash prizes. For the best ole Mass [sic] $200." The individual who depicted "An Overloaded Bus" won the prize for best costume.[46]

The disastrous Broad Street pedestrian mall of the first year had been scrapped, but the barge shows continued. In 1975, thousands of people had gathered at night to enjoy free performances of their favourite bands and hear Alfred Pragnell, the much-loved actor and storyteller. In 1976, similarly large crowds attended the scheduled three shows, standing in boats and on the swing bridge as well as the allocated paved areas for the performances.[47]

The Crop Over Queen Show was also introduced in 1975. It was reported: "A huge crowd witnessed the crowning of Miss Paula Hunte as the 'Queen of the Crop' last Thursday evening, 29th May, at Marine House. Miss Hunte took the title from five other finalists, to 'reign' for the month-long June festival sponsored by the Board of Tourism."[48]

Staged for two years, the Crop Over Queen Show was a beauty pageant, though the organizers insisted that factors such as "costume, poise, personality and a knowledge of the tourism and agricultural industries" be given equal weight. However, both competitions were fraught with controversy. In the inaugural year, the designer of the winner's costume was accused of copying a Trinidadian carnival design. Paula Hunte, the first queen, distinctly remembers that both black and white Barbadians, as well as some tourists, lined the streets to see her in costume as she stood on the back of an army truck. Some applauded, some stared, some booed and some even threw eggs at her, shouting: "De costume come from Trinidad!" The following year, the official result was challenged, as all the points had not been included in the final total. Chaos ensued two days after the event when it was revealed that the judges' score sheets had gone missing and that one of them had designed the costume of a participant.[49]

The committee also faced severe criticism regarding the relevance of a beauty pageant to the festival. One critic wrote ". . . without prejudice to any of the contestants, I ask, have any of these 'beauties' ever bent under the boiling sun to plant, cultivate, cut and load sugar canes? Then what is the criteria (*sic*) used to select 'Crop Over' candidates?" Another advised the committee to have plantations ". . . sponsor the Crop Over Queens competition selecting the girls from the children of the people who are employed with the crop. If this cannot be done another name should be given to this event."[50]

The other new event in 1975, the Crop Over Calypso King contest, also began with controversy. It was organized by the Mighty Dragon and was won by the Mighty Destroyer. It was also the first time that calypso was included, as the committee had deemed both spouge and calypso part of bacchanalia-type activity that was unsuitable. However, it was poorly marketed, as the calypso contest was not advertised on the radio, television or in the official Crop Over calendar. As a result, only forty people attended the show. The board faced criticism regarding the "rough treatment" and lack of respect for the art form: "It is a proven fact that Barbadians like calypso, but the problem is that we don't get enough promotion or exposure. For instance, following the Crop Over King contest the Tourist Board could have introduced us to the hotels and given us that necessary exposure."[51] In 1976, there was a marked difference in the staging of the Calypso King contest. It was held at Culloden Farm, the residence of Prime Minister Errol Walton Barrow, under his patronage. It was widely marketed and even the rules of the contest were published.[52] The Mighty Grynner was crowned king with the song "Crop Over". The competition would become one of the staples of the festival.

Yet, though attempting to be more inclusive of the public for some events, the board and the committee continued to stage events that deliberately marginalized most of the Barbadian public. These events reflected the culture of the Barbadian elite, drew minimum crowd attendance and had little to do with the plantation origins of the festival. In 1976, one of the most controversial events was staged. Promoted as the Gala Fancy Costume Ball, it was held at the Sandy Lane Hotel, the most expensive and exclusive hotel on the island. Priced at an exorbitant fee of BBD$25, participants were required to wear Edwardian and Georgian period costumes. A competition for the best costume would see the winners enjoying such prizes as complimentary accommodation and dinners at Sandy Lane.[53]

With its excessive entrance fee, elite space and the nature of the activities, the ball drew its fair share of comments, perhaps best captured here in verse:

> De ball did keep at
> one o' de big
> Wes' Coas' hotels, firs' to begin,
> An' den agen, yuh had to pay,
> Twenty-five dollars to get in!
> Dah time, I c'n help cacklin' –
> An' 'nough people laugh wid me,
> 'Cause de people dat went in costume
> Din number nuh mo' dan t'ree!
> **Dah serve de organisers right!**
> **'Stead o' holin' a big-time ball,**
> **Duh should arrange de kin' o' events**
> **Dat woulda suit one an' all!** (poet's emphasis)[54]

The marginalizing nature of the activities and the high entrance fees had continually drawn criticism from the public. In an article entitled "Crop Over Charade", the writer posed the rhetorical but pertinent question: "Is the revenue earned from Crop-over, especially the high-priced events, to be channelled into other areas of the agricultural economy or for amenities for the workers?"[55] The response would have been not likely – not with the tourism mandate.

Other events marginalized most of the Barbadian public, more so because of the venues in which they were held and the nature of the activities. In 1974, the Barbados Kennel Clubs had staged an All-Breed Championship Dog Show, featuring Irish Setters, English Springer Spaniels, Great Danes and Pembroke Welsh Corgis. Then in 1975, the German

Shepherd Dog Club held a Canine Carnival at Hastings Rocks, a venue and event that, at the time, would not have immediately drawn a mass audience. A fashion show featuring "the Great Gatsby look" was held over eight nights for two weekends and organized by Jeanne Cipolato.[56] An air rally was held in 1975 and 1976, attracting pilots and parachutists from Barbados, England, Venezuela, St Lucia, Martinique and Grenada. It was reported that only three hundred people witnessed the air race at Seawell Airport.[57] Thus it became one of those events, as the poet emphasized, that did not "suit one an' all".

The ultimate rub came in 1975 when the committee opted to add a gymkhana to the mix. Often a two-day affair, gymkhanas were an equestrian cultural practice emanating from the British imperial sport genre. Deemed a feature of high society, gymkhanas were the sport of the British and Barbadian white elite. As Moxly had observed in 1886: ". . . a portion of the ground is occasionally borrowed for their sports by a local athletic club, and here the garrison athletic meetings, pony races, and frequent 'gymkhanas' come off." He also noted that when the North American and West Indian fleets were in port, there would be ". . . the outburst of every description of Barbadian gaiety . . . a succession of balls, dinners, picnics, gymkhanas, regattas and shamfights take place".[58]

In the twentieth century, gymkhanas remained the sport of the elite. They owned the horses and stables, and had access to venues required for the event. It was the elite who had occasionally staged a gymkhana at the popular agricultural exhibition held every Christmas in Queen's Park. Moreover, Marryshow, the key voice in Crop Over, was an active participant in gymkhanas, and in 1975, was also a competitor.[59]

Consequently, when looking for the ultimate spectacle for the final weekend of Crop Over that did not reflect the dreaded bacchanalia or 'jump-up' activity, the committee thought it fit to showcase the gymkhana. In doing so, they called upon an elitist cultural practice deeply ingrained in their construct of identity. They also presumed that the gymkhana would be an attractive activity for visitors that most African-Barbadians would also enjoy. With reference to the latter, they were greatly mistaken.

The gymkhana was held at Brighton Riding Stables and was staged on the final weekend over a period of two days. Riders were invited from the United Kingdom, Canada, Guadeloupe, Martinique and Trinidad to compete. The Barbados Police Band staged a musical ride. Other activities were 'trick training' by Geoff Chandler on his Shetland pony, Pleasure; Anne Hassell jumping through a ring of fire on her horse, Polly Flinders; and an inter-club competition. The entrance fee was BBD$2, the equivalent price to what was charged for the plantation fairs that same year.[60]

Though affordable for all who wanted to witness the equestrian spectacle, again it was the nature of the activity and the venue that drew lines of separation. The gymkhana found few supporters among the public and was singled out by Layne-Clarke for criticism, along with other events determined as the culture of the elite: "The relevance of a high-class dog show to a festival rooted in the traditions of sugar cultivation really escapes me. Similarly, I'm totally at a loss to understand the inclusion in the programme of a Gymkhana to say nothing of a regatta – activities preserved and reserved for the privileged and their imitators."[61]

Margaret Gordon noted that the "new events . . . while not exclusively Barbadian in character, were arranged by local organizations". However, she made the following plea: "If it (the festival) can incorporate more of the features of the original Crop Over . . . It will appeal to all the more Barbadians and thus all the more to the visitor, who comes here, after all, to experience something which is different from what he experiences at home, and to give his life a wider, and in this case, a Barbadian dimension."[62] The committee ignored their critics. In 1976 and 1977, they staged the gymkhana again.

On the other hand, it was also in the period 1975–1976 that the committee made an inexplicable move and centralized the burning of "Mr Harding". The burning of this effigy in the plantation yard on the last day was a feature of traditional Crop Over on several plantations. In the revived festival, Mr Harding was burnt at the fair at Spencers Plantation, despite the rain. However, in 1975, the committee moved the event to Bridgetown and he was burnt at the Garrison Savannah. Paula Hunte, the Crop Over queen, recalls lighting the fire. By 1976, a "large crowd of revellers" jumping to the music of three steel bands followed the truck bearing Mr Harding from Pelican Village to the Garrison. The distance provided the revellers at least an hour's 'jump-up'. At the Garrison, the crowds celebrated as they witnessed the "fatal end" of the effigy.[63]

The inclusion of Mr Harding was a controversial move for the board and the committee. In the oral narrative, Mr Harding represented more than the hard times that followed the out-of-crop season due to limited work opportunities. He also symbolized the cruel activities of the colonial/imperial authority or the white planter/overseer elite on the plantations. Even Gordon remarked on the decision: "... where else would it be possible to burn the effigy of a white overseer or gangleader, on account of his cruel treatment of those black people under his control without provoking some kind of reaction from one section or other of the community?"[64]

The public embraced the revived narrative of the effigy, as well as the accompanying bacchanalia or jump-up. However, there were immediate rumblings of disapproval from sections of the elite as well as some from the middle class. These served to further fuel the tensions manifested in the festival.[65] Hence, it is interesting to observe this ultimate twist to the narrative. With the burning of Mr Harding, the committee had approved the inclusion of African-Barbadian masquerade for the final moment of spectacle. They had also unwittingly engineered the very bacchanal atmosphere that they had so steadfastly rejected.

MAJOR CHANGES DEMANDED

By December 1976, public pressure demanded that major changes be made to programme.[66] Yet, in 1977, the Board of Tourism continued to organize the festival with Denise Hope, the newly appointed deputy chair, on the committee. Marryshow, not Straker, was made chair. The organizers immediately declared their intention of "pruning, shaping and developing the festival along lines acceptable to Barbadians". First to be pruned was the Crop Over queen competition that, in view of the debacle of previous years, Marryshow reportedly described as "unpopular, a bother".[67] Moreover, the board issued a much-revised statement as to the identity of the festival. Their role was: "to stage every June and throughout the month of June a performance of cultural, artistic, and sporting activities that would so capture the fascination, the cooperation, and the involvement of the people of Barbados, that it would within a matter of years be accepted as an established institution, and in the long run influence greater and greater numbers of visitors to come to Barbados during this month, the month with the lowest levels of visitors, traditionally."[68]

When compared to their 1974 statement, this was a major overhaul. The board no longer touted that the primary purpose of the festival was to attract tourists. Emphasis was placed on gaining the consent of the community, so it would "be accepted as an established institution".[69] The tourism narrative was demoted to the rank of secondary objective. The committee also signalled a significant change to the festival programme: "More emphasis will be placed this year on activities to be held outside the Bridgetown area. In addition to the now traditional fairs at plantations (in St Lucy, St John and Christ Church), Military night at King George V Park, a night with Miss Maxwell at Bathsheba, and talent shows in Christ Church, St James, St Lucy, and St Andrew."[70]

Consequently, the public could view activities in other towns and was also invited to contribute to the festival. For example, an art and craft market normally staged in Bridgetown, was also held in Oistins and Holetown. A Crop Over essay contest was organized by the Gemini Youth Group of St Philip for the children of Christ Church and the rural parishes of St George, St John and St Philip. A "Bajan Night", featuring Barbadian musical groups, was staged at the National Stadium. This event replaced the "International Night" with the foreign talent of previous years.[71]

Events exploring the new nationalist agenda were also included. *Pampalam*, the multimedia theatre piece written by Janet Layne-Clarke that used Bajan Creole, was first staged in 1977. With well-known icons such as the Mighty Gabby, Marva Manning and Patrick Gollop as cast members, as well as scenes from the popular radio play *Okras in de Stew*, *Pampalam* aimed to reflect "the roots and rhythms of Barbadian life". Performances were staged in Bridgetown as well as in the rural parishes of St George and St Philip.[72] The shows were well received. Yoruba House, the Afrocentric cultural group that the board had deliberately ignored in the early years of the festival, was included.

These innovations were welcomed by the populace and gave renewed focus to the festival. Yet, it continued to be plagued by criticism, especially regarding the issue of finances. The board maintained that Crop Over was unprofitable. In 1976, they had spent BBD$100,000 and had only taken in BBD$40,000 in gate receipts. Moreover, the costs of running the festival, including mounting and dismantling stages, theatrical lighting and the rental of performance spaces ". . . will be drastically reduced or eliminated if there were a national auditorium which would have, of necessity, all these facilities".[73] Unimpressed, the public continued to question the integrity of the board.

In addition, the anti-tourism narrative had grown stronger. Barbadian

Jean Holder, Executive Director of the Caribbean Tourism Centre, had (ironically in view of his post) publicly rejected that slant for the festival. He argued that it should not be judged by whether it attracted "any tourists at all". In a personal interview, Holder emphasized that at the time the tourism focus had alienated the needs of the populace and "was not going anywhere". Yet, Crop Over had the tremendous potential to become a national festival that would help to develop a national identity.[74] Other voices of protest resounded, including the editor of *The Nation*. He argued that to ". . . attempt to build it as a tourist attraction from its inception, is to prostitute a festival that is of great significance to the country".[75]

THE DEMOCRATIZATION OF CROP OVER

In 1978, a definitive change occurred. Responsibility for the festival was moved to the Culture Division of the Ministry of Education. The Board of Tourism was deemed incompetent in view of the ". . . severe criticism of the way it was organised and who were mostly attracted and involved".[76] Furthermore, with Louis Tull as the new Minister of Education, Nigel Harper as chair of the organizing committee, and both Elombe Mottley of Yoruba House and Jean Holder as members, a Barbadian-centred agenda was created, specially designed to involve a wide cross-section of the public. On reflection, Tull called this process "the democratization of Crop Over".[77]

Key events were introduced to the festival, including Kadooment[78], the masquerade street celebrations that had been long denied by the committee. Held on the last day, the results were overwhelming. With thirty masquerade bands and a membership of sixty to three hundred per band, what Kadooment did was to provide a twelve-hour spectacle of thousands of costumed Barbadians jumping in the streets.[79] These masqueraders defied those who accused Barbadians of lacking creativity or being too conservative to participate in Caribbean-styled celebrations.

What must be emphasized is the genuine surprise experienced by all. Indeed, anything involving gatherings on the street received an overwhelming response. In that year, the organizers staged an event in the streets of Bridgetown. To everyone's amazement, some ten thousand people turned up. Kamau Brathwaite captures the general feeling at the time: "[I]t was a national explosion (people didn't believe it was possible to have 10,000 people in the streets)."⁸⁰ The Barbadian example of the street carnival in Brathwaitian terms re/emerged, soon to be strengthened in the ensuing years.

However, it was in the Kadooment celebrations that the occupation of the street reached its zenith. In 1979, Kadooment Day was proclaimed a national holiday. Costumed revellers paraded in front of spectators at the National Stadium, before jumping along the parade route. This time the scene was chaotic:

> Kadooment was one mass of confusion from beginning to end, with long waits by the masqueraders, and crowd bottle-necks along the route, which was too long, and not well controlled by the authorities. At the Stadium the crowd, variously estimated at 12, 15, 20,000 even, spilled over from the stands and on to the parade track, jostling masqueraders, obstructing the view of the spectators in the stands. The route-judging was made meaningless by the crush of spectators, and the onset of darkness.⁸¹

Confusion or not, Kadooment was judged a success. In the ensuing years, the organizers experimented with various routes in an effort to address the congestion. The Culture Division also ensured that the tradition of calypso came into its own. With the advent of Kadooment, the Barbadian calypso art form was given space to thrive and Crop Over quickly became "a festival marked by the proliferation of calypsos".⁸² Utilizing many of the rhythms of the fife and drum/bumbatuk/tuk band, as well as other music forms, a distinctly Barbadian genre emerged. Two music competitions were created for the festival: Pic o' de Crop, in which the winner was proclaimed Calypso Monarch, and Tune of the Crop, the title awarded to the most popular song played on the route on Kadooment Day. Yet, the new organizers did not escape criticism. Complaints were made about the parade starting late and that the route had the masqueraders jumping uphill. One observer noted that at the Folk Nite, four nuns had to suffer through dirty jokes and being the target of a calypsonian. The Cohoblopot Festival Queen Show was also criticized for its failure to deliver its promise, especially with reference to the national dress.⁸³

Overall, the changes were viewed as positive. Marshall argued that the festival had become "mass national theatre" as the Culture Division had "visibly changed its form and its meaning". Gilkes defiantly exclaimed: "[T]hose days are gone. The whole concept of Crop-Over being something for tourists passed when the ministry took it over to convert it into a cultural activity by Barbadians for Barbadians. And this, more than any other factor, has been responsible for the festival's growth over the past two years."[84]

However, an old narrative plagued the new organizers. As the gymkhana had been abandoned, the burning of Mr Harding became the final event. He was burned at the end of Kadooment in the presence of enthusiastic crowds. At 20ft in height, he created quite a spectacular climax. But the rumblings of protests had grown over the years, forcing the organizers to reexamine his relevance. Though popular with most Barbadians, questions arose regarding the perception of burning an entity that represented the ethnic group (white) of most tourists that the festival hoped to attract, as well as much of the elite in society. Additionally, concerns were expressed about reactions to the burning, which included the throwing of coconut shells and other items at Mr Harding.[85] In 1982, the protests reached a crescendo and Mr Harding was officially rejected by the state, never to be burnt again. In this way the tourism narrative, with its entangled strands of history, ethnic and cultural identities, continued to adversely impact the festival.

CONCLUSION

Kamau Brathwaite celebrated the reawakening of African-Barbadian creative energies in the independence period, despite centuries of oppression. He observed that the "success of Crop Over ... points to a society with the kind of communal wealth capable of such public/ritual celebration". These energies were not allowed to surface in the early years of the festival as "they did not apparently exist", and the organizers refused to engage them.[86] A blatant act of discrimination, it served to reveal the conflicting identities within the Barbadian cosmos.

Furthermore, the question of whose construct of identity should guide the revived festival became the central tension. The Board of Tourism and its committee determinedly designed a festival based on the oligarchic narrative. Subsequently, their colleagues and Euro/American visitors would experience what was determined as the best examples of culture. These featured the cultural practices of the elite, such as the gymkhanas, balls, dog shows, regattas, and the entertainment by international musical acts. With little regard to the national narrative, they were attempting to strengthen the colonial discourse in the independence era.

Yet, the revived Crop Over unwittingly granted spaces for the marginalized narrative to further emerge, challenging the traditional Anglocentric conservative discourse that presumed to speak for all African Barbadians. The continued questioning by the populace as they voiced their objections to the imposed cultural narrative effectively shook the confidence of the old guard and reclaimed those moments of "public/ritual celebration".[87] Hence, what was dismissed as *mere* entertainment, such as the plantation fairs, the examples of performances of African-Barbadian masquerade, including landships and the burning of Mr Harding, served as instances of celebration and cultural resistance that had endured through slavery and emancipation into independence.

Indeed, this chapter has demonstrated that when those examples of African-Barbadian masquerade culture were fully included, the festival gained momentum. These local cultural expressions anchored the enterprise, sanctioning it. Until then, the general opinion was that Crop Over, as engineered by the elite and their supporters, lacked depth and a sense of the authentic. Consequently, the very traditions that had been marginalized and excluded served to energize and create new avenues for the exploration of Barbadian cultural identities.

NOTES

1. Bridgetown is the capital of Barbados.
2. Eric Hobsbawm, "Introduction: Inventing Traditions," in *The Invention of Tradition*, ed. Eric Hobsbawm and Terence Ranger (Cambridge: Cambridge University Press, 1983), 2.
3. Margaret Gordon, "Crop Over Festival Barbados 1974," in *The Bajan and South Caribbean*, July 1974, 1; Jerome Handler, "Taking Exception," in *West Indies Chronicle*, November/December 1974, 337.
4. See discussion in Marcia Burrowes, "Treat to Labourers: Plantation Crop Over from Slavery to Independence," *Journal of the Barbados Museum & Historical Society* Vol. LVII (Dec 2011): 54–76. For marginalization of African-Barbadian traditions, see Flora Spencer, "Crop-Over; an Old Barbadian Plantation Festival" (Bridgetown: Commonwealth Caribbean Centre, 1974).

5. Hobsbawm, "Introduction," 4–5.
6. See the editorial, "Whites should Adjust to Change: Whites Going 'Down Under'," *The Advocate News*, 26 November 1974, 2.
7. Personal interview with Jean Holder, 12 October 2012.
8. See Harold Hoyte, "Yoruba," *The Bajan and South Caribbean*, February (1973), 36–37 and 40.
9. Personal interview with Ian Estwick, 19 June 1997. Estwick served as chairman of the National Cultural Foundation.
10. Mikhail Bakhtin, *Rabelais and His World*, trans. Helen Iswolsky (Massachusetts: MIT Press, 1968), 6–7.
11. *Sixteenth Annual Report 1974–75: Barbados Board of Tourism* (Bridgetown, Letchworth Press, 1975), 17.
12. ibid.
13. Burrowes, "Treat to the Labourers," 54–76.
14. "Crop Over: A Festival in the Making," *The Bajan*, June 1975, 12.
15. A correspondent: "Barbados Crop-Over Festival, 1975," *Bulletin of East Caribbean Affairs* 1, no. 5 July (1975): 6–7.
16. ibid., 6.
17. Andrea King, "Marryshow in First Crop-Over," *Weekend Nation*, 29 June 2001, 15. See also *Fifteenth Annual Report, Barbados Board of Tourism, 1973–74*, 3.
18. ibid.
19. Frederick Smith, *Eulogy for Morgan*, as quoted by Davidson Bowen in "Well Done," *The Nation*, 1 June 2005, 1.
20. Morgan was president of the Barbados Hotel Association in 1957, 1958 and 1962. See "Morgan Receives Queen's Honours," *The Traveller: Tourist Board Barbados*, January-March 1970, 1.
21. Attempts to locate correspondence, such as minutes of meetings, for this period of the festival have to date been unsuccessful. Both the Ministry of Tourism and the National Cultural Foundation maintain that the documents were destroyed. Reliance has been placed on oral testimony, newspaper articles, reports from the board and other printed matter.
22. Jeanette Layne-Clarke, "As I was Saying," *The Nation*, 6 June 1976, 14.
23. Latoya Burnham, "It's Al good!" *Weekend Nation*, 25 July 2003, 18.
24. Personal interview with Al Gilkes, 3 November 2012. Personal interview with Elombe Mottley, 24 October 2011.
25. Jeanette Layne-Clarke, "As I was Saying," *The Nation*, 6 June 1976, 14.
26. Livvy Burrowes, chairman of the Barbados Tourist Board, was a member, along with Anna Bjerham of Trinidad, Al Gilkes and Leroy Trotman.
27. Personal interview with Jean Holder, 12 October 2012.

28. *Sixteenth Annual Report 1974–75: Barbados Board of Tourism*, 17.
29. Margaret Gordon, "Crop Over Festival Barbados 1974," in *The Bajan and South Caribbean*, July 1974.
30. ibid.
31. "Morgan delighted over the Response," *The Advocate News*, 2 June 1974, 1.
32. See Burrowes, "Treat to the Labourers," 54–76.
33. "John Wickham's Roundabout" in *The Bajan and South Caribbean*, July 1974, 25.
34. Frank Odle was the Director of Tourism. "Response Overwhelming to Festival in St. Lucy," *The Advocate News*, 11 June , 1974, 3.
35. Colvin Rock, "Mall was a Big Blunder," *The Advocate News*, 10 July 1974, 2.
36. Ulric Rice, "Lessons from Crop Over '74," *The Advocate News*, 18 May 1975, 5.
37. "Ambakaila Dancers Coming to Barbados," *The Advocate News*, 16 June 1974, 10; "Crop Over Calendar," *The Advocate News*, 26 May 1974, 13.
38. Roy Ward, "Crop Over – Its Pros and Cons," *The Advocate Magazine*, 7 July 1974, 7.
39. ibid. See also Jeannete Layne-Clarke, "Ambakaila and Crop-Over . . . in passing," *The Nation*, Sunday, 7 July 1974, 9.
40. Ann Hewitt and Lucene Bishop, "Crop Over Charade," *The Advocate News*, 6 June 1975, 4.
41. "Preparing for bigger Festival," Editorial, *The Advocate News*, 4 June 1975, 4.
42. "Crop Over Festival 1975 is on," *Tourism Newsletter*, 15 February 1975, 1.
43. Conversation with Emile Straker, 29 November 2012.
44. Young Bajan, "Crop Over Festival should be More Bajan," 16 June 1975, 2.
45. "Small fire breaks out at programme," *The Advocate News*, 21 June 1976, 1.
46. See advertisement, *The Advocate News*, 31 May 1976, 7; and 28 June 1975.
47. Other performers were the Nightingale Home Steelband, calypsonian the Mighty Dragon, and gospel singer Joseph Niles.
48. "Crop Over Festival 1975 into High Gear," *Tourism Newsletter*, 31 May 1975, 2.
49. *Tourism Newsletter*, 15 April 1975, 1. Personal interview with Paula Hunte, 3 October 2011. Ingrid Settles, "Disgusted with recent Crop-Over pageant," *The Advocate News*, 21 June 1976, 4.
50. Omowale Stewart, "The Irony of Crop Over as a Community Thing," *The Nation*, 1 June 1975, 5. See also Concerned, "Is the North Forgotten?" *The Advocate News*, 20 June, 1975, 2
51. "What about Calypsonians?" *The Advocate News*, 9 July 1975, 2; and 28 June 1975, 6.

52. See advertisement for rules, *The Nation*, 18 April 1976, 7. See advertisement for the contest, *The Advocate News*, 24 May 1976, 2.
53. See advertisement in *The Advocate News*, 18 April 1976, 11.
54. Jeanette Layne-Clarke, "Out of my head," *The Nation*, 30 June 1978, 14.
55. "Crop-Over Charade," *The Advocate News*, 6 June 1975, 4.
56. See advertisement in *The Advocate News*, 15 June 1974, 5; and 9 June 1974, 7.
57. "Air show defies grey conditions," *The Advocate News*, 27 June 1976, 1.
58. J.H. Moxly, *An Account of a West Indian Sanatorium and a Guide to Barbados* (London: Sampson Low, 1886), 48, 51.
59. "Gymkhana at Mangrove," *The Bajan and South Caribbean*, July 1975, 43.
60. See advertisement in *The Advocate News*, 26 June 1976, 8.
61. Layne-Clarke, "As I was Saying," *The Nation*, Sunday, 6 June 1976, 14.
62. Gordon, "Crop Over Festival 1975," 4.
63. "Mr. Harding ends festival," *The Advocate News*, 29 June 1976, 6. Personal interview with Paula Hunte. Personal interview with Al Gilkes, who hired the steel bands to facilitate the jump-up, 3 November 2012.
64. Gordon, "Crop Over Festival 1975".
65. Dawn Morgan, "Bury Mr. Harding", *The Pelican Magazine, The Nation*, 29 April 1983, 4.
66. "Call for changes in Crop-Over Festival," *The Advocate News*, 3 June 1976, 1. Also see *Tourism Newsletter*, 15 and 31 May 1977. 2.
67. Carol Cadogan was made festival coordinator and Denise Hope, deputy chair, became a member of the committee. Also see "No Queen Contest," *The Nation*, 29 May 1977, 3.
68. "Idea Behind the Festival," *Tourism Newsletter*, 15 and 31 May 1977, 2.
69. ibid.
70. "Idea Behind the Festival," 2.
71. "Crop Over Essay Contest," *The Nation*, 5 June 1977, 9. "Several Innovations for Crop Over '77," *The Advocate News*, 25 May 1977, 8. Personal interview with Elombe Mottley.
72. "Pampalam: Naughty but nice," *The Nation*, 12 June 1977, 3.
73. "No auditorium so festival costs go up," *The Advocate News*, 24 May 1977, 1.
74. "CTRC Director Opens Academy of Art," *The Advocate News*, 1 June 1976, 1. Personal interview with Jean Holder, 15 October 2012.
75. "Crop-Over Has a New Significance," Editorial, *The Nation*, 16 June 1978, 4.
76. "It's With Us: Crop-Over 1978," *The Nation*, 16 June 1978, 14.
77. Telephone conversation with Louis Tull, December 2013.

78. Kadooment is the Barbadian word for confusion and merriment.
79. "Thousands of Bajans Jump Up: Kadooment draws Carnival Spirit," *The Advocate News*, 4 July 1978, 1, Trevor Marshall, "Crop-Over Harvest," 9.
80. Kamau Brathwaite, *Bajan Cultural Report and Plan* (Bridgetown: UNESCO/Ministry of Education and Culture, 1979), 11.
81. Trevor Marshall, "An Evaluation of Crop Over," *The Bajan*, 14–16 August 1979, 16.
82. Curwen Best, *Barbadian Popular Music and the Politics of Caribbean Culture* (New York: Alterations Consultants, 1995), 61.
83. "Two things I did not like about Crop-Over Folknite," *The Advocate News*, 1 July 1978, 4. Also, "Cohoblopot a nonsense show," *The Advocate News*, 12 July 1978, 5.
84. Trevor Marshall, "Crop-Over Harvest," 9; Al Gilkes, "The Future of Crop-Over," *The Nation*, 4 July 1979, 5.
85. Lickmout Lou, "Bare Confusion at Kadooment," *The Nation*, 29 June 1979, 5.
86. Kamau Brathwaite, *Bajan Cultural Report and Plan* (Bridgetown: UNESCO/Ministry of Education and Culture, 1979), 41.
87. ibid.

[18]

CONTESTING NARRATIVES OF TRINIDAD AND TOBAGO'S HISTORY
The Contribution of Bridget Brereton and an Exploration of the Syrian/Lebanese Narrative

[FIONA ANN RAJKUMAR]

PROFESSOR BRIDGET BRERETON IS UNDOUBTEDLY ONE OF THE Caribbean region's most prolific social historians. She has written and presented on many pivotal topics in Caribbean history, including race and race relations, gendered history and oral testimony. Her work has inspired and encouraged criticality in her many students; teachers of Caribbean history in Trinidad and Tobago and the wider Caribbean; and international academia. It is hoped that educators will take up the challenge to build on the foundation of her research, which has provided critical analytical tools for the conceptualization of multi-ethnic and multi-cultural societies such as Trinidad and Tobago. This chapter is one such venture. Its purpose is to expand Brereton's research on ethnic narratives within the context of Trinidad and Tobago, by bringing to the fore the Syrian/Lebanese community, on which there is a paucity of academic research.

In an address to History and Social Studies teachers, titled "Histories and Myths: The Case of Trinidad and Tobago", at the Rudranath Capildeo Learning Resource Centre in Couva, Trinidad, in May 2002, Brereton drew from the concept of the 'narrative', as proposed by postmodernist theorists, as she examined its role in the reconstruction of historical memory in the twin-island republic. It was my introduction to Brereton's work on some of the various narratives and myths that formed an essential part of the history of Trinidad and Tobago.

In her presentation, she quite accurately stated: "I'm not so rash as to attempt a definition, but post modernists propose that there can never be one singly universally accepted narrative about the past, never one story of the history of France, of the USA, of Trinidad and Tobago. Instead, they insist there are always many narratives, many stories, all needing to be told."[1]

She proposed: "Reconstructing a nation's history must involve bringing together many different narratives rather than attempting a single linear account."[2] However, she admonished the educators in attendance to update themselves constantly with new knowledge, while assisting students in interrogating what was myth or downright falsehood in their own understanding of the past. This is insightful since narrative histories are often not produced by professionally trained historians. As a result, these narratives sometimes tend to be centred on the ideologies of the producers and the groups they represent, and not empirical historical evidence. She concluded by stating that "... our accounts of the past must be firmly grounded on carefully assessed evidence. If not, we will be entering into the realm of myth, and it is the historian's duty to expose myths of all kinds."[3] Brereton outlines how this could be achieved in her work on historical narratives.[4]

The comprehensive documentation of the history of the Syrian/Lebanese in Trinidad and Tobago is an ongoing process. Much of the work done on the community, thus far, is largely general in nature, focusing on their introduction into the society, their adjustment to life in the land of their adoption, their cultural traditions and practices, and their propensity for business. In this area, Enid Lewis was the pioneer, with her general study, which was written in 1970.[5] Also, in the same vein are articles by Angela Laquis and Gerard Besson.[6] Two full-length texts have also contributed to our general knowledge on the group. The first text, published by Besson, focuses on the philanthropic activities of the Syrian-Lebanese Women's Association,[7] while the second is a family history based on the life and contribution of the prominent businessman Abdou Sabga.[8]

The works of Sarah McCracken,[9] Lou-Ann Barclay[10] and Fiona Rajkumar[11] on the Syrian/Lebanese community are a departure from the above historiographical trend. They all attempted to analyze facets of the economic dimension of their experience. McCracken began the process of documenting the community's economic progress, while Barclay's analysis attempted to incorporate an introductory assessment of the role that culture might have played in their financial success. Rajkumar's PhD dissertation analyzed the economic progress of the Portuguese, Chinese and Syrian/Lebanese communities in Trinidad, interrogating some of the stereotypes pertaining to their economic position in the context of Trinidad and Tobago. It also investigated links between ethnicity and socio-economic progress by focusing on areas such as ethnic associations and informal networks, attitudes to the language, education and religion, marriage practices and the socialization of children. Members of the community, including Annette Rahael and Ramon Mansoor, have written introspective papers on their adaptation to the country.[12] Topics include the contribution of the Syrian/Lebanese to Trinidad and Tobago, ethnic endogamy, citizenship, stereotyping and diasporic double consciousness.

From a perusal of the historiography on this minority group, despite increased interest, there are still many areas left to be examined. Many have speculated about the inner workings of this tight-knit community, but this has not always translated into dedicated research. This work, therefore, seeks to contribute to the body of existing knowledge. According to Brereton, "Post colonialist states struggle to create a 'universalistic' historical narrative, a singular linear story which captures the 'whole' past of the nation." The result is "the creation of ethnic and/or sub-regional narratives of the past which challenge the hegemonic national narratives so often created around the time of formal independence in the formerly colonial countries".[13] This has certainly been the case in Trinidad and Tobago, which consists predominantly of diasporic communities from Europe, Africa, India, China, Syria and Lebanon. Brereton outlined and critiqued many of the emerging ethnic narratives in her work, including those of the imperialist; the anti-colonialist Afro-creole; the Afro-Trinidadian; the Indo-Trinidadian; the Hindu-centric; the Kalinago; and Tobago.[14] The aim of this study is to continue in the same vein by establishing and then critiquing some of the more prominent emergent themes in the Syrian/Lebanese narrative.

TRINIDAD'S SYRIAN/LEBANESE COMMUNITY – EARLY HISTORY

The Syrian/Lebanese community belonged to the final wave of new immigrants to enter Trinidad. They came from the area commonly known as Greater Syria, currently the modern countries of Syria, Lebanon, Jordan and Palestine. For centuries, it was a crossroads of traffic and commerce. Syria comprised Muslims, Christians and others, a mixture that caused endemic religious conflict. For nearly four hundred years, between 1516 and 1918, the Ottoman Turks ruled Syrians with an iron fist. Non-Muslims were unlikely to aspire to political office and faced discrimination from their Turkish superiors. The welfare and economic prosperity of non-Muslims were, therefore, inextricably linked to their religious affiliation. It was also difficult for them to travel freely because Christians were subjected to hostility from the Muslim Turks.

The precarious social situation was further compounded by economic difficulties for peasants, who seldom owned the land they cultivated. By the 1860s, many Maronite Christians were leaving Greater Syria for the Americas, namely North America, Brazil and the Argentine.[15] Immigrants from Syria and Lebanon were present in Trinidad from as early as the 1890s, and by the turn of the century, there was a small population of Syrian/Lebanese families in the British colony. These included the Habib, Galy, Akat and Abraham families. In 1909, Abdou Sabga arrived in Trinidad, en route to the United States in search of his wife and young cousin. His story is similar to many others who came to Trinidad in search of family members and decided to stay, because of the perceived economic opportunities in the colony. These and other families from Syria and Lebanon would become the foundation of the community during the first two decades of the twentieth century.[16] Their number was always small. In 1946, the census recorded 889 Syrians and "Asiatics", not including Chinese. In 1960, the community peaked at 1,590 and declined to 993 in 1970, then 951 in 1980.[17]

The majority who came to Trinidad were farmers and had little prior knowledge of formal business. A few middle-class professionals arrived, such as Abraham Hadeed's grandmother, who was a teacher.[18] In Trinidad, most of the Syrian and Lebanese immigrants became peddlers who would walk for miles with bundles of dry goods and fabric on their backs, in search of customers. They were also willing to extend credit to their African and Indian customers, which earned them the added trust of villagers. Peddling was particularly suited to the newly arrived immigrants because it needed no fixed capital; stock could be obtained on credit; little skill was necessary; and a few basic words of English would suffice.[19] Also, according to Besson, "They made their first homes in the boarding houses along Marine Square and the old and dilapidated mansions of George, Duke, Duncan and Charlotte Streets."[20]

The period 1945–1955 saw many Syrian/Lebanese in the dual economic role of peddlers and store owners. As their assets grew, some were able to purchase automobiles to transport their goods to areas far removed from the urban centres. According to Enid Lewis, one of the earlier writers on the group, by 1953 "nearly all of the small stores in Port of Spain and San Fernando were owned by Syrians while a few of the larger and medium-sized ones belonged to them also".[21] The early 1950s saw the community growing in prosperity, and by the 1970s, they owned at least twenty per cent of the garment factories in Trinidad.[22] These included Glamour Girl Lingerie (on the Churchill-Roosevelt Highway), Eagles Shirt Factory (in San Fernando), Premiers Garments Limited, makers of Greyhound garments for men, and Odette's, for women's clothing (Port of Spain). Other prominent businessmen in the community were – Anthony Sabga, founder of the Ansa Group (now deceased); George Matouk, whose contribution to the food industry and experimentation with local fruits and spices was tremendously successful; the Hadeed brothers, owners of Francis Fashions and Shoe Locker chain of stores; Jimmy Aboud, "The Textile King", as well as many others. After the oil boom of the 1970s, many members of the community began investing heavily in real estate and property development, which further consolidated their economic position into the 1980s.

This qualitative study focuses on the Syrian/Lebanese group with the aim of determining and analyzing their historical narrative. Articles in newspapers provide core information about the group, as they reflect the perspectives of various community members. These articles can be broken down into two broad categories: The first encompasses stories written in the 1990s after the 1990 attempted coup d'état by the Jamaat al Muslimeen. Many Syrian/Lebanese businesses were vandalized and they were linked to the illicit drug trade. They were called "clannish foreigners who married themselves" and who needed to return "home". These newspaper articles, often based on interviews, and containing lengthy verbatim quotations, were attempts by members of the community to share their story and clear the air on some of the notions circulating about them. The second category was found in a newspaper supplement titled "A Century of Giving" in the *Trinidad Guardian* on 25 July 2010. The supplement, comprising twenty-five pages, commemorated the centennial anniversary of the arrival of the earliest immigrants and contained the nucleus of their narrative. It reflected how the group chronicled its existence in and contribution to Trinidad and Tobago, and how it wanted to be portrayed. Themes included a triumph over poverty through hard work and dedication, citizenship and charity. More controversial topics such as endogamy and intermarriage were not addressed.

THE SYRIAN/LEBANESE NARRATIVE

This section outlines and evaluates the main components of the Syrian/Lebanese narrative, considering the historical evidence with the view of exposing any myths. Firstly, it addresses the image of the itinerant peddler that characterized the community at the beginning of the twentieth century. Secondly, it interrogates their portrayal as economic pioneers through hard work. Thirdly, it examines their representation as citizens and nation-builders, especially through their charitable organizations. Finally, it explores issues of identity and belonging, illustrating their dual pledge of allegiance to Trinidad and Tobago, and simultaneous embrace of Mother Syria or Lebanon. As was stated earlier, particular emphasis is placed on the analysis of interviews in the supplement "A Century of Giving: The Syrian/Lebanese Community in Trinidad and Tobago", which contains the essence of their narrative or self-representative history.

One essential aspect of the narrative is its emphasis on the early history of the group and its pioneers. In the *Guardian* supplement, Abdou Sabga was imbued with the title "Father of the Syrian/Lebanese community". Although he was not the first to arrive, the date of his landing in 1909 was used as the benchmark for the centenary celebratory events that unfolded in 2010.[23] One of the two published texts generated by the Syrian/Lebanese community, *A Life Worth Remembering – Abdou Joseph Sabga 1898–1985: A Chronicle of the Sabga Family and One of Its Most Distinguished*

Members, written by Abdo and Natayla Sabga, attests to the crucial role that Abdou and his family played in the lives of many early Syrian/Lebanese immigrants. The story of Abdou Sabga mirrored that of many of the earliest immigrants. When he arrived in Trinidad in 1909, at the age of ten, he was unable to speak English. He quickly learned it, and by the time he was a teenager, he was peddling his bundles from door to door. Eventually, he founded Joseph Sabga and Sons at No. 18 Henry Street in Port of Spain. It was from his home and business that many immigrant families were able to eke out a living as peddlers.[24]

In the article titled "Their Legacy Lives On", the author outlines a comprehensive list of the early families and their economic trajectories, from peddling to the establishment of businesses. Members of these families included Elias Galy, who arrived in 1909; Wahid Matouk, who came in 1925; Nagib Elias, who arrived in 1929; Anthony Sabga, who arrived at the age of seven in 1930 and worked in his father's haberdashery business; Joseph Nahous, who landed in 1937; as well as Abraham Moses and Roy Joseph who arrived in the 1930s.[25] Chain migration was the concept used by historian David Nicholls to describe the initial entry and growth of the Syrian community in Jamaica. Nicholls made the distinction between systems of migration such as indentureship, which were impersonally organized, compared to chain migration, where prospective immigrants learned of opportunities, and had initial accommodation and employment arranged by previous immigrants. The first migrants in the chain usually emigrated on their own initiative, thus constituting the first link of the chain. This is a viable framework that can also be used to theorize about the growth and economic expansion of the early Syrian/Lebanese community in Trinidad and Tobago, where many of the initial immigrants named above were either encouraged to come to Trinidad by relatives or brought their relatives to live and work with them once they, the first link, had been established.[26] Joseph Nahous, for instance, sent for his children fourteen years after he arrived, and placed them in his business to work.

Also prominent in their early history are accounts of immigrants who were tricked by unscrupulous individuals selling tickets in Beirut and Marseilles to "America". Many hapless victims of these schemes only realized, when it was too late, that the tickets were of insufficient value to transport them to their desired destination. As a result, many were deposited on the shores of Caribbean islands, including Trinidad and

Tobago. Amusing stories were recounted of how some Arabs overslept and missed their intended destination, only to find themselves in Trinidad.

The image of the itinerant peddler was also pervasive in the early narrative. Those who peddled soon became known as the *kasheek*, meaning those who sold goods from door to door. The peddler was a symbol of the humble beginnings of the community, as well as a powerful embodiment of their hard work, industry and perseverance. Many early members shared similar 'peddler' stories. Newspaper articles with headlines such as "The Mighty Trinis", "Lebanese Cedar", "Hard Work Don't Kill" and "Their Legacy Lives On" provide details about the lives of the immigrants and their initial poverty. It was reiterated that many had arrived penniless, with nowhere to live, little formal education and no means of employment. Anthony John Aboud, for instance, recounted the story of his own father, who started peddling at fifteen in the 1930s, and with the support of other Syrian/Lebanese, was able to build a life for his family.[27] In 2010, the image of the peddler was used on a souvenir stamp to commemorate the centennial anniversary of their arrival.[28]

Linked to the story of the peddler was an unwavering work ethic credited as being responsible for their evolution into successful entrepreneurs. Most articles written on and by members of the Syrian/Lebanese community stressed the traits of hard work, industry and perseverance as foundational to their economic success. "Hard Work Don't Kill: Secret of Migrants Success", published in the *Trinidad Express* in 1996, went into painstaking detail to demonstrate that what was then seen as the economic success of the Syrian/Lebanese community had been built through the sweat, toil and sacrifice of the previous generations.[29] In "Syrians Deal with Change", Emile Elias mentioned that although many descendants of the pioneers owned profitable businesses, not all of them possessed the traits of a successful entrepreneur. He also attempted to debunk the myth that all of the members of their community were wealthy, and went on to give examples of relatives who returned to the Middle East because it was just too hard to make it in Trinidad.[30]

Existent works outlined in the historiography confirm the prominent role that entrepreneurs of Syrian and Lebanese descent play in the economy of Trinidad and Tobago.[31] As was previously seen in the community's narrative, this is primarily attributed to dedication, hard work and a willingness to sacrifice. However, the research points to additional factors at play, in tandem with hard work and perseverance. To interrogate this aspect of the Syrian/Lebanese narrative, two additional explanations for their burgeoning presence in the economic arena, brought to the forefront by my prior research into minority entrepreneurial groups in Trinidad and Tobago, will be highlighted. One perspective explores the role of ethnicity in the success of ethnic entrepreneurs, while the other examines the role of the state in the entrenchment of the Syrian/Lebanese in the economy of Trinidad and Tobago.

In "To Be or Not to be Chinese", Thomas A. Shaw argued that in the correct environment, ethnicity could be used as a tool for achieving economic success. According to him, "the use of ethnicity as a strategy may not be conscious, or even voluntary, but like any cultural 'tool' in a given situation it may be the best way of occupying and using an environment".[32] Case studies presented in *Ethnic Communities in Business: Strategies for Economic Survival* by Robin Ward and Richard Jenkins, and *Ethnic Entrepreneurs: Immigrant Business in Industrial Societies* by Roger Waldinger, Howard Aldrich, and Robin Ward, have revealed that migrant groups often activated strong ties to kin, and co-ethnics, in order to mobilize the resources needed to form and maintain a business. In this way, ethnic solidarity provided an avenue that assisted immigrants in occupying their new environment. On arrival in the new society, the immigrant naturally gravitated towards those of his kind who were already settled. It was from this reservoir that many immigrant firms sourced their labour force. The employment of kin, and co-ethnics, served as an entry point into the new society, while simultaneously providing a safe haven for new immigrants. Furthermore, in the business arena, it was, and still is, significant that labour costs be kept lower than those of competitors. Those entrepreneurs who depended on their ethnic group for support often employed relatives and other community members at both the lower and managerial levels, which allowed them to reduce their expenditure on salaries. Meanwhile, in small, family-owned enterprises, family members were most times unpaid labourers. In this way, the employment of kin or co-ethnics provided employers with cheap, dependable, homogenous and loyal labour – a very valuable resource in small enterprises.[33] This type of labour force was, therefore, imperative to the survival and growth of businesses with low profit margins or limited access to mainstream sources of credit or technical assistance.

In the Portuguese and Chinese communities in Trinidad and Tobago, there is documentation of formal group associations. The research does not reveal the existence of longstanding formal ethnic associations within the Syrian/Lebanese community, equitable to the Chinese district associations;[34] however, it does highlight strong internal networking ties that functioned similarly to these associations. Interviews conducted with members of the Sabga and Hadeed families revealed that family and community networks were indispensable to the economic development of the community. Joseph Abdou Sabga opened his home to numerous immigrants and gave them goods on credit. His three sons – Abdou, Ayoub and Assad – continued this tradition. In fact, Abdou gained a reputation as the leader of the community and the Sabga home became a symbol of hope and courage for numerous new immigrants. An interview with a member of the Sabga family, who is also a Hadeed by marriage, revealed that prominent families, such as the Matouks and Gabriels, all started out living in and working out of the Sabga home and store on Henry Street, Port of Spain, which was like a station for all the Arabs during the first decades of the twentieth century.[35] The above examples from the Syrian/Lebanese community substantiate Shaw's claim that drawing upon ethnicity and ethnic ties was a successful way of occupying and benefitting from the economic environment.

Entering into business was often seen as a viable occupation for immigrants that allowed them to progress economically in a foreign environment, where they had little education and language skills. In fact, in the right circumstances, entrepreneurs who depended on their ethnic group for support had the potential to accumulate wealth, since they were not dependent on outside sources. The result was that for some immigrant groups, such as the Syrian/Lebanese, business was not just a way to make a living, but evolved into a way of life, a tradition passed from one generation to another. Thus, some Syrian/Lebanese families developed what can be termed a "merchant ideology". This was particularly evident in many Syrian/Lebanese businesses that retained second- and third-generation family members in management positions.[36]

Dependence on the ethnic group and the development of a trading ethic resulted in the concentration of the small Syrian/Lebanese community in the business arena. Prior to the 1960s, these businesses were relatively small-scale in nature. Between the 1960s and 1980s, however, many

Syrian/Lebanese businesses transitioned into larger, more lucrative establishments. This transition was facilitated by factors external to the ethnic group. The 1950 Pioneer Ordinance, engineered by the People's National Movement (PNM) government, as part of its economic strategy to facilitate the emergence of a local manufacturing industry, was one such factor. This initiative and other mechanisms that allowed for tax incentives and import substitution behind tariff walls were integral to the PNM's consecutive five-year plans that were meant to transform Trinidad's post-independence economy. According to Brereton, the traditional white commercial interests were the primary benefactors of legislation deployed by the PNM government to assist in the expansion of the local business and manufacturing industry. Thus, although these initiatives were meant to assist those who were not traditionally part of the business elite in getting a foothold, the elites were better poised to take advantage of the government incentives.[37] An economic analysis conducted on the Portuguese, Chinese and Syrian/Lebanese in the 1950s and 1960s also revealed that Syrian/Lebanese entrepreneurs were concentrated in industries that benefitted from the economic policies implemented by the state industries, including manufacturing, textiles, clothing and construction. They greatly profited from the proposals of the government in its Pioneer Industry legislation, and consecutive five-year economic plans during the decades of the 1960s and 1970s. These were areas in which the Chinese and Syrian/Lebanese were concentrated, and were, therefore, able to take advantage of the aforementioned avenues for the growth and expansion of their businesses.[38]

Access to the economic incentives offered by the state would, in part, explain the rapid growth and expansion of many Syrian/Lebanese businesses, particularly in the areas of food, clothing, textiles, manufacturing, construction and real estate between the 1960s and 1970s. It was then that they truly entrenched their position in the national economy – by crossing over into industrial areas. Many Syrian/Lebanese businessmen had hitherto amassed relative wealth without large-scale employment. By the 1960s, many moved from being the owners of small and medium-sized establishments to being the proprietors of larger, more aesthetically pleasing buildings in urban centres which they used for their own retail outlets or rented out. In "The Syrian/Lebanese in T&T", Jeremy Matouk stated that his father, George, had been inspired by Prime

Minister Eric Williams' desire to see local business come to the fore. He eventually moved away from trade and entered the food industry, taking on the multinational brands that had long dominated the local market.[39] The receptivity of Syrian/Lebanese businessmen to the government's call to entrepreneurs to provide large-scale employment, assist in the diversification of the local economy, and development of an indigenous manufacturing industry, was a strategic economic move that allowed access to resources that elevated the level of business they did. The industrial thrust of the Syrian/Lebanese was, therefore, aimed predominantly at the production of necessities for modern Trinidad and Tobago, such as food, clothing, entertainment complexes and shopping malls, electrical appliances, furniture and cars, which targeted the entire country as a guaranteed market. Additionally, the 1970s oil boom provided a further boost to the economy that benefitted businessmen. A businessman who was interviewed said that his father had told him: "... you hear all those things about how wonderful businessmen are, how great their acumen ... none of us would have done that well if we did not have that oil boom in the 1970s. Money passed through the economy and went to the businessmen ... this provided the jolt we needed."[40]

Thus far, it is evident that the essence of the early narrative of the Syrian/Lebanese group focused on the arrival and economic progress of various immigrant families. Central themes included the trickery that brought some of them to the Caribbean, the poverty of their peddler predecessors, their hard work and determination to succeed and their impeccable work ethic, which ultimately resulted in their phenomenal economic success. The historical research is beginning to show, however, that it was more than hard work and acumen that propelled the transition from peddler and small businessman to large-scale entrepreneur. Previous works on the success of ethnic minority groups in Trinidad and Tobago have also pointed to the need for more probing investigation into the role of state initiatives, and incentives, in the consolidation of entrepreneurial groups, such as the Syrian/Lebanese, within the local context.[41]

Another theme for consideration is the emphasis on the group as nation-builders and their legitimacy as citizens of Trinidad and Tobago. In the *Trinidad Guardian* supplement, "A Century of Giving", the title itself could be seen as contesting their portrayal as outsiders who had contributed little to the national community. The 'outsider' label was evident during both the 1970s Black Power Revolution and the 1990 Jamaat-al-Muslimeen's attempted coup d'état. However, this way of viewing the community had emerged as early as the second half of the 1930s.

In 1936, parliamentarian Timothy Roodal called for modification to the immigration laws to stem what was seen as the bane of Chinese and Syrian/Lebanese immigrants because they only employed "their own" and were a drain on national resources.[42] During the 1990 attempted coup, Syrian/Lebanese businesses were targeted and taunts such as "Go back where you came from, Syrian" were hurled at them. As they attempted to grapple with these responses during the 1990s, the themes of citizenship and nation-building began to emerge strongly in their narrative. According to John Rahael in 1991, ". . . although many were shaken and wondered when the next attack would be, no one was deciding to leave. No one was throwing in the towel."[43] The Mighty Trini, Syrian calypsonian/songwriter Robert Elias, composed two patriotic calypsos, "Sailing" and "We are the Citizens", which members of the community stated, captured their sentiments about their adopted homeland, in spite of sometimes being treated as "second-class" citizens. In 2012, "Sailing" was deemed one of the most patriotic calypsos by newspaper journalist Peter Ray Blood in "Patriotism Through Calypso". In the song, Elias reiterates his unrelenting love for the country, stating that, regardless of what happens to the good ship of Trinidad and Tobago, he is "sailing with the boat – sink or float".[44]

Among the main reasons that the Syrian/Lebanese community was seen as clannish was their perceived cliquishness, the society's negative view of intermarriage, and their propensity for marrying "their relatives". Discussions relating to parallel cousin marriage or family endogamy and marrying within one's ethnic group, or ethnic endogamy, are reflected in the historiography and newspaper articles generated during the 1990s, after the attempted coup. It is evident from the research that during the early decades of the twentieth century, Syrian and Lebanese parents encouraged their children to return to their villages and tribes in search of a spouse, who was often a parallel cousin. Community leader Abdou Sabga, for instance, found his wife in Syria, after breaking off a clandestine relationship with a young lady outside of the community. A reading between the lines of this account indicates that his family members were relieved when he married Linda Aboud, thus initiating the long-standing relationship between the Sabgas and the Abouds.[45]

The practice of returning to the homeland for a spouse continued to be evident as late as the 1990s. The fresh injection of Middle East-born individuals into the community up to the 1970s was one factor that accounted for the persistence of, not just ethnic endogamy, but family endogamy. An article in the *Trinidad Express,* dated 12 August 1996, records an interview with Nino Tommy, who stated that: "It is true that that's how the family liked it. From young my mother always told me that she wants to take me to Lebanon to get married. I had different views but now, when I really think about it . . . if I am going to live with someone for the rest of my life, I would want someone of my own kind."[46]

At the time of the interview, Tommy was involved with a woman of Indian descent, who had expressed her desire that they marry. Tommy, on the other hand, had doubts, and appeared torn between his feelings and the wishes of his parents. This brings to the forefront the influence of parents who were from the Middle East. Tommy was born in Trinidad; but his mother was from Lebanon. Although his father had been born in Trinidad, he had made a trip to Lebanon and returned with a bride. His mother was keen to continue this practice to preserve the family's culture.

The views of members of the Syrian/Lebanese community appear to be divided on the topic of ethnic endogamy and what has been termed 'integration'. By the 1990s, the number of mixed marriages had increased. The article, "Syrians Deal with Change", revealed some of their opinions on marrying outside the group. Peter Elias commented that he saw the Syrian/Lebanese community becoming more assimilated into the society. He drew reference to their counterparts in Jamaica, whose Syrian/Lebanese community was older than Trinidad's, as an example of change and integration due to the higher occurrence of mixed marriages. According to Elias: "As time goes by marriage will be based more on background than on race. I see the future of our community integrating more, not because it is a conscious effort, but because it is a natural course of our future. More and more people's taste will widen. I mean you adapt to a community – it is inevitable."[47]

Others who were born here, such as Emile Elias, for instance, echoed his views. It was evident that intermarrying with other races was much easier in the 1980s and 1990s than during his parents' era. For Emile, it was less threatening and no longer created that much discomfort because there was a greater sense of belonging to the society.[48] In the same article, and in direct contrast to the above ideas, others, who chose to remain anonymous, still "admitted to a strong prejudice against others outside their community". In another article, prominent members were adamant that "they will not become a callaloo".[49]

The above issues on marriage, endogamy and integration, which featured in discussions on and by the members of the group during the 1990s, were largely absent from their emerging narrative in 2010 in the newspaper supplement marking the centennial anniversary of their arrival. Instead, strong sentiments of nation-building and citizenship were espoused. The newly appointed honorary consul for Syria, Marwan Yousef, wrote an article "A Pledge to Build, Contribute and Respect", in which he stated, "I was born in Syria, and I am proud to be a Syrian. I am just as proud to be a citizen of this nation. The Syrian/Lebanese Community is committed to nation-building. We are committed to total integration into the national community, while the culture of a people never leaves them." Yousef went on to give examples of ways in which the business community had invested much of its time and finances in developing the nation so that all could benefit. Using the newspaper as a medium, Yousef, therefore, sought to contest ideas that they were clannish and exploitative, while reinforcing the image of them as nation-builders. His article also spoke about the issues of belonging and diasporic double consciousness, which are integral to the experiences of migrant groups. This is captured in his statement, "Firstly, we belong to Trinidad and Tobago, but like other diasporic communities in the society, we have not forgotten our ties to the Motherland . . . We and our children are real 'Trinis', involved in the music, dance, drama, language, food and other aspects of culture in this nation." Yousef also stressed the group's success in areas other than business that contributed to the nation's development and productivity, such as various professions, the arts and sports.[50]

In their narrative on nation-building, their role in the economy is also highlighted as complementary and not exploitative. Jeremy Matouk recalled that his grandfather, Wahid, told him that, early on, it was not possible to purchase commercial property on the major streets of Port of Spain, such as Frederick and Henry Streets. Those streets were reserved for the longer established and more upstanding British, French creole and European communities. The Syrian/Lebanese had to conduct their business on Charlotte, George and Nelson Streets. Even in the import trade, they were not offered the same goods as the established businesses by the foreign salesmen. According to Matouk, it was the prejudices and second-class citizenship they experienced in the economic arena that caused many members of the community to offer support to the independence movement and the PNM. He stated that many believed in Williams' vision to develop the economy using local businesspeople who could create an indigenous manufacturing sector. Matouk, therefore, saw their financial success as a community as a triumph for the local economy, which had benefitted many.[51]

The final theme within the Syrian/Lebanese narrative is also linked to nation-building. Prominence is given to the charitable work of their community. Charity, or giving back, is an integral theme in their narrative. Aside from the contribution of the business community, charity is predominantly personified in the work done by the Syrian-Lebanese Women's Association. It looms large in the narrative, as it represents the foremost way in which the group has given back to society. The association, which was initially called the Mediterranean Star, has worked on numerous projects alongside organizations that assist disadvantaged children.

The 1970s Black Power Movement also impacted the Mediterranean Star. In the article, "The Work of the Syrian/Lebanese Women's Association", the author stated that the women were torn between sympathizing with the frustrated disenfranchised, and the fear of people in their community. They decided that the best way to combat their negative image was to make their work known via a well-organized public relations programme and the media. The idea was successful and soon they were participating in public events alongside other service organizations. It was at this time that they approached the governor-general's wife, Lady Thelma Hochoy, with a tremendous pledge of BBD$30,000 towards the setting up of the Lady Hochoy Home for disabled children, a project that took them two years to complete. By 1975, founding member, Minerva Sabga, was awarded the Hummingbird Medal Gold for community service.[52]

After a lull in the 1970s and early 1980s, the Mediterranean Star witnessed a changing of the guards as the younger women, many of them Trinidad-born, were encouraged by their mothers to take over the association. This new generation wrote by-laws and added structure to the organization. They changed its name to the Syrian-Lebanese Women's Association of Trinidad and Tobago to reflect their commitment to both the country and their culture. They placed emphasis on three areas: social, cultural and charitable outreach. Over the six decades of its existence, the association grew steadily from eight founding members to encompass three hundred. Their work was featured across two pages in the 2010 *Trinidad Guardian* supplement. Moreover, in the 1990s, many articles highlighted and endorsed the association's contribution, while also paying tribute to members' husbands for their support.

It is worth mentioning that one of the other two texts on the community highlights the association's genesis, development and contributions. *The Voyage of the Mediterranean Star: The Syrian/Lebanese Women's Association of Trinidad and Tobago* was published in 2002 by Paria Publishing Company, as part of the commemoration of its fiftieth anniversary. The group's initiatives to raise the standard of living of citizens from all walks of life was seen by Syrians and Lebanese as truly mirroring the concern that they as a community had for their compatriots.

CONCLUSION

The Syrian/Lebanese community has been part of the population of Trinidad and Tobago for over a century. Yet, as one of the smaller ethnic communities, they continue to strive to create a space for themselves within the broader narrative of citizenship. The narrative or 'history' emerging out of the community could, therefore, be seen as part of a dialogue geared towards demystifying the group, while also portraying it in a favourable light. As a result, the themes of economic diligence, nation-building, patriotism, inclusion and charitable work were foundational to the recasting of their role as citizens of Trinidad and Tobago by 2010. Issues of race relations and ethnic endogamy, especially the controversial practice of intermarriage, were not prominent features. According to Brereton, there will always be myths about the past that serve individual or group interests. As she has advocated, this work aimed to provide a narrative of the past grounded in available evidence, and which offers interesting, socially progressive, and perhaps novel, perspectives on the topic.[53]

NOTES

1. Bridget Brereton, "Histories and Myths: The Case of Trinidad and Tobago" (presentation at the Rudranath Capildeo Learning Resource Centre, Couva, Trinidad, May 2002).
2. Brereton, "Histories and Myths," 2.
3. ibid., 13–14.
4. See Bridget Brereton, "Contesting the Past: Narratives of Trinidad and Tobago," *New West India Guide* 2&3 (2007): 169–96; "'All Ah We Is Not One': Historical and Ethnic Narratives in Pluralist Trinidad," *Global South* 4 (2010): 227–63; and "Ethnic Histories: The Indocentric Narrative of Trinidad's History" (paper presented at Conference on Global South Asian Diaspora, University of the West Indies, St Augustine, 2011).
5. Enid Lewis, "The Syrian/Lebanese Community of Trinidad" (Caribbean Studies Paper, University of the West Indies, St Augustine, 1970).
6. Angela Laquis, "The Syrian/Lebanese Community in Trinidad" (Caribbean Studies Paper, University of the West Indies, St Augustine, 1980); Gerard Besson, "The Syrians of Trinidad," in *The Book of Trinidad*, ed. Gerard Besson and Bridget Brereton (Port of Spain: Paria Publishing, 1992).
7. Gerard Besson and Alice Besson, *The Voyage of the Mediterranean Star: The Syrian/Lebanese Women's Association of Trinidad and Tobago* (Port of Spain: Paria Publishers, 2001).
8. Abdo Sabga and Natayla Sabga, *A Life Worth Remembering: Abdou Joseph Sabga 1898–1985: A Chronicle of the Sabga Family and One of its Most Distinguished Members* (Laventille: Zenith Service, 2001).
9. Sarah McCracken, "The Contribution of the Syrian/Lebanese to the Economy of Trinidad and Tobago" (Caribbean Studies Paper, University of the West Indies, St Augustine, 1998).
10. Lou Ann Barclay, "The Syrian/Lebanese Community: A Preliminary Study of a Commercial Ethnic Minority," in *Entrepreneurship in the Caribbean, Culture, Structure and Conjuncture*, ed. Selwyn Ryan and Taimoon Stewart (St Augustine: Institute for Social and Economic Research, University of the West Indies, 1994).
11. Fiona Rajkumar, "Ethnicity and Economy: The Portuguese, Chinese and Syrian/Lebanese in Trinidad 1945–1981" (PhD diss., University of the West Indies, St Augustine, 2007).
12. Ramon Mansoor, "Cross Culturalism and The Caribbean Canon" (presentation at University of the West Indies, St Augustine, 2004).
13. Brereton, "'All Ah We Is Not One'," 5.
14. Brereton, "Histories and Myths,"; "Contesting the Past Narratives, 169–96; "'All ah we is not one'"; "Ethnic Histories".

15. Besson, *Book of Trinidad*, 400.
16. ibid.
17. Statistics taken from Rajkumar, "Ethnicity and Economy," 125.
18. Abraham Hadeed, personal interview, 2004.
19. Barclay, "The Syrian/Lebanese Community," 217.
20. Besson, *Book of Trinidad*, 402.
21. Lewis, "The Syrian/Lebanese," 6.
22. ibid., 8.
23. "Syrian/Lebanese Influence in Trinidad: Celebrating 100 years of contribution", *Trinidad Guardian*, 25 July 2010, 9.
24. Abdo Sabga and Natayla Sabga. *A Life Worth Remembering – Abdou Joseph Sabga 1898–1985: A Chronicle of the Sabga Family and One of Its Most Distinguished Members* (Laventille: Zenith Services, 2001)
25. "Their legacy Lives On," *Trinidad Guardian*, 25 July 2010, 16.
26. David Nicholls, "The Syrians of Jamaica," *Jamaican Historical Review* 4, no. 4 (1986): 51.
27. Anthony J. Aboud, "Defining a Purpose," *Trinidad Guardian*, 25 July 2010, 21.
28. "Commemorating 100 years presence of the Syrian/Lebanese community," *Trinidad Guardian,* 25 July 2010, 4.
29. "Hard Work Don't Kill: Secret of Migrants Success," *Trinidad Express*, 1996.
30. Anna Walcott, "Syrians Deal with Change," *Trinidad Guardian*, 1992.
31. See Barclay, "The Syrian/Lebanese Community"; McCracken, "The Contribution of the Syrian/Lebanese"; Rajkumar, "Ethnicity and Economy".
32. Thomas Shaw, "To Be or Not to Be Chinese: Differential Expressions of Chinese Culture and Solidarity in the British West Indies," in *Caribbean Ethnicity Revisited*, ed. Stephen Glazier (New York: Gordon and Breech Science Publishers) 1985, 95.
33. Roger Waldinger, Howard Aldrich, and Robin Ward, "Opportunities, Group Characteristics and Strategies," in *Ethnic Entrepreneurs: Immigrant Businesses in Industrial Societies,* ed. Roger Waldinger, Howard Aldrich, Robin Ward and Associates (London: Sage, 1990), 35.
34. The research on early members of migrant groups, such as the Chinese and Syrian/Lebanese within the context of Trinidad and Tobago during the first half of the twentieth century, contains many examples showing dependence on the ethnic group for economic success. In a paper that examines the evolution of Chinese associations in Trinidad and Tobago, I looked at the socio-economic role of Chinese district associations prior to the 1970s. Associations such as Chung Shan, Fui Toong On and Sun Wai were both social and economic in scope. They often provided meals and lodging

for new immigrants without a place of abode, small interest-free loans to members, and often linked new immigrants with Chinese businessmen looking for workers. Fiona Rajkumar, "The Emergence and Evolution of Chinese Associations in Trinidad," *Journal of Caribbean History* 46 (2012).

35. Rajkumar, "Ethnicity and Economy".
36. Rajkumar, "Ethnicity and Economy," Chapter 5: Family Life and Socialization.
37. Brereton, "The White Elite," 42.
38. See Rajkumar, "Ethnicity and Economy," Chapter 3: A Socio-Economic Analysis 1945–1981.
39. Jeremy Matouk, "The Syrian/Lebanese in Trinidad and Tobago", *Trinidad Guardian*, 25 July 2010, 19.
40. Personal interview in Rajkumar, "Ethnicity and Economy," 64. (The interviewee preferred to remain anonymous).
41. Rajkumar, "Ethnicity and Economy".
42. Timothy Roodal, Hansard Report, Trinidad and Tobago Parliament, 1936.
43. Judy Diptee, "The Mighty Trinis," *Trinidad Express*, 30 June 1991.
44. Peter Ray Blood, "Patriotism Through Calypso," *Trinidad Guardian*, 31 August 2012.
45. Sabga and Sabga, *A Life Worth Remembering*, 64.
46. "Young Cloth Store Syrian: We're not the Mafia," *Trinidad Express*, 12 August 1996, 7.
47. Anna Walcott, "Syrians Deal with Change," *Trinidad Guardian*, 15 November 1992.
48. Walcott, "Syrians Deal with Change," *Trinidad Guardian*.
49. Diptee, "The Mighty Trinis," *Trinidad Express*, 2.
50. Information for this paragraph was taken from Marwan Yousef, "A Pledge to Build, Contribute and Respect," *Trinidad Guardian*, 25 July 2010, 7.
51. Information for this paragraph was taken from Matouk, "The Syrian/Lebanese in Trinidad and Tobago," *Trinidad Guardian*, 19.
52. "The Work of the Syrian/Lebanese Women's Association," *Trinidad Guardian*, 25 July 2010, 12.
53. Brereton, "Histories and Myths," 13.

[Part Six]
THE HISTORIAN AND HER CRAFT

[19]

BRIDGET BRERETON AND THE NARRATIVES OF MODERN TRINIDAD
An Assessment of Three Volumes

[MICHAEL TOUSSAINT]

"Break a vase, and the love that reassembles the fragments is stronger than that love which took its symmetry for granted when it was whole."
—Derek Walcott[1]

IN THIS CHAPTER, I OFFER MY ASSESSMENT OF the critical role that Bridget Brereton has played in the development of historiography regarding the islands of Trinidad and Tobago. I propose to start with an examination of some of the historiographical works that preceded her entry into this arena, and those that were contemporaneous with her offerings. Then, I will review three of her publications: *Race Relations in Colonial Trinidad, 1870–1900*,[2] *A History of Modern Trinidad, 1763–1863*[3] and *Law, Justice and Empire: The Colonial Career of John Gorrie, 1829–1892*.[4] They will be discussed in terms of their order of importance in relation to the social history of Trinidad. Each text is examined individually to determine its significance in understanding Trinidad's social history. Then, an overall appraisal of Brereton's work, as reflected in these texts, will be offered. Of necessity, there is commentary on the work of other writers, and other works of Brereton. It was the Jamaican-born Franklin W. Knight, today a leading African-American historian and scholar, who reminded us only recently that "the Caribbean has always had a history" and that "historians have tried to capture that since Columbus wrote his famous journal in 1492".[5] Shortly afterwards, the explorer commissioned Father Ramon Pane to write an account of the early inhabitants they had found on the island of Hispaniola. Furthermore, some people consider Pane's *An Account of the Antiquities of the Indians* to be the first book written on the First Peoples and the island they inhabited. The work is unique: it was the first to be written about the region and its people by a European, and on Caribbean, New World or American soil. Today, we know far more about the First Peoples than before,[6] and about the societies that succeeded them. Pane's voice was Euro-centred in tone and texture. Knight's observations, which are not lost on resident (Trinidad and Tobago) scholars, constitute a Caribbean challenge. Where necessary, we are to disturb our neighbourhood.[7]

Selwyn Cudjoe, in *Beyond Boundaries: The Intellectual Tradition of Trinidad and Tobago in the Nineteenth Century,* informs us of "an existent tradition of writing, cultural practices, custom, use of language etc., evident in tracts, novels, newspapers, travel writing, dramatic performances, open-air theatre, sermons and poetry that scholars seldom examine".[8] George Lamming well-intentionally forewarned that "a whole planet collapsed in the Caribbean archipelago". Furthermore, he maintained that "As we [meaning scholars, academics and activists] reflect on the whole range of the region's political culture we attempt to colonise an enterprise which starts us on multiple journeys towards nurturing a whole." It is one which he claims "we recognise but can't very readily define, and whose definition a correct self-knowledge could make irrelevant".[9] He avers: "The wider we cast the net the more conscious we are of the omissions we would be guilty of." Faltering cognizance of this reality has often been one of the shortcomings of reconstructing the Caribbean's past. It is particularly so with respect to efforts regarding the history of particular islands and mainland territories of the regions, as illustrated in the historiography of Trinidad (and Tobago).

It is not that the historians have not been doing their work nor have they been oblivious to the challenge. Much has been written, and they have also devoted attention to many phenomena and issues. Yet, Las Casas' *Aqui si contiene una disputa, o controversia* and *Brevíssima Relación de la destrucción de las Indias*[10] ought to have forewarned that the history of the region would constitute a contentious space, leaving much for future generations of historians to haggle over.

It is often from contentions in historiography that its scholars shift emphasis from the general to the specific and vice versa. But always the major challenge for them, and for those that will in future muse on their thoughts, is the balance in their synthesis. Even if it can be argued that the balancing rather than the skewing of historicity is not necessarily the forte on which many famous historians have built their celebrity, or that inevitably they would have written from the vantage point of their second record, it would be necessary at least to acknowledge these quirks in the historiography on Trinidad. Las Casas wrote its history from an anti-mercantilist, Amerindo-centric consciousness. Pierre-Gustave-Louis Borde's *Histoire de l'ile de la Trinidad sous le gouvernement espagnol, Dieuxieme partie (1622–1798)*, published in Paris in 1876, was in no small measure committed to the romanticization of the island's predominantly French culture during the last years of Spanish rule.[11] Pierre M'Callum's *Travels in Trinidad during the months of February, March and April 1803* is described aptly by E.L. Joseph as little other than a collection of scurrilously levelled accusations against Picton, the colony's first British governor.[12] Joseph's *History of Trinidad* itself was, by the publisher's own admission, the result of its author's distinctive, staunch British attitude, and essentially pro-Spanish, anti-French comportment. Remarkably, the publisher perceived it to be the first accurate history of the island.[13]

In 1961, Gertrude Carmichael, the librarian at the Imperial College of Tropical Agriculture, published *History of the West Indian Islands of Trinidad and Tobago*,[14] an inarguably invaluable text, all the more because, as K.S. Wise surmised, most of the previous works only covered the history up to 1837. Wise would have known. A medical doctor by profession, and the surgeon-general of Trinidad and Tobago, he was the founder of the Trinidad and Tobago Historical Society. He failed to notice, though, that essentially, for Carmichael, the history of these islands started only with the arrival of Columbus, which, of course, it absolutely did not. Still, no one can impose a premium on her contribution. Before and even after her, writers approached the writing of the colony's history from various kinds of vantage points, some credible, others suspect, though hardly any to be totally discredited. Accreditation is after all a matter of epoch, zeitgeist, and the social milieu and cultural compulsives of groups.[15] Such influences, call them what we may, are perennially there.

Historians can often reveal more than intended through what they knowingly or unknowingly overlook or obliviate. This is seen in historical accounts before and after Carmichael's, some well-known, others less familiar, even to historians. Lionel Mordaunt Fraser's two-volume *History of Trinidad*, published in 1891, was virtually an ode to the governor, for the most part limited to the relations between Trinidad and Afro-revolutionary St Domingue.[16] It is, notwithstanding, part of the historiography of both the island and the region.

Evaluative criteria, even in our time, raise questions of their own. Like the writing of history, its reading also constitutes socially shaped or acquired taste: for the reader responds according to how the historical recounting meets the nurtured palate. So, when Eversley wrote *The Trinidad Reviewer for the Year 1900*,[17] one ought to determine by what yardstick he would have been measuring developments and events: that of the stubborn colonial mind or those restive reformers who were to storm against the barriers to constitutional change in the next century?

Similar types of questions could be asked randomly in *A Collection of Papers Historical, Social and Descriptive about Trinidad and its People* by Lewis Osborn Innis'.[18] Likewise, one might be solicitous regarding John Bierly's *Trinidad then and now being a series of sketches in connection with the progress and prosperity of Trinidad, and Personal Reminiscences of Life in that Island, 1874–1912*, if only to determine the level of connection to or differentiation from J.H. Collen's *Handbook of Trinidad: For the Use of Settlers* and his *Guide to Trinidad and Tobago: A Handbook for Tourists and Visitors*. Sometimes, when writers put pen to paper, the masses and their enterprises, if not left out, are treated with derision.[19]

Carmichael's history was, therefore, certainly the most important in terms of the period it covered and its reach into social domains. By the same token, it is no wonder Eric Williams' first historical text on the island found such fertile soil for the cultivation of an anti-colonial history. All of the lived history of the bulk of the people of the region, and the developments of the century after emancipation – with its mounting crescendo of dissent, resentment and defiant militancy, intensified almost at the very start of the century and certainly during the interwar years – suggested the need for such a text. Williams himself had been well prepared for materializing it. Tried and tested through the interregnum and by 1944 with *Capitalism and Slavery*,[20] he slammed into colonialism. It was the age of decolonization and British colonio-imperial vulnerability. There was the manifest success of his academic peers and colleagues – Nehru in India, Nkrumah in Ghana; the collapse of the British-contrived regional federation idea; and the rising tide of black nationalism. Once developments at Malborough House had signalled the all-clear for the independence of Trinidad and Tobago, Williams abandoned forthwith his work on the first of a three-volume series on primary written sources pertaining to West Indian history and began the construction of a text on Trinidad and Tobago's history.

The result was *History of the People of Trinidad and Tobago*. Completed and published on the eve of the country's acquisition of political independence, it was the first wide-ranging and chronologically extensive, local history narrative written by a black nationalist of Trinidad and Tobago. It was a polemical work, mobilized by a nationalist agenda, which still offers little regarding the contribution of Europeans to the society, even if some of his criticism against colonialism was justified. But it was not only the Europeans. Williams was kind to his friends and devastating to his enemies.[21] Anticipating his critics, he warned that the aim of writing the book was not literary perfection or conformity with scholastic canon, but to provide the people of Trinidad and Tobago on their Independence Day with a national history, and furthermore, "If some do not like the book, that is their business."[22]

This reminds us of a similar comment from his mentor, C.L.R. James in *The Black Jacobins*.[23] To this author, such bombast subtracts neither from James nor Williams. The latter's 1962 publication constitutes a Herculean achievement by any measure. Williams' diaries, today still largely unexplored by historians, points to his tireless work on the text – from start to finish – over a mere two months.[24] Moreover, having charted new territory, the book has intrinsic value, even if his critics might contend that it only sealed his messianic fate at the helm of Trinidad and Tobago's politics for almost two additional decades after its publication. At any rate, the written history of Trinidad and Tobago has always been articulated through various voices who were hardly disinterested: the hunter, the hunted, the apologist, the protagonist and so on. Few scholars have attempted to give adequate expression to the lay and working classes in the society, or the people from these strata, via a democratic historicity. Brereton is one of them. Her attempt to ventilate the different narratives, to allow the constituencies themselves to have their presence and say, – rather than to stage-manage the acting and commentary of key players, and how they ought to be interpreted historically, must be applauded.

Accordingly, I have opted to consider her work through the three volumes mentioned: a general history of Trinidad; a social history of the island; and the history of a judicial official who served in other British colonies before coming to Trinidad and Tobago. The selections allow us to consider, in various ways, Brereton's treatment of the relationship between the rulers and the ruled, and to a significant extent, that of the notable characters and groups, and their roles and functions. Moreover, in one instance, some of the characters overlapped as dramatis personae, and provided an extensive and far-reaching context for understanding her treatment of colonial authority, authority figures and subject-people. This arrangement allows us to place Brereton on trial, even if it could only amount to a preliminary hearing. There is a case to be made for seeing her work in a particular light over the past few decades, today, and in the future – especially if the region sustains its interest in developing its historiography.

I shall begin with *Race Relations in Colonial Trinidad*, the first to be published, and the text most singularly devoted to her explication of the island's social history. This book emerges directly from Brereton's doctoral thesis and contains ten chapters, which attempt to document the social history and resulting race relations of nineteenth-century Trinidad. The early chapters detail the social environment in terms of data on the demographics; the geographical distribution of principal towns and communities; the over-concentration on the western littoral fringe of the island; and communication problems between the urban and rural areas. She elaborates the economic environment, alludes to the evolution of the colonial state's policy on Crown lands, and discusses the conflict between the sugar interests and the small man as it related to the accessibility of these lands. The colonial agricultural economy is explained: sugar and cocoa, operating against the background of Crown colony government, cyclical depression in the global cane sugar market, attempts at diversifying local agriculture, and efforts to create saving institutions for the labouring classes. All of these are set against the backdrop of the determination of the white community to continue to control the local economy in a land regarded nonetheless by the typical European-descended mind as "no colony for British settlers",[25] and who believed that "All labour performed by the hands under the sun must be left to men of the coloured races."[26] The remaining chapters elaborate on the social conflicts, challenges and achievements of the various social groups, and of the society as a whole. Remarkably, throughout the volume Brereton's data presents itself, stridently probing, logically conceptualized, and neither distracted nor detained by deference or disdain for any group.

In discussing the "The White Elite", meticulous attention is paid to the differentiations within that group. Brereton's commentary on the complexity of white local colonial society during Victorian times is striking and witty. What is interesting is that Brereton allows the African-descended to speak virtually unplugged. Hitherto, they were perceived in such a subaltern manner that in the local historiography, when it came to discussion on white issues, their opinions were absent, muted or obfuscated. In Brereton's offering, however, readers are brought face to face with the "birds of passage", those British men who stayed a few years, earned large salaries and then moved on.[27] Alluding to J.J. Thomas of *Froudacity* fame, she willingly concedes that these were Froude's Anglo-West Indians, who believed that "being Anglo-Saxon they had a divine right to dominate any country in which they found themselves".[28] Satirically, she tantalizingly cites an editorial which surmised that among such Englishmen, those "with capital went to Australia, with brains to India, with neither to the West Indies".[29] The British government, more particularly the Colonial Office, we are informed, "brought them out and it was their delight to lord it over the people who paid their salaries".[30]

Brereton also introduces us to other categories of whites, who, again, after Thomas, belonged neither to the official class nor remnants of the slave-holding class, with its Bourbon mentality, but were forced to depend on their brain, capital and energy to make a living in Trinidad. They had come to Trinidad, settled down and identified with the creoles (as opposed to the "birds of passage").[31] Then there were the creoles themselves, whom one is skilfully admonished to regard as an integral part of the society, "native" as much as the non-white population, but whom, although a great many of them had the physical characteristics of the white race, were, in sociological terms, marginal – not to the local society,[32] but to the metropole. Considerable attention is therefore devoted to the French creoles, the leading sector within the white creole community, and their exaggerated deference to birth and breeding.[33] Brereton differentiates them from the British creoles, alerting us also to the conflicts and tension between the white expatriate and creole communities.[34]

With Brereton, it is not merely what is said but how images are conveyed. We are provided with graphic allusions to the white creole community, with the French at the forefront in terms of exhibiting their pomposity at various levels: driving through the streets in their carriages; gathering in the afternoons for tea and dinner; the males appearing in court to be made to honour their responsibilities to their coloured children born out of wedlock.[35] We see them as constantly challenging the white expatriates for control over the economic and political institutions, and over issues of governance and administration.[36]

The white creoles – whether French, British or otherwise – were also challenged by the rising black and coloured middle class. Brereton explored the role of education in the evolution and upward mobility of this class; and how persons of mixed colour and hardworking, self-made blacks fanned out into a number of professions – law, medicine, teaching, the clergy, journalism and the civil service. She distinguished between those of "French free coloured origin" and those who were not descendants of the established free coloured planters, arguing that the latter had to strive to establish themselves through education and ability. We are introduced to many prominent descendants from the French free coloured lineage, but equally to those blacks and coloureds who pulled themselves up by their own bootstrap, without the head start of having a partially white ancestry: the "J.J. Thomases"[37] and the "Samuel Carters".[38]

Pervasiveness of late nineteenth-century discrimination is thus well brought out in the text: European whites discriminated against white French creoles, who in turn discriminated against descendants of the French free coloureds, who joined them in discriminating against the blacks. Numerous cases are presented of discrimination against, and prosecution of, prominent blacks and coloureds, and of their resentment. Interestingly, we are introduced to one of the earliest calypso bards, Hannibal, who was himself given to ridiculing blacks. Here is Brereton quoting Hannibal:

> I ain't black, I ain't white
> If it comes to blows or a fight
> I'll kick the black man to save the white . . .
> God, you is a white man
> I want to know the truth
> Who but the devil
> Could mek these nigger brutes?[39]

Having cited this example of the late-nineteenth-century-type exposition of the Curse of Ham, Brereton moved quickly to point out that some blacks and coloureds did not practise discrimination against their black kith and kin, but instead devoted their energies to the promotion of black pride and achievement.[40]

Several areas of the text preoccupy themselves with the pursuit of this agenda, firstly in the urban and then rural communities, and in the context of African cultural continuities. Accordingly, the development of black urban enclaves is examined against the background of increased African inter-island migration to Trinidad in the 1870s and 1880s, and newly emergent urban communities and challenges are accounted for.[41] There is, for example, discussion of Afro-Barbadian immigrants in the island and their tendency to attract opprobrium for every ill in the society, notwithstanding the arrival of large numbers of immigrants from other Caribbean colonies, and the fact that unplanned and disorganized urban development was bound to exacerbate destitution and criminal activity in the capital and surrounding areas.[42] Brereton paints a vivid picture of unplanned housing (barrack yards, juvenile delinquency, vagrancy, petty crimes, prostitution, the neglect of family institutions, and the loose association of unemployed men and women formed into bands for drinking, gambling and fighting – bands that took over the annual carnival parade during the 1870s and 1880s.[43]

But for Brereton, it was not all negative. Many blacks had been drawn to the city in search of work. Many women had found employment as domestics, washerwomen and seamstresses, or had established small businesses as petty traders, shopkeepers and hucksters. Likewise, men had found jobs as porters, janitors, messengers and cab-drivers. Some worked in bakeries and breweries, or as dockworkers. According to Brereton, most were employed as construction workers or artisans, and were skilled craftsmen, such as carpenters, masons, mechanics, tailors, shoemakers and printers. However, life in the capital was compounded by the fact that many had no employable skills, and therefore had little or no prospect of getting a job. Some ran afoul of the law and were often in violent confrontations with the police. The judicial system they faced was itself unaided by an inadequate, inefficient magistrate court system plus urban overcrowding. For Brereton, the result was "epidemics, death and a mass of human misery".[44] The rural scenario was primarily agricultural and less depressing. It was presented as the habitat of a wide range of different ethnic groups: First Peoples, Venezuelan peons, African descendants and Indian immigrants. With the ultimate exemption of this last group, all were frustrated by land alienation policies, and land and other taxes whose objective was preserving the interests of the planter class.[45] Brereton makes a strong attempt to illuminate their individual experiences and conceptualizations of their reality.

Notwithstanding her representation of the whites throughout the text as the dominant culture, she contends that, on the basis of sheer demographics, longevity within the society, and reinforcement through various streams of immigration, blacks were, at a certain level, the most dominant cultural grouping, although theirs was not the culture of the hegemonic dominant classes.[46] Given this, despite the pandering to white culture, the African-descended community succeeded in maintaining many aspects of their ancestral practices.[47] This provided the basis for her exploration of the "soul of the black folk", including their more African religious traditions and their syncretism with Roman Catholicism and Protestantism.[48] Brereton found it necessary to discuss the Shango, the Shouter Baptists, the Rada community, wakes, obeah, the many African drum dances, tamboo bamboo, and emerging genres of calypso, including those with Venezuelan influence.[49] She was able to differentiate between calypsonian and *chantwell*,[50] jamette and pimp, 'bad John'[51] and stick fighter.[52]

Towards the end, Brereton discusses the Indian immigrant community, which she describes as a new element in the Caribbean society, whose language, physical appearance and culture were so strikingly different that they were considered to be separate and apart from mainstream society. Brereton recognized from the onset the many difficulties and challenges confronting this group: the exploitative conditions of their indenture; their evolution as another segment in an already divided society; the perception of the Indian by others; and the difficulties provoked initially by internal differentiation among them – some were Hindus, others were Muslim. She also discusses their protest and agitation, the opening up of Crown lands to the Indians and the development of conflicts between Indians and blacks during the 1870s and 1890s. She explores how, despite the many challenges, the Indians held fast to their religion and culture. She also recounts the commutation of their return passages into individual land holdings, the establishment of villages, and the formation of settled rural communities. The India-born Indian eventually gave way to the Trinidad-born Indian – the creole Indian. For Brereton, both as an immigrant community and an expanded one by natural increase, and on account of their contribution to the sugar industry, the Indians constituted the most important group to have migrated to the island in the nineteenth century.[53]

The final chapter brings the various strands of the preceding discourses together, reflecting Trinidad as a significantly divided society during the last decades of the nineteenth century. However, Brereton analyzes this development as not only the result of local dynamics but, more importantly, of their interplay with international developments and conceptualizations regarding race. Her attention here is focused on the development of social Darwinism, social anthropology and scientific racism.[54] Her canvas is wide, but one gets a sense of the intensified imbibition by some of the notions of the natural inferiority of the non-white community, more particularly of the blacks, and the uncritical acceptance of this view as the persistent cause of the poverty of Haiti.[55] Given all of this, it is clear to the reader that marriage between a white and a black person was to nearly all of the local white population an untenable proposition.[56]

But for Brereton, complexities regarding a range of seemingly self-evident propositions emerged from the dominant white culture. In terms of the international perspective, for example, whites saw significant distinctions between the capability of northern Europeans and Iberian Europeans, and for many, it was difficult to locate the French within the hierarchy. But for some in Trinidad, French culture was the more progressive.[57] And in plural Trinidad, where some coloureds had done significantly well, the racist discourse carried on in international circles had to be conducted locally in hushed tones.[58] But what was more, not all whites believed in the inferiority of the African-descended, and many among the latter did not believe this about themselves.[59]

For Brereton, the purpose of the study would have been to examine the nature of society and race relations in Trinidad during the last three decades of the nineteenth century, with special reference to the white, coloured and black groups.[60] These were years which, she admitted, saw "few striking and momentous events" and were not obviously "formative".[61] Yet, she appears to have explored a number of sources that were hitherto less utilized in published historiographical works, including newspapers and the writings of contemporary historians and other scholars. Clearly, Brereton canvassed a wide range of sources and commentaries to solicit official, private, popular, individual, scholarly and less-than-scholarly opinions on Trinidad and its variegated society.

This is true of many of her publications. Paradoxically, although her sources are not fully cited in the second publication under review, the effect of this prior wide-ranging foraging of source material is clearly reflected in *A History of Modern Trinidad*. The book explores the history of the island from pre-Columbian times to independence in 1962. In terms of both the style of writing and the visual layout of the text, the book is remarkably reader-friendly. It indexes all the topics and themes, and gives a chronology of the major events between 1498 and 1962, as well as a rather undersized but obviously carefully selected bibliography. Given the range of developments and issues covered, it can be regarded as a rather compact text without compromising the quality of its scholarship or relevance. Following a brief preface, which introduces the book as an attempt to provide a scholarly and interpretive history of Trinidad since the 1780s, Brereton opens the very first chapter with an instantaneous and absolute dismissal of one of the most misleading and distortive historiographical myths. She writes: "Christopher Columbus did not of course discover Trinidad on 31 July 1498,"[62] and she continues, correctively: "Trinidad was discovered by Amerindian people of the Arawak group, who had lived there for many centuries, and by (Kalinago) Caribs who had begun to raid the island long before 1498 . . ."[63] This provides the opening salvo for a rather inclusive, discursively democratic text.

Compared to *Race Relations,* which discusses three decades of social history, this volume explores developments in Trinidad over a far more extensive period and attempts to incorporate all the major economic, social and political happenings. Yet, this allowed Brereton the opportunity to provide snippets and glimpses of the social history of Trinidad. She begins with a discussion of the First People, following up with an examination of Spanish colonial policy, inclusive of the unfolding of the relationship between the two groups. The book discusses the Arena massacre, the ultimate response of the First People to the atrocities perpetrated by the Spanish missionaries.[64] There is also an appreciation of the developing conflictual relationship between the emerging Spanish creole community and Spanish officials sent out occasionally from the metropole to assert the Crown's authority and interest. This social discourse sets the basis for an understanding of the contemporary demographic and economic problems, and provides the background for a discussion of the 1783 Royal Cedula of Population.[65]

The latter, as is well articulated in the historiography on Trinidad, laid the foundation for the development of a plantation economy and society,[66] but more importantly, for our discussion, one made up largely of French white and coloured planters and their enslaved African-descended labourers. According to Brereton, the arrival of these French immigrants from Grenada, St Lucia, Martinique and Cayenne virtually transformed the island into a French colony, although under the control of the Spanish government.[67] However, the framework for additional social conflicts and tensions was set from the time of the arrival of the Cedulants. For, like the white French immigrants, the free coloured population permitted to settle on the island were also given grants of land, albeit in smaller quantities; they were more numerous. Moreover, given the land grants and other concessions they received, they were certain to pose a threat to both white French and Spanish colonists on the island, especially as many of them were of republican persuasion and aspired to equality with whites on the island.

These are the kinds of issues raised by Brereton who continued to focus on the issue of race-based social conflicts, as these developed following the capitulation of the island to the British in 1797, and certainly during Colonel Picton's administration, and throughout the period of slavery and afterwards. Many notable historians have explored this race-based reality of the island's history. What is remarkable, however, is Brereton's ability to sustain interest in this dimension of her socio-historical observations. She does so, while simultaneously providing visibility and salience to myriad issues affecting the various social groups throughout the lengthy period covered in the text.

To be sure, the issues and developments facing the First People, the Spanish, the French and the British, as well as the African-descended population, and later, Indian and Chinese immigrants, are all discussed. It is noteworthy that neither the voice of the imperial and colonial authorities nor that of any particular ethnic group is rendered dominant.[68] This is also the approach she adopted in taking readers to the post-emancipation nineteenth century.⁶⁹ Furthermore, as she explores this period, and approaches the early twentieth century, a similar orientation is in train: no political, economic or social agency is accorded paramountcy. This makes it possible for her to move easily into a discussion of issues prior to 1937–38, and from thence to the years in the run-up to independence.⁷⁰

In discussing Trinidad on the road to political independence, all the key political parties and pressure groups – including labour and various ethnic organizations and their leading personalities – are foregrounded.⁷¹ The political leadership of the country, both government and opposition, are projected all the way to Malborough House. Thus, in elaborating existing or evolving scenarios, Brereton is able to assume historiographical legitimacy, even in discussing race and politics in modern Trinidad (issues over which communities on the island remain significantly polarized to this day).⁷² This is so primarily because Brereton's modus operandi is clear from the onset: the issues facing contending groups are juxtaposed, their respective positions solicited and represented to counterbalance claims of one group against another. More importantly, she is never unwilling to identify their biases and is equally adept in this text, if not all others, at ridiculing with polished politeness, the prejudices and biases of the various classes and constituencies.⁷³

The third text, *Law, Justice and Empire: The Colonial Career of John Gorrie 1829–1892*, has to be seen as a continuity of the very important exercise of democratizing historiography. Here, the critical link is Brereton's treatment of Justice Gorrie. One of her more recent major publications, the book is devoted to a discussion of this very colourful, feisty and fiery judicial official of Scottish birth, whom she often described as a radical chief justice. From her own accounts, she had a long-standing preoccupation with Gorrie. As a historical character and personality, she first introduced him in her 1972 PhD dissertation,⁷⁴ and then *Race Relations in Trinidad*.⁷⁵ Gorrie was a member of the bench who was perceived by whites to be too sympathetic to the cause of the black, coloured and Indian masses.

In one chapter, he is presented as lashing out on behalf of an African-descended, middle-class court official who committed suicide after being accused of removing records from the court in Gorrie's interest. At the time he was the subject of an investigation regarding his conduct as the Chief Justice. He protested vehemently, arguing that the official was treated in this way because of his colour.[76] For Brereton, Gorrie was evidently radical. For, as she pointed out, during his time it was rare to find a white British official as prepared to publicly challenge and chastise his white compatriots. He took them on in the courts, the legislative chambers and elsewhere, in pursuit of the cause of blacks, coloureds and Indians unfairly treated by the colonial system. In Trinidad, it was difficult to find any other white public official as determined to champion their causes to secure the rights and privileges to which they were entitled as free men. The book, therefore, comes across as commentary on the struggle of these communities as much as on the contributions of this colourful white liberal. It is to Brereton's credit that she is guilty of this historiographical commitment. For, in polarized societies, writers are given to writing under the spell of their ethnicity, an aspect of their second record that often renders it difficult for them to peer beyond the blind spot on their intellectual retina where other ethnic groups are concerned.

But Brereton went further. She reflects on Gorrie's commitment to the oppressed masses, not merely in respect of Tobago and Trinidad, but in a much wider international context. His earliest appearance on the legal scene in the Caribbean region was in connection with the Morant Bay Rebellion. He surfaced then, not as a member of the Jamaica Royal Commission, but before it as a lawyer, serving as an invitee of the Jamaican Committee, and on behalf of the victims of the reprisals. Then, between 1866 and 1868, he took part in the efforts in Britain to bring Eyre to trial.[77] Subsequently, Gorrie served as a high-level judicial official in several British multi-racial colonies. From 1869 to 1876, he functioned firstly and briefly as a substitute procureur-general,[78] and then as a puisne judge in Mauritius.[79] From 1876 to 1882, he served as chief justice in Fiji in the South Pacific and also as the chief judicial officer of British territories across the Western Pacific, and at one time even additionally as the British high commissioner over the various islands involved.[80] Between 1882 and 1886 he was the chief justice of the Leeward Islands.[81] In 1885 he was appointed chief justice of Trinidad.[82] Following its unification with Tobago in 1889 he became responsible for both islands. Brereton's book therefore explores both Gorrie's life and the struggle of the man in an international context. That struggle was (and still is) relevant everywhere. It is worth considering that everywhere, more than one ethnic group, represented either through the effort of individuals or communities, contributed inextricably to that struggle. This, too, is reflected in the manner in which data is presented in *Law, Justice and Empire*.

The introduction of the text provides a short but encompassing synopsis of Gorrie's life through which Brereton's major assumptions about his character and orientation are presented.[83] Essentially, he is introduced, perhaps intoned, as a "maverick colonial official" who tried to serve the interest of "subject people;"[84] to ensure their protection and assistance from the government; and that they enjoyed "absolute equality" before the law.[85] The rest of the book tests these assumptions, verifying Brereton's perspectives through a rather expansive array of sources, including primary, official documents and newspapers pertaining to the various colonies; private family correspondences; and other documents, including the writings of Gorrie who was himself a journalist, poet and novelist.[86]

After discussing Gorrie's family background and early childhood, all of which reflect him as being nurtured in the religio-political liberalism of Scottish radicals, Brereton shows us Gorrie, as a people-centred legal advocate in the 1865–8 royal commission of inquiry into the Morant Bay rebellion. Next, the reader is exposed to Gorrie's activism in Mauritius between 1869 and 1876 and Fiji from 1876 to 1892. If Brereton is to be seen as adept in discussion of the struggle of the oppressed races, in Trinidad and Tobago, she is to be considered no less so for her discussion of their struggle in the Indian Ocean and the Pacific. In the Caribbean, the oppressed were of varied types: First Peoples, Africans, Indians, Chinese and those of mixed descent. In Mauritius, they included the formerly enslaved blacks and the Indian indentured immigrants who formed the overwhelming majority of the population. The principal obstacle in the way of equality was the island's French creoles and their jaundiced presupposition that theirs was an inalienable right to abuse Africans as though slavery had not been abolished, and Indians as though indentureship was to be unquestionably another legitimized form of enslavement.[87] In Fiji, the masses were the Fijians, Tongans and other Polynesians together with Indian immigrants, pitted against white immigrants from Australia and New Zealand and the prejudice and land hunger these last groups had nurtured since arriving in the South Pacific.[88] Here, as in the British Caribbean, Gorrie regularly and irritatingly gobsmacked them.[89]

For Brereton, it was this resolute but experienced official who committed himself to a similar quality of jurisprudential responsibility in the Leeward Islands between 1883 and 1886.[90] There, the downtrodden and oppressed were the formerly enslaved and their offspring who remained fettered by its discriminatory, overstayed riders.[91] In Trinidad between 1886 and 1889, and both Tobago and Trinidad from 1889 to 1892, they faced comparable challenges. In Tobago, for example, it was particularly the black peasant *metayers*, to whom he gravitated in administering and dispensing justice.[92] His commitment to their cause led Brereton to caption him as "ah we judge", an expression denoting the high esteem in which he was held by the African-descended of Tobago.[93]

Far more than most other white men, Gorrie was about the democratization of the law and even-handed justice, and Brereton has brought to the fore both the struggle of the masses and this hitherto unsung hero. Such is the nature of the democratization of historiography, and it is worth considering that many of the early and later historical texts written on Trinidad would have fallen short of any such agenda. Many early histories focused on government and politics, and valorizing or diminishing certain imperial and colonial administrations.[94] Many family histories were also written as panegyrics to British- and French-originated households. While the early twentieth century saw the emergence of more inclusive narratives, this was also coterminous with the proliferation of an anti-colonial, polemic genre, which peaked on the road to independence, and in the immediate post-independence period during the build-up to the Black Power Revolution of the early 1970s. The last century has also seen its share of ethnic-based, racially polarized historical narratives.[95]

Brereton entered the arena, providing readers with a more balanced recounting. Over the years she has operated skilfully, and perhaps so uneventfully and unassumingly, across the battleground of scholarship and dialectics that one can miss out on certain meaningful implications.

Firstly, when Brereton started her postdoctoral contribution to the reconstruction of Trinidad's past, the nationalist history of the Caribbean was in its infancy.[96] In the 1960s, analytical books of a high quality on the Caribbean were rare. Both the University of the West Indies (UWI) and its academic domain of Caribbean history were, at best, pubescent.[97] Courses on Caribbean history were made compulsory only during that decade. Undoubtedly, though, there were academics at these institutions who were acutely aware of the complexity of the Caribbean, and the fact that this reality of the region had been overlooked by self-acclaiming, metropolitan academicians and equally extreme local challengers.[98] Moreover, if for all of the seeming authorities – on both sides – the Caribbean was to be seen in black-and-white terms, then for the new breed of Caribbean scholars striving to understand the unyielding complexity of the region's texture, tone and tenets, this approach seemed to represent one of the best hopes for development and progress.

Brereton's entry into the field occurred at a significant conjuncture. The age of the colonialist writer had passed, but the metropolitan-trained nationalist was on the rise. The UWI was being called upon to match its scholarship against what had been benighted by greater metropolitan grounding. Deservedly or not, the latter had about it an aura and boast, sometimes baseless, of incomparability. Brereton was also immersing herself in historiographical work at a time when the various streams of narratives emerging from ethnic and social plurality, locally and elsewhere, were advancing in their own scholarship with demands for legitimacy.[99] Merely to engage in a social history of Trinidad in the late 1960s was to take on the challenge of historiographical democracy.

It is not merely a matter of race or ethnicity. In 1961 when Carmichael, a white woman, wrote, there was very little mention of non-white women, except for Louisa Calderon, who was fleetingly explored in her work.[100] In Williams' *History of the People of Trinidad and Tobago*, women are similarly scantily treated.[101] Much remained to be written about them, labour, the arts, the narratives of the various social classes – all of which loom large in Brereton's many offerings. When she essayed history, she did so, not in the patriarchal tradition, or as a contemporary bystander recording contemporary times for posterity.[102] She wrote primarily as part of a new generation of locally bred Caribbean career historians, concerned with modernist balance, inclusivity and rationality.

In *Race Relations* she makes a noteworthy observation concerning overcoming the bias of the past without infusing, far less invoking, those of the present. She writes: "The problems historians encounter point to the analysing of the interaction of races and classes in a complex West Indian society of a century ago."[103] Accordingly, she warns "What the historian must not do is to attribute to the black masses of Trinidad in the 1870s the beliefs, prejudices and attitudes of their descendants a century later, and this is just as true of other groups in the society."[104] She contended further "... it was not possible that white, coloured and black people in the 1870s had a set of values and attitudes identical to those held during the period of slavery".[105] This notwithstanding, she acknowledged that the pattern of race relations established then had not changed much until the 1930s, but reckoned that investigating the relations covered by her study would help in laying the historical foundation for understanding the society at the time of her writing, and was of expository relevance to Trinidad of today. Within this was the recognition of the necessity to probe nuances and manners not so well recorded of groups who operated through prejudice, as well as those who felt they were discriminated against. The result, in comparison with what had gone before, was a greater, more broad-based inclusivity in the search for and incorporation of records in the historiography of both Tobago and Trinidad; in particular, the giving of voice to the voiceless, subalterns, and those treated to elision.

Brereton does this in fine style. In *Race Relations*, her penchant for satirical commentary could make one overlook, however momentarily, its seriousness and germane quality. *Law, Justice and Empire* constitutes a formidable discourse on jurisprudence and empire. It brings to the fore an appreciation of Brereton's deep understanding of law and justice as tools of empire and the ruling classes. It provides invaluable insights into the nature and operations of the British colonial system, including differentials between the de jure and de facto with which the masses had to contend. *History of Modern Trinidad* remains one of the most inclusive and democratic historical texts about the island, although, as with other general histories, there are oversights or opportunity costs. The treatment of Tobago's related historical context is a case in point.

In a manner almost characteristic of the written history regarding Trinidad and Tobago, those who write about either of the islands usually operate out of one of two models. They generally acknowledge, firstly, the politico-territorial dimension shaped by their unification between 1889 and 1898. However, beyond this, they either proceed to treat the successive social history of the two islands to some measure of mutual exclusivity or to one of oversimplification, as though after unification they then melded into an indivisible community. Many, including Brereton, acknowledge Trinidad's society as being significantly affected by the arrival of immigrants from many territories, including the Anglophone

Caribbean. However, with respect to the last, very little attention has been paid to the impact on Trinidad's immigration from Tobago. Developments today betray that historiographical overlook, and, on reflection, the complexities that have underscored the social, political and economic relationship between the two islands. More attention has been paid to migration from Barbados to Trinidad,[106] despite Tobago's comparatively closer proximity to Trinidad and the fact that migration from the former to the latter began as a form of resistance to slavery and preceded the unification process. Tobago's impact on Trinidad remains in need of greater historical focus.

A reader might also say that *A History of Modern Trinidad* is not based on original sources. However, Brereton herself readily tells us this, so that what might be perceived as a negative can also be appreciated as more of an attempt to draw from streams of consciousness constituted in other historiographical authorities.

On a more general basis, others might be wont to accuse Brereton of the absence of theoretical exposition. Admittedly, such a focus is not the ground on which she stands out, or generally frames her historical offering. Therein lies her sophistication. Her work is often presented primarily against the background of the complexity of differing historical narratives and theoretical praxes. Not surprisingly, she has introduced many issues and themes neglected by historians. It is primarily in this context that her work is evaluated here as a rather significant contribution to the history of Trinidad and Tobago, and the Caribbean. Her body of work is certainly an important component of the region's historiography. It is an important part of the creation of our own Caribbean narrative and has inspired many others to do so. After forty years of her teaching and writing out of the UWI, the premiere English-speaking Caribbean institution of higher education, our world of historiography owes her a debt for a distinctive methodological and epistemological orientation, and a value proposition that can aptly be described as Breretonism. Probing this assertion is likely to be instructive and beneficial for tenaciously and even-handedly reassembling the fragments of our Caribbean history with love.[107]

NOTES

1. "The Antilles: Fragments of Epic Memory," Nobel Lecture, 7 December 1992. https://www.nobelprize.org/prizes/literature/1992/walcott/lecture/.
2. *Race Relations in Colonial Trinidad 1870–1900* (Cambridge: Cambridge University Press, 2002).
3. *History of Modern Trinidad, 1973–1962* (Oxford: Heinemann International, 1981).
4. *Law, Justice and Empire: The Colonial Career of John Gorrie, 1829–1892, Vol. 2* (Kingston: University of the West Indies Press, 1997).
5. Franklin W. Knight, "Eric Williams and the Construction of a Caribbean". Paper presented at a centenary conference "New Perspective on the Life and Work of Eric Williams", St Catherine's College, Oxford University, 24–25 September 2011).
6. Basil Reid, *Myths and Realities of Caribbean History* (Tuscaloosa: University of Alabama Press, 2009).
7. Verene A Shepherd, *I Want to Disturb my Neighbour: Lectures on Slavery, Emancipation and Postcolonial Jamaica* (Kingston: Ian Randle Publishers, 2007).
8. Selwyn Cudjoe, *Beyond Boundaries: The Intellectual Tradition of Trinidad and Tobago in the Nineteenth Century* (Massachusetts: Calaloux, 2003).
9. See George Lamming, ed. *Enterprise of the Indies* (Port of Spain: Trinidad and Tobago Institute of the West Indies, 1999), vii.
10. Bartolome de Las Casas, *Aqui si contiene una disputa, o controuersia* (Seville: Sebastian Trugillo, 1522) and *Brevíssima Relación de la destrucción de las Indias* (Seville: Sebastian Trugillo, 1552).
11. Pierre-Gustave-Louis Borde, *Histoire de l'Ile de la Trinidad sous le Gouvernement Espagnol, Premiere Partie (1498–1622)* (Paris: Maisonneuve et Cie, Libraires-Editeurs, 1876). See English translation, *The History of the Island of Trinidad under the Spanish Government, First Part (1498–1622)* (Port of Spain: Paria Publishing, 1982), xiii–xix; and *Histoire de l'Ile de la Trinidad sous le Gouvernement Espagnol, Dieuxieme Partie (1622–1797)* (Paris: Maisonneuve et Cie, Libraires-Editeurs, 1882). English translation *The History of the Island of Trinidad under the Spanish Government, Second Part (1622–1797)* (Port of Spain: Paria Publishing, 1982).
12. Pierre Franc M'Callum, *Travels in Trinidad, during the Months of February, March, and April, 1803* (Liverpool: W. Jones, 1805); and *A Political Account of the Island of Trinidad from its Conquest by Sir Ralph Abercrombie* (London: Cadell and Davies, 1807).
13. E.L. Joseph, *History of Trinidad* (London: H.J. Mills, 1838. Republished London: Frank Cass, 1970).

14. Gertrude, Carmichael, *The History of the West Indian Islands of Trinidad and Tobago, 1498–1900* (London: Alvin Redman, 1961).
15. V.F. Calverton, *The Making of Man: An Outline of Anthropology* (New York: The Modern Library, 1931), 1–37.
16. Lionel Mordaunt Fraser, *History of Trinidad Vol. 1 – 1781 to 1813* (London: Frank Cass, 1891 and 1896. Republished in 1971); and *History of Trinidad Vol. II – 1814–1839* (London: Frank Cass 1891 and 1896. Republished in 1971).
17. T. Fitz-Evan Eversley. *The Trinidad Reviewer 1900* (London: 1900)
18. Published by the Mirror Printing Works in 1910.
19. J.H. Collens, ed. *Handbook of Trinidad and Tobago: For the Use of Settlers* (Port of Spain: Government Printing Office, 1912). Also, for an exposition on J.H. Collins, *A Guide to Trinidad and Tobago: A Handbook for Tourists and Visitors* (London: R.E. Stock, 1888); Melise Thomas-Bailey, "E-Consciousness: Economic Black Consciousness in Nineteenth and Twentieth Century Trinidad and Tobago," in *Beyond Tradition: Reinterpreting the Caribbean Historical Experience*, ed. Heather Cateau and Rita Pemberton (Kingston: Ian Randle Publishers, 2006), 224–47.
20. Eric Williams, *Capitalism and Slavery* (Capitol Hill and London: University of North Carolina Press, 1994), xi–xxii.
21. Kirk Meighoo, *Politics in a Half-Made Society: Trinidad and Tobago 1925–2001* (Kingston: Ian Randle Publishers, 2003).
22. Eric Williams, *History of the People of Trinidad and Tobago* (Port of Spain: PNM Publishing, 1962).
23. C.LR. James, *The Black Jacobins: Toussaint L'Ouverture and the San Domingo Revolution* (New York: Random House, 1963), xi.
24. Michael Toussaint, "The Eric Williams' Diaries," in *The Fires of Hope Vol. 2*, ed. Debbie Mc Collin (Kingston: Ian Randle Publishers, 2016), 142–68.
25. Brereton, *Race Relations in Colonial Trinidad*, 17.
26. ibid.
27. ibid., 34.
28. ibid.
29. ibid.
30. ibid.
31. ibid., 35.
32. ibid.
33. ibid., 35–59.
34. ibid., 53–89.
35. ibid., 60–61.
36. ibid., 64–109.

37. See J.J. Thomas, The Theory and Practice of Creole Grammar (Port of Spain: Chronicle Publishing Office, 1869), and Froudacity: West Indian Fables Explained (London: T. Fisher Unwin, 1889). The latter was a reply to J.A. Froude's The English in the West Indies: Or, The Bow of Ulysses (London: Longman Green and Company, 1888). Through the last publication by Thomas, a crafty dismissal of the Eurocentric baubles of Froude, Thomas, according C.L.R. James, wrote himself into the history of Trinidad and Tobago for all times.
38. Samuel Carter was a coloured printer, owner and publisher of several newspapers, including *The New Era* and *San Fernando Gazette*. Allusion to the "Samuel Carters" is in reference to several other coloured newspaper proprietors who, from a philosophical and business perspective, operated just like him. See *Race Relations*, 86–109; and Melise Thomas-Bailey, "E-Consciousness," in *Beyond Tradition*, ed. Cateau and Pemberton, 224–47.
39. Brereton, *Race Relations*, 104.
40. ibid., 104–9.
41. ibid., 130–51.
42. ibid., 110–29.
43. ibid., 116–75.
44. ibid., 118.
45. ibid., 130–51
46. ibid., 152–53.
47. ibid.
48. ibid., 153–59.
49. ibid.
50. A singer of early calypsos, which were sung in French Creole, whose role was that of a griot.
51. Trinidadian slang for a violent or aggressive person. The term was coined after a well-known Barbadian criminal called John Archer living in Trinidad, whose nickname was Bad John.
52. ibid.
53. ibid., 170.
54. ibid., 194–95
55. ibid., 196–98.
56. ibid., 205.
57. ibid., 204–5.
58. ibid., 205–8.
59. ibid., 63–109.
60. ibid., 1.
61. ibid., 196.

62. Brereton, *History of Modern Trinidad*, 1.
63. ibid.
64. ibid., 1–7.
65. Brereton, *History of Modern Trinidad*, 7–12 and 13–15.
66. See Carl C. Campbell, *Cedulants and Capitulants* (Port of Spain: Paria Publishing, 1992).
67. Brereton, *History of Modern Trinidad*, 13–17.
68. ibid., 22–75.
69. ibid., 76–176.
70. ibid., 76.
71. ibid., 157–222.
72. This is a reality of which Brereton remains unendingly conscious. See Brereton's "All ah we is not one" (2010), and "Contesting the Past: Narratives of Trinidad and Tobago History" (2007).
73. Brereton, *History of Modern Trinidad*, 223–49.
74. See B.M. Brereton, "A Social History of Trinidad 1870 to 1900" (PhD Diss., University of the West Indies, 1972).
75. See Brereton, *Law, Justice and Empire*, xi–xix.
76. Brereton, *Race Relations,* 102–3.
77. Brereton, *Law, Justice and Empire*, 32–65.
78. ibid., 67.
79. ibid.
80. ibid., 104–92.
81. ibid., 193–226.
82. ibid., 206.
83. ibid., i–xix.
84. ibid., xii.
85. ibid., xiii.
86. ibid., 102–203.
87. ibid., 66–103.
88. ibid., 104–92.
89. ibid., 218–219.
90. ibid., 193–226.
91. ibid., 200–205.
92. ibid.
93. ibid., 227–58.
94. Borde, *History of Trinidad, Volume 1*, xxii–xxxvii; and *History of Trinidad, Second Part*, 236–343.
95. J.G. La Guerre, "Afro-Indian Relations in Trinidad and Tobago," University of the West Indies Extra-Mural Department, *Caribbean Issues: A Journal of*

Caribbean Affairs Race and Colour 1 no. 1. (April 1974): 59–61; and edited by the same author, *Calcutta to Caroni. The East Indians of Trinidad* (New York: Longman Caribbean, 1974); David G. Nicholls, "East Indians and Black Power in Trinidad," *Race* 12 (1970–71): 443–45; Bridget Brereton, "The Foundations of Prejudice: Indians and African in the 19th Century," University of the West Indies Extra-Mural Department, *Caribbean Issues. A Journal of Caribbean Affairs Race and Colour* 1, no. 1 (April 1974): 15–22.

96. Bridget Brereton, *From Imperial College to University of the West Indies: A History of the St. Augustine Campus* (Kingston: Ian Randle Publishers, 2011), 60; and Woodville Marshall, *From Plantation to University Campus: The Social History of Cave Hill Barbados* (Kingston: University of the West Indies Press, 2013), 1–7.
97. Gordon K. Lewis, *The Growth of the Modern West Indies* (Kingston: Ian Randle Publishers, 2004), xi; and Franklin K. Knight, "Introduction," xiii–xxxv, in same work.
98. Brereton, *From Imperial College*, 60.
99. Patrick Manning, *Navigating World History: Historians Create a Global Past* (New York: Palgrave Macmillan, 2003), 145–56.
100. Carmichael, *History of the West Indian Islands*, 51.
101. Williams, *History of the People*, 1–4. His primary discourse on women was in relation to the indigenous groups.
102. See, for example, Karina Williamson, "Mrs Carmichael: A Scotswoman in the West Indies, 1820–1826," in *International Journal of Scottish Literature* (Spring/Summer 2008): 9–17. http://www.ijsl.stir.ac.uk/issue4/issue4digest.pdf.
103. Brereton, *Race Relations*, 3.
104. ibid., 4.
105. ibid.
106. Howard Johnson, "Barbadian Migration in Trinidad 1870–1897," *Caribbean Studies* 13, no. 3 (October 1973): 5–30.
107. An earlier abridged version of this article was published in *History in Action* 5 no.1 (2016). This is the journal of the History Department, University of the West Indies, St Augustine.

[20]

CALLED TO ACTION
Caribbean Historians and the Preservation of Primary Sources for the History of the Region

[JOHN A. AARONS]

IT IS APPROPRIATE WHEN HONOURING PROFESSOR BRIDGET BRERETON to reflect on the important and pioneering role that historians, and in particular historians at the University of the West Indies (UWI), have played in promoting the preservation of the primary sources for the history of the region. These materials are the archival records which contain information found nowhere else and are therefore indispensable for historical enquiry and research. Brereton's role in promoting the value and importance of archival materials has been demonstrated in two significant ways.

The first has been her strong advocacy of the importance of preserving historical records, based on her extensive experience in trying to locate primary sources for her many publications. In this context, one recalls her pleas in October 2010 for the proper preservation of the archival records of the UWI's St Augustine campus at the launch of her book on the history of the campus, held at the Central Bank auditorium in Port of Spain. Secondly, her role in the decision-making process relating to libraries and archives, in particular, her chairmanship of three bodies – the board of the National Library and Information System Authority (NALIS) from 2002 to 2005, the Library Committee of the St Augustine Campus from 1995 to 1999 and the UWI's cross-campus University Archives and Records Management Advisory Committee (UARMAC) from 2000 to 2008.

Brereton's involvement with the UARMAC has special significance in the context of this chapter. This is because the committee not only has oversight responsibility for the unified archives and records management programme of the UWI, but it performs an advocacy role in the promotion and development of archival activities in the region. Coupled with this is the responsibility to advise the university on the "preservation and accessibility of the Archives of the former Federation of the West Indies".[1] The inclusion of these regional responsibilities in the committee's terms of reference when they were revised in 1998 was at the urging of then chair, Woodville Marshall (now professor emeritus).

In proposing the expansion of the terms of reference, Marshall's intention was to ensure some continuity between the university's early involvement with the historical archives of the region and the establishment of its own records management and archives programme, which included the appointment of the advisory committee in the 1990s. This involvement by the university in regional archival activity dated back to June 1948, shortly after the University College (forerunner to the independent university) was established, and even before teaching started in October of that year. It was formalized in 1958 when the University senate appointed a committee on archives to oversee a preliminary survey of the historical records of the region.

In the years that followed, the university proved a catalyst in the development of archival programmes, the highlights being the microfilming of the records in the Eastern Caribbean and the co-sponsorship with the government of Jamaica of the first conference on Caribbean archives. Much of this has been documented by Marshall as he traced the development of the teaching of history at the university. Very appropriately, his article on this subject was included in the publication honouring Sir Roy Augier (Professor of History), who was the only surviving member of the original university's Senate Committee on Records.[2]

Marshall indicated the leading roles that members of staff of the UWI's History Department have played in safeguarding West Indian archival materials and making them available for research purposes. This in itself should not be surprising, for historians depend on the existence of primary source materials for their investigations. Thanks to the advocacy work of many of these historians, irreplaceable records dating back to the early days of colonial rule have been salvaged, restored or microfilmed and made available for research purposes. National archives have been established in most of the region and the UWI, as an institution, can take some credit for these achievements.

The purpose of this chapter, though, is not just to reflect on the achievements in securing records of the colonial era, however significant these initiatives have been. Rather, it is also to look to the future and the role that historians can play in helping to ensure the identification and preservation of archival records produced over the past thirty to fifty years, which covers the period in which most of the region gained independence.

With independence, the former colonies became responsible for managing their own affairs. This meant, among other things, becoming responsible for the preservation of the records of their administrations. No longer would administrative matters be referred to the Colonial Office in London for ratification, decision-making, or simply information purposes. Records of these matters contained in letters, telegrams, minutes of meetings, memoranda and so on would in time be transferred to the British National Archives – or to use the name familiar to the older generation of historians – the Public Records Office. Although not all the records of the colonial era are available in London, a significant proportion are there and this provides a safety net for researchers of the pre-independence era.

The danger now is that there is a gap in the historical record which exists from roughly the 1960s onwards, since many post-independence records are not finding their way into appropriate archival custody. This is happening even in a country such as Jamaica, which has a well-developed records management and archival infrastructure. The problems are due to the absence in many countries of organized records management programmes, inadequate or non-existent archival facilities, lack of trained staff, or simply a lack of commitment on the part of their governments to this critical task. It could also be due to the fact that our societies are small and governments are reluctant to have the records of their operations open for scrutiny.

This all means that historians, and scholars in general, should not assume that locally generated primary source materials are available for their research projects. It is, therefore, in the interest of historians at the UWI – either as individuals or working through their departments – to become more active in promoting the value of records to the governments of the region to ensure the preservation of records with archival value. Proactive action by present-day historians would be in keeping with the initiatives taken by the UWI in its early days as a university college in securing the preservation of the records of the colonial era. The situation is no less urgent now than then and action has to be taken if the primary sources for the history of the post-independence era are to be safeguarded.

THE UWI'S INVOLVEMENT IN PRESERVING WEST INDIAN ARCHIVES

The development of Caribbean archives from the middle of the twentieth century is closely linked with the establishment and growth of the UWI itself, particularly from 1949, when the first professor of history was appointed and the Department of History was established. However, in June 1948, Thomas Taylor (later Sir), principal of the then University College of the West Indies (UCWI), started thinking about the archival resources of the region in his plans for a history department. He stated, with reference to the staff who would work there, that "these people will be keenly interested in Caribbean archives and will know much more about archives in general than almost anyone in the area. We hope to build up an active school in Caribbean history where archives would be put to their proper use, i.e. historical research . . .".[3]

Taylor was so concerned about the conditions under which the historical archives were being housed in the various territories that the fledging University College considered housing them temporarily at Mona. While realizing that this was not an ideal situation, Taylor noted that "whatever we do with them cannot be worse than the things which have happened already".[4] In this regard, he noted the loss of records in British Guiana (now Guyana) as a result of a fire and the manner in which the Vice Admiralty records in Jamaica had been transported – "by the use of the shovel, wheelbarrow, and lorry . . ."[5] The idea at the time was to house the region's archives in an annex to the new library, which was then under construction. A brief was prepared and an architectural plan drawn up for an archives section at the Mona library.

Taylor said, "If there is any possibility of erecting archival storage as a part of the library in the first stage, I should certainly do it, and would then at once approach the Governments of all the Caribbean Colonies."[6]

Eventually, nothing came of this idea as funds were insufficient for a storage area. Governments in the territories were also understandably reluctant to agree to the idea of sending their valuable records to Jamaica – even for temporary storage.

However, Taylor was not prepared to abandon his plan to do something for the archives, even though the British Public Office and the Librarian of the Colonial Office did not support his idea of a central repository for Caribbean records. He said that they had "dug their heels in on what they consider an ideal solution. This is to set up a miniature Public Records Office in each of the colonies staffed by a trained archivist."[7] The Colonial Office was not prepared, however, to fund the venture.

Taylor turned to the idea of microfilming the records, with copies to be deposited at the university. In 1952, he approached the Carnegie Foundation, but this was not an area of interest to them at the time and nothing came of the proposal. Taylor's initiatives were, nevertheless, important, for they not only laid the foundation for later interventions, but they forced the colonial administrations to at least consider the state of their records.

Taylor's successor as principal, Walter Grave, continued efforts to find a solution and in January 1957, he appointed an informal committee, which he chaired, to discuss the matter. A paper prepared for the committee by the librarian, William Gocking, and Clinton Black, the Government Archivist of Jamaica, noted, "The College has seen it as part of its duty in the field of education to take all possible steps to make archives in the area a matter more of fact than of guess work, and their availability to scholars an accepted amenity, no longer involving them in a pioneering expedition."[8] This paper was later expanded into a project proposal that was submitted to the Rockefeller Foundation.

As a result of the agitation by a number of historians concerned over the condition of the historical records in the region, several influential persons and institutions in Britain were made aware of the situation. Sir Philip Morris, Vice Chancellor of the University of Bristol, felt that in view of the historical links between his city and the region, his university had a vested interest in the future of the records. He proposed to Grave the establishment of a "single West Indian record office where the archives of all the colonies could be properly housed".[9] After stating that the UCWI was the best place for this centre, he suggested – in language carefully crafted – that if it was unable to handle the responsibility, then the University of Bristol could assist. He suggested that his university "should act as an agent for the UCWI... and should for a limited period of perhaps five or seven years receive the archives, undertake a certain amount of repair work... and make them as far as possible available for study..."[10]

Not surprisingly, Grave rejected outright the suggestion that the records should be sent to England. However, this external pressure might have spurred the UCWI to take some action on its own. It decided that a survey should be carried out on the condition of the records in the region, and in March 1958, Grave wrote to all governors and administrators of the colonies, apprising them of this move and requesting their support.

In underlining the university's interest in becoming a centre of study and research into questions affecting the region as a whole, he said that "the work that is being done on an authoritative history of the West Indies has emphasised the interest of the College in the preservation and care of historical material".[11] Although, by this time, UCWI had dropped plans to house the records on a permanent basis, the principal did offer to accept any records on a temporary basis until such time "as more adequate accommodation could be provided for them in their place of origin".[12]

In May 1958, the senate recommended, and it was later approved by the Finance and General Purposes Committee, that the accumulated income from the Nuffield Benefaction should be used to fund the preliminary survey of the records. Consequently, the senate appointed a planning committee to work out the details of "a preliminary survey of the archives of the region". This committee, which became known as the Senate Committee on Archives, was chaired by A.P. Thornton, professor of history, and among the members were William Gocking, the university librarian, Elsa Goveia (Professor of West Indian History) and Augier from the Department of History.

The work of the committee ultimately resulted in the appointment in 1959 of archivist Michael Chandler, who was attached to the Department of History. His tasks were to undertake a survey of the archival records of the region and to have them microfilmed. This project, over which the Senate Committee on Records had oversight responsibility, was funded by a grant of £13,840 sterling from the Rockefeller Foundation. Contact was also established with the National Archives of the United States, which provided Chandler and a technician with training in microfilming techniques.

The results of Chandler's work are well known – the publication of the guide to the records of Barbados, the groundwork he laid for the Barbados Archives Department (of which he was the first archivist), and the microfilming of the records of Barbados and other territories in the Eastern Caribbean. Chandler was succeeded by E.C. Baker, who, interestingly enough, was described as the "University Archivist". He continued work on the records of the Windward and Leeward Islands, and produced a guide to the records of the latter.

The university's involvement in the preservation effort showed that it was prepared to take up a challenge, about which Hector Wynter (then Assistant Registrar) said in 1959, historians had been calling for over "the past 30 years". This was to ". . . make the preservation of West Indian archives part of the public business, as well as part of the public conscience of the West Indies".[13] In 1963, the University Council proposed that a conference be held to discuss the state of archival development in the region and it appointed a committee to work out the details.

This led to the first Caribbean Archives Conference, held at the Mona campus in September 1965, which was sponsored by the university and the government of Jamaica. As noted by Woodville Marshall, the conference was a university project in its original concept, but "it was the Department of History which was mainly responsible for the final formulation and execution".[14] Department staff served on the planning committee, which was chaired by Elsa Goveia, who also chaired the conference.

As a result of the conference, the Caribbean Archives Association, forerunner to the Caribbean Regional Branch of the International Council on Archives, was established. This association has since played a leading role in promoting archival development in the region. Members of staff of the University Archives and Records Management Programme are very involved in its activities.

CARIBBEAN ARCHIVES TODAY

As a result of the initiatives of the UWI and the support of governments, national archives have been established in most of the territories in the region. The exceptions are countries such as Dominica and Grenada, where the archives are under the control of, or part of, the public library. At least ten of the contributing countries of the university (Antigua, Bahamas, Barbados, Belize, Bermuda, the Cayman Islands, Jamaica, St Kitts and Nevis, St Lucia, and Trinidad and Tobago), have trained archivists responsible for their programmes. Not surprisingly, the first task of these archival institutions has been to acquire all surviving materials, chiefly from government bodies and to ensure their preservation. These records tend to be those dealing with land, slavery, immigration, church institutions and administrative matters, for example, correspondence with the colonial authorities in London.

These archival institutions have worked on organizing and publicizing their material. Several of them came together to nominate their collections of slave registers for listing on UNESCO's Memory of the World Register, aimed at publicizing and safeguarding the documentary heritage of mankind. Finally, in 2009, the registers in the Bahamas, Belize, Dominica, Jamaica, St Kitts, and Trinidad and Tobago, along with those in the United Kingdom, were inscribed on the register, under the title "Register of Slaves of the British Caribbean 1817–1834". Overseas assistance has also been forthcoming. For example, Jamaica, St Kitts and Grenada received assistance in surveying and digitizing some of their colonial records under the British Library's Endangered Archives Programme.

However, many of the archival institutions – particularly those in the smaller countries – are ill-equipped to deal with modern official records, those produced by their governments over the past thirty to fifty years and which by now should have achieved archival status. This period from the 1960s is significant as it covers the era of the West Indian Federation and the aftermath, when most territories had some form of internal self-government or independence. All the countries in the former federation, have been independent for at least thirty years, with Jamaica and Trinidad and Tobago commemorating over sixty years of independence.

In many territories no regulations govern the disposal of official records, and even when they exist, they are often ignored. To complicate matters further, many of the archival institutions lack staff trained in archival administration as well as adequate accommodation to house the records. The current archivist of St Kitts and Nevis, and the former archivist of St Vincent both identified a lack of space as the major impediment to their programmes. Among the consequences of this is that they cannot fully implement retention schedules.[15]

The absence of national archival legislation in most countries limits archival development as only the Bahamas, Belize, Barbados, Bermuda, the Cayman Islands, St Lucia and Jamaica have laws governing the operations of their national archives. Trinidad and Tobago, while not having a law, has a well-developed archival institution. The Government Archivist, however, noted that there is "no official transfer policy which identifies a standard date for transfer of records when they were identified as having archival value or were at risk".[16] Jamaica has an act, but there is no compulsion for government bodies to transfer records to the national archives on a regular basis.

For the transfer of records to archival custody on a systematic basis, a records management programme with clearly defined retention/disposal schedules is essential. Very often these programmes do not exist or, if they exist, they are in a rudimentary state. A constant complaint from archivists and records managers in the region is that governments do not recognize the importance of records management and its contribution to transparency and good governance. Freedom/Access to Information legislation has shown the value of records management, but comparatively few jurisdictions have laws in place.

A cursory survey of the regional archives reveals that, on the whole, only a small percentage of the post-independence records of archival value have been transferred to archival custody. Naturally, this varies from institution to institution, but in many instances, records are transferred when the particular department has run out of space to store them. Most institutions report receiving publications such as Hansards, gazettes, laws, annual reports and so on, but although they are important, they are no substitute for original records, such as minutes of meetings, correspondence, memoranda and so on. The statement by the Chief Librarian of Grenada regarding records that "there is no obligation for anything to go anywhere" could well apply to many other countries.[17]

In cases where records, such as Cabinet papers, have been transferred, they are often covered by the thirty-year closed period, and permission has to be sought to make them available for researchers. The Jamaica Archives has abandoned the thirty-year closed period since it is inconsistent with the country's Access to Information Act, but this has had no real impact.

Although the Cabinet Office has transferred some of its records to the Jamaica Archives, such as submissions and notes, it has not up to now transferred the minutes of post-1962 Cabinet meetings, in spite of promises to do so.

As a result of these issues, the historian and social scientist interested in researching events over the past fifty or so years face problems in locating primary source materials in national archival institutions. It is not surprising that researchers working on subjects such as biographies of public figures, and political, social and economic matters in the post-Independence era have to rely heavily on published materials (including newspapers), unpublished government documents, private papers and oral sources. Although there is nothing wrong with using these sources, they do not give the full picture of events. How much fuller these accounts would be if the authors had access to minutes of Cabinet meetings and the official records (correspondence, memoranda and so on) of the offices of the prime ministers and other ministries.[18]

THE ROLE OF THE HISTORIAN

Faced with situations where little or no attention is paid to records management and archival programmes, historians, working through their institutions, organizations and societies, should be conscious of the need to make representations to the appropriate government bodies for more attention to be paid to these areas. In doing this, historians should be aware of the fact that if there is no demand for archival records, governments might not take seriously their value for research purposes and therefore be convinced of the need to make adequate provision for their preservation. In countries with freedom of information legislation, historians could use the provisions of those laws to request information on topics they are researching.

Of particular concern is the situation in countries such as Dominica and Grenada, which do not have any ongoing archival and records management programmes. Without any policies or systems in place, records are not maintained and disposed of in a systematic way, and this will have long-term consequences, not only for efficient government operations, but for the historical consciousness of the population. There is also the danger, felt by many archivists, of records being deliberately destroyed. There is need to prevent unwarranted destruction of materials.

The historian acting alone can play an important role. If the archival records covering the areas of their research agenda are not available in the appropriate archival institution, representations should be made to the originating department (the department which created the records) for access to them. These actions by historians could prove beneficial not only to themselves, but to other researchers. For example, in the early 1970s, some confidential records from the former Colonial Secretariat in Jamaica for the 1930s and 1940s (outside of the closed period at the time) were transferred to the Jamaica Archives, when a particular historian researching the period noted their absence and made representations (which were successful) for access to them.[19]

Historians – and this is easier in the four campus territories of the UWI – can also assist archival institutions in promoting the value of their repositories by assisting in the mounting of exhibitions to commemorate significant events in their nation's history. An exhibition or a lecture around the anniversary of a particular event in the modern history of a country might lead to interest in locating the records related to it.

Proactive approaches by historians, some of which have been discussed in this paper, should demonstrate to governments and to societies in general, the value of archival records and the importance of ensuring their preservation for posterity. These actions are necessary as government officials are often unaware of the value of archival materials due to many factors, including their own lack of understanding of the contribution of records management to effective administration, and the low visibility that archival institutions tend to have. Historians, therefore, have a vested interest in doing all they can to assist archivists in promoting archives and in encouraging the use of their materials. In doing this, they could follow the example set by Professor Emerita Bridget Brereton, who has built on the activities of her distinguished predecessors at the UWI in promoting the use of archival resources in "reassembling the fragments" of our history.[20]

NOTES

1. Position paper on "Principles, Policies and Procedures, Plans and Priorities of the University Archives and Records Management Programme," rev. 1998 (stencilled), 16.
2. Woodville Marshall, "History Teaching in the University of the West Indies," in *Before and After 1865: Education, Politics and Regionalism in the Caribbean. In honour of Sir Roy Augier*, ed. Brian Moore and Swithin Wilmot (Kingston: Ian Randle Publishers, 1998), 47.
3. Taylor to C.Y. Carstairs, Barbados, 17 June 1948, University Archives, Mona, 92.1, box 104, L4/563.
4. ibid.
5. ibid.
6. Taylor to R.H. Garvey, Grenada, 7 June 1948, University Archives, Mona, 92.1, box 104, LA/563.
7. Taylor to Whitney Shephardson, New York, 2 April 1952, University Archives, Mona, 92.1, box 104, LA/563.
8. "Survey and Preservation of Archives in the West Indies," stencilled, n.d., University Archives, Mona, 92.1, box 104 L4/563.
9. Sir Philip Morris to Dr W. Grave, 5 August 1957, University Archives, Mona, 92.1, box 104 L4/563.
10. ibid.
11. Dr W. Grave to governors and administrators of colonies, 6 March 1958, University Archives, Mona, 92.1, Box 104 L4/563.
12. ibid.
13. Hector Wynter to L.G. Maxwell, Secretary, Inter University Council or Higher Education, Overseas, 24 April 1959. In enclosing the advertisement for the post of archivist, Wynter said, "The scheme calls for the services of a professional archivist of high standing. The job will prove an intricate one, and the man who carries it out will need other qualifications beside the merely professional, as he will have to deal with governors, prime ministers, business firms and the like: he must do his work in a social and political atmosphere, and remain on an even keel. In a word, he must be a man of presence and personality."
14. Marshall, "History Teaching," 73.
15. Personal communication from the archivists.
16. Personal communication from the Government Archivist.
17. Personal communication from the Chief Librarian.
18. Biographies have been published of Jamaican prime ministers Donald Sangster, Hugh Shearer and Edward Seaga. Only in the biography of Seaga

are official records used as sources, but these are chiefly from his collection, a large portion of which has been deposited in the library at the Mona campus of the UWI.

19. Personal knowledge while working at the Jamaica Archives.
20. Although the situation in archival institutions has hopefully improved since this paper was written, the importance of historians playing advocacy roles is still very relevant. Professor Emerita Brereton continues to play a leading role in this, as shown by the emphasis in her writings on the value and importance of primary source materials to our history. See her book *History Matters: Selected Newspaper Columns, 2011–2021* (Port of Spain, Paria Publishing, 2022).

SELECTED BIBLIOGRAPY

Abénon, Lucien-René. *La Guadeloupe de 1671 à 1759: Étude Politique, Economique et Sociale*, 2 vols. Paris: L'Harmattan, 1987.
Adelaîde-Merlande, Jacques. *Histoire Générale des Antilles et des Guyanes: des Précolombiens à nos Jours*. Paris: Editions Caribéennes, 1994.
Adelman, Jeremy. *Sovereignty and Revolution in the Iberian Atlantic*. Princeton and Oxford: Princeton University Press, 2006.
Al Azan. *An Organ Devoted to the Cause of Islam* 1, no. 1 (1944).
Ali, Shameen. "A Social History of East Indian Women in Trinidad since 1870" (MPhil diss., The University of the West Indies, St Augustine Campus, 2002).
Anon. "Spirit of West Indian Society – Outrage in Barbados," *Edinburgh Review*, Aug. 1825, 479–99.
Anon. Remarks on the insurrection in Barbados, and the bill for the Registration of Slaves (Lon.) 1816.
Anthias, Floya, and Nira Yuval-Davis, eds. *Woman- Nation- State*. Basingstoke: Macmillan 1989.
Anthony, Michael. *The Making of Port of Spain: Volume I: 1757–1939*. Port of Spain: Key Caribbean Publications, 1978.
Ardener, Shirley. "Muted Groups": The Genesis of an Idea and its Praxis," *Women and Language* 28 no. 2 (Fall 2005): 50–54, 72.
Artola, Miguel. La Burguesía Revolucionaria (1808–1869), Historia de España Alfaguara V. Madrid: Alianza Editorial-Alfaguara, 1973.
Auguste Lacour, *Histoire de la Guadeloupe*, 4 vols. (Basse-Terre: Editions de diffusion de la culture antillaise, 1976).
Bakhtin, Mikhail. *Rabelais and His World*, trans. Helen Iswolsky. Massachusetts: MIT Press, 1968.
Banbuck, C.A. *Histoire Politique, Economique et Sociale de la Martinique sous L'Ancien Régime, 1635–1789*. Paris: Librairie des Sciences Politiques et Sociales, 1935.
Barclay, Lou Ann. "The Syrian/Lebanese Community: A Preliminary Study of a Commercial Ethnic Minority." In *Entrepreneurship in the Caribbean, Culture, Structure and Conjuncture*, edited by Selwyn Ryan and Taimoon Stewart. St Augustine: Institute for Social and Economic Research, University of the West Indies, 1994.
Bayard de Volo, Lorraine. *Women and the Cuban Insurrection: How Gender Shaped Castro's Victory*. New York: Cambridge University Press, 2019.

Beaumont, Augustus. *Compensation to Slave Owners Fairly Considered.* London: Effingham Wilson, 1826.

Beckles, Hilary McD. "An Unfeeling Traffic; The Inter-Colonial Movement of Slaves in the British Caribbean, 1807–1833." In *The Chattel Principle: Internal Slave Trades in the Americas*, edited by Walter Johnson. Yale: Yale University Press, 2004.

Beckles, Hilary McD. "Emancipation by Law or War? Wilberforce and the 1816 Barbados Slave Rebellion." In *Abolition and Its Aftermath, 1790–1916*, edited by David Richardson. London: Frank Cass, 1985.

Beckles, Hilary McD. *Britain's Black Debt: Reparations for Caribbean Slavery and Native Genocide.* Mona: University of the West Indies Press, 2013.

Beckles, Hilary. *Chattel House Blues. Making of a Democratic Society in Barbados, from Clement Payne to Owen Arthur.* Kingston: Ian Randle Publishers, 2004.

Beckles, Hilary. *Natural Rebels: A Social History of Enslaved Black Women in Barbados.* New Brunswick, New Jersey: Rutgers University Press, 1989.

Belénus, René. *L'Esclave en Guadeloupe et en Martinique du XVIIe au XIXe Siècle.* Pointe-à-Pitre: Editions Jasor, 1998.

Bellance, Hurard. *La Police des Noirs en Amérique (Martinique, Guadeloupe, Saint-Domingue) et en France aux XVIIe et XVIIIe Siècles* (Matoury, Guyane: Ibis Rouge Editions, 2011).

Besson, Gerard, and Alice Besson. *The Voyage of the Mediterranean Star: The Syrian/Lebanese Women's Association of Trinidad and Tobago.* Port of Spain: Paria Publishers, 2001.

Besson, Gerard. "The Syrians of Trinidad," In *The Book of Trinidad*, edited by Gerard Besson and Bridget Brereton. Port of Spain: Paria Publishing, 1992.

Best, Curwen. *Barbadian Popular Music and the Politics of Caribbean Culture.* New York: AC Inc., 1995.

Bethel, Nicolette. "Aunt Selma's Dilemma". A Poem originally published in *Junction: An Anthology of Bahamian Poetry and Prose*, edited by Eunice Bethel Humblestone. London: Macmillan Caribbean and Bahamas Poetry Society, 1987.

Blérald, Alain-Phillipe. *Histoire économique de la Guadeloupe et de la Martinique du XVIIe à nos Jours.* Paris: Karthala, 1986.

Bolland, Nigel. *The Politics of Labour in the British Caribbean: The Social Origins of Authoritarianism and Democracy in the Labour Movement.* Kingston: Ian Randle Publishers, 2001.

Bolt, Christine. *Victorian Attitudes to Race.* London: Routledge and Kegan Paul, 1971.

Boomert, Arie. *The Indigenous Peoples of Trinidad and Tobago: From the First Settlers Until Today.* Leiden: Sidestone Press, 2016.

Borde, Pierre-Gustave-Louis. *Histoire de l'Ile de la Trinidad sous le Gouvernement Espagnol. Premiere Partie (1498–1622)*. Paris: Maisonneuve et Cie, Libraires-Editeurs: 1876.
Brading, D. A. *The First America: The Spanish Monarchy, Creole Patriots, and the Liberal State 1492–1867*. Cambridge: Cambridge University Press, 1991.
Braithwaite, Lloyd. "Stratification in Trinidad." In *Slaves, Free Men, Citizens. West Indian Perspectives,* edited by Lambros Comitas and David Lowenthal. New York: Anchor Press, 1973.
Brathwaite, Kamau. *Bajan Cultural Report and Plan*. Barbados: UNESCO/Ministry of Education and Culture, 1979.
Brereton, Bridget, M. "A Social History of Trinidad 1870 to 1900." PhD Diss., University of the West Indies, 1972.
Brereton, Bridget. "'All Ah We Is Not One': Historical and Ethnic Narratives in Pluralists Trinidad," *Global South* 4 (2010): 227–263.
Brereton, Bridget. "A Social History of Emancipation in the British Caribbean: The First 50 Years." In *August First, the Celebration of Emancipation Day*, edited by Patrick Bryan. Kingston: Fredrich Ebert Stifrung and The Department of History, UWI, 1994.
Brereton, Bridget. "Contesting the Past: Narratives of Trinidad & Tobago History," *Nieuwe West-Indische Gids* 81, nos. 3&4 (2007): 179–82.
Brereton, Bridget. "Contesting the Past: Narratives of Trinidad and Tobago," *New West India Guide* 2&3 (2007): 169–196.
Brereton, Bridget. "Family Strategies, Gender and the Shift to wage Labour in the British Caribbean." In *Engendering Caribbean History Cross Cultural Perspectives,* edited by Verene Shepherd. Kingston: Ian Randle Publishers, 2011.
Brereton, Bridget. "Gender and the Historiography of the English-speaking Caribbean." In *Gendered Realities: Essays in Caribbean Feminist Thought* (pp. 129–144). Mona, Jamaica: University of the West Indies Press, 2002; *Clio, Women, Gender, History* 29:2, no. 50 (2019): 211.
Brereton, Bridget. "Gendered Testimony: Autobiographies, Diaries and Letters by Women as Sources for Caribbean History." Department of History, Mona, Jamaica: The University of the West Indies, 1994.
Brereton, Bridget. "Post-Emancipation Protest in the Caribbean: The 'Belmanna Riots' in Tobago, 1876," *Caribbean Quarterly* 30, nos. 3/4 (1984): 114.
Brereton, Bridget. "Society and Culture in the Caribbean, The British and French West Indies, 1870–1980," in *The Modern Caribbean*, edited by Franklin Knight and Colin Palmer. Chapel Hill, NC: The University of North Carolina Press, 1989.
Brereton, Bridget. "The Foundations of Prejudice: Indians and African in the 19th Century," *Caribbean Issues. A Journal of Caribbean Affairs Race and Colour* 1 no. 1 (April 1974): 15–22.

Brereton, Bridget. "The White Elite of Trinidad, 1838–1950." In *The White Minority in the Caribbean*, edited by Howard Johnson and Karl Watson. Kingston: Ian Randle Publishers, 1998.

Brereton, Bridget. *A History of Modern Trinidad, 1793–1962*. Oxford: Heinemann International, 1989.

Brereton, Bridget. *A History of Modern Trinidad: 1783–1962* (Kingston: Heinemann Caribbean, 1981).

Brereton, Bridget. *From Imperial College to University of the West Indies: A History of the St. Augustine Campus*. Kingston/Miami: Ian Randle, 2011.

Brereton, Bridget. *Gendered Testimony: Autobiographies, Diaries and Letters by Women as Sources for Caribbean History. The 1994 Elsa Goveia Memorial Lecture.* Jamaica: University of the West Indies, 1994.

Brereton, Bridget. *History Matters: Selected Newspaper Columns, 2011–2021.* Port of Spain: Paria, 2022.

Brereton, Bridget. *History of Modern Trinidad, 1973–1962.* Oxford: Heinemann International, 1981.

Brereton, Bridget. *Race Relations in Colonial Trinidad 1870–1900.* Cambridge: Cambridge University Press, 1979.

Brereton, Bridget. *Race Relations in Colonial Trinidad 1870–1900.* Cambridge: Cambridge University Press, 2002.

Brereton, Bridget. *Law, Justice, and Empire: the Colonial Career of John Gorrie, 1829–1892.* Vol. 2. Mona, Jamaica: University of the West Indies Press, 1997.

Brewer, W. M. "Review of *The Negro in the Caribbean*, by Eric Williams," *Journal of Negro History* 28, no. 2 (1943): 238.

Burn, W.L. *Emancipation and Apprenticeship in the British West Indies.* London: Jonathan Cape, 1937.

Burnard, Trevor. *Mastery, Tyranny and Desire Thomas Thistlewood and His Slaves in the Anglo Jamaican World.* Chapel Hill and London: University of North Carolina Press, 2004.

Burrowes, Marcia. "Treat to Labourers: Plantation Crop Over from Slavery to Independence," *The Journal of the Barbados Museum & Historical Society, JBMHS*, Vol. LVII (Dec 2011): 54–76.

Bush, Barbara. *Slave Women in Caribbean Society 1650–1838.* Kingston: Ian Randle Publishers, 1990.

Butel, Paul. *Histoire des Antilles Françaises, XVIIe-XXe Siècle.* Paris: Editions Perrin, 2002.

Butler, Kathleen. *The Economics of Emancipation; Jamaica and Barbados, 1823–1843.* Chapel Hill: University of North Carolina Press, 1995.

Butler, Mary. "A Fair and Equitable Consideration: The Distribution of Slave Compensation in Jamaica and Barbados," *Journal of Caribbean History* 22, nos. 1–2 (1988): 138–52.

Butt-Thompson, Frederick William. *West African Secret Societies: Their Organisation, Officials and Teaching*. London: Witherby, 1929.
Calder-Marshall, Arthur. *Glory Dead*. London: Michael Joseph, 1939.
Calverton, V. F. *The Making of Man: An Outline of Anthropology*. New York: The Modern Library, 1931.
Campbell, Carl C. *Cedulants and Capitulants*. Paria: Publishing, 1992.
Canning, Kathleen, and Rose O. Sonya. *Gender, Citizenships and Subjectivities*. Oxford: Blackwell, 2002.
Carmichael, Gertrude. *The History of the West Indian Islands of Trinidad and Tobago, 1498–1900*. London: Alvin Redman, 1961.
Carnegie, Charles V. "The Anthropology of Ourselves: An Interview with Sidney W. Mintz," *Small Axe* 19, no. 19 (2006): 106–179.
Carr, E.H. "Review of World Revolution: The Rise and Fall of the Communist International, 1917–1936, by C.L.R. James," *International Affairs* 16, no. 5 (1937): 819–820.
Carter, Henderson. *Labour Pains: Resistance and Protest in Barbados, 1838–1904*. Kingston: Ian Randle Publishers, 2012.
Chace, Russell. "Protest in Post-Emancipation Dominica: The" Guerre Negre" of 1844." *The Journal of Caribbean History* 23, no. 2 (1989): 118.
Chamberlain, Mary. "Gender and the Moral Economy." In *Empire and Nation-building in the Caribbean* (pp. 76–98). Manchester University Press, 2013.
Chamberlain, Mary. *Narratives of Exile and Return*. London and Basingstoke: Macmillan Press, 1997.
Chamberlain, Mary. *Narratives of Exile and Return*. New Brunswick: Transaction Publishers, 2004 [1997].
Chapman, J.K. *The Career of Arthur Hamilton Gordon: First Lord Stanmore 1829-1912*. Toronto: University of Toronto Press, 1964.
Choucoutou, Lydie Ho-Fong-Choy "Littérature et Esclavage: Quelques Considérations." In *De l'esclavage aux Réparations*, edited by Serge Chalons, Christian Jean-Etienne, Suzy Landau and André Yebakima. Paris: Karthala, 2000.
Clarke, Roberta. "Women's Organisations, Women's Interests," *Social and Economic Studies* 35, no. 3 (1986):107–55.
Cobbett, W., ed. *The Parliamentary History of England*, Vol. 36, 1820.
Coco, Lémy Lémane. *Histoire de l'Esclavage dans les Colonies Françaises*. Chevilly-Larue: Éditions Monde Global, 2008.
Collens, J. H. ed. *Handbook of Trinidad and Tobago: For the Use of Settlers*. Port-of-Spain: Government Printing Office, 1912.
Collins, J. H. *A Guide to Trinidad and Tobago: A Handbook for Tourists and Visitors* (London: R. E. Stock. 1888),

Comma-Maynard, Olga. *The Brierend Pattern: The Story of Audrey Jeffers O.B.E. and the Coterie of Social Workers*. Port of Spain: Busby's Printerie, 1971.

Cook, A. Val Lorwin, and Arlene Kaplan Daniels, eds. *Women and Trade Unions in Eleven Industrialized Countries*. Philadelphia: Temple University Press, 1984.

Cottman, Evans W. (with Wyatt Blassingame), *Out Island Doctor*. London: Hodder and Stoughton, 1987. (First printed in 1963).

Craig-James, Susan E. *The Changing Society of Tobago, 1838–1938: A Fractured Whole, Volume 1: 1838–1900*. Arima: Cornerstone Press, 2008.

Craig-James, Susan E. *The Changing Society of Tobago, 1838–1938: A Fractured Whole, Volume 11: 1900–1938*. Arima: Cornerstone Press, 2008

Craig-James, Susan. *The Changing Face of Tobago, 1838–1938: A Fractured Whole*, Volume I 1838–1900. Volume II, 1900–1938. Arima: Cornerstone Press, 2008.

Craton, Michael, and Gail Saunders. *Islanders in the Stream*, 2. London: University of Georgia Press, 1998.

Cudjoe, Selwyn. *Beyond Boundaries: The Intellectual Tradition of Trinidad and Tobago in the Nineteenth Century*. Massachusetts: Calaloux, 2003.

D'Aguilar, Jacquelyn. *Thicker Than Blood. The deGregorys of The Bahamas. An Island Family Story*. Bahamas: Media Enterprises Ltd., 2014.

Daniel, George T. "Labor and Nationalism in the British Caribbean," *Annals of the American Association of Political and Social Sciences* 310, no. 1 (1957): 162–71.

Davin, Anna. "Imperialism and motherhood," *History Workshop Journal* 5 (1978): 9–66.

de Savornin Lohman, Anna. *Herinneringen*. Amsterdam: P.N. van Kampen, 1909.

Debien, Gabriel. "Les Esclaves." In *Histoire des Antilles et de la Guyane*, edited by Pierre Pluchon. Toulouse: Privat, 1982.

Debien, Gabriel. *Les Esclaves aux Antilles Françaises, XVIIe-XVIIIe Siècle*. Basse-Terre: Société d'histoire de la Guadeloupe, 1974.

Delon, Danielle, ed. *The Letters of Margaret Mann: With the Cazabon-Mann Watercolours of 19th Century Trinidad*. Port of Spain: National Museum and Art Gallery of Trinidad and Tobago, 2008.

Domínguez, Jorge I. *Insurrection and Loyalty: The Breakdown of the Spanish Empire*. Cambridge: Harvard University Press, 1980.

Draper, Nicholas. "Compensation for Barbados Slaveowners," The 29th Elsa Goveia Memorial Lecture, Cave Hill Campus, UWI, 16 Oct. 2013; also,

Draper, Nicholas. "Slave Ownership and the British Country House; The Records of the Slave Compensation Commission as Evidence." In *Slavery and the British Country House*, edited by Madge Dresser and Andrew Hann. Swindon: English Heritage, 2013.

Draper, Nicholas. "The Rise of a New Planter Class? Some Countercurrents from British Guiana and Trinidad, 1807–1833," *Atlantic Studies* 9, no. 1 (2012): 65–83.

Draper, Nicholas. *The Price of Emancipation: Slave Ownership, Compensation, and British Society at the End of Slavery.* Cambridge: Cambridge University Press, 1980.

Du Tertre, Jean-Baptiste (Père). *Histoire Générale des Antilles Habitées par les Français,* 4 vols. 1671, reprint Fort-de-France, Éditions des horizons caraïbes, 1973.

Dubois, Laurent. *Avengers of the New World: The Story of the Haitian Revolution.* Cambridge, Mass: Belknap Press of Harvard University Press, 2004.

Dunn, Richard. *Sugar and Slaves.* Jamaica: The University of the West Indies Press, 2000.

Eastman, Scott. *Preaching Spanish Nationalism across the Hispanic Atlantic, 1759–1823.* Baton Rouge: Louisiana State University Press, 2012.

Eccles, Karen. "Trinidadian Women and World War II." PhD diss., The University of the West Indies, St Augustine Campus, 2013.

Edwards, Brent Hayes. *The Practice of Diaspora: Literature, Translation and the Rise of Black Internationalism.* Cambridge, MA: Harvard University Press, 2003.

Edwards, Bryan. *History, Civil and Commercial, of the British Colonies in the West Indies in Three Volumes.* London: Stockdale, Piccadilly, 1801.

Engerman, Stanley. "Some Considerations Relating to the Property Rights in Man," *Journal of Economic History* 33 (1973): 113–50.

Eudell, Demetrius L. *The Political Languages of Emancipation in the British Caribbean and the U.S. South.* Chapel Hill: The University of North Carolina Press, 2002.

Fallope, Josette. *Esclaves et Citoyens: Les Noirs à la Guadeloupe au XIXe siècle.* Basse-Terre: Société d'histoire de la Guadeloupe, 1992.

Fanon, Frantz. *Black Skin, White Masks.* London: Paladin, 1970.

Fick, Carolyn, *The Making of Haiti: The Saint Domingue Revolution from Below.* Knoxville: University of Tennessee Press, 1990.

Fogel, Robert William, and Stanley L. Engerman. "Philanthropy at Bargain Prices: Notes on the Economics of Gradual Emancipation," *Journal of Legal Studies* 3, no. 2 (1974): 377–401.

Fouchard, Jean. *Les Marrons de la Liberté.* Paris: Editions de l'école, 1972.

Fouchard, Jean. *The Haitian Maroons: Liberty or Death,* trans. A Faulkner Watts. New York: Edward W. Blyden Press, 1981.

Franklin K. Knight, "Introduction," *The Growth of the Modern West Indies.* Kingston: Ian Randle Publisher, 2004

Fraser, Lionel Mordaunt. *History of Trinidad Vol. 1. 1781 to 1813.* London: F. Cass 1891 and 1896. Republished in 1971.

Fraser, Lionel Mordaunt. *History of Trinidad Vol. I1. 1814–1839.* London: F. Cass 1891 and 1896. Republished in 1971.

Froude, James Anthony. *The English in the West Indies: Or, The Bow of Ulysses.* London: Longman Green and Co., 1888.

Froude, James Anthony. *The English in the West Indies, or, The Bow of Ulysses*. Illinois: Scribner, 1888.

Gautier, Arlette. "Genre et Esclavage aux Antilles Françaises: Bilan de l'Histographie." In *L'Esclave et les Plantations: De l'Etablissement de la Servitude à son Abolition*, edited by Philippe Hroděj. Rennes: Presses Universitaires de Rennes, 2009.

Gautier, Arlette. *Les Sœurs de Solitude: La Condition Féminine dans l'esclavage aux Antilles du XVIIe au XIX siècle*. Paris: Éditions Caribéennes, 1985.

Geggus, David and David Barry Gaspar, eds. *A Turbulent Time: The French Revolution and the Greater Caribbean*, 1997.

Geggus, David, ed. *The Impact of the Haitian Revolution in the Atlantic World*. Columbia: University of South Carolina Press, 2001.

Geggus, David, ed., *Haitian Revolutionary Studies*. Bloomington: Indiana University Press, 2002.

Geggus, David. *Slavery, War and Revolution: The British Occupation of Saint-Domingue, 1793–1798*. London: Oxford University Press, 1982.

Genovese, Elizabeth Fox. *Within the Plantation Household Black and White Women of the Old South*. North Carolina: University of North Carolina Press, 1988.

Gisler, Antoine. *L'Esclavage aux Antilles Françaises XVIIe-XIXe siècles*. Paris, Karthala, 1981.

Goodridge, Richard A. "Women in Public Sector Unionism in Barbados 1944 to 1975." In *New Gender Studies from Cameroon and the Caribbean*, edited by J. Endeley et al. Buea: University of Beau, 2004.

Gordon, Margaret. "Crop Over Festival Barbados 1974." In *The Bajan and South Caribbean* (July 1974).

Goveia, Elsa V. *A Study of the Historiography of the British West Indies to the End of the Nineteenth Century*. Mexico City: Instituto Panamericano de Geografia e Historia, 1956.

Graham, Lawrence Otis. *Our Kind of People. Inside America's Black Upper Class*. New York: Harper Collins Publishers, 1999.

Green, W.A. "James Stephen and British West India Policy, 1844–1847," *Caribbean Studies* 13–14 (1974): 33–56.

Green, William A. "The Apprenticeship in British Guiana, 1834–1838," *Caribbean Studies* 9 (1969): 44–66.

Green, William A. *British Slave Emancipation: The Sugar Colonies and the Great Experiment, 1830–1865*. Oxford: Clarendon Press, 1976.

Greenbaum, Susan D. "Economic Cooperation among Urban Industrial Workers: Rationality and Community in an Afro-Cuban Mutual Aid Society, 1904–1927," *Social Science History* 17 no. 2 (1993): 173–93.

Groenewoud, Margo. "Hidden Strengths: Intellect and Ideology behind the

Women's Movement in Curacao and Aruba, 1946–1995" in eds. Rose Mary Allen and Sruti Bala *Handbook of Gender Studies in the Dutch* Caribbean. Boston: Brill, 2024, 114–133.

Guppy, Nicholas Guppy, ed. *Child of the Tropics, Victorian Memoirs.* London: Collins and Harvill, 1980.

Hall, Catherine. *Gendered Nations: Nationalisms and Gender Order in the Long Nineteenth Century.* Oxford: Berg, 2000.

Hall, Douglas. "The Apprenticeship Period in Jamaica, 1834–1838," *Caribbean Quarterly* 3 (December 1953): 142–66.

Hamilton, J. Taylor, and Kenneth G. Hamilton. *History of the Moravian Church: The Renewed Unitas Fratrum, 1722–1957.* Pennsylvania: International Board of Christian Education, Moravian Church in America, 1967.

Handler, Jerome S., and JoAnn Jacoby. "Slave Names and Naming in Barbados, 1650–1830," *William and Mary Quarterly* 53, no.4 (1996): 685–728.

Haraksingh, Kusha. "Labour Movements in Caribbean History." In *General History of the Caribbean Volume VI: Methodology and Historiography of the Caribbean*, edited by B.W. Higman. London: UNESCO Publishing/Macmillan Education, 1999.

Hastings, S.U., and B. L MacLeavy. *Seedtime and Harvest: A Brief History of the Moravian Church in Jamaica 1754–1979.* Kingston: Moravian Church Corporation, 1979.

Heuman, Gad J. *Between Black and White: Race, Politics and the Free Coloreds in Jamaica, 1792–1865.* Westport, CT: Greenwood Press, 1981.

Heuman, Gad. "'Is This What you Call free?' Riots and Resistance in the Anglophone Caribbean." In *Contesting Freedom: Control and Resistance in the Post-Emancipation Caribbean*, edited by Gad Heuman and David Trotman. Oxford: MacMillan, Caribbean, 2005.

High, Steven. *Base Colonies in the Western Hemisphere, 1940–1967.* New York: Palgrave Macmillan, 2009.

Higman, B.W. *UNESCO General History of the Caribbean*, 6 vols. New York: Palgrave Macmillan, 2003.

Higman, Barry W. "The West India 'Interest' in Parliament, 1807–1833," *Historical Studies* 13, no. 49 (1967): 1–19.

Higman, Barry. "Demographic Trends." In *The Cambridge World History of Slavery*, edited by David Eltis, Stanley Engerman, Seymour Drescher and David Richardson. United Kingdom: Cambridge University Press, 2017.

Higman, Barry. "Demography and Family Structures." In *The Cambridge World History of Slavery*, edited by David Eltis and Stanley Engerman. New York: Cambridge University Press, 2011.

Higman, Barry. *Slave Populations of the British Caribbean 1807–1834.* Baltimore, The John Hopkins University Press, 1984.

Hill, Robert, "In England, 1932–1938," In *C.L.R. James: His Life and Work*, edited by Paul Buhle. London: Allison and Busby, 1986.

Hobsbawm, Eric. "Introduction: Inventing Traditions." In *The Invention of Tradition*, edited by Eric Hobsbawm and Terence Ranger. Cambridge: Cambridge University Press, 1983.

Hoefte, Rosemarijn. "The Lonely Pioneer: Suriname's First Female Politician and Social Activist, Grace Schneiders-Howard," *Wadabagei* 10 no. 3 (2007): 87.

Hogsbjerg, Christian. *C.L.R. James in Imperial Britain*. Durnham: Duke University Press, 2014.

Holt, Thomas C. *The Problem of Freedom: Race, Labor, and Politics in Jamaica and Britain, 1832–1938*. Baltimore: The Johns Hopkins University Press, 1992.

Hoppit, Julian. "Compulsion, Compensation, and Property Rights in Britain, 1688-1938," *Past and Present* 201 (2011): 93–128.

Hoyte, Harold. 'Yoruba', The Bajan and South Caribbean, February (1973).

Hroděj, Philippe, ed., *L'Esclave et les Plantations: De l'établissement de la Servitude à son Abolition*. Rennes: Presses Universitaires de Rennes, 2008.

Hughes, Colin. *Race and Politics in the Bahamas*. St Lucia: University of Queensland Press, 1981.

Ishemo, Shubi L. "From Africa to Cuba: An Historical Analysis of the Sociedad Secreta Abakuá (Ñañiguismo)," *Review of African Political Economy* 29 no. 92 (2002) 253–72;

Ives, Charles. *The Isles of Summer or Nassau and the Bahamas* (New Haven: Self-published 1880),

James, C.L.R. "A National Purpose for Caribbean Peoples," At the Rendezvous of Victory, 143–50.

James, C.L.R. *A History of Negro Revolt*. London: Fact, 1938.

James, C.L.R. *Beyond a Boundary*. London: Hutchinson of London, 1963.

James, C.L.R. *Learie Constantine, Cricket and I*. London: P. Allan, 1933.

James, C.L.R. *Mariners, Renegades and Castaways: The Story of Herman Melville and the World We Live In*. New York: Privately Printed, 1953.

James, C.L.R. *The Black Jacobins: Toussaint L'Ouverture and the San Domingo Revolution*. New York: Random House, 1963.

James, C.L.R. *The Life of Captain Cipriani: An Account of British Government in the West Indies, with the Pamphlet The Case for West Indian Self-Government*. Durham: Duke University Press, 2014.

James, C.LR. *The Black Jacobin, Toussaint L'Ouverture and the St. Domingue Revolution*. New York: Random House, 1963.

Jaurès, Jean. *Histoire Socialiste de la Révolution Française, tome I, La Constituante*. Paris: Éditions de la Librairie de L'Humanité, 1927.

Jayawardena, Kumari. *Feminism and Nationalism in the Third World*. New Delhi: Kali for Women, 1986.

Jemmott, Jenny M. *Ties That Bind: The Black Family in Post-Slavery Jamaica, 1834–1882*. Kingston: University of the West Indies Press, 2015.
Johnson, Howard. "Barbadian Migration in Trinidad 1870–1897," *Caribbean Studies* 13 no.3 (October 1973): 5–30.
Jordon, G.W. *An Examination of the Principles of the Slave Registry Bill*. London: Cadell and Davies, 1816.
Joseph, E. L. *History of Trinidad*. H. J. Mills, 1838. Republished 1970.
Kadish, Doris Y., ed., *Slavery in the French Caribbean world: Distant Voices, Forgotten Acts, Forged Identities*. Athens: University of Georgia Press, 2000.
Kerr-Ritchie, Jeffrey. *Rites of August First: Emancipation Day in the Black Atlantic World*. Baton Rouge: Louisiana State University Press, 2007.
Kingsley, Charles. *At Last: A Christmas in the West Indies*. London: Macmillan, 1871.
Kipling, Rudyard. *Complete Verse*. New York: Doubleday, 1939.
Kuyk, Betty M. "The African Derivation of Black Fraternal Orders in the United States," *Comparative Studies is Society and History* 25 no. 4 (1983): 559–92.
La Guerre, J. G. *Calcutta to Caroni. The East Indians of Trinidad*. New York: Longman Caribbean, 1974.
La Guerre, John G. "Afro-Indian Relations in Trinidad and Tobago," *Caribbean Issues: A Journal of Caribbean Affairs Race and Colour*, 1 no. 1. (April 1974): 59–61.
La Guerre, John Gaffar, and Cherita Girvan. "The General Election of 1946 in Trinidad and Tobago," *Social and Economic Studies* 21, no 1. (1972): 184–204.
Lacour, Auguste. *Histoire de la Guadeloupe*, 4 vols. Basse-Terre: Editions de Diffusion de la Culture Antillaise, 1976.
Lambert, David. *White Creole Culture: Politics and Identity during the Age of Abolition*. Cambridge: Cambridge University Press, 2005.
Lamming, George, ed. *Enterprise of the Indies*. Port of Spain: The Trinidad and Tobago Institute of the West Indies, 1999.
Lara, Oruno. *La Guadeloupe dans l'Histoire*. Paris: L'Harmattan, 1979.
Lawrence, K.O., ed. "The Trinidad Water Riot of 1903: Reflections of an Eyewitness," *Caribbean Quarterly* 15, no. 4 (1969):5–22.
Lee Boggs, Grace. "C.L.R. James: Organizing in the U.S.A., 1938–1953," In *C.L.R. James: His Intellectual Legacies*, edited by Selwyn R. Cudjoe and William E. Cain. Amherst: University of Massachusetts Press, 1995.
Levy, Claude. "Barbados: The Years of Slavery, 1823–1833," *Journal of Negro History* 44 (1959): 308–45.
Levy, Claude. *Emancipation Sugar and Federalism: Barbados and the West Indies, 1833–1876*. Gainesville: University of Florida Press, 1980.
Lewis, Gordon K. *Main Currents in Caribbean Thought*. Baltimore: Johns Hopkins University Press, 1983.
Lewis, Gordon K. *The Growth of the Modern West Indies*. Kingston: Ian Randle Publisher, 2004.

Lewis, Gordon K. *The Growth of the Modern West Indies*. New York: NYU Press, 1968.
Lewis, Matthew Gregory. *The Journal of a West Indian Proprietor Kept During a Residence in the Island of Jamaica*. London: John Murray, 1834.
Lightfoot, Natasha. "'Their Coats were Tied Up like Men': Women Rebels in Antigua's 1858 Uprising," *Slavery & Abolition: A Journal of Slave and Post-Slave Studies* 31 (December, 2010): 527–45.
Ligon, Richard. *A True and Exact History of the Island of Barbados*. London: Humphrey Moseley, 1657.
Look Lai, Walton. "C.L.R. James and Trinidadian Nationalism," In *C.L.R. James's Caribbean*, edited by Paget Henry and Paul Buhle. Durham: Duke University Press, 1992.
Louis, Roger. *Imperialism at Bay: The United States and the Decolonization of the British Empire, 1941–1945*. New York: Oxford University Press, 1978.
Luke, Learie. *Identity and Secession in the Caribbean: Tobago versus Trinidad, 1889–1980*. Kingston: The UWI Press, 2007.
Lynch, Louis. *West Indian Eden: The Book of Barbados*. Glasgow: Robert Maclehouse, 1959.
M'Callum, Pierre Franc. *A Political Account of the Island of Trinidad from its Conquest by Sir Ralph Abercrombie*. London, 1807.
M'Callum, Pierre Franc. *Travels in Trinidad, during the Months of February, March, and April, 1803*. Liverpool, W. Jones, 1805.
Mahase, Anna. *My Mother's Daughter. The Autobiography of Anna Mahase Snr 1899–1978*. Claxton Bay: Royards, 1992.
Maingot, Anthony P. "Politics and Populist Historiography in the Caribbean," In *Intellectuals in the Twentieth Century, vol. 2, Unity and Variety: The Hispanic and Francophone Caribbean*, edited by Alistair Hennessy. London: Macmillan Caribbean, 1992.
Malik, Yogendra K. *East Indians in Trinidad: A Study in Minority Politics*. London: Institute of Race Relations, Oxford University Press, 1971.
Mam-Lam-Fouck, Serge. *L'Esclavage en Guyane entre l'Occultation et la Revendication*. Cayenne: Ibis Rouge Editions, 1998.
Mam-Lam-Fouck, Serge. *La Guyane Française au temps de l'Esclavage: de l'or et de la Francisation*. Petit-Bourg: Ibis Rouge, 1999.
Manning, Patrick. *Navigating World History Historian Create a Global Past*. New York: Palgrave Macmillan, 2003.
Marshall, Trevor. "An Evaluation of Crop Over," *The Bajan*, August 14–16, 1979.
Marshall, W.K. "Apprenticeship and Labour Relations in Four Windward Islands," in *Abolition and Its Aftermath: The Historical Context*, edited by David Richardson. London: Frank Cass, 1985.

Marshall, Woodville. "History Teaching in the University of the West Indies," In *Before and After 1865: Education, Politics and Regionalism in the Caribbean. In honour of Sir Roy Augier,* edited by Brian Moore *and* Swithin Wilmot. Kingston: Ian Randle, 1998.

Marshall, Woodville. "Metayage in the Sugar Industry of the British Windward Islands 1838–1865," *Jamaica Historical Review* 3, no.1 (May 1965): 28–29.

Martin, Gaston, *Histoire de l'Esclavage dans les Colonies Françaises*. Paris: Presses Universitaires de France, 1948.

Martin, Tony. "Vote for a Woman! Audrey Jeffers and the 1936 Entry of Women into Trinidad Politics." In *Before and After 1865: Education, Politics and Regionalism in the Caribbean,* edited by Brian Moore and Swithin Wilmot. Kingston: Ian Randle Publishers, 1998.

Martin, Tony. "Revolutionary Upheaval in Trinidad, 1919: Views from British and American Sources," *Journal of Negro History* 58, no. 3 (July, 1973): 323.

Martineau, Alfred, and L. May, *Trois Siècles d'Histoire Antillaises: Martinique et Guadeloupe de 1635 à nos Jours*. Paris: Société d'histoire des Colonies Françaises, 1935.

Mascoll, Clyde. "Modelling Two Caribbean Economies with a Fiscal Emphasis: Barbados and Jamaica 1973–2010." PhD diss., University of the West Indies, 2014.

Mathurin Mair, Lucille. *The Rebel Woman in the British West Indies during Slavery.* Kingston: Institute of Jamaica Publications Limited, 1975.

Maudslay, Alfred P. *Life in the Pacific Fifty Years Ago.* London: George Routledge and Sons, 1930.

Mawby, Spencer. *Ordering Independence: The End of Empire in the Anglophone Caribbean.* London: Palgrave Macmillan, 2012.

Mayer, Tamar, ed. *Gender Ironies of Nationalism: Sexing the Nation.* Routledge, 2012.

McClintock, Anne, Aamir R. Mufti, and Ella Shohat, eds. *Dangerous Liaisons: Gender, Nation and Post-Colonial Perspectives.* St. Paul: University of Minnesota Press, 1997.

McIntosh, S.C.R. *Fundamental Rights and Democratic Governance: Essays in Caribbean Jurisprudence.* Kingston: Caribbean Law Publishing, 2005.

McIntosh, Simeon. "A Wretched Judgement," *Barbados Advocate,* Monday, 16 May 1994.

McPherson, J.M. "Was West Indian Emancipation a Success," *Caribbean Studies* (1964): 28–34.

Meighoo, Kirk. *Politics in a Half-made Society: Trinidad and Tobago 1925–2001.* Kingston: Ian Randle, 2003.

Millette, James. "C.L.R. James and the Politics of Trinidad and Tobago," In *C.L.R. James: His Intellectual Legacies,* 328–347.

Minto-Coy, Indira. "The Grit that Makes the Pearl: Collaborative Problem Solving in the Midst of National Crisis," *Systems Research and Behavioral Science* 29 (2012): 221–26.

Mohammed, Patricia. *Gendered Realities Essays in Caribbean Feminist Thought*. Mona: University of the West Indies Press, 2002.

Mohammed, Patricia. *Imaging the Nation*. Basingstoke: Macmillan Caribbean, 2007.

Moitt, Bernard, *Women and Slavery in the French Antilles, 1635–1848*. Bloomington: Indiana University Press, 2001.

Moitt, Bernard. "In the Shadow of the Plantation: Women of Color and the *Libre de Fait of Martinique and Guadeloupe, 1685–1848*." In *Free Women of Color in the Americas*, edited by David Barry Gaspar and Darlene Clark Hine. Bloomington: Indiana University Press, 2004.

Montague, Ludwell Lee, "Review of *The Black Jacobins: Toussaint L'Ouverture and the San Domingo Revolution*, by Cyril Lionel Robert James," *Hispanic American Historical Review* 20, no. 1 (1940): 130.

Morrissey, Marietta. *Slave Women in the New World: Gender Stratification in the Caribbean*. Kansas: University Press of Kansas, 1989.

Morton, Sarah E., ed., *John Morton of Trinidad: Pioneer Missionary of the Presbyterian Church in Canada to the East Indians in the British West Indies*. Toronto: Westminster Company, 1916.

Moxly, J.H. *An Account of a West Indian Sanatorium and a Guide to Barbados*. London: Sampson Low, 1886.

Nicholls, David G. "East Indians and Black Power in Trinidad," *Race* 12 (1970–71): 443–45.

Nurse, Lawrence, and Dwayne Devonish. "Worker Participation in Barbados: Contemporary Practice and Prospects," *The International Journal of Human Resource Management* 19, no. 10 (2008): 1911–28.

Nurse, Lawrence. *Trade Unionism and Industrial Relations in the Caribbean: History, Contemporary Practice and Prospect*. Westport, Conn: Greenwood, 1992.

Olwig, Karen Fog. *Caribbean Journeys: An Ethnography of Family and Home in Three Family Networks*. Durham: Duke University Press, 2007.

Ortiz, Fernando. *Cuban Counterpoint: Tobacco and Sugar*. New York: Alfred Knopf, 1947.

Pago, Gilbert, *Les Femmes et la Liquidation du Système Esclavagiste à la Martinique, 1848–1852*. Pointe-à-Pitre: Ibis Rouge, 1998.

Palmiste, Clara, and Michelle Zancarini-Fournel. "Caribbean Worlds: A Space Apart." Translated by Siân Reynolds. *Clio Women, Gender, History* 50, no. 2 (2019): 9–18.

Pateman, Carole. "The Patriarchal Welfare State." In *Defining Woman: Social Institutions and Gender Divisions*, edited by Linda McDowell and Rosemary

Pringle. Cambridge: Polity Press in association with The Open University, 1992.

Paton, Diana. *No Bond but the Law: Punishment, Race, and Gender in Jamaican State Formation, 1780–1870*. Durham: Duke University Press, 2004.

Peabody, Sue, and Tyler Stovall. *The Color of Liberty: Histories of Race in France*. Durham: Duke University Press, 2003.

Pemberton, Rita, Debbie Mc Collin, Gelien Matthews and Michael Toussaint. *Historical Dictionary of Trinidad and Tobago*. Lanham, Maryland: Roman and Littlefield, 2018.

Penn, Rosalyn Terborg. *African American Women in the Struggle for the Vote, 1850–1920*. Indiana: Indiana University Press, 1988.

Pessar, Patricia R., and Sarah J. Mahler, "Transnational Migration: Bringing Gender," *International Migration Review* 37 no. 3 (2003), 812–46.

Petraud, Lucien. *L'Esclavage aux Antilles Françaises Avant 1789*. Paris: Hachette, 1897.

Phillip, Nicole Laurine. "Women in Grenadian History from Slavery to People's Revolution 1783–1983." PhD diss., The University of the West Indies, St Augustine Campus, 2002.

Phillips, David. *La Magdalena: The Story of Tobago 1498–1898*. New York: iUniverse, Inc. 2004.

Phillips, Glen. "The Changing Role of the Merchant Class in the British West Indies, 1834–1867," (PhD diss., Howard University, 1976).

Pierre-Louis, Jessica. "Free women of colour and property donations in Martinique 1806–1830." *Clio Women, Gender, History* 50, no. 2 (2019): 109–123.

Pierson, Ruth Roach, Nurpur Chaudhuri, and Beth McAuley, eds. *Nation, Empire, Colony: Historicising Gender and Race*. Bloomington: Indiana University Press, 1998.

Pocock, J. G. A. "Languages and their Implications: The Transformation of the Study of Political Thought," In *Politics, Language & Time: Essays on Political Thought and History*. Chicago: University of Chicago Press, 1989.

Powles, L.D. *The Land of the Pink Pearl. Recollections of Life in the Bahamas*. London: Samson Low, Marston, Searle and Rivington, 1888.

Pratt, F.G. "Review of *The Case for West Indian Self-Government*, by C.L.R. James," *International Affairs* 12, no. 5 (1933), 674.

Price-Mars, Jean. *Ainsi Parla L'Oncle*. Port-au-Prince: Imprimerie de Compiègne, 1928.

Rajkumar, Fiona. "Ethnicity and Economy: The Portuguese, Chinese and Syrian/Lebanese in Trinidad 1945–1981." PhD diss., University of the West Indies, St. Augustine, 2007.

Ramsoedh, Hans. "Politieke Strijd, Volksopstand en Antisemitisme in Suriname Omstreeks 1890," *Tijdschrift voor Sociale Geschiedenis* 18 no. 4, (1992): 479–501.

Reddock, Rhoda, *Women, Labour and Politics in Trinidad and Tobago: A History.* London: Zed Books, 1994.

Reddock, Rhoda. *Women's Movements and Organisations in the Process of Revolutionary Transformation: The Case of Grenada.* n.p., 1983.

Reid, Basil. *Myths and Realities of Caribbean History.* Tuscaloosa: University of Alabama Press, 2009.

Rennie, Bukka. *History of the Working-Class in the 20th Century – Trinidad and Tobago.* Toronto: New Beginning Movement, 1973.

Riccucci, N.M. *Women, Minorities and Unions in the Public Sector.* New York: Greenwood, 1990.

Rivere, William. "Labour Shortage in the British West Indies after Emancipation," *Journal of Caribbean History* 4 (May 1972).

Rodríguez O, and E. Jaime. *The Independence of Spanish America.* Cambridge Latin American Studies 84. Cambridge: Cambridge University Press, 1998.

Rowbotham, Sheila. *Hidden from History. Three hundred years of Woman's Oppression and the Fight Against it.* London: Pluto Press, 1973.

Ryan, Selwyn. *Eric Williams: The Myth and the Man.* Mona: University of the West Indies Press, 2009.

Ryan, Selwyn. *Race and Nationalism in Trinidad and Tobago.* Toronto: University of Toronto Press, 1972.

Sabga, Abdo, and Natayla Sabga, *A Life Worth Remembering: Abdou Joseph Sabga 1898–1985 – A Chronicle of the Sabga Family and one of its Most Distinguished Members.* Laventille: Zenith Service Limited, 2001.

Sala-Molins, Louis. *Le Code Noir ou le Calvaire de Canaan.* Paris: Presses Universitaires de France, 1987.

Samaroo, Brinsley, ed. *The Blackest Thing in Slavery was Not the Black Man: The Last Testament of Eric Williams.* Kingston, Jamaica: University of the West Indies Press, 2022.

Samaroo, Brinsley. "Constitutional and Political Development of Trinidad 1898–1925." PhD diss., University of London, 1969

Samaroo, Brinsley. "The Trinidad Disturbances of 1817–20: Precursor to 1937," In *The Trinidad Labour Riots of 1937: Perspectives 50 Years Later*, edited by Roy Thomas. Trinidad: Extra Mural Studies Unit, University of the West Indies, 1987.

Schœlcher, Victor. *Histoire de l'Esclavage Pendant les Deux Dernières Années*, 1847 reprint, 2 vols. Pointe-à-Pitre: Émile Désormeaux, 1973.

Scott, James C. *Domination and the Arts of Resistance. Hidden Transcripts.* New Haven: Yale University Press, 1990.

Scott, JoanWallach. *Gender and the Politics of History.* New York: Columbia University Press, 1988.

Scully, Pamela, and Diana Paton, eds., *Gender and Slave Emancipation in the Atlantic World*. Durham: Duke University Press, 2005.

Seabrook, W.G. "Review of *The Black Jacobins,* by C.L.R. James," *Journal of Negro History* 24, no. 1 (1939): 125–27.

Serrera, Ramón María. "Sociedad Estamental y Sistema Colonial," In A. Annino, L. Castro Leiva and F. X. Guerra, dir., *De los Imperios a las Naciones: Iberoamérica, Forum International des Sciences Humaines*. Zaragoza: IberCaja, 1994.

Shaw, Thomas. "To Be or Not to Be Chinese: Differential Expressions of Chinese Culture and Solidarity in the British West Indies." In *Caribbean Ethnicity Revisited*, edited by Stephen Glazier. New York: Gordon and Breech Science Publishers.

Sheller, Mimi. "'You Signed My Name, But Not My Feet': Paradoxes of Peasant Resistance and State Control in Post-Revolutionary Haiti." In *Contesting Freedom: Control and Resistance in the Post-Emancipation Caribbean*, edited by Gad Heuman and David Trotman. Oxford: MacMillan Caribbean, 2005.

Sheller, Mimi. "Acting as Free Men: Subaltern Masculinities and Citizenship in Postslavery Jamaica." In *Gender and Slave Emancipation*, edited by Pamela Scully and Diana Paton. Durham, North Carolina: Duke University Press, 2005.

Sheller, Mimi. "Quasheba, Mother, Queen: Black Women's Public Leadership and Protest in Post-emancipation Jamaica, 1834–1865," *Slavery & Abolition: A Journal of Slave and Post-Slave Studies* 19 no. 3 (December, 1998): 90–117.

Shepherd, Verene A. *I Want to Disturb my Neighbour. Lectures on Slavery, Emancipation and Postcolonial Jamaica*. Kingston: Ian Randle Publishers, 2007.

Shepherd, Verene, and Hilary Beckles. *Caribbean Slavery in the Atlantic World*. Kingston: Ian Randle Publishers, 2002.

Shepherd, Verene. *Women in Caribbean History*. Kingston: Ian Randle Publishers, 1999.

Shepherd, Verne, Bridget Brereton, and Barbara Bailey, eds. *Engendering History. Caribbean Women in Historical Perspective*. Kingston: Ian Randle Publishers, 1995.

Silvestrini, Blanca and Maria de los Angeles Castro Arroyo. "Sources for the Study of Puerto Rican History: A Challenge to Imaginative Research," *Latin American Research Review* 16, no. 2 (1981): 156–171.

Smith, Faith. *Creole Recitations: John Jacob Thomas and Colonial Formation in the Late Nineteenth-Century*. Charlottesville: University of Virginia Press, 2002.

Smith, Howard L. and Mary Grenier, "Sources of Organizational Power for Women: Overcoming Structural Obstacles." *Sex Roles* 8, no. 7 (1982): 773–846.

Stedman, John Gabriel. *Narrative, of a Five Year's Expedition Against the revolted Negroes of Surinam, in Guiana, on the Wild Coast of South America, from the Year 1772 to 1777*. London: J. Johnson and J. Edwards, 1796.

Stepan, Nancy. *The Hour of Eugenics: Race, Gender and Nation in Latin America.* Ithaca: Cornell University Press, 1996.

Stroble, Margaret. "Gender and Race in the Nineteenth- and Twentieth-Century British Empire." In *Becoming Visible: Women in European History*, edited by Renate Bridenthal, Claudia Koonz and Susan Stuard. Boston: Houghton Mifflin Company, 1987.

Sturge, Edmund. *West India Compensation to the Owners of Slaves: Its History and Results.* Gloucester: John Bellows, 1893.

Sturge, John, and Thomas Harvey, *The West Indies in 1837.* London: Hamilton, Adams & Co., 1838.

Sutton, Paul, comp. *Forged for the Love of Liberty: Selected Speeches of Dr. Eric Williams.* Port-of-Spain: Longman, 1981.

Taylor, Bruce. "Emancipation in Barbados, 1830–1850" (PhD diss., Fordham University, 1975).

Teelucksingh, Jerome. *Labour and the Decolonization Struggle in Trinidad and Tobago.* New York: Palgrave Macmillan, 2015.

Thélier, Gérard and Pierre Alibert, *Le Grand Livre de l'Esclavage: Des Résistances et de l'Abolition.* Réunion: Les Editions Orphie, 1998.

Thomas, J. J. *Froudacity: West Indian Fables Explained.* London: T. Fisher Unwin, 1889.

Thomas, J. J. *The Theory and Practice of Creole Grammar.* Port-of-Spain: The Chronicle Publishing Office, 1869.

Thomas-Bailey, Melise. "E-Consciousness: Economic Black Consciousness in Nineteenth and Twentieth Century Trinidad and Tobago." In *Beyond Tradition: Reinterpreting the Caribbean Historical Experience*, edited by Heather Cateau and Rita Pemberton. Kingston: Ian Randle Publishers, 2006.

Titmuss, Richard M. "The Social Division of Welfare: Some Reflections on the Search for Equity." In *The Philosophy of Welfare,* edited by Richard M. Titmuss. London: Allen and Unwin, 1987.

Titus, N.F. *The Development of Methodism in Barbados, 1823–1883.* Berne: Peter Lang, 1994.

Toussaint, Michael. "The Eric Williams' Diaries." In *The Fires of Hope* Vol. 2 edited by Debbie Mc Collin. Kingston: Ian Randle Publishers, 2016.

Trollope, Anthony. *The West Indies and the Spanish Main,* 4th ed. London: Chapman & Hall, 1860.

Trotman, David. "Capping the Volcano: Riots and their Suppression in Post-emancipation Trinidad," In *Contesting Freedom: Control and Resistance in the Post-Emancipation Caribbean,* edited by Gad Heuman and David Trotman. Oxford: MacMillan Caribbean, 2005.

Tyson, George F. "'Our Side': Caribbean Immigrant Labourers and the Transition

to Free Labour on St. Croix, 1849–79." In *Small Islands, Large Questions: Society, Culture and Resistance in the Post-Emancipation Caribbean*, edited by Karen Fog Olwig. London: Frank Cass, 1995.
van der Walle, Johan. *Een oog Boven Paramaribo: Herinneringen*. Amsterdam: Querido, 1975.
Voight-Graf, Carmen. The Journal of Pacific Studies 27, no.2 (Nov. 2004): 180.
Walcott, Derek. *The Star Apple*. New York: Farrar, Strauss and Giroux, 1977.
Waldinger, Roger, Howard Aldrich, and Robin Ward. "Opportunities, Group Characteristics and Strategies." In *Ethnic Entrepreneurs: Immigrant Businesses in Industrial Societies*, edited by Roger Waldinger, Howard Aldrich, Robin Ward and Associates. London: Sage, 1990
Walvin, James. *An African's Life: The Life and Times of Olaudah Equiano 1745–1797*. New York: Cassell, 1998.
Wastell, R.E.P. "The History of Slave Compensation, 1838–1845" (master's thesis, University of London, 1932).
White, Deborah Gray. *Too Heavy a Load: Black Women in Defense of Themselves 1894*. New York: W.W. Norton, 1999.
Wilberforce, Robert I., and Samuel Wilberforce. *The Life of William Wilberforce*. London: John Murray.
Williams, Bronty Liverpool. "A Historical Study of Women in Twentieth Century St Vincent and the Grenadines." MPhil diss., The University of the West Indies, St Augustine Campus, 2002.
Williams, Eric and E. Franklin Frazier, eds. *The Economic Future of the Caribbean*. Washington, DC: Howard University, 1944.
Williams, Eric, ed. and comp. *Documents Illustrating the Development of Civilization*, 3 vols. Washington, DC: Kaufman Press Inc., 1947–1948.
Williams, Eric. "Manifest Destiny of the United States: Review of The Caribbean Policy of the United States, 1890–1920, by W. H. Calcott", *Journal of Negro Education* 12, no. 1 (1943): 85.
Williams, Eric. "The Impact of the International Crisis upon the Negro in the Caribbean," *Journal of Negro Education* 10, no. 3 (1941): 543.
Williams, Eric. *Capitalism and Slavery*. Capitol Hill and London: University of North Carolina Press, 1994.
Williams, Eric. *Documents of West Indian History*, vol. I: 1492–1655. Port-of-Spain, P.N.M. Publishing, 1963.
Williams, Eric. *Education in the British West Indies*. Port-of-Spain: Teachers' Economic and Social Association, 1950.
Williams, Eric. *From Columbus to Castro*. London: Andre Deutsch, 1970.
Williams, Eric. *From Columbus to Castro: The History of the Caribbean, 1492 to 1969*. London: André Deutsch, 1970.

Williams, Eric. *History of the People of Trinidad and Tobago*. Port of Spain: PNM Publishing, 1962.

Williams, Eric. *Inward Hunger*. Chicago: University of Chicago Press, 1969.

Williams, Eric. *The Economic Aspect of the Abolition of the West Indian Slave Trade and Slavery*, edited by D. Tomich and W. Darity. New York: Rowman and Littlefield, 2014.

Williams, Eric. *The History of the People of Trinidad and Tobago*. Port-of-Spain: P.N.M. Publishing, 1962.

Williams, Eric. *The Negro in the Caribbean*. Washington, DC: Associates in Negro Folk Education, 1942.

Willson, F. M. G. *A Strong Supporting Cast: The Shaw Lefevres 1789–1936*. London: The Athlone Press, 1993.

Wilmot, Swithin. "Not 'Full Free': The Ex-Slaves and the Apprenticeship System in Jamaica, 1834–1838," *Jamaica Journal* 17 (1984): 2–10.

Woodcock, Henry Isles. *A History of Tobago*. London: Frank Cass, 1971.

Worcester, Kent. *C.L.R. James: A Political Biography*. Albany: State University of New York Press, 1996.

Worrell, R. "Leroy Harewood Pan-African Humanist," *IDEAZ* 1, no. 2 (2002): 29–35.

Worrell, R. "Leroy Harewood: Pan-African Humanist." In *Pan-Africanism, Pan-Africanists, and African Liberation in the 21st Century*, edited by H. Campbell and R. Worrell. Washington, DC: New Academia Publishing, 2006.

Yuval-Davis, Nira. *Gender and Nation*. London: Sage, 1997.

CONTRIBUTORS

EDITORS

HEATHER CATEAU is a senior lecturer in Caribbean History at The University of the West Indies, St Augustine Campus. She has held the positions of Dean of the Faculty of Humanities and Education, Head of the History Department and University Dean. Her research focus has contributed to a revisionary approach to plantation and enslavement systems in the Caribbean. She is also a past president of the Association of Caribbean Historians. She has co-authored and co-edited: *Turning Tides Caribbean Intersections in the Americas and Beyond*; *Beyond Tradition: Reinterpreting the Caribbean Historical Experience*; *The Caribbean in the Atlantic World* and *Capitalism and Slavery Fifty Years Later*.

RONALD C. NOEL lectures in the History Department of The University of the West Indies. He came into academia after a career in industry which spanned three decades. He previously worked as a Senior Chemical Sales Representative for George F. Huggins & Co. Ltd in charge of some of the major chemical manufacturers and distributors in the world. It was in this community of extensive business dealings that Dr Noel saw the inner workings of the North Atlantic world and this environment comprised of colleagues who had both imperial and colonial dispositions. It was between these two broad worlds that Dr Noel found at times that he had to act as an agent and at times as a mediator in trade disputes. The saving grace was always history. History was his Greatest Collaborator. Dr Noel is the holder of a PhD in history from Howard University, Washington, DC. His areas of special research interest include: The Black Diaspora, African Initiatory Rites and Secret Societies, Rural Development and Public Policy in Africa, Pan-Africanism with special emphasis on Henry Sylvestre-Williams, Caribbean and Latin American History ,History of the United States and Industricism.

RITA PEMBERTON is a former Senior Lecturer, Head of the Department of History and Deputy Dean, Student Affairs in the Faculty of Humanities and Education at The University of the West Indies, St Augustine Campus. She is also past president of the Association of Caribbean Historians and former Chief Examiner Caribbean History. She was a Member of the Working Committee of the Sub-Committee to Revise the Tobago House of Assembly Act and the Position of Tobago in the Constitution of Trinidad and Tobago from 2008 to 2012 and currently serves as Chairman of the Committee to review the Placement of Statues, Monuments and Signage in Trinidad and Tobago. She researches Caribbean Health and Environment and the History of Trinidad and Tobago.

CONTRIBUTORS

JOHN AARONS is a former University Archivist, The University of the West Indies, Government Archivist, Jamaica Archives and Records Department and Executive Director of the National Library of Jamaica. Since his retirement, he has co-edited with two colleagues two volumes on Caribbean Archives

SIR HILARY McD. BECKLES is the Vice-Chancellor of The University of the West Indies. He was the Principal and Pro Vice-Chancellor of The University of the West Indies, Cave Hill Campus from 2000 to 2015. Sir Beckles is an eminent university administrator and economic historian. He is an esteemed internationally recognized historian who has led the intellectual call for reparatory justice from colonial powers. His books, *Britain's Black Debt: Reparations for Caribbean Slavery and Native Genocide* (2013), and *How Britain Underdeveloped the Caribbean: A Reparation Response to Europe's Legacy of Plunder and Poverty* (2021) have brought specificity to his activism while pursuing this challenging issue. Sir Beckles has an extensive and impressive list of distinguished academic credits, and his scholarship is a natural and essential part of compulsory readings when studying themes such as enslavement and freedom in Caribbean history. It is in this regard, his contribution to this volume delivers a revealing revisionist perspective on who actually paid for the freedom of enslaved Africans with particular emphasis on Barbados.

MARCIA BURROWES is Deputy Dean in the Faculty of Culture, Creative and Performing Arts at The University of the West Indies, Cave Hill Campus.

She conceptualized and implemented the Taught UWI Cultural Studies Programme at the graduate level (MA, MPhil, PhD) and the undergraduate level (Minor in Cultural Studies). Her research interests include Caribbean Cultural Identities, Diaspora and Windrush narratives, and Caribbean Traditional Masquerade.

MARY CHAMBERLAIN is Emerita Professor of History at Oxford Brookes University. From 1987 to 1991, she lived in Barbados, and began working in Caribbean history. Using oral history, she published two pioneering studies of migration and families, *Narratives of Exile and Return* and *Family Love in the Diaspora: Migration and the Anglo Caribbean Experience*, and a further study of decolonization, *Empire and Nation-building in the Caribbean: Barbados 1937–1966*.

HUMBERTO GARCÍA-MUÑIZ Senior Researcher, Institute of Caribbean Studies, University of Puerto Rico, is the author of *Sugar and Power in the Caribbean: The South Porto Rico Sugar Company in Puerto Rico and the Dominican Republic, 1900–1921* and *La Ayuda Militar como Negocio: Estados Unidos y el Caribe*. His latest article, published in the *Revue d'Histoire Haïtienne*, discusses the establishment of the Haitian American Sugar Company in Haiti in early twentieth century.

RICHARD GOODRIDGE is Lecturer in History at the Cave Hill Campus of The University of the West Indies. His research interests include women and labour history in Cameroon and the Caribbean. His focus is on the legacy of the African presence in Barbados and the way it is taught. This body of research is evidenced in several publications which include *A History of Public Sector Unionism in Barbados*.

JUAN R. GONZÁLEZ MENDOZA has a PhD in History from the University of Stony Brook in New York, USA. Four years ago, he retired from Interamerican University of Puerto Rico, San Germán, after thirty-six years of service. He is a member of the Academia San Germeña de la Historia and a life member of the Association of Caribbean Historians (ACH). As a member of the ACH he served in the Executive Committee on several occasions, and was Vice-President and Secretary-Treasurer, as well as member of the Nominating Committee and the Antonio Ramos Mattei-Neville Hall Prize for best article on Caribbean history. His publications have centred on Puerto Rican nineteenth century history, ecological history, and historiography, among others.

GAD HEUMAN is Professor Emeritus at the University of Warwick. He is the author of *Between Black and White: Race, Politics, and the Free Coloreds in Jamaica*; *The Killing Time: The Morant Bay Rebellion in Jamaica*; and *The Caribbean: A Brief History*. He has also edited several books and is the editor of the journal, *Slavery & Abolition*.

ROSEMARIJN HOEFTE is a senior researcher at KITLV/Royal Institute of Southeast Asian and Caribbean Studies in Leiden, the Netherlands and professor of the history of Suriname after 1873 at the University of Amsterdam. She is also the editor-in-chief of the *New West Indian Guide*.

GELIEN MATTHEWS is Head of the Department of History of The University of the West Indies, St Augustine Campus. Her major publications include *Caribbean Slave Revolts and the British Abolitionist Movement*, *Historical Dictionary of Trinidad and Tobago* (co- authored), *History of the Church of the Nazarene Trinidad and Tobago* and *The Church of the Nazarene in Four of the Windward Islands*. She lectures in Caribbean, Latin American and US History; and is the recipient of the prestigious UWI/Guardian Life Premium Teaching Award.

BERNARD MOITT is a professor at Virginia Commonwealth University. Born and raised in Antigua, his research focuses on slavery in French West Africa, primarily Senegal, and the French Antilles. Among his numerous publications are *Women and Slavery in the French Antilles, 1635–1848* (2002) and *Child Slavery and Guardianship in Colonial Senegal* (2024).

DANE MORTON GITTENS is an experienced Part-time Lecturer and former Principal with a demonstrated history of working in the education management industry. He is skilled in Lecturing, Editing, Educational Technology, Curriculum Development, and Research. He is a noted education professional with a Bachelor of Arts (BA), Master of Arts (MA), Doctor of Philosophy (PhD) focused in History from The University of the West Indies, St Augustine Campus.

RITA PEMBERTON is a former Senior Lecturer, Head of the Department of History and Deputy Dean, Student Affairs in the Faculty of Humanities and Education at The University of the West Indies, St Augustine Campus. She is also past president of the Association of Caribbean Historians and former Chief Examiner Caribbean History. She was a Member of the Working Committee of the Sub-Committee to Revise the Tobago

House of Assembly Act and the Position of Tobago in the Constitution of Trinidad and Tobago from 2008 to 2012 and currently serves as Chairman of the Committee to review the Placement of Statues, Monuments and Signage in Trinidad and Tobago. She researches Caribbean Health and Environment and the History of Trinidad and Tobago.

FIONA ANN RAJKUMAR is an Associate Professor of History at the University of the Southern Caribbean and alumni of The University of the West Indies, St Augustine Campus. She has worked in tertiary education for the past 17 years. Her areas of research interest include ethnic minorities, economic and migration history in the Caribbean, advocacy for history education, home-schooling and youth mentorship in the context of Trinidad and Tobago.

RHODA REDDOCK is Emerita Professor of Gender, Social Change, and Development at The University of the West Indies, St Augustine Campus. Widely published, her most recent publication is *Decolonial Perspectives on Entangled Inequalities* (2021) (with Encarnación Guttierez-Rodriguez). She is currently an executive member of the International Sociological Association (ISA) and an elected expert of the UN Committee for the Elimination of Discrimination against Women (CEDAW).

JAMES ROSE was born in Guyana. He studied history at the University of Guyana and King's College, London. Had has taught history at the Polytechnic of North London [PNL] [London Metropolitan University] and the University of Guyana.

BRINSLEY SAMAROO (decd), was a professor of history in the Department of History at The University of the West Indies, St Augustine Campus, and a former Head of the Department of History. In his long professional career, Professor Samaroo was known for his contributions to public history, politics, and activism. As an author, he wrote on many topics and was a pioneering researcher on the Indian diaspora. Among some of his other academic interests were: class, caste and labour struggles, the history of Trinidad and Tobago, and the lives of two late politicians of Trinidad and Tobago, former prime minister Dr Eric Eustace Williams and former prime minister and president, Arthur Napoleon Ray Robinson. Professor Samaroo was also a Senior Research Fellow of the University of Trinidad and Tobago. Some of his notable works included: *India in the Caribbean* (1987), editor; *The Art of Garnett Ifill: Glimpses of the Sugar Industry* (2003);

Adrian Cola Rienzi: The Life and Times of an Indo-Caribbean Progressive (2021); *The Price of Conscience: Howard Noel Nankivell and Labour Unrest in the British Caribbean in 1937 and 1938* (2015); and *The Blackest Thing in Slavery was Not the Black Man: The Last Testament of Eric Williams* (2022), editor. Professor Samaroo will also be remembered for his consistent and dedicated research visits to the Alma Jordan West Indiana Division of the Main Library at The University of the West Indies, St Augustine Campus.

GAIL SAUNDERS (decd) OBE, Order of Distinction and Honorary doctorate UWI, 2004, was a renowned, Bahamas historian, archivist and athlete. She established, then became Director of the National Archives of the Bahamas from 1971 to 2004. She was a member of the 1962 Bahamas National Relay team, a former scholar in Residence of the College of the Bahamas and Director General of Heritage for the Bahama Archives until 2008. She served as president of the Bahamas Historical Society, the Association of Caribbean Historians, the Caribbean Archives Association, was an executive member of the International Council on Archives and is an inductee to the Bahamas National Sports Hall of Fame. Her publications include *Historic Nassau, Islanders in the Stream: A History of the Bahamian People, Vols. 1 and 2* (with Michael Craton), and *Bahamian Society After Emancipation* and *Race and Class in the Colonial Bahamas, 1880–1960*.

MICHAEL TOUSSAINT is a former lecturer in the Department of History at the St Augustine Campus of The University of the West Indies, where he taught Caribbean History, European Imperialism and Historiography of the African Diaspora and served as Editor of *History in Action*, the journal of the Department of History. He has pioneered research on African and Indian outmigration from the Caribbean to Latin America and the Legacy of slavery and indentureship. He has published numerous book chapters, papers in peer reviewed journals and entries in global-based diasporic encyclopaedias. His publications include: *Historical Dictionary of Trinidad and Tobago* (Joint Author); "Post-Abolition Trinidad-Venezuela Relations in the Nineteenth Century: The Problem of the Manumisos and Aprendizajes" in *The Arts Journal* (2007); "Trinidad and Tobago, Anti-Colonial Movement" and "Trinidad and Tobago, Parliamentary Crisis" in *The International Encyclopaedia of Revolution and Protest* (2009); and "Chambers, George Michael" and "Peoples National Movement" in Encyclopedia of African-American Culture and History.

PEDRO L V WELCH, Professor of Social and Medical History, was a retired former Dean, Faculty of Humanities and Education, and Deputy Principal, at The University of the West Indies, Cave Hill Campus. He published extensively on various themes of Caribbean history, particularly on the urban context of the slave plantation system, with his text, *Slave Society in the City*, receiving multiple citations. He lectured by invitation throughout the Caribbean, in Europe, and in North America and was a historical consultant to media outlets BBC and MSNBC. He served as an Editorial Consultant to the *Journal of Caribbean History* and was the editor of the *Journal of the Barbados Museum*. Professor Welch was a former Chair of the Barbados Task Force on Reparations and previously served for six consecutive terms as Secretary-Treasurer of the Association of Caribbean Historians.

INDEX

Abénon, Lucien, 235, 240–41
African Institute, abolitionist (1807), 10
Andina, Miguel de, 106, 112
Anti-slavery campaign(s), 3, 7, 13, 256
Apprenticeship (Calculation), xvi, 24–26, 37, 40, 44, 255–59
Archibald-Crichlow, Beryl, 288
Audrey Jeffers campaign, 287

Barbados Assembly, 10
Barrow, Errol, 293, 360, 367
Beckles, John (Speaker of the House, 1815), 10
Bissette, Cyrille, 247
Blérald, Phillipe, 240
Board of Tourism, xxv, 355–56, 360, 366, 371, 373, 375,
Bogle, Paul, 262–66
British Guiana Constitutional Commission Report (1957), 96
Burnard, Trevor, 180
Bush, Barbara, 180
Butel, Paul, 239
Butler, Mary, 24, 180
Butler, Tubal Uriah "Buzz", 282, 288
Buxton, Thomas, 14–17, 22–24

Canning, George, 10, 23
CARICOM
  establishment of, 169
Chamberlain, Joseph, 90

Churches
  Anglican, 66, 68, 81, 83, 345
  Methodist, 68, 75, 345–46
  Moravian, 75
  Presbyterian, 68, 345
  Roman Catholics, 89, 97, 125, 412
Cipriani, Arthur Andrew, 168, 280
Clarke, Denis, 328
Clarke, Roberta, 322–23
Clarkson, Thomas, 10
Colonial administration
  Constitution (1812) Spain, 101, 105, 115, 117
  Constitution (1924), Trinidad and Tobago, 279
  Constitution (1946) Trinidad and Tobago, 92
  Constitution (1953) British Guiana, 128
  Constitution (Article 22), Spain, 109
  Constitution (Article 70), Spain, 110
  Constitution (Article 74), Spain, 111
  Constitution (Article 97), Spain, 112
  Constitution Act (1876), Tobago, 49
  Constitution Reform Committee (1955) Trinidad and Tobago, 97, 288
  Constitution, Barbados, 334
  Constitution, Trinidad and Tobago, 462

469

Crown Colony, xix, 89, 90–91, 93, 96, 97–98, 127, 153, 157, 271–73, 275–76, 278, 408

Committees
Colonial Policy Committee (1956), 141
Constitution Reform Committee (1955), 97
Constitutional Reform Committee, 288
Crop Over Festival Committee, 361
Franchise Committee, 285–86
Judicial Committee, 335
Legislative Reform Committee, 274, 278
Library Committee, 428
University Archives and Records Management Advisory Committee (UARMAC), 428
West India Committee, 17
Women's Affairs Committee, 330–31

Constitutional Cortes (1810), 117
Coterie of Social Workers, 280, 282–85
Crichlow, Patsy, 330
Crop Over, 355–63
Cuba, 102, 115–17, 158, 160, 164, 166, 294
Cyprus, 92–93

Dalgleish, Andrew, 134
Dalrymple, Annice, 330
de Savornin Lohman, Anna, 193–95, 198–99, 201–203, 205–207
Deane Commission, 297, 300, 305, 307–308
Debien, Gabriel, 239, 243–44
Donghi, Halperin, 116,

Emancipation, xvi, xxiv, xxv, xxvii, 15, 17, 19, 20, 22, 24–27, 32, 36–37, 40–41, 44–46, 52, 57–58, 75, 80–81, 154, 186, 255, 298, 376
call for, Buxton, 23
Day (Trinidad and Tobago), xvii, 33, 39–40, 46
French Antilles, 247
onset of, 272
process of, xv, 23
Tobago, 37

Ethnicity
Bahamian whites, 345
French Creoles, 95, 277, 409–410, 418

Fiji, 90, 92–93, 216, 417–18
Finlayson, Rosanna, 264
First Peoples, 272, 404, 412, 418
Fitzpatrick, George, 92

Franchise
(for women), xxiii, 273, 279
Adult franchise, 35, 255, 259, 270–74, 283–89
Political Franchise, xxiii, 270
Royal Franchise Commission – establishment of, 278–79,

Froude, James Anthony, 90, 409

Gandhi, Mahatma, 93, 153
Garvey, Marcus, 155, 294
Geoghegan, 264, 266
Gollop, Patrick, 372
Gordon, George William, 262
Goveia, Elsa, 235, 295, 433–34

Governance
Code Noir, 236–37, 241–42, 246
House of Assembly (Bahamas), 348
House of Assembly (Barbados), 12, 327

House of Assembly (Jamaica), 255, 259
House of Assembly (Tobago), 49, 88, 272
Self-government, xxiii, 97, 115, 142, 270, 289,
call for, 157, 159
transition to, xviii
Guyana, 93, 127, 182, 183, 188, 431, 465

Hamilton-Gordon, Arthur, 213, 215, 221
Harlem Renaissance, 295
Huggins, George, 92,
Huggins, John, Sir, 160
Hutson, Katherine, 330–31

Idenburg, Cato, 193, 196–202, 205
Independence, xii, xxiv, 143, 153, 164, 166, 168, 293, 296, 311–12, 357–58, 375–76, 383, 396, 407, 416, 419, 430
'political' – movement for women, 270, 289
Caracas, declaration of, 102, 116
Haiti, 235
Hispanic America, 101
Square, 362
Trinidad and Tobago (1962), 35, 168, 407, 414
International Bank for Reconstruction and Development (IBRD), 130
International Labour Organization, 324
International Year of [the] Woman, 323

Jagan, Cheddi, 93, 141–42, 166
Jagan, Janet, 140, 141–42
James, C.L.R. (Black Jacobins), 155, 156–75, 245, 250, 407

James, C.L.R., xix, xx, 93, 151, 152, 153, 154, 445, 450, 452, 453
Jeffers, Audrey Lane, 280–81, 286–89

King, Gladwyn Ophelia, 319, 320, 321, 331, 332, 334, 335, 337
Knight, Franklyn W., 403, 404

Laws
American Constitution (1776), 96
Constitution (Barbados) (Amendment) 1995, 337
Constitution 1924 (Trinidad and Tobago), 279
Constitution 1953 (British Guiana), 128, 144, 149
Emancipation Act, xvi, 22
Emancipation Law, passing of, 21
Mackau Law (1847), 241, 247
Protection of Wages (Amendment) Act (1975), 333
Registration Act, xvi
Registry Act (Barbados), 8–9
Registry Bill (1815) (Barbados), 9
Spain's Constitution (1812), 101, 117, 122
Tobago Constitution Act (1876), 49
Trinidad and Tobago Constitution (1946), 92
Waddington Constitution, 128
Laws (Local)
Bastardy Ordinance, 280, 283
Ordinance (1888) (Tobago), 56
Ordinance (1914) (Trinidad), 276
Pioneer Ordinance (1950), 391
Layne-Clarke, Jeanette, 361, 370, 372
L'Ouverture, Toussaint, 9
Lewis, Gordon K., 234

Manners-Sutton, 218, 222, 226
Manning, Marva, 372
Maroons, 264
Marronnage, 241, 242–44
Marryshow, Julian, 359, 360, 361, 369, 371
Marryshow, T.A, 152
Mathurin Mair, Lucille, 180
McLaren, 222
Meléndez, 102, 105, 106, 109, 110, 111, 112, 115
Meléndez, Salvador, 102
Metayers, Metayage
Mighty Gabby, 372
Missionaries, 15, 40, 242, 304
    Methodist, 15
    Moravian, 68, 202
    Spanish, 414
Moitt, Bernard, 180
Morgan, Peter, 359–62
Morris, Philip, 432
Morris, Robert, 332
Morrisey, Marietta, 180, 183
Mottley, Elton Elambe, 358, 260, 361, 373
Moyne Commission, 282, 285,

Naming practice, 64, 66, 67, 68, 71, 72, 75, 80, 83
    Maroon naming practice, 71
Navarro, Marysa, 180
Negro Welfare, Cultural and Social Association (NWCSA), 275, 282–83

Olaudah Equiano, 65

Pan-African Association, 274, 277
Pan-African movement, 294
Pensions, 299, 300, 327

People's Education Movement of the Teacher's Economic and Cultural Association (Trinidad and Tobago), 96
People's Progressive Party (Guyana), 127
People's National Movement (PNM), 97, 152, 164–69, 391, 396
Post Office Savings Bank, 133
Post-Emancipation, xvii, xxii, xxiv, 36, 44–46, 49, 52–53, 58, 63, 67, 75, 83, 183, 185, 259–61, 265–66, 271, 305, 343, 406, 415
Pre-Emancipation, 63–64, 81, 83, 185
Pre-Independence, 430
Post-Independence, xxiv, 335, 391, 419, 430–31, 435
    Archival records, 436
    Societies, xxvii
Protests, 59, 255, 259
    Arouca Riots (1891), 43
    Barbados (1937), 303, 307, 308
    Belmanna War (1876), 48, 90, 261
    Black Power Revolution (1970) (Trinidad and Tobago), 169, 393, 419
    Bolshevik Revolution (1917), 277
    Coup d'état – Jamaat al Muslimeen, 385, 393
    Dog Tax Riot (1867), 48
    Fabrique Nationale (1966) (Belgium), 321
    French Industrial Revolution, 160
    General Bussa; Bussa Rebellion, 9, 15, 65, 293
    Haitian Revolution, 155, 235, 245, 246–47
    Indian Revolt (1857), 89, 92
    Industrial Revolution, 91, 151
    John Canoe (1840) (1841), 259

Labour Riots in Trinidad (1937), 39, 43, 60
Labour Struggle (1919) (Tobago), 50, 51
Land Tax Riot (1952), 46
Morant Bay Rebellion (1865), 90, 262, 264–66, 417–18
North American War of Independence, 101
Riots (Puerto Rico), 118
Riots in Antigua (1858), 260
Riots in Barbados, 28
Riots in Dominica (1844), 260
Riots in St. Croix (1878), 261
Riots, 41, 43, 45, 46, 48
Sam Sharpe-led rebellion (1831), 19
Water Riots (1903), 43, 274–76

Quinones, de Nicolás, 102, 104–107, 109–14, 117

Racism, 237, 244, 245, 293, 294, 343, 413
French and US, 237
Ramirez, Don Francisco, 113
Religion
Hindu, 68, 92–93, 97, 165, 168, 383
Muslim, 92–93, 97, 384, 412
Shango, 412
Shouter Baptists, 412
Rienzi, Adrian Cola, 286
Roxborough Estate, 49
Roy-Camille, Alex, 236

Scott, R.M, 288
Seven Years War, 102
Sharpe, William Frances, 82
Shepherd, Verene, 180
Smith, Lionel, 22

Smith, Roslyn, 319
Smith, William, 16
Statutes
Amelioration Act, xvi
Apprenticeship Act, 256
Appropriations Bill, 332
Emancipation Act, xvi, 22, 23

Trade Unions, 33, 41, 45, 296, 319, 320–23, 326, 333, 335–37
Bahamas Trade Union Congress, 330
Bahamas Trade Union, 330
Barbados Civil Service Association (BACSA), 323, 325–27
Barbados Workers Union, 319, 321
British Trade Union, 134
Butler Movement, 289
Caribbean Labour Congress, 134
Caribbean Women Trade Unionist, 330
Oilfield Workers Trade Union (OWTU), 169
Trade Union Council, 134
Trinidad and Tobago Unified Teachers' Association (TTUTA), 322
World Federation of Trade Unions, 134

Sylvester Williams, Henry, 274, 277
Syrian/Lebanese in Trinidad
Elias, Emile, 388, 394
Elias, Galy, 387
Elias, Nagib, 387
Elias, Peter, 394
Elias, Robert, 393
Sabga, Abdou, 382

Tobago Constitution Act 1876, 49
Trinidad and Tobago Constitution, 92
Trinidad and Tobago, xi, xii, xiii, xiv, xviii, xix, xx, xxiii, xxvi
Trollope, Anthony, 89

United Democratic Party, 129, 142
Universal Adult Suffrage, 140, 274, 282, 284, 286–87

West India Royal Commission, 38, 292
Westminster model, 93
Wilberforce, William, 3, 4, 8, 9, 10–14, 37

Williams, Chief Justice, 334
Williams, Denys, 335
Williams, Eric, xx, 93, 96–98, 151–69, 170, 197, 239, 406-407
    Pro-independence leader of the British Caribbean, 152
Williams, Nathaniel, 44, 51
Women in the Caribbean Project, 322
Wood Commission (1921), 272, 277
Woodcock, George, 134, 137–38
Woodcock, Henry Isles, 36, 37, 38,
Workingmen's Association, Trinidad, 45, 51, 274
Workingmen's Reform Club, 274
World War I, 277, 280
World War II, 285, 360

www.ingramcontent.com/pod-product-compliance
Lightning Source LLC
Chambersburg PA
CBHW021414300426
44114CB00010B/490